THE LAW OF EVIDENCE

SIXTH EDITION

ESSENTIALS OF
CANADIAN LAW

THE LAW OF EVIDENCE

SIXTH EDITION

DAVID M. PACIOCCO

Justice of the Ontario Court of Justice

LEE STUESSER

Professor of Law, Bond University

The Law of Evidence, sixth edition
© Irwin Law Inc., 2011

Published in 2011 by

Irwin Law Inc.
14 Duncan Street
Suite 206
Toronto, ON
M5H 3G8

www.irwinlaw.com

ISBN: 978-1-55221-218-9
e-book ISBN: 978-1-55221-219-6

Library and Archives Canada Cataloguing in Publication data

Paciocco, David M.
    The law of evidence / David M. Paciocco and Lee Stuesser

(Essentials of Canadian law)
Published: Toronto, 2nd. ed 1999–
Every 2–3 years

[1st ed. (1996)–]
ISSN 1493-4833
ISBN 978-1-55221-218-9 (6th edition)

1. Evidence—Law (Canada)   I. Stuesser, Lee II. Title III. Series

KE8440.P33   347.71   C00-300565-8
KF8935.ZA2P33

The publisher acknowledges the financial support of the Government of Canada
through the Canada Book Fund for its publishing activities.

We acknowledge the assistance of the OMDC Book Fund, an initiative of
Ontario Media Development Corporation.

Printed and bound in Canada.

 2 3 4 5   15 14 13

SUMMARY
TABLE OF CONTENTS

DETAILED
TABLE OF CONTENTS

CHAPTER 2:
THE BASICS OF ADMISSIBILITY AND THE EVALUATION OF EVIDENCE   24

CHAPTER 4:

HEARSAY 103

CHAPTER 6:

OPINION AND EXPERT EVIDENCE 181

CHAPTER 11:

SECONDARY MATERIALITY AND YOUR OWN WITNESS *487*

I dedicate my contribution to this book to Michael D. Edelson,
an exceptional advocate, for his friendship and mentorship

—David M. Paciocco

FOREWORD
to the Fifth Edition

Some years ago, I agreed to write the foreword to the first edition of this book with enthusiasm. Even without seeing the manuscript, I felt confident that with a "Paciocco" and "Stuesser" stamp of quality on it, the book would be excellent. From my very first reading, I thought it was even better than an excellent piece of writing—it had all the makings of a very useful tool for all consumers of the law of evidence. Several editions later, I know that it is.

Any experienced legal writer will appreciate what a challenging task it is to distill a massive body of jurisprudence into a seemingly simple set of principles. The challenge is particularly daunting when it comes to the constantly-evolving law of evidence. Yet Professors Paciocco and Stuesser have succeeded, with brilliance. The authors have not only extricated from our Canadian jurisprudence a concise, yet scholarly, summary of the current "rules" of evidence, they have made the law intelligible by relating those rules to the underlying governing principles. Realistic examples bring the rules to life and make the book immensely readable. The organization of the material is very user-friendly, making it a valuable guide for law students, practitioners, academics, and judges.

I have often used this textbook in my daily work over the years. In 2003–2004, I took a six-month leave from my regular judicial duties to prepare an electronic bench book on the law of evidence for the National Judicial Institute for use by Canadian trial and appellate judges. I could think of no better text to use as a backdrop for the project. With the permission of the authors and the publisher, the textbook was therefore adapted to meet the particular requirements of sitting judges. The format of the book may have been adapted to suit the electronic version of the bench book, but at no time did I see any need to change the substance of it. The bench book is now available to all judges across Canada. We are grateful to Professors Paciocco and Stuesser and their publisher.

The Honourable Louise Charron
Justice of the Supreme Court of Canada

PREFACE

This book has been written in an effort to simplify, and record concisely, the main rules and principles of the law of evidence. It is an attempt to explain the basic concepts of evidence to the law student. At the same time, it is an effort to provide the practitioner with a simple and accessible catalogue of the authority that is most frequently needed in the conduct of trials or hearings. We are pleased that this work has been adapted by the National Judicial Institute as the "bench book" that has been distributed to judges of all courts across Canada to assist in their evidentiary rulings.

In an effort to simplify the law of evidence, we have chosen to reduce the most important rules into proposition form. These propositions or statements of law can be found italicized throughout the text above the discussions to which they relate. We are aware that there will occasionally be controversy over the proper statement of rules of law and that the law of evidence has proven particularly resistant to efforts at codification. We are nonetheless of the view that our efforts at stating the law in clear terms can be of value to both students and practitioners by simplifying and focusing the discussion. Where major controversies exist, we have attempted to note them. We have also used many examples in an effort to illustrate the operation of the rules.

In this sixth edition, we have adhered to the organizational plan that we adopted for the first five editions. The general concepts of the law of evidence are introduced in chapter 1. The introduction supplies an opportunity to describe generally the function of the law of evidence, to make observations about the trend in recent authority, and to present foundational material that should assist in understanding the discussions contained in the main body of the work.

Chapters 2 through 9 deal with the rules of admissibility. The methods of presenting evidence, which might appear to come logically before the rules of admissibility, have been relegated to chapter 10. We felt it preferable to acquaint the uninitiated with what kind of information can be presented, before describing how it can be presented. Chapter 12 deals with rules relating to the use that the trier of fact can make of admissible evidence. The conclusions, which are found in chapter 13, provide a general thematic discussion of the forces that have moved the law of evidence and that will continue to do so in the foreseeable future.

The rules of admissibility are organized according to two criteria. First, a distinction is drawn between those rules that relate to the admission of evidence about the factual event in issue and those dealing with the admission of evidence that is about other evidence in the case. This latter kind of proof, which we call "secondarily material" because it is not about the primary issues, provides the trier of fact with information about such things as the credibility of witnesses. The law of evidence has taken a more restrictive approach to the admission of this kind of proof than it has with proof relating directly to the event in issue. We have treated this topic in both chapters 10 and 11.

The second criterion that we used in organizing the admissibility discussion was to order the chapters generally according to the main purpose for which relevant and material information might be excluded. Chapters 3 (Character Evidence), 4 (Hearsay Evidence), 5 (Hearsay Exceptions), and 6 (Opinion Evidence) describe cases where admissibility is restricted mainly out of a desire to improve the quality of fact finding. For better or for worse, potentially misleading information is excluded in an effort to enhance the accuracy of the fact-finding process. Chapters 7 (Privilege), 8 (Self-incrimination), and 9 (Improperly Obtained Evidence) describe exclusionary rules that are concerned less with the accuracy of the evidence[1] than with the pursuit of policies and principles considered to be more important than the accurate determination of facts.

As is commonly the case, most of the discussion in this book relates to rules of criminal evidence. The rules emerged from criminal cases, and continue to develop in them. Frequently, where there are material and important differences, reference is made to non-criminal rules. The civil rules of evidence for Quebec have been disregarded, not because we consider those rules to be unimportant or uninteresting, but because of limitations in our expertise.

---

1   With the notable exception of the voluntariness rule related to admissions by an accused person in a criminal case.

CHAPTER 1

INTRODUCTION

1. THE ROLE OF THE LAW OF EVIDENCE

Few cases ultimately turn on disagreements about the law and what it requires. Most cases come down to disputes about facts. Typically, the parties disagree over what happened. As a result, most cases turn on "evidence," which, of course, is the data factual decision-makers (referred to as "triers of fact") use when resolving factual controversies. This is true whether the trier of fact is an adjudicator in an administrative hearing, a judge in a "judge alone" trial, or the jury in a jury trial.

The law of evidence is therefore crucial. It determines what data can be considered, how it can be proved, and the use to which it can be put. If its rules prevent data from being proved or used by the trier of fact, the law of evidence can prevent a litigant from winning. There is no sense having a contract, for example, if the party you are trying to bind denies you have a contract and you cannot prove that you do. You will not enjoy the contract because you do not have the evidence necessary to trigger the law you want to rely upon. The gateway to the application of law is therefore evidence, and the law of evidence is the key that opens that gateway.

We make this point not only to punctuate the importance of the law of evidence. This point also demonstrates that the law of evidence does not exist for its own sake. The law of evidence exists to provide a process for gaining access to the benefits provided by substantive rules. Its role is therefore facilitative, secondary or "adjectival"—it is meant to serve the application of the substantive law. To assist in demonstrating this it is helpful to introduce the three kinds of evidentiary rules that serve the substantive law, "rules of process," "rules of admissibility," and "rules of reasoning." The operation of these rules is determined by the presiding judicial official (referred to as the "trier of law"), either the adjudicator in an administrative hearing, or the judge in a "judge alone" or jury trial.

1.1) Rules of Process

Evidence law's rules of process serve the substantive law by outlining how evidence is presented to triers of fact. Those rules provide procedures designed to enhance the prospects that witnesses will tell the truth, such as the "promise to tell the truth," the oath, and the affirmation. And they describe how information is to be communicated to the court. The law of evidence, therefore, controls the manner in which questions are posed, the way exhibits are presented, and the conduct of in-court demonstrations.

1.2) Rules of Admissibility

Where the law of evidence plays its most controversial role is in determining "admissibility"—in identifying what information triers of fact are allowed to consider. Ideally, the rules of admissibility should be generous. Given its role in serving the application of the substantive law, the law of evidence should ideally enable triers of fact to have orderly access to any information that could help them make an accurate determination about whether the substantive law applies.

This basic "principle of access to evidence" is well recognized. In R. v. Jarvis the Supreme Court of Canada elevated it to a constitutional level in criminal cases, referring to the "principle of fundamental justice that relevant evidence should be available to the [trier of fact] in the search for the truth."[1] This principle is not, however, pursued single-mindedly. The rules of evidence frequently impede access to information. For example, the rule of solicitor-client privilege prevents lawyers from testifying about what their clients have said, even though solicitor-client conversations may produce the most frank and complete account of the client's information. The law of evidence has judged that a competing policy—protecting the confidentiality of solicitor-client communications so that clients can be candid and secure proper legal

---

1   [2002] 3 S.C.R. 757.

advice relevant to their actual situation—is generally more important than the principle of access to evidence. Many rules of evidence "exclude" information from consideration entirely, in this way.

Other rules of evidence—rules of "restricted admissibility"—allow information to be considered but purport to impose limits on the use that can be made of that information even where logically that information may have a range of possible uses. This is achieved by requiring triers of fact to avoid using restricted evidence for improper purposes in their decisions. If they do, they will have erred in law. In jury trials where evidence has been admitted for restricted purposes the judge must provide "limiting instructions regarding the permissible inferences that may be drawn from the evidence."[2]

The hearsay rule is an example of a rule of restricted admissibility. It does not prohibit the admissibility of everything that has been said prior to court. It simply holds that ordinarily courts must not treat what has been said out of court as though it is the equivalent of in-court testimony. In other words, courts should not use out-of-court statements as a narrative account of what happened—as proof of the truth of its contents. On the other hand, if those out-of-court statements are relevant for other purposes they can be admitted and used for those limited purposes. For example, it is permissible to use an out-of-court statement made by a testifying witness to show that, in their current testimony, the witness has now changed their story from what they said before. The prior statement can be used to prove the contradiction, but not as proof of the facts it asserts. Most exclusionary rules work this way. They do not bar a particular kind of information. Instead, they restrict the uses to which information can be put when it is admitted.

We find it helpful in instructing students of the law of evidence to suggest that there are three categories that can assist in understanding why the law of evidence excludes evidence or restricts admissibility—"rules of practical exclusion," "rules of subordinated evidence," and "rules of non-evidence."

Rules of practical exclusion reject evidence in order to encourage trial efficiency. There are rules, for example, limiting the number of expert witnesses that can be called, absent special permission to call more.

Rules of subordinated evidence exclude data from consideration because of competing considerations of policy or principle. Solicitor-client privilege, introduced above in this chapter, is an example. Another example is the rule that excludes some unconstitutionally obtained evidence.

---

2   *R. v. Starr* (2000), 147 C.C.C.(3d) 449 at 523 (S.C.C.).

Rules of non-evidence exclude information that will not help the trier of fact—information that is not really evidence at all, hence the name "non-evidence." Irrelevant information is an obvious example of non-evidence. Other rules of non-evidence are more subtle. They exclude information that seems helpful on its face but which may in fact be unhelpful because it can distort the truth. The hearsay rule, introduced above, is an example. Experience shows that we typically know too little to judge rationally the accuracy of a speaker's information if the speaker is not present in court to answer questions about their honesty, their opportunity to observe, their memory, or what precisely they meant to communicate. A hearsay statement that may seem tremendously useful on its face will be dangerous to act upon without more information from the person who made that hearsay statement. The interesting thing about rules of non-evidence is that, despite the common impression that the rules of evidence tend to exclude useful information, these rules of exclusion are meant to improve the accuracy of fact-finding.

These three categories of exclusionary rule are not, of course, airtight. The objectives achieved by many rules fall into more than one of these categories. The exclusion of irrelevant evidence, for example, occurs not only because it is "non-evidence," but also because excluding irrelevant evidence serves the needs of practical exclusion by making trials more efficient. Even though the three categories of exclusion are imperfect, they are useful in answering the most important question in understanding the rules of exclusion—"why." If lawyers do not understand why a rule of exclusion exists they will not use it properly.

Only common law systems like our own make heavy use of rules of admissibility. Most legal systems have few such rules. They trust triers of fact to sort through the information, choose what is useful, and give it the "weight" or importance it deserves. The difference in approach is not only a matter of philosophical disagreement about how best to determine the truth. It is an inevitable consequence of the disparate processes that are employed. Non-common law systems tend to use "inquisitorial" practices in which triers of fact or their assistants participate actively in finding the data for decision-making. These systems tend not to use the contained, oral hearings employed by common law systems to gather information. In inquisitorial systems decisions are often made based on court files that will include transcripts or summaries of earlier witness interviews. As a result, inquisitorial procedures tend not to be conducive to exclusion, which is much easier to achieve in a contained oral hearing with a presiding official where the presentation and content of information can be controlled. The exclusionary function is therefore one of the distinguishing characteristics of common law systems.[3]

1.3) Rules of Reasoning

Just because evidence has been admitted does not mean it will influence the outcome. The trier of fact may not trust the admitted evidence. The witness who delivers it may not be believable, or the evidence may not conform to common sense, or may conflict with other more compelling proof. Often, by the end of the case, the evidence proves to be unimportant even if it is believed. There are therefore two stages at which evidence is evaluated: (1) the admissibility stage where it is evaluated for compliance with rules of admissibility, and (2) the deliberation stage where the trier of fact makes the ultimate decision in the case by "weighing" the evidence and applying its finding to the relevant rules of substantive law.

The law of evidence does have some "rules of reasoning" to assist during this deliberation stage. There are rules, for example, that describe the standards required for success by the competing parties by establishing burdens and standards of proof. There is also case law on the evaluation of the testimony of children, or the demeanour of witnesses. And there are rules that warn triers of fact that certain kinds of proof will often be dangerous to rely upon.

Rules of reasoning, however, comprise the smallest category of evidentiary rules. This is because the law of evidence is about facts, and facts are infinitely variable. The significance that facts have as proof varies from case to case and is often the subject of reasonable debate. For example, it is generally believed that convicted criminals tend to be less trustworthy than others. The law therefore permits the criminal record of a witness to be proved so that the trier of fact knows who they are being asked to believe. In spite of the law's assumption that his information is generally helpful, some people, when judging testimony, will think the past criminal record of the witness has little impact on whether the witness is telling the truth in a particular case. And not all criminal convictions are equal. Convictions can be imposed in a variety of circumstances and vary in nature. Some are for minor offences that say little about honesty. Rather than preordain the effect that a criminal conviction will have on the credibility of witnesses by developing a rule, the law of evidence therefore leaves that up to the good

---

3   J.B. Thayer, *A Preliminary Treatise on Evidence at the Common Law*, reprint of 1898 ed. (New York: Augustus M. Kelly, 1969) at 264.

sense of individual triers of fact to evaluate in context. This is how the law of evidence generally behaves. Since the evaluation of evidence is more a matter of common sense than of law, and since different people tend to see the world differently, the law of evidence tends to stay out. The "weight" triers of fact choose to give to items of evidence is generally a matter of discretion.

The lawyer's role in all of this is to use the opportunity for argument at the close of the case to point out the strengths and contribution of its own evidence, and the problems and perils of evidence presented by opposing lawyers. A firm understanding of the law of evidence can assist immeasurably in making good legal argument on these points. This is because the careful evaluation of factual data turns on concepts commonly encountered in the law of evidence, things such as "weight," "probative value," "credibility," and "reliability." The exclusionary rules of non-evidence can also assist in planning legal argument for they work to identify evidence that may seem to be helpful but which on critical examination is not; even when evidence passes the threshold of admissibility of these rules, it will still suffer to a degree from the underlying problems those exclusionary rules are meant to address. Triers of fact should be alerted to these problems. Understanding why evidence is excluded therefore assists in crafting cogent legal arguments about what use should be made of the evidence that has been admitted.

1.4)   The Challenge of the Law of Evidence

The rules of evidence designed to achieve these various roles tend to be highly conceptual. They often require subtle but crucial distinctions to be made between kinds of reasoning or inferences. This makes them difficult to apply. So, too, does the mission of the law of evidence in regulating the proof of facts. Since facts are infinitely variable, the rules of evidence aim at moving targets and always require the exercise of judgment to apply. The rules are therefore as complex in design and as difficult to apply as they are important. Master them and enjoy a tremendous litigation advantage. Misunderstand them at your peril and the peril of your clients.

2. THE SOURCES OF EVIDENCE LAW

Most of the law of evidence in Canada consists of common law rules. Each jurisdiction within Canada, including Canada itself, has an evidence act.[4] The application of each evidence act is determined by the constitutional division of powers. The *Canada Evidence Act* applies in the federal courts, in criminal matters, in non-criminal federal prosecutions, in federal administrative proceedings, in bankruptcy matters, and in other civil proceedings over which the federal government has jurisdiction. The provincial Evidence Acts apply to matters within provincial jurisdiction, including provincial prosecutions, provincial administrative proceedings, and in most civil litigation.

These evidence acts are not codes purporting to include the heart of the law of evidence. They merely supplement the common law. They consist of provisions that modify some common law rules, such as those relating to when witnesses qualify to give testimony or when they can be forced to testify. The evidence acts touch most areas of the law of evidence, but do so selectively. Since they are an overlay on the common law it is often necessary to understand the relevant common law rules to appreciate how these provisions operate.

Apart from the evidence acts, there are many specialized statutes that have provisions relating to the proof of facts. For example, land registration acts typically provide for the issuance and admissibility of certificates to assist in proving real estate transactions,[5] while professional registration statutes also provide for the use of certificates to prove membership in the profession.[6] Rules of practice established within each province also include provisions relating to the law of evidence.[7] It is important for counsel to be familiar with the relevant statutory provisions in their area of practice that could affect evidentiary issues.

3. TRENDS IN THE LAW OF EVIDENCE

Three related trends have marked the progress of evidence law in Canada over the last two decades: (1) the move to a contextual or "purposive" approach, (2) the development of the overarching exclusionary discretion, and (3) increased admissibility. Since these trends define

---

4   For a list and citations to these statutes, see Table of Canadian Evidence Acts following chapter 13.

5   See, for example, *Land Titles Act*, R.S.O. 1990, c. L.5, ss. 113, 117, 165, & 166.

6   See, for example, *Registered Nurses Act, 1988*, S.S. 1988–89, c. R-12.2, s. 18(3).

7   See, for example, Rule 51.11 of the Nova Scotia *Civil Procedure Rules*, created under the authority of the *Judicature Act*, R.S.N.S. 1989, c. 240, s. 46, providing for proof of documents and electronic information in civil proceedings before the Nova Scotia Supreme Court.

the current culture of the law of evidence their early description serves the introductory discussion that follows.

3.1) The Purposive Approach

In the past, the law prized certainty. It gave priority to providing clear, predictable rules that would apply equally in all cases. The doctrine of precedent, in turn, ensured that once a rule was recognized, it would become entrenched in the law. As a result, evidentiary rules purporting to provide clear answers proliferated. For example, there were dozens of rules that operated as exceptions to the hearsay rule; if a litigant could fit the out-of-court statement into a pre-existing exception, the out-of-court statement could be used for a hearsay purpose, but not otherwise.

This kind of approach provided a veneer of technical precision and predictability to the process of proof but there were problems. The rules of evidence that were produced were invariably overinclusive or underinclusive. In other words, they either failed to catch those situations they were created to catch, or they caught situations they were not meant to catch. This is in part because the human capacity to design perfect rules — rules that will invariably and only accomplish their underlying goal — is limited. This is true of all rules, including substantive rules. Yet the problem of imperfect rules has always been particularly acute for rules of proof. This is because the law of evidence is about facts and, as indicated, facts are infinitely variable, compounding the challenge of perfect design. The law of evidence therefore works best if a purposive and flexible approach is taken.

The law of evidence was already moving to more flexible standards as part of a general trend to make the law more functional and less technical. In Canada, however, two particular social developments accelerated and amplified the shift to a "purposive" or principled, context-based approach. The sexual offence awakening and the *Canadian Charter of Rights and Freedoms* each showed the underperformance of the law of evidence to be intolerable and led to a wholesale change in the way the rules of proof operate.

In the 1980s the prevalence of sexual offences, long under the social radar, was exposed, particularly for child victims. Meanwhile feminists and law reformers were showing how inhospitable the rules of evidence were to the prosecution of these offences. Many of these rules, including rules of evaluation that called for corroboration (strict technical confirmation) of the testimony of sexual assault complainants and children, were intended to protect accused persons against false sexual offence allegations. But these rules rested in stereotype and dull assumptions about women, children, and sexual offences. Appropriately, they have now been replaced by practices designed to repel stereotype and to focus on the merits of the individual case.

The increased sensitivity to sexual victimization also played a leading role in tearing down imperfect rules that had more neutral objectives. The leading example is *R. v. Khan*.[8] The hearsay rule would have resulted in exclusion in that case of an overwhelmingly reliable out-of-court complaint made by a young victim about being sexually assaulted by the family doctor. Without this reliable hearsay her version of events would not be available. The hearsay rule was never intended to produce this kind of result. It was meant to exclude unreliable out-of-court statements. The Supreme Court of Canada rectified the overinclusive nature of the hearsay rule by adopting a general "purposive exception" that now permits courts to examine admissibility by assessing whether, in the context of the particular case, exclusion will advance the goals the hearsay rule is intended to achieve. Similar contextual approaches followed. They are now used for most major rules of evidence, including the law of opinion evidence, the main character evidence rules, the law of privilege, and unconstitutionally obtained evidence.

At the same time the second influence, the *Canadian Charter of Rights and Freedoms*, also encouraged the movement towards more flexible rules of admissibility.[9] Some rules of evidence, if applied rigidly, had the effect of denying access to information that might raise a reasonable doubt about guilt in particular criminal cases. Other rules of evidence had the potential to admit evidence that could operate unfairly against accused persons. If those rules applied when producing such results, they would be vulnerable to *Charter* challenge. The solution has been to loosen the rules of exclusion to allow for the proof of important defence evidence, and to provide judges with the discretion to avoid admitting prosecution evidence that could undermine the fairness of the trial, even where admissibility is provided for by statute.[10]

Although not as central, the movement to more purposive rules of proof has also been encouraged by access to justice concerns in the context of historical litigation, most specifically involving aboriginal rights claims. This form of litigation can require proof relating to events that are hundreds of years old. Typically the only source of aboriginal

---

8 (1990), 59 C.C.C.(3d) 92 (S.C.C.).

9 *Canadian Charter of Rights and Freedoms*, Part I of the *Constitution Act, 1982*, being Schedule B to the *Canada Act 1982* (U.K.), 1982, c. 11 [*Charter*].

10 See chapter 2, section 5, "The Exclusionary Discretion."

information is oral history passed on from generation to generation, and often imbued with spiritual content. The traditional bias in the law of evidence for proof through in-court testimony of live witnesses with personal knowledge would make it impossible to adjudicate such claims if traditional rules of evidence were insisted upon. As a result, the Supreme Court of Canada has adopted an approach whereby it has affirmed "the continued applicability of the rules of evidence [to such litigation], while cautioning that these rules must be applied flexibly, in a manner commensurate with the difficulties posed by such claims."[11] Three simple principles or ideas underlying the admissibility of evidence are used to permit admissibility determinations to be made on a case-by-case basis:

> First, the evidence must be useful in the sense of tending to prove a fact relevant to the issues in the case. Second, the evidence must be reasonably reliable; unreliable evidence may hinder the search for the truth more than help it. Third, even useful and reasonably reliable evidence may be excluded in the discretion of the trial judge if its probative value is overshadowed by its potential for prejudice.[12]

The movement to make the rules responsive to the needs of the particular case has not come without a cost. Flexibility is being achieved at the expense of certainty. The rules of evidence have never been easy to apply. Yet many of those rules of evidence now require more detailed evaluation and produce less predictable results than ever before. The hope is that ultimate outcomes are improved.

3.2) The Development of a General Exclusionary Discretion

Again, because of the imperfect design of the law it is not uncommon for technically admissible evidence to create problems if it is received. The evidence may not be worth hearing because it will take too much time, or be confusing, or surprise one of the parties, or it may cut too deeply into privacy interests, or assault the dignity of individuals unduly. Technically admissible evidence may even be so inflammatory or prone to invite emotional reaction or stereotypical thinking that it can distort the outcome of a case. Until recently the allure of precedent and certainty caused courts to deny judges the authority to keep such evidence out in an effort to avoid these problems. The same influences

---

11   *Mitchell v. Canada (M.N.R.)*, [2001] S.C.J. No. 33 at para. 29.
12   *Ibid.* at para. 30.

that led to the adoption of a purposive approach have now changed the law. Judges now have the discretion to exclude evidence, even if it is technically admissible, based on a cost-benefit analysis. If the "probative value" of the evidence is outweighed by the "prejudice" [or costs] its admission will cause, it can be excluded.[13] This formula for discretion has become ubiquitous in the law of evidence. As will be seen, not only do judges have this omnipresent authority relating to technically admissible evidence, a number of key rules of exclusion incorporate this formula. In effect, many of the rules of admissibility call for much the same kind of evaluation of the evidence that was once confined to the deliberation stage.

3.3) Increased Admissibility

The development of purposive rules of admissibility has resulted in increased admission. There is also a discernible legislative movement away from reliance on strict rules of proof. It has been true for many years, for example, that hearsay and other technically inadmissible evidence can be used in bail hearings. This kind of practice is becoming widespread. We now permit judges to incarcerate people who were initially permitted to serve their sentences in the community on the basis of hearsay documents.[14] Amendments to the *Extradition Act*, a statute that applies when a foreign jurisdiction seeks to remove a suspect from Canada for trial, have reduced reliance on rules of evidence.[15] Recent amendments have even endorsed the use of technically inadmissible evidence during preliminary hearings.[16] Courts are permitted to make a host of important national security-based decisions, including deporting suspects,[17] listing persons and entities as "terrorist organizations,"[18] and deciding on privilege and non-disclosure,[19] all on the basis of otherwise technically inadmissible information. These regimes assume that important decisions can be made after exposure to, or the evaluation of, information that the common law of evidence had been so distrustful of, or so concerned about, that it would have been rejected out of hand.

This movement has been spurred on largely by concerns about efficiency, but there are other influences. Undoubtedly, international

---

13   See chapter 2, section 5 "The Exclusionary Discretion."
14   *Criminal Code*, R.S.C. 1985, c. C-46, ss. 742.6(4) & (5).
15   S.C. 1999, c. 18, ss. 32 & 33.
16   *Criminal Code*, above note 14, ss. 540(7)–(9).
17   *Immigration and Refugee Protection Act*, S.C. 2001, c. 27, ss. 173 and 175(1)(b).
18   *Criminal Code*, above note 14, s. 83.06(6.1).
19   *Canada Evidence Act*, ss. 38.06(3.1) and 38.131(5).

co-operation in the security and extradition context, coupled with exposure to many legal systems that do not have rules of exclusion, is also reducing our historical attraction to technical rules of admission. Whatever the genesis of this movement, access to information is loosening, including under common law rules. The trend is towards increased admissibility.

4. THE VARIABLE APPLICATION OF THE LAW OF EVIDENCE: COURTS AND TRIBUNALS

It is sometimes said that "[t]here is no difference, as to the rules of evidence, between civil and criminal cases."[20] This is not entirely so. Evidence may be admissible in civil proceedings but not in a criminal case. For example, because of special statutory treatment, the admission of bad character evidence is not as restricted in child protection proceedings as it is in a criminal prosecution involving the same allegation of abuse.[21] The *Charter* does not apply *per se* to the admission of unconstitutionally obtained evidence when it is being used in private, civil proceedings. Evidence that may have to be excluded under the *Charter* in a criminal case is therefore generally admissible in a civil case.[22]

The common law rules can also differ between civil and criminal cases. Self-incrimination protection available to the accused in a criminal case does not apply in civil cases because persons are not "incriminated" in civil cases.[23] Involuntary confessions, inadmissible in a criminal case, may be admissible in a civil case.[24] The test for protecting therapeutic records differs between civil and criminal cases.[25]

Even when the same general rules apply, their application may well be affected according to whether they are being applied in civil or criminal cases. For example, in determining the admissibility of expert opinion evidence a court must determine whether the benefits of its

---

20   *Baker v. Hutchinson* (1976), 13 O.R. (2d) 591 at 596 (C.A.).

21   See *Child and Family Services Act*, R.S.O. 1990, c. C.11, s. 50(1).

22   See, for example, *Monsanto Canada Inc. v. Schmeiser* (2002), 218 D.L.R. (4th) 31 (Fed. C.A.); *Cat Productions Ltd. v. Macedo*, [1985] 1 F.C. 269 (T.D.); and *P.(D.) v. Wagg* (2004), 184 C.C.C. (3d) 321 at para. 64 (Ont. C.A.).

23   See, for example, *Knutson v. Saskatchewan Registered Nurses' Assn.* (1990), 46 Admin. L.R. 234 (Sask. C.A.).

24   See, for example, *Bains v. Yorkshire Insurance Co.* (1963), 41 W.W.R. 555 (B.C.S.C.).

25   Compare the tests adopted in *M.(A.) v. Ryan*, [1997] 1 S.C.R. 157 and *R. v. O'Connor*, [1995] 4 S.C.R. 411. The *O'Connor* test has been overtaken by legislation. Section 278.1 of the *Criminal Code*; as am., above note 14, for criminal cases.

admission outweigh the costs. That decision can vary depending on whether the case is a civil or criminal one.[26] The same is true of the application of the balancing process employed to determine the admissibility of similar fact evidence in civil and criminal cases.[27] This is invariably so because the interests, and even the mode of trial, will differ.

Indeed, within different kinds of criminal proceedings the rules of evidence differ. The rules that apply during a criminal trial do not apply at bail hearings, or preliminary inquiries, or extradition hearings. None of these proceedings involve a final determination of guilt of the accused and therefore fewer restrictions apply on proof. Hearsay, for example, will be more readily admitted at these types of hearings than at a trial.

In *Germany (Federal Republic) v. Ebke* the accused argued that a statutory provision permitting an extradition judge to act on evidence inadmissible in Canada but admissible in the country seeking to try the accused was contrary to the *Charter*. In essence, the accused argued that the Court was constitutionally compelled to use Canadian evidence rules in making the extradition decision. The Court held against this argument, emphasizing that "our [particular] rules of evidence are not fundamental principles of justice" that must be applied at every kind of hearing. What is required to achieve fairness and to meet the policy needs in a given context varies, and so too do the rules of proof.[28]

For this reason practices unacceptable during a criminal trial may be permissible at the sentencing hearing.[29] It is evident that at the sentencing hearing the character of the accused becomes important, permitting proof of prior criminal convictions even though the same evidence would be inadmissible during the guilt phase of the trial. At the sentencing phase proof of uncharged criminal conduct forming part of the circumstances of the offence can be proved as an aggravating circumstance;[30] and even uncharged criminal conduct occurring on other occasions may prove relevant and admissible, for example, to show that expressions of remorse are not genuine, or to demonstrate the risk of reoffence in order to decide whether a community sentence is fitting.[31] Where the issue is whether the accused breached a conditional sentence, there are even statutory provisions permitting a breach

---

26   See the discussion in chapter 6, section 4.3, "Precondition 2 — Relevance."

27   See the discussion in chapter 3, section 16, "Character Evidence in Civil Cases."

28   (2003), 173 C.C.C. (3d) 261 at paras. 16 & 17 (N.W.T.C.A.).

29   *Criminal Code*, above note 14, s. 724(3); *R. v. Gardiner* (1982), 30 C.R. (3d) 289 (S.C.C.).

30   *R. v. Larche* (2006), 214 C.C.C. (3d) 289 (S.C.C.), *Criminal Code, ibid.*, s. 725.1(c).

31   *R. v. Angelillo* (2006), 274 D.L.R. (4th) 1 (S.C.C.).

to be established by filing a supervisor's report outlining the alleged breach, something totally unheard of when an initial determination of guilt is being considered.[32] So long as the report includes witness statements or information that the supervisor could testify to directly in court, this kind of summary documentary proof will be accepted, subject to the accused applying and persuading the judge that cross-examination would serve a useful purpose.[33]

Not only do the rules of evidence vary within a criminal case according to the nature of the issue being tried, the same set of rules can function differently in jury trials than they do in a trial by judge alone. This is because many rules of admissibility require a judge to exclude evidence if it is too "prejudicial" in the sense that it is apt to be misused by a trier of fact. Judges, familiar with the risks associated with such evidence, are less likely to misuse these kinds of proof than juries. There is therefore less risk in admitting prejudicial proof in a judge alone trial, resulting in a looser operation of the rules than in jury trials. Clear examples are, utilizing the prior convictions of the accused to show his lack of credibility, section 276 applications involving proof of the sexual experiences of a complainant,[34] and the admission of similar fact evidence revealing discreditable conduct by the accused.[35]

The rules of evidence differ, as well, among civil proceedings. Hearsay evidence, for example, not admissible in civil trials before the superior court of Ontario, would be admissible in a small claims court proceeding held in that province.[36] Administrative tribunals tend not to be subject to the same rules of proof used in court-based litigation. Administrative tribunals are meant to apply accessible, informal procedures that should remain unencumbered by technical rules such as the laws of evidence. Policy considerations differ. Statutes, therefore, tend to exonerate administrative boards from the strict application of the rules of evidence. For example, the Ontario *Statutory Powers Procedure Act*[37] allows tribunals to admit as evidence and act on any oral testimony or any document or other thing relevant to the subject matter of the proceedings, whether admissible as evidence or not in a court of law. This is not to say that the

---

32   *Criminal Code*, above note 14, s. 742.6(5).

33   *R. v. McIvor*, 2008 SCC 11.

34   *R. v. Temertzoglou* (2002), 11 C.R. (6th) 179 at para. 31 (Ont. S.C.J.).

35   See *R. v. Sutherland* (2001), 146 O.A.C. 53 (C.A.); *R. v. Vrdoljak* (2002), 1 C.R. (6th) 250 at 260–61 (Ont. S.C.J.); *R. v. W.(L.)*, [2004] O.J. No. 4163 (C.A.).

36   *Courts of Justice Act*, R.S.O. 1990, c. C.43, s. 27(1).

37   R.S.O. 1990, c. S.22, s. 15.

rules of evidence are ignored in such proceedings. Established rules of evidence are consulted for guidance, but need not be slavishly followed.

The point is that in deciding what rules to apply, attention must be paid to the nature of the proceeding and the kind of issue being resolved. Care should be taken not to apply common law criminal rules unnecessarily in civil cases, and it is necessary to gain familiarity with relevant, specialized statutory provisions. Even when dealing with rules that apply to both the civil and criminal domain, care should be taken. With context and purposive application becoming increasingly important in the law of evidence,[38] and with more and more rules of admissibility requiring a preliminary weighing of the value and "costs" of calling the evidence, one can expect differences in the way that those rules are applied in each of those domains.

5. PUTTING THE RULES OF EVIDENCE IN A CONTEXT

It is helpful in understanding the operation of the laws of evidence to put them in their context by describing the process of the hearing within which they operate. The processes vary depending on whether the hearing is criminal, civil, or administrative. For illustrative purposes we have chosen to describe the model of a criminal trial. Before doing so the *voir dire* or "trial within a trial" should be described since *voir dires* are held in both civil and criminal cases and are an important vehicle for resolving controversies on evidentiary issues.

5.1) The *Voir Dire*

In the conduct of a hearing, it often becomes necessary to settle subsidiary legal disputes such as whether particular evidence is admissible. Some of those legal disputes will turn on questions of fact. For example, the Crown in a criminal trial may wish to prove a confession made by the accused. As a matter of law that confession will be admissible only if the Crown can prove that, as a matter of fact, it was voluntarily made. Absent the agreement by the parties that the confession was voluntary, an evidentiary hearing will therefore have to be held. Hearings of this kind — "trials within a trial" conducted to settle discrete legal issues — are called *voir dires*.

---

38   See the discussion in section 3, above in this chapter, "Trends in the Law of Evidence."

Technically, the *voir dire* is a separate hearing. This is in part because it may be necessary in resolving the *voir dire* issue to hear evidence that is not admissible at the trial itself. Evidence heard during the voir dire is therefore not part of the general trial record and cannot be relied upon in coming to an ultimate decision, unless the parties agree. In the confession example, if the confession was not proved to be voluntary there would be no such agreement. The criminal trial would simply commence again after the failed *voir dire* application as if no confession had ever been mentioned. If the confession was proved to have been voluntary, however, the parties could agree to make the voir dire proceedings part of the trial record so as not to have to repeat the same evidence again. Failing that agreement, the Crown would have to prove that confession again at the trial and a good deal of the evidence would be repeated.

In judge alone trials it is common for the parties to agree to have the *voir dire* evidence admitted as part of the main trial record. In a jury trial an agreement to admit *voir dire* evidence in this way is not generally possible. This is because, ordinarily, the jury will be removed from the courtroom during *voir dires*. Jurors are removed both to protect them from becoming tainted by inadmissible evidence and because *voir dires* are about questions of law for the presiding judge—the trier of law—to resolve. These legal issues do not ordinarily concern the jury.

In judge alone trials the judge is both the trier of law responsible for conducting the *voir dire*, and the trier of fact responsible for ultimately deciding the case. It is obviously not possible to insulate the judge from voir dire evidence. Unless it becomes part of the trial record on consent, the judge is legally required to disregard evidence presented during the *voir dire* when deciding the case.

5.2) The Criminal Trial Process—An Illustration

The criminal trial begins when the accused is placed in the charge of the trial court by pleading "guilty" or "not guilty" to the specific allegations or charges that are contained in the "information" or "indictment."[39] If a plea of "not guilty" is made to any of the charges, the trial commences.

---

39 An "information" is the document containing the sworn allegation of an informant, usually a police officer, that the accused has committed an offence. This legal document gives the court jurisdiction over the alleged offence. An "indictment" is the document that is prepared for indictable or more serious offences after the accused has been committed to stand trial before the superior court of criminal jurisdiction within a province. It is signed by the Crown Attorney as agent for the Attorney General and gives the superior court jurisdiction over the offence.

In a jury trial, some preliminary legal issues are settled before the jury attends court. A judge may agree to conduct some admissibility *voir dires* at this time to convenience jurors provided the admissibility decisions can properly be made without the benefit of hearing all of the evidence in the case. When these preliminary matters are completed, the jury is called in. The judge provides opening remarks about how the trial will be conducted to assist the jury, and the presentation of evidence begins.

The Crown presents its evidence first. In jury trials, and in judge alone trials where the alleged facts are complex, the Crown will be permitted to make an opening statement before doing so. This statement will outline the case in general terms and will indicate what the Crown will be attempting to prove. The purpose of this statement is to place the Crown's general theory of the case before the trier of fact in a comprehensible manner, since the actual evidence will normally be presented in a piecemeal fashion that may be difficult to follow without the kind of blueprint provided in the opening remarks. Nothing said in the opening statement constitutes evidence in the case. In other words, the trier of fact cannot rely on any of the facts alleged in the opening statement unless those facts are proved to its satisfaction by admissible evidence.

When the Crown's opening statement is complete, the evidence begins. Formal admissions of fact may be made by the accused or the Crown. The jury, or the judge in a judge alone trial, is simply told that these admitted facts exist, and will take them into account in rendering a verdict.

Most contested evidence will be introduced in the form of the testimony of witnesses, although physical items may be introduced from time to time as exhibits. Each witness who is called by the Crown is "examined in chief" by the Crown. In this examination, the information the witness has is presented to the trier of fact in the form of responses elicited by neutral questions designed to organize the presentation of information and to keep it relevant.

Once the examination in chief is completed, defence counsel cross-examines the Crown's witness. Questions posed in cross-examination need not be neutral and can suggest facts or challenge the testimony of the witness. They will be designed to reveal information helpful to the accused, to qualify harmful information presented in chief by the witness, or to reveal problems with the reliability of the testimony of the witness. When the cross-examination is completed, the Crown can re-examine the witness if new matters have been raised that could not reasonably have been anticipated, or to "explain, clarify or qualify answers given in cross-examination that are considered damaging to the examiner's case."[40] In exceedingly rare cases, re-cross-examination[41] and possibly a second re-examination may be allowed. This process is followed for each witness until the case for the Crown is complete. It is possible that at the end of the Crown's case, the judge may, after motion by defence counsel, remove the case from the jury by directing a verdict of acquittal. This outcome occurs solely where the Crown's evidence does not make out a "*prima facie* case."[42]

If the case is not removed from the trier of fact, the defence will elect whether to call evidence. If it chooses to do so, it may make an opening statement that is subject to the same limits, and serves the same purpose, as the Crown's opening statement. The defence's opening statement normally takes place at the close of the Crown's case, although some courts allow the defence to make a statement after the Crown's opening statement if it so chooses. The presentation of defence evidence follows the same basic format as the Crown's evidence, with defence counsel examining its witnesses in chief, and the Crown cross-examining them. Re-examination by defence counsel takes place, where appropriate.

At the close of the defence's case, the Crown may be allowed to present reply evidence, although there are restrictions on the kind of evidence that can be called at this stage of the trial. Reply evidence should be allowed solely where the defence evidence raises relevant matters that could not reasonably have been anticipated by the Crown,[43] or where something occurring during the defence case makes otherwise inadmissible Crown evidence admissible. For example, if the accused puts her character into issue by claiming during her testimony that she is not the type to commit the offence, the Crown will be allowed to call certain kinds of evidence to rebut this assertion.

Where the defence has called evidence, it must make its closing submissions first. Where the defence does not call evidence, it makes its submissions last. There is no jurisdiction in a court to vary this order, which is provided for by subsection 651(3) of the *Criminal Code*. In a jury trial, if the Crown makes its submission last and does so in a manner that causes unfairness to the accused, the trial judge has a duty to remedy this with appropriate instructions to the jury. Some judges of the Supreme Court of Canada are of the view that, in extreme cases, the trial judge can even give the defence a limited right of reply.[44]

---

40   R. v. *Candir*, [2009] O.J. No. 5485 at para. 148 (C.A.).
41   R. v. *Moore* (1984), 15 C.C.C. (3d) 541 at 568 (Ont. C.A.).
42   See the discussion in chapter 12, section 3.5, "The *Prima Facie* Case Standard."
43   R. v. *Anderson*, [2009] A.J. No. 176 at paras. 37–43 (C.A.); R. v. *Pasqua*, [2009] A.J. No. 702 at paras. 11–27 (C.A.).
44   R. v. *Rose* (1998), 129 C.C.C. (3d) 449 (S.C.C.).

After the submissions have been completed, it then falls to the judge in a jury trial to direct the jury as to the pertinent points of substantive and procedural law, including the operation of the burden and standards of proof and the restricted uses that can be made of admissible evidence. The judge will summarize the major items of evidence for the jury, although it is jury members' recollection of the evidence and not the judge's that is to govern. The judge will provide counsel with an opportunity, in the absence of the jury, to comment on the propriety and sufficiency of the direction. This is an area where counsel should be well prepared. A failure to object to a misdirection or a nondirection can prevent a successful appeal in some cases, despite errors by the judge.[45] After receiving the comments of counsel, the judge may recall the jury and redirect them in light of any legitimate objections that have been raised.

The case is then given to the jury for deliberation. If it can reach a unanimous decision, it will return with a "general verdict," where no reasons for decision are provided. The verdict is supposed to be based on findings of fact arrived at according to admissible evidence after applying the appropriate standards and burdens of proof. This finding of fact is then applied to the relevant rules of substantive law as outlined in the judge's direction.

In a non-jury trial, the judge simply renders a decision or adjourns the matter for decision. Unlike a jury, the judge will give reasons for the decision, sometimes in writing. Those reasons may be brief, so long as they are sufficient to enable an appeal court to understand the basis for the decision, and demonstrate that the judge has not misapprehended or misunderstood the evidence.[46]

45　See section 6.2(b), below in this chapter, "Where the Party Appealing Did Not Object."

46　*R. v. Sheppard*, [2002] S.C.C. 26; *R. v. Braich*, 2002 SCC 27; *R. v. Walker*, [2008] 2 S.C.R. 245; *R. v. M.(R.E.)*, [2008] 3 S.C.R. 3. *R. v. Wadforth*, [2009] O.J. No. 4176 (C.A.) is a good illustration of the duty applying to credibility findings. The duty to provide reasons can apply not only to the ultimate decision but to evidentiary rulings taken during *voir dires*. That duty will not arise if the evidentiary ruling is supportable on the evidence or its basis is apparent, unless the evidentiary issue is so crucial or pivotal or decisive that the failure to provide reasons undermines procedural fairness: *R. v. Woodward* (2009), 67 C.R. (6th) 152 (Man. C.A.). An example of where such duty arose was *R. v. Chappell* (2003), 15 C.R. (6th) 350 (Ont. C.A.) relating to a key hearsay statement admitted under the principled hearsay exception.

6. ENFORCING THE LAW OF EVIDENCE

6.1) Enforcement at the Hearing

Enforcement of the rules of evidence begins with the party who wishes to present the evidence. Given the risks that judges or juries can become tainted by hearing inadmissible evidence, it is unethical for lawyers to blurt inadmissible information out before juries, or to present evidence to judges where there is no air of reality to its admissibility. Where the propriety of a question or the admissibility of evidence is contentious, counsel should alert opposing counsel and the judge so that admissibility can be properly determined.[47]

Judges and administrative adjudicators have the authority to enforce the laws of evidence even when the party entitled to rely on them does not ask that they be enforced. Judges may therefore do such things as stop leading questioning, or direct witnesses not to offer hearsay evidence, or enforce other rules of proof, even in the absence of objection. Yet judges and administrative adjudicators will not always enforce the rules of evidence where there has been no objection. This is because hearings in which the laws of evidence apply are adversarial, and adversarial proceedings permit tactical choices to be made by the parties. If tactically a party does not want the benefit of a rule of evidence, the adjudicator may respect that decision. For example, a party who can demonstrate inadmissible testimony to be false may choose to sit back and let the opposing witness offer it so that the credibility of the witness can be demonstrated.[48]

Since adjudicators may not enforce the rules of evidence on their own motion it is important for lawyers wishing to enjoy the benefits of the rules of evidence to "object." Objection will force the judge or adjudicator to rule. Objections can be taken to the improper form of questions, to the admission of inadmissible evidence, to improper submissions of opposing counsel, or, in a jury trial, to errors in the judge's charge to the jury.

An objection is made by standing, waiting to be recognized by the court, and concisely stating the objection and arguing why the rule is being breached.[49] In a jury trial, unless the objection is merely to the

---

47   See Canadian Bar Association, *Code of Professional Conduct*, Appendix — Principles of Civility for Advocates, rules 48 and 54.

48   See, for example, *R. v. Bomberry* (2010), 78 C.R. (6th) 191 at para. 29 (Ont. C.A.).

49   See Canadian Bar Association, *Code of Professional Conduct*, Appendix — Principles of Civility for Advocates, rules 50, 51, and 55.

form of a question, the jury will be asked to leave the courtroom before argument is made and the party who is making the objection should be careful not to alert the jury to the content of the contentious evidence.

Unfortunately objections are an imperfect way of enforcing the rules of evidence. Frequently by the time the objection is made the inadmissible information is out or the improper comment has been made. If a jury becomes exposed to inadmissible information in this way, the judge should give a prompt and clear instruction to ignore that evidence entirely.[50] In a judge alone trial even timely and effective objection may not prevent the judge from hearing inadmissible evidence for it may be necessary to hear it before resolving its inadmissibility. The judge, of course, is required to disregard such evidence.

6.2) Enforcement on Appeal

6.2 (a) Where the Party Appealing Did Object

If a party has objected and a judge or adjudicator makes an incorrect decision in applying the evidentiary rule, a legal error will have occurred. Where there is an appeal process available for legal errors, as there is in criminal cases and in civil litigation before courts, an appeal will succeed unless the appeals court decides the error was harmless. In criminal cases the "proviso" or "curative provision" in section 686 of the *Criminal Code* can be invoked to reject an otherwise meritorious appeal where "the verdict would necessarily have been the same if such error had not occurred,"[51] in other words, where there can be no reasonable possibility that the verdict would have been different.[52] This can occur where the error is minor or otherwise could have had no effect on the verdict.[53]

Although the rules vary from province to province, the same holds true in civil cases. An appeal will not succeed from an error that could have made no difference to the outcome. In Ontario, for example, the *Courts of Justice Act* prevents an appeal court from directing a new trial "unless some substantial wrong or miscarriage of justice occurred."[54]

6.2 (b) Where the Party Appealing Did Not Object

The failure to object cannot make inadmissible evidence admissible; nor does the failure to object relieve the judge of the obligation of get-

---

50   *R. v. Siu* (1998), 124 C.C.C. (3d) 301 at 327 (B.C.C.A.); *R. v. Colas* (2001), 161 C.C.C. (3d) 335 at para. 30 (Ont. C.A.).

51   *R. v. Bevan*, [1993] 2 S.C.R. 599 at 616.

52   *R. v. Hunter* (2003), 181 C.C.C. (3d) 26 (Alta. C.A.).

53   *R. v. Arradi*, [2003] 1 S.C.R. 280 at para. 42.

54   Above note 36, s. 134(6).

ting evidentiary rules right.[55] Similarly, "counsel's position cannot justify treating an instruction that is wrong in law as a correct statement of the law."[56] For this reason a failure to object to an outright evidentiary error will not ordinarily be fatal, particularly not where the error is a material one that raises issues of fairness or presents a risk of a miscarriage of justice.[57]

Still, in some cases an appeal from an evidentiary error will fail because the appealing party failed to object in a timely fashion. The law does not offer a definitive formula for determining when this will happen. There are two clear trends in the case law as to when this might occur.

The first is predicated on what might be termed "estoppel" reasoning, in which the actions of the litigant make it unreasonable to appeal the error. For example, unless the error is significant, an appeal is unlikely to succeed if the appeal court concludes that the failure to object was a tactical[58] or conscious decision;[59] or if the appellant used the same evidentiary practices that he is now complaining about his opponent having used;[60] or if he sought to use the inadmissible evidence to his advantage;[61] or if the failure to object prevented the court from canvassing the issue fully to see whether the complaint would have had merit.[62]

The second basis for holding a failure to object to be fatal to an appeal rests on "immateriality" reasoning. If the error is minor and a party does not object, or if the party rests content to challenge the credibility

---

55 *R. v. D.(L.E.)*, [1989] 2 S.C.R. 111 at para. 26; *R. v. Wilks* (2005), 201 C.C.C. (3d) 11 at para. 48 (Man. C.A.).

56 *R. v. Austin* (2006), 214 C.C.C. (3d) 38 at para. 15 (Ont. C.A.). In contrast, the *Austin* court explained at para. 14 that where the complaint is that a jury direction was unclear or inadequate or unbalanced or otherwise unfair, rather than erroneous, the failure to object at the time will be a "significant consideration" on appeal.

57 *R. v. B.(G.D.)* (2000), 143 C.C.C. (3d) 289 at 299 (S.C.C.); *R. v. C.(J.D.)* (2003), 11 C.R. (6th) 192 (Ont. C.A.); *R. v. Jumuga* (1976), 29 C.C.C. (2d) 269 (S.C.C.).

58 *R. v. Johnson* (2002), 166 C.C.C. (3d) 44 (Ont. C.A.); *R. v. Austin* (2006), 214 C.C.C. (3d) 38 at para. 14 (Ont. C.A.); *R. v. Cuming* (2001), 158 C.C.C. (3d) 433 at para. 38 (Ont. C.A.).

59 *R. v. Edwards* (2004), 72 O.R. (3d) 135 at 149 (C.A.). In *Edwards*, the accused contributed to the erroneous charge by agreeing to it in a "pre-charge" conference with the judge. By contrast, if the judge causes the failure to object by discouraging objections, the failure to object will not undermine an appeal: *R. v. Ejiofor* (2002), 5 C.R. (6th) 197 (Ont. C.A.).

60 *R. v. Paul* (2002), 7 C.R. (6th) 30 (Ont. C.A.).

61 *R. v. B.(F.F.)*, [1993] 1 S.C.R. 697 at paras. 32–33; *R. v. Reid* (2003), 18 C.R. (6th) 350 (Ont. C.A.).

62 *R. v. Bero* (2000), 151 C.C.C. (3d) 545 (Ont. C.A.).

or reliability of the evidence[63] "it can . . . be assumed that he did not think [the error] was important."[64]

It is evident that a party identifying an evidentiary error should object not only to ensure the proper application of the rules of evidence, but to secure an effective right to appeal.

---

63   R. v. Trochym (2004), 186 C.C.C. (3d) 417 (Ont. C.A.).
64   R. v. Dupras (2003), 173 C.C.C. (3d) 55 (B.C.C.A.), and see R. v. Gravino, [1995] O.J. No. 3109 (C.A.), where the failure to object was taken as confirmation that careful scrutiny was in fact being given by the trial judge to dangerous evidence.

CHAPTER 2

THE BASICS OF ADMISSIBILITY AND THE EVALUATION OF EVIDENCE

1. THE BASIC RULE OF ADMISSIBILITY

Information can be admitted as evidence only where it is relevant to a material issue in the case.

There is a "basic rule" that all evidence must satisfy in order to gain admission. This rule requires that all evidence must be relevant to a material issue in the case. Even if evidence meets this "basic rule," it may not ultimately be admitted. Evidence that is relevant to a material issue may still be caught by an exclusionary rule, of which there are many, or it may be rejected through the operation of an exclusionary discretion. Relevance and materiality are therefore necessary but not sufficient conditions for admissibility. Whether evidence satisfies the basic preliminary condition for admissibility of relevance and materiality is a matter to be decided by the trial judge as an issue of law.

Often lawyers fail to distinguish between the separate concepts of relevance and materiality, referring to "immaterial" evidence as being "irrelevant."[1] In *R. v. Truscott* the Ontario Court of Appeal subsumed materiality in its definition of relevance, noting that "[e]vidence will be irrelevant either if it does not make the fact to which it is directed more or less likely, or if the fact to which the evidence is directed is not material

---

1   See, for example, *R. v. Arp* (1998), 129 C.C.C. (3d) 321 at 338 (S.C.C.).

to the proceedings."[2] The first concept described by the Court—whether the evidence makes a fact it is directed to more or less likely—describes the concept referred to in this text as "relevance." The second concept described by the Court—whether the evidence is directed to a material issue in the proceedings—is referred to in this text as "materiality." While it is by no means wrong to use the term "relevance" to capture both concepts, it is useful analytically to distinguish between them.[3]

2. MATERIALITY

Evidence that is not directed at a matter in issue in the case is "immaterial." To identify immaterial evidence, ask, "What is my opponent trying to prove?" and then decide whether the thing sought to be proved is a matter in issue.

2.1) The Concept Explained

Regardless of the kind of proceeding, courts or tribunals resolving issues of fact are being asked to settle particular controversies. They are not interested in information about matters other than those that need to be settled. Evidence that is not directed at a matter in issue is inadmissible because it is "immaterial." By contrast, "[evidence] is material if it is directed at a matter in issue in the case."[4]

2.2) Primary Materiality

Evidence is material if it relates to a primary issue that arises for decision. For example, if the accused is charged only with robbery, proof that the police found child pornography when executing a search warrant at his residence is immaterial. A court will, however, be interested in evidence about whether the accused threatened the victim with bodily harm when taking the money since the substantive law of robbery includes as one of its elements proof that the accused used violence or the threat of violence. If the accused person asks for evidence to be excluded because of an unconstitutional search, the court will become

---

2   *R. v. Truscott* (2006), 213 C.C.C. (3d) 183 at para. 22 (Ont. C.A.).
3   See *R. v. Collins* (2001), 160 C.C.C. (3d) 85 at paras. 18–19 (Ont. C.A.), for a description of materiality and relevance, and a general summary of the role these notions play in determining admissibility.
4   *R. v. B.(L.)* (1997), 9 C.R. (5th) 38 at 48 (Ont. C.A.).

interested in proof about how the search was conducted. As these examples show, the primary issues that a tribunal has to determine are defined by the pleadings in the case, the substantive laws that pleaded allegations or claims turn on, and those procedural rules that arise during the case that require facts to be determined. Since these are the things the court or tribunal has to resolve to adjudicate the matter before it, evidence about these issues is primarily material and the law of evidence will be receptive to its admission.

2.3) Secondary Materiality

A trier of fact cannot resolve primarily material questions of fact without first deciding whether the information it is receiving is accurate. It must therefore assess or judge the quality of the material evidence. Often other evidence can assist the trier of fact in undertaking this assessment. Assume, for example, that the trier of fact is to resolve the material issue of whether the Crown has proved beyond a reasonable doubt that the accused is the perpetrator of the offence. In making this decision it would be useful for the trier of fact to learn that the key identification witness has been bribed, or was not wearing her glasses at the time, or uses the expression "tall" to describe anyone over five feet, six inches. Even though this information is not directly about the primarily material issue that the trier of fact is there to resolve, it is clearly useful. It is indirectly or secondarily material in that it assists the trier of fact in resolving the primarily material issue. The term "secondary materiality" can therefore be used to describe evidence that is about other evidence in the case.

Although courts do not formally distinguish between primary and secondary materiality, it is helpful to draw the distinction. Whereas the law of evidence is receptive to primarily material evidence, there are strict limits on the admission of secondarily material evidence. These limits are imposed chiefly because of legitimate concern about undue consumption of time and about unnecessarily complicating matters.[5] This is not to say that secondarily material information is unimportant. Most cases turn on whether primarily material evidence is trustworthy. As will be seen, the law of evidence prefers to rely on cross-examination as its main tool for producing secondarily material information, rather than inviting other forms of secondarily material evidence.

---

5   See the discussion in chapter 6, section 3.3, "The Rule against Oath-helping"; chapter 10, section 6.2, "Cross-examination on Credibility"; section 6.5, "The Collateral Facts Rule"; section 6.6, "Cross-examination on Prior Convictions"; section 6.7, "Prior Inconsistent Statements"; and chapter 11, "Secondary Materiality and Your Own Witness."

2.4)   The Reception of Immaterial Evidence

In practice, some evidence that is, strictly speaking, immaterial is admitted. This occurs because it is not always easy to identify in advance what the proposed use of evidence is. Or parties may not object because the immaterial evidence does not matter. Occasionally, however, immaterial information can influence the trier of fact. Consider the child pornography example used above. This evidence could cause an emotional reaction against the accused and prejudice him in the eyes of the trier of fact even though it has no legal bearing on the material issues. Where immaterial evidence will take significant time to develop, or where it might influence the outcome of the case, it should be objected to.

3. RELEVANCE

3.1)   The Concept Explained

Evidence is relevant where it has some tendency as a matter of logic and human experience to make the proposition for which it is advanced more likely than that proposition would appear to be in the absence of that evidence. To identify logically irrelevant evidence, ask, "Does the evidence assist in proving the fact that my opponent is trying to prove?"

While the concept of materiality describes the relationship between evidence and the matters in issue, logical "relevance" is about the relationship between evidence and the fact it is offered to prove. There is no legal test for identifying relevant evidence. Relevance is a matter of logic. To identify logically irrelevant evidence, ask, "Does the evidence assist in proving the fact that my opponent is trying to prove?" For example, evidence that the alleged robber had downloaded a map of the area where the bank that was robbed was located would be relevant in linking the accused to the robbery. Evidence that he had downloaded movies about bank robbers would not.

3.2)   Direct Evidence, Circumstantial Evidence, and Relevance

"Direct evidence is evidence which, if believed, resolves a matter in issue."[6] For example, on the issue of whether the man with the teardrop tattoos

---

6   *R. v. Cinous*, 2002 SCC 29 at para. 88.

had a gun, testimony of a witness saying, "I saw the man with the tear-drop tattoos holding a gun" is direct evidence. Direct evidence establishes a material fact without the need for any inferences to be drawn.

Circumstantial evidence "is evidence that tends to prove a factual matter by proving other events or circumstances from which [either alone or in combination with other evidence] the occurrence of the matter in issue can be reasonably inferred."[7] Unlike direct evidence, circumstantial evidence requires inferences to be drawn before it is of use in resolving material issues. Testimony that, "like the accused, the robber had a tattoo of a stream of tears on his right cheek," is circumstantial evidence that the accused is the robber. To find this evidence useful, the trier of fact must infer that, because such tattoos are rare, the accused and the robber may well be one and the same person. Combined with the other evidence, the coincidental, unusual tattoos may be enough to prove the identity of the accused as the robber beyond a reasonable doubt.

It can be readily seen that the concept of relevance is important only for circumstantial evidence. Information that is direct evidence of a material issue does not require a bridging inference before it is useful; therefore, no inquiry into a logical nexus between the evidence and the fact sought to be proved is required.

3.3)   The Standard of Logical Relevance

Evidence is relevant where it has some tendency as a matter of logic and human experience to make the proposition for which it is advanced more likely than that proposition would be in the absence of that evidence.[8] As the Supreme Court of Canada has said:

> To be logically relevant, an item of evidence does not have to firmly establish, on any standard, the truth or falsity of a fact in issue. The evidence must simply tend to "increase or diminish the probability of the existence of a fact in issue." . . . As a consequence, there is no minimum probative value required for evidence to be relevant.[9]

For example, imagine that the evidence offered is that, like the accused, the robber had brown eyes. "While such evidence may have little . . . probative value, given the prevalence of brown-eyed people in the relevant

---

7   *Ibid.* at para. 89.
8   Definition approved in *R. v. J.(J.-L.)*, [2000] 2 S.C.R. 600 at para. 47, and *R. v. B.(L.)*, above note 4 at 47–48. See the American *Federal Rules of Evidence*, Rule 401, and the decision of La Forest J. in *R. v. Corbett*, [1988] 1 S.C.R. 670.
9   *R. v. Arp*, above note 1 at 338.

population, nonetheless, it is still relevant to identity" since it is a point of consistency between the accused and the robber.[10] It is important to appreciate that "[t]he threshold of relevance is not high."[11] Relevance need not establish a material fact on its own. It is enough to pass the relevance threshold to admissibility that the evidence has a logical tendency to contribute to a finding about that material fact.

3.4) Logical Relevance and Context

"Relevance is contextual in that it depends on the facts in issue, the position taken by the parties in respect of those facts, and the other evidence adduced in relation to those facts."[12] For example, in *Monteleone v. R.*,[13] the Crown wanted to prove that the accused, charged with arson, told police that he had placed a hot vacuum cleaner in the basement of his premises near some boxes. This evidence alone does not have any tendency to prove that he caused the fire intentionally, since it suggests that the fire was accidental. Other evidence, however, proved that the vacuum cleaner had not overheated. Together, these two items of evidence gave rise to the inference that the accused fabricated an innocent account of how the fire started, perhaps to conceal the fact that the fire had been started intentionally. Relevance may become apparent only when other evidence is adduced, and even then it may depend on a chain of inferences.

Similarly, apparently relevant evidence may prove to be irrelevant when taken in context. In *R. v. Ferris*[14] the accused, charged with murder, was overheard to say "I killed David." David was the victim. In isolation, this statement appears to be fine evidence for the Crown. In fact, a police officer heard the accused say something inaudible, then "I killed David," and then something else inaudible. He may have said, "They think I killed David but I did not." In context, the utterance was simply irrelevant as it could assist in establishing nothing. It follows that if the desired inference is "speculative or unreasonable" or too equivocal the evidence is irrelevant.[15] In *R. v. Arcangioli*[16] the accused and a number of men attacked the victim, who was stabbed. Arcangioli, who was charged with aggravated assault by stabbing, admitted to punching the

---

10   *R. v. Powell* (2006), 215 C.C.C. (3d) 274 at para. 22 (Ont. S.C.J.).
11   *R. v. Candir*, [2009] O.J. No. 5485 at para. 48 (C.A.).
12   *R. v. Truscott*, above note 2 at para. 23.
13   (1987), 59 C.R. (3d) 97 (S.C.C.).
14   (1994), 34 C.R. (4th) 26 (S.C.C.).
15   *R. v. White*, [2011] S.C.J. No. 13 at para. 167.
16   (1994), 27 C.R. (4th) 1 (S.C.C.).

victim but denied stabbing him. The Crown wished to rely on evidence that Arcangioli ran from the scene to prove he was the stabber. There are cases where flight from the scene of a crime can support the inference that the accused was attempting to escape after committing the crime charged, but here Arcangioli's flight was irrelevant in showing what he did. Arcangioli may have fled because he had committed an assault on the victim by punching him. A trier of fact could only act arbitrarily if it chose to believe that he fled because he had stabbed the victim; hence, the evidence was irrelevant on the issue for which it was offered.

Relevance concepts also apply to lines of reasoning. For example, for the same reason the flight evidence is generally impermissible, it is ordinarily inappropriate for judges to rely on the motivation of accused persons to gain acquittal as a reason to disbelieve their evidence. The motive to gain acquittal is shared equally by the guilty and innocent. There are cases, however, where the potential motive of the accused to lie to secure an acquittal can become relevant. In *R. v. Laboucan* the accused defended himself by pointing to the motivation of Crown witnesses to lie to avoid their own guilt, and he was being tried with a co-accused person who wanted to defend himself by showing why Laboucan should not be believed.[17]

3.5) The Controversy about Logic and Human Experience

Not everyone sees the world the same way. In *R. v. White* the Supreme Court of Canada split badly because of this. Some judges found that the failure of the accused to hesitate before running away after his illegal handgun discharged was logically more consistent with an intentional shooting than the accidental shooting the accused claimed. Other judges found this inference to be entirely speculative. "It seems to me every bit as plausible to conclude," said Justice Binnie, "that a person in possession of an illegal handgun that just shot a stranger—accidentally or otherwise—would run away as fast and as far as he could without any hesitation."[18]

Not only can our perceptions of the logical relationship between facts be affected by our own understandings of the world on mundane

17   [2010] S.C.J. No. 12. This kind of evidence also implicates the presumption of innocence. Reliance on the motivation of the accused to lie, even where relevant, is permissible solely where it does not undermine the presumption of innocence in all of the circumstances. In other words, the inference must address real issues in the case and not be taken simply because of the assumption that accused persons have a motive to lie because they are guilty.

18   *R. v. White*, above note 15 at para. 181.

matters, but there are some who claim that our ability to perceive objective or absolute truth in areas of controversy is hopelessly tainted by our biases and perspectives. During the 1990s when traditional assumptions relating to sexual assault were being challenged, for example, positions about relevance polarized, particularly in debates about the relevance of the psychiatric history of a complainant or their prior sexual experiences.

Divorced from the inflamed emotion of sexual offence litigation, however, there are numerous sage passages that suggest that triers of fact should be given access to information they may find utility in, even if others would disagree. After all, triers of fact are to render decisions according to their oaths and their consciences, and they should have all the information they consider of importance available to them. If an inference is not "speculative or unreasonable" the relevance standard will be met even if a judge would not personally rely on the evidence if she was the trier of fact. As La Forest J. said in R. v. Corbett:

> . . . at the stage of the threshold inquiry into relevancy, basic principles of the law of evidence embody an inclusionary policy . . . .
>
> In the absence of cogent evidence establishing that evidence . . . is irrelevant . . . the fact that reasonable people may disagree about its relevance merely attests to the fact that unanimity in matters of common sense and human experience is unattainable.[19]

Judges may, however, exclude evidence as irrelevant after relying on "the accumulated knowledge from courts and studies to the effect that certain types of evidence can appear probative when they are not."[20] There are cases where inferences have been resolutely rejected as resting unreasonably on inappropriate stereotypes. For example, in R. v. Seaboyer[21] the Court rejected as impermissible "twin myths" the beliefs that the past consensual sexual experiences of a complainant are relevant (1) to her credibility because they show her to be of discreditable character, or (2) to her readiness to consent to sex because she has shown herself to be the type to consent. For the overwhelming majority of issues of fact arguments about myth are unlikely to arise and an indulgent approach will be taken in determining relevance.

---

19   Above note 8 at 720.
20   R. v. White, above note 15 at para. 44.
21   (1991), 7 C.R. (4th) 117 (S.C.C.).

4. EVALUATING OR WEIGHING THE PROBATIVE VALUE OF EVIDENCE

It is important not to confuse the "relevance" and "weight" of evidence. While relevance describes the tendency of evidence to support logical inferences, the concept of "weight" relates to how "probative" or influential the evidence is. As the foregoing discussion demonstrates, the basic rule of admissibility requires relevance and materiality, but not weight. "Once evidence is found to be relevant [to a material issue] it is generally admissible and the [trier of fact] is left to decide how much weight to give a particular item of evidence."[22]

Even though the law of evidence has relatively few "rules of reasoning" to assist decision-makers in weighing evidence, it is worthwhile examining the concept of weight closely and in a structured way. Thinking about weight this way will assist in preparing cross-examination, in making arguments, and in the judicial evaluation of evidence that is admitted. As will be seen shortly, this exercise is also useful in understanding the exclusionary discretion, about to be discussed, as well as several exclusionary rules of evidence described later in this chapter. This examination is not complex as the weight of evidence is simply a function of how believable and how informative the trier of fact considers it to be.

4.1) How Believable Is the Evidence?

Assume a witness testifies that the robber with the gun was the person with a face tattoo of a stream of tears. If the trier of fact is concerned that the witness may be lying, or may be mistaken about this, the evidence may be given little if any weight. Believability affects weight.

When deciding whether evidence is believable, legal theory draws a helpful distinction between "credibility" and "reliability."[23] "Credibility" is about the honesty of the witness. Evidence showing that a witness has been corrupted, has a motive to mislead, or has a discreditable character will be relevant to credibility. For example, evidence that the witness identifying the robber was an accomplice who has made a deal with the police could cause a trier of fact to give the testimony little weight.

---

22   R. v. White, above note 15 at para. 54.
23   See, for example, R. v. Norman (1993), 26 C.R. (4th) 256 at 274 (Ont. C.A.); S.D. v. Criminal Injuries Compensation Board (2010), 262 O.A.C. 216 at para. 13 (Div. Ct.).

"Reliability" is the term used to describe the accuracy of evidence. It can relate to the accuracy of a scientific or forensic process, but when applied to witnesses, reliability captures the kinds of things that can cause even an honest witness to provide inaccurate information. The reliability of witness testimony can be affected, for example, by (1) inaccurate observations, (2) memory problems, or (3) a failure by the witness to communicate observations accurately. Our witness may, for example, have been too far from the scene to conclude dependably that it was the tattooed man who held the gun, or he may not recall sufficient details of the event to instill confidence that he is right about this. Although credible, his evidence will be given little weight because it is unreliable.

4.2) How Informative Is the Evidence?

The ability of particular evidence to inform depends upon (1) how live the issue it addresses is, and (2) how cogent the evidence is in proving the thing it is offered to prove. Assuming the fact it describes is a live issue, "direct evidence" is completely informative since it directly asserts the very thing that is of interest. On the live issue of which robber held the gun, direct evidence that "I saw the man with the teardrop tattoos holding a gun" is definitive if the witness is believed. The only thing affecting the weight of material direct evidence is therefore its believability.

For circumstantial evidence the strength of the logical inference yielded by the evidence is critical in determining weight. For example, evidence of a fingerprint found at the scene is better circumstantial evidence that the accused was there than proof that a common type of fibre consistent with the carpets in the home of the accused was found at the scene. The inference from fingerprint to presence is stronger than the inference from common fibre to presence. Hence, a trier of fact will give more "weight" to the fingerprint evidence.

Together the believability and informativeness of evidence are often referred to as "probative value." The trier of fact is free to decide how believable or important evidence is, so long as their findings are not wholly unreasonable. There is therefore no presumption that witnesses tell the truth.[24] It is up to the trier of fact to decide whether that is so.

4.3) The "Legal Relevance" Concept

There are scholars and judges who take a different view of relevance than the one described here. As explained by Justice Doherty, those

---

24 R. v. Thain (2009), 243 C.C.C. (3d) 230 at para. 32 (Ont. C.A.).

who ascribe to the "legal relevance" view believe that the relevance concept is not just about whether there is a logical connection between the evidence and a fact in issue; it includes an evaluation of whether the evidence is "sufficiently probative to justify its admission despite the prejudice [or costs] that might flow from its admission."[25] Exceptionally, this is the meaning that "relevance" is given when it is considered under the "*Mohan* test" dealing with the admissibility of expert opinion evidence.[26] In *R. v. White* at one point Justice Binnie appeared to endorse a halfway proposition about relevance. He said that it was not enough in that case "simply to evaluate whether evidence . . . might be portrayed as relevant to the issue of murderous intent merely 'as a matter of logic and human experience.' Rather . . . relevance depends on the evidence having probative value in relation to a live issue."[27] The better view and the more conventional view is that, apart from the *Mohan* test where relevance inquiry does engage probative value as well as "prejudice" evaluations, "the . . . cogency of the inferences that may be drawn from the item of evidence have no place in the inquiry into relevance."[28] It is cleaner and more in keeping with the principle of access to evidence to treat logically relevant evidence about material issues as admissible, subject to the rules of exclusion and the exclusionary discretion.

5. THE EXCLUSIONARY DISCRETION

5.1) The Nature of the Discretion

Apart altogether from fixed rules of exclusion, judges have the discretion to exclude relevant and material evidence where its probative value is outweighed by its "prejudice." In considering the exclusionary discretion, a judge must determine the value of the evidence, based on both its believability and the strength of the inferences it leads to, against the costs presented by such evidence, including things as diverse as the practicalities of its presentation, the fairness to the parties and to witnesses, and the potentially distorting effect the evidence can have on the outcome of the case. Because of full answer and defence considerations, defence evidence

---

25   *R. v. Abbey* (2009), 246 C.C.C. (3d) 301 at para. 82 (Ont. C.A.). See *Cowles v. Balac* (2006), 83 O.R. (3d) 660 at 713 (C.A.).
26   See chapter 6, section 4.3, "Precondition 2 — Relevance."
27   *R. v. White*, above note 15 at para. 180.
28   *R. v. Candir*, above note 11 at para. 48.

should be excluded solely where the risks of prejudice substantially outweigh its probative value.

Even in the absence of an exclusionary rule requiring its rejection, logically relevant evidence may be excluded through the exercise of judicial discretion. The extent to which the Supreme Court of Canada has endorsed the existence of this discretion has varied over time. For most of the past century judges were considered to have little or no discretion to exclude technically admissible evidence.[29] This was because the "rule of law" and common law theory are intrinsically wary of discretion. Discretion imports choice, and it is better that persons be ruled by law and not by the choices of other people. Moreover, discretion can confuse the roles of the trier of law and the trier of fact.

In spite of these concerns, for the reasons described above,[30] we are currently in an era of strong discretion in which the judge is often given a vital role to play in evaluating evidence as a prelude to admissibility. The law has now come to recognize two, sometimes overlapping, kinds of exclusionary discretion.

One gives judges the discretion in criminal cases "to exclude evidence obtained in circumstances such that it would result in unfairness if the evidence was to be admitted at trial."[31] This discretion gained its feet in Canada through the influence of the *Charter* and is now said to be grounded both in the constitution and the common law. Since this discretion is most likely to be invoked where evidence has been unfairly or illegally obtained,[32] it is discussed in this book along with the exclusionary remedy.[33]

The other form of discretion, more intimately linked to questions of relevance, permits judges to exclude otherwise technically admissible evidence in criminal, civil,[34] and administrative law cases,[35] where the benefits of its admission cannot justify the negative effects its admission will cause. In *R. v. Mohan*, Sopinka J. spoke of a "cost-benefit analysis" — "that is 'whether its value is worth what it costs,'"[36] with the

---

29   See *R. v. Wray*, [1971] S.C.R. 272.
30   See chapter 1, section 3.2, "The Development of a General Exclusionary Discretion."
31   *R. v. Buhay*, [2003] 1 S.C.R. 631 at para. 40.
32   See *R. v. Hape* (2007), 220 C.C.C. (3d) 161 at paras. 108–10 (S.C.C.).
33   See the discussion in chapter 9, section 8, "Excluding Unfairly Obtained Evidence in the Absence of a *Charter* Violation."
34   *Gray v. Insurance Corp. of B.C.* (2010), 326 D.L.R. (4th) 564 at para. 1 (B.C.C.A.).
35   *Lavallee v. Alberta (Securities Commission)* (2010), 317 D.L.R. (4th) 373 at paras. 9 and 16 (Alta. C.A.).
36   (1991), 29 C.R. (4th) 243 at 252 (S.C.C.).

"costs" concept describing the vast array of negative implications admission can cause. In the language of the cases, evidence can be excluded as a matter of discretion where its prejudice (or costs) outweighs its probative value, even where that evidence otherwise complies with the rules of admissibility.[37]

Judges even retain the discretion to exclude evidence that satisfies the technical requirements of statutory rules of admissibility, such as section 715[38] (providing for the admission of prior testimony) and section 715.1 of the *Criminal Code*[39] (providing for the admission of videotaped statements by children about sexual offences), and section 12 of the *Canada Evidence Act*[40] (providing for the convictions of a witness to be proved).

At common law, there had been no recognized discretion to exclude technically admissible *defence* evidence.[41] In *R. v. Seaboyer*, the Supreme Court of Canada changed the law by recognizing that such discretion exists, but emphasized that it is to be applied in an extremely guarded fashion. The Court noted that defence evidence should not be excluded simply because its probative value is outweighed by the prejudice it could cause. It can be excluded solely where its probative value is *substantially* outweighed by the prejudice it could cause.[42] The more imposing standard for excluding defence evidence is related to the long-standing belief that it is better to produce an inaccurate acquittal than a wrongful conviction. This requires that the accused be given the benefit of every doubt, including in the application of rules of proof. As Justice Rosenberg explained in *R. v. Clarke*, the protection of the innocent and the right to present full answer and defence depend on the ability to call evidence.[43]

While there is discretion to exclude otherwise admissible evidence, the law of evidence furnishes no "inclusionary" discretion. In other words, if evidence does not satisfy the rules of admissibility, a judge is

---

37   A slightly different formula for exclusion is used for defence evidence in criminal cases, as described later in this chapter.

38   *Criminal Code*, R.S.C. 1985, c. C-46; *R. v. Potvin* (1989), 68 C.R. (3d) 193 (S.C.C.).

39   *R. v. L.(D.O.)* (1993), 25 C.R. (4th) 285 (S.C.C.).

40   R.S.C. 1985, c. C-5; *R. v. Corbett*, above note 8.

41   See *R. v. Sang*, [1979] 2 All E.R. 1222 (H.L.); *R. v. Hawke* (1975), 22 C.C.C. (2d) 19 at 54–55 (Ont. C.A.).

42   Above note 21 at 137–40.

43   (1998), 18 C.R. (5th) 219 at 231 (Ont. C.A.). For a time the notion that the discretion to exclude defence evidence arises only where its probative value is *substantially* outweighed by the prejudice it may cause was under serious attack. In *R. v. Shearing* (2002), 165 C.C.C. (3d) 225 at paras. 103–9 (S.C.C.), however, the Supreme Court of Canada strongly reaffirmed the *Seaboyer* approach for determining questions of the admissibility of defence evidence.

not empowered to receive it. Having said this, the exclusionary rules
are, in some cases, applied more leniently in order to allow the admission of important defence evidence. Martin J.A. recognized in *R.
v. Williams* that "a court has a residual discretion to relax in favour of
the accused a strict rule of evidence where it is necessary to prevent a
miscarriage of justice and where the danger against which an exclusionary rule aims to safeguard does not exist."[44] To be clear, this is not
to say that the rules of proof do not apply to accused persons. They do.
It is just that there will be cases where we can reduce the risk that we
will convict innocent people by applying the rules of evidence loosely
rather than strictly.

In *R. v. Felderhof*[45] Justice Rosenberg raised the interesting possibility that while the law of evidence does not allow technically inadmissible evidence to be received, the *Charter* might. He suggested
that inadmissible defence evidence could perhaps be admitted by way
of *Charter* remedy, if doing so would remedy state action that made a
trial unfair. A possible example might be if state action were to deprive
the accused of the testimony of a defence witness. A court in such circumstances might be prepared to accept hearsay evidence as a substitute, even where that hearsay evidence would not otherwise have been
admissible. In appropriate cases this could be a preferable remedy to
staying the proceedings entirely.

5.2) The Exclusionary Discretion and Weighing "Probative Value"

To decide whether the costs outweigh the benefits, or whether the probative value of evidence outweighs its prejudice, a judge must come to
some appreciation of the probative value of the evidence. This evaluation presents the risk in jury trials that the judge will do the jury's job.
As indicated, the weight to be given to evidence has generally been
considered as a matter for the trier of fact or the jury. What is a judge
to consider, then, in assessing the probative value of evidence? Can the
trial judge evaluate both the "believability" and the "informativeness"
of the evidence?

There is no controversy that the judge is to assess how "informative" the evidence is. If it does not address a live issue or its cogency is
questionable, or even if the evidence is redundant, exclusion is more
likely. The controversy relates to "believability" since assessments of

---

44   (1985), 18 C.C.C. (3d) 356 (Ont. C.A.).
45   (2003), 17 C.R. (6th) 20 at para. 74 (Ont. C.A.)

credibility and reliability are for the ultimate determination of the trier of fact, not the trier of law.

The Supreme Court of Canada has long battled with whether judges should be permitted to consider credibility and reliability when determining whether to withdraw a case from the jury where the Crown finishes its evidence without presenting a *"prima facie* case." In order to avoid confusing the function of trier of law and trier of fact, the Court has settled that the judge considering a motion to remove the case from the jury is not to assess how believable Crown witnesses are but is to proceed on the assumption that the evidence they have related is true. Credibility and reliability are for the trier of fact, the jury, to decide. Similar thinking prompted the New Brunswick Court of Appeal to hold in R. v. *Duguay*[46] that a trial judge erred when using the exclusionary discretion to reject relevant evidence because of concern about the credibility of the witness.[47]

The problem with the *Duguay* view is that credibility and reliability of the witness is integral to the probative value of the evidence offered. If the objective of the discretion is to avoid admitting prejudicial information unless it is worth enduring the costs, it is artificial and self-defeating to ignore credibility and reliability problems that would seriously diminish the value of the evidence. So long as judges in jury trials exercise restraint by asking whether a reasonable trier of fact could find the evidence credible and reliable, instead of whether they themselves find it credible or reliable, the division of responsibility between triers of law and triers of fact can be respected, while at the same time costly evidence of little real value can be excluded.

Not surprisingly, there is authority holding that credibility and reliability can and should be considered in exercising exclusionary discretion. In R. v. *D.(A.S.)*, the Ontario Court of Appeal held that in assessing probative value for the purposes of section 276 of the *Criminal Code*, the so-called rape-shield provision, the trial judge "must take credibility into account in order to arrive at a proper conclusion."[48] The Supreme Court of Canada agreed. In dismissing an appeal from the decision, the Court spoke of the importance of a judge, called upon to assess the probative value of proposed testimony for the purpose of determining its admissibility, being able to assess the credibility of the witness offering

---

46   (2007), 50 C.R. (6th) 378 (N.B.C.A.).

47   The *Duguay* court found support for its conclusions in now-overruled case law which had prevented trial judges from considering the reliability of hearsay declarants in deciding whether their hearsay statements were reliable enough to admit. See Lisa Dufraimont, "Annotation" (2007) 50 C.R. (6th) 380.

48   (1998), 13 C.R. (5th) 283 at 306 (Ont. C.A.), aff'd R. v. *Darrach*, [2000] 2 S.C.R. 443.

the proposed testimony.[49] In *R. v. Handy* the Supreme Court of Canada recognized that "where admissibility is bound up with, and dependent upon probative value [as it is where the Crown wants to lead evidence about the uncharged misconduct of the accused on other occasions] the credibility of the evidence is a factor that the trail judge . . . is entitled to take into consideration."[50] In *R. v. Post*[51] the British Columbia Court of Appeal held that a judge was right to exercise discretion to exclude a hearsay statement offered by the defence, even though it satisfied the *K.G.B.* hearsay exception, in part because the person making the statement had been using drugs and alcohol heavily at the time the statements were made. The Ontario Court of Appeal accepted in *R. v. Humaid*[52] that exclusionary discretion could be used to reject evidence of a hearsay statement because the *witness* to the statement was so unreliable. And in the leading opinion evidence decision, *R. v. Mohan*, Sopinka J. explained: "Evidence that is otherwise logically relevant may be excluded . . . if it is misleading in the sense that its effect on the trier of fact, particularly a jury, is out of proportion to its reliability."[53]

The better view is therefore that in considering the exclusionary discretion, whether in a criminal trial or a civil trial, a judge should determine the value of the evidence based on the strength of the inferences, the credibility of the evidence where it is testimony, and the reliability of the evidence.

5.3) The Concept of Prejudice

The "prejudice" that is to be weighed against probative value includes any adverse costs associated with the presentation of evidence. Until the recent growth in the exclusionary discretion, it was most common to see the term used more restrictively. "Prejudice" described the prospect that parties to a case would be "prejudged." Evidence would operate "prejudicially" solely where, by its nature, it had a tendency to be given more weight by the triers of fact than it deserved. For example, graphic photographs could prejudice a defendant by creating sympathy for the plaintiff, and thus distort accurate fact-finding.[54] Similarly, proof of misconduct by the accused on other occasions could cause the trier

---

49   *R. v. Darrach, ibid.* at para. 63.
50   (2002), 164 C.C.C. (3d) 481 at para. 134 (S.C.C.). See chapter 3, section 5.1, "The Strength of the Evidence That the Similar Acts Occurred."
51   (2007), 46 C.R. (6th) 344 at para. 56 (B.C.C.A.).
52   (2006), 37 C.R. (6th) 347 (Ont. C.A.).
53   Above note 36 at 252.
54   See *Draper v. Jacklyn*, [1970] 2 S.C.R. 92.

of fact to dislike him, thereby judging him more harshly than the evidence in the case would allow. In criminal cases, "prejudice" was a concept confined to the accused. Evidence that could cause a hostile and even distorting judgment about the victim was not considered "prejudicial" for the purposes of potential exclusion; since only the accused was being judged in the case, only he could be "prejudged."[55]

Now, "prejudice" can describe both the distorting impact that evidence can have on the finding of fact, and the fairness in allowing evidence to be presented. In *R. v. Potvin*, for example, Wilson J. for the Court said that it would be prejudicial for the Crown to rely on a rule that allows for the admission of a transcript of the former testimony of an unavailable Crown witness, where the Crown itself has contributed to the unavailability of that witness.[56] Moreover, we now speak of evidence being prejudicial to witnesses or to the Crown. In *R. v. Osolin* the Supreme Court of Canada held that lines of questioning undertaken in the cross-examination of sexual assault complainants can be denied, even if relevant, if the questioning is unduly prejudicial.[57]

The concept of "prejudice" also embraces other adverse practical consequences of receiving evidence. It can include such things as the undue consumption of time, unfair surprise depriving a party of the opportunity to respond, the creation of distracting side issues, and the potential to confuse the trier of fact. In short, any potential that evidence has to undermine an accurate result, to complicate or frustrate the process, or to assault the dignity of witnesses or parties can agitate in favour of the exclusion of technically admissible evidence. The judge must consider these factors to gauge how prejudicial the admission of the evidence would be.

5.4) The Balancing

Once determined, probative value—the "believability" and "informativeness" of the evidence—is to be weighed against the costs or prejudice of admitting the proof. The judge should not speculate about prejudice, but consider the actual or likely costs presented by such evidence,[58] including things as diverse as the practicalities of its presentation, the fairness to the parties and to the witnesses, and the potentially distorting effect the evidence can have on the outcome of the case. In a

---

55   See, for example, *R. v. Valley* (1986), 26 C.C.C. (3d) 207 (Ont. C.A.), leave to appeal to S.C.C. refused (1986), 26 C.C.C. (3d) 207n (S.C.C.).

56   Above note 38 at 237.

57   (1993), 26 C.R. (4th) 1 at 24 (S.C.C.).

58   *Landolfi v. Fargione* (2006), 79 O.R. (3d) 767 at 782 (C.A.).

jury trial, the judge should even consider whether judicial direction can remove prejudice. Based on these considerations, a judgment call is made on whether to receive it.

So stated, this exclusionary power has the theoretical potential to render all other rules of evidence obsolete and to undermine the role of the trier of fact. In practice, courts exercise restraint in applying the discretion. Considerations of full answer and defence for defence evidence in criminal cases, the basic principle of access to evidence in all other situations, respect for the role of the jury in jury trials, and the importance of judging evidence in context in judge alone trials all combine to encourage sparse use of the exclusionary discretion.

A clear example of the exclusionary discretion occurred in *R. v. Powell*.[59] The person who committed the robbery that Powell was charged with had a handgun which was never discovered. Witnesses could not describe the gun with any precision. Powell was found to be in possession of a handgun sometime later. At the robbery trial the Crown wanted to prove this arguing that it provided some circumstantial evidence of identity since even if it could not be shown to be *the* handgun it at least proved that Mr. Powell, like the robber, had access to handguns. The trial judge held that linking Mr. Powell to a possibly unrelated handgun would be far too prejudicial to warrant admitting, given the limited probative value of the inference being offered, and so proof of his possession of the handgun was excluded.

It is evident that the application of the exclusionary discretion is context-based and fact-specific, regardless of whether it operates in criminal, civil, or administrative cases. By its very nature, this process involves the exercise of judgment or discretion. The relative weight to be assigned to the factors requires an ad hoc judgment and is not a process that can be captured by a bright line rule capable of yielding a single correct result.[60]

Given that it is a discretion, "[t]he trial judge's conclusions informed by correct legal principles are entitled to deference."[61] In *R. v. Terry*,[62] for example, the trial judge was held not to have erred by admitting a poem written by the accused referring to the taking of a life. While its connection to the crime was said to be "tenuous" and its potential prejudice "considerable," the Supreme Court of Canada held that the trial judge's careful instruction ameliorated the risk that the poem would be misused. By contrast, where a court believes that the discretionary decision has

---

59   *R. v. Powell*, above note 10 .
60   *R. v. Pilon* (2009), 247 O.A.C. 127 at para. 54 (C.A.).
61   *R. v. Candir*, above note 11 at para. 58.
62   (1996), 48 C.R. (4th) 137 at 147–48 (S.C.C.).

caused prejudice, a reversible error might be found to have occurred. In *R. v. Savoy* the trial judge permitted the Crown to present evidence that the accused had access to drugs that could cause death, even though there was no medical evidence as to how the deceased died. The British Columbia Court of Appeal held that this evidence was of little or no probative value and was highly prejudicial, and, given the prominence it was given by the Crown, may well have been a decisive factor in the circumstantial case. The conviction was overturned.[63]

Ordinarily where a judge determines that the probative value of evidence is outweighed by its prejudicial effect, exclusion of the evidence in its entirety will occur. Even where a judge realizes in a jury trial that the probative value of evidence already admitted is outweighed by its prejudice, the jury should be directed to disregard it.[64] There are cases, however, where judges are able to remedy the problem by editing prejudicial information out of otherwise admissible statements or documents,[65] or by permitting the evidence to be led but cautioning jurors about potentially prejudicial evidence and giving them instructions on where the problem may lie.[66]

6. RELEVANCE, MATERIALITY, AND NARRATION

It is inevitable that in narrating a story, even in response to questions, witnesses will include minutiae that do not meet the tests of relevance and materiality. For example, the trier of fact is likely to learn what a police officer was doing when a call was received, or whether the police officer was in a marked or an unmarked police vehicle. This is harmless background material, and reference to it is generally tolerated because it improves comprehension by presenting a total picture and makes it easier for the witness to recount the evidence.[67]

At times information that forms part of the natural narrative of an event is not simply trivial background information. Narrative information can be extremely prejudicial. In *R. v. Smith*,[68] for example, events

---

63   *R. v. Savoy*, [1997] B.C.J. No. 449 (B.C.C.A.). See also *R. v. O'Connor* (2002), 170 C.C.C. (3d) 365 at paras. 47–51 (Ont. C.A.).

64   See *R. v. White*, above note 15 at para. 50..

65   See *R. v. White*, [2006] A.J. No. 1548 (Q.B.).

66   *R. v. White*, above note 15 at para. 33. See below chapter 12, section 2.5, "Warnings (Cautions) in Lieu of Discretionary Exclusion."

67   *Ibid.* at para. 47.

68   (2007), 225 C.C.C. (3d) 278 (Alta. C.A.). Smith appealed his conviction, claiming that the discreditable background information should not have been admit-

could not be described without narrating the "daily" criminal pursuits of the accused, charged with murder. As a result, the jury learned as part of the narrative about discreditable conduct by the accused that would otherwise have been immaterial and inadmissible. Care must be taken with the narrative doctrine; prejudicial information should gain this kind of "back door" entry only where significant testimony cannot be recounted meaningfully and fairly without its disclosure. Even then, the testimony should be edited pursuant to the judge's exclusionary discretion to the extent it can be, to minimize any damage that may be done. When immaterial, prejudicial or otherwise immaterial information does piggy-back its way into the record as part of the narrative, judges must avoid relying on it for improper purposes; and in jury trials, if there is any risk that jurors could misuse the evidence, judges must give limiting instructions directing those jurors as to the limitations on the use that the evidence can be put to.[69]

The idea that some things are part of the story has influenced the development and application of a number of rules of evidence. The *res gestae* hearsay exceptions, for example, are premised to differing degrees on the relationship in time between the statements and the events those statements describe or reveal.[70] Prior consistent statements made by a witness are not normally admissible, although the doctrine of "narrative" is sometimes used to justify leading some evidence that the witness made statements out of court.[71] Fortunately, more is required to justify admission in these cases than the simple fact that the statements form part of the story. Each of the rules has its own criteria and limitations, which are discussed in the chapters that follow.

7. STANDARDS OF ADMISSIBILITY OF EVIDENCE

Care has to be taken not to confuse the ultimate standards of proof that the law requires before facts are found in a case, with the standards that have to be met before individual items of evidence are admissible. For example, while the Crown in a criminal case must prove the guilt of the accused beyond a reasonable doubt to secure a conviction, it need

---

ted, but both the indispensability of the information to a coherent narrative, and Smith's own decision to fold some of it into his defence theory, thereby making it material, undermined his appeal.

69   See *R. v. Mariani* (2007), 220 C.C.C. (3d) 74 (Ont. C.A.).
70   See chapter 5, section 10, "Spontaneous Statements (*Res Gestae*)."
71   See chapter 11, section 4.8, "Narrative."

not prove each piece of its evidence beyond a reasonable doubt for that evidence to be received. A blood-stained shirt will be admissible if there is some evidence on which a reasonable trier of fact could conclude that it was the victim's, even if it is not established beyond a reasonable doubt that it was. The trier of fact is left to decide whether the shirt assists in proving anything, in light of all the other evidence in the case. In the end, guilt can be established beyond a reasonable doubt when all the evidence is assessed together, even though, individually, none of the pieces would establish guilt beyond a reasonable doubt. It is therefore an error of law for the judge to direct a jury to apply the ultimate burden of proof to individual items of evidence[72] unless that item of evidence is the only proof of an essential part of the Crown case.[73]

While the ultimate standards of proof relate to whether facts are proved, rather than whether evidence is admissible, there are standards that do apply as preconditions to the admissibility of evidence. It would be easier if there were only one such standard, but, unfortunately, there is not. The standards of admissibility vary with different kinds of evidence, and even in some cases to the same kind of evidence. It is therefore important to consult applicable rules, using the following guidelines:

7.1)   Testimony Where No Exclusionary Rule Is in Issue

Most often there will be no rule of exclusion to consider. In such cases the only standard of admission that will apply is compliance with the basic rule — that the evidence has some tendency as a matter of human experience to advance a material inquiry. Evidence meeting this modest standard will be received unless its probative value is outweighed by the prejudice it may cause if admitted. Nothing is to be gained by complicating the matter by asking whether a particular item of evidence is relevant on the balance of probabilities or whether its probative value probably outweighs the risk of prejudice it presents. If there is a dispute, a judge will simply judge whether the evidence is worth hearing given these competing concerns.

7.2)   Exhibits or "Real Evidence"

A similar approach is taken where a party wishes to have a physical item admitted into evidence and made an exhibit in the trial.[74] This "real evidence" is generally admissible where it is both relevant on the

---

72   *R. v. Morin* (1988), 66 C.R. (3d) 1 (S.C.C.).

73   *R. v. Kyllo* (2001), 48 C.R. (5th) 46 (B.C.C.A.).

74   See chapter 10, section 7, "Real Evidence."

standard just described, and "authentic" — in other words, where it is, in fact, what it is purported to be. The party producing the real evidence need not establish, however, that it is probably authentic or that it is authentic beyond a reasonable doubt. It is enough if there is some evidence on which a reasonable trier of fact could conclude that the item is authentic.

7.3)   Rules Having "Factual Triggers"

7.3 (a)   Proving Factual Triggers on the Balance of Probabilities

Many of the rules of evidence about to be examined have "factual triggers." In other words, these rules outline one or more factual preconditions that must exist before the rule applies. For example, solicitor-client privilege does not apply unless the target evidence is a communication between a solicitor and client, of a confidential nature, relating to the seeking, forming, or giving of legal advice. A party seeking to invoke the privilege has to prove that each of those elements existed. The general rule is that the party seeking to have such a rule of evidence applied must establish each of the factual prerequisites on the balance of probabilities.

Accordingly, in R. v. U.(F.J.), the Supreme Court of Canada noted that, in applying the general hearsay exception allowing for the proof of "necessary" and "reliable" hearsay evidence, the party calling the evidence has to prove that the out-of-court statement is probably reliable before it can be admitted.[75] If the claim that hearsay is necessary is based on the death of the witness, the party presenting the evidence has to prove on the balance of probabilities that the witness really is dead.

The "similar fact evidence" rule applies where the Crown wants to rely on discreditable uncharged conduct of the accused to support a prosecution. One of the triggers for admission of such evidence requires the Crown to connect the accused to that other act of misconduct. Anomalously this precondition to admission does not have to be proved on the balance of probability. It is enough if there is sufficient evidence of that link that a reasonable trier of fact could act upon.[76]

7.3 (b)   Proving Factual Triggers beyond a Reasonable Doubt

It has been said "the general rule that preliminary findings of fact may be determined on a balance of probabilities is departed from [in criminal cases] in those certainly rare occasions when admission of the

---

75   (1995), 42 C.R. (4th) 133 (S.C.C.). See also R. v. Evans (1993), 25 C.R. (4th) 46 (S.C.C.).

76   See chapter 3, section 5.2 (a), "Connection to the Accused."

evidence may itself have a conclusive effect with respect to guilt."[77] Do not be misled by the generality of this observation. There are some examples that bear it out, but most often the "beyond a reasonable doubt" standard will not apply, even where evidence is terminal to the case for the accused. Even where the Crown leads devastating opinion evidence that the suspect DNA and the DNA of the accused have identical characteristics leading to overwhelming odds that the suspect DNA belonged to the accused, the preconditions to the admission of the opinion evidence need be established only on the balance of probabilities.[78] It is best, then, to look to the specific authorities rather than to this general principle.

The most well-known involves statements made by the accused to a person in authority. Before a statement made by the accused to a person in authority can be admitted, the Crown must first prove beyond a reasonable doubt that the statement was voluntarily made.[79]

If the statement of a young person is offered by the Crown in a criminal case, the Crown must not only prove voluntariness beyond a reasonable doubt. The Crown will also have to prove beyond a reasonable doubt that the statutory requirements in the *Youth Criminal Justice Act*[80] have been complied with, including the right to have their rights explained to them in a language they understand, and the right to have a parent or support person present when the statement is made. If the Crown claims the youth waived the rights provided by these statutory requirements this waiver, too, must be proved beyond a reasonable doubt.[81]

There are other rules of evidence, known as presumptions, where preliminary facts will sometimes have to be proved beyond a reasonable doubt. A "presumption" works this way. If a party proves that a basic fact exists, the trier of fact is then to presume that another fact also exists. Normally, the basic fact need merely be proved on the balance of probabilities for the presumed fact to arise. Where a finding that the presumed fact exists will be conclusive of guilt, however, the Crown must establish that basic fact beyond a reasonable doubt. For example, where the Crown presents a certificate of analysis from a

---

77   *R. v. Arp*, above note 1 at 352.

78   *R. v. Terciera* (1998), 15 C.R. (5th) 359 (Ont. C.A.), aff'd [1999] 3 S.C.R. 866.

79   *R. v. Pickett* (1975), 31 C.R.N.S. 239 (Ont. C.A.). To be clear, the Crown need not prove beyond a reasonable doubt that the statement was made. It need only prove voluntariness to this high standard. See chapter 8, section 5.4 (d), "the Crown must establish beyond a reasonable doubt, in light of all the circumstances . . . ."

80   *Youth Criminal Justice Act*, S.C. 2002, c. 1.

81   *R. v. L.T.H.*, [2008] S.C.J. No. 50.

qualified breathalyzer technician recording the blood-alcohol level of the accused, it is presumed that the blood-alcohol content of the accused at the time of driving was as represented on that certificate. Since this presumption virtually determines an essential element of the offence on a blood-alcohol driving charge, the statutory preconditions to admitting a certificate, including among other things that it was served on the accused, must be proved beyond a reasonable doubt.[82]

7.4)   Basic Common Law Rules of Exclusion Pertaining to the Nature or Effect of the Evidence

Other rules of evidence, including some of the most basic common law rules of exclusion (hearsay, opinion, character evidence), do not have factual triggers. Their operation depends on the nature of the evidence. There is no sense in discussing standards of proof relating to admissibility for such rules. For example, a question is either leading or it is not. No evidence is required to show it to be so. Similarly, evidence is either being offered to perform a hearsay purpose or it is not. It is either opinion evidence or it is not. It either raises issues of character, or it does not. These are matters of legal characterization for the adjudicator or judge to make about the nature of the evidence, not matters turning on the proof of preliminary facts susceptible to standards of proof.

The same is true where the rule turns on the "effect" of admitting the evidence, as rules sometimes do. For example, whether prejudice outweighs probative value is not susceptible to proof—it is a matter of judgment relating to the nature of the evidence in the context of the case. Similarly, unconstitutionally obtained evidence is excluded where its admission would have the effect of bringing the administration of justice into disrepute. Whether it will do so is a matter of legal characterization, not proof. Unfortunately, the case law concerning this rule tends to speak about the onus being on the party seeking exclusion to establish that its admission would bring the administration of justice into disrepute. Such comments are best understood as requiring the party seeking to exclude evidence to establish the factual scenario he relies upon on the balance of probabilities. Whether admitting evidence given that factual scenario, once established, would bring the administration of justice into disrepute is a question of legal characterization, not proof.

---

82   *R. v. Egger* (1993), 21 C.R. (4th) 186 at 202 (S.C.C.).

7.5) Statutory Modifications

Sometimes statutes alter the standards of proof that would otherwise apply in determining admissibility. For example, unlike other real evidence, computer records cannot be authenticated using the generous standard described above. They will be admissible under the *Canada Evidence Act* only where designated prerequisites are met.[83] If the party presenting the evidence proves that the electronic document was stored in the usual and ordinary course of business, for example, it will be admissible as authentic unless the opposing party rebuts the presumption that the document is genuine and accurate. Obviously where statutes spell out standards of admissibility, they govern.

In sum, it is necessary for the individual rules to be examined to determine the appropriate standard of proof for admissibility, always bearing in mind that it is not necessary to speak in terms of standards of proof when a rule of evidence turns on the legal characterization of the evidence or the effect of its admission.

---

83   *Canada Evidence Act*, above note 40, ss. 31.1–31.3.

CHAPTER 3

CHARACTER EVIDENCE: PRIMARY MATERIALITY

1. INTRODUCTION

1.1) Generally

"Character evidence" is any proof that is presented in order to establish the personality, psychological state, attitude, or general capacity of an individual to engage in particular behaviour. It can take a number of forms. Character may be established circumstantially—for example, by proving the particular acts of a person on other occasions. This can be done through the testimony of witnesses to those events, through admissions by the person whose character is being explored, through certificates proving his criminal convictions, or in other ways. Character can also be proved compendiously through statements of opinion ("In my view Joan is dishonest") or by proof of reputation ("Joan's reputation in the community for honesty is poor"). "Character" in its broader sense can even be proved through expert opinion ("Simon is a sexual psychopath").

Not all of these kinds of evidence will be admissible in all cases. Indeed, the rules of evidence are extremely guarded about the admission of character evidence. This kind of evidence often presents serious risk of prejudice and can create distracting and time-consuming side issues; moreover, where the character of a person is not a matter directly in issue in a proceeding,[1] there is often insecurity about its relevance and true probative value.

---

1   "Character" in a broad sense is directly in issue in proceedings such as danger-

Because of the shifting importance of these considerations, character evidence rules vary depending on whether the evidence is being presented in a criminal or a civil case, or whether it relates to a party or a non-party. They vary, as well, depending on whether the character evidence is being adduced on a primarily material issue (such as what happened) or a secondarily material issue (such as to challenge the credibility of a witness). In criminal cases, the rules vary depending upon whether it is the accused or the Crown calling the evidence. This chapter deals solely with character evidence that is primarily material, in the sense that it is being introduced as circumstantial evidence to assist in determining what happened.[2]

1.2) Character and Relevance

The relevance of character evidence is often controversial because, by its very nature, it is general information about a person that is being presented for the purposes of leading to specific conclusions about behaviour on a particular occasion. Its probative value often depends on the proposition that persons tend to act consistently with their character. We know from human experience, however, that this is only sometimes true. The fact that there is an increased tendency for a person to act in a particular way does not mean that he always acts that way, nor does it necessarily mean that he acted that way on the occasion in question. Not only is the probative value of character evidence often controversial, the generalizations involved in character typing tend to be pejorative and judgmental. The spectacle of attacking a person's character is therefore distasteful. More important, it presents the risk of prejudice and opens general issues that may distract the trial from the material issues. There are therefore a number of rules preventing or controlling the admission of this kind of evidence.

1.3) Character and Habit

"Character" evidence rules are concerned with drawing inferences based on the kind of person the relevant individual is. Those rules are therefore disinterested in activities that do not lead to type-casting. It

---

ous offender applications, in inquiries into fitness to stand trial, in s. 16 mental disorder defences, or in defamation suits.

2   For discussion of secondarily material character evidence see chapter 10, section 6.5, "The Collateral Facts Rule," and chapter 11, "Secondary Materiality and Your Own Witness."

is therefore important in applying these rules to distinguish between "character" and "habit." A habit, being the tendency of a person to engage repeatedly in a particular kind of conduct, may or may not reflect on one's character. Where it does not, the rationales underlying the character evidence rules do not apply, and the admission of evidence about that habit should turn solely on its relevance and on the application of general exclusionary considerations. Where, however, a habit can colour the impression held by others of the kind of person the subject is the character evidence rules should determine admissibility. Character evidence rules should therefore govern the admission of the accused person's habit of carrying a gun. By contrast, they should not apply to evidence that the accused was in the habit of smoking a particular brand of cigarette that was found at the scene of the crime.

For this reason, in *R. v. B.(L.)* the Ontario Court of Appeal ruled that where the Crown seeks to lead evidence about the practices or propensities of the accused, it is essential to ask whether "the proposed evidence [is] discreditable to the accused?"[3] If not, the character evidence rules do not apply. To be clear, evidence of practice or propensity need not reveal criminal conduct to be discreditable. Discreditable evidence includes any conduct or information about the accused that is morally objectionable or apt to demonstrate that he or she has a contemptible or reprehensible character.[4] It even extends beyond this to include proof of a stigmatizing condition such as mental illness[5] or sexual preference. As society becomes more liberal in its attitudes, proof of sexual preference is likely to fall outside of the bad character evidence rule, just as evidence of marital infidelity after separation now has.[6] By the same token the "good character" evidence rules apply solely where the evidence, by its nature, attracts favourable judgments about the kind of person the subject is. Proof that a person is never late is not good character evidence, but a history of philanthropy would be.

---

3   *R. v. B.(L.)* (1997), 9 C.R. (5th) 38 at 49 (Ont. C.A.). For this reason, Justice Charron suggests that we should be referring to "evidence of discreditable conduct" rather than to "similar fact evidence."

4   *R. v. Robertson* (1987), 58 C.R. (3d) 28 at 46 (S.C.C.).

5   *R. v. Morin* (1988), 66 C.R. (3d) 1 (S.C.C.).

6   *R. v. Walizadah* (2007), 223 C.C.C. (3d) 28 at paras. 19–23 (Ont. C.A.).

2. DISCREDITABLE CONDUCT EVIDENCE CALLED BY THE PROSECUTION IN A CRIMINAL CASE

Evidence that the accused has engaged in discreditable or criminal acts, or is otherwise of a discreditable character is presumptively inadmissible. The onus is on the prosecution to satisfy the trial judge on the balance of probabilities that in the context of the particular case the probative value of the evidence in relation to a particular issue outweighs its potential prejudice and thereby justifies its reception.

In assessing the probative value of the evidence, consideration should be given to such things as:

- *the strength of the evidence that the discreditable or criminal act occurred;*
- *(1) the connection between the accused and the similar act event, and (2) the extent to which the discreditable or criminal act supports the inferences sought to be made, relating to a specific issue in the case (a.k.a. the "connectedness" of the evidence to the "questions in issue"); and*
- *the extent to which the matters it tends to prove are at issue in the proceedings (the materiality of the evidence).*

In assessing the risk of prejudice caused by the evidence, consideration should be given to such things as:

- *"moral prejudice," being the risk that the evidence will be used to draw the prohibited inference that the accused is the kind of bad person likely to commit the offence charged; and*
- *"reasoning prejudice," which includes the risk that:*
  - » *the trier of fact may be distracted from deciding the issue in a reasoned way because of the inflammatory nature of the proposed evidence;*
  - » *the trier of fact may become confused about what evidence pertains to the crime charged, and what evidence relates to the alleged similar act;*
  - » *the trial will begin to focus disproportionately on whether the similar act happened; and*
  - » *the accused will be unable to respond to the allegation that the similar act occurred, because of the passage of time, surprise, or the collateral nature of the inquiry.*

If this rule is applied properly as a strict rule of admissibility, evidence that does no more than invite the general inference that the accused is the kind of person to commit the offence will not be admitted. This rule is designed to avoid such general inferences, as they are "prohibited" by law. Even when evidence disclosing the discreditable character of the accused is admitted to support other proper, specific inferences, it is only to be used for those inferences, and not to draw the prohibited general inference.

3. THE PROHIBITED INFERENCE

As stated by the Supreme Court of Canada, "[i]t is trite law that 'character evidence [called by the Crown] which shows *only* that the accused is the type of person likely to have committed the offence in question is inadmissible.'"[7] Moreover, even where it logically follows it is impermissible to infer from admissible evidence that the accused may be guilty because he is the kind of person who would commit the offence. This "prohibited inference" has been described as a "primary rule of exclusion,"[8] "one of the most deeply rooted and jealously guarded principles of our criminal law."[9] Hence, it is not permissible in a burglary trial to prove that, because he has a history of burglary, the accused is the kind of person likely to have committed the burglary in question.

Justice Binnie explained why the prohibited inference exists in the unanimous Supreme Court of Canada decision in *R. v. Handy*, now the leading Canadian case on character evidence:

> Proof of general disposition is a prohibited purpose. Bad character is not an offence known to law. Discreditable disposition or character evidence at large, creates nothing but "moral prejudice" and the Crown is not entitled to ease its burden by stigmatizing the accused as a bad person.[10]

This is not to say that general disposition or general character is entirely without relevance. Surely it is easier to believe an allegation that the accused committed a burglary, knowing that, because he has committed burglaries before, he is the kind of person who would do so. Yet the relevance of this general character evidence is modest when it comes

---

7   *R. v. G.(S.G.)* (1997), 8 C.R. (5th) 198 at 226 (S.C.C.) [emphasis in original].
8   *R. v. Morris* (1983), 36 C.R. (3d) 1 at 14 (S.C.C.), Lamer J. [as he then was].
9   *Maxwell v. D.P.P.*, [1935] A.C. 309 at 317 (H.L.).
10 *R. v. Handy* (2002), 164 C.C.C. (3d) 481 at para. 72 (S.C.C.).

to resolving whether the accused committed the particular burglary alleged. More importantly, relying on inferences arising from general disposition or general character is dangerous. It is apt to add more heat than light.[11] It may cause the trier of fact to convict, not because of the natural strength of the kind of evidence, but as a reaction to the discreditable, contemptible, or stigmatizing character of the accused. For these reasons, in spite of its modest relevance, evidence that does no more than invite the prohibited inference is inadmissible.

Even though the existence of the prohibited inference is "not controversial,"[12] its precise contours have been the source of confusion. Until *Handy*, it was common for judges and legal commentators to use the misleading short form of "propensity reasoning" to describe the prohibited inference. They said that propensity reasoning is not allowed. Yet a moment's reflection makes clear that not all propensity reasoning is impermissible. For example, proof that the accused has a propensity to make distinctive lipstick markings on the mirrors of homes he burgles does not depend for its relevance on the prohibited inference that he is, by virtue of his general character, the kind of person dishonest enough to burgle. The distinctive nature of the burglaries suggests, as a matter of common sense, that the same person did each burglary where such markings are found. If the accused can be linked to one such burglary, it follows that he is likely to have committed the other similar and distinctive burglaries as well. Since this evidence would unquestionably be admissible, it is clear "that propensity reasoning in and of itself is not prohibited."[13] Only a certain kind of propensity reasoning is impermissible. In particular, "it is propensity reasoning that is based solely on the general bad character of the accused . . . which is prohibited,"[14] or as the Supreme Court of Canada calls it, proof of "general disposition," or "bad personhood."[15] If all the evidence does is to "paint the [accused] as a 'bad person,'"[16] thereby capable in character of committing the crime charged, it will be inadmissible. By contrast, "situation specific evidence of propensity"[17] is not *per se* impermissible. As will be seen below, "situation specific evidence of propensity" may be admitted, depending on its probative value and the risk of prejudice it presents.

---

11   *D.P.P. v. Boardman*, [1975] A.C. 421 at 454 (H.L.), Hailsham L.J.

12   *R. v. Handy*, above note 10 at para. 36.

13   *R. v. B.(L.)*, above note 3 at 60, quoted with approval in *R. v. Handy, ibid.* at para. 68.

14   *R. v. B.(L.), ibid.* at 60, also quoted with approval in *R. v. Handy, ibid.* at para. 68.

15   *R. v. Shearing* (2002), 2 C.R. (6th) 213 at para. 57 (S.C.C.).

16   *Ibid.* at para. 48.

17   *R. v. Handy,* above note 10 at para. 65.

The distinction between the impermissible "general" variety of propensity reasoning, and the permissible "specific" variety, can be difficult to discern in a particular case. One of the things that makes the distinction obscure is that any evidence of the bad character or discreditable conduct of the accused will reveal something about "general character" or "general disposition" even if that evidence is of the "specific" admissible variety. To return to the example of the robber with the lipstick markings, the specific propensity to use this distinctive *modus operandi* cannot be communicated to the trier of fact without also revealing that the accused is, by his character, the type to burgle, or "the type of person likely to have committed the crime." Impermissible inferences can therefore arise from permissible evidence. Thus, as its name suggests, the prohibited inference does not purport to cause the exclusion of a kind of evidence, but rather seeks to prevent a kind of inference from being drawn. It does this in two ways. It supports a rule that excludes, *ab initio*, any evidence that demonstrates no more than the general bad character of the accused and it prevents general bad character inferences from being relied on when permissible evidence betrays that general character. The similar fact evidence rule is therefore both a rule of exclusion and a rule of restricted admissibility.

4. THE "SIMILAR FACT EVIDENCE" RULE DESCRIBED

4.1) The Scope of the "Similar Fact Evidence Rule"

The rule that is designed to prevent reliance on this impermissible inference and to identify when discreditable conduct evidence is important enough to admit in spite of the risks it presents is generally known as the "similar fact evidence rule." The rule has been given this label because it developed in cases where the Crown was attempting to prove that the accused person had committed similar acts before. The term "similar fact evidence rule" can, however, be misleading. This is because "the rule also extends to criminal or otherwise discreditable acts that bear no similarity to the offence with which the accused is charged."[18] It applies, and must therefore be satisfied, in every case where the Crown is presenting evidence to establish the guilt of the

---

18   *R. v. Mahalingan* (2008), 61 C.R. (6th) 207 at para. 160 (S.C.C), and see *R. v. D.(H.)*, [2000] S.J. No. 209 (C.A.).

accused[19] that either directly or indirectly reveals the discreditable or stigmatizing character of the accused. The similar fact evidence rule applies whether the discreditable conduct is criminal or not,[20] and whether the evidence recounts specific acts or relates directly to who the accused is, rather than to what the accused has done.[21] The rule is triggered by discredit, not similarity.

4.2) The "Similar Fact Evidence Rule" Stated

The "similar fact evidence rule" was stated with clarity in *R. v. Handy*:

> Similar fact evidence is . . . presumptively inadmissible. The onus is on the prosecution to satisfy the trial judge on the balance of prob-abilities that in the context of the particular case the probative value of the evidence in relation to a particular issue outweighs its poten-tial prejudice and thereby justifies its reception.[22]

Although this concise articulation of the rule does not speak about the prohibited inference, as will be explained, if this rule is applied prop-erly the prohibited inference will be avoided. The *Handy* decision is important because it sweeps aside years of confusion in Canada.

4.3) The Development of the Rule

The classic approach to similar fact evidence, inspired by *Makin v. A.G. for New South Wales*,[23] was for courts to determine the admissibility of similar fact evidence by attempting to identify permissible inferences, in order to avoid the impermissible inference. In an era of formalized precedent, it was not long before courts neglected the difficult challenge of trying to articulate the precise inferences the evidence yielded on the particular facts of the case; instead they relied on the example of previ-ous decisions. This caused courts to develop categories for admission

---

19 Related but distinct rules apply where the Crown calls the evidence for other purposes, such as rebutting defence evidence suggesting that the accused is of such good character that she is not the type to commit the offence (see the discussion in this chapter, section 14, "Good Character Evidence and Crown Rebuttal Evidence"), or to undermine the credibility of the accused as a witness (see the discussion in chapter 10, section 6, "Cross-examination").

20 *R. v. Handy*, above note 10 at para. 34.

21 See *R. v. Pascoe* (1997), 5 C.R. (5th) 341 (Ont. C.A.), where expert evidence was excluded in reliance on this rule, because it purported to show the general, discreditable characteristic of the accused as a homosexual pedophile.

22 Above note 10 at para. 55.

23 (1893), [1894] A.C. 57 (P.C.).

to simplify things. The most familiar categories involved using similar fact evidence to establish "design," to rebut "accident" or "innocent association,"[24] and to show identity or the *actus reus* of an offence by demonstrating a "system," or "hallmark," or some "striking similarity." While each of these categories encompasses situations that can, depending on their particular facts, meet the test articulated in *Handy*, courts often used these categories as a substitute for thought. Instead of analyzing the evidence closely, they simply used labels as the "open-sesame" to admissibility. A spectacular example is *R. v. Clermont*,[25] a rape prosecution, where the trial judge allowed the Crown to prove that Clermont had been convicted of rape before. Even though the sole issue was consent, and the facts were materially different in each case, the judge justified admissibility by noting that the evidence was adduced to establish a "pattern of similarity" and "to rebut the defence of innocent association or a defence of mistake." He went on to state that the "similarities" were such that the acts in both cases were committed by the same person and that the intention was the same in both cases. Fittingly, the Supreme Court of Canada ordered a new trial.

The similar fact evidence rule was gradually "reformulated" in an effort to improve the quality of analysis. Courts, most notably in *Director of Public Prosecutions v. Boardman*,[26] and in *R. v. B.(C.R.)*,[27] began to require the balancing of probative value against prejudice in determining admissibility. This had the virtue of making the inquiry case-specific. Courts using this approach also began to speak about the permissible use of propensity reasoning, while at other times affirming the existence of a prohibited inference. This caused confusion for those who misunderstood the prohibited inference as preventing propensity reasoning *ab initio*. The contribution that *Handy* makes to the jurisprudence is that it clarifies the distinction between general propensity reasoning and specific propensity reasoning. In doing so, it reconciles the two branches of authority, while articulating the standard of proof for admissibility, explaining in clear terms the approach that should be taken to determining the admission of similar fact evidence.

---

24 This is the "defence" that applies where the accused concedes that he was in the company of the complainant, but asserts that nothing illegal happened. His association with the complainant was entirely innocent. In effect, "innocent association" is nothing more than a contrivance that was used, particularly in homosexual offences, to convert a simple denial into a foundation for the proof of character evidence.

25 (1986), 53 C.R. (3d) 97 (S.C.C.).

26 Above note 11.

27 [1990] 1 S.C.R. 717.

4.4) The Similar Fact Rule and the Avoidance of General Propensity Reasoning

To repeat, in stating the rule concisely the Court in *Handy* holds that:

> Similar fact evidence is . . . presumptively inadmissible. The onus is
> on the prosecution to satisfy the trial judge on the balance of prob-
> abilities that in the context of the particular case the probative value
> of the evidence in relation to a particular issue outweighs its poten-
> tial prejudice and thereby justifies its reception.[28]

How does this approach seek to prevent the admission of evidence
that does no more than to invite the prohibited inference if, unlike the
classic approach to admissibility, it does not ask directly whether the
evidence is being used for a prohibited purpose? It does so in two ways.

First, there is the presumption that similar fact evidence is inadmissible unless the prosecution shows that its probative value outweighs
its potential prejudice. This was described in *R. v. Arp*, in the Supreme
Court's last foray into the similar fact evidence rule before *Handy*, as a
"strict test for admissibility."[29] By applying it as a strict test, evidence that
does no more than to prove the general propensity of the accused will
not gain admission for it will invariably have greater potential prejudicial effect than probative value.[30] Indeed, there is much to be said for
the proposition that to be admissible, the probative value of similar fact
evidence must significantly outweigh the risk of prejudice it presents.[31]

Second, in *Handy* the Court emphasized the need for the evidence
to be evaluated "in relation to a particular issue." The Court observed
that evidence of general criminal disposition or bad character will have
no cogency, as it does not have any specific connection with or relation
to the issues for decision in the subject case.[32] "[G]eneral disposition of
the accused does not qualify as 'an issue in question.'"[33] It is therefore
incumbent on the Crown to identify a live issue in the trial to which
the evidence of disposition relates.[34] If the evidence truly does relate to
a material issue, then it will go beyond simply demonstrating general
propensity. By insisting on the identification of the specific issue that

---

28   Above note 10 at para. 55.
29   *R. v. Arp* (1998), 129 C.C.C. (3d) 321 at 353 (S.C.C.).
30   *Ibid.*
31   *R. v. Pickton* (2009), 260 C.C.C. (3d) 132 at para. 77 (B.C.C.A.).
32   Above note 10 at para. 92.
33   *Ibid.* at para. 71.
34   *Ibid.* at para. 74. See *R. v. Pickton*, above note 31 at para. 78; *R. v. Johnson* (2010),
      262 C.C.C. (3d) 404 at para. 92 (Ont. C.A.).

the evidence is relevant to, the risk of the admission of evidence that depends for its relevance on the prohibited inference is reduced.

4.5) Categories of Cases

The call in *Handy* for the identification of issues in assessing admissibility is not an invitation to return to a categories approach.[35] Evidence will not necessarily be admissible simply because it is tendered for a familiar purpose. The Crown must still meet its burden of showing that in the particular circumstances of the case at hand, the probative value of the evidence in relation to the issue in question outweighs its potential to cause prejudice.

Having said this, what is required to meet the rule can depend on the nature of the issue that the evidence is being used to resolve. Where the question in issue is different, the criteria required to meet the rule will differ. For example, in "identity cases" in which the Crown attempts to identify the accused as the perpetrator of the crime by proving that the accused committed another act, there must be evidence connecting the accused to that other act, and that other act must bear a high enough degree of similarity to the crime charged to support the conclusion that the same person likely committed both offences. If this link and the high degree of similarity are missing, the evidence does not bear sufficient probative value to outweigh the risk of prejudice.[36] By contrast, there is no need for a high degree of similarity between the similar fact incidents and the crime charged where the Crown is simply trying to prove other acts of violence by the accused against a complainant in order to show that the accused had a particular animus against the complaint, and therefore intended to harm her.[37] This does not mean that there is one rule for identity cases and another for animus cases. Differences in the application of the rule simply reflect that similar fact evidence will have to exhibit different characteristics in different contexts in order to reach the level of probative value required to satisfy the *Handy* rule. This is not surprising because the probative value and prejudicial potential evidence has in a particular case is a question of logic and fact, and varies too widely to accommodate the use of simple, general rules of admissibility.

---

35   *R. v. Handy, ibid.* at para. 75.

36   See section 9, "The Special Case of Proving Identity through Similar Fact Evidence," below in this chapter, for a discussion of this use of the similar fact evidence rule.

37   See section 5.2 (g), "Discreditable Conduct Relating to the Alleged Victim," below in this chapter, for a discussion of this use of the similar fact evidence rule.

How, then, does one go about applying this variable rule in a given case? The key to applying it successfully is to understand and apply the concepts of probative value and prejudice to the precise facts of a given case.

5. STEP 1 IN THE ANALYSIS: WEIGHING PROBATIVE VALUE

Probative value is the product of a number of factors. Although the similar fact evidence rule does not require judges to follow any particular step-by-step approach, a measure of the probative value of the similar fact evidence can be gained by examining

1) the strength of the evidence that the similar acts actually occurred;
2) (a) the connection between the accused and the similar act event, and (b) "the extent to which the proposed evidence supports the inferences sought to be made"[38] in relation to a specific issue in the case (a.k.a. the "connectedness" between the similar fact evidence and the "questions in issue");[39] and
3) the extent to which the matters it tends to prove are live issues in the proceedings [the materiality of the evidence].[40]

5.1) The Strength of the Evidence That the Similar Acts Occurred

5.1 (a)   Generally
"Where admissibility is bound up with, and dependent upon, probative value, the credibility of the similar fact evidence is a factor that the trial judge, exercising his or her gatekeeping function, is . . . entitled to take into consideration."[41] In other words, the more believable it is that the similar fact event occurred, the more probative value the evidence has. Occasionally, the similar act will have resulted in a conviction, in which case the incident has already been proved beyond a reason-

---

38   R. v. B.(L.), above note 3 at 50.
39   R. v. Handy, above note 10 at para. 76.
40   R. v. B.(L.), above note 3 at 50. In R. v. Mahalingan, above note 18 at para. 163, Justice Charron endorsed the list of factors described in this book as an appropriate framework for evaluating probative value under the similar fact evidence rule.
41   R. v. Handy, above note 10 at para. 134. See also R. v. MacCormack, [2009] O.J. No. 302 at para. 54 (C.A.).

able doubt.[42] In other cases it may emerge from circumstantial evidence alone, as in *Makin v. A.G. for New South Wales* where the *actus reus* of murder of a particular baby could be inferred from the fact that the Makins had buried twelve babies in the backyards of homes they had lived in over the course of several years.[43] Where the similar fact evidence depends on the credibility of a witness, a judge should consider whether the testimony is "reasonably capable of belief" before admitting the evidence.[44] Even then, the more problematic the proof is, the less probative it will be and the less likely admissibility will occur. In *R. v. Handy* the probative value of the evidence was diminished by serious questions about the credibility of the similar act witness, including material inconsistencies in her account,[45] and her financial and personal motives to mislead.[46]

5.1 (b) Acquittals and Stays

Where the accused has been prosecuted for and acquitted of a prior act of misconduct, it will ordinarily be impermissible to use that prior act as similar fact evidence.[47] This is because an acquittal is a finding that the accused was innocent of the prior act,[48] and because the rule of "issue estoppel" bars "the Crown from re-litigating an issue that has been determined in the accused's favour in a prior criminal proceeding, whether on the basis of a positive finding or reasonable doubt."[49] There are exceptions to this rule.

---

42 See *R. v. Fisher* (2003), 179 C.C.C. (3d) 138 (Sask. C.A.), where proof of the similar fact incidents was "strong" because the accused had pled guilty to charges relating to the incidents.

43 Above note 23.

44 *R. v. Handy*, above note 10 at para. 133.

45 *Ibid.*

46 This is mentioned by the Ontario Court of Appeal in *R. v. Handy*, [2000] O.J. No. 1373, but not mentioned when that decision was affirmed in *R. v. Handy*, above note 10.

47 *R. v. Mahalingan*, above note 18.

48 *R. v. Grdic*, [1985] 1 S.C.R. 810; *R. v. Arp*, above note 29.

49 *R. v. Mahalingan*, above note 18 at para. 31. The law is not so clear where a charge alleging the prior act of misconduct has been "stayed." There is authority treating a stay of proceedings as tantamount to an acquittal, triggering the bar: see, for example, *R. v. Rulli*, [1999] O.J. No. 966 (C.A.), leave to appeal to S.C.C. refused, [1999] S.C.C.A. No. 284. On the other hand, proceedings are stayed for a variety of reasons. Most stays are unrelated to the merits of the allegation. The Supreme Court of Canada therefore suggested in *Mahalingan* that a more flexible approach having regard to the purposes of issue estoppels may be appropriate (at para. 77).

The first is known as the *Ollis* exception, after the illustrative decision.[50] Ollis was acquitted of false pretences for cashing a cheque when there was no money in his account. He claimed when tried subsequently for passing another dishonoured cheque that he thought there was money in the account at the time. Yet this second event occurred after the first criminal complaint had been made against Ollis making it most unlikely that Ollis would honestly believe there was money in the account. Since the Crown in *Ollis* was not challenging the earlier acquittal when proving the earlier charge, the Supreme Court of Canada endorsed the *Ollis* exception in *R. v. Mahalingan*, holding that the Crown can "lead evidence underlying a previous acquittal to establish the accused's state of mind in relation to a subsequent charge."[51] The better view is the broader one that if the *fact* of the prior charge is relevant—whether to the state of mind or any other live issue in the case—the Crown can lead evidence about it even where there has been an acquittal.

The second exception is the *Arp* anomaly. This anomaly applies to multi-count indictments—cases where the accused is tried at the same time for more than one act of alleged misconduct. Where this happens and the similar fact evidence rule is satisfied, the Crown can rely on evidence about one charge as similar fact evidence helping to prove another charge.[52] This is so even though the accused may ultimately be acquitted on one or more of those charges. In other words, a trier of fact will not err in using an allegation as similar fact evidence even where the accused will be acquitted of that allegation at the end of the case. This *Arp* anomaly is a pragmatic exception. Were it not recognized, it would be perilous to jointly try charges that the Crown wishes to use as similar fact evidence. Judges are expected to reduce the risk that the principles of issue estoppel will be compromised by directing jurors that they should not use counts that they have already decided to acquit on, as similar fact evidence on the remaining charges.[53]

5.1 (c)   Collaboration

Where evidence depends for its probative value on the unlikelihood that two or more persons would be making similar false allegations, collaboration or "collusion" between those persons undermines entirely the probative value of the evidence.[54] "Collusion can arise both from

---

50   *R. v. Ollis*, [1900] 2 Q.B. 758.
51   *R. v. Mahalingan*, above note 18 at para. 62.
52   See section 10, "The Problem of Multi-Count Indictments or Informations," below in this chapter
53   *R. v. Mahalingan*, above note 18 at paras. 71–72.
54   *R. v. Shearing*, above note 15 at para. 40 (S.C.C.).

a deliberate agreement to concoct evidence as well as from communication among witnesses that can have the effect, whether consciously or unconsciously, of colouring and tailoring their description of the impugned events."[55] Where there is an air of reality to the prospect of collusion "it is not incumbent on the defence to prove collusion."[56] "[T]he Crown is required to satisfy the judge on the balance of probabilities that the evidence is not tainted with collusion," failing which the similar fact evidence will not be admitted.[57]

For there to be an air of reality to the prospect of collusion there must be more than proof of opportunity because "[t]he issue is concoction or collaboration, not contact."[58] Each case will be highly fact dependent. In *R. v. Shearing* the fact that there were communications between some of the thirteen complainants and that civil proceedings had been commenced by two sisters did not furnish an air of reality that was "sufficiently persuasive to trigger the trial judge's gatekeeper function."[59] By contrast, in *R. v. B.(C.)*[60] the Ontario Court of Appeal found an air of reality where the complainants, who were the daughter and granddaughter of the accused, had discussed their allegations and filed a joint lawsuit after the accused punished them financially by firing the daughter and ceasing payments for the granddaughter's education expenses.

5.2)   The Extent to Which the Proposed Evidence Supports the Desired Inferences

The extent to which the similar fact evidence supports the desired inferences has two components: (1) "connection to the accused" (Is the prior conduct linked to the accused?) and (2) "'connectedness' to a properly defined issue" (How informative is the similar fact evidence?).

5.2 (a)   Connection to the Accused
The relevance of similar fact evidence is predicated on the proposition that the accused did the discreditable acts sought to be proved. If there is insufficient evidence rationally to connect the accused to the simi-

---

55   *R. v. B.(C.)* (2003), 171 C.C.C. (3d) 159 at para. 40 (Ont. C.A.).

56   *R. v. Handy*, above note 10 at para. 113; see Christopher W. Morris, "The Possibility of Collusion as a Bar to the Admissibility of Similar Fact Evidence" (2003) 11 C.R. (6th) 81.

57   *Ibid.* at para. 112.

58   *Ibid.* at para. 111.

59   *R. v. Shearing*, above note 15 at paras. 39–45.

60   Above note 55.

lar fact event, it can yield no logical inferences. In *R. v. Sweitzer*,[61] for example, the Crown sought to use eleven allegations of sexual assault committed with the same *modus operandi*, as mutual similar fact evidence proving that Sweitzer was the perpetrator of each of the assaults. The problem was that none of these incidents could logically prove Sweitzer's identity because there was no evidence linking him to any of these allegations. There were however, three other allegations that Sweitzer could be linked to. Since the *modus operandi* was similar, these allegations could be used as similar fact evidence to infer that Sweitzer committed all fourteen similar attacks. Connectedness to the accused of the similar fact episode is a necessary condition to admissibility.

This does not mean that the trial judge has to go so far as to decide that the accused is probably the perpetrator of the similar act. Since the ultimate decision whether to use the similar fact evidence is for the trier of fact, at the admission stage the judge need merely be satisfied that there is some evidence upon which a reasonable trier of fact can make a proper finding that the accused committed that similar act. It will be enough if the evidence linking the accused to the similar act establishes more than a "mere possibility" that he committed it.[62]

Nor does the linking evidence need to be entirely independent of the similar fact evidence. In *R. v. MacCormack* the similar fact evidence included surveillance tapes showing mannerisms and physical characteristics that helped link the accused to the similar fact events. It would have been "unduly antiseptic" to disregard this and insist that only independent evidence can establish the requisite link.[63]

5.2 (b) "Connectedness" to a Properly Defined Issue

Even if a similar fact event did happen and the accused can be linked to the event, the probative value of proving that event will depend on the extent to which, as a matter of human experience, proof of that event supports the desired inference about the matter in issue. In *Handy* the Court referred to this as the "connectedness (or nexus) that is established between the similar fact evidence and the offences alleged" and called it the "principal driver of probative value in the case."[64] The key to undertaking this evaluation is to identify properly the issue the similar fact evidence informs, to identify the inferences the Crown is seeking to use to inform that issue, and to assess the cogency or per-

---

61   *R. v. Sweitzer*, [1982] 1 S.C.R. 949.

62   *R. v. Arp*, above note 29 at 347. See *R. v. Lacroix* (2008), 302 D.L.R. (4th) 13 at 15 (Que. C.A.), rev'd on other grounds (2008), 302 D.L.R. (4th) 13 at 13 (S.C.C.).

63   *R. v. MacCormack*, above note 41.

64   Above note 10 at para. 76.

suasiveness of those inferences.[65] The cases of *R. v. Handy*[66] and *R. v. Shearing*[67] can be used to demonstrate.

In *Handy* the complainant alleged that the accused sexually assaulted her in a painful and degrading manner. The Crown argued that testimony by the former wife of the accused about acts of violence perpetrated against her by the accused was relevant to the credibility of the complainant's account. The Crown urged that the evidence would help establish the credibility of the complaint by showing, consistent with what the complainant was describing, that the accused derived pleasure from sex that is painful to his partner and would not take no for an answer. The Court began its analysis by stressing the importance of properly identifying the issue in question. It rejected the Crown's claim that the evidence helped establish the "credibility of the complainant." What the Crown was really trying to use the similar fact evidence to prove was the *actus reus*. On this kind of issue, "since it is the improbability of a like result being repeated by mere chance that carrie[s] the probative weight, the essence of this probative effect is the similarity of the instance[s]."[68] The Court then identified seven non-exhaustive factors that would assist in assessing similarity:

1) proximity in time of the similar acts
2) the extent to which the other acts are similar in detail
3) number of occurrences of the similar acts
4) circumstances surrounding or relating to the similar acts
5) any distinctive features unifying the incidents
6) intervening events
7) any other factor which would tend to support or rebut the underlying unity of the similar acts.[69]

Using this approach, it became apparent that the similar acts were insufficiently connected to the case to yield real probative value as to whether the accused committed the acts alleged. It was true that the similar acts were sufficiently close in time to the event to support an inference of ongoing propensity, and that they were numerous enough to establish a propensity, but substantial dissimilarities diluted the probative value of the evidence.[70] One of the incidents, choking his

---

65 See *R. v. Johnson*, above note 34 at para. 92.
66 Above note 10.
67 Above note 15.
68 *R. v. Handy*, above note 10 at para. 81, quoting J.H. Chadbourn, ed., *Wigmore on Evidence*, vol. 2 (Boston: Little, Brown, 1979) at 245–46.
69 *R. v. Handy*, *ibid*. at para. 82.
70 *Ibid*. at para. 127. "Not every dissimilarity is fatal . . . but substantial dissimilarities may dilute probative strength."

ex-wife, was simply irrelevant because it was not sexual misconduct. The other incidents involving the ex-wife occurred in the context of a long dysfunctional relationship, whereas the complainant was alleging a "one night stand." None of the acts alleged by the ex-wife began as consensual, as the complainant was alleging in her case, and, although not a condition prerequisite to the admission of sexual activity,[71] there was nothing highly distinctive in the kind of conduct in question that could supply cogency. While the evidence was capable of raising the first desired inference, that the accused derived pleasure from sex that is painful to his partner and would not take no for an answer, the second inference, that this character or propensity supports the inference that the accused proceeded willfully and knowingly in forcing himself on a non-consenting complainant, was "a good deal more problematic" as a proposition of common sense.[72] On balance, neither inference was probative enough to admit because the evidence was not connected sufficiently to the facts of the offence charged to yield probative value on whether the acts allegedly occurred.

R. v. Shearing[73] dealt with a series of jointly charged allegations against the leader of a "marginal cult," the Kalabrian sect. Shearing denied the repeated acts of intercourse alleged by the two "G" sisters who had lived at the Kalabrian residence with their mother and he claimed that the sexual touching of eleven other complainants who came to the residence for religious training was consensual. The Crown was ultimately permitted to rely on all other allegations as similar fact evidence to prove the *actus reus* for each of the allegations — in the case of the "G" sisters to help prove the act, and in the case of the other complainants, to prove non-consent. In examining the nexus or connectedness of all of the counts to each count the Court asked whether "the similar fact is . . . strong enough to be capable of properly raising in the minds of the jury the double inference contended for by the Crown,"[74] namely, that Shearing had a "situation specific propensity to groom adolescent girls for sexual gratification by exploiting pseudoreligious elements of the Kalabrian cult,"[75] and that he proceeded that way with each complainant. The Court analyzed the case according to the same seven-factor list identified in *Handy*. It found that while the numerous sexual act

---

71   *Ibid.* "It should be repeated that the search for similarities is a question of degree. Sexual activity may not show much diversity or distinctiveness" [footnote omitted].

72   *Ibid.* at para. 135.

73   Above note 15.

74   *Ibid.* at para. 38.

75   *Ibid.* at para. 31.

allegations differed, there was sufficient similarity in the *modus oper-andi* Shearing used to create each sexual opportunity, to support the double inferences sought by the Crown. In particular, each of the witnesses described Shearing as securing participation through a distinctive combination of "spiritualist imagery" (using the sexual contact to achieve a higher state of awareness), "horror stories" (invasion of the young girls by disembodied minds), "and the prophylactic power of [his] sexual touching to ward off these horrific threats." The testimony demonstrated a "sexually manipulative personality with a spiritual twist" that, when coupled with the age of the majority of complainants, and with the insistence in each case on confidentiality or silence, was sufficiently situation-specific to support the relevant inferences.[76]

Where the probative value of similar fact evidence depends on similarities, care has to be taken not to act on "generic similarities," or the kinds of features likely to be present in most instances of the same crime. Generic similarities do not yield appropriate inferences. They also increase the risk that the improper inference from "bad person-hood" will be drawn, and they may mask important dissimilarities between the similar fact evidence and the crime charged.[77]

As indicated above in this chapter, what it takes to provide sufficient "connectedness" to the "question in issue" varies according to what that question is. Since the impact of inferences is being examined, connectedness is a matter of logic, not law. As is always true, the logical connection must be evaluated in the entire context of the case. In *R. v. Pickton* the trial judge took too narrow a view of the context. As a result he failed to see how the discreditable conduct evidence that included the use of handcuffs supported the credibility of a witness who recounted strikingly similar admissions he claimed that Pickton had made.[78]

There are no shortcuts or categories that save reasoning. Still, it is informative to explore the most common range of issues that can be advanced through the admission of similar fact evidence.

The first use examined in the text that follows, "Discreditable Conduct That Is Directly Relevant," does not require a close evaluation of relevance. All other uses of similar fact evidence require careful assessment of whether, logically, in the context of the case, the discreditable evidence truly informs the target issue identified.

---

76   *Ibid.* at paras. 51–63.
77   *R. v. Blake* (2003), 181 C.C.C. (3d) 169 at paras. 61–63 (Ont. C.A.), aff'd (2004), 188 C.C.C. (3d) 428 (S.C.C.).
78   Above note 31 at para. 127.

5.2 (c)   Discreditable Conduct That Is Directly Relevant

Sometimes discreditable conduct evidence will be sufficiently connected to a question in issue because it will be "directly relevant" in the
broad sense that the Crown cannot prove the offence charged without
also revealing that the accused has engaged in discreditable conduct
other than the crime charged. For example, it is often necessary to disclose discreditable conduct by the accused on other occasions in order
to establish a motive for a crime, such as proof that a robbery accused
is a drug addict who committed the offence to feed a habit.[79] In R. v.
G.(S.G.)[80] the Crown theory was that the accused ordered the murder
of her son's friend because he was suspected of being an informant
who was going to disclose that there were stolen goods and drugs at her
house. The Crown could not therefore present its murder case without
proving the discreditable fact that the accused possessed stolen goods
and drugs. Naturally, the Court endorsed the admission of this important evidence. It noted that "[e]vidence which is directly relevant to the
Crown's theory of the case is admissible even though it may also demonstrate the bad character of the accused, as long as its probative value
outweighs its prejudicial effect."[81]

For this reason, discreditable gang associations are invariably
proved where the Crown prosecutes the accused for a criminal organization offence, which requires as a matter of law proof that the offence prosecuted is gang-related. A judge should nonetheless be astute
in such cases to limit the proof linking the accused to the gang to evidence that is more probative than prejudicial.[82]

5.2 (d)   Discreditable Conduct Establishing *Mens Rea*

Prior discreditable conduct by an accused person can have significant
probative value in demonstrating the mental state of the accused, be
it knowledge or intent. In such cases, the evidence can be sufficiently
connected to the issue in question as a matter of common sense, even
in the absence of real similarity between the events in question. R. v.
Francis is a case where previous acts of alleged discreditable conduct

---

79   R. v. *Lessard* (2005), 199 C.C.C. (3d) 322 (B.C.C.A.).

80   Above note 7.

81   *Ibid.* at 227. See also R. v. *Beattie* (1996), 94 O.A.C. 363 (C.A.). See also. R. v.
      Bomberry (2010), 78 C.R. (6th) 191 (Ont. C.A.), where the killing occurred
      when the accused was prostituting herself, and where the narrative disclosed
      intravenous drug abuse.

82   See R. v. *Terezakis* (2007), 223 C.C.C. (3d) 344 at para. 46 (B.C.C.A.), where the
      court recognized the broad scope for the exercise of this exclusionary discre-
      tion in criminal organization offences.

assisted in proving knowledge. The accused was charged with false pretences. He claimed to have believed that the crystal ring he was selling was in fact a diamond, as he had represented it to be. Proof that he had previously sold crystal, representing it to be diamond, weakened his defence of mistake of fact. The coincidence that he would do this unwittingly on more than one occasion supported the Crown theory that he knowingly used this particular technique to perpetrate fraud.[83]

Similarly, when a question arises as to whether the accused intended a consequence or caused it by accident, discreditable conduct evidence can be probative. In *R. v. McLean*, where the defence suggested on three occasions that it was implausible to think that the accused would have shot the victim intentionally with other persons in the house, the Ontario Court of Appeal held that the Crown was entitled to rebut this argument by proving that on another occasion the accused did shoot someone while other persons were in the house.[84] In *R. v. Stewart* evidence that a physician had a propensity to sexualize his relationship with a number of patients helped to rebut his claim that some of the touching was accidental.[85]

5.2 (e) Discreditable Conduct Establishing *Actus Reus*

As *Shearing* demonstrates, similar fact evidence can be used to prove that a crime occurred, or, to put the matter more technically, to establish the *actus reus* of an offence. So, too, does the classic case of *Makin v. A.G. for New South Wales*.[86] Evidence that a number of babies found buried in three properties linked to the Makins was admitted to establish that the alleged murder victim, the baby Horace Murray, had been killed. The prospect that Horace Murray had died of natural causes was significantly reduced by the evidence of the deaths and of the secreted burial of twelve other babies whom the Makins had also secured from their mothers by placing an ad in the paper and accepting modest and inadequate payment to care for the children.[87] By contrast, in *R. v. Watkins* the Crown's attempt to prove the *actus reus* of the offence by using similar fact evidence failed because the similar fact event was too different from the event charged to support the inferences sought. The Crown had tried to support its theory that the deceased was strangled

---

83   (1874), L.R. 2 C.C.R. 128. This kind of case is sometimes analyzed as turning on the existence of a "systematic course of conduct," of which the offence charged is but one example. See, for example, *R. v. Foley* (1996), 75 B.C.A.C. 195 (C.A.).

84   *R. v. McLean* (2002), 170 C.C.C. (3d) 330 (Ont. C.A.).

85   *R. v. Stewart* (2004), 183 C.C.C. (3d) 421 (B.C.C.A.).

86   Above note 23.

87   See also *R. v. Pickton*, above note 31, for a comparable contemporary example.

by the accused and then tied with a phone cord to a doorknob to simu-
late a suicide, by calling evidence from a former girlfriend of the accused that he had restrained her hands for several minutes by pulling
on a phone cord that he had wrapped around her wrists.[88]

5.2 (f)   Discreditable Conduct and the Credibility of Complainants

Similarities in the particular features of *independent* allegations by
two or more persons can reach the point where it would defy common sense to think that such similarities are merely coincidental. It is
possible where this is so to use independent allegations to support the
credibility of the complainant who is making an allegation. Independent allegations can yield probative value on credibility in this way even
where there is nothing strikingly similar or unique in the allegations,
provided a network of features is shared between the allegations that
is significant enough to undermine the suggestion of chance. For example, in *R. v. G.(M.A.)*,

> [e]ach [witness] described predatorial behaviour that was facilitated
> by the appellant's exploitation of the student/teacher relationship.
> Like the complainants, the witnesses on the prior conduct described
> what could be regarded as a pattern of "grooming" by the appellant
> through his unorthodox displays of affection toward his students,
> and the atypical extent to which he cultivated personal relationships
> with his students by, for example, encouraging them to regard him
> as their confidant.[89]

Does it not enhance the credibility of each complainant to learn that
several complainants were not just making allegations but allegations
that share these materially similar features? This kind of reasoning
depends entirely on being able to discount any collaboration or contamination between those witnesses,[90] for if the similar fact witness
has become exposed to the complainant's version, the "unlikelihood
of coincidence between stories" reasoning that animates the credibility
inference will be undermined.

The Court in *R. v. Shearing* warned that particular care must be
taken when attempting to use similar fact evidence to support the
credibility of witnesses. This can be done properly only where there
is an improbability of coincidence given the *particular features* of the

---

88   *R. v. Watkins* (2003), 181 C.C.C. (3d) 78 (Ont. C.A.).

89   *R. v. G.(M.A.)* was dealt with by the Ontario Court of Appeal as a companion
      case to *R. v. B.(L.)*, above note 3 at 72, with the reasons being delivered in a
      single judgment.

90   See section 5.1(c), "Collaboration," above in this chapter.

respective allegations. It would be an error to use proof that merely "blackens the character of the accused . . . [to] enhance the credibility of a complainant['s allegation]. Identification of credibility as the 'issue in question' may, unless circumscribed, risk the admission of evidence of nothing more than general disposition ('bad personhood')."[91]

5.2 (g) Discreditable Conduct Relating to the Alleged Victim

Courts often permit the Crown to prove the violent or abusive nature of the prior relationship between the accused and an alleged victim.[92] In *R. v. MacDonald*, for example, the complainant described how her relationship with the accused, charged with possessing a weapon and threatening her, had become increasingly abusive leading up to the incident. She was allowed to recount specific, uncharged acts of violence that he committed against her. The Ontario Court of Appeal held that "evidence of the nature of the relationship . . . provided context that was essential to an accurate interpretation of the event."[93] Where such evidence demonstrates a "strong disposition"[94] to act violently or sexually[95] towards the victim, it is not being used to prove the "bad personhood" of the accused but, as *R. v. Batte* explained, to support the specific inferences that the accused is disposed to act violently (or sexually) *towards the victim* and that he had that disposition on the occasion in question.[96] While it is common to describe this evidence as demonstrating motive or animus,[97] these labels do not detract from the fact that the evidence is being used for permissible propensity reasoning that can enlighten a court about either the *actus reus* of an offence,[98] or the *mens rea*.[99]

---

91   *R. v. Handy*, above note 10 at paras. 115–16.

92   See *R. v. Cudjoe* (2009), 68 C.R. (6th) 86 at para. 64 (Ont. C.A.).

93   *R. v. MacDonald* (2002), 170 C.C.C. (3d) 46 (Ont. C.A.).

94   *R. v. C.(D.A.R.)* (2002), 170 C.C.C. (3d) 64 at para. 45 (P.E.I.C.A.).

95   In *R. v. H.(J.)* (2006), 44 C.R. (6th) 136 (Ont. C.A.), the "strong disposition" threshold was not met by evidence of three prior sexual episodes between the accused and his younger sister that were different in nature than the crime alleged, particularly given the long delay between those episodes and the alleged crime.

96   (2000), 49 O.R. (3d) 321 at paras. 102–3 (C.A.).

97   See, for example, *R. v. F.(D.S.)* (1999), 132 C.C.C. (3d) 97 (Ont. C.A.).

98   For example, *R. v. MacDonald*, above note 93, as to whether words spoken were threatening, and *R. v. C.(D.A.R.)*, above note 94, as to whether the assault alleged occurred.

99   For example, in *R. v. Dupré* (1994), 25 W.C.B. (2d) 85 (Que. C.A.), evidence of harassment and a prior attack on the shooting victim helped demonstrate that the shooting was not accidental. In *R. v. Millar* (1989), 71 C.R. (3d) 78 (Ont. C.A.), evidence of a course of violent conduct against a child supported proof of intent to injure in a baby-shaking case. In *R. v. De La Cruz* (2003), 174 C.C.C. (3d) 554

This is not to say that evidence of prior acts of violence or sexual aggression by the accused against a victim will always be admissible. The evidence is still presumptively inadmissible and should be allowed only where a court concludes that the probative value of the evidence in relation to a particular issue, which the Crown must identify,[100] outweighs its prejudice. For example, in *R. v. Johnson* a prior physical assault related to the victim's "misbehaviour" offered no "real insight in the background and relationship between the accused and the victim" that could help prove that the accused was the one responsible for her sexual killing.[101]

5.3) The Materiality of the Evidence

The issue that the similar fact evidence is tendered to establish must be "live" or material. "If the issue has ceased to be in dispute, as for example when the fact is admitted by the accused, then the evidence is [immaterial] and must be excluded."[102] In *Handy* the Supreme Court of Canada also noted how the relative importance of the issue in the particular trial may also have a bearing. "Similar fact evidence that is virtually conclusive of a minor issue may still be excluded for reasons of overall prejudice."[103]

5.4) Confirmation by Other Evidence

The relevant inquiry is into the probative value of the inference yielded by the similar fact evidence, not the probative value of the Crown's case. For this reason the probative value of the similar fact evidence is not enhanced because other evidence supports the same inference the similar fact evidence is offered to promote. *R. v. Arp*[104] illustrates the point. There the Crown presented similar fact evidence, arguing that similarities in the *modus operandi* between two killings showed that

---

(Ont. C.A.), the evidence revealed that the accused, charged with criminal harassment, had an animus towards the complainant and a need to dominate and control her. In *R. v. Reid* (2003), 18 C.R. (6th) 350 (Ont. C.A.), evidence of past abuse of his former common-law partner supported the Crown theory that he killed her male friend because of his violent, possessive, and jealous relationship with her.

100   *R. v. C.(D.A.R.)*, above note 94 at para. 44.

101   *R. v. Johnson*, above note 34 at para. 101.

102   *R. v. Handy*, above note 10 at para. 74. See *R. v. Proctor* (1991), 11 C.R. (4th) 200 at 210 (Man. C.A.).

103   *R. v. Handy, ibid.*

104   *R. v. Arp*, above note 29.

the same person committed both killings. If Arp could be linked to one killing, this similar fact *modus operandi* inference would therefore help show that he committed both murders. As it happens, the Crown had other evidence linking Arp to each killing. He possessed the first murder victim's jewelry and his DNA was linked to the second killing. Along with the similar fact evidence this other evidence certainly made the Crown's case against Arp stronger. Yet the discovery of the jewelry and the DNA did nothing to enhance the similar fact inference itself. As indicated, that inference derived from the similarities in the manner in which the victims were killed and the jewelry and DNA evidence had nothing to do with *modus operandi*. Since the admissibility question is about the probative value of the similar fact evidence, the Supreme Court of Canada therefore evaluated the probative value of the similar fact evidence independently of the other evidence that happened to point in the same direction.

In *R. v. James*[105] the Ontario Court of Appeal did not apply the *Arp* principle. It found that similar fact evidence demonstrating that seven years earlier the accused had lured a woman into a secluded area and sexually assaulted her, could be used as evidence that his homicide of the victim, also lured into a remote area, was sexual in nature. The court held that the probative value of the similar fact evidence was enhanced because other evidence also suggested the killing was sexual. With respect, this is not so. That other evidence enhanced the strength of the Crown's case but did nothing to make the similar fact evidence more probative. The *Arp* principle should have governed. The probative value inquiry should focus on the contribution of the similar fact evidence alone.

6. STEP 2 IN THE ANALYSIS: ASSESSING PREJUDICE FOR THE PURPOSE OF ADMISSIBILITY

"[P]otential prejudice to the accused may be assessed in the following manner:

- by considering the potential for 'moral prejudice' against the accused. 'Moral prejudice' means the risk of convicting the accused because he is a 'bad person' rather than based on proof that he committed the offence; and

---

105 (2007), 213 C.C.C. (3d) 235 (Ont. C.A.).

- *by considering the potential for 'reasoning prejudice' against the accused, meaning the risk of distracting or confusing the jury, or of undue consumption of time, and the danger that the jury may have difficulty disentangling the subject matter of the charges from the similar fact evidence."[106]*

6.1) Moral Prejudice

Moral prejudice refers to the risk that the evidence will be used to infer guilt based on the "forbidden chain of reasoning . . . from general disposition or propensity."[107] Of interest, Justice Binnie noted that model jury behaviour studies call into question the effectiveness that a judge's limiting instruction not to use the forbidden chain of reasoning will have. In *R. v. Last* Justice Deschamps cautioned that jury directions do not remove but only reduce the risk of moral prejudice.[108] The limits on what restricted admissibility doctrines can achieve reinforce the need to maintain a high awareness of the potential prejudicial effect of admitting similar fact evidence, particularly where the similar fact conduct is reprehensible.

The Supreme Court of Canada cautioned in *Shearing* that where the similar fact evidence reveals a "morally repugnant act" its potentially poisonous nature will require a correspondingly high probative value to overcome its impact.[109] In *Shearing* itself the evidence was deeply disturbing, revealing a pattern of the misuse of religious authority to sexually exploit adolescents. It took highly probative evidence to justify running the risks of moral prejudice this proof would cause.

Similar fact evidence will also raise a real risk of moral prejudice where, as in *R. v. Handy*, the similar fact incidents are more reprehensible than the charge before the court.[110] By contrast, where the offence charged is significantly more troubling than the similar fact evidence, the risk of moral prejudice is diminished. In *R. v. Talbot* proof that the accused plied young boys with alcohol without sexually assaulting them caused only a modest risk of prejudice where he was charged with intoxicating and then sexually assaulting other boys.[111]

---

106 *R. v. K.(C.P.)*, [2002] O.J. No. 4929 at para. 30 (C.A.).
107 *Ibid.* at para. 139.
108 [2009] S.C.J. No. 45 at para. 46.
109 *R. v. Shearing*, above note 15 at paras. 71–72, and see *R. v. B.(C.R.)*, [1990] 1 S.C.R. 717 at 735, and *R. v. Pascoe*, above note 21.
110 Above note 10 at para. 141.
111 *R. v. Talbot* (2002), 161 C.C.C. (3d) 256 (Ont. C.A.).

The risk of moral prejudice is considered to be modest where the similar fact evidence involves prior acts of aggression against the victim of the crime charged. This is because of the theory that the evidence of prior threats or abuse of the victim is so closely connected to the specific charge that it is unlikely a jury would resort to the prohibited inference.[112]

6.2) Reasoning Prejudice

Reasoning prejudice has to do with the distraction of the trier of fact from its proper focus on the charge itself. "Distraction can take different forms."[113] The first kind of distraction is much like "moral prejudice" in that it describes how the trier of fact can be deflected from engaging in a rational assessment of the case by sentiments of revulsion and condemnation. The second form of distraction arises from the risk that the court will be caught up in a conflict about the similar fact evidence. Where this happens, the accused may be unable to respond effectively, because of the lapse of time or surprise, or the distraction of having to defend the charge as well as litigate collateral issues requiring full side-trials into whether the similar fact event has even occurred.[114] In *R. v. McDonald*, prejudice sufficient to require the exclusion of the evidence arose because the allegations made by the similar fact witness were more complex and more difficult to try than the offence charged. It was therefore too prejudicial to expect the accused to respond to the similar fact allegations.[115] "Thus the practical realities of the trial process reinforce the prejudice inherent in the poisonous nature of the propensity evidence itself."[116] Finally, there is the danger where many separate but similar incidents are being proved that the trier of fact might "mix up the matters of consideration (the similar acts) with the matters of decision (the charge)."[117]

6.3) Factors Reducing the Impact of Prejudice

The risk of prejudice is considered to be less in a judge alone trial than in a jury trial.[118] This does not mean it disappears entirely. Even judges

---

112 *R. v. Dupras* (2003), 173 C.C.C. (3d) 55 (B.C.C.A.); *R. v. Pasqualino* (2008), 233 C.C.C.(3d) 319 (Ont. C.A.); *R. v. Sandhu* (2009), 63 C.R. (6th) 1 (Ont. C.A.).

113 *R. v. Handy*, above note 10 at para. 145.

114 *Ibid.* at para. 146.

115 [2000] O.J. No. 3315 at para. 33 (C.A.).

116 Above note 10 at para. 146.

117 *R. v. Shearing*, above note 15 at para. 69.

118 *R. v. B.(T.)* (2009), 95 O.R. (3d) 21 at paras. 26–29 (C.A.).

can struggle to overcome the tainting effect that discreditable information which is given undue focus during a trial can have. As for reasoning prejudice, the superior ability of judges to focus on material issues does little for the impact admission can have on the length and complexity of the trial. The admission of similar fact evidence can also prejudice accused persons. Attention and resources that can otherwise be expended addressing the charged allegations may be diverted to respond to the similar fact evidence. Depending on its nature and vintage there are even cases where it is more difficult to defend against the similar fact allegations than against the crime charged. It would therefore be wrong to assume that the prejudice in admitting similar fact evidence disappears entirely in judge alone trials.

Where prejudice can be diminished by editing the evidence and leading it in a more restrictive form, this may be appropriate to reduce the risk of prejudice.[119] Moreover, in assessing prejudice, attention should be paid to whether the discreditable information is going to gain admission in some other way; if the problematic information will be admitted in any event through another mode of proof, such as by confronting the accused as a witness under section 12 of the *Canada Evidence Act* with his prior convictions,[120] the degree of prejudice caused by admission of the similar fact evidence may be reduced.

6.4) Factors Enhancing the Impact of Prejudice

It has often been said that "where the similar fact evidence is required to bear the whole burden of connecting the crime charged . . . a very high degree of similarity is required."[121] This is because the consequences of the misuse of similar fact evidence, should it occur, are apt to be higher when it stands alone

7. THE BALANCING

Once probative value is assessed and the risk of prejudice is identified in the context of the particular case, the final step is to balance the two, always bearing in mind that the similar fact evidence is *prima facie*

---

119 *R. v. Shearing*, above note 15 at para. 142; *R. v. McLean*, above note 84 at para. 20.
120 *R. v. McLean*, *ibid.* at para. 20.
121 *R. v. Dickenson* (1984), 40 C.R. (3d) 384 at 389 (Ont. C.A.), and see *R. v. Paul* (2002), 7 C.R. (6th) 30 (Ont. C.A.), and *R. v. Warren*, [1999] O.J. No. 4555 at para. 5 (C.A.).

inadmissible, and that admission will be an exception that must be established as appropriate, on the balance of probabilities, by the Crown. As indicated, to prevent the prohibited inference there is merit in looking for probative value to exceed significantly the risk of prejudice that admission would present.[122]

In *R. v. Handy*, Justice Binnie observed that a challenge in balancing probative value and prejudice is that there is no necessary inverse relationship between probative value and prejudice. When probative value increases, prejudice does not necessarily decrease.[123] Given that there is always a risk of prejudice when similar fact evidence is admitted, perhaps the best way to conduct the balancing exercise is to ask whether the similar fact evidence has been demonstrated to be sufficiently probative to justify running the risks of prejudice presented by the evidence.

This assessment is not scientific. The exercise is one of balancing competing considerations. Different judges can therefore come to different conclusions on the same facts without an error occurring.[124] Accordingly, the decision of the trial judge is entitled to "substantial deference," always bearing in mind that "[a] trial judge has no discretion to admit similar fact evidence whose prejudice outweighs its probative value,"[125] and has no power to admit similar fact evidence that can do no more than raise the prohibited inference. An appeal court will interfere only if there has been a material error in principle in applying the law or where there is only one reasonable answer and the judge fails to arrive at it.[126]

8. THE MANDATORY DIRECTION

When similar fact evidence is admitted its use is restricted. Judges err if they misuse it and jurors must be trained not to do so. Although no specific wording is required, a proper jury direction should ordinarily:

- direct the jury to avoid relying on the prohibited inference.[127] The jury must be told "that they may not use the similar fact evidence to

---

122 *R. v. Pickton*, above note 31 at para. 77.

123 *R. v. Handy*, above note 10 at para. 149.

124 *R. v. Harvey*, (2001), 48 C.R. (6th) 247 at para. 42 (Ont. C.A.), aff'd (2002), 7 C.R. (6th) 1 (S.C.C.).

125 *R. v. Handy*, above note 10 at para. 153.

126 *R. v. Harvey*, above note 124 at para. 50 (Ont. C.A.).

127 *R. v. B.(F.F.)* (1993), 18 C.R. (4th) 261 at 275; *R. v. N.(R.K.)* (1997), 114 C.C.C. (3d) 40 at 47–48 (Ont. C.A.).

reason from general disposition or character to guilt"[128] by "infer[ring] that the accused is a person whose character or disposition is such that he or she is likely to have committed the offence or offences charged";[129]

- direct the jury that they are not to "punish the accused for past misconduct [revealed by the discreditable conduct evidence] by finding the accused guilty of the offence or offenses charged";[130]
- provide direction on the appropriate, non-prohibited use to which the discreditable conduct evidence may be put in the case at hand,[131] including by describing for the jury the issue the evidence addresses and instructing them that they are not to use it for any other purpose;[132]
- advise the jury not to use the evidence unless they are satisfied that the similar fact incident occurred;[133]
- direct the jury on the frailties of the similar fact evidence;[134] and
- (where the desired inference depends upon coincidence reasoning) direct the jury to consider whether that apparent coincidence can be explained away by collaboration or contamination between witnesses.[135]

The most critical aspect is the "limiting instruction" described in the first bullet. The failure to provide it normally results in a successful appeal. There are exceptions. Where the discreditable conduct evidence relates to the victim of the alleged offence a judge may not be required to train the jury to avoid the prohibited inference since the risk of moral prejudice is believed to be low.[136] Similarly, where the misconduct evidence describes a "completely different type of wrongdoing," the failure to give a direction may not be fatal if the misconduct is materially less offensive than the conduct charged,[137] or is presented in a non-inflammatory way.[138]

---

128 R. v. B.(C.), above note 55 at para. 35.
129 R. v. Arp, above note 29 at 356.
130 R. v. B.(C.), above note 55 at para. 35.
131 R. v. Rulli, above note 49.
132 R. v. Handy, above note 10 at para. 70.
133 R. v. B.(C.), above note 55 at para. 29.
134 R. v. Anderson (2003), 19 C.R. (6th) 152 at paras. 28–29 (Ont. C.A.).
135 R. v. B.(C.), above note 55 at para. 44.
136 R. v. Krugel (2000), 143 C.C.C. (3d) 367 (Ont. C.A.). See this chapter, section 6.1, "Moral Prejudice."
137 R. v. M.(R.), [1998] O.J. No. 3922 (C.A.).
138 R. v. C.(N.P.) (2007), 86 O.R. (3d) 571 at para. 23 (C.A.).

9. THE SPECIAL CASE OF PROVING IDENTITY THROUGH SIMILAR FACT EVIDENCE

Sometimes the similar way that two or more crimes are committed supports the conclusion that they were each committed by the same person. Although identity cases are resolved using the general similar fact evidence rule described above, the Supreme Court of Canada in *R. v. Arp* provided extremely formalized suggestions for analyzing such cases.

Two inquiries must be undertaken before this kind of similar fact evidence can be admitted. First, the judge is to "assess the degree of similarity demonstrated by the manner in which the acts in question were committed to determine whether it is *likely* the same person committed the alleged similar acts."[139] As the Court noted, "[g]enerally . . . a high degree of similarity between the acts is required . . . . The similarity between the acts may consist of a unique trademark or . . . a series of significant similarities."[140] It is important to remember that in answering the predicate question of whether the same person likely committed both acts, the focus must be on the acts themselves and not on other evidence of the accused's involvement in those acts. As explained, the probative value of the similar fact inference turns on similarity between the events, not on other evidence.[141]

The case of the lipstick robber described earlier in this chapter would pass this part of the test for admission because the "unique trademark" employed by the robber renders it unlikely that different persons would, by coincidence, be acting in this same unusual fashion. By contrast, in *R. v. Trochym*, proof that the accused had in the past banged aggressively and incessantly on the door of another girlfriend after their relationship ended, was too generic to yield the "improbability of coincidence" required to enable the trier of fact to infer that it must have been Trochym who was heard knocking on the door of his deceased former girlfriend the day she died.[142]

Although on the outer edge of admissibility, the *Arp* case itself illustrates how even a series of "significant similarities" short of a "unique trademark" can, on the basis of coincidence reasoning, establish that

---

139 Above note 29 at 344 [emphasis in original].

140 *Ibid.* at 345. *R. v. Nicholas* (2004), 70 O.R. (3d) 1 (C.A.), is a case where a series of significant but non-unique similarities between offences helped identify the accused as the perpetrator.

141 See the discussion in section 5.4, "Confirmation by Other Evidence," above in this chapter.

142 *R. v. Trochym* (2007), 216 C.C.C. (3d) 225 (S.C.C.).

the same person likely committed both offences. The facts were these. Approximately three and one-half years apart, two lone, young, intoxicated females went missing in the early-morning hours. Each was transported to a remote location near Prince George, B.C. Each was killed and left naked. In each case the victim's clothes were scattered about by a killer who used a sharp implement to cut some of the clothing. The Supreme Court of Canada chose not to disturb the trial judge's finding that these homicides were sufficiently similar that they were likely committed by the same person.

Where the judge has determined that the crime charged and the similar act offence were likely committed by the same person, the judge is then to ask a second question. The judge is to determine whether there is some evidence linking the accused to the similar act.[143] If these two tests are met the probative value of the similar act will outweigh the prejudice of the evidence.[144] It can therefore go to the jury on the issue of identity. It is then up to the jury to decide whether to use that evidence. The "jury should be instructed that . . . [if] they have concluded that there is sufficient likelihood that the same person committed the alleged similar acts, they may consider all the evidence relating to the similar acts in considering whether the accused is guilty of the act in question."[145] If they so conclude, they may choose to infer that "[t]he unlikelihood of an accused's twice being implicated in two very similar offences may furnish circumstantial evidence of his or her guilt for both."[146]

Where it can be shown that a gang used a unique or distinctive *modus operandi* in committing other offences, this can serve as similar fact evidence to establish that a gang was responsible for a specific crime where that same *modus operandi* was used. In *R. v. Perrier* the *modus operandi* used in committing each home invasion was so distinct that it was improbable that the home invasions had been committed by independent gangs. The "signature" consisted of having one gang member pose as a postman to gain entry to the home of East Asian women, who would then be overpowered by two other gang members and bound by duct-tape. This evidence linked the gang to the crime charged.[147]

Similar fact proof that the gang committed the offences is not, however, proof without more that a particular member of the gang

---

143 See section 5.2 (a), "Connection to the Accused," above in this chapter.
144 *R. v. Arp*, above note 29 at 345.
145 *Ibid.* at 353–54.
146 *Ibid.* at 351.
147 *R. v. Perrier* (2004), 188 C.C.C. (3d) 1 (S.C.C.).

participated. The Crown can use distinctive gang crimes as proof of individual identity only if the Crown shows that the composition of the gang never changed and the accused was a member, or by showing that the accused played such a distinctive role that no other member of the group could have performed it during the offence charged, or by furnishing independent evidence linking the accused to each of the offences.[148] In *Perrier* there was no basis to link the accused to the crime, even though he was a gang member. The trial judge therefore erred in using proof of the gang crimes as evidence to prove his involvement.

10. THE PROBLEM OF MULTI-COUNT INDICTMENTS OR INFORMATIONS

Often accused persons will face several criminal allegations during the same trial. This occurs when the "information" or the "indictment" contains more than one charge or "count." Most often the counts arise out of the same event. Where this is so it is permissible to use evidence presented about one of those counts when disposing of the other accounts.[149] At times, however, different counts will relate to different events. Shearing, for example, was charged in one indictment with twenty sexual offences against eleven different complainants that happened on different occasions, while Arp was charged in the same indictment with two separate sexual slayings.[150] Multi-count informations and indictments that allege *separate incidents* immediately raise the risk of prejudice, given that the triers of fact will be learning during the same trial about separate allegations of misconduct by the accused. The similar fact evidence rule influences how this risk is dealt with. There are three relevant scenarios.

First, the accused may apply for an order "severing" the counts so that they will be tried in separate proceedings. If the court rules that the counts can be used as similar fact evidence this "will favour a joint trial since the evidence on all incidents would have to be introduced in

---

148 *Ibid.* See also *R. v. Chan* (2004), 188 C.C.C. (3d) 14 (S.C.C.).

149 For example, if an accused uses a gun during a robbery and touches the bank teller in a sexual manner, the accused could be charged with separate offences of robbery, sexual assault, and use of a weapon in the commission of an offence. Naturally, since the evidence presented about each of those counts relates to the same event—the way the accused acted when in the bank—it can be considered when resolving each of the related counts.

150 *R. v. Shearing*, above note 15, and *R. v. Arp*, above note 29.

any event."[151] The severance motion will likely fail. If the similar fact evidence rule is not satisfied and there are no compelling reasons to try the multiple counts together (such as a meaningful legal and factual nexus between counts, the risk of inconsistent verdicts, potential prejudice caused by delay, or efficiency and cost effectiveness) severance may be required to prevent the pointless risk of prejudice.[152]

It is important for accused persons opposing the use of similar fact evidence to apply for severance of counts rather than to simply object to admissibility. Not only will severance prevent the trier of fact from hearing about the other alleged misconduct, but also courts have held that where unrelated incidents are going to be tried jointly in any event, the gateway for admission of similar fact evidence is more welcoming. This is because most of the "reasoning prejudice" concerns that might impel exclusion in separate trials do not apply.[153]

The second scenario applies where the evidence relating to one or more different event counts is not admissible as similar fact evidence on the other counts but where the counts are not severed. In these cases it is not possible to exclude proof of misconduct on other occasions so we take a restricted admissibility approach and rely on jury directions to ameliorate the risk of prejudice. The trial judge must direct the trier of fact not to consider the evidence pertaining to one event as proof that the accused committed an allegation made in a separate account. This bar does not apply to credibility determinations. Observations about the credibility of a witness made when that witness is testifying about one event can be used by the trier of fact in deciding whether to believe what that witness says about a different event charged in the same information or indictment.[154]

The third scenario involves cases where the evidence on one or more of the counts is admissible as similar fact evidence on the other counts. The trial judge must ensure in such cases that the evidence is used properly. In jury trials this requires complex jury directions in which juries are trained on how to apply similar fact evidence, and cautioned where necessary not to invoke the prohibited inference.[155]

---

151 R. v. Last, above note 108.
152 Ibid.
153 See R. v. MacCormack, above note 41 at para. 56 (C.A.); R. v. B.(T.) (2009), 95 O.R. (3d) 21 at paras. 27–32 (C.A.).
154 R. v. C.(P.E.) (2005), 196 C.C.C. (3d) 351 (S.C.C.).
155 See the jury direction provided for in R. v. Arp, above note 29 at 356.

11. CHARACTER EVIDENCE CALLED BY AN ACCUSED (AGAINST A CO-ACCUSED)

> *Subject to the discretion of the trial judge to exclude evidence where its prejudicial effect is greater than its probative value, an accused person may establish that, by reason of his character, a co-accused is the more likely perpetrator of the crime with which they are charged. In doing so, however, the accused will be taken to have put his own character in issue.*

Jointly accused persons may attempt to deflect the blame to each other and, in doing so, may be allowed to adduce evidence about a relevant character trait of the other to suggest that he is the more likely perpetrator. This would include evidence that the Crown could not have called.[156] It is even permissible for an accused person to rely upon the otherwise prohibited inference that the co-accused is, by reason of his character, the type of person to commit the offence.[157] The sole fixed limitation is that an accused cannot try to establish the propensity of a co-accused by relying on acts for which the co-accused has been acquitted.[158] Where an accused does call evidence suggesting that the co-accused is the kind of person to commit the offence that inference can be relied on by the accused in defending himself, but not by the Crown in proving the guilt of the co-accused. Nor can evidence of the co-accused's character be used by the Crown on the issue of the co-accused's credibility as a witness.[159] In a jury trial, both the positive use to which the evidence can be put, and the limits on its use, must be explained to the jury.[160]

The right of an accused to make full answer and defence does not automatically trump the rights or interests of a co-accused.[161] The judge retains the discretion to exclude character evidence about a co-accused where its probative value to the case for the accused does not warrant the serious prejudice it will cause to the co-accused. In order to permit the judge to undertake this balancing, the accused should notify the judge of his intention to prove evidence demonstrating a co-accused's

---

156 R. v. *Kendall* (1987), 57 C.R. (3d) 249 (Ont. C.A.).

157 R. v. *Suzack*, [2000] O.J. No. 100 (C.A.), leave to appeal to S.C.C. refused, [2000] S.C.C.A. No. 583.

158 R. v. *Akins* (2002), 5 C.R. (6th) 400 (Ont. C.A.).

159 R. v. *Diu*, [2000] O.J. No. 1770 at para. 142 (C.A.).

160 R. v. *Suzack*, above note 157 at para. 127 (C.A.).

161 R. v. *Creighton* (*sub nom. R. v. Crawford*) (1995), 37 C.R. (4th) 197 at 213 (S.C.C.); R. v. *Akins*, above note 158.

bad character. The judge should ensure that there is a real evidentiary foundation in the case for the proof that is probative enough to "be legitimately and reasonably capable of assisting the [trier of fact] in arriving at a just verdict." The judge should also ensure that the risk of prejudice does not substantially outweigh that probative value on the basis that the evidence would "mislead the [trier of fact because it would be given too much weight], would involve an inordinate amount of time, would unduly distract the jury from the real issues in the case, or would cause unfair surprise to [the co-accused's] defence."[162]

Moreover, accused persons who urge that their co-accused is the type to have committed the offence put their own character in issue; the suggestion implicit in their evidence is that they are not the type. If they are in fact the type, this propensity can be shown.[163]

12. "GOOD" OR EXCULPATORY CHARACTER EVIDENCE CALLED BY AN ACCUSED: INTRODUCED

The accused may prove that she is not the kind of person who would commit the offence with which she is charged. This proof can be done through

- *reputation witnesses;*
- *admissible expert testimony;*
- *the accused's own testimony;*
- *similar fact evidence; and*
- *according to some authorities, the opinion evidence of lay witnesses who are familiar with the accused.*

Where an accused presents this kind of evidence, she will be taken to have placed her own character in issue, enabling the Crown to present evidence about her character for the purpose of neutralizing the character evidence of the defence. This can be done through

- *the cross-examination of the character witnesses and of the accused;*

---

162 R. v. *Pollock* (2004), 23 C.R. (6th) 98 (Ont. C.A.).

163 R. v. *McMillan* (1975), 29 C.R.N.S. 191 (Ont. C.A.), aff'd (*sub nom. McMillan v. R.*), [1977] 2 S.C.R. 824. See the discussion in section 4.15.1 "Generally," for a more detailed description of the same principle, applied to evidence of the character of third parties other than the accused.

- *rebuttal reputation witnesses;*
- *proof of the previous convictions of the accused;*
- *admissible expert testimony; and*
- *otherwise admissible similar fact evidence.*

There is authority suggesting that rebuttal can be done by using relevant prior inconsistent statements made by the accused.

"Good" or exculpatory character evidence is proof presented by the accused to suggest that he or she is not the type to have committed the offence. Typically the character trait proved by the accused is a positive one such as honesty, or passivity. For this reason the term "good character" is used to describe the relevant rules. Those rules embrace, however, proof that the accused possesses an unappealing character trait that, on the peculiar facts of a case, may make the commission of the offence less likely, such as "homophobia"[164] or suicidal tendency.[165] The term "good character" should therefore be understood as including any character trait that may help exculpate the accused.

Proof of good character is generally considered to be relevant; we may not be surprised to hear of criminal allegations against some acquaintances, but might thoroughly disbelieve a similar allegation if directed at others. Since the trier of fact does not know the character of the accused, the rules of evidence allow this kind of proof, although for some offences, such as sexual assaults, its probative value may be slight,[166] including in the case of sexual offence allegations involving adult victims.[167] It is nonetheless an error for the trial judge to ignore good character evidence or to fail to direct a jury that it may consider good character evidence relating to the accused, both to raise a reasonable doubt on the charges and, if he testifies, to assess his credibility as a witness.[168]

The common law is guarded about the admission of this kind of evidence because of concern that it will take an inordinate amount of time to present, raising as it does the entire life of the accused. As the following modes of proving good character demonstrate, strict limits have traditionally been placed on how it can be presented. When the accused calls such evidence, he puts his character into issue and the Crown becomes entitled to use various techniques to rebut that evidence. However, where the defence uses an inadmissible method of presenting

---

164 *R. v. Lupien*, [1970] S.C.R. 263.
165 *R. v. Morrissey* (2003), 12 C.R. (6th) 337 (Ont. S.C.J.).
166 *R. v. Profit* (1993), 24 C.R. (4th) 279 (S.C.C.).
167 *R. v. R.(B.S.)* (2006), 212 C.C.C. (3d) 65 at 83 (Ont. C.A.).
168 *R. v. Norman* (1993), 26 C.R. (4th) 256 (Ont. C.A.); *R. v. Millar,* above note 99.

good character evidence, such as by cross-examining Crown witnesses to elicit answers reflecting their opinion that he is not the type to commit the offence, the Crown cannot rebut this evidence. The appropriate response is for the judge to direct the jury to disregard it.[169]

13. GOOD CHARACTER EVIDENCE AND MODES OF PRESENTATION

13.1) Reputation Evidence

The accused cannot call witnesses to show that he has engaged in specific acts demonstrating his good character. This is to avoid mini-trials into those specific claims. Instead, the common law allows the compendious and concise technique of calling reputation witnesses. Witnesses who know the accused and are familiar with her reputation because they share a relevant circle of acquaintances with her are permitted to testify that her reputation is good.[170] The reputation testified to must be relevant, be it for morality in a sexual offence case,[171] peacefulness in a violence case, or honesty in a dishonesty prosecution.

13.2) Opinion Evidence

It has long been established that a character witness must confine himself to the community's perceptions of the accused, and cannot express his or her own opinion about the accused's character.[172] Occasionally courts ignore this limitation. In *R. v. Millar*, for example, without discussing its earlier decisions, the Ontario Court of Appeal held that a trial judge erred by not directing the jury properly in a baby-shaking case as to how it could use the personal opinions expressed by the family members, friends, and neighbours of the accused that he was a calm, gentle, caring, thoughtful, and nurturing person.[173]

In some cases expert witnesses may be allowed to testify that the accused has some distinctive characteristic that would make it less likely

---

169   *R. v. Close* (1982), 68 C.C.C. (2d) 105 (Ont. C.A.); *R. v. Demyen (No. 2)* (1976), 31 C.C.C. (2d) 383 (Sask. C.A.).

170   *R. v. Levasseur* (1987), 56 C.R. (3d) 335 (Alta. C.A.). It was once required that the witness reside in the same neighbourhood as the accused, a relic of bygone days.

171   *R. v. Lizzi* (1996), 2 C.R. (5th) 95 (Ont. Gen. Div.).

172   *R. v. Close*, above note 169; *R. v. Demyen (No. 2)*, above note 169; *R. v. Clarke* (1998), 18 C.R. (5th) 219 at 235–36 (Ont. C.A.).

173   *R. v. Millar*, above note 99.

that the accused committed the offence. *"Reliable"* expert evidence of this type would be admissible if "the trial judge . . . [is] satisfied, as a matter of law, that either the perpetrator of the crime or the accused has distinctive behavioural characteristics such that a comparison of one with the other will be of material assistance in determining innocence or guilt."[174] Most attempts by accused persons to lead evidence of this kind have failed because behavioural science tends not to provide reliable correlations between character types and incapacity to commit particular kinds of crime.[175]

13.3) The Testimony of the Accused

The accused can assert his good character when testifying. In *Morris v. R.*, for example, the accused advised the jury that he had never been convicted or even arrested.[176] The accused is even permitted to relate specific acts that suggest he is not the kind of person to commit the offence. In *R. v. Samuel*, the accused, charged with larceny, testified that he twice found property and returned it.[177]

When an accused person asserts his good character in either of these ways, even during cross-examination, he will be taken to have put his character in issue, opening the door for the Crown to lead rebuttal evidence showing the accused is not of good character. The prerogative of asserting one's good character can therefore operate as a trap for accused persons, opening the door to proof of bad character.

When, then, will an accused be taken to have placed his character into issue? An accused will put his character in issue only when he raises the issue by initiating evidence intended to suggest that he is not the type to commit the offence charged.[178]

The accused need not directly assert good character. As the foregoing examples illustrate, if the clear inference invited by the accused is that he would not commit such a crime, his character will fall into issue. That determination can be influenced by things as evanescent as the inflection of the voice used by the accused; in *R. v. H.(E.D.)* the accused put his character into issue by asserting, "I did not and would not do that."[179] In *R. v. McFadden*, the accused did so while being prosecut-

---

174   *R. v. Mohan* (1994), 29 C.R. (4th) 243 at 264 (S.C.C.).

175   See chapter 6, section 4.5, "Precondition 4—The Absence of an Exclusionary Rule."

176   (1978), 6 C.R. (3d) 36 at 59 (S.C.C.).

177   (1956), 40 Cr. App. Rep. 8 (C.C.A.).

178   *R. v. McNamara (No. 1)* (1981), 56 C.C.C (2d) 193 at 346 (Ont. C.A.).

179   *R. v. H.(E.D.)*, [2000] B.C.J. No. 1928 (C.A.).

ed for indecently assaulting and murdering a woman, when he stated, "I have the most beautiful wife in the world."[180] The implication was that he would not be the type to have committed such an offence because of his personal situation. In *R. v. McNamara (No. 1)*, the accused put his character in issue by suggesting that his mandate was to run the company "[l]ike any company should be run, legally."[181] With that statement he was effectively affirming his own honesty.

By contrast, accused persons do not put their character in issue simply by denying the allegation, explaining a defence, or repudiating parts of the Crown's case. In *R. v. P.(N.A.)*, for example, the Crown, in giving context to the assault and threatening charges relating to the wife and daughter of the accused, painted him as a terrible husband and father. The accused did not put his character in issue when, in response, his testimony took on the "moral tone" of a loving and caring spouse.[182] Nor will the accused be considered to have done so because of answers furnished by other defence witnesses during cross-examination. If the Crown could use clever cross-examination of defence witnesses as a way of opening the door to proving the bad character of the accused, it would effectively prevent the accused from exercising his right to choose whether to make character an issue in the case.[183] Nor will the accused have put his character in issue by making statements asserting his good character to the police outside of court, even where it should be clear to the accused that the police will want to use that statement as evidence during his trial.[184]

13.4) Similar Fact Evidence Indicative of Innocence

The accused can rely on exculpatory similar fact evidence, so long as it is sufficiently situation specific. If the evidence proves only a general character trait such as honesty or passivity it will not be admissible because of the prohibition on the accused using specific acts to demonstrate "good character" traits. If, however, the similar fact evidence reveals a specific disposition that suggests the accused may have acted innocently on the occasion in question the accused will be permitted to call that proof. In *R. v. Morrissey*[185] the accused, who was charged with murder, was allowed to support his claim that he accidentally shot

---

180   (1981), 28 C.R. (3d) 33 at 35 (B.C.C.A.).
181   *Ibid.* at 343.
182   (2003), 8 C.R. (6th) 186 (Ont. C.A.).
183   *R. v. A.(W.A.)* (1996), 3 C.R. (5th) 388 (Man. C.A.).
184   *R. v. Wilson*, [1999] M.J. No. 239 at para. 40 (C.A.).
185   *R. v. Morrissey*, above note 165.

his girlfriend while attempting suicide, by proving that he had also attempted suicide when two previous relationships were breaking up.

Where the defence calls similar fact evidence, the rule differs from the ordinary similar fact evidence rule. This is because concerns about moral prejudice tend not to apply where the accused wants exculpatory similar fact evidence adduced. Accordingly, when the accused calls such evidence, subject to the narrow general judicial discretion to exclude defence evidence, the only issue is whether the evidence is relevant in supporting the specific disposition claimed.

14. GOOD CHARACTER EVIDENCE AND CROWN REBUTTAL EVIDENCE

Where the accused places his character in issue in one of the permissible fashions, the Crown may call evidence tending to show that the accused is not of good character. This "evidence may be used to refute the assertion of good character and on the issue of the accused's credibility [as a witness], but may not be used as a basis for determining guilt or innocence."[186] A jury must be instructed to this effect. Still, the risk that this bad character evidence will be applied prejudicially is obvious. Just as the defence is limited in the techniques it can employ, so too is the Crown.

14.1) Cross-examination

The Crown can cross-examine the accused, or the witness who has provided the good character evidence, in a fashion that suggests that the accused does not possess the good character that is claimed. In *R. v. O.(D.)*, a sexual abuse case involving his stepdaughter, the accused claimed that he was a good parent. This enabled the Crown to cross-examine him about whether he took proper care of his son, about his lack of interest in the whereabouts of his own daughter, and that he had allowed his stepdaughter to move back in with her mother even though he knew the mother was not looking after her.[187]

The cross-examination of reputation witnesses is particularly dangerous for the accused. Since reputation is the product of what is said about another, it is, by its very nature, hearsay information. Hearsay can therefore be used to rebut it. In particular, the reputation witness

---

186 *R. v. H.(E.D.)*, above note 179 at para. 19.
187 *R. v. O.(D.)* (2001), 156 C.C.C. (3d) 369 (Ont. C.A.).

can be asked whether he has heard rumours involving the accused, ostensibly to test his familiarity with the reputation of the accused or his judgment about the quality of that reputation.[188]

14.2) Rebuttal Reputation Evidence

The Crown can call witnesses to suggest that the reputation of the accused for the relevant character is in fact bad.[189]

14.3) Section 666 of the *Criminal Code*

This provision allows the previous convictions of the accused to be proved whenever he puts his good character in issue. Even subsequent convictions can be established provided the conduct was close enough in time to reflect on the relevant disposition.[190] Since the accused has put his character into issue, unlike in the case of section 12 of the *Canada Evidence Act*,[191] the Crown is entitled not only to prove the convictions, but also to question the accused about the specifics underlying the criminal convictions.[192]

14.4) Expert Evidence

In *R. v. Tierney* the accused said that he was not the kind of person to sexually assault the complainant. A Crown psychiatrist was allowed to be called in rebuttal to demonstrate the abnormal disposition of the accused to react violently to rejection by women.[193]

14.5) Similar Fact Evidence

Ordinarily, where similar fact evidence is admitted the prohibited inference prevents the trier of fact from using it to draw conclusions about the general character of the accused. Where an accused puts their good character in issue, things change. Admissible similar fact evidence can be used both for the specific purpose for which it was admitted and to

---

188 *Michelson v. United States*, 335 U.S. 469 (1948). See *People v. Laudiero*, 192 N.Y. 304 (Ct. App. 1908) for an interesting illustration.

189 *R. v. Rowton* (1865), 169 E.R. 1497 (C.C.R.).

190 *R. v. Close*, above note 169.

191 See the discussion in chapter 10.6.6 "Cross-examination on Prior Convictions," dealing with a related but distinct evidentiary use of prior convictions.

192 *R. v. P.(N.A.)*, above note 182 at para. 32.

193 (1982), 70 C.C.C. (2d) 481 (Ont. C.A.).

neutralize the general suggestion by the accused of good character.[194] It stills remains impermissible for a trier of fact to convict the accused because of his bad character, however. In effect, the general bad character shown by the similar fact evidence can be used to knock evidence of general good character off the scales, but as a matter of law, the general bad character inference is not to be treated as adding affirmative weight to the Crown case.

14.6) Prior Inconsistent Statements

In *R. v. Dussiaume*,[195] the accused teacher testified that he was a happily married man. This was clearly done to invite the inference that, given his circumstances, he was unlikely to have committed a sexual assault on a student. To rebut this evidence the Crown called three persons whom the accused had told of marital problems he was having. The Ontario Court of Appeal, without discussing limits on the methods of rebutting good character evidence, held that this testimony was permissible. This result is sensible. Proving prior inconsistent statements made by the accused is a compendious or expeditious way of presenting relevant rebuttal evidence.

14.7) Testimony Relating to Specific Acts Not Satisfying the Similar Fact Evidence Rule

In *R. v. Brown*, the accused, charged with aggravated assault in a baby-shaking case, testified that he had saved two brothers who were at risk of drowning, and had never abused his own children. The trial judge erred by permitting the Crown to call the son of the accused to testify to specific acts of abuse perpetrated by the accused against him.[196] The Court of Appeal recognized, however, that where an accused has testified to specific acts of good character and the Crown demonstrates that permissible methods of rebuttal will not suffice to prevent a distorted picture from being created by that testimony, the trial judge has the discretion to permit witnesses to be called by the Crown to contradict the accused on those specific assertions. The trial judge did not exercise that discretion properly in *Brown* because the accused's good character evidence was not probative enough to warrant the degree of prejudice this would cause, and because the trial judge had not cautioned the

---

194 *Ibid.*; *R. v. McFadden*, above note 180 at 48.
195 (1995), 98 C.C.C. (3d) 217 (Ont. C.A.).
196 *R. v. Brown*, [1999] O.J. No. 2983 (C.A.).

unrepresented accused that if he chose to defend himself in this manner he was putting his character in issue.

15. THE CHARACTER OF THIRD PARTIES IN CRIMINAL CASES

Where the character of persons other than the accused is relevant to a primarily material issue, it can be proved, subject to sections 276 and 277, which impose limits in the case of sexual offence complainants.

15.1) Generally

15.1 (a) Admissibility of a Third Party's Character

Third parties, including complainants, are not being judged formally and are not at risk of losing their liberty. They are not the subject of state-based allegations. They do not, therefore, benefit from the presumption of innocence. Accordingly, they do not have the same degree of protection that accused persons have. Where their character is relevant on a primarily material issue, particularly when it can assist the accused in making full answer and defence, evidence about their character will generally be admissible.

For example, in self-defence cases where there is a foundation for suggesting that the deceased was the aggressor, it is relevant to the reasonableness of the accused's actions that he was aware that the deceased had a reputation for violence. In such cases it is easier to believe that the accused feared bodily harm and therefore felt the need to use force in self-defence. Evidence about the reputation of the victim for violence is therefore admissible.[197] So too are specific acts of violence known to the accused, such as where the accused was the victim of that violence.[198]

Proof that the victim has a violent disposition as demonstrated through specific acts of violence unknown to the accused is also relevant according to the theory that violent people are more likely to react violently than those who do not have a violent disposition.[199] Provided the evidence establishing the propensity for violence of the victim is strong enough, it is admissible even if it does not satisfy the similar

---

197 R. v. *Dubois* (1976), 30 C.C.C. (2d) 412 (Ont. C.A.).
198 R. v. *Ryan* (1989), 49 C.C.C. (3d) 490 (Nfld. C.A.).
199 R. v. *Scopelliti* (1981), 63 C.C.C. (2d) 481 (Ont. C.A.).

fact evidence test. The accused may also call evidence of the victim's reputation for violence, in order to support the inference that it was the victim who acted aggressively.[200]

Although these principles developed in self-defence cases, evidence about the discreditable propensities of non-victims can be led where the accused defends himself on the basis that the act was committed by another person who had the opportunity to do so,[201] or when such evidence is otherwise relevant. For example, in *R. v. Khan* it was recognized that in an appropriate case, a past practice of racial profiling by police officers would be admissible.[202]

Judges, of course, retain discretion to exclude evidence called by an accused person about the character of another, where the potential for prejudice to the Crown's case substantially outweighs the probative value of the defence evidence.[203] Such discretion was used in the self-defence case of *R. v. Pilon* to exclude evidence of the deceased's habit of carrying a gun because other evidence already showed this. The proof offered was also remote in time and could have raised collateral issues.[204] Because the evidence is called by the accused and does not involve a co-accused who is in jeopardy at the same trial, however, that discretion is to be exercised in a guarded fashion.

In *Khan* the trial judge evaluated whether to exercise that discretion by consulting the *Handy* factors that operate under the similar fact evidence rule before ultimately excluding testimony about a past act of alleged racial profiling by police officers. This is an appropriate way to structure the analysis so long as it is remembered that the rules differ in this important respect—unlike similar fact evidence called by the Crown, relevant third-party character evidence is *prima facie* admissible when called by the accused.

15.1 (b) Rebuttal Evidence and the Character of the Accused

Accused persons who defend themselves by "pointing a finger at a third party [and] suggesting that that person has a propensity to commit the crime charged" will generally be taken to have put their own character in issue.[205] To be clear, the accused persons will not be taken to have

---

200 *R. v. Hamilton* (2003), 180 C.C.C. (3d) 80 (B.C.C.A.).

201 *R. v. Arcangioli* (1994), 27 C.R. (4th) 1 (S.C.C.); *R. v. Pollock*, above note 162 at paras. 100–1.

202 *R. v. Khan* (2004), 189 C.C.C (3d) 49 (Ont. S.C.J.).

203 *R. v. Yaeck* (1991), 10 C.R. (4th) 1 (Ont. C.A.).

204 *R. v. Pilon* (2009), 247 O.A.C. 127 (C.A.).

205 *R. v. Wilson*, above note 184 at para. 45. See *R. v. McMillan*, above note 163; *R. v. Bourguignon* (1997), 118 C.C.C. (3d) 43 (Ont. C.A.).

put their character into issue simply by pointing the finger at another; the accused is apt to lose their bad character shield only if the accused attempts to cast blame on another by pointing to that other's general propensity to commit the crime.[206] The same result can arise in a self-defence case where the accused leads evidence demonstrating the propensity of the deceased for violence in an effort to paint the deceased as the aggressor.[207] The thinking is that when it comes to determinations of who the responsible actor is, it would be misleading for the trier of fact to learn only about the character or capacity of the third party while being left in the dark about the character or capacity of the accused.[208]

Not all judges agree. In *R. v. Wilson*, Wilson had claimed in his own defence that the deceased had threatened him with a gun on other occasions, and had done so on the evening she died. The Court held that Wilson was entitled to present evidence about the deceased "with impunity," and could not thereby be taken to have put his own character into issue.[209] That position is not entirely without merit. Even someone with criminal propensity can be a victim or be wrongfully charged; should they lose the protection of the bad character shield by attempting to rely on relevant evidence supporting their claim of innocence?

Instead of accepting that accused persons can lead such evidence with impunity, most courts handle the risks this strategy poses to accused persons by using judicial discretion. Judges may prevent the Crown from leading rebuttal evidence where the potential prejudice of doing so outweighs its probative value.[210] In *R. v Williams*, for example, the Crown was prevented from proving Williams' criminal record even though he supported his self-defence claim by proving the victim's record for violence. The trial judge reasoned that there was already evidence on the record that revealed the violent disposition of both men, and that admitting the record of the accused would be unduly prejudicial.[211]

Even when the accused does open the door to proof of his own bad character in this way, proof of his bad character is to be used solely to neutralize any express or implicit suggestion the accused has made that he is not the type to commit the offence. It cannot be used as affirmative evidence of his guilt.

---

206 *R. v. Vanezis* (2006), 213 C.C.C. (3d) 449 (Ont. C.A.).
207 *R. v. Scopelliti*, above note 199.
208 *R. v. Parsons* (1993), 84 C.C.C. (3d) 226 at 238 (Ont. C.A.).
209 *R. v. Wilson*, above note 184 at para. 40.
210 *R. v. Fudge* (1997), 103 O.A.C. 153 (C.A.).
211 *R. v. Williams* (2008), 233 C.C.C. (3d) 40 (Ont. C.A.).

15.1 (c) Third-party Evidence Called by the Crown

It is possible for the Crown to present relevant evidence about the character or personality of third parties. This can be done to rebut any character submissions made by the defence.[212] The Crown can even initiate proof of the character or personality of third parties, including the complainant, in some cases. In *R. v. Jack*, where the accused was prosecuted for murder without the body of the alleged victim having been found, evidence was called to show that the alleged victim was a good mother who would not have abandoned her children and therefore must have been the victim of foul play.[213] In *R. v. Diu*, the Ontario Court of Appeal accepted that in some self-defence cases, evidence of the peaceable character of the deceased could be initiated by the Crown, provided its probative value outweighed its prejudicial effect.[214] In *Diu*, the trial judge erred in admitting such evidence because the probative value of the reputation evidence that had been led was exceedingly low, coming as it did from the parents of the deceased, while prejudice was high given the tendency of that evidence to evoke sympathy. In *R. v. Dejong*, the British Columbia Court of Appeal has held that it is impermissible for the Crown to initiate such evidence where it would suggest inferentially that, given the peaceable character of the victim, the accused must be the type to have committed the offence charged.[215]

15.2) Complainants in Sexual Offence Cases

Because of chronic underreporting of sexual offences, sensitivity to the privacy interests of complainants, and concerns about relevance, special statutory limitations have been created that restrict the kind of character evidence that can be called about complainants in sexual offence prosecutions.

At common law the accused could call witnesses who would testify as to the *poor reputation* of a sexual offence complainant for chastity. The chastity of the complainant was considered to be relevant on both the issues of consent and credibility. A sexually experienced woman was considered to have demonstrated a propensity to consent, increasing the likelihood that she consented on the occasion in question. Since "sexual permissiveness" by women was considered to be misconduct, it was also believed that the evidence said something about

---

212 *R. v. Soikie*, [2004] O.J. No. 2902 (S.C.J.), and see *R. v. Soares* (1987), 31 C.C.C. (3d) 403 (Ont. C.A.).

213 (1992), 70 C.C.C. (3d) 67 (Man. C.A.).

214 *R. v. Diu*, above note 159 at para. 49.

215 (1998), 16 C.R. (5th) 372 (B.C.C.A.).

the complainant's character, and discreditable character was seen to be relevant to credibility. Obviously, these "twin-myth" inferences are pejoratively judgmental and premised on a simplistic and anachronistic worldview. Fittingly, the common law assumptions and their supporting rules have been eviscerated by legislation.

Sexual reputation evidence is no longer admissible. Section 277 of the *Criminal Code* makes sexual reputation evidence inadmissible on the issue of credibility. Subsection 276(2)(a) makes sexual reputation evidence inadmissible on the issue of consent as well, since the only sexual experience evidence allowed under the section is evidence "of specific instances of sexual activity."

Meanwhile, section 276 imposes strict limits on the admissibility of proof about specific instances of a complainant's sexual activity. As the classic similar fact evidence rule did, it imposes a two-part hurdle to the admission of such evidence. First, subsection 276(1) prohibits absolutely the use of sexual experience evidence for certain enumerated purposes. Then, subsection 276(2) provides that even if proof of the sexual activity of the complainant is not being used for a prohibited purpose, it will still be inadmissible unless the judge determines that the evidence has "significant probative value" that is not outweighed by competing considerations.

15.2 (a) The Prohibited Purposes
Subsection 276(1) provides in relevant part that

> evidence that the complainant has engaged in sexual activity, whether with the accused or with any other person, is not admissible to support an inference that, by reason of the sexual nature of that activity, the complainant
>
> (a) is more likely to have consented to the sexual activity that forms the subject-matter of the charge; or
>
> (b) is less worthy of belief.

Section 276 does not prevent all sexual activity evidence from being used to inform the issues of consent or credibility. Instead, it prohibits only certain kinds of *inferences* about consent and credibility from being drawn. In particular, only the "twin myth" inferences relating to consent or credit which draw on "the sexual nature of the activity" for their relevance are prohibited. This prevents the defence from relying on inferences that the complainant is, by reason of the sexual nature of her activity, *the kind of person* to consent, or *the kind of person* who cannot be believed. If the evidence is being used to support these general character inferences, it is absolutely inadmissible. If the sexual experience evidence is being used for some other purpose, even on the issues of consent or credibility, it may or may not be admissible. Its admission will be determined by weighing the probative value of the evidence against the prejudice its admission might cause, according to the formula provided in subsection 276(2)(c).[216]

15.2 (b) Probative Value and Prejudice

Even if specific, relevant evidence passes this first hurdle it may still be excluded by the operation of subsection 276(2)(c). First, it will be excluded by that subsection if it does not have "significant" probative value. In order to be "significant" the evidence must "not be so trifling as to be incapable, in the context of all the evidence, of raising a reasonable doubt."[217] Second, even if the evidence is "significant" in this sense, the evidence may still be excluded if its "significant probative value" is "substantially outweighed by the danger of prejudice [it presents] to the proper administration of justice." On its face, this provision seems to contemplate that even evidence capable of raising a reasonable doubt could be denied to an accused. This is a troubling proposition, inconsistent both with the presumption of innocence and full answer and defence principles. In practice, if evidence is probative enough to raise a reasonable doubt, it would be admitted. It is where its probative value is insufficient to raise a reasonable doubt on its own that competing considerations can cause the evidence to be excluded, even though it is relevant. Subsection 276(3) provides a non-exhaustive list of the competing considerations that a court must take into account in making this assessment, including the right of the accused to make full answer and defence and the need to protect the complainant's personal dignity and right of privacy.

R. v. Crosby[218] provides an example of the operation of section 276. The complainant denied that she went to the home of one of two men accused of sexually assaulting her so that she could have sex with one of them. She had earlier told the police, in effect, that this is in fact why she had gone there. The Supreme Court of Canada held that the accused could prove that she had made this prior inconsistent statement. The statement was relevant to her credibility, but not because of "the sexual nature of the activity" that it disclosed. It was relevant for the permissible purpose of showing that she had made a previous statement inconsistent with material testimony that she had provided

---

216 R. v. Darrach (2000), 148 C.C.C. (3d) 97 at 116–18 (S.C.C.).
217 Ibid. at 119.
218 (1995), 39 C.R. (4th) 315 (S.C.C.).

at the trial as to why she had gone to the house. The prejudicial impact of admitting this evidence did not substantially outweigh its significant probative value.

The prevalent practice in cases involving proof of a prior sexual history *between the accused and the complainant* is to admit the evidence where the nature of the complainant's claim of non-consent would appear more likely than it should as a result of the misleading impression that would otherwise be left that the two were sexual strangers at the time.[219] Whether sexual history evidence can make the possibility of consent between the complainant and the accused more tenable is context-specific. For example, proof of a past sexual relationship with one of several men alleged to have forcibly confined and sexually assaulted the complainant in a motel room would do nothing to enlighten the trier of fact about whether she consented to have sex under these circumstances, even with her former lover.[220] By contrast, learning that a man in his forties and a seventeen-year-old girl had been intimate in the past may help debunk doubts that such a young woman would have consented to go to a motel room with him for the purpose of sex, or may assist him in explaining why he would remove his clothing after bringing along the same kind of condom she preferred because of an allergic condition.[221]

Because of lingering distaste from an era when judgmental character inferences were used to suggest consent, judges tend to explain the admission of sexual experience evidence in such cases as providing "context" or "narrative." There is little doubt, however, that the issue the proof typically bears upon is consent.[222] Since it does not engage the prohibited inference there is nothing wrong with acknowledging this. Where, in such cases, the relevant picture can be cast without embarrassing intimate details or repetition, it should be.

16. CHARACTER EVIDENCE IN CIVIL CASES

Unless the character of a party to a civil proceeding is directly in issue, or unless the civil case raises allegations of a criminal nature, good character evidence cannot be called.

---

219 See, for example, *R. v. Strickland* (2007), 45 C.R. (6th) 183 (Ont. S.C.J.), and the cases cited therein.
220 *R. v. Rarru* (1995), 60 B.C.A.C. 81 (C.A.).
221 *R. v. Temertzoglou* (2002), 11 C.R. (6th) 179 (Ont. S.C.J.).
222 See Don Stuart, "Annotation" (2007) 45 C.R. (6th) 185.

> *Evidence demonstrating the bad character of a party that is*
> *presented as circumstantial proof of what happened must satisfy*
> *the similar fact evidence rule to be admissible, although that rule*
> *tends to operate more generously and subject to different consider-*
> *ations than in a criminal case*

16.1) Generally

Character evidence tends not to play as large a role in civil litigation as it does in the prosecution of criminal offences. Where the character of a litigant is directly in issue, as in a defamation action, character evidence is admissible, although the methods by which it can be adduced are controlled.[223]

Where character is not directly in issue, some of the civil evidence rules are more restrictive than those that apply in criminal cases.

16.2) The Good Character of Parties: Primary Materiality

Proof that a party is of good character is not generally admissible. This restriction has been explained historically on the questionable basis of irrelevance; whereas a person of good character would not commit a crime, the same cannot be said of civil wrongs.[224] Better rationales include that in criminal cases we allow such proof because of the liberty interest of accused persons, while in civil cases priority is given to keeping litigation manageable, to avoiding the confusion of issues, and to preventing unfair surprise to the litigants. Exceptionally, where the civil suit alleges what are in substance criminal acts, a party may be permitted to prove their good character in response. In *Plester v. Wawanesa Mutual Insurance Co.*, for example, an arson allegation by an insurance company made against the plaintiff opened the door to good general reputation evidence about the plaintiff.[225]

16.3) The Bad Character of Parties: Primary Materiality

The admission of evidence demonstrating the bad character of parties in a civil case is governed by the similar fact evidence rule, where that evidence is presented as circumstantial evidence about what happened. There is a tendency, however, to overuse the rule, just as there is in

---

223 *Plato Films Ltd. v. Speidel*, [1961] 1 All E.R. 876 (H.L.).
224 *A.G. v. Radloff* (1854), 10 Exch. 84 (Ex. Ch.).
225 *Plester v. Wawanesa Mutual Insurance Co.*, [2006] O.J. No. 2139 (C.A.).

criminal cases. *Kotylak v. McLean's Agra Centre Ltd.* was a products liability case.[226] Evidence was offered by other farmers that, like the plaintiff's crops, their crops were also damaged by the "seed boot" supplied by the defendant. The trial judge admitted the evidence, but not before applying the similar fact evidence rule. The testimony of the other farmers was not, however, about the character of the defendant. It was about the functioning of a product supplied by the defendant. There was therefore no need to consult the similar fact evidence rule. The similar fact evidence rule should be consulted solely where the evidence in question demonstrates or implies that one of the parties has a discreditable character.

Although there are few reported cases, it is common to see criminal decisions cited and for courts to proceed on the basis that the rule is identical in both criminal and civil cases. There is even authority for the proposition that, as in criminal cases, character evidence cannot be used in civil litigation to establish general disposition.[227] In *Sego v. Sudbury (Regional Municipality) Police Force*, for example, in a civil battery case, the court denied a plaintiff the right to prove the proclivity of a police officer for aggression because that proclivity was relevant only to general disposition.[228] In *Johnson v. Bugera* the British Columbia Court of Appeal expressed doubt that there was any difference between admissibility of evidence in civil and criminal cases, with the possible exception that courts would have a heightened concern about admitting such evidence in criminal cases.[229] In spite of this, the court held that proof of a substantial history of speeding by the defendant should be admitted in a tort action and relied on that evidence to help establish that he was speeding at the time of the accident. If the rule is indeed the same in civil and criminal cases, it is difficult to see how this evidence could have been admitted. By its nature, it could do nothing other than show that the accused was the type to speed and therefore was probably speeding on this occasion. This is precisely the inference that the criminal rule purports to disallow.

With respect, the rules should not be treated as identical, even with the proviso that the rule is applied more liberally in civil cases.[230] First, the nature of the "prejudice" differs significantly between civil and criminal cases. In criminal cases, there is a prohibited inference.

---

226 *Kotylak v. McLean's Agra Centre Ltd.*, [2000] S.J. No. 554 (Q.B.).
227 *Greenglass v. Rusnovick*, [1983] O.J. No. 40 (C.A.).
228 *Sego v. Sudbury (Regional Municipality) Police Force*, [1999] O.J. No. 697 (Gen. Div.).
229 *Johnson v. Bugera*, [1999] B.C.J. No. 621 (C.A.).
230 See, for example, *Dhawan v. College of Physicians and Surgeons (Nova Scotia)* (1998), 168 N.S.R. (2d) 201 at 217 (C.A.).

It operates to exclude what is often relevant evidence because of those distinctively criminal principles that relate to the presumption of innocence and the fear of wrongful conviction. There is no need for a prohibited inference in civil cases where the presumption of innocence does not operate. Fittingly, in *S.(R.C.M.) v. K.(G.M.)* the trial judge admitted evidence of spousal abuse against a former partner by the father in a custody dispute after using an inference that clearly would have been impermissible in criminal cases: "Spousal abuse is a pattern of conduct. Human experience tells us that generally people act consistently."[231] Moral prejudice is not as crucial a factor in civil cases.

Second, in criminal cases the similar fact evidence rule applies solely to the Crown. It does not prevent the accused from calling relevant, general disposition evidence. This lack of symmetry is a familiar thing in criminal cases. In a civil case, the right of access to evidence is not skewed in this same way. The parties have equal rights in a civil case to the accurate determination of facts and to access to relevant evidence. There should be no presumption of inadmissibility as there is in criminal cases. Admission should turn on relevance, subject to the ordinary exclusionary discretion. Courts should do as Lord Denning did in *Mood Music Publishing v. DeWolfe Ltd.*:[232] determine admissibility in a civil case without regard to the immaterial prohibited inference, and do so on the basis of a weighing process that does not presume inadmissibility. In a civil case, the judge should simply decide whether the evidence is relevant and if so, whether its probative value is outweighed by its prejudicial effect. The evaluation of probative value can be guided by the structure and example of criminal precedents, as it was in *G.(J.R.I.) v. Tyhurst*[233] where the evaluation of the evidence was enriched by using the step-by-step approach and the collusion discussions found in *Handy* and *Shearing*, provided the presumption of inadmissibility is not applied. The consideration of prejudice should emphasize matters of importance in civil litigation—typically reasoning prejudice considerations, including unfair surprise, the undue consumption of time, and whether the opposing party litigant is in a fair position to respond.

---

231 *S.(R.C.M.) v. K.(G.M.)*, [2005] S.J. No. 443 (Q.B.).
232 *Mood Music Publishing Co. v. De Wolfe Ltd.*, [1976] 1 All E.R. 763 (C.A.). See also *K.N. v. Alberta*, [1999] A.J. No. 394 (Q.B.), and *College of Physicians and Surgeons of Ontario v. K.* (1987), 59 O.R. (2d) 1 (C.A.).
233 (2003), 226 D.L.R. (4th) 447 (B.C.C.A.).

16.4) Character of Third Parties

Provided it has sufficient relevance and will not take undue time to develop, evidence of the disposition of third parties can be proved by specific acts to show how that person may have acted on the occasion in question.[234]

---

234 *Joy v. Phillips, Mills & Co. Ltd.*, [1916] 1 K.B. 849 (C.A.); *McKenna v. Greco (No. 1)* (1981), 33 O.R. (2d) 595 (C.A.).

CHAPTER 4

HEARSAY

Hearsay is an out-of-court statement that is offered to prove the truth of its contents. The essential defining features of hearsay are: (1) the fact that an out-of-court statement is adduced to prove the truth of its contents and (2) the absence of a contemporaneous opportunity to cross-examine the declarant.

An out-of-court statement includes previous statements made by a witness who testifies.

An out-of-court statement also includes an "implied statement," which is any assertion revealed through actions and not words. Where the actions are intended to communicate a message, they are treated the same as a verbal or a written statement. Where the actions are not intended to communicate a message, courts are divided as to whether or not these statements fall under the hearsay rule.

1. RECOGNIZING HEARSAY

The rule is simple to state: Absent an exception, hearsay evidence is not admissible. In other words, hearsay evidence is presumptively inadmissible. The difficulty lies in identifying what is or is not hearsay. The Supreme Court of Canada has told us that the essential defining features of hearsay are: (1) the fact that an out-of-court statement is adduced to prove the truth of its contents and (2) the absence of a contemporaneous opportunity to cross-examine the declarant.[1] The Court, in another case, provided the following simple, yet most work-able, definition: Hearsay is (1) an out-of-court statement, (2) which is admitted for the truth of its contents.[2]

In order to understand hearsay one needs to understand the under-lying concerns that give rise to the exclusionary rule. The fundamental concern is the inability to test the reliability of hearsay statements. Our adversary system rests upon the calling of witnesses, who give their evidence under oath, whose demeanour can be observed, and who are subject to cross-examination by opposing counsel. These trial safe-guards assist in the weighing and testing of the witness's testimony. Statements made out of court may not be so tested. Justice Charron, writing for the full Court in R. v. Khelawon, provided the following explanation:

> Without the maker of the statement in court, it may be impossible to inquire into that person's perception, memory, narration or sincer-ity. The statement itself may not be accurately recorded. Mistakes, exaggerations or deliberate falsehoods may go undetected and lead to unjust verdicts. Hence, the rule against hearsay is intended to enhance the accuracy of the court's findings of fact, not impede its truth-seeking function.[3]

To illustrate hearsay and the need for cross-examination, consider the following example:

In a prosecution for drunk driving, witness (W) testifies that a passenger (P) in the car driven by the accused, stated that "the accused had been drinking and was drunk." Assume that P is not called to testify.

W is testifying as to P's out-of-court statement and that statement is being offered for its truth—that the accused had been drinking and was drunk. W's testimony is hearsay. Why? Consider on what matters you might cross-examine W. The cross-examination would be limited to the accuracy of what W heard P say, largely a futile exercise. Nor does it get to the heart of the issue, which is the accuracy of what is contained in the statement. P, as the maker of the statement, should be cross-examined. What did P observe the accused drinking? How did P know it was alcohol? Over what period of time did P observe the accused? Why did P conclude that the accused was drunk? And so

---

1   R. v. Khelawon (2006), 215 C.C.C. (3d) 161 at para. 35 (S.C.C.).
2   R. v. Evans (1993), 25 C.R. (4th) 46 at 52 (S.C.C.).
3   Above note 1 at para. 2.

the questioning goes. Without P, the statement is untested and its real value as evidence cannot be assessed.

2. STATEMENTS OFFERED FOR THEIR TRUTH

Only those statements offered for their truth offend the rule against hearsay. In other words, hearsay evidence is not identified by the nature of the evidence, but by the use to which the evidence is to be put. When an out-of-court statement is offered simply as proof that the statement was made, it is not hearsay, and it is admissible as long as it has some probative value. The person relating that the statement was made is in court and can be cross-examined. For example, take the following scenario:

The plaintiff fell on steps leading into the defendant's store and sues in negligence for injuries caused. A delivery driver is called. The driver testifies that one hour prior to the accident a customer came into the store and told the manager, "Your steps are covered with ice and need to be cleared." The customer cannot be located.

Consider the use to which the delivery driver's testimony is to be put. Knowledge of a potential hazard relates to what is reasonable or unreasonable in the circumstances. The customer's statement amounts to a warning that a hazard existed. Its significance is that it was made and presumably heard by the manager. The delivery driver can be cross-examined on these points. Now if the statement were offered to prove that ice indeed covered the steps, it would be hearsay and, in order to test the truth of this statement, the customer would need to be cross-examined.

The question becomes one of relevancy: What relevant purpose does the statement have aside from its truth? If the statement has some probative value, it may be admissible for that limited purpose, though it is incumbent upon the trial judge to caution the jury as to its limited relevancy and to the fact that it is not admissible for its truth. Juries should not be left to determine the proper and improper uses of evidence.[4] In the example above, the jury would need to be told that the delivery driver's statement was admissible as evidence of notice of an ice hazard, but was not admissible to prove that the ice hazard actually existed.

Relevancy is a broad concept, and little is to be gained by grouping or listing possible non-hearsay uses. Nevertheless, a few examples are

---

4   R. v. Starr (2000), 147 C.C.C. (3d) 449 at 524 (S.C.C.).

helpful to illustrate the point. Take the case of *Subramaniam v. Public Prosecutor.*[5] The accused was charged with possession of twenty rounds of ammunition, an act that was contrary to an emergency decree to counter terrorism then in place in Malaysia. The accused was found wounded by security forces, was searched, and the ammunition discovered. The accused's defence was duress, and he took the stand. He described how he was captured by terrorists and was about to relate conversations with them. The trial judge interjected to rule that what the terrorists said was hearsay—unless the terrorists were called to testify. Of course, the terrorists were not called. Subramaniam was convicted and sentenced to death. Fortunately for him, the Privy Council allowed his appeal on the grounds that the trial judge had erred in preventing him from telling the court what the terrorists had said. Subramaniam's defence of duress would be made out if he had been compelled to do the acts by threats that gave rise to a reasonable apprehension of instant death. Of importance in the law of duress is the fact that threats are made. In Subramaniam's case, it was of no significance whether the terrorists would have acted on their threats. The relevancy of these statements had nothing to do with their being true.

An understanding of the substantive law is required, in the case of *Subramaniam*, the law of duress. An excellent Canadian example comes from a leading case on subsection 24(2) of the *Charter* — *R. v. Collins.*[6] In this case, Ruby Collins was seated in a pub when she was suddenly seized by the throat and pulled down to the floor by a man who said to her, "police officer." The police officer noticed that Collins had her hand clenched around an object. The object was a green balloon containing heroin, and Collins was charged with possession for the purpose of trafficking. A *voir dire* was held into the admissibility of the heroin. At issue was the reasonableness of the officer's search and seizure of the drugs. The officer was called and admitted that nothing he had observed in watching Collins had aroused his suspicion that she was handling drugs. His suspicions were based on what he was told by other officers. As he was about to testify as to what he was told, the defence objected on the basis of hearsay. The objection was upheld and, as a result, the Crown failed to establish a reasonable basis for the officer's suspicion and actions. The problem is that the hearsay objection was "groundless." The issue in the *voir dire* was whether the officer was acting reasonably, given the information he had at the time. Therefore, the important thing was what he was told, and not whether that information was true. The

5   [1956] 1 W.L.R. 965 (P.C.).
6   (1987), 56 C.R. (3d) 193 (S.C.C.).

Supreme Court of Canada ordered a new trial, and presumably in that new trial the officer was allowed to testify as to what he was told.

3. PRIOR STATEMENTS OF WITNESSES: ABSENCE OF CONTEMPORANEOUS CROSS-EXAMINATION

Hearsay is concerned with out-of-court statements—any statement made other than by the witness while testifying in court. What of out-of-court statements made by the witness who does testify? The maker of the statement is present and can be cross-examined. For example, in our drunk-driving scenario, assume that P is called as a witness. P testifies as to having observed the accused drinking. However, P cannot recall exactly how many drinks the accused had or the various signs of intoxication that he had exhibited. P does recall telling W all these details. Is it hearsay for W to relate P's out-of-court statement? After all, P is present in court, under oath, can be observed, and can be cross-examined on the making of that statement. Is P's out-of-court statement hearsay? Yes.

The Supreme Court of Canada in R. v. Khelawon has made it clear that the traditional law of hearsay extends to out-of-court statements made by the witness who does testify in court when that out-of-court statement is tendered to prove the truth of its contents.[7] The rationale for the general exclusionary rule lies in the difficulty in testing the reliability of the out-of-court statement. A premium is placed on in-court testimony. The witness who testifies in court is under oath, can be observed by the trier of fact and is available for cross-examination. Cross-examination is the key and is the fundamental tester of truth. Subsequent cross-examination may not be sufficient to test the reliability of the out-of-court statement. It is important to note that this does not mean that the out-of-court statements made by witnesses are always excluded. Identifying the statement as hearsay is but a starting point. The statements may well be admitted under a hearsay exception, where difficulties in assessing the reliability of the out-of-court statements are addressed.

When a witness repeats or adopts his or her earlier out-of-court statement no hearsay issue arises.[8] For example, assume that the passenger in the drunk-driving case earlier in this chapter is called as a witness. She

---

7   Above note 1 at para. 37.
8   See R. v. Khelawon, ibid. at para. 38.

cannot recall the number of drinks that the accused had prior to driving. In an earlier statement to the police she told the officer that the accused had five to six drinks. Crown counsel may refresh her memory using her out-of-court statement. She reads over her statement and recalls the five to six drinks, which is now her evidence. The out-of-court statement triggered her in-court testimony and there is no hearsay concern.[9]

Hearsay concerns do arise when the witness either recants her earlier out-of-court statement or testifies that she has no memory of making the statement. In our drunk-driving example, the passenger witness testifies that she only saw the accused have one drink before driving. The Crown seeks to tender the out-of-court statement as proof of the fact that the accused had five to six drinks. In these circumstances the trier of fact is asked to accept the out-of-court statement over her sworn testimony in court. The out-of-court statement is being tendered for its truth and reliability.[10]

Even more problematic is when the witness testifies that she has no memory of making the statement, or worse still, has no memory of the entire incident including talking to the police. Faced with a "no memory" witness, no cross-examination at trial is possible on why she is now giving inconsistent testimony or why she told the police that the accused had five to six drinks. In this situation cross-examination at trial is rendered largely futile.

Therefore, to clarify, any out-of-court statement that is tendered for its truth is hearsay. The fact that the witness testifies in court does not matter. The prior statement is still hearsay and for it to be admitted for its truth, a hearsay exception needs to be found. The statement may, of course, be admitted for purposes other than its truth. For example, a prior inconsistent statement may be put to the witness to attack credibility, or a prior consistent statement of the witness may be introduced to rebut any suggestion of recent fabrication.[11]

4. IMPLIED STATEMENTS

An out-of-court statement may be verbal, written, or implied. An "implied statement" is any assertion that is not expressed by language, but

---

9   Refreshing of memory is found in chapter 10, section 5.

10 Admitting prior inconsistent statements for their truth is found in chapter 5, section 2.

11 See chapter 10, section 6.7, "Prior Inconsistent Statements," and chapter 11, section 4.3, "Recent Fabrication."

rather is revealed through action. The nod of the head or the pointing of a finger speak loudly and are intended to communicate a message. These are assertions by conduct and are treated the same as a spoken or written statement.[12]

For example, in R. v. Perciballi the Crown wanted to prove that a co-accused had made a 911 call from a doughnut shop.[13] The intent of the call was to divert the police from the scene of an armoured car robbery. The Crown called a witness, who had earlier taken the police to the donut shop and pointed to two phones where he had seen the co-accused make a phone call the night of the robbery. At trial the witness denied pointing anything out to the police. The Crown then called a police officer who testified as to the witness's act of pointing. The Ontario Court of Appeal agreed that this pointing amounted to an assertion by conduct.

A more difficult question, and one where there is no unanimity, concerns "implied statements" that are not intended to be communicative. Sometimes a person's belief in a state of facts is apparent from his conduct, even though he does not consciously wish to communicate that belief. In such cases it can be said that the existence of that state of fact is an "implied statement" inherent in his conduct. For example, from your office window you observe a line of cars stopped at an intersection below. You cannot see the traffic lights, but you then observe the cars proceed through the intersection. From this you conclude that the light has turned green. In coming to this conclusion you are drawing a common-sense inference from the conduct of the drivers in moving their cars. But break that common-sense inference down. You are effectively concluding that since people tend to move their cars into an intersection only when they know the light has turned green, the light must have turned green. What you are doing is treating the conduct of the drivers as evidencing their knowledge that the light is green, so in forming your conclusion you are relying on what they seem to know. You are treating the conduct of each driver as an implied assertion by each driver that the light is green. Now, if one of the drivers via a cell-phone was talking to you and said, "Got to go; the light just turned green," this statement would be hearsay if it was offered to prove that fact. Since the express statement is hearsay, the argument holds that the implied statement flowing from the conduct should also be hearsay.

---

12   R. v. MacKinnon (2002), 165 C.C.C. (3d) 73 at 79 (B.C.C.A.).
13   R. v. Perciballi (2001), 154 C.C.C. (3d) 481 at 520–21 (Ont. C.A.), aff'd [2002] 2 S.C.R. 761.

Implied assertions can be contained in verbal or written statements. The classic case is *Wright v. Doe d. Tatham*.[14] At issue was whether the will of John Marsden was valid. Wright was Marsden's steward and the principal beneficiary under the will. Tatham was Marsden's cousin and sole heir-at-law should the will be overturned. Tatham alleged that Marsden was not mentally competent at the time that he executed the will. To support Marsden's sanity, Wright sought to tender into evidence letters written to Marsden by three different acquaintances. The tone and content of the letters implied that the writers believed Marsden to be sane. The House of Lords excluded the letters because they were being used for this implicit assertion. Had the writers said in their letters — "Marsden, you competent fellow" — this express assertion of competency would be hearsay. Simply put, the House of Lords was not prepared to allow the evidence to do indirectly what it could not do directly.

The House of Lords equated unintended assertions with intended assertions. But are they the same? When a person intends to make a statement, concerns are raised as to why. Is the person intending to be truthful or deceitful? Unintended assertions are far more likely to be sincere. For this reason the trend in the United States is to treat unintended assertions as not hearsay.[15]

Even though it may be unlikely that unintended assertions are insincere, there remain other areas of concern that ought to be tested, for example, the person's perception of the events. Consider the case of *R. v. Wysochan*.[16] Wysochan was convicted of the murder of Anita Kropa and sentenced to death. Anita had been shot. At the time, the only people present were her husband, Stanley Kropa, and the accused. According to Stanley, the accused did the shooting. According to Wysochan, the shooting must have been done by Stanley. At issue were words spoken by Anita after the shooting. Anita said to a friend, "Tony, where is my husband?" and when Stanley came near her she stretched out her hand to him and said, "Stanley, help me out because there is a bullet in my body." The Court of Appeal ruled that these statements were not hearsay; they merely showed her belief and feelings towards her husband. Yet the implied assertion is obvious — "Wysochan shot me" — but if

---

14   (1837), 112 E.R. 488 (Ex. Ch.), aff'd (*sub nom. Wright v. Tatham*) (1838), 7 E.R. 559 (H.L.).

15   Under the *Federal Rules of Evidence* 801(a), a "statement" is "(1) an oral or written assertion, or (2) nonverbal conduct of a person, if it is intended by the person as an assertion." See also E.W. Cleary, ed., *McCormick on Evidence*, 3d ed. (St. Paul, MN: West, 1984) s. 250.

16   (1930), 54 C.C.C. 172 (Sask. C.A.).

she had said that it would be hearsay. In this case, is it not critical to know first of all whether she actually saw who shot her?

Implied assertions are difficult to identify and, as in *Wysochan*, are often overlooked or ignored by the courts. However, the English House of Lords in *R. v. Kearley* reaffirmed *Wright v. Tatham*.[17] In *Kearley* the police raided the accused's apartment, which he shared with his wife and another man. Drugs were found but not in sufficient quantity to raise the inference that Kearley was a dealer. The police remained in the apartment for several hours after the search, and during this time they intercepted ten telephone calls in which the callers asked for Kearley and asked for drugs. Seven other people arrived at the door asking for Kearley and asking for drugs. At trial the Crown was unable or unwilling to call the telephone callers or visitors. Instead, the police officers were called to testify as to what they were told to prove the charge of possession with intent to supply. A majority in the House of Lords found that the statements made to the police were implied assertions that Kearley was a drug dealer and, accordingly, were inadmissible.

Given the facts in *Kearley*, the decision of the House of Lords is technical, rigid, precedent driven, and defies common sense. Fortunately, we are not bound by it. The prevailing view in Canadian courts is that such evidence is not hearsay. Rather, incoming calls such as in *Kearley* are treated as original circumstantial evidence. They are statements of intention by the callers relevant for the fact the calls are made, which when combined with other evidence goes to prove trafficking.[18] In a fact situation almost identical to *Kearley* the Ontario Court of Appeal concluded that the intercepted telephone calls were not hearsay and were admissible.[19] The court also went on to say that even if the calls were hearsay, given the reliability surrounding their being made, they were admissible as a hearsay exception.

What then is the status of implied assertions? Are they hearsay or not? What is important to keep in mind is that today, in the law of evidence, this question is not an "in or out" proposition. If the evidence is treated as non-hearsay, this does not mean that the evidence is automatically admissible. The trial judge retains a discretion to exclude otherwise admissible evidence where the potential prejudice outweighs the probative value of the evidence. For example, say that in *Kearley*, instead of ten calls there was but one. The probative value of the evidence pointing to dealing in drugs is much reduced. Referring to

---

17 *R. v. Kearley*, [1992] 2 All E.R. 345 (H.L.).

18 See *R. v. Ly*, [1997] 3 S.C.R. 698; *R. v. Williams*, 2009 BCCA 284; *R. v. Bui*, 2003 BCCA 556.

19 *R. v. Edwards* (1994), 34 C.R. (4th) 113 (Ont. C.A.).

this scenario, Lord Browne-Wilkinson, writing in *Kearley*, concluded: "The possible prejudice to the accused by the jury drawing the wrong inference would be so great that I would expect a judge in his discretion to exclude it."[20] In turn, if the evidence is treated as hearsay, it is not automatically excluded. The evidence may well be admitted as a hearsay exception where it is found to be reasonably necessary and sufficiently reliable.[21]

---

20 Above note 17 at 390.
21 See *R. v. Wilson* (1996), 47 C.R. (4th) 61 (Ont. C.A.).

CHAPTER 5

HEARSAY EXCEPTIONS

1. PRINCIPLES UNDERLYING THE EXCEPTIONS

Hearsay evidence may be admissible under an existing hearsay exception or may be admitted on a case-by-case basis according to the principles of "necessity and reliability." "Necessity and reliability" are the guiding principles for the admissibility of all hearsay. The existing hearsay exceptions must comply with these principles. If the hearsay exception does not conform to the principled approach it should be modified, where possible, to bring it into compliance.

The "necessity" requirement is satisfied where it is "reasonably necessary" to present the hearsay evidence in order to obtain the declarant's version of events. "Reliability" refers to "threshold reliability," which is for the trial judge. The function of the trial judge is limited to determining whether the particular hearsay statement exhibits sufficient indicia of reliability so as to afford the trier of fact a satisfactory basis for evaluating the truth of the statement.

The hearsay exceptions are governed by the same principles that underlie the hearsay rule. The hearsay rule is in place to improve accurate fact finding by excluding hearsay statements that may well be unreliable or that cannot be adequately tested. In this way the hearsay rule facilitates the search for truth. Hearsay exceptions are also in place to facilitate the search for truth by *admitting* into evidence hearsay statements that are reliably made or can be adequately tested.

What has evolved over time is a long list of hearsay exceptions under common law and statute. Unfortunately, formalism often prevailed as counsel strove to fit evidence within an existing hearsay exception. This led to pigeon-holing of the evidence. Precedent prevailed over principle and evidence was wrongly admitted or excluded. Wigmore observed:

> The needless obstruction to investigation of truth caused by the hearsay rule is due mainly to the inflexibility of its exceptions, to the rigidly technical construction of those exceptions by the courts, and to the enforcement of the rule when its contravention would do no harm, but would assist in obtaining a complete understanding of the transaction.[1]

Wigmore urged greater flexibility based upon two guiding principles: necessity and reliability. The principle of necessity arose from the choice of either receiving the evidence untested or losing the evidence entirely. In assessing the reliability of the evidence, what was looked for was some substitute for cross-examination to support the trustworthiness of the statement.

The Supreme Court of Canada in *R. v. Khan* accepted Wigmore's approach.[2] Khan was a doctor charged with sexually assaulting a three-and-a-half-year-old patient. The child and her mother went to Dr. Khan, who was their family doctor. The child was examined first, in her mother's presence. Dr. Khan then had the child wait in his private office. Dr. Khan and the child were alone for some five to seven minutes while the mother got undressed in the examining room. Dr. Khan then examined the mother. Some thirty minutes after the child had been left alone with Dr. Khan, the mother and child had essentially the following conversation:

Mrs. O: So you were talking to Dr. Khan, were you? What did he say?

T: He asked me if I wanted a candy. I said yes. And do you know what?

Mrs. O: What?

T: He said "open your mouth." And do you know what? He put his birdie in my mouth, shook it, and peed in my mouth.

---

1   *Wigmore on Evidence*, 3d ed., vol. 5 (Boston: Little, Brown, 1940) at para. 1427.
2   (1990), 59 C.C.C. (3d) 92 (S.C.C.).

Mrs. O: Are you sure?

T: Yes.

Mrs. O: You're not lying to me, are you?

T: No. He put his birdie in my mouth. And he never did give
          me my candy.[3]

The mother noted that the child was picking at a wet spot on her sleeve; subsequent tests showed that the spot was produced by semen and a mixture of semen and saliva. At trial, the judge ruled that the child was not competent to testify and refused to admit the above out-of-court statement made to the mother.

The child's out-of-court statement was being tendered for its truth. In order to be admitted, a hearsay exception needed to be found. No existing exception applied, although arguably the child's statement could have been force-fitted into the category of spontaneous declarations. Madam Justice McLachlin, writing for the court, found that to do so in the circumstances would deform the spontaneous declaration rule beyond recognition. Rather, she turned to principle. The principles turned to were necessity and reliability. Necessity was interpreted as being "reasonably necessary." In terms of reliability, that determination would vary in the circumstances and was best left to the trial judge. Applying these principles to the case on appeal, the Court ruled that the child's statement to her mother should have been received.

Arguably, *Khan* could have been confined to children's evidence and to child abuse cases. This was not to be. Within two years the Supreme Court of Canada in *R. v. Smith* made it abundantly clear that the principles identified in *Khan* were of a general application.[4]

Khan and *Smith*, therefore, expanded the admissibility of otherwise inadmissible hearsay evidence. They created a principled approach, which was in addition to the existing exceptions and available on a case-by-case basis. What was left unclear was the impact that the principled approach would have on the existing hearsay exceptions.

In *R. v. Starr* the Supreme Court of Canada reaffirmed the continued relevance of the existing hearsay exceptions.[5] The Court recognized the primacy of the principled approach. Necessity and reliability are now the touchstones for the admissibility of all hearsay evidence. Having said this, Justice Iacobucci, writing for the majority, was not prepared to abolish the existing exceptions. He recognized several important func-

---

3   *Ibid.* at 95.
4   (1992), 15 C.R. (4th) 133 at 148 (S.C.C.).
5   *R. v. Starr* (2000), 147 C.C.C. (3d) 449 (S.C.C.). See also *R. v. Khelawon* (2006), 215 C.C.C. (3d) 161 at para. 60 (S.C.C.).

tions served by the hearsay exceptions. First, they add predictability and certainty, which leads to greater efficiency of court time. Second, they serve a valuable educative function by providing a useful guide as to the admissibility of hearsay in specific factual contexts. Third, they assist in reinforcing that "necessity" is really a search for the best evidence available. For these reasons Justice Iacobucci chose to "rationalize" the traditional exceptions with the principled approach. In other words, the traditional exceptions are to be tested against the principles of necessity and reliability, and where the exceptions are found to be wanting they will need to be modified or abolished. For example, in *Starr*, the traditional exception that admitted hearsay statements of "state of mind" or of "present intentions" was found to be in conflict with the principled approach in that it had the potential to admit unreliable hearsay. The exception, as it stood, simply required that the statements be of "present intentions." There was no requirement that such statements be made in circumstances of reliability. Accordingly, the exception was modified to conform to the principled approach and additional indicia of reliability were imposed. The modified exception now requires that the statement of "present intentions" must appear to have been made in a natural manner and not under circumstances of suspicion.[6]

Based on the *Starr* decision, and affirmed by the Supreme Court of Canada in R. v. Khelawon,[7] the following is a framework for considering the admissibility of hearsay evidence:

1) Hearsay evidence is presumptively inadmissible unless it falls under an exception to the hearsay rule. The traditional exceptions to the hearsay rule remain presumptively in place.

2) A hearsay exception can be challenged to determine whether it is supported by indicia of necessity and reliability, required by the principled approach. The exception can be modified as necessary to bring it into compliance.

3) In "rare cases," evidence falling within an existing exception may be excluded because the indicia of necessity and reliability are lacking in the particular circumstances of the case.[8]

4) If hearsay evidence does not fall under a hearsay exception, it may still be admitted if indicia of reliability and necessity are established on a *voir dire*.

---

6   R. v. Starr, *ibid.* at 518. Statements of present intention are discussed in section 10.2.

7   Above note 5 at para. 42.

8   See R. v. Simpson, 2007 ONCA 793, leave to appeal to S.C.C. refused, 2008 CanLII 33807 (S.C.C.).

There are two additional considerations. First, even where the evidence is admissible under an exception to the hearsay rule or under the principled approach, the judge may still refuse to admit the evidence if its prejudicial effect outweighs its probative value.[9]

R. v. Nicholas is an example of the misapplication of the judicial discretion.[10] In Nicholas the trial judge exercised his residual discretion to exclude statements made by a complainant notwithstanding that these statements were both necessary and reliable. The complainant was sexually assaulted in her home. She made a 911 call approximately ten minutes after the attack. The call was audiotaped. She then made a videotaped statement to the police some six hours later. At trial it was accepted that she was too traumatized to testify. The trial judge, however, excluded the statements because the defence could not cross-examine her—even though the trial judge remarked that it was difficult to imagine the utility of any cross-examination. Of importance, the complainant's evidence would only establish that she was sexually attacked. She could not identify her attacker because her face was covered with a pillow. Identity was going to be established through DNA evidence. The Court of Appeal reversed the trial judge's ruling. There was no prejudice to the accused in that there really would be little or no point to be served in cross-examination of the complainant. What Nicholas underscores is that trial judges need to weigh the probative value of the hearsay evidence against any valid articulated prejudice. We need to be reminded that hearsay evidence often presupposes that the declarant is unavailable or cannot be effectively cross-examined. In R. v. Smith the Supreme Court concluded: "[W]here the criteria of necessity and reliability are satisfied, the lack of testing by cross-examination goes to weight, not admissibility, and a properly cautioned jury should be able to evaluate the evidence on that basis."[11] Cross-examiners, when faced with hearsay evidence, will always complain about the lack of cross-examination as a matter of rote. A complaint without substance is not enough.

Second, it must be remembered that admitting evidence under a hearsay exception does not trump other rules of evidence. For example, a hearsay statement that contains inadmissible opinion or repeats inadmissible hearsay should not be admitted into evidence. This was the problem in R. v. Couture where, in the circumstances of that case, the

---

9 For an example of a trial judge using the residual discretion to exclude hearsay statements see R. v. M.M. (2001), 156 C.C.C. (3d) 560 (Ont. C.A.).

10 R. v. Nicholas (2004), 182 C.C.C. (3d) 393 (Ont. C.A.).

11 Quoted in R. v. Nicholas, ibid. at para. 96.

hearsay evidence also violated the spousal incompetency rule.[12] Another very common situation is in domestic homicide cases where the prosecution seeks to introduce statements made by the deceased showing past abuse by the accused. In these cases the evidence must overcome both the hearsay and character hurdles.[13] Before admitting hearsay statements under the principled approach, the trial judge must determine on a *voir dire* that necessity and reliability have been established on a balance of probabilities. In a criminal context, concerns for necessity and reliability take on a constitutional dimension. Justice Iacobucci emphasized that it is a principle of fundamental justice, protected by the *Charter*, that the innocent must not be convicted and to allow the Crown to introduce unreliable hearsay against an accused would compromise trial fairness, and raise the spectre of wrongful convictions.[14] "Trial fairness" is not just a one-way street. In *R. v. Khelawon* the Court noted that society too has an interest in seeing that the trial process arrives at the truth and that "the criterion of necessity is founded on society's interest in getting at the truth."[15]

It is recognized that where hearsay evidence is tendered by an accused, a trial judge can relax the strict rules of admissibility where it is necessary to prevent a miscarriage of justice.[16] Such preferential treatment acknowledges the liberty interest of the accused. But this is not to say that the necessity/reliability concerns are swept aside for the defence. A close review of the cases where this proposition is applied shows that the evidence sought to be admitted by the defence was close to the line in terms of admissibility. Fairness concerns, therefore, merely tipped the reliability/necessity analysis in favour of the accused; the rules were relaxed but not abandoned.[17]

Similarly, should the principled approach be applied in a more liberal fashion in civil cases? In England, for example, the hearsay rule has been abolished in civil cases and hearsay concerns are dealt with by way of notice requirements and weight.[18] It is also true that expediency in introducing evidence is a valid concern given the costs of litiga-

---

12   *R. v. Couture* (2007), 220 C.C.C. (3d) 289 (S.C.C.).

13   *R. v. Moo*, 2009 ONCA 645.

14   *R. v. Starr*, above note 5 at 529.

15   *R. v. Khelawon*, above note 5 at paras. 48–49.

16   See, for example, *R. v. Sunjka* (2006), 80 O.R. (3d) 781 at para. 23 (C.A.); *R. v. Folland* (1999), 132 C.C.C. (3d) 14 at 31–32 (Ont. C.A.); *R. v. Post*, 2007 BCCA 123, leave to appeal to S.C.C. refused, 2007 CanLII 37200 (S.C.C.).

17   *R. v. Kimberley* (2001), 157 C.C.C. (3d) 129 at 156 (Ont. C.A.).

18   For a discussion of the English law, see Hodge M. Malek, *Phipson on Evidence*, 16th ed. (London: Sweet & Maxwell, 2005) c. 29.

tion and there is no countervailing concern about protecting the liberty interest of an accused.[19] There is much wisdom, however, in treating the law of hearsay the same. A general across-the-board relaxing of the hearsay rules in civil cases is too blunt an approach. Admitting hearsay without due scrutiny would impair the fact-finding process. The search for truth remains important in civil cases where much can be at stake. What is recommended is a case-by-case consideration of the hearsay evidence in the context of the issues in the case and the potential impact of receiving the evidence in hearsay form.[20] "Context" and "impact" include: the seriousness of the case, importance of the evidence, consequences to the parties and costs or efforts required to secure the original evidence. These factors primarily go to the necessity arm of the principled approach and it is here that "expediency" may well be more of a factor in civil cases. If requiring the maker of a statement to be called would be prohibitively expensive or burdensome given the role the evidence would play in the case, it may not be reasonable to expect the party to produce the witness. On the other hand, in terms of assessing the reliability of the hearsay statements, the indicia of reliability do not change whether it is a civil or criminal case.[21]

1.1)   Reasonable Necessity

"Necessity" is founded on the need to get at the truth; in substance it is a form of the "best evidence" rule. Hearsay evidence may be necessary to enable all relevant and reliable information to be placed before the court, so justice may be done.[22] It does not mean that the evidence is "necessary to the prosecution's case." Nor is necessity to be equated with the unavailability of the witness. Certainly if the witness is deceased or not competent or too traumatized to testify there is necessity. Necessity, however, is to be given a more flexible meaning. Justice McLachlin in *Khan* used the phrase "reasonable necessity." The key is the unavailability of the witness's courtroom testimony. The witnesses may be available, but through the passage of time their testimony may no longer be complete, or they may have changed their testimony and an earlier out-of-court statement arguably should be put to the trier of fact in determining the truth. In *Smith*, Chief Justice Lamer turned to

---

19   See, for example, *Clark v. Horizon Holidays Ltd.* (1993), 45 C.C.E.L. 244 (Ont. Gen. Div.), and *Dodge v. Kaneff Homes Inc.*, [2001] O.J. No.1141 (S.C.J.).

20   See *R. v. Khelawon*, above note 5 at para. 57, and *R. v. Couture*, above note 12 at para. 76.

21   See *Jung v. Lee Estate*, [2007] 5 W.W.R. 577 (B.C.C.A.).

22   *R. v. F.(W.J.)* (1999), 138 C.C.C. (3d) 1 at 15 (S.C.C.).

Wigmore's articulation of necessity, which encompasses not only un-availability but "an expediency or convenience." He quoted the following from Wigmore:

> The assertion may be such that we cannot expect, again or at this time, to get evidence of the same value from the same or other sources . . . . The necessity is not so great; perhaps hardly a necessity, only an expediency or convenience, can be predicated. But the principle is the same.[23]

The case of *Khan v. College of Physicians and Surgeons* illustrates the point.[24] Dr. Khan, besides the criminal prosecution, faced disciplinary action brought by the college. At the disciplinary hearing, the tribunal heard from the young girl, now eight years old, who testified as to the incident that had occurred more than four years before. The child's mother also testified and repeated the child's statement given to her shortly after leaving Dr. Khan's office. Various other persons were called and they too repeated what they had been told by the child. In these circumstances, where is the necessity? The Ontario Court of Appeal adopted a flexible case-by-case approach. The court stated that "[t]he fact that the child testifies will be relevant to, but not determinative of, the admissibility of the out-of-court statement."[25] The court then engaged in a detailed analysis of the transcript and found that the child could not provide a full and candid account of the events. It then became reasonably necessary to admit the out-of-court statement of her mother. It was not, however, reasonably necessary to admit the subsequent statements made to other persons.

"Reasonable necessity" requires that "reasonable efforts" be undertaken to obtain the direct evidence of the witness. The requirement of necessity is there in part to protect the integrity of the trial process. Without a requirement of necessity the introduction of out-of-court statements could replace the calling of witnesses, which would deprive the opposing party of the opportunity to test the evidence through cross-examination, even where effective cross-examination is entirely possible. In *R. v. Khelawon*, necessity was conceded. The witness had died. However, at the time of making his statement he was elderly and frail. There was no evidence that the Crown attempted to preserve his evidence under sections 709 to 714 of the *Criminal Code*, which provide for the taking of evidence on commission. The Court was critical of this

---

23   Above note 4 at 149.
24   (1992), 9 O.R. (3d) 641 (C.A.).
25   *Ibid.* at 656.

and noted, "[I]n an appropriate case, the court in deciding the question of necessity may well question whether the proponent of the evidence made all reasonable efforts to secure the evidence of the declarant in a manner that also preserves the rights of the other party."[26]

As a general proposition, therefore, where a witness is physically available, and there is no evidence that he or she would suffer trauma in testifying, then the witness should be called.[27] There is a spectrum of trauma. Proof of severe trauma is not required.[28] On the other hand, it is not enough that a witness is unwilling to testify. "Fear or disinclination without more, do not constitute necessity."[29]

There is no presumption of necessity and it is not to be lightly assumed.[30] The trial judge must determine, in the given case, why it is necessary to receive a statement untested by cross-examination. Where the necessity claim rests on the contention that a witness could be traumatized if required to testify, the Crown does not have to demonstrate that psychological trauma is certain; it is enough to show "a real possibility of psychological trauma."[31] In most instances the Crown will need to rely on an assessment of the witness undertaken by a qualified expert. For example, in R. v. Nicholas the complainant in a break and enter and sexual assault was not called to testify.[32] Instead her psychologist was called and testified that the complainant suffered from post-traumatic stress disorder, which made it "impossible" for her to testify. In fact there was a risk that she would commit suicide if forced to testify. Necessity was established.

There is no absolute rule that a particular kind of evidence, or indeed any evidence, need be called in all cases. Necessity may be self-evident. For example, the test of necessity may be met by the very fact of the young age of the child witness, or from the facts and circumstances as they arise at trial.[33] This is what occurred in R. v. F.(W.J.).[34] The accused was charged with sexually assaulting a five-year-old girl. The complainant was six years and eight months old at trial. The girl was called to testify and she "clammed up." The Crown then sought

---

26   R. v. Khelawon, above note 5 at para. 104. See also R. v. Mohammed, 2007 ONCA 513.

27   R. v. Parrott (2001), 150 C.C.C. (3d) 449 at 476–77 (S.C.C.).

28   R. v. Rockey (1996), 110 C.C.C. (3d) 481 at para. 28 (S.C.C.).

29   R. v. F.(W.J.), above note 22. See also R. v. Pelletier (1999), 30 C.R. (5th) 333 (B.C.C.A.).

30   R. v. Rockey, above note 28 at para. 17.

31   R. v. Robinson (2004), 189 C.C.C. (3d) 152 at para. 41 (Ont. C.A.).

32   R. v. Nicholas, above note 10.

33   See R. v. P.(J.) (1992), 74 C.C.C. (3d) 276 (Que. C.A.), aff'd [1993] 1 S.C.R. 469.

34   Above note 22.

to introduce the girl's out-of-court statements. The trial judge refused to admit these hearsay statements on the basis that necessity was not established. What concerned the trial judge was that the Crown had failed to provide the court with some explanation as to why the child refused to testify. In the Supreme Court of Canada the majority held that an explanation was not required. On the facts it was obvious that the child was "unable" to testify.

A final point is that necessity relates to the particular witness's evidence. The fact that there is other evidence from other witnesses on the same point is of no moment and does not render the hearsay evidence "unnecessary."[35] "Necessity" is concerned with obtaining the relevant direct evidence from a particular witness. In *R. v. Smith*, Chief Justice Lamer made the point this way:

> The criterion of necessity, however, does not have the sense of "necessary to the prosecution's case." If this were the case, uncorroborated hearsay evidence which satisfies the criterion of reliability would be admissible if uncorroborated, but might no longer be "necessary" to the prosecution's case if corroborated by other independent evidence. Such an interpretation of the criterion of "necessity" would thus produce the illogical result that uncorroborated hearsay evidence would be admissible, but could become inadmissible if corroborated.[36]

What of multiple statements? If a witness testifies, the law generally does not allow for the admission of other prior consistent statements; such repetition violates the rule against oath-helping. Things should be no different for unavailable witnesses. Repetitious statements made by unavailable witnesses should not each be admitted or the rule against prior consistent statements will be subverted. What should be needed before multiple hearsay statements made by an unavailable witness are admitted is additional information or context to support the "necessity" in admitting additional statements, or portions of those statements.[37]

1.2)   Threshold Reliability

"The criterion of reliability is about ensuring the integrity of the trial process. The evidence, although needed, is not admissible unless it is sufficiently reliable to overcome the dangers arising from the difficulty of testing it."[38] In considering "reliability," a distinction is made between

---

35   *R. v. Woodard*, 2009 MBCA 42 at para. 48.

36   *R. v. Smith*, above note 4 at para. 35.

37   See *R. v. Cansanay*, 2010 MBQB 81 and *R. v. Candir*, 2009 ONCA 915.

38   *R. v. Khelawon*, above note 5 at para. 49.

"threshold" and "ultimate" reliability.[39] This distinction reflects the important difference between admission and reliance. Threshold reliability is for the trial judge and concerns the admissibility of the statement. The trial judge acts as a gatekeeper whose function "is limited to determining whether the particular hearsay statement exhibits sufficient *indicia* of reliability so as to afford the trier of fact a satisfactory basis for evaluating the truth of the statement."[40] So long as it can be assessed and accepted by a reasonable trier of fact, then the evidence should be admitted. Once admitted, the jury remains the ultimate arbiter of what to do with the evidence and deciding whether or not the statement is true.

In *Starr* the Supreme Court of Canada limited the factors that a trial judge could look to in determining threshold reliability to those circumstances surrounding the statement itself.[41] This became the "threshold box.". All external considerations fell outside the box and could only be used by the trier of fact in determining ultimate reliability. Most troubling, the trial judge was not to consider the presence of corroborating or conflicting evidence.

To highlight the issue, consider the facts in *Khan*. Semen and saliva were found on the little girl's sleeve. Surely this evidence corroborates what she said; however, it is not a circumstance under which the statement was made. It does not impact on her ability to accurately or sincerely make the statement. It simply shows that what she said was probably true. Following *Starr*, the trier of fact may take the semen and saliva into account in assessing the truth of her statement, but the trial judge may not do so in determining admissibility. Boxing of the evidence in such a way proved difficult and led to inconsistent application of the law across the country. The Supreme Court of Canada abandoned this approach in *Khelawon*.[42] A functional approach was endorsed. All relevant factors going to the reliability of the statement can now be looked to by the trial judge. This is a welcome reversal by the Supreme Court. It accords with practical common sense and by allowing trial judges to consider all indicia of reliability or unreliability it best ensures that sufficiently reliable evidence goes before the trier of fact.

There is concern, however, that the *voir dire* on the admissibility of the hearsay evidence could well overtake the trial. Appellate courts

---

39   See *R. v. Hawkins* (1996), 111 C.C.C. (3d) 129 (S.C.C.), and *R. v. Khelawon, ibid.* at paras. 50–52.

40   *R. v. Hawkins, ibid.* at para. 75.

41   *R. v. Starr*, above note 5 at paras. 215–17.

42   Above note 5 at para. 93.

call for restraint.[43] The difficulty is where to draw the line and the reality that there is no fixed line. A functional approach by its nature is case-specific. The most important point of reference is that trial judges need to be mindful "that the question of ultimate reliability not be predetermined on the admissibility *voir dire*."[44]

Just as with necessity, reliability too is to be given a flexible meaning. Wigmore referred to "some degree of trustworthiness more than ordinary" as being sufficient.[45] Because hearsay comes in a wide variety of forms and contexts, there is no set list of factors that may influence reliability. However, in *Khelawon*, the Court observed that the reliability requirement will generally be met on the basis of two different grounds, neither of which excludes consideration of the other. First, the statement is made in circumstances that speak to its truth and accuracy. The statement is inherently trustworthy. Second, another way of fulfilling the reliability requirement is to show that its truth and accuracy can be adequately tested.[46] This second factor is not so much about reliability as it is about "testability." The hearsay evidence is admitted because the trier of fact is in a position to test the evidence and assess its true worth.

1.2 (a)   Inherent Trustworthiness

"Common sense dictates that if we can put sufficient trust in the truth and accuracy of the statement, it should be considered by the fact finder regardless of its hearsay form."[47] The perfect case is *Khan*. The little girl's statement to her mother about being sexually molested by Dr. Khan was inherently trustworthy. The child's statement was made shortly after the incident. The statement was made innocently, without prompting or suggestion. The child had no motive to lie; she really did not know what had actually happened to her. Finally, there was the semen stain on the child's clothing.

A second case to illustrate the point is that of *R. v. U.(F.J.)*.[48] In this case a complainant told the police that the accused, her father, was having sex with her "almost every day" and provided considerable details. The interviewing police officer then spoke with the father and he too admitted to the sex and described similar details. At trial the complain-

---

43   See *R. v. T.R.* (2007), 220 C.C.C. (3d) 37 (Ont. C.A.); *R. v. Lowe*, 2009 BCCA 338
     at para. 78.
44   *R. v. Khelawon*, above note 5 at para. 93.
45   Above note 1 at para. 1420.
46   Above note 5 at para 49.
47   *Ibid.* at para. 62.
48   *R. v. U.(F.J.)* (1995), 42 C.R. (4th) 133 (S.C.C.).

ant recanted and denied any sexual acts had occurred. In response the Crown was allowed to introduce her prior out-of-court statement for its truth. "The striking similarities between her statement and the independent statement made by her father were so compelling that the only likely explanation was that they were both telling the truth."[49]

In terms of factors that go to inherent trustworthiness consider whether the statement was made:

- spontaneously,
- naturally,
- without suggestion,
- reasonably contemporaneously with the events,
- by a person who had no motive to fabricate,
- by a person with a sound mental state,[50]
- against the person's interest in whole or in part,
- by a young person who would not likely have knowledge of the acts alleged,
- whether there is corroborating evidence.

In addition, consider whether there are any safeguards in place surrounding the making of the statement that would go to expose any inaccuracies or fabrications. For example:

- was the person under a duty to record the statements,
- was the statement made to public officials,
- was the statement recorded,
- did the person know the statement would be publicized.

Motive is an important factor to consider in determining reliability. Proved evidence of motive to fabricate goes to the very heart of the reliability of any statement made; so too does proved absence of motive. In between, where there is no proved motive or proved absence of motive, then motive is a neutral factor. *R. v. Czibulka* provides an excellent discussion on motive as applied to threshold reliability.[51] The accused was convicted of second-degree murder in the killing of his wife. The key issue on appeal was the admissibility of a letter written by the deceased some three months prior to her death. In the letter the deceased described a life of abuse, violence, and hate at the hands of the accused

---

49   *R. v. Khelawon*, above note 5 at para. 86.

50   The Ontario Court of Appeal in *R. v. Khelawon* (2005), 194 C.C.C. (3d) 161 (C.A.), recognized that expert psychiatric evidence as to the declarant's mental state was admissible in determining threshold reliability.

51   *R. v. Czibulka* (2004), 189 C.C.C. (3d) 199 (Ont. C.A.), leave to appeal to S.C.C. refused, [2004] S.C.C.A. No. 502.

and of her fear and wish to leave him. The trial judge admitted the letter in part because the deceased had no apparent motive to lie. Justice Rosenberg took issue with this finding. He noted, "Lack of evidence of motive to fabricate is not equivalent to proved absence of motive to fabricate."[52] Evidence is needed.

"Relationship" evidence is another factor. The relationship may concern the topic of the statement. In *Czibulka* the deceased wrote about her husband, the accused. Evidence of animus or malice in the relationship may taint the reliability of any statements made about him. Similarly, the relationship between the declarant and the receiver of the communication is also important. Judges need to consider whether the declarant would have any reason to lie to the receiver. For example, a young woman phones her mother to tell her that she will be late but that Bobby will give her a ride home. There is evidence that the mother likes and trusts Bobby. In this situation, the girl may well simply be telling her mother what she wants to hear.[53]

In the above example the mother is the receiver of the statement. There is some disagreement over whether the credibility and reliability of the receiver is a factor to be considered under threshold reliability. The Supreme Court of Canada has made it clear that threshold reliability is concerned with the reliability of the declarant and not with the receiver.[54] This position makes sense. The principled approach is concerned about the trustworthiness of what the hearsay statement is claiming. In the preceding example the evidence is being admitted to prove that Bobby would be giving the declarant a ride home. What the mother heard tells us nothing about the truth of this statement. Moreover, the mother presumably is available to testify and can be subjected to full cross-examination. Having said this, the reliability and credibility of the receiver may well become a factor under the residual discretion to exclude evidence where its potential probative value is exceeded by the potential prejudicial effect.[55] In exercising this discretion, confidence that the statement was indeed made goes to its potential probative value.

How satisfied must the trial judge be of the trustworthiness of a hearsay statement? In *Khelawon* the Court quoted from Wigmore and the need for "sceptical caution."[56] In *R. v. Couture* the Court went on to

---

52   *Ibid.* at para. 44. See also *R. v. Blackman*, 2008 SCC 37 at para. 39.

53   See *R. v. Czibulka*, above note 51 at para. 51.

54   *R. v. Blackman*, above note 52 at para. 50. See also *R. v. Humaid* (2006), 208 C.C.C. (3d) 43 (Ont. C.A.).

55   See *R. v. Duguay*, 2007 NBCA 65.

56   Above note 5 at para. 62.

explain that "what must be shown is a certain cogency about the statements that removes any real concern about their truth and accuracy."[57] The test is certainly a high one and it should be noted that in both *Khelawon* and *Couture* the statements were not admitted.

1.2 (b)   Can the Evidence be Tested?

"Common sense tells us that we should not lose the benefit of the evidence when there are adequate substitutes for testing the evidence."[58] The optimal way of testing evidence is to have the declarant state the evidence in court, under oath and subject to contemporaneous cross-examination. This second aspect of reliability considers whether there are any substitutes that address the hearsay dangers arising from lack of oath, presence, and cross-examination. They include:

- was the person under oath when making the statement;
- was the making of the statement audio- or videotaped;
- at the time of making the statement, was the person cross-examined;
- is the person now available to be cross-examined in court on making the out-of-court statement.

The focus under this ground is not so much on whether there is reason to believe the statement is true, but rather whether the trier of fact will be in a position to rationally evaluate the evidence. A good example is found in the case of *R. v. Hawkins*.[59] Hawkins, a police officer, was charged with obstructing justice and corruptly accepting money. His then girlfriend, Graham, testified at his preliminary inquiry, which spanned a period of time. Initially she implicated Hawkins; then she recanted much of what she had said. By the time of trial Hawkins and Graham were married and Graham was incompetent to testify for the prosecution. The Crown was allowed to introduce into evidence her preliminary inquiry evidence, notwithstanding that Graham could hardly be regarded as a trustworthy witness. Her evidence was riddled with internal contradictions. However, at the time of testifying at the preliminary she was under oath, in a court of law, the evidence was transcribed, and she was subject to cross-examination. The process provided a means to assess the trustworthiness of the evidence. Internal contradictions in Graham's evidence went to the actual probative value of her testimony—a matter for the trier of fact. "When the reliability requirement is met on the basis that the trier of fact has a

---

57   *R. v. Couture*, above note 12 at para. 100.

58   *R. v. Khelawon*, above note 5 at para. 63.

59   *R. v. Hawkins*, above note 39.

sufficient basis to assess the statement's truth and accuracy, there is no need to inquire further into the likely truth of the statement."[60]

In terms of testing the evidence, the availability of cross-examination is always a critical factor. In *R. v. Couture* the majority emphasized how important this factor is by noting that "in the usual case, the availability of the declarant for cross-examination [at trial] goes a long way to satisfying the requirement of adequate substitutes."[61]

Although there are no hard-and-fast rules about the manner of conducting the hearsay admissibility inquiry, there are good reasons to look first at whether there are adequate substitutes for testing the evidence. The presence or absence of adequate substitutes is a fairly narrow inquiry. Further, whenever the reliability requirement is met on the basis of adequate means to test the statement, there is no need to inquire further into the likely truth of the statement, which is a much broader examination.[62]

It is also the case that these separate grounds for determining threshold reliability are not to be considered in isolation to one another. Factors may overlap and a far more functional, flexible approach is required. The grounds ought not to become rigid categories.

The factors considered in *Khelawon* are fluid and each may bear on the other.

A final point on the principled approach that may assist in applying the law is that necessity and threshold reliability are interrelated.[63] Professor Irving Younger provided this "rule of thumb": necessity plus reliability equals one. What this means is the greater the necessity, the less the reliability. Conversely, the greater the reliability, the less the necessity.[64] Wigmore, for example, was prepared to reform the hearsay rule to admit all statements of deceased persons, absolute necessity alone dictating admissibility.[65]

---

60 *R. v. Khelawon*, above note 5 at para 92.

61 *R. v. Couture*, above note 12 at para. 92.

62 See *R. v. Couture*, *ibid.* at para. 87.

63 *R. v. Wilcox* (2001), 152 C.C.C. (3d) 157 at 186 (N.S.C.A.). See also *R. v. Khelawon*, above note 5 at paras. 46 and 77.

64 Irving Younger, *An Irreverent Introduction to Hearsay*, American Bar Association Section of Litigation Monograph Series No. 3 (Chicago: American Bar Association, 1977) at 20–21.

65 Above note 1 at para. 1427. See also *Modonese v. Delac Estate*, 2011 BCSC 82.

2. PRIOR INCONSISTENT STATEMENTS

Prior inconsistent statements of non-party witnesses may be admitted for their truth on a case-by-case basis using the principled approach. Necessity is accepted whenever a witness recants his or her earlier out-of-court statement. Reliability is found either when the process in taking the prior inconsistent statement is sufficient to allow the trier of fact to assess its value against the witness's in-court testimony or the statement is inherently trustworthy.

At common law, prior inconsistent statements made by a non-party witness, if offered for their truth, were not admissible unless adopted as true by the witness. They were admissible only as to credibility to show that on a prior occasion the witness said something inconsistent with the testimony now given.[66] The trial judge typically would charge the jury as follows:

Ladies and gentlemen of the jury, as to the evidence concerning what was said in the statement, I must ask you to bear in mind that the only evidence you can consider from the witness is the evidence given in this courtroom. I must direct you that what was said in that statement is not to be taken as evidence of the truth. The statement serves only to test the credibility of the witness.

Such a limiting instruction has been described as "pious fraud."[67] Yet, there are valid concerns underlying the orthodox rule. First, there is something incongruous about accepting as true the prior inconsistent statement of a witness whose sworn testimony at trial is not believed. Second, there is concern about pressures and inducements brought to bear in the making of these statements. Both of these concerns are readily seen in the Supreme Court of Canada's decision in *R. v. B.(K.G.)* (commonly referred to as *K.G.B.*), where the Court recognized that in appropriate circumstances prior inconsistent statements could be admitted for their truth.[68]

K.G.B. presented a clear case for the court. Simply put, the prior inconsistent statements were needed to be introduced for their truth, or the Crown had no case. The accused, a young offender, was charged with murder in a stabbing death. The victim and his brother were walking home in the early-morning hours when they got into a fight with

---

66   See *R. v. Deacon* (1947), 3 C.R. 265 (S.C.C.).
67   E.M. Morgan, "Hearsay Dangers and the Application of the Hearsay Concept" (1948) 62 Harv. L. Rev. 177 at 193.
68   (1993), 79 C.C.C. (3d) 257 (S.C.C.).

four young male occupants of a car. In the course of the fight, the victim was stabbed and killed by one of the youths. The Crown called the three other occupants of the car. Each had given separate statements to the police. Each was videotaped. Each was made with a parent present, and in one case the mother, a brother, and a lawyer were present. Each statement implicated the accused. At trial, each recanted. Each admitted making the statement, but denied that it was true. The trial judge found that each had lied on the stand and, in turn, he had no doubt that the out-of-court statements were true. But under the existing law these statements could not be admitted for their truth. Accordingly, there was insufficient evidence to establish the accused's identity, and the charge against him was dismissed.

In the Supreme Court of Canada Chief Justice Lamer, for the majority, applied the principles of necessity and reliability from *Khan* and *Smith*. Obviously in the circumstances, necessity could not be equated with unavailability. The makers of the statements were present and could be cross-examined. Necessity arose from the fact that the statements were important evidence going to prove what actually occurred, which otherwise would be lost. Chief Justice Lamer explained:

> In the case of prior inconsistent statements, it is patent that we cannot expect to get evidence of the same value from the recanting witness or other sources: as counsel for the appellant claimed, the recanting witness holds the prior statement, and thus the relevant evidence, "hostage." The different "value" of the evidence is found in the fact that something has radically changed between the time when the statement was made and the trial.[69]

And in subsequent cases, the Supreme Court has confirmed that the necessity criterion is met whenever a witness recants.[70]

The question of reliability was more troubling for the Court, notwithstanding the fact that the maker of the statement was present and could be cross-examined. The problem is that the trier of fact is being asked to choose between two statements—one made out of court and the other made in court with all the trial safeguards. In these circumstances, Chief Justice Lamer stated that the reliability concern was "sharpened" and he called for "comparative reliability" between the two statements. Ideally he wanted to replicate *all* the trial safeguards of oath, presence, and cross-examination. In this way the trier of fact would be in the best position to test the out-of-court statement against

---

69   *Ibid.* at 296.
70   *R. v. U.(F.J.)*, above note 48 at 155.

the inconsistent in-court testimony. Therefore, according to the Chief Justice, the requirement of reliability would be satisfied where,

- the statement is made under oath or solemn affirmation following a warning as to the existence of sanctions and the significance of the oath or affirmation;
- the statement is videotaped in its entirety; and
- the opposing party has a full opportunity to cross-examine the witness respecting the statement.

These represent optimal conditions. They are not prerequisites to admissibility. In *Khelawon* Justice Charron explained that *K.G.B.* was never intended to create a new categorical exception. Rather, the admissibility of prior inconsistent statements for their truth was to be determined using the principled case-by-case approach. The criteria outlined in *K.G.B.* are not fixed, but provide guidance.[71] Indeed, flexibility has become the rule. Subsequent case law shows that rarely are all the *K.G.B.* criteria met. In fact, there are instances where the courts have found reliability absent all the *K.G.B.* criteria.[72]

A key variable with respect to prior inconsistent statements is the availability of the declarant to be cross-examined on his or her prior inconsistent statement.[73] Emphasis is on "effective cross-examination." "In order for this factor to weigh in favour of admission, there must be a 'full opportunity to cross-examine the witness' at trial."[74] When a witness denies or cannot recall making the statement, cross-examination at trial is thwarted. A testing of the witness's recantation is only possible when the witness admits making the earlier statement and provides a story for his or her recantation. Certainly, the effectiveness of any in-court cross-examination is a factor, but it should not be the determining factor; otherwise the admissibility of a recanting witness's out-of-court statement would rest on how he recanted. Having said this, as a guide, when cross-examination is of limited value, the need for other indicia of reliability increases, and when effective cross-examination is possible, the need for other indicia of reliability decreases.

---

71   See *R. v. Khelawon*, above note 5 at para. 45.

72   *R. v. Letourneau* (1994), 87 C.C.C. (3d) 481 (B.C.C.A.), leave to appeal to S.C.C. refused, [1995] S.C.C.A. No. 163. See also *Jung v. Lee Estate*, above note 21, which applied the law to a civil case.

73   In *R. v. Couture*, above note 12 at para. 95, Justice Charron for the majority stated: "[T]he opportunity to cross-examine is the most powerful factor favouring admissibility."

74   *R. v. Devine*, 2008 SCC 36 at para. 26.

In searching for alternative indicia of reliability, the specific concerns surrounding the admissibility of prior inconsistent statements need to be kept in mind. There is the fear of fabrication. Oral statements are far too easy to manufacture. Professor McCormick first voiced concern about "the hazard of error or falsity in the reporting of oral words."[75] McCormick proposed that only statements made in writing or signed by the declarant, or given as prior testimony in an official hearing, or oral statements acknowledged by the declarant, were to be admitted for their truth. The unacknowledged oral statement was to be excluded.

There is also the fear of untoward pressures being brought to bear on witnesses to provide desired statements. In criminal cases the particular concern lies with police interrogations. After all, it is the police who investigate crimes, it is the police who take witness statements, and it is the police and prosecution who would benefit most from a rule of law allowing such statements to be introduced for their truth. For these reasons, the police should see to it that statements are taken properly. A trial judge has discretion to refuse to admit a statement for its truth "when there is any concern that the statement may be the product of some form of investigatory misconduct."[76]

Videotaping is desirable and should be encouraged. It should be noted that Chief Justice Lamer in his opening paragraph in *K.G.B.* expressed the view that the time had come to replace the orthodox rule precisely because of the availability of videotaping. Yet, in subsequent cases the courts rarely take the police to task for not videotaping statements. Courts ought not to excuse police forces from following the dictates of *K.G.B.* unless there are special circumstances.[77]

The *K.G.B.* case is about "testability." The Court was looking for indicia of reliability in the "process" so that the trier of fact is in a suitable position to assess the out-of-court statement against the in-court testimony. It should not be forgotten that prior inconsistent statements can also be admitted because of their inherent trustworthiness. As we have already seen, in *R. v. U.(F.J.)* a prior inconsistent statement was admitted for its truth based on its inherent trustworthiness.[78] Reliability was to be found in the fact that the daughter's out-of-court statement alleging incest was "strikingly similar" to her father's confession and,

---

75   C.T. McCormick, "The Turncoat Witness: Previous Statements as Substantive Evidence" (1947) 25 Tex. L. Rev. 573 at 588.

76   *R. v. Khelawon*, above note 5 at para. 81.

77   *R. v. Conway* (1997), 121 C.C.C. (3d) 397 at 409 (Ont.C.A.). See also *R. v. Wilson* (2006), 210 C.C.C. (3d) 23 (Ont. C.A.).

78   *R. v. U.(F.J.)*, above note 48.

in the absence of improper suggestion or of collusion, it was fair to assume that both were telling the truth. Furthermore, in the case, the daughter admitted making the statement and she could effectively be cross-examined on it and on her recantation.

When admitting prior inconsistent statements for their truth on the basis of "striking similarity" it is contemplated that the comparison statements are both admissible. For example, in *U.(F.J.)* the daughter's statement could be compared to the father's confession. However, if the father's statement was ruled inadmissible for whatever reason there would be no "comparison" statement. The triers of fact would be assessing reliability without the key indicia of reliability. In *U.(F.J.)* Chief Justice Lamer held that the comparison statements needed to be admissible.[79] This seems logical, as Justice Rosenberg concluded in a subsequent case: "It would seem odd that evidence the trial judge relied upon to find that the statement was reliable (threshold reliability) would not be available to the jury when it comes to make its decision on ultimate reliability."[80]

Reliability concerns are reflected in the procedural safeguards that accompany the *K.G.B.* application. The application normally would follow upon the calling party invoking section 9 of the *Canada Evidence Act*.[81] A section 9 hearing is by way of a *voir dire* and allows for a party to prove that a witness it called made a prior inconsistent statement and, if permitted by the court, allows it to cross-examine the witness on that statement. The *K.G.B.* application becomes an additional phase of the *voir dire*. The procedure outlined is as follows:

- The calling party must state its intention in tendering the statement. If the party gives notice that it will seek to have the statement admitted for its truth, the *voir dire* will continue on that issue.
- The calling party bears the burden of proof to establish on a balance of probability the admissibility of the prior inconsistent statement for its truth.[82]
- The calling party must establish threshold reliability on a case-by-case basis.

---

79 *Ibid.* at para. 51.

80 *R. v. Khelawon*, above note 50 at para. 130.

81 Note a *K.G.B.* application is not confined to situations where one's own witness recants. It is also available to the cross-examining party who seeks to prove the truth of an earlier statement recanted by an opposing side's witness. See *R. v. Eisenhauer* (1998), 14 C.R. (5th) 35 (N.S.C.A.), leave to appeal to S.C.C. refused, [1998] S.C.C.A. No. 144.

82 Justice Cory, in dissent, would place the threshold of proof at beyond a reasonable doubt. *R. v. B.(K.G.)*, above note 68.

• The calling party must also establish that the statement was made voluntarily, if to a person in authority, and that there are no other factors that would tend to bring the administration of justice into disrepute if the statement is admitted for its truth. "Voluntariness" in this context does not equate to the voluntariness requirement for the admission of confessions. In particular, the threshold of proof of voluntariness is the balance of probabilities, not proof beyond a reasonable doubt.[83] The voluntariness rule for confessions is influenced by self-incrimination considerations that are not relevant in this context.

At the end of the *voir dire* the trial judge makes a ruling. Reasons are required. This is especially important where the criteria as outlined in *K.G.B.* are not met and the Crown is relying on substitute indicia of reliability.[84]

A last point, often overlooked, is that not all prior inconsistent statements can be admitted for their truth—even if they comply with the *K.G.B.* criteria. The prior inconsistent statement has to be otherwise admissible. In other words, if the witness could not testify as to the statement in court, it is not rendered admissible simply because it was made out of court.[85] For example, consider the *K.G.B.* situation. Suppose that one of the youths in his videotaped statement to the police said: "I was told by X that Keith stabbed the victim four times." This is a hearsay statement. The youth would not be allowed to repeat this statement in court, and the party calling the youth should not be allowed to repeat it using *K.G.B.* In the actual case, the videotaped statement could be admissible for its truth in that the youths were repeating an "admission" made by the accused; admissions are a well recognized hearsay exception.[86]

3. PRIOR IDENTIFICATIONS

Out-of-court identifications made by a witness may be admitted for their truth and for credibility where the witness makes an in-court identification.

Out-of-court identifications may also be admitted for their truth where the witness makes no in-court identification, but can

---

83   See *contra R. v. Ducharme* (2000), 151 Man. R. (2d) 288 (Q.B.).
84   See *R. v. Chappell* (2003), 172 C.C.C. (3d) 539 (Ont. C.A.).
85   See *R. v. Devine*, above note 74 at paras. 13–14.
86   See section 6 of this chapter.

*testify that he or she previously gave an accurate description or
made an accurate identification.*

*Where the identifying witness makes no in-court identification
and does not testify as to the accuracy of any prior identification,
then the situation is the same as if he or she has not testified. The
out-of-court identification is hearsay and is not admissible under
the hearsay exception for prior identification.*

As a general rule a witness is not permitted to testify as to his own previous consistent statements because they add nothing to the in-court
testimony. Prior statements of identification are an exception.[87] This is
because in-court identifications are inherently suspect. After all, the
witness expects to see the perpetrator in court, and the accused usually is conspicuously present. For these reasons, the so-called dock
identification is accorded little value.[88] A case in point is *K.G.B.*, where
the brother of the stabbing victim identified the accused as the knife-
wielding assailant. The trial judge attached little probative value to this
identification, which he termed a "naked opinion given 19 months after
the event."[89]

The problem in *K.G.B.* was that there had been no pre-trial identification. The courts have long recognized that witnesses should be
asked to identify an accused at the earliest opportunity and under the
fairest of circumstances.[90] These identifications are the far better test of
the witness's evidence. Therefore, as a matter of common sense, courts
readily admit prior identifications to give credence to the in-court identifications. Are the prior identifications hearsay? There is no consensus.
Some courts treat the out-of-court identifications as hearsay statements,
but admissible pursuant to a hearsay exception; other courts treat the
statements as non-hearsay original evidence.[91] In the circumstances
where the witness has made a dock identification and the out-of-court
identification is consistent, the question really does not matter. The
two identifications are intertwined. They corroborate each other and
are admissible to give credence to the in-court testimony.

However, it should not be accepted that every statement of prior
identification is admissible for its truth. There may be inconsistencies
between the in-court testimony of the witness and the out-of-court

---

87   *R. v. Starr*, above note 5 at 536.
88   See *R. v. D.R.H.*, 2007 MBCA 136 at para. 54.
89   L. Stuesser, "Admitting Prior Inconsistent Statements for Their Truth" (1992) 71
      Can. Bar Rev. 47 at 51.
90   D. Deutscher & H. Leonoff, *Identification Evidence* (Toronto: Carswell, 1991) at 110.
91   See *R. v. Tat* (1997), 14 C.R. (5th) 116 at paras. 31–32 (Ont. C.A.).

statement. For example, on the stand the witness testifies that her assailant had no facial hair, but in a statement to the police she described the assailant as having a moustache. The accused at the time did have a moustache. If the out-of-court statement is to be admitted for its truth the witness will have to adopt and accept the statement in her evidence. Otherwise you are left with the inconsistency and it is not admissible for its truth.[92] The situation is also different when the eyewitness makes no identification in court. Obviously, the evidence of the prior identification is not going in for consistency; nevertheless, such evidence is regularly admitted when the identifying witness can testify that he or she previously made an accurate identification. *R. v. Swanston* provides a good example.[93] In this case the accused was charged with robbery. The victim identified the accused in a line-up and at the preliminary inquiry held shortly after the robbery. At trial, a year and a half after the robbery, the victim was unable to positively identify the accused, who no longer sported a beard or a moustache. The victim recalled the earlier identifications, and the Crown proposed to call police witnesses to confirm that the man identified on these two occasions was the accused. The trial judge refused to allow this evidence. The British Columbia Court of Appeal found this to be an error and ordered a new trial. The court accepted that the prior identification was admissible as independent evidence, given that the eyewitness was present, could be cross-examined, and could attest to the accuracy of the earlier identification. In *R. v. Langille*, the Ontario Court of Appeal expanded upon this principle to allow police officers to testify as to prior *descriptions* of a robber that they were given by an eyewitness.[94]

Some believe that hearsay is being admitted when a prior identification is proved. This may or may not be so. Since prior identifications are acts, their relevance does not always require reliance on words spoken out of court. For example, witness A testifies that she identified the assailant at the scene to Officer B, who then arrested him. Officer B then testifies that the man he arrested is the accused before the court. Together, the evidence of A and B leads to the circumstantial inference that the man before the court is the assailant. This inference is based entirely on in-court testimony and no hearsay is relied upon. That same principle should apply to identifications occurring later at the police station.[95] So long as the identification witness testifies that the person

---

92   *R. v. Campbell*, 2006 BCCA 109.
93   (1982), 25 C.R. (3d) 385 (B.C.C.A.).
94   (1990), 59 C.C.C. (3d) 544 (Ont. C.A.).
95   See *R. v. Tat*, above note 91.

she identified was the assailant, there is no hearsay problem.[96] If, in the circumstances, the inference of identification is so weak that its probative value is outweighed by its prejudice, the exclusionary discretion can be used to exclude it.[97]

Whether prior identifications are hearsay being admitted pursuant to an exception, or non-hearsay, there are limits that must be observed. As a matter of principle, the eyewitness must testify that she selected the perpetrator during the identification, and the earlier identification must be a reliable one. Consider what happens when either of these factors is absent. Where the witness makes no in-court identification and is unable to recall making a prior identification, the situation is the same as if he or she has not testified. Meaningful cross-examination on the making of the alleged identification is not possible. In these circumstances, to allow another witness to testify as to what the "identifying" witness said is clearly hearsay and is not admissible under this exception.

Concerning the reliability of the earlier identifications, McCormick wrote: "Justification is found in the unsatisfactory nature of courtroom identification and the safeguards which now surround staged out-of-court identifications."[98] What if those safeguards are absent? Should the evidence still be admitted where it is tainted by improper staging procedures? Once again, we are assuming that the witness makes no in-court identification and is not able to purify the tainted evidence. If we go back to principle, the reliability threshold may not be met and the evidence ought to be excluded.

A further question arises if the witness in court recants the earlier identification. Does this situation fall within the prior identification exception or within the K.G.B. exception for prior inconsistent statements? In *R. v. Devine* at issue was a recanted statement of identification and the Supreme Court of Canada dealt with its admissibility under K.G.B.[99] An identification is a form of statement and K.G.B. should be the guiding authority, not to be circumvented by simply labelling the exception as one of prior identification.

Where there is no recantation, but merely a failure of recollection, then *Khan* and not K.G.B. applies. This was the case in *Starr*, where the Crown actually failed to examine the witness on making a prior

---

96   *Contra* R.J. Delisle, "Annotation to *R. v. Tat*" (1997) 14 C.R. (5th) 118 at 119.
97   See *R. v. Coutu*, 2008 MBCA 151 at paras. 66–92.
98   E.W. Cleary, ed., *McCormick on Evidence*, 3d ed. (St. Paul, MN: West, 1984) s. 251 [footnotes omitted].
99   *R. v. Devine*, above note 74.

identification.[100] Instead the Crown chose to call two police officers to tell the jury about the witness's out-of-court identification. The Court found that the police testimony was inadmissible both under the hearsay exception for prior identification and under the principled approach.

4. PRIOR TESTIMONY

Testimony given at a prior proceeding, if offered for its truth, is hearsay. Wigmore disagreed. In his view, prior testimony was not hearsay and no exception need be created because the evidence had already been subjected to cross-examination.[101] Arguably *Khelawon* supports Wigmore's position in that the Court defined hearsay in terms of (1) a statement tendered for its truth and (2) the absence of a contemporaneous opportunity to cross-examine the declarant. The Court, however, in its reasons did address *R. v. Hawkins*, which is a prior testimony case, and treated it as hearsay and in need of a hearsay exception. Certainly in terms of the present hearing, the earlier testimony is an out-of-court statement, and the current trier of fact is denied an opportunity to observe the witness give evidence.

The existing hearsay exception for prior testimony is shaped by the general principles of necessity and reliability. The necessity for admitting the prior testimony is grounded in the unavailability of the witness. Reliability rests on the fact that at the prior hearing the witness was under oath, and was available for cross-examination, and there is an accurate transcript of the testimony to be tendered. One might assume that, given these safeguards, any and all prior testimony ought to be admissible. Such is not the case. The common law rule is crafted in far narrower terms.

4.1) The Common Law Exception

At common law, evidence given in a prior proceeding by a witness is admissible for its truth in a later proceeding provided

- *the witness is unavailable;*
- *the parties, or those claiming under them, are substantially the same;*

---

100 *R. v. Starr*, above note 5.
101 See *Wigmore on Evidence*, above note 1 at para. 1370.

- *the material issues to which the evidence is relevant are substantially the same; and*
- *the person against whom the evidence is to be used had an opportunity to cross-examine the witness at the earlier proceeding.*

The common law exception is confined to testimony from prior proceedings where the issues and parties are substantially the same as in the present hearing. The requirements that there be "identity of issues" and "identity of parties" go to ensure that the party against whom the evidence is offered had an adequate opportunity to cross-examine the witness at the earlier proceeding. An actual cross-examination is not needed; the opportunity is enough[102] — but it must have been an adequate one. In terms of "identity of issues," it is not necessary that all the issues in the two actions correspond; nor is it necessary that the causes of action be the same. What is required is that "the evidence relates to any material issues that are substantially the same in both actions."[103] This ensures that the cross-examining party in the earlier proceeding was motivated to challenge the evidence in the same way as the present party. The key, then, is identity of issues and of motive.

In terms of "identity of parties," the common law rule speaks of "the same parties." Why? In principle the requirement that all parties be the same is unnecessary. It really should not matter who is offering the evidence. The fundamental concern lies with the party against whom the evidence is being offered. This is the party now being denied the opportunity to cross-examine the witness, and this is the party who needed to be present or represented at the prior proceeding.

To illustrate the scope and application of the common law rule, consider the following example:

D is charged with criminal negligence causing death. His defence is that it was not he who was driving the car at the time of the accident, but the deceased. Y testified at the criminal trial that he saw D driving just prior to the accident. Y dies. A civil case is now brought by the parents of the deceased against D for wrongful death. D, once again, claims that he was not the driver. Should Y's prior testimony be admitted on this issue?

The parties are different, yet insistence that all parties be the same serves no real purpose. The fundamental point is that D had an opportunity to conduct an adequate cross-examination. True, the issues in the criminal and civil trials are different, but this, too, does not have an impact on the cross-examination of Y. The matter of identification

---

102   *R. v. Potvin* (1989), 68 C.R. (3d) 193 (S.C.C.).
103   *Town of Walkerton v. Erdman* (1894), 23 S.C.R. 352 at 366.

is the same in both trials and it is difficult to see how the cross-examination of Y in the criminal trial would be any different at the civil trial. Would it make any difference if, for example, at the civil trial D wanted to introduce Y's testimony that the deceased was driving? This is a stronger case for exclusion, in that the parents of the deceased, against whom this evidence is now offered, were not parties at the criminal trial. They had no opportunity to cross-examine Y and are bound by the cross-examination undertaken by Crown counsel. Yet, Crown counsel presumably was motivated in the same way as the parents to discredit Y's testimony.[104] In both these examples, rote application of the common law rule results in exclusion of the prior testimony. However, in principle, the prior testimony ought to be admitted, and this is a case where application of the principled approach is warranted.

4.2) Admissibility under the Rules of Court

In civil cases the various rules of court provide an alternative basis for admitting prior testimony. Most of the rules are drafted in narrow terms. For example, in Ontario the rule applies only to the admission of examinations for discovery.[105] In the above illustration where Y's testimony at the criminal proceeding is sought to be admitted at the civil trial, recourse would have to be made to the common law or possibly to the Ontario *Evidence Act*.[106] By contrast, it is most unlikely that any such recourse is necessary in British Columbia, where the *Supreme Court Civil Rules* provide for a far broader exception than was contemplated under the common law. The British Columbia rule allows for the admitting of a transcript of any evidence "taken in any proceeding, hearing, or inquiry . . . whether or not involving the same parties."[107]

4.3) Admissibility under the *Criminal Code*

> *[Section] 715(1) Where, at the trial of an accused, a person whose evidence was given at a previous trial on the same charge, or whose evidence was taken in the investigation of the charge against the accused or on the preliminary inquiry into the charge, refuses to be sworn or to give evidence, or if facts are proved on oath from which it can be inferred reasonably that the person*

---

104 See *Cottrell v. Gallagher* (1919), 16 O.W.N. 76 (C.A.).
105 *Rules of Civil Procedure*, R.R.O. 1990, Reg. 194, r. 31.11(6).
106 Ontario, *Evidence Act*, s. 5. See also *Manitoba Evidence Act*, s. 27.
107 *Supreme Court Civil Rules*, B.C. Reg. 168/2009, r. 12-5(54).

(a) is dead,

(b) has since become and is insane,

(c) is so ill that he is unable to travel or testify, or

(d) is absent from Canada,

and where it is proved that the evidence was taken in the presence
of the accused, it may be admitted as evidence in the proceedings
without further proof, unless the accused proves that the accused
did not have full opportunity to cross-examine the witness.

In criminal cases, the common law rule is embodied in section 715 of
the *Criminal Code*. First, the witness must be unavailable, which under
the section includes when a person refuses to testify. Second, the prior
testimony sought to be admitted into evidence must relate to the same
charge and must have been taken in the presence of the accused and
after the accused has had full opportunity to cross-examine the witness. The leading case on section 715 is *R. v. Potvin*.[108] Potvin and two
others were charged with second-degree murder. The Crown proceeded
against Potvin first. One of the others testified at Potvin's preliminary
inquiry, but refused to testify at the trial. The Crown succeeded in having the witness's testimony taken at the preliminary inquiry admitted
into evidence. The defence argued that this prior testimony ought not
to have been admitted because the accused had a fundamental right
under section 7 of the *Charter* to cross-examine the witness at trial before the trier of fact. The Supreme Court of Canada rejected this argument. The Court confirmed that it is the opportunity to cross-examine,
and not the fact of cross-examination, that is crucial. In *Potvin*, the
accused had full opportunity to cross-examine the witness at the preliminary inquiry. The fact that defence counsel, for tactical reasons,
might conduct the cross-examination at the preliminary inquiry differently than at trial did not deprive the accused of a "full opportunity" to
cross-examine the witness.

Nor is the accused deprived of "full opportunity" to cross-examine
a witness resulting from a failure to disclose information that could
have been used in cross-examination. "Full opportunity" is applied to
situations where counsel has an intention to pursue certain questions
and is frustrated in so doing. This will occur when a witness refuses
to answer questions in cross-examination, a witness dies or disappears
during the cross-examination, or the judge curtails the cross-examination by imposing improper limitations or restrictions. "It should *not*
apply where the failure to cross-examination stems from an accused

---

108 Above note 102.

person's ignorance of potentially useful information, no matter the cause or reason."[109] Lack of disclosure is better raised as a matter of trial fairness discussed below in this chapter. Under the common law, once a full opportunity to cross-examine is found, the prior testimony is admitted. Under section 715, this procedure is not necessarily the case. The word "may" in subsection 715(1) confers on the trial judge a statutory discretion to exclude the prior testimony notwithstanding the fact that the conditions are met in circumstances where a purely mechanical application of the section would operate unfairly to the accused. The discretion to exclude the evidence may be exercised: (1) where there was unfairness in the manner in which the evidence was obtained; or (2) where the admission would affect the fairness of the trial itself—that is, where it is highly prejudicial to the accused but only of marginal probative value. This discretion, however, is not a blanket authority to undermine the object of the subsection.

In *Potvin*, the witness's evidence was critically important. Here was an eyewitness to the murder who testified that the accused beat the victim to death. The Manitoba Court of Appeal in *R. v. Sophonow* had suggested that section 715 was never intended to apply to crucial testimony.[110] The Supreme Court of Canada rejected this hard-and-fast rule. Nevertheless, the Court certainly left it open to a trial judge to exclude testimony where, as in *Potvin*, the credibility of the unavailable witness is critical. This was precisely the situation in *R. v. Daviault*.[111] The Supreme Court of Canada had ordered a new trial following upon its controversial ruling with respect to the defence of extreme intoxication.[112] In the meantime, the elderly victim of the assault had died. She was the Crown's key witness. The complainant had made a statement to the police that differed from her testimony at the trial. In particular, she had said in the statement that Daviault was drunk, but at trial she testified that it did not appear that he was drunk. The Crown had not disclosed this statement to the defence prior to the first trial. Such disclosure is now required, following the Supreme Court of Canada's decision in *R. v. Stinchcombe*.[113] Defence counsel at the first trial asked the complainant only three questions. In the circumstances, the trial judge held that the cross-examination would have been different had the statement been disclosed; he exercised the discretion provided in

---

109 *R. v. Lewis*, 2009 ONCA 874 at para. 68.
110 (1986), 50 C.R. (3d) 193 (Man. C.A.).
111 (1995), 39 C.R. (4th) 269 (C.Q.).
112 *R. v. Daviault* (1994), 33 C.R. (4th) 165 (S.C.C.).
113 (1991), 8 C.R. (4th) 277 (S.C.C.).

Potvin and did not allow the Crown to read into evidence the woman's testimony from the first trial.

Where the prior testimony does not fit within section 715, recourse can be had to the principled approach. Section 715, therefore, does not occupy the field with respect to admitting prior testimony in criminal cases. The principled approach has been used to admit prior testimony from different proceedings involving the accused and even in cases where the accused was not present and had no opportunity to cross-examine the witness.[114]

5. PRIOR CONVICTIONS

A party to a civil proceeding may prove that the other party or a third party has been convicted of a criminal offence for the purpose of establishing prima facie *that such person committed the offence charged.*

As we have seen, prior testimony may be admitted. It would seem that the logical next step would be to admit prior convictions as evidence of the material facts underlying the charges. Return to the example given in the previous section:

D is charged and convicted of criminal negligence causing death. His defence was that it was not he who was driving the car at the time of the accident, but the deceased. A civil case is now brought by the parents of the deceased against D for wrongful death. D, once again, claims that he was not the driver. Can the parents introduce into evidence D's conviction?

In order to support the conviction the criminal court must have found as a fact that D was the driver; he was driving with wanton or reckless disregard for the lives and safety of other persons; and as a result he caused the death. Essentially these same issues are before the court in the civil action.[115] Moreover, the evidence has high assurances of reliability. There are the usual criminal trial safeguards, including the fact

---

114 See *R. v. Backhouse* (2005), 194 C.C.C. (3d) 1 at paras. 176–88 (Ont. C.A.), which involved testimony from an unrelated Highway Traffic trial; *R. v. Wilder*, 2006 BCCA 1, leave to appeal to S.C.C. refused, 2007 CanLII 5098 (S.C.C.), which admitted evidence given by a witness at the trial of co-accused. Justice Southin, in dissent, lamented the use of the principled approach as "doing an end run around Parliament" at para. 58. See also *R. v. Lewis*, above note 109 at paras. 84–96.

115 See *Betterton v. Turner* (1982), 133 D.L.R. (3d) 289 (B.C.S.C.).

that the Crown must prove its case beyond a reasonable doubt. Notwithstanding the logic in admitting such evidence, the English Court of Appeal in *Hollington v. Hewthorne* ruled to the contrary.[116]

Hollington v. Hewthorne is not followed in Canada. Moreover, a number of provinces now in their Evidence Acts expressly provide for the admissibility of prior convictions.[117] Evidence of a prior conviction may be used "offensively" by a plaintiff to prove the basis of a claim. For example, in *Simpson v. Geswein* the plaintiff brought an action in assault and battery against the defendant.[118] In the criminal court the defendant was convicted of assault with a weapon concerning the same incident. The plaintiff filed the certificate of conviction as *prima facie* proof of the assault, subject to rebuttal.

Evidence of a prior conviction may be used "defensively" by a defendant to resist a claim. *Demeter v. British Pacific Life Insurance Co.* is the classic example.[119] Demeter was convicted of the murder of his wife. He then brought an action to recover as beneficiary under various insurance policies taken out on her life. The insurers defended on the basis that Demeter could not now benefit from his own criminal act, and they introduced the murder conviction into evidence. The conviction was admitted as *prima facie* proof that Demeter was the murderer, subject to rebuttal.

Justice Sharpe in *F.(K.) v. White* explained that the *prima facie* standard affords a convicted party the opportunity to explain why the conviction should not be taken as proof of the underlying facts.[120] If there is a good explanation, the matter may proceed to trial. However, if there is no explanation and the convicted party simply wants to put forth the same evidence that was rejected and seeks to relitigate the same issue then this should not be permitted.

"What is improper is to attempt to impeach a judicial finding by the impermissible route of relitigation in a different forum."[121] The fundamental concern is that baseless relitigation undermines the integrity of

---

116 [1943] 2 All E.R. 35 (C.A.).

117 See the *Alberta Evidence Act*, s. 26; *British Columbia Evidence Act*, s. 71; and the Ontario *Evidence Act*, s. 22.1.

118 *Simpson v. Geswein* (1995), 103 Man. R. (2d) 69 (Q.B.). See also *Q. v. Minto Management Ltd.* (1984), 46 O.R. (2d) 756 (H.C.J.). Note that in Ontario the *Victims' Bill of Rights, 1995*, S.O. 1995, c. 6, s. 3 provides that a person convicted of a prescribed crime is liable in damages for emotional distress and bodily harm. In other words, proof of the conviction establishes liability and the only issue then is damages.

119 (1983), 43 O.R. (2d) 33 (H.C.J.).

120 (2001), 198 D.L.R. (4th) 541 at 564 (Ont. C.A.).

121 *Toronto v. C.U.P.E. Local 79* (2003), 232 D.L.R. (4th) 385 at para. 46 (S.C.C.).

the judicial system and amounts to an abuse of process.[122] The *Toronto v. C.U.P.E. Local 79* case is a good example. The City of Toronto fired a unionized youth worker because he was convicted of the sexual assault of a boy whom he had supervised. His union grieved his dismissal. The City relied on the conviction and transcript of the trial proceedings to establish its case. The boy did not testify. The labour arbitrator did hear from the accused and, based upon the evidence he heard, it was obvious that he was not satisfied that the worker had committed the sexual assault upon the boy. This was a clear attack upon the prior criminal conviction and amounted to a "blatant" abuse of process in that it would undermine the integrity of the criminal justice system.

In subsequent cases courts have used abuse of process and the principle of maintaining the integrity of the judicial process to extend admissibility of prior court findings beyond criminal convictions. In *Skender v. Farley* the Court prevented a party from relitigating an issue that had already been adjudicated in a prior civil proceeding.[123] And the Supreme Court of Canada applied these same principles to find that judgments of prior civil or criminal courts are admissible in subsequent interlocutory proceedings.[124]

Unlike a criminal conviction, it is accepted law that an acquittal is not admissible in a subsequent civil trial to prove that the party did not commit the offence. Because of the high burden of proof on the Crown in a criminal case, the fact that an accused is acquitted is no evidence that the accused did not commit the offence on a civil standard.[125]

When will rebuttal be allowed? The answer is — rarely. As a general rule a party will be barred from relitigating a prior criminal conviction. Relitigation, however, may be permitted when it "enhances" rather than "impeaches" the integrity of the judicial system. For example:

- when the first proceeding is tainted by fraud or dishonesty;
- when fresh, new evidence, previously unavailable, conclusively impeaches the original results; or
- when fairness dictates that the original result should not be binding in the new context. Unfairness may arise, for example, if the stakes in the original proceeding were too minor to generate a full and robust response, while the subsequent stakes are considerable.[126]

---

122 *Ibid.* at para. 43.
123 *Skender v. Farley* (2007), 289 D.L.R. (4th) 111 (B.C.C.A.).
124 *British Columbia (Attorney General) v. Malik*, 2011 SCC 18.
125 See *Rizzo v. Hanover Insurance Co.* (1993), 103 D.L.R. (4th) 577 (Ont. C.A.).
126 *Toronto v. C.U.P.E. Local 79*, above note 121 at para. 52.

In *Becamon v. Wawanesa Mutual Insurance Company* the court refused to rely on guilty pleas entered to Highway Traffic offences.[127] The court relied on the comments above and concluded that it would be unfair to apply the doctrine of issue estoppel where the original proceedings were minor but the stakes in the new proceeding could involve hundreds of thousands of dollars.

6. ADMISSIONS OF A PARTY

A party may introduce into evidence against an opposing party any relevant

- *statement made by the opposing party;*
- *act of the opposing party;*
- *statement made by a third person which is expressly adopted by the opposing party or where it may be reasonably inferred that the opposing party has adopted it;*
- *statement by a person the opposing party authorized to make the statement, or where the statement was made by the opposing party's agent or employee concerning a matter within the scope of the agency or employment, during the existence of the relationship; and*
- *statement made by a co-conspirator in furtherance of a conspiracy.*

Admissions are acts or words of a party offered as evidence against that party.[128] Professor Younger provides this rule of thumb: "Anything the other side ever said or did will be admissible so long as it has something to do with the case."[129] Often the phrase "admission against interest" is used. Beware. The phrase invites confusion between an admission made by a party and the completely different hearsay exception for "declarations against interest" made by non-parties.[130] An admission does not require that a party knowingly make a statement against interest. The evidence is "against interest" simply because the opposing side has decided to introduce it at trial against the party. *R. v. Evans* illustrates the point.[131] Evans was charged with armed robbery. Identity was at issue. The getaway car was purchased from a couple two

---

127 *Becamon v. Wawanesa Mutual Insurance Company*, 2009 ONCA 113.
128 *McCormick on Evidence*, above note 98, s. 262.
129 Younger, above note 64 at 24.
130 See section 7, "Declarations against Interest by Non-parties," below in this chapter.
131 (1993), 25 C.R. (4th) 46 (S.C.C.).

days prior to the robbery. The couple were unable to positively identify the purchaser, but did recall that the man told them that he worked in chain-link fencing, had a big dog, and that the dog was going to have pups. These statements are innocent enough. At the time it could be said that the man had no intent of making them "against interest." The statements became "against interest" because the Crown now sought to admit them into evidence, along with evidence that Evans also had worked in chain-link fencing and owned a large, pregnant dog.

For our purposes, we have classified admissions as hearsay. This interpretation is open to debate. Wigmore was of the view that admissions were not hearsay at all, in that they passed the gauntlet of the hearsay rule because the party against whom the evidence is being admitted has no need to cross-examine himself.[132] However, the prevailing view, and one accepted by the Supreme Court of Canada in *Evans* and in *R. v. Couture*[133] is that an admission is an exception to the hearsay rule. We need not resolve this debate since under either view an admission is admissible. Nevertheless, this distinction is important as it may put admissions outside the analytical framework set out in *Starr*. As noted by Justice Sopinka in *R. v. Evans*:

> The rationale for admitting admissions has a different basis than other exceptions to the hearsay rule. Indeed, it is open to dispute whether the evidence is hearsay at all. The practical effect of this doctrinal distinction is that in lieu of seeking independent circumstantial guarantees of trustworthiness, it is sufficient that the evidence is tendered against a party. Its admissibility rests on the theory of the adversary system that what a party has previously stated can be admitted against the party in whose mouth it does not lie to complain of the unreliability of his or her own statements.[134]

Flowing from this, the Ontario Court of Appeal in *R. v. Foreman* found that admissions are admitted "without any necessity/reliability analysis."[135]

---

132 J.H. Wigmore, *Evidence in Trials at Common Law*, rev. by J.H. Chadbourn, 3d ed., vol. 4 (Boston: Little, Brown, 1972) s. 1048.

133 Above note 12 at para. 75.

134 Above note 131 at 54.

135 (2002), 169 C.C.C. (3d) 489 at para. 37 (Ont. C.A.), leave to appeal to S.C.C. refused, [2003] S.C.C.A. No. 199. This view was accepted in *R. v. Osmar* (2007), 217 C.C.C. (3d) 174 at para. 53 (Ont. C.A.), leave to appeal to S.C.C. refused, [2007] S.C.C.A. No. 157; and in *R. v. Terrico*, 2005 BCCA 361 at para. 49 (C.A.), leave to appeal to S.C.C. refused, [2005] S.C.C.A. No. 413. However, this approach must be read in light of the Supreme Court of Canada decision in *R. v. Mapara*, 2005 SCC 23. See section 6.6, below in this chapter.

Most admissions take the form of statements—written or oral. These statements may be used to impeach the party by way of showing a prior inconsistent statement, and they are admissible for their truth. There is no need to comply with the dictates of *K.G.B.*, which applies to prior inconsistent statements made by non-parties.

Confessions of an accused in a criminal prosecution are a type of admission governed by special rules.[136] A confession is where the accused makes a statement to "a person in authority." When this occurs the "confessions rule" applies and the Crown bears the onus of proving the voluntariness of the statement beyond a reasonable doubt. Determining voluntariness is usually dealt with in a *voir dire*. An admission is when an accused makes a statement to ordinary persons; in this case the statements are presumptively admissible without the necessity of a *voir dire*.[137]

6.1) Formal and Informal Admissions

Admissions are either "formal" or "informal." "Formal" admissions dispense with the need to prove a fact in issue. In other words, a party is prepared to concede the particular point. The formal admission, once made, is binding on the party and is not easily withdrawn. For example, in a personal injury action it is quite common to see the defendant admit liability but contest the quantum of damages. Liability is no longer in dispute, and any evidence subsequently sought to be introduced on that point ought to be excluded as irrelevant; the formal admission has conclusively resolved that issue. In civil cases, formal admissions may be made by way of the pleadings, in agreed statement of facts, or by submissions of counsel. In criminal cases the most common "formal" admission is that of the guilty plea. Section 655 of the *Criminal Code* also allows an accused to admit any fact alleged by the Crown against him. We will primarily be concerned with "informal" admissions. An "informal" admission is not conclusive proof of an issue, nor does it in any way bind the parties; it is always open to be contradicted or explained.[138]

The distinction between formal and informal admissions came to the fore in *R. v. Korski* where certain witness statements were introduced by consent as "agreed facts." Defence counsel argued that the

---

136 See chapter 8, section 5, "Pre-trial Rights to Silence."

137 *R. v. S.G.T.*, 2010 SCC 20 at para. 20.

138 For a discussion of "formal" and "informal" admissions, see the judgment of Huddart J.A. in *R. v. Desjardins*, 1998 CanLII 6149 (B.C.C.A.); and *R. v. Baksh* (2005), 199 C.C.C. (3d) 201 (Ont. S.C.J.).

jury ought to have been instructed to accept as fact what was said by the witnesses in their statements. Madam Justice Steel, writing for the Court of Appeal, disagreed. The statements were not going in as "formal" admissions of fact; rather they were "merely agreements as to what the witnesses would have said, not that what they say is necessarily true."[139] Counsel need to be mindful of the distinction and clearly put on the record what is agreed to.

6.2)   Admissions Need Not Be Based on Personal Knowledge

An admission need not be based on personal knowledge. A party may accept what others say and, if so, the party is deemed to have adopted those statements. The case of *R. v. Streu* is a classic illustration.[140] The accused was charged with possession of stolen tires and rims. The Crown needed to prove that the items were actually stolen and relied on certain admissions made by the accused. In selling the items to an undercover police officer, Streu said: "My friend ripped them off. . . . Well, I know they're hot and all but they're his tires." Streu presumably was relying on what he was told by his friend. The Crown had no other proof that the tires and rims were stolen property. Streu's statements of belief needed to be accepted as statements of fact. The Supreme Court of Canada held that they were. Sopinka J. wrote:

> The rationale underlying the exclusion of hearsay evidence is primarily the inherent untrustworthiness of an extrajudicial statement which has been tendered without affording an opportunity to the party against whom it is adduced to cross-examine the declarant. This rationale applies equally in both criminal and civil cases. It loses its force when the party has chosen to rely on the hearsay statement in making an admission. Presumably in so doing, the party making the admission has satisfied himself or herself as to the reliability of the statement or at least had the opportunity to do so.[141]

The party must in some way indicate an acceptance or belief in the truth of the hearsay statement. The value to be attached to the belief, of course, is a matter of weight for the trier of fact. "On the other hand, if the party simply reports a hearsay statement without either adopting

---

139   *R. v. Korski*, 2009 MBCA 37.
140   (1989), 70 C.R. (3d) 1 (S.C.C.).
141   *Ibid.* at 8.

it or indicating a belief in the truth of its contents, the statement is not admissible as proof of the truth of the contents."[142]

6.3) Admissions by Conduct

Admissions may be implied from a party's conduct. As Professor Younger stated in his rule of thumb, admission includes "[a]nything the other side ever said or *did*." For example, an accused person can effectively be signalling or acknowledging their guilt by fleeing from the scene of a crime or by lying when confronted with the accusations.[143] Or, an admission of negligence may be inferred from evidence of subsequent remedial measures taken after an accident.[144] The issue really is one of relevancy. Courts must be satisfied as to the validity of the inference from the conduct to the alleged admission. For example, in *Walmsley v. Humenick*, the five-year-old defendant shot an arrow that caused his playmate, the plaintiff infant, to lose his right eye.[145] The defendant's parents helped to pay for the plaintiff's medical bills. The plaintiff now claimed that this act was an admission of liability. The trial judge rejected this argument. On the evidence, the two families were friends and neighbours and the payments could just as easily have been a gesture of compassion, which in the circumstances should not be construed as an admission of liability.

6.4) Admissions by Silence

Admissions also may be implied from a party's silence. Certain preconditions must exist: (1) a statement, usually an accusation, is made in the presence of the party; (2) in circumstances such that the party would be expected to respond; (3) that the party's failure to respond could reasonably lead to the inference that, by his silence, the party adopted the statement; and (4) the probative value of the evidence out-

---

142   *Ibid.* at 9.

143   See *R. v. Arcangioli* (1994), 27 C.R. (4th) 1 (S.C.C.), re: flight; and *R. v. Guyett* (1989), 72 C.R. (3d) 383 (Ont. C.A.), re: deliberate lies.

144   In the United States under rule 407 of the *Federal Rules of Evidence* subsequent remedial measures taken by a party are not admissible to prove negligence. The rule of exclusion rests on the social policy of encouraging parties to take measures to reduce further injury. The Ontario Divisional Court, in *Algoma Central Ry. v. Herb Fraser & Assoc. Ltd.* (1988), 66 O.R. (2d) 330 (Div. Ct.), termed this policy concern "a fallacious argument" and went on to admit evidence of subsequent remedial measures. See also *James v. River East School District No. 9*, [1976] 2 W.W.R. 577 (Man. C.A.).

145   [1954] 2 D.L.R. 232 (B.C.S.C.).

weighs its prejudicial effect.[146] One must be cautious in inferring adoption through silence. A party's silence may be ambiguous. For example, the driver of a car involved in an accident consoles and cares for an injured passenger. The passenger says to the driver, "I told you that you were going too fast." The driver says nothing in reply. The statement is hearsay, unless admitted as an admission. In this situation, is it reasonable for the driver to deny? Before admitting such evidence a *voir dire* is needed so that the trial judge can thoroughly assess the circumstances under which the statement was made and the alleged adoption by silence.[147] *R. v. Tanasichuk* provides a good example of the law at work. The accused was charged with the murder of his wife. Whilst in prison he phoned a long-time friend and neighbour. He complained that the prison authorities would not permit him to attend his wife's funeral. The friend became angry and said to the accused that as far as she was concerned he had killed his wife, the only person who had ever loved him. The accused did not respond. Was this an adopted admission by silence? Unfortunately, because of how the statement came out at trial — it actually was first raised by counsel for the accused — there was no *voir dire* and specific details as to the conversation were not examined. Without such an evidentiary foundation the adoptive admission by silence ought not to have been put to the jury.

The principle of adoption by silence does not apply where an accused is confronted with the allegations by a person in authority; in these circumstances an accused has a right to remain silent, and invoking that right cannot be used against him.[148] The common law right to silence exists at all times against the state, whether or not the person asserting it is within its power or control. An accused's right to silence applies any time he or she knowingly interacts with a person in authority.[149] In fact the law also protects "selective silence." In *R. v. Turcotte* the accused chose to answer some police questions. In so doing he did not waive his right to silence when he chose not to answer certain other questions. As the Court noted, "Refusing to do what one has a right to refuse to do reveals nothing."[150]

---

146 *R. v. Tanasichuk*, 2007 NBCA 76 at para. 110 (C.A.), leave to appeal to S.C.C. refused, 2009 CanLII 8412 (S.C.C.). See also *R. v. Mariani* (2007), 220 C.C.C. (3d) 74 at para. 76 (Ont. C.A.).

147 See *R. v. Tanasichuk, ibid.* at para. 121.

148 *R. v. Eden*, [1970] 3 C.C.C. 280 (C.A.); *R. v. Cones* (1999), 143 C.C.C. (3d) 355 (Ont. C.A.).

149 *R. v. Turcotte*, 2005 SCC 50 at para. 51.

150 *Ibid.* at para. 55.

6.5) Vicarious Admissions

When a party authorizes another person to speak on her behalf, obviously the party is bound by any admissions made. Such authority, however, is rarely bestowed. The more common situation is where an agent or employee makes an unauthorized statement that the opposing side now seeks to have admitted as an admission against the party. Take the following example:[151]

The plaintiff went to see a movie. Upon leaving the theatre she slipped and fell in the lobby injuring herself. She alleged that she fell because of wet spots on the floor. A key issue was whether the theatre had actual or constructive notice of the wet spots. The plaintiff seeks to introduce the following statement made by an usher to the theatre's janitor shortly after the fall: "Now you come when it's too late, after someone falls. Why didn't you come a half hour ago when I called you?" Is this statement admissible as an admission against the theatre?

On this issue there is no consensus. The prevailing view in England is that such unauthorized statements are not admissible against the party. This position was accepted by the majority of the Ontario Court of Appeal in *R. v. Strand Electric Ltd.*[152] Laskin J.A. dissented. For him it was sufficient that the agent/employee had authority to "act" on behalf of the party; there was no need for express authority to "speak" on behalf of the party.[153] Accordingly, he would admit an employee's statements against his or her employer under the following conditions. First, there must be proof of the agency/employment. The party offering the evidence cannot rely on the out-of-court assertions by the agent of the agency — this is inadmissible hearsay. Proof of the agency requires the agent to testify, the testimony of someone else who knows, or other circumstantial evidence. Second, the admissions of the agent/employee tendered against the principal must have been made to a third party within the scope of his authority during the subsistence of the agency/ employment.

Laskin J.A.'s approach is consistent with the prevailing law in the United States.[154] Statements by agents or employees have certain guar-

---

151 *Rudzinski v. Warner Theatres Inc.*, 114 N.W. 2d 466 (Wis. S.C. 1962).

152 [1969] 1 O.R. 190 (C.A.).

153 This dissenting view was accepted in *Morrison-Knudsen Co. v. British Columbia Hydro & Power Authority* (1973), 36 D.L.R. (3d) 95 (B.C.S.C.). See also *Christensen (Estate) v. Proprietary Industries Inc.*, 2004 ABQB 399 at para. 44; *Ault v. Canada (Attorney General)*, 2007 CanLII 55359 at para. 27 (Ont. S.C.J.).

154 *Federal Rules of Evidence*, Rules 801(d)(2)(C) & (D) make admissible both authorized and unauthorized statements of agents and servants. They provide:

antees of trustworthiness. The agent is well informed about acts in the course of his employment. It is also unlikely that the agent, while still employed by the principal, would make a statement against the principal's interest—unless it were true. Adherence to a narrow test of admissibility, therefore, results in excluding much valuable and reliable evidence—such as the usher's statement in the problem above. A wider approach is preferable, as the following comment attests:

> The test of admissibility should not rest on whether the principal gave the agent authority to make declarations. No sensible employer would authorize his employee to make damaging statements. The right to speak on a given topic must arise out of the nature of the employee's duties. The errand boy should not be able to bind the corporation with a statement about the issuance of treasury stock, but a truck driver should be able to bind his employer with an admission regarding his careless driving. Similarly, an usher should be able to commit his employer with an observation about a slippery spot on the lobby floor.[155]

In the above problem, the usher was speaking to another employee of the theatre, and the statement was not made to an outside third party. In order to be an admission, must the statement be made to a third party? Once again, there is disagreement. Certainly under the narrow "authority to speak" criterion, such statements are not admissible; however, they may be admissible under the wider test if made in the scope of employment. In *Morrison-Knudsen Co. v. British Columbia Hydro & Power Authority* MacDonald J. thoroughly reviewed the authorities on this question and concluded that statements made by agents to their principals were admissible as admissions against the principals.[156] This conclusion is consistent with the notion that an admission is "anything the other side ever said or did," there being no requirement that the party's act or statement be made to the outside world. For example, diary entries made by a party may well be introduced into evidence as admissions.

A statement is not hearsay if –
. . .

The statement is offered against a party and is . . . (C) a statement by a person authorized by the party to make a statement concerning the subject, or (D) a statement by the party's agent or servant concerning a matter within the scope of the agency or employment, made during the existence of the relationship.

155 *Rudzinski v. Warner Theatres Inc.*, above note 151 at 471.
156 Above note 153. See also *Ault v. Canada (Attorney General)*, above note 153 at para. 28.

6.6) Admissions by Parties in Furtherance of a Common Design

As a general proposition, an admission is evidence only against its maker. Therefore, the confession of one co-accused is not admissible against the other co-accused.[157] For example, A and B are charged with murder. A in a statement to the police confesses to the murder: "We killed him. I stabbed him and B hit him with a baseball bat." The confession, although implicating both, is evidence only against A, and the jury must be so instructed. In fact, B may move to have a separate trial from A because of the prejudicial impact of admitting A's statement.[158]

If the participants are tried separately the above rule does not apply. In our example, if A and B are tried separately then A is a competent witness at B's trial and vice versa. Should A refuse to testify at B's trial or recants on the stand his prior statement may be admitted for its truth under the principled approach.[159] The key concern with accomplice statements lies in their questionable reliability. All too often, especially when caught, it may well be in the best interests of one criminal to minimize his own involvement and betray his partners in crime. Denial is the first refuge of a scoundrel; passing blame is the second.[160] Yet, under the principled approach should this concern be addressed and the statement is found to be sufficiently reliable then it may be admitted into evidence. "There simply is no rule of evidence that precludes the admission of the statement of an accomplice who is tried separately."[161]

A second exception to this general proposition is for statements made by those involved in a common design. As we saw in the section above, if we treat the statement of the usher as a vicarious admission, it may be used in evidence against the theatre; if not, it is inadmissible against the theatre and would only be admissible against the usher, provided he was made a party to the action. Another exception to the rule applies for statements made by those involved in a common design. A partnership is a legitimate example. Once a partnership is proven by

---

157 *R. v. Rojas*, 2008 SCC 56; *R. v. MacDonald*, 2010 ONCA 178.

158 *R. v. Guimond* (1979), 44 C.C.C. (2d) 481 (S.C.C.).

159 See *R. v. Naicker*, 2007 BCCA 608, leave to appeal to S.C.C. refused, 2008 CanLII 18941 (S.C.C.); *R. v. Goodstoney*, 2007 ABCA 88, leave to appeal to S.C.C. refused, [2007] S.C.C.A. No. 365.

160 In *Lilly v. Virginia*, 119 S. Ct. 1887 (1999), the Supreme Court of the United States refused to admit such statements, citing the confrontation clause and real concern over the reliability of such accomplice evidence that could not be cross-examined upon by the accused.

161 *R. v. Naicker*, above note 159 at para. 44 (C.A.).

independent evidence to exist, the admission of one partner acting in the scope of the partnership is evidence against all the partners. A form of illicit partnership involves those in criminal or civil conspiracies. The exception is not limited to conspiracies *per se*; rather, it applies to all offences involving a common design. In *R. v. Samuels* the relationship of a seller and buyer of drugs was capable of giving rise to a finding of a common design.[162]

Not every statement of a co-conspirator is admissible. Only those statements made during the course of the conspiracy and in furtherance of the conspiracy fall within the exception. A co-conspirator's guilty plea is not admissible. Nor is the full confession of a co-conspirator made to the police. In both instances, the statements are made after the fact and not in furtherance of the conspiracy.

The difficulty with the "co-conspirator exception" is that it applies only if there is evidence that the accused was a member of a conspiracy, and this issue is the very one before the court. The American courts have moved to a two-stage approach whereby the trial judge, as a preliminary matter, first determines the admissibility of the co-conspirator declarations. In the second stage it is for the jury to determine whether the evidence, including the co-conspirator declarations, is sufficient beyond a reasonable doubt.

This is not the approach in Canada. Essentially, the trier of fact is left to decide what to do with the co-conspirator declarations. In charges involving common design, all evidence, including the hearsay statements of co-conspirators, is conditionally admissible. It is then for the trier of fact to review the evidence and to determine whether to invoke the co-conspirator exception. The law in this regard is complex, requiring a four-part jury instruction. The first two parts address the question of when the statements of one conspirator can be used against a co-conspirator. Part one of that two-part instruction relates to what is required to prove the existence of a conspiracy, and part two relates to proof of the involvement of the accused in the conspiracy. The "co-conspirator exception" applies only when these two parts, parts one and two, have been met. Parts three and four of the jury direction explain to the jury how to use those co-conspirator statements that do meet the exception. Hence, a trial judge is to instruct the jury as follows:

(1) The jury is to consider whether on all the evidence they are satisfied beyond a reasonable doubt that the alleged conspiracy in fact existed. If they are not so satisfied, then the accused must be acquitted.

---

162 *R. v. Samuels*, 2007 ONCA 608.

(2) If they find that a conspiracy as alleged did exist, they must then review all the evidence that is directly admissible against the accused and decide on a balance of probabilities whether or not he is a member of the conspiracy.

(3) If this conclusion is reached, they then become entitled to apply the hearsay exception and consider the acts and declarations made by the co-conspirators in furtherance of the conspiracy as evidence against the accused on the issue of his guilt beyond a reasonable doubt.

(4) They should be told that this ultimate determination is for them alone and that the mere fact that they have found sufficient evidence directly admissible against the accused making his participation in the conspiracy probable, and to apply the hearsay exception, does not make a conviction automatic. They must be clearly satisfied beyond a reasonable doubt as to the existence of the conspiracy and the accused's membership in it.[163]

A key issue is, what does the reference to "all the evidence" mean in part one? When the Crown is seeking to invoke the exception to use the statements of A as proof during the trial against B, does the reference to "all of the evidence" in part one include all statements made by A?

It is settled that all acts and statements made by the alleged co-conspirators in the formation of, or apparent furtherance of, a conspiracy, are included in the phrase "all of the evidence," and can be considered during the part one inquiry. At first blush it may appear circular to allow statements made by A to be used as part of the co-conspirators test, when that test is being employed to determine whether those very same statements by A should be used against B during the trial. Bear this in mind, though: The issues are different. In the part one inquiry, the issue is not whether A's statements in furtherance of the conspiracy can be used to prove B's guilt, but whether there is a conspiracy. There is nothing circular in treating evidence differently on different issues.

The fact that the material issue is different when applying part one of the co-conspirator test also helps explain why statements alleged to be made in formation or furtherance of the conspiracy by a co-conspirator are admissible. Those statements that are made in the formation of the conspiracy are not hearsay at all. They are circumstantial evidence of the existence of the conspiracy because their relevance lies in the fact that they were said. They are direct evidence of the formation of an agreement to commit an offence, and their admission does not depend

---

163   R. v. *Carter* (1982), 31 C.R. (3d) 97 (S.C.C.).

on the truth of their contents.[164] This will also be true of most statements made in furtherance of a conspiracy. On the issue of whether a conspiracy exists, their relevance will lie in the fact they were made, not in their truth. Even those statements made by a co-conspirator in furtherance of a conspiracy that are being relied on for the truth of their contents will tend to have sufficient indicia of reliability to justify admitting *on the issue of the existence of the conspiracy*. They will tend to be statements accompanying or explaining acts done in furtherance of the conspiracy and, like statements caught by the *res gestae* exceptions, their context will assist in evaluating their reliability. So, as a general rule, statements made by a co-conspirator in furtherance of a conspiracy can be considered during the part one inquiry of the co-conspirators exception. Of course, like all hearsay, these statements may be excluded from consideration under the principled approach.

There is greater controversy about statements by A that are not made in furtherance of the conspiracy, but are statements *about* the conspiracy. For example, after being arrested A makes a full confession to the police: "I was involved in a conspiracy with B." Are such statements to be included in the phrase "all the evidence," such that they can be considered during the part one inquiry? The courts are divided.[165] Ordinary principles of hearsay would say no. Absent a hearsay exception applying, narrative statements are admissible only against the maker as admissions, but not against anyone else.[166]

In spite of this, in *R. v. Viandante*,[167] the Manitoba Court of Appeal held that a declaration of conspiracy by one is direct evidence of the existence of the conspiracy, and can be used on that issue. It is best not to take an all-or-nothing approach, however. If the confession of A as to the existence of the conspiracy is attended with indicia of reliability, and necessity is satisfied (as it will be in a joint trial), then the statement should be admissible.

Turning to step two, it is incumbent upon the trial judge to point out to the jury what evidence is or is not directly admissible against the accused. The jury is not to consider the evidence against the accused

---

164 *R. v. Cook* (1984), 39 C.R. (3d) 300 (Ont. C.A.).

165 See the discussion in *R. v. Sutton* (1999), 140 C.C.C. (3d) 336 (N.B.C.A.), aff'd without addressing this issue (2000), 148 C.C.C. (3d) 513 (S.C.C.). An excellent discussion is also found in *R. v. Pilarinos*, [2002] B.C.J. No. 1324 (S.C.).

166 See *R. v. Guimond*, above note 158, and *R. v. Baron and Wertman* (1976), 31 C.C.C. (2d) 525 (Ont. C.A.). For a good discussion on statements of co-accused see *Lilly v. Virginia* (1999), 119 S.Ct. 1887.

167 (1995), 40 C.R. (4th) 353 (Man. C.A.). See also *R. v. Collins* (1999), 133 C.C.C. (3d) 8 (N.L.C.A.).

in isolation. Context is needed, and the jury is entitled to consider the evidence of the actions and declarations of co-conspirators for the limited purpose of establishing the context in which the accused's own acts and statements are to be understood.

There is even greater concern in two-person conspiracy cases in that there is a real danger that a jury will assume guilt purely after stage one; the finding beyond a reasonable doubt of the conspiracy means both parties must be guilty. There is enhanced need for a trial judge to instruct the jury that it is still possible in a two-person conspiracy case for one party not to be convicted. Justice Rosenberg puts forth this hypothetical:[168]

> Assume a conspiracy allegedly involving only an agreement between A and B in which A gives a statement to the police in which he says that he and B conspired to traffic in cocaine. Using all the evidence at stage one, including the statement, the jury could conclude beyond a reasonable doubt that a conspiracy involving A and B to traffic in cocaine existed. However, the statement has a limited use. It could be used to establish the existence of the conspiracy at stage one, and can also be used to show A's probable membership in the conspiracy at stage two. However, as against B, the statement cannot be used to show that B was a probable member of the conspiracy at stage two.

A very careful jury instruction indeed is required.

From the foregoing it is obvious that the admissibility of evidence of co-conspirators is complex—even for judges. Yet, under *Carter* the question of admissibility is left to the jury. The jury is expected to sift through the evidence, compartmentalize it, and correctly apply two different standards of proof. Perhaps we expect too much.[169] Moreover, we now add on the further complexity that certain pieces of evidence may be admissible under the principled approach. There is much to be said for the American approach, where admissibility of co-conspirator evidence is determined by the trial judge. The jury is then left to decide, on the basis of the admissible evidence, whether the prosecution has proven that the accused was a member of a conspiracy beyond a reasonable doubt.

Overturning *Carter* and adopting the American approach was expressly rejected by the Supreme Court of Canada in *R. v. Mapara*.[170] The

---

168 *R. v. Bogiatzis*, 2010 ONCA 902 at para. 25.

169 See the comments of the High Court of Australia in *Ahern v. R.* (1988), 165 C.L.R. 87 (H.C.A.).

170 *R. v. Mapara*, above note 135. The Court applied much of the reasoning from the Ontario Court of Appeal in *R. v. Chang* (2003), 173 C.C.C. (3d) 397 (Ont. C.A.).

Court was loath to modify *Carter* and turn the admissibility of co-conspirator statements over to trial judges for two reasons. First, the *Carter* approach was seen to be better suited to bring home to the jury the need for independent evidence of the accused's participation in the conspiracy. And, second, to modify *Carter* would increase delay and difficulties in trial procedure;[171] the Court envisaged co-conspirator trials becoming dominated by a series of hearings on the admissibility of such statements.

The defence in *Mapara* also challenged the co-conspirator exception as being inconsistent with the principled approach. One argument raised in reply by the Crown was that the principled approach had no application because the exception was based on the law of admissions and was not hearsay in the first place. As noted earlier, Wigmore never regarded admissions as hearsay. The Chief Justice, writing for the majority, gave this argument short shrift. In her view, the introduction of co-conspirator statements were hearsay and they raised valid hearsay concerns. She then went on to examine the *Carter* rule for conformity with the principles of necessity and reliability.

Necessity was found based on three factors:

- co-accused declarants are not compellable by the Crown;
- the undesirability of trying alleged co-conspirators separately; and
- the evidentiary value of contemporaneous declarations made in furtherance of an alleged conspiracy.

Reliability was found in that:

- The trier of fact must be satisfied beyond a reasonable doubt that the conspiracy in fact existed.
- The state must establish on a balance of probabilities through evidence directly admissible against the accused that the accused was a member of the conspiracy.
- The trier of fact is also only to consider out-of-court declarations made in furtherance of the conspiracy.
- Statements made in furtherance of the conspiracy generally will be made spontaneously and contemporaneously with the events at a time where there would be little reason to lie.

The Court's conclusion: the *Carter* rule meets the requirements of the principled approach and stands.

The Court's decision in *Mapara* represents a very practical approach that respects the wisdom and experience of the common law. The Court was not going to lightly overturn *Carter* without good cause.

---

171 *R. v. Mapara, ibid.* at para. 30.

Conspiracies are difficult to prove. Co-conspirators are by nature a deceitful and secretive lot. A totality of evidence is often needed to fit the pieces of a conspiracy together. Thus, there is a practical wisdom that admits such evidence.

What the Court did keep open was the "rare case" where evidence falling within the accepted co-conspirator exception should nevertheless not be admitted because the required indicia of necessity and reliability are lacking. The Court opined that this would only apply to the "most exceptional cases."[172]

7. DECLARATIONS AGAINST INTEREST BY NON-PARTIES

The common law recognizes a hearsay exception for statements made against the declarant's interest. Essentially the exception applies to nonparties. Declarations against interest made by parties are admissions, and, as we have seen, fall under their own exception. The assumption underlying this exception is that people do not readily make statements that admit facts contrary to their interests unless those statements are true. The common law judges confined the exception to declarations made against pecuniary or proprietary interests, and the courts were loath to extend the exception to statements made against penal interest. This attitude changed in Canada with the Supreme Court's decision in *R. v. O'Brien.*[173] However, declarations against penal interest are treated with far more caution than is the case for declarations against pecuniary or proprietary interest.

7.1) Declarations against Pecuniary and Proprietary Interests

A declaration against pecuniary or proprietary interest may be admitted where

1) *the declarant is unavailable to testify;*
2) *the statement when made was against the declarant's interest; and*
3) *the declarant had personal knowledge of the facts stated.*

---

172   *Ibid.* at para. 34. For an example of an "exceptional case," see *R. v. Simpson*, above note 8.

173   (1977), 38 C.R.N.S. 325 (S.C.C.).

Necessity flows from the unavailability of the declarant. Reliability is founded on the fact that the declarant, who is aware of adverse facts, admits them. The clearest case is the acknowledgment of a debt owed. Yet, acknowledgment of a debt paid is also accepted as against the declarant's interest, in that the declarant is admitting that the debt has been extinguished or reduced. In civil cases, the courts seem to seize upon any statement against pecuniary or proprietary interest—regardless of the amount owed. In *Gromley v. Canada Permanent Trust Co.* a statement admitted as against interest involved $4.[174] More rigorous scrutiny of reliability is warranted in a criminal case. An appropriate threshold for reliability is found under rule 804(b)(3) of the *Federal Rules of Evidence* in the United States, where a statement against interest is one that is "so far contrary to the declarant's pecuniary or proprietary interest . . . that a reasonable person in the declarant's position would not have made the statement unless believing it to be true."

In principle the declarant need not realize that the statement may be used against him. For example, an entry in a diary states, "I just borrowed $100 from John and I have no intention of paying him back." This is a statement against interest, notwithstanding that the writer never ever considered that the diary entry would be used against him.

Professor Morgan explained the exception in the following terms:

> The theory on which the rule rests is that a person will not concede even to himself the existence of a fact which will cause him substantial harm, unless he believes that the fact does exist. Whether he realized that in making the statement he was creating evidence against himself is immaterial upon the question of admissibility, however pertinent it may be in determining the persuasive value of the declaration.[175]

Not all declarations against interest are clear-cut. They may in fact contain statements quite favourable to the maker's interest. For example, suppose that the entry in the diary read: "I just borrowed $100 from John and I have no intention of paying him back because he still owes me $10,000." Is this a declaration against interest? The statement in its entirety is far more favourable than unfavourable, and one approach is to balance the good against the bad to determine whether the statement, as a whole, is against interest. If so, it is admissible; if not, it is inadmissible. A second approach is to admit the statement in its entirety if any portion of it is against the declarant's interest. Most of the authorities adhere to this view, and it is premised on the theory that

---

174 (1969), 5 D.L.R. (3d) 497 (H.C.J.).
175 E.M. Morgan, "Declarations against Interest" (1952) 5 Vand. L. Rev. 451 at 476.

the statement as a whole was made within the same frame of mind as the declaration against interest and therefore carries with it a measure of trustworthiness.[176] The value to be attached to the connected portions is a matter of weight for the trier of fact.

Accordingly, courts have admitted "all matters involved in or knit up with the statement."[177] The declaration against interest may, in fact, be completely irrelevant to the proceeding but is the means through which a relevant collateral fact is admitted into evidence. *Higham v. Ridgway* is the classic example.[178] At issue was the date of birth of a child. Entries made by a midwife were admitted. The entries were "against interest" to the extent that they showed amounts paid on the ledger (meaning that the maker no longer had a claim for that money). Whether this money was paid was irrelevant. However, the ledger also contained the notation that the payment was for a birth attendance on a certain day, which was the collateral fact sought to be proven, and the court admitted this evidence.

7.2)   Declarations against Penal Interest

A declaration against penal interest may be admitted where:

1) *The declaration is made in such circumstances that the declarant should have apprehended a vulnerability to penal consequences as a result.*

2) *The vulnerability to penal consequences cannot be remote.*

3) *"[T]he declaration sought to be given in evidence must be considered in its totality. If upon the whole tenor the weight is in favour of the declarant, it is not against his interest."*

4) *In a doubtful case a Court might properly consider whether or not there are other circumstances connecting the declarant with the crime and whether or not there is any connection between the declarant and the accused.*

5) *The declarant is unavailable by reasons of death, insanity, or grave illness which prevents the giving of testimony even from a bed, or absence in a jurisdiction to which none of the processes of the Court extends. A declarant would not be unavailable [where he or she refuses to testify].*[179]

---

176   For a thorough review of this issue, see *Alberta (Public Trustee) v. Walker* (1981), 122 D.L.R. (3d) 411 (Alta. C.A.).

177   *Ibid.* at 439.

178   (1808), 103 E.R. 717 (K.B.).

179   *Lucier v. R.*, [1982] 1 S.C.R. 28 at 43.

The common law long excluded statements against penal interest. The primary reason was a concern about false confessions. This suspicion · regarding the trustworthiness of such declarations permeates the penal interest exception.[180]

We see this suspicion in the Supreme Court of Canada's decision in *R. v. O'Brien*, which purported to sweep aside the "arbitrary and tenuous" distinction between pecuniary or proprietary interests and penal interests.[181] All declarations against interest were supposed to stand on the "same footing." The reality is that the Supreme Court of Canada has created a far more stringent exception for declarations against penal interests than for pecuniary or proprietary statements against interest.

The Court applied five principles (as noted above). Given these principles, the penal interest exception is far different from those for pecuniary or proprietary interests. Under principle 1, the declarant must know that the *statement* will be held against him. It is not sufficient merely to accept the adverse fact; there must be vulnerability flowing from the making of the statement. The Court accepted the following:

> In ordinary circumstances where a declaration is made for instance to an unestranged son, wife or mother, the psychological assurance of reliability is lacking because of [sic] risk of penal consequences is not real and the declarant may have motives such as a desire for self-aggrandizement or to shock which makes the declaration unreliable.[182]

In *R. v. Underwood* the Alberta Court of Appeal adopted a rather charitable view of "vulnerability."[183] The accused was involved in the drug trade and was charged with the murder of one of his associates. At his trial he sought to lead evidence that another of his associates, "P," now dead, had confessed to the killing. Another associate would testify that P had confessed to the killing. Even though this was a statement made to a fellow member involved in the drug trade the Court of Appeal found that P should have felt vulnerable to penal consequences. With respect this finding rings hollow and means essentially that vulnerability is likely to be found whenever a supposed confession is made to anyone. The court's ruling fails to reflect the long-held suspicions and

---

180 Rule 804(b)(3) of the *Federal Rules of Evidence* in the United States admits declarations against penal interest provided "corroborating circumstances clearly indicate the trustworthiness of the statement."

181 Above note 173 at 331.

182 See *R. v. Kimberley*, above note 17 at 150–57 for a good analysis of the need to apprehend penal consequences. For a rare example of where a declaration against penal interest was admitted see *R. v. Kociuk*, 2009 MBQB 162.

183 (2002), 170 C.C.C. (3d) 500 (Alta. C.A.).

concerns about such evidence particularly when presented through the testimony of gang associates.

Principle 3 adopts an approach where the trial judge must weigh all the evidence to determine whether, on balance, the declaration is or is not against interest. This restriction runs counter to the prevailing view found when dealing with statements against pecuniary or proprietary interests, which is to include a declaration in its entirety so long as a portion of it is against interest. Principle 4 reflects further caution. Before admitting such declarations in doubtful cases, the court wants additional guarantees of trustworthiness. Here, once again, is the fear of collusion and fabrication.

The Supreme Court of Canada's subsequent decision in *Lucier v. R.* further reflects the suspicion that the Court has with declarations against penal interest.[184] The Crown wanted to introduce a declaration against penal interest made by a witness to incriminate the accused. The deceased witness admitted setting a fire and that he had been paid to do so by the accused. The statement was incriminating and, logically, should be admissible in its entirety. However, the Supreme Court of Canada ruled that the exception could only be used to *exculpate* and not to *inculpate* an accused, who is "robbed" of the opportunity to cross-examine the witness. Yet, every hearsay exception when used by the Crown denies the accused an opportunity to cross-examine the witness. What we see in *Lucier* is a lingering concern about the reliability of such statements, and what the Court is really saying is that it would be unfair to convict an accused using such evidence.

The decision of the Ontario Court of Appeal in *R. v. Kimberley* may well be a harbinger of what to expect with respect to this exception.[185] In deciding whether to admit a "declaration against penal interest" the court focused exclusively on the requirements of necessity and reliability and ignored the exception. The court did, however, refer to the principles underlying the exception to determine threshold reliability.

8. DYING DECLARATIONS

In a criminal case, a dying declaration of a deceased person is admissible for the prosecution or the defence when

- *the deceased had a settled, hopeless expectation of almost immediate death;*

---

184 Above note 179.
185 Above note 17.

- *the statement was about the circumstances of the death;*
- *the statement would have been admissible if the deceased had been able to testify; and*
- *the offence involved is the homicide of the deceased.*

With respect to this exception, there is necessity. The witness is dead. Reliability is said to derive from the belief that a person who knows that he or she is about to die will be motivated to speak truthfully. The classic statement of the rationale for the rule is as follows:

> Now the general principle on which this species of evidence is admitted is, that they are declarations made in extremity, when the party is at the point of death, and when every hope of this world is gone: when every motive to falsehood is silenced, and the mind is induced by the most powerful considerations to speak the truth; a situation so solemn, and so awful, is considered by the law as creating an obligation equal to that which is imposed by a positive oath administered in a Court of Justice.[186]

Death must be near and certain, and the deceased must be aware of this fact. The test is subjective. Each case falls to be decided on the facts. The mere likelihood or probability of impending death is not enough. In *R. v. Aziga* the accused was charged with 2 counts of first degree murder and 13 counts of aggravated sexual assault for having knowingly transmitted HIV.[187] The police took statements from two of his victims who were about to die. One woman died 18 hours after giving the statement and the second woman died 18 days later. The trial judge was satisfied that both women when they made the statements had a settled, hopeless expectation of death and the statements were admitted as dying declarations and under the principled approach.

If the common law had left the exception based on the above principles, it would be justifiable. Actually, these principles did guide the courts prior to the nineteenth century, when dying declarations were admitted in both the criminal and the civil courts.[188] Instead, through misguided adherence to precedent, courts have fashioned an exception that defies logic and is truly absurd.[189]

The exception is now confined to cases of homicide. Yet, if we accept the underlying rationale for the rule, then dying declarations

---

186 *R. v. Woodcock* (1789), 168 E.R. 352 at 353 (K.B.), Chief Baron Eyre.
187 *R. v. Aziga*, 2006 CanLII 38236.
188 *McCormick on Evidence*, above note 98, s. 283.
189 See R.J. Delisle & D. Stuart, *Evidence: Principles and Problems*, 8th ed. (Scarborough, ON: Carswell, 2007) at 813–14.

should be admissible in all cases where relevant. As the law now stands, the dying declaration of a passenger involved in an automobile accident is admissible against the driver of the car only if that driver is charged with criminal negligence causing death (a recognized form of homicide) involving that passenger. That very same declaration would not be admissible in a civil wrongful death suit brought against the driver by the deceased passenger's family. Nor would it be admissible if the charge were simply one of dangerous driving. Nor would it be admissible if the driver were charged with criminal negligence causing death to another passenger; the exception requires that the declarant's death be the subject matter of the charge. These limitations are both unnecessary and unprincipled. What is needed is a return to principle. Either we accept the rationale underlying the rule or we do not. If we do, then dying declarations have an indicia of reliability, which may lead to their admissibility in a given case. If we do not, then such declarations have no additional indicia of reliability and probably should be excluded. In any event, admissibility for dying declarations should fall to be determined under the principled approach.

9. DECLARATIONS IN THE COURSE OF DUTY

The admissibility of declarations made in the course of duty is based on the presumed reliability with their making. First, most records are of a "mechanical" nature. They are prepared as a matter of routine, where there is little reason or motive to fabricate. Under the common law, where a declarant had a motive or an interest to misrepresent, the records would not be admitted into evidence. Second, businesses rely on these records, and it is the job of the maker to be accurate. Should the employee prove to be inaccurate, there exists the threat of dismissal. Third, the entries are prepared reasonably contemporaneously with the events or transactions recorded.

A declaration in the course of duty is different from an admission. Declarations that fall under this exception may be admitted by the party responsible for the record in order to support his or her case, unlike an admission that is tendered by the opposing party *against* the party who made the statement. This exception is also different from declarations against interest, in that courts have held that collateral or extraneous statements that accompany the declaration are not admissible.

9.1)   At Common Law

> *Declarations, oral or written, are admissible for their truth where*
> *(1) made reasonably contemporaneously; (2) in the ordinary course*
> *of duty; (3) by persons having personal knowledge of the matters;*
> *(4) who are under a duty to make the record or report; and (5) there*
> *is no motive to misrepresent the matters recorded.*

At common law, the maker of the statement had to be dead. This requirement made sense when the rule developed and most of the records related to small shop owners and tradesmen, but it makes no sense given our modern business community. This absurdity is well illustrated by the decision of the House of Lords in *Myers v. D.P.P.*[190] The case involved stolen cars, and the Crown sought to prove ownership of the cars through records kept by the manufacturer. The records, prepared by unknown employees, contained the cylinder block numbers of the engines installed in the cars. A majority of the House of Lords held that this evidence was hearsay and not admissible under any exception. The majority completely ignored the inherent reliability of the records and the total impracticality and futility in calling the employees responsible. The majority was not prepared to relax the common law requirements; it held that such a change was for Parliament, and not the courts.

The Supreme Court of Canada in *Ares v. Venner* made the change that the House of Lords in *Myers* was unwilling to make.[191] *Ares v. Venner* involved a case of medical malpractice. The plaintiff's leg, which had been broken, had to be amputated below the knee, and the plaintiff blamed the attending physician. At issue was the admissibility of notes made by nurses. The notes contained statements such as: "Quiet evening, complained of discomfort, relieved by sedation, numbness in all toes, toes now swollen and blue." The Court chose to follow the dissenting Lords in *Myers* and changed the law. Hall J. concluded the judgment of the Court with the following statement of the law:

> Hospital records, including nurses' notes, made contemporaneously
> by someone having personal knowledge of the matters then being
> recorded and under a duty to make the entry or record should be re-
> ceived in evidence as *prima facie* proof of the facts stated therein.[192]

---

190 [1965] A.C. 1001 (H.L.).
191 *Ares v. Venner* (1970), 12 C.R.N.S. 349 (S.C.C.).
192 *Ibid.* at 363.

Now, in *Ares v. Venner* the nurses were in court and available for cross-examination, but this fact was not central to the Court's decision.[193] *Ares v. Venner* expanded the common law exception for declarations in the course of duty. The case is not confined to "nurses' notes"; it has general application and is available in criminal cases as well as in civil cases.

The Alberta Court of Appeal dealt with this exception in *R. v. Monk-house*.[194] There a witness brought a document to court which he had produced by summarizing information contained in the company payroll records. He, of course, had no personal knowledge about the accuracy of that information. The document was nonetheless used to prove the earnings of an employee. The court held that the common law rule that the maker of the declaration must have personal knowledge of the matter recorded was satisfied if the information originally was recorded by a person or persons acting under a duty to compile the information. There is no need to identify the specific recorder; a document will be admissible so long as the court is satisfied that the maker was acting under a duty to record the information.[195]

9.2) Business Records

Legislative reform followed in the wake of the decision in *Myers v. D.P.P.* An exception for "business records" was created in the *Canada Evidence Act* and in most of the provincial Evidence Acts.[196] These provisions eclipse, but do not replace, the common law.[197] The common law exception remains an important adjunct to the statutes. It applies to both "oral and written" statements, whereas the statutes are confined to "writings" or "records." It does not require that notice be given, whereas some of

---

193 See *R. v. Khan*, above note 2 at 105, where McLachlin J. wrote: "I add that I do not understand *Ares v. Venner* to hold that the hearsay evidence there at issue was admissible where necessity and reliability are established only where cross-examination is available."

194 (1987), 61 C.R. (3d) 343 (Alta. C.A.).

195 *Trang v. Alberta (Edmonton Remand Centre)*, 2006 ABQB 824 at para. 11 (Q.B.).

196 See, for example, *Canada Evidence Act*, s. 30; *Manitoba Evidence Act*, s. 49; Ontario, *Evidence Act*, s. 35. Only Alberta and Newfoundland and Labrador do not have business records provisions.

197 See *Canada Evidence Act*, s. 30(11), which states that the section is "in addition to and not in derogation of . . . b) any existing rule of law under which any record is admissible in evidence." Most of the provincial statutes contain a similar statement. See, for example, *Manitoba Evidence Act*, s. 49(5), and the Ontario *Evidence Act*, s. 35(5).

the statutes contain notice requirements.[198] Moreover, in *Ares v. Venner* the Court admitted much evidence that could be termed "opinion," whereas certain courts have held that, given the wording of the statute, only statements of "fact" may be admitted.[199]

Unfortunately, although the various statutes have a similar purpose, there is no uniformity. For example, consider the admissibility of records made when the maker had a motive to fabricate. Under the common law, when such a motive is found, the records are inadmissible. The statutes deal with this issue in a variety of ways. Under the *Canada Evidence Act*, records are not admitted when made in the course of an investigation or inquiry, obtaining or giving legal advice, or in contemplation of a legal proceeding.[200] By contrast, the Manitoba and Ontario statutes provide that the circumstances of the making of any writing or record may affect its weight but not its admissibility.[201] Given this wording, Griffiths J. in *Setak Computer Services Corp. v. Burroughs Business Machines Ltd.* concluded that once the record complied with the criteria under the statute, the court had no discretion to exclude the evidence, but could in the circumstances attach no weight to it.[202] Obviously, this approach will have to be re-evaluated in light of the fundamental principle that only sufficiently reliable hearsay is to be admitted into evidence in the first place.

Despite the differences, there are certain common interpretative questions that arise and need to be considered. All the statutes in fairly similar terms speak of the need for the record or writing to be made in the "usual and ordinary course of any business." Although "business" is broadly defined in all the statutes, some of the definitions are broader than others. For example, the Ontario statute does not include "government" in its definition, with the result that one Ontario court ruled that a police officer's notes could not be admitted under the section.[203] The decision would be different in Manitoba and some other provinces,

---

198 See *R. v. Laverty* (1979), 9 C.R. (3d) 288 (Ont. C.A.), and *Kaban v. Sett* (1993), 90 Man. R. (2d) 26 (Q.B.).

199 See *Adderly v. Bremner*, [1968] 1 O.R. 621 (H.C.J.), and *Augustine Estate v. Inco.*, 2006 CanLII 21783 at para. 9 (Ont. S.C.J.).

200 *Canada Evidence Act*, s. 30(10).

201 *Manitoba Evidence Act*, s. 49(4); Ontario *Evidence Act*, s. 35(4).

202 (1977), 15 O.R. (2d) 750 (H.C.J.).

203 *Woods v. Elias* (1978), 21 O.R. (2d) 840 (Co. Ct.). It should be noted that a number of child welfare cases in Ontario do admit police occurrence reports. See, for example, *Children's Aid Society of London and Middlesex v. K.*, 2006 CanLII 22129 (Ont. S.C.J.).

where "business" includes activities "carried on by or as part of the operation of government."[204]

It is not enough that the record simply be made by a business. The record must be made in the "usual and ordinary course" of the business. The leading case is that of *Palmer v. Hoffman*, a decision of the United States Supreme Court.[205] The defendant railroad company sought to introduce, as a business record, a railway accident report prepared by its engineer, since deceased. The applicable statute required that the record be made in "the regular course of any business." The Court ruled that the inherent nature of the business needed to be examined. In the case on appeal, although accident reports were regularly prepared following each and every incident, they were not made with respect to the "railroad business." In the words of Mr. Justice Douglas, the report's primary purpose was "in litigating, not in railroading," and the report was ruled inadmissible.[206] The Court's narrow construction of the statute was no doubt prompted by concern with the self-serving nature of the evidence in the case. Here the defendant railroad company was tendering, in its defence, a report on the accident prepared at its request by its own employee. In the words of Justice Douglas, this would be a "real perversion of a rule designed to facilitate admission of records which experience has shown to be quite trustworthy."

In *Setak Computer Services Corp. v. Burroughs Business Machines Ltd.*, Griffiths J. refused to follow *Palmer*. He wrote:

> With respect, I believe that *Palmer* imposes an unreasonable and unnecessary limitation on the wording of the enactment. To draw a distinction between records relating to the principal business and those relating only to an auxiliary feature of the business, is not justified by the plain wording of the section. So long as the records are made in the usual and ordinary course of some phase of the business, whether principal or auxiliary, they should be admitted, in my view, according to the plain meaning of s. 36 [now s. 35].[207]

Besides requiring that the record be made in the "usual and ordinary course" of business, half the provincial statutes impose a further requirement that "it was in the usual and ordinary course of business to make the writing or record." This additional requirement is true to the common law. A "duty to make the record" reinforces the guarantees of reliability since without it there may be less impetus on the employee to

---

204 *Manitoba Evidence Act*, s. 49(1).
205 63 S. Ct. 477 (1943).
206 *Ibid.* at 481.
207 Above note 202 at 760.

be careful and accurate in making the record. Cromwell J.A. examined this issue in *R. v. Wilcox*.[208] In dispute was the admissibility of a secretly kept "crab book." The employee keeping the record was under no duty to do so and specifically had been instructed to keep computer records rather than handwritten records. Under the common law the crab book failed the "duty to record" requirement. Next Justice Cromwell turned to section 30 of the *Canada Evidence Act*, which has no "duty" requirement.[209] Although in his view the crab book could be said to have been made in the ordinary course of business, Justice Cromwell was not prepared to admit it under section 30. He felt that in so doing the ambit of the section would be extended too broadly and he preferred to apply the principled approach. Ultimately he found that the crab book had sufficient guarantees of trustworthiness to be admitted.

Most of the provisions provide that the writing or record be made of "any act, transaction, occurrence or event." This phrasing has been interpreted to mean that only statements of "fact" are admissible. Statements of opinion are inadmissible.[210] Keep in mind, however, the distinction between "fact" and "opinion" is a difficult if not artificial one to make. Referring back to *Ares v. Venner*, arguably many of the comments made by the nurses in that case would be admissible under our more flexible opinion rule. Moreover, otherwise admissible opinion found in the records should be allowed, so long as the opinion falls within the declarant's usual course of duties. For example, the autopsy report of a deceased coroner or the laboratory results found by a deceased forensic scientist may be admitted.[211]

A final problem concerns "double hearsay." The record itself is a hearsay statement and, in turn, if the record relies on the hearsay statements of others, it becomes "double hearsay." For example, the record of the cylinder block numbers in *Myers* may have been made by an employee who relied on information received from another employee, who actually took the numbers off the cylinders. Does this render the record inadmissible? Most of the statutes state that "lack of personal knowledge by the maker" may affect weight but not admissibility. Such wording contemplates the admissibility of hearsay within the record.

---

208 *R. v. Wilcox*, above note 63.

209 See also New Brunswick, *Evidence Act*, s. 49; Prince Edward Island, *Evidence Act*, s. 32.

210 See, for example, *Adderly v. Bremner*, above note 199; *Augustine Estate v. Inco*, above note 199; *Setak Computer Services Corp. v. Burroughs Business Machines Ltd.*, above note 202.

211 *R. v. Larsen* (2001), 42 C.R. (5th) 49 (B.C.S.C.), aff'd 2003 BCCA 18, and *R. v. West* (2001), 45 C.R. (5th) 307 (Ont. S.C.J.).

In the situation where one employee relies on the observations of other employees, all are under a duty to be accurate, and the underlying rationale for the exception is preserved. We see this recognized under common law,[212] and under the *Canada Evidence Act*, even though it does not have a "lack of personal knowledge" qualifier.[213]

The situation is quite different when the person who gives the information is not under any business "duty" at all. Take the common scenario where an eyewitness to an accident gives a statement to the police. The police officer has a duty to record accurately the information given, but the witness has no comparable duty to be accurate. This was the very fact situation in *Johnson v. Lutz*, where the New York Court of Appeal ruled that the accident report was inadmissible. The court established the principle that both the giver and the taker of the information needed to act in the regular course of business.[214] A majority of American decisions follow *Johnson*, as do a number of Canadian decisions. The following statement of the law captures the principle:

> Moreover, the section is intended to make admissible records which, because they were made pursuant to regular business duty, are presumed to be reliable. The section was not intended to make hearsay evidence of any third party admissible. Hearsay statements should only be admitted where the maker of the writing and the informant or informants are both acting in the usual and ordinary course of business.[215]

The principle is sound. The reliability of the records is premised on the notion that they are prepared by persons under a "business duty"; where a person provides information gratuitously, the record loses its stamp of trustworthiness.

The trend appears toward increased reliance on the principled approach when difficulties arise in admitting "business records." In *R. v. Larsen* an autopsy report was admitted where the contemporaneous requirement was missing.[216] In *R. v. Wilcox* the crab book was admitted notwithstanding the lack of a "duty to record."[217]

---

212 See *R. v. Monkhouse*, above note 194.

213 *R. v. Martin* (1997), 8 C.R. (5th) 246 (Sask. C.A.).

214 253 N.Y. 124 (C.A. 1930).

215 *Olynyk v. Yeo* (1988), 33 B.C.L.R. (2d) 247 at 254 (C.A.), reflecting the statement of Griffiths J. in *Setak Computer Services Corp. v. Burroughs Business Machines Ltd.*, above note 202. See also *Trang v. Alberta (Edmonton Remand Centre)*, above note 195; *Children's Aid Society of London and Middlesex v. K.*, above note 203.

216 Above note 211.

217 Above note 63.

9.3) Electronic Records

There is no doubt that today many documents are stored electronically. Accordingly, most of the jurisdictions have enacted specific legislation to deal with electronic documents.[218] Importantly the legislation does not create any new hearsay exception. Rather the concern with electronic records is authenticity and maintaining confidence in the integrity of the stored information. Electronic documents therefore need to be admitted under existing common law and statutory hearsay exceptions. For example, a deceased's online diary—if admissible for its truth—is still hearsay. What this does mean is that business records, electronically stored, will need to comply with the business record exception, in terms of hearsay, and meet statutory or common law requirements in terms of authenticity.[219]

10. SPONTANEOUS STATEMENTS (*RES GESTAE*)

"*Res gestae*," literally defined, means the "facts surrounding or accompanying a transaction." Unfortunately, in the words of Wigmore, the phrase is "not only entirely useless, but even positively harmful."[220] It is harmful because it invites tying admissibility to a "transaction," which creates an unprincipled limitation. It is useless because actually there is no specific *res gestae* exception; rather, the term embraces a number of distinct hearsay exceptions. These exceptions include statements of present physical condition, statements of present mental state, excited utterances, and statements of present sense impression.

The better phrase to use to encompass these exceptions is that of "spontaneous statements": the common principle underlying each of these exceptions is that reliability is founded on the *spontaneous* making of the statement before there is time for concoction. Necessity is based on expediency, "in the sense that there is no other equally satisfactory source of evidence either from the same person or elsewhere."[221] Accordingly, unavailability of the declarant is not a prerequisite; the declarant may testify, and the spontaneous statement may also be admitted into evidence.

---

218   See the *Canada Evidence Act*, s. 31.1; Ontario *Evidence Act*, s. 34.1; *Alberta Evidence Act*, s. 41. Most notably British Columbia has not enacted such legislation and relies on common law principles.

219   See *McGarry v. Co-operators Life Insurance Co.*, 2011 BCCA 214 at paras. 54–77.

220   Wigmore, *Evidence in Trials at Common Law*, above note 132, vol. 6, s. 1767.

221   *Ibid.*, s. 1714.

10.1) Statements of Present Physical Condition

Where a person claims to be experiencing a particular physical condition, the statement containing that claim is admissible but only to prove that the person was experiencing the condition at the time and to establish its duration.

This exception is confined to natural expressions that usually accompany and provide evidence of an existing injury or illness. Consider the following situation:

A homeowner involved in landscaping his yard shovels and carts load after load of dirt. He sits down to rest and then complains of severe back pain.

In the circumstances, the homeowner's "statement of pain" is admissible.

The homeowner goes to see his doctor. During the examination, the homeowner grimaces and cries out whenever the doctor touches his back area.

This "statement of pain" too is admissible within the present exception, provided that the duration of the injury is relevant.

During the examination the doctor asks, "How long have you been like this?" and the homeowner responds, "For two days." The doctor also asks, "How did this happen?" and the homeowner responds, "I hurt my back working in the yard carting dirt."

The statement of "past" pain is not admissible; nor is the homeowner's statement as to the cause of the pain. Neither of these statements are spontaneous reactions to a physical condition. As the British Columbia Court of Appeal, after a thorough examination of this exception, concluded: "The hallmark of such statements is their spontaneity. The common law exception for such statements rests on the circumstantial guarantee of reliability that may be presumed from the spontaneous utterance as to the declarant's bodily sensation."[222]

In the United States, statements of "past" pain and of its "cause" that are made for purposes of medical diagnosis or treatment are admissible under a specific hearsay exception.[223] The reliability of such

---

222 *Samuel v. Chrysler Credit Canada Ltd.*, 2007 BCCA 431 at para. 36 (C.A.).

223 Rule 803(4) of the *Federal Rules of Evidence* reads:

The following are not excluded by the hearsay rule, even though the declarant is available as a witness:

(4) **Statements for purposes of medical diagnosis or treatment.** Statements made for purposes of medical diagnosis or treatment and describing medical history, or past or present symptoms, pain, or sensations,

statements is grounded on the assumption that persons seeking medical care would provide accurate information related to their treatment. The Ontario Court of Appeal in *R. v. Czibulka* did not accept this position; it held that statements as to the cause of a condition are inadmissible under this exception.[224]

10.2) Statements of Present Mental State

Where a person describes his or her present state of mind (emotion, intent, motive, plan), the person's statement to that effect is admissible where the state of mind is relevant and the statement is made in a natural manner and not under circumstances of suspicion.

Many statements going to a person's state of mind are not hearsay at all. They are admissible, not for their truth, but for the fact they were said. Only where the statements as to state of mind are going in for their truth is there need to resort to the hearsay exception. Therefore, "the first question to be asked is whether the intended use of the evidence requires that the trier accept as true the declaration of mental state."[225] Doherty J., in an excellent summary of the law, explained this distinction in the following terms:

> If the statements are explicit statements of a state of mind, they are admitted as exceptions to the hearsay rule. If those statements permit an inference as to the speaker's state of mind, they are regarded as original testimonial evidence and admitted as circumstantial evidence from which a state of mind can be inferred. The result is the same whichever route is taken.[226]

For example:

In a murder case the defence is that the victim killed herself. She died of a drug overdose. A few weeks prior to her death she made the following statements:

1) "No one likes me; no one would miss me."
2) "I intend to kill myself."

The defence seeks to have these statements admitted into evidence.

---

or the inception or general character of the cause or external source thereof insofar as reasonably pertinent to diagnosis or treatment.

224 Above note 51 at para. 18.
225 G. Lilly, *An Introduction to the Law of Evidence*, 2d ed. (St. Paul, MN: West, 1987) at 249.
226 *R. v. P.(R.)* (1990), 58 C.C.C. (3d) 334 at 341 (Ont. H.C.J.).

Statement 1 is not being tendered for its truth; it is admissible as "original" evidence from which it may be inferred that she was depressed and potentially suicidal. Statement 2 is being admitted for its truth; it is an "explicit" statement of her intention and must be admitted under this hearsay exception. The statement also affords circumstantial evidence that she did in fact carry out her intention and kill herself. Statements of intention are not admissible to show the state of mind of persons other than the declarant, nor may they be admitted to show that persons other than the declarant acted in accordance with the declarant's stated intention.[227] The statements are also not admissible to establish past acts or events referred to in the utterances. Returning to our example:

The deceased in her diary wrote:

1) **"John [the accused] intends to kill me."**
2) **"I tried to kill myself last night, but the drugs didn't take effect."**

Statement 1 is not admissible as proof of John's intent. Statement 2 is not admissible as evidence that the deceased had tried to kill herself previously.

R. v. Starr, above, is now the leading case on statements of intention. The Supreme Court of Canada modified the exception to comply with the principles of necessity and reliability. In particular, the Court imported the requirement that in order for such statements to be admissible they had to be made in a natural manner and not in circumstances of suspicion.

At issue in the case was the admissibility of a statement made by a murder victim to his girlfriend. In the early-morning hours, the girlfriend found the deceased in a car with another woman and another couple. The girlfriend wanted the deceased to come home with her. He said that he could not, because he "had to go and do an Autopac [insurance] scam with Robert [the accused]." The majority of the Court excluded the statement because, in their view, the deceased may well have been lying in order to explain why he was with the other woman.

The Court also held that it is generally impermissible to use the statement of intention of one person to prove the intention of another. Accordingly, the majority found that it was improper to admit the deceased's statement to show Robert's intention. Chief Justice McLachlin disagreed. For her, the deceased's statement was not being used to prove joint intention; it was simply one piece of circumstantial evidence, which, along with other circumstantial evidence, supported the inference that the deceased was with Robert that night. Simply put, the

---

227 R. v. Starr, above note 5.

intention of the deceased to meet with Robert made it more likely that he did meet with Robert, than if he had had no such intention.

The Supreme Court of Canada re-examined this question in *R. v. Griffin*.[228] The accused was on trial for murder. It was the prosecution's theory that the deceased was killed over a drug debt. At issue was the deceased's statement to his girlfriend, "If anything happens to me it's your cousin's family [meaning Griffin]." The only issue at trial was the identity of the killer. Since the deceased was heavy into the drug trade the defence suggested that others could well have wanted to kill him. The statement was accepted as going to the deceased's state of mind. It described a specific fear of the accused. It was also accepted that the statement could not go to prove Griffin's state of mind. In other words, it was not directly admissible to prove identity. However, the statement was relevant indirectly to prove identity. The Court held that the deceased's fear went to motive. If we accept the deceased's fear of the accused it goes to establish the relationship between the two; it goes to establish Griffin's animus towards the deceased, from which the jury could infer that Griffin was the killer. Further, by showing the deceased's particularized fear of Griffin it went to rebut the defence suggestion that someone other than Griffin might have had a motive to kill the deceased. The statement was relevant to show that as far as the deceased was concerned—in his state of mind—Griffin was the only person with cause to do him harm. Standing alone, the statement cannot prove that Griffin was the killer, but when tied to other evidence such as Griffin's intense search for the deceased in the days leading up to the killing it provided circumstantial evidence identifying Griffin as the killer. A careful limiting instruction is required. In admitting the statement for this purpose it is necessary for the trial judge to caution the jury against using the statement to impute Griffin's state of mind.[229]

10.3) Excited Utterances

A statement relating to a startling event or condition may be admitted to prove the truth of its contents if it is made while the declarant is under the stress of excitement caused by the event or condition.

For far too long this exception was bedevilled by the phrase *res gestae*, in that courts held that in order to be admissible the statements had to be "part of the story" or "part of the transaction." The classic case is

---

228   *R. v. Griffin*, 2009 SCC 28.
229   See also *Walton v. R.* (1989), 166 C.L.R. 283 (H.C.A.).

that of *R. v. Bedingfield*.[230] The accused, known as "Harry," was charged with murder. The defence was suicide. The accused was seen to go into a house. A minute or two later the deceased rushed out of the house with her throat cut and said to her aunt, "See what Harry has done!" This statement was not admitted because the "transaction"—the stabbing—was over. The Ontario Court of Appeal came to the same conclusion in *R. v. Leland*.[231] At issue was the admissibility of a statement made by the deceased shortly after being stabbed. The deceased called out to his wife, "Rose, she stabbed me." The statement was not admitted. The court noted that the statement "did not form any part of the *res gestae*. The fighting had ceased. No one was pursuing the deceased or seeking to continue the struggle." What a ludicrous requirement! Presumably a statement would be admissible had the deceased cried out while being attacked, "Rose, she *is stabbing* me."

Fortunately, our courts have abandoned the "transaction" requirement and have returned to principle. The key principle is that the statement is made in response to an event where the possibility of concoction can be disregarded. In *R. v. Clark*, the Ontario Court of Appeal reversed *Leland*.[232] The court admitted the statement of the victim, who cried out: "Help! Help! I've been murdered! I've been stabbed!" The court referred to the decision of the Privy Council in *Ratten v. R.* and cited the following as the correct statement of the law:

> [T]he test should be not the uncertain one whether the making of the statement was in some sense part of the event or transaction. This may often be difficult to establish: such external matters as the time which elapses between the events and the speaking of the words (or vice versa), and differences in location being relevant factors but not, taken by themselves, decisive criteria. As regards statements made after the event it must be for the judge, by preliminary ruling, to satisfy himself that the statement was so clearly made in circumstances of spontaneity or involvement in the event that the possibility of concoction can be disregarded.[233]

---

230 (1879), 14 Cox C.C. 341.
231 (1950), 11 C.R. 152 (Ont. C.A.).
232 (1983), 35 C.R. (3d) 357 (Ont. C.A.).
233 *Ratten v. R.*, [1971] 3 All E.R. 801 at 807 (P.C.), quoted in *R. v. Clark* (1983), 35 C.R. (3d) 357 at 373 (Ont. C.A.). This test for spontaneous utterances was approved of in *R. v. Folland* (1999), 132 C.C.C. (3d) 14 (Ont. C.A.). See as well *R. v. Lawson*, [1998] Crim. L. Rev. 883 (Eng. C.A.), where Lord Bingham referred to Julius Caesar's famous utterance "*Et tu, Brute*," as falling within the exception.

In *R. v. Andrews* the House of Lords went on to craft the following guidelines for trial judges when faced with applications to admit such evidence:

1. The primary question which the judge must ask himself is — can the possibility of concoction or distortion be disregarded?

2. To answer that question the judge must first consider the circumstances in which the particular statement was made, in order to satisfy himself that the event was so unusual or startling or dramatic as to dominate the thoughts of the victim, so that his utterance was an instinctive reaction to that event, thus giving no real opportunity for reasoned reflection . . . .

3. In order for the statement to be sufficiently "spontaneous" it must be so closely associated with the event which has excited the statement, that it can be fairly stated that the mind of the declarant was still dominated by the event. Thus the judge must be satisfied that the event, which provided the trigger mechanism for the statement, was still operative. The fact that the statement was made in answer to a question is but one factor to consider under this heading.

4. Quite apart from the time factor, there may be special features in the case, which relate to the possibility of concoction or distortion . . . .

5. As to the possibility of error in the facts narrated in the statement, if only the ordinary fallibility of human recollection is relied upon, this goes to the weight to be attached to and not to the admissibility of the statement and is therefore a matter for the jury. However, here again there may be special features that may give rise to the possibility of error.[234]

Andrews provides a good example of the principles. In *Andrews* the victim of a stabbing identified his attackers to two police officers. The officers had been called to the scene approximately ten to fifteen minutes after the stabbing. While they were tending the victim's wounds, one of the officers asked how he had received his injuries and the accused was named. This statement was ruled admissible, notwithstanding the time lag and the officer's solicitation of the response.

R. v. Nicholas provides a recent Canadian example.[235] The victim of a sexual assault made a 911 call some ten minutes after the attack. She was unable to testify at trial owing to post-traumatic stress disorder, however, the audio tape of the 911 call was admissible as a spontaneous utterance.[236]

---

234 [1987] 1 A.C. 281 at 300–1.
235 Above note 10.
236 See also *R. v. Dakin* (1995), 80 O.A.C. 253 (C.A.).

10.4) Statements of Present Sense Impression

A statement that describes or explains an event or condition made while the person was perceiving the event or condition, or immediately thereafter, may be admitted for its truth.

Under the excited utterance exception, the key principle is that a person is so dominated by the stress and excitement of an event that concoction or fabrication is unlikely. One of the criticisms of the exception is that a person who is excited, although perhaps not prone to concoction, may actually be more prone to inaccuracies. It may well be preferable that the person be unexcited and therefore able to observe in a cool and rational manner. Herein lies the rationale for the admissibility of statements of "present sense impressions," an exception recognized in the United States, but as yet not expressly accepted in Canada.[237] Consider the example below:

In an automobile accident case the plaintiff alleges that the defendant was driving at an excessive rate of speed. The plaintiff seeks to introduce into evidence a statement made by the driver of a car who observed the defendant's car shortly before the accident. The driver stated at the time: "Look at that red Corvette. It passed me like I was standing still and I'm going the speed limit." A passenger in the car is called to testify as to this statement.

The statement is not prompted by excitement; it is a simple statement of observation and is admissible as a present sense impression—whether the driver is called or not.[238] The statement is reliable since it was made contemporaneously or immediately thereafter, which means there is little time for fabrication or forgetfulness. Moreover, there is the added safeguard that in most cases either the declarant is available to be cross-examined on the statement, or the recipient of the statement, who also was present as the events unfolded, is available for cross-examination. A present sense impression amounts to a narrative by the person reporting what she is observing. Therefore, the statement must be made contemporaneously. This time requirement is far stricter than for excited utterances.

---

237 See Rule 803(1) of the *Federal Rules of Evidence*.
238 In *R. v. Fattah*, 2006 ABQB 85 at para. 21 (Q.B.), there was no "panic" and hence no spontaneous utterance.

CHAPTER 6

OPINION AND EXPERT EVIDENCE

1. THE GENERAL EXCLUSIONARY RULE AND ITS EXCEPTIONS

"In the law of evidence, an opinion means an 'inference from observed fact.'"[1] In our system of trial, it is the neutral, impartial trier of fact who is to determine what inferences to draw from facts. "A basic tenet of our law is [therefore] that the usual witness may not give opinion evidence, but testify only to facts within his knowledge, observation and experience."[2]

In spite of this general exclusionary rule, opinion evidence is often offered. It is therefore more instructive to focus on when opinion evidence will be allowed. As will be developed in this chapter, there are two categories of admissible opinion evidence, one for lay witnesses and one for expert witnesses. In simple terms, we let lay witnesses offer opinions when there is no other meaningful way for them to communicate ordinary knowledge that they possess. We let expert witnesses offer opinions where triers of fact do not have the special training or experience required to make the relevant and worthwhile observations that the witness is offering.

It is therefore a straightforward matter as to which set of rules apply in a given case. If all that is required to form the opinion is ordinary

---

1   *R. v. Collins* (2001), 160 C.C.C. (3d) 85 at para. 17 (Ont. C.A.).
2   *R. v. D.(D.)*, [2000] S.C.R. 275 at para. 49.

experience, the lay opinion rule should be used. For example, the lay opinion evidence rule governed whether a police officer could testify to the direction the person who made footprints in the snow was running, since "any school child would deduce this from the tracks . . . observed."[3] By contrast if special training or experience is needed to form the opinion, the expert opinion rules apply. For example, evidence predicting the effects that the pharmaceutical "antabuse" would have on alcohol abuse by an alcoholic had to meet the expert evidence rules.[4]

The expert evidence rules are, of course, intended to determine when individuals can offer testimony about things that lay persons do not have the special training or experience to observe. As a result, the expert evidence rules that govern opinion evidence are not confined to opinions *per se*. Any time a witness offers observations — even descriptive ones — that cannot competently be made without special training or experience, the expert evidence rules described in this chapter apply. For example, a lay witness would not be permitted to describe the anatomy of the eyeball.

Confusion can be avoided if it is remembered that the issue in determining which rules to apply is not whether the witness is an expert. It is whether the witness, expert or not, is offering information that requires special training or experience to observe. Accordingly in *R. v. Collins* the expert evidence rules did not apply to testimony about the results of an experiment conducted by police officers to determine whether bullets would ricochet off the water, striking a target on the opposite shore.[5] The experiment did not require expertise to conduct, and no scientific principles were required to observe the results. Even if the police officers conducting the experiment had been ballistic experts, expert evidence rules would not have applied. By contrast, had the officers offered testimony about the speed the bullets travelled when fired from the gun their testimony would have to comply with the expert evidence rules. It is the substance of the evidence that matters, not the status of the witness.

---

3   *R. v. Lee* (2010), 251 C.C.C.(3d) 346 (Alta. C.A.), aff'd 2010 SCC 52 at para. 6.
4   *Children's Aid Society of Simcoe County v. J.D.* (2010), 265 O.A.C. 197 (Div. Ct.). Still, care has to be taken not to apply the wrong set of rules. In *R. v. Ilna* (2003), 172 C.C.C. (3d) 240 (Man. C.A.), for example, the lay opinion rule was used to admit the opinion of police officers that the crime scene had been "staged" to look like a break-in. Given that the court remarked (at para. 79) that professional experience enabled the officers to assess the crime scene, it is arguable that the expert evidence rule should have applied. And see *Arctic Foundations of Canada Inc. v. Mueller Canada Inc.*, [2010] 6 W.W.R. 732 (Man. Q.B.) where the trial judge improperly used the lay opinion rule to examine the admission of testimony about the failure of a thermosyphon system on the stability of structures.
5   Above note 1.

2. LAY WITNESSES

Lay witnesses may present their relevant observations in the form of opinions where

- *they are in a better position than the trier of fact to form the conclusion;*
- *the conclusion is one that persons of ordinary experience are able to make;*
- *the witness, although not expert, has the experiential capacity to make the conclusion; and*
- *the opinions being expressed are merely a compendious mode of stating facts that are too subtle or complicated to be narrated as effectively without resort to conclusions.*

Even for lay witnesses, the general exclusionary rule disallowing opinion evidence is often not applied. This is because the stark dichotomy between fact and opinion that is presupposed by the general rule is unrealistic. As Dickson J. said in *Graat v. R.*: "Except for the sake of convenience there is little, if any, virtue in any distinction resting on the tenuous and frequently false antithesis between 'fact' and 'opinion.' The line between 'fact' and 'opinion' is not clear."[6] For example, when a witness identifies the driver of the vehicle by pointing her out in court, he is stating as a fact that she is the driver. Yet, in a real sense he is offering his opinion that the person in court is the same person who was driving the vehicle. Numerous apparent statements of fact are arguably no more than expressions of opinion; things like age, height, weight, the identification of people or things, the speed of vehicles, distance, whether someone is happy or angry, all call for judgment to be made about what has been observed and for conclusions to be drawn. Obviously, it is common for witnesses to testify about such things. The fact is that lay witnesses do offer opinions.

We once proceeded on the basis that there was a general exclusionary rule prohibiting lay witnesses from testifying about their opinions, to which there were numerous particular exceptions allowing for proof of the kinds of things that have just been described. In *Graat*[7] the Supreme Court of Canada adopted a more general, sensible, and less technical approach. Graat was charged with impaired driving, and the trial judge had permitted a series of witnesses to offer opinion evidence about whether the ability of Graat to drive a motor vehicle was im-

---

6   (1982), 31 C.R. (3d) 289 at 305 (S.C.C.).
7   *Ibid.*

paired. Dickson J. held that it was appropriate to allow such testimony, but not because the degree of impairment of an individual is one of those established, exceptional cases where laypersons can offer their opinion. Rather, Dickson J. decided that the evidence was admissible on the more general basis that lay witnesses can present their observations as opinions where they "are merely giving a compendious statement of facts that are too subtle and too complicated to be narrated separately and distinctly."[8]

To understand this distinction, attempt to describe the difference between a vehicle travelling at forty kilometres an hour and one travelling at seventy kilometres an hour without expressing what will clearly be conclusions that capture the series of indescribable and internalized observations that enable most people to provide fair estimates of speed. Or, consider the recognition of faces. The compendious statement of fact, "That is Aunt Sally," subsumes myriad subtle characteristics observed and digested by the witness, attributes that could not be communicated effectively without resort to conclusions.

Except in those common areas where this kind of opinion evidence is routinely admitted, the admissibility of lay opinion evidence is a matter of judicial discretion. Based on the reasoning in *Graat*, an important consideration is whether it is necessary to have the lay witness express an opinion. In exercising that discretion, the trial judge should therefore assess whether the trier of fact is in as good a position as the witness to form the relevant conclusion. If so, the lay opinion should not be admitted unless the lay opinion evidence can, without prejudicing the case, assist in the orderly presentation of information. In *R. v. Walizadah*,[9] for example, it was useful to permit a police officer to give jurors a fair and balanced guided tour through a video re-enactment even though they were capable of seeing what was there to be seen.

It is clear from *Graat* that in determining whether lay opinion evidence is needed, the trial judge should consider whether, given the nature of the observation or the deficiencies of language, it is necessary for the witness to resort to "compendious" statements in order to communicate effectively what has been observed. Where the witness can communicate the information adequately by describing with particularity what has been observed, the witness should generally not be permitted to express an opinion.

The judge will consider whether the conclusion is one that people with ordinary experience are able to make. Persons of ordinary experi-

---

8   *Ibid.* at 310.
9   (2007), 223 C.C.C. (3d) 28 at paras. 44–46 (Ont. C.A.).

ence may be able to estimate the speed of a motor vehicle, for example, but not the speed of an airplane. A judge will also consider whether the particular witness has the requisite "experiential capacity" to form the relevant opinion. A young child will not likely have the ordinary experience needed to comment even on the speed of a motor vehicle. This is different than requiring "expertise." To offer lay opinion evidence, no special training or skill is required. Ordinary experience suffices. As indicated, if the information requires more than ordinary experience to identify, use the expert evidence standards.

3. THE ULTIMATE ISSUE RULE

3.1) General

It was once said that "an opinion [whether lay or expert] can never be received when it touches the very issue before the [court]."[10] The concern was that to allow a witness to express her "verdict" on the very issue that the trier of fact had to decide would be "usurping the functions of the jury." Put more simply, there was fear that the trier of fact might be influenced unduly by the opinion, accepting it uncritically regardless of the actual evidence in the case. There is no longer an "ultimate issue" rule that absolutely bars qualified witnesses from offering opinions on the ultimate issues in a case. The ultimate issue rule was put to rest for lay witnesses in *Graat v. R.*[11] There the accused attempted to use the ultimate issue rule to oppose the admission of lay opinions about his impairment. He argued that impairment was the very issue before the court and that to let witnesses say that his ability to drive was impaired might cause the judge simply to accept their judgment, rather than deciding the case on the evidence. Dickson J. criticized the ultimate issue rule and said that so long as the opinions were not superfluous, they were properly heard. He remarked that witnesses cannot "usurp" the role of the trier of fact because the trier is free to accept all, or part, or none of their testimony. It is the trier of fact who renders the verdict, not the witnesses.

Even though the fear of undue influence is more compelling where the opinion witness is an "expert," it has since been resolved that the ultimate issue rule is also gone for expert witnesses; there is no rule of general application preventing expert witnesses from offering opinions

---

10   *Graat v. R.*, above note 6 at 297.
11   *Ibid.*

on the ultimate issues in a case.[12] As will be seen later in this chapter, however, the fact that an expert is about to testify on one of the ultimate issues in the case will sometimes be a *factor* to consider in determining whether the testimony will be admitted.[13]

Although the ultimate issue rule itself is gone, two of its cousins survive. The first of those rules provides that a witness cannot offer an opinion on a pure question of domestic law. The second has come to be known as the rule against oath-helping.

3.2)   Opinions on Pure Questions of Domestic Law

No witness, expert or otherwise, can provide an opinion on a pure question of domestic law.[14]

The rule is easy to state and to understand — evidence is to be about questions of fact, not law. The law is for lawyers to argue, not witnesses to offer. It was therefore an error for a trial judge to permit a taxpayer to call a family law lawyer to explain that a clause in a separation agreement was legally enforceable,[15] it was an error for the trial judge to allow an expert witness to interpret the word "appreciates" in section 16 of the *Criminal Code*, pertaining to the mental disorder defence,[16] and it was wrong for an expert to offer an opinion on whether the accused was "guilty."[17] Occasionally, however, a legal standard does not have its own technical definition and requires nothing more than a conclusion of fact to resolve. For example, the concept of impairment in the offence of impaired driving refers to nothing more than the fact of impairment. Because it holds the same legal meaning as the term would have for laypersons, it is not a pure question of law and there is no problem in allowing witnesses to state opinions on that ultimate issue.

It is appropriate for a court to receive expert evidence about foreign law. Foreign laws are not laws here. The content of foreign law is therefore treated as a question of fact. And since domestic judges are not trained in foreign law, they require the assistance experts in the foreign law can offer.[18]

---

12   *R. v. Mohan* (1994), 29 C.R. (4th) 243 at 255 (S.C.C.); *R. v. R.(D.)* (1996), 107 C.C.C. (3d) 289 at 304 (S.C.C.).

13   See the discussion in this chapter, section 5, "Novel and Challenged Science."

14   *Graat v. R.*, above note 6 at 309.

15   *Syrek v. Minister of National Revenue* (2009), 387 N.R. 246 (Fed. C.A.).

16   R.S.C. 1985, c. C-46; *R. v. Skrzydlewski* (1995), 103 C.C.C. (3d) 467 at 471 (Ont. C.A.).

17   *R. v. Van*, [2009] S.C.J. No. 22.

18   See, for example, *Friedl v. Friedl* (2009), 95 B.C.L.R. (4th) 102 (C.A.).

3.3) The Rule against Oath-helping

> *A properly qualified witness can provide general information relevant in judging the credibility of a witness, but is prevented by the rule against oath-helping from expressing an opinion about whether a particular witness is telling the truth.*

"The rule against oath-helping prohibits the admission of evidence adduced solely for the purpose of proving that a witness is truthful."[19] The rule exists because "[i]t is a basic tenet of our legal system that judges and juries are capable of assessing credibility and reliability of evidence."[20] Triers of fact can discharge their central function of deciding the ultimate issue of whether witnesses are providing accurate testimony without the need for the opinions of others about whether those witnesses are being truthful. It is not just that such opinions are superfluous or unnecessary. Even though laypeople are capable of assessing credibility, determinations of credibility are notoriously difficult. There is fear that if experts, or even laypersons familiar with witnesses,[21] are permitted to express their opinions as to whether witnesses are telling the truth or furnishing accurate information, triers of fact might simply defer to those opinions rather than assessing credibility and reliability themselves. It was therefore wrong in *R. v. P.(W.A.)* for the mother of the complainant to testify, "I knew she wasn't lying [when she disclosed the sexual abuse to me]."[22]

The "rule against oath-helping" is not confined to opinions offered in support of the credibility or reliability of witnesses. It is also offended when witnesses offer an opinion that another witness is incredible or unreliable.[23] Moreover, the rule is not confined to overt opinions about credibility or reliablity. It also catches cases where, as a matter of substance, the relevance of the evidence lies only or primarily in the implication that the witness is,[24] or is probably,[25] giving accurate testimony. For example, a trial judge erred in *R. v. W.(A.W.)* by permitting an experienced police officer to intimate her belief in the credibility of the

---

19   *R. v. Llorenz*, [2000] O.J. No. 1885 at para. 27 (C.A.).

20   *R. v. Béland (sub nom. Béland v. R.)* (1987), 60 C.R. (3d) 1 at 41 (S.C.C.).

21   *R. v. Clarke* (1998), 18 C.R. (5th) 219 (Ont. C.A.); *R. v. Sauvé* (2004), 182 C.C.C. (3d) 321 (Ont. C.A.); *R. v. B.(F.F.)* (1993), 79 C.C.C. (3d) 112 at 135 (S.C.C.).

22   [2010] 2 W.W.R. 51 (N.W.T.C.A.).

23   *R. v. Rogers* (2005), 198 C.C.C. (3d) 449 (B.C.C.A.).

24   *R. v. Llorenz*, above note 19 at para. 15.

25   See *R. v. K.(P.V.)* (1993), 22 C.R. (4th) 332 (N.S.C.A.), where it was held that the rule was offended by testimony that 90 percent of children claiming to have been abused are being truthful.

complainant by recounting how thorough the investigation was, and how she did not lay a complaint in all cases.[26] The rule is also breached where a witness offers an opinion on how to interpret apparent reliability problems with the testimony of another witness. In *R. v. Reid*, for instance, an expert crossed the line by testifying that the inconsistencies in a murder witness's evidence could be accounted for because she suffered battered woman's syndrome.[27] And the rule can be breached by a witness bolstering their own testimony by invoking hearsay support. In *R. v. Ranger*, for example, a "crime scene expert" violated the rule by stating that she had her opinion verified by ten colleagues similarly trained.[28] Simply put, evidence cannot be offered for the purpose of sharing an opinion about how believable testimony is.

It is important to understand the limits on the rule against oath-helping. First, the rule is not violated where the testimony of a witness expressing their own observations or admissible opinions happens to lend support to the testimony of another witness.[29] Otherwise, two witnesses independently making the same observation could not both testify.

Second, if there is utility apart from simple oath-helping in having a witness express an opinion on the credibility or reliability of another witness, and the probative value of that opinion outweighs the risk of prejudice it presents, an opinion on the credibility or reliability of another witness can be received.[30] For example, in *R. v. Burns*[31] the expert based his opinion largely on what he was told by the witness. The expert would not have formed the opinion he did if he had not believed her. The Supreme Court of Canada concluded that when he expressed his belief in the complaint he did so not to bolster the complainant's testimony but to explain the foundation for his own opinion.

A third and important limit on the rule against oath-helping permits experts to offer opinion evidence that is relevant to the credibility or reliability of other witnesses. In such cases the expert does not comment on the truthfulness or reliability of the witness, but offers the trier of fact background information outside the competence of the trier of fact that the trier of fact can then use in making its own conclusions about whether to credit the witness. For example, witnesses may possess psychological or physical characteristics that could diminish

---

26   [2001] A.J. No. 347 (C.A.), and see *R. v. Sauvé*, above note 21, and *R. v. Dove* (2008), 55 C.R.(6th) 182 (B.C.C.A.).
27   (2003), 177 C.C.C. (3d) 260 (Ont. C.A.).
28   *R. v. Ranger* (2003), 178 C.C.C. (3d) 375 at para. 65 (Ont. C.A.).
29   *R. v. B.(F.F.)* (1993), 79 C.C.C. (3d) 112 at 135 (S.C.C.).
30   *R. v. Llorenz*, above note 19 at paras. 30–31.
31   [1994] 1 S.C.R. 656.

their credibility or reliability where those characteristics would not be apparent to or understood by triers of fact without expert assistance. Expert evidence might reveal, for example, that a witness suffers from a delusional mental illness or hysterical condition that could cause them to misperceive events.[32] Or there may be common assumptions triers of fact are apt to make about credibility that are wrong or prone to overgeneralization. Where this is so expert evidence may be necessary to assist the trier of fact in properly evaluating the credibility of witnesses. Recognized examples include the significance of recantations of allegations of sexual abuse by children,[33] or the relevance of continued association by a complainant with the abuser.[34] In order to permit triers of fact to become educated about the possible implications of such matters, the law therefore draws a distinction between opinion evidence "about credibility" (which is inadmissible because of the rule against oath-helping) and opinion evidence "relevant to credibility." Opinion evidence relevant to credibility will be admissible where the *Mohan* requirements are satisfied, "even though it will likely have some bearing on the trier of fact's ultimate determination of the question of credibility."[35] For this reason the expert in *R. v. Reid* would not have violated the rule against oath-helping had he confined himself simply to educating the trier of fact about the nature of battered woman's syndrome and its possible effects on disclosure patterns (evidence relevant to credibility), instead of expressing his own opinion that inconsistencies in a witness's evidence could be discounted on this basis (evidence about credibility).[36]

The often elusive distinction between evidence about credibility and evidence relevant to credibility, coupled with restrictions on how evidence is to be used where it does reveal the opinion of one witness about the credibility of another, gives rise to two obligations on trial judges. First, where a witness embarks on evidence relevant to credibility, the trial judge must ensure that the evidence presented is confined to its proper purpose[37] and that the expert does not stray into

---

32 See *Toohey v. Metropolitan Police Commissioner*, [1965] A.C. 595 (H.L.), and *R. v. Hawke* (1975), 29 C.R.N.S. 1 (Ont. C.A.).

33 See, for example, *R. v. J.(F.E.)* (1990), 74 C.R. (3d) 269 (Ont. C.A.).

34 *R. v. F.(D.S.)* (1999), 43 O.R. (3d) 609 (C.A.); *R. v. Meyn* (2003), 176 C.C.C. (3d) 505 (B.C.C.A.). Experts will testify that the continued association of complainants with their abusers is not uncommon and is not, therefore, a dependable indication that the abuse did not happen.

35 *R. v. K.(A.)* (1999), 137 C.C.C. (3d) 225 at para. 96 (Ont. C.A.).

36 *R. v. Reid*, above note 27.

37 See *R. v. K.(A.)*, above note 35.

offering opinions about credibility and reliability.[38] In *R. v. Llorenz* the testimony of a witness offended the rule against oath-helping because he was allowed to cast that testimony in a fashion that had more impact in revealing his belief of the complainant than it did in educating the trier of fact about the behaviour and characteristics of sexual offence victims.[39] Second, the trial judge has an obligation to direct the jury in a jury trial on the limited use that is to be made of the evidence.[40]

4. EXPERT WITNESSES

4.1) The Test for Admissibility

Expert opinion evidence is presumptively inadmissible. It can be admitted only if the party calling it satisfies the following four preconditions to admissibility, on the balance of probabilities:

- *the expert evidence must be "necessary" in the sense that the expert deals with a subject-matter that ordinary people are unlikely to form a correct judgment about without assistance;*
- *the expert evidence must be logically relevant to a material issue;*
- *the witness must be qualified to offer the opinion in the sense that the expert possesses special knowledge and experience going beyond that of the trier of fact in the matters testified to; and*
- *the proposed opinion must not run afoul of any exclusionary rule apart entirely from the expert opinion rule ("the absence of an exclusionary rule")*

Even if these four preconditions are met, the trial judge, as the "gatekeeper," must decide whether the expert evidence is sufficiently beneficial to the trial process to warrant its admission despite the potential harm to the trial process that may flow from the admission of the expert evidence.

4.1 (a) The *Mohan* Standards of Admission

In *R. v. Mohan* the Supreme Court of Canada held that the "[a]dmission of expert evidence depends on the application of the four following criteria": (1) necessity in assisting the trier of fact, (2) relevance, (3) a properly qualified expert, and (4) the "absence of an exclusionary

---

38   *R. v. G.(P.)* (2009), 63 C.R. (6th) 301 (Ont. C.A.).
39   *R. v. Llorenz*, above note 19.
40   *R. v. K.(A.)*, above note 35.

rule" that would be offended by the admission of the evidence. The burden is on the party calling the evidence to establish that each of these components is satisfied, on the balance of probabilities.[41] The precise meaning of those four components, which reflect the prior common law,[42] will be explained below in this chapter. What is crucial to appreciate, however, is that these components are not to be applied as rigid, technical rules but rather as context-specific criteria for admissibility.[43] In applying them the trial judge has an important gate-keeping function to perform to ensure that expert evidence is admitted only where warranted. Specifically, the judge is to evaluate whether the "costs" or problems caused by admitting the expert evidence would outweigh the benefits in doing so.[44] If so, the expert evidence will be inadmissible, in whole or in part.

As will be explained, the "benefits" of expert testimony mean nothing more than the probative value of the evidence. As for the "costs of admission," in *R. v. D.(D.)* the Supreme Court of Canada commented that these relate to the "distracting and time-consuming thing expert testimony can become."[45] Concern was expressed about the difficulty courts can have in understanding and evaluating expert evidence and the time and resources it can require. The Court also noted that the status or credentials of the expert, or the scientific or technical content of expert testimony, can cause triers of fact simply to adopt the expert evidence without adequate scrutiny.[46]

The *Mohan* standards apply in civil litigation,[47] administrative cases where rules of evidence are applied,[48] and in criminal cases. They also

---

41 This is consistent with general principles about the standards of proof applicable to prerequisite conditions for admissibility. See *R. v. Terceira* (1998), 15 C.R. (5th) 359 at 378 (Ont. C.A.), aff'd [1999] 3 S.C.R. 866; *R. v. J.(I.)*, [1999] O.J. No. 1192 (C.A.), and see *R. v. J.(J.-L.)*, [2000] 2 S.C.R. 600 at para. 40, where this was the standard described as applying to the third *Mohan* criteria.

42 *R. v. Terceira, ibid.* at 368.

43 *R. v. Mohan,* above note 12 at 251–52.

44 *R. v. J.(J.-L.),* above note 41 at paras. 28–29.

45 *R. v. D.(D.),* above note 2 at para. 57.

46 *Ibid.*

47 *Drumonde v. Moniz* (1997), 105 O.A.C. 295 (C.A.). In *Dulong v. Merrill Lynch Canada Inc.* (2006), 80 O.R. (3d) 378 (S.C.J.), the court noted at para. 9:

    There is no question that, in civil cases at least, the path of least resistance . . . seems to be to admit the evidence and then compensate for its weaknesses by attaching less weight to the opinion. But such an approach is an abdication of the proper function of a trial judge [as a gatekeeper].

48 *Deemar v. College of Veterinarians of Ontario* (2008), 298 D.L.R. (4th) 305 (Ont. C.A.).

apply in both jury and judge alone trials.[49] It is possible for one rule to operate in such varied kinds of cases because the gate-keeping component of the *Mohan* test makes its application highly contextual. Different outcomes can occur depending on the nature and forum of the litigation. In *Pro-Sys Consultants Ltd. v. Infineon Technologies AG*, for example, the British Columbia Court of Appeal applied a less rigorous admissibility evaluation in a class action case because disclosure under the *Rules of Civil Procedure* had yet to take place.[50] A human rights tribunal admitted expert evidence about racial profiling noting that the same evidence may not make the grade in a criminal case, because of the subtle nature of discrimination and the special role performed by human rights tribunals.[51] Even within criminal cases the intensity of the *Mohan* test vacillates. In light of the reluctance of criminal courts to deprive accused persons of defence evidence[52] courts are inclined to apply the standards of admissibility for expert evidence in a more generous fashion than for Crown evidence.[53]

It follows that although prior decisions are useful as illustrations, whether evidence will satisfy the *Mohan* test is not a matter of strict precedent.[54] A brand of expert evidence admissible in one case may not be admissible in another. Admissibility is to be determined on a case-by-case basis, because the needs of the case or even the quality of the evidence presented about the expertise will vary. Moreover, the state of learning can progress. Expert techniques or science, such as DNA evidence, can gain trust as learning improves, while "with further study or experience [theories] may prove less reliable than once believed."[55] In *R. v. Burns*, for example, the Supreme Court of Canada had approved of the admission of expert psychological evidence diagnosing a complainant as having been sexually assaulted, although no concerted challenge had been mounted to demonstrate the shortcomings of the theory sup-

---

49   *R. v. J.(J.-L.)*, above note 41 at para. 40.

50   (2009), 98 B.C.L.R. (4th) 272 (C.A.).

51   *Nassiah v. Peel Regional Police Services Board*, [2006] O.H.R.T.D. No. 18 (Ont. Human Rights Trib.).

52   *R. v. D.(D.)* above note 2 at para. 29.

53   *R. v. Bell* (1997), 8 C.R. (3d) 107 (N.W.T.C.A.); *R. v. B.(M.)*, [1998] O.J. No. 4359 (C.A.). Having said this, when it comes to evaluating the weight to be given to expert evidence that has been admitted, both Crown and defence evidence should be assessed employing the same standards: *R. v. Collins*, above note 1 at para. 46. Defence evidence should not be assigned more importance or reliability than it fairly bears simply because it is defence evidence.

54   *R. v. K.(A.)*, above note 35 at para. 76.

55   *R. v. Trochym* (2007), 43 C.R. (6th) 217 at para. 32 (S.C.C.).

porting that diagnosis.[56] As a result, in R. v. Olscamp, Justice Charron, then a trial judge, did not consider herself bound on the question of whether similar evidence tendered in that case was admissible.[57] She examined the state of learning critically, and found that child abuse accommodation syndrome could not reliably diagnose sexually abused children. This same example also shows how expert evidence may be admissible when presented for one purpose but not another. In R. v. K.(A.) child abuse accommodation syndrome evidence was subsequently held to be inadmissible for the purpose of proving that the child was assaulted, but aspects of it were admissible in order to educate the jury that the very factors that the defence were relying on to show the complainant not to be credible could be nothing more than the sequelae of sexual abuse.[58] The Mohan standards therefore invite a highly contextual approach to the admission of expert evidence.

4.1 (b)   The Abbey Restructuring of the Mohan Test

In R. v. Abbey the Ontario Court of Appeal felt the need to retool the admissibility test that had been articulated in Mohan.[59] This is because the Mohan standards include preconditions to admissibility that are necessary conditions to admission (necessity, relevance, the absence of any other exclusionary rule, and a qualified expert), as well as a gate-keeping function that requires a contextual examination and balancing of costs and benefits. Analytically, it is therefore better to undertake the analysis in two stages—preconditions to admissibility first and balancing second. Yet Mohan failed to separate them when describing the test.

Mohan authority had also developed a redundant structure for performing the gate-keeping function. In Mohan itself the Court seemed to contemplate that this cost-benefit analysis would be part of the "relevance" inquiry. Yet in R. v. D.(D.) the Court suggested that even the necessity component of the test required an evaluation of relative costs and benefits.[60] This seemed to replough the same ground as the relevance inquiry. Indeed, in R. v. D.(D.) the court went further and identified a residual "probative value/prejudice" discretion to exclude evidence that meets the Mohan test, even though the Mohan test itself will have already engaged these considerations during the cost-benefit analysis.[61]

---

56   Above note 31.

57   (1994), 95 C.C.C. (3d) 466 (Ont. C.A.).

58   R. v. K.(A.), above note 35.

59   R. v. Abbey, [2009] O.J. No. 3534 at paras. 76–79 (C.A.), leave to appeal to S.C.C. refused, [2010] S.C.C.A. No. 125.

60   Ibid.

61   R. v. D.(D.), above note 2 at paras. 11 and 29.

Abbey therefore invites judges to examine the four preconditions to admissibility first, without engaging in a contextual evaluation, and only then to apply the gate-keeping function of balancing competing interests. This adds to the clarity of the evaluation and avoids redundancy.

Given the rules of *stare decisis* the Ontario Court of Appeal cannot, of course, change the *Mohan* test. Only the Supreme Court of Canada can. Yet the *Abbey* approach is sensible, and to the extent that it simply reorganizes the same legal standards used by the Supreme Court of Canada in *Mohan* it is adopted here. The italicized proposition of law at the opening of this section on "Expert Witnesses" therefore sets out the *Mohan* standards but uses the *Abbey* structure.

4.1 (c)   Applying the Expert Witness Test

The admissibility of expert evidence is determined during a *voir dire*.[62] There are no rigid rules about how detailed or formal the inquiry must be. What is required will vary with the nature of the evidence in the case.[63] To enable the judge to decide properly whether the proposed expert evidence will be admissible, it is essential for the party proposing the expert to indicate with precision what the scope and nature of the expert testimony will be and what facts it is intended to prove.[64] If admissibility is contested, information relating to each of the *Mohan* preconditions should be presented, as well as all information required to enable the judge to perform the gate-keeping function.

4.2)   Precondition 1 — Necessity in Assisting the Trier of Fact

4.2 (a)   The "Necessity" Test

"The same understanding of necessity applies in both criminal and civil cases."[65] Essentially, expert evidence will be "necessary" where the expert deals with a subject-matter that ordinary people are unlikely to form a correct judgment about without assistance (such as the cause of a fire,[66] or the interpretation of forensic clues as to the cause of a motor vehicle accident[67]), where the expert provides information likely outside the ex-

---

62   Where the issue can be determined on the basis of counsel's submissions alone, it may not be necessary to hold a *voir dire*: *R. v. K.(A.)*, above note 35 at para. 73.

63   *R. v. Terceira*, above note 41 at 373.

64   *R. v. Nahar* (2004), 181 C.C.C. (3d) 449 (B.C.C.A.).

65   *Taylor v. Sawh*, [2000] O.J. No. 257 at para. 18 (C.A.).

66   *Hung-Huong Enterprises Ltd. v. Sovereign General Insurance*, [2001] O.J. No. 2678 (S.C.J.).

67   *Taylor v. Sawh*, above note 65.

perience and knowledge of the judge or jury (such as parliamentary procedures and the scope of MLA's duties[68]), or where the technical nature of information requires explanation (such as the analysis of DNA,[69] or the airworthiness of an aircraft[70]).[71] By contrast, if normal experience enables triers of fact to cope, expert evidence should not be received. For example, evidence from a psychologist that witnesses have problems of perception and recall when events are brief and stressful is not outside the normal experience of triers of fact,[72] nor are the conclusions of a psychologist about whether a person intended to cause death to another,[73] or of a sociologist to indicate whether a person's actions are provoked.[74] While the "necessity" standard is not to be applied "too strict[ly],"[75] the *Mohan* court stressed that expert evidence will not be admissible simply because it may be helpful. It must truly be "necessary."[76]

The "necessity" inquiry includes examining whether substitutes for the expert testimony are available to address a trier of fact's knowledge gap. Judges must consider such things as whether a jury direction can make expert evidence unnecessary.[77] The fact that the point in issue can be established adequately without expert evidence can also make the presentation of expert evidence unnecessary. In *R. v. C.(G.)*, for example, the complainant gave a compelling explanation as to why she had not complained to her mother at the time of the assault, rendering expert evidence about why sexual abuse victims might delay reporting superfluous.[78] And in *R. v. Osmar*[79] the jury did not require expert assistance to understand and appreciate Mr. Osmar's direct claim that he confessed because of the powerful inducement offered him. Both his evidence and the testimony of the police recounted the inducement, giving the jury all that they required.[80]

---

68 *Goddard v. Day*, [2000] A.J. No. 1377 (Q.B.).

69 *R. v. Terciera*, above note 41 at 373.

70 *Allen Estate v. Interlake Aviation*, [1997] M.J. No. 566 (Q.B.).

71 *R. v. Currie* (2002), 166 C.C.C. (3d) 190 at para. 67 (Ont. C.A.).

72 *R. v. McIntosh* (1997), 117 C.C.C. (3d) 385 (Ont. C.A.).

73 *R. v. Currie*, above note 71.

74 *R. v. Nahar* above note 64.

75 *R. v. Currie*, above note 71 at para. 67.

76 *R. v. D.(D.)*, above note 2 at para. 57.

77 *Ibid.; R. v. B(M.)*, [1998] O.J. No. 4359 (C.A.).

78 *R. v. C.(G.)* (1997), 8 C.R. (5th) 21 (Ont. Gen. Div.). This kind of expert evidence will rarely, if ever, satisfy the necessity requirement, as a result of the decision in *R. v. D.(D.)*, above note 2.

79 (2007), 217 C.C.C. (3d) 174 (Ont. C.A.).

80 By contrast in *R. v. Phillion* (2009), 241 C.C.C.(3d) 193 at para. 218 (Ont. C.A.) the impact that Phillion's personality disorder would have on his readiness to falsely confess went beyond ordinary knowledge and required expert testimony.

Having said this, the fact that other experts are available to testify on a matter cannot undermine the necessity of an expert opinion on the same matter. In *Taylor v. Sawh*, the Ontario Court of Appeal reversed a trial judge's decision that because two engineers were going to provide accident reconstruction testimony, it was unnecessary for a qualified police officer to offer an opinion on the cause of the accident.[81] And in *R. v. Klymchuk* that same court held that the necessity test cannot be used to impel a party to call "less impressive" evidence; the defence had argued that a crime scene specialist who had not attended the scene was not needed as the police officers who were at the scene could adequately identify the indicia that the crime scene had been staged to look like a break in.[82] Necessity is to be judged according to whether the particular kind of evidence being offered meets the necessity requirement, not according to whether other experts have already filled the need for expert testimony.

4.2 (b)   *Abbey* on "Necessity"

In *R. v. Abbey*[83] the Ontario Court of Appeal treats "necessity" not as a precondition to admissibility but as a "cost-benefit" factor to be evaluated at the second or gate-keeping stage. The *Abbey* court envisaged a sliding scale in which the more "necessary" the evidence is, the more likely it will be admitted. This sliding scale would permit expert evidence that "could assist the jury" even, apparently, where the jury is equipped to decide the point without the opinion, provided the evidence scores high enough on other benefit factors and its costs are few.[84]

This may be a realistic description of what occurs in practice. After all, even the line between common sense and expertise is not always clear. As the Alberta Court of Appeal has said:

> [E]ach case must be assessed to determine whether it meets the *Mohan* requirements, bearing in mind the fallibility of myths and stereotypes, the inconstancy of common sense, and the tension between the role of the expert and the function of the trier of fact in determining the . . . issue based on judicial notice of human behaviour.[85]

"Necessity" is therefore a judgment call and not a precise measure that can be identified with precision. There is no doubt that expert evidence is at times admitted even where its true "necessity" can be debated.

---

81   Above note 65.
82   *R. v. Klymchuk* (2005), 203 C.C.C. (3d) 341 at para. 61 (Ont. C.A.).
83   *R. v. Abbey*, above note 59.
84   *Ibid.* at paras. 93–95.
85   *R. v. R.A.N.*, [2001] A.J. No. 294 at para. 22 (C.A.).

Still, it is inconsistent with Supreme Court of Canada authority to sub-stitute a sliding scale of utility for a necessity test, even one that should not be applied "too strictly." The Supreme Court of Canada was un-equivocal. In *R. v. D.(D.)* it said that expert evidence should be admitted "[o]nly when lay persons are apt to come to a wrong conclusion without expert assistance, or where access to important information will be lost unless we borrow from the learning of experts."[86] Unless and until the Supreme Court of Canada reconsiders its position, necessity is a prerequisite to admission.[87]

4.3) Precondition 2—Relevance

In *R. v. Mohan* the Court treated the "relevance" component of the ad-missibility test as requiring a "legal relevance" inquiry. In other words, it called for judges to look for more than just logical relevance. Judges finding opinion evidence to be logically relevant were directed to go on and consider whether the information warrants admission in law, given its costs and benefits.[88] *Mohan* therefore contemplated that judges would perform their gate-keeping function when evaluating relevance.

As indicated, the *R. v. Abbey* structure sensibly separates the pre-conditions for admission from this gate-keeping function. Using *Abbey*'s analytical structure, the relevance admissibility precondition calls only for logical relevance.[89] Cost-benefit can be evaluated later. This modifi-cation is not inconsistent with *Mohan*. All of its components are intact.[90] The analysis is simply more orderly.

The "logical relevance" precondition is straightforward. It embraces both the concepts of relevance and materiality that comprise the basic rule of admissibility, described in chapter 2. It merely means that expert evidence that has no tendency as a matter of human experience and logic to make the existence of a fact in issue more or less likely than it would be without that evidence, will be strictly inadmissible.[91] For example, in *R. v. Haynes*, expert evidence about the accused's dependent personality disorder was not relevant to a material issue since it was not directed at either his intention or to a mental disorder defence. Why he joined in the killing was not material, making the expert evidence inadmissible.[92]

---

86   Above note 2 at para. 57.
87   This is why we continue to treat "necessity" as a precondition to admissibility, even though we have otherwise adopted *Abbey*'s analytical structure.
88   *R. v. Mohan*, above note 12 at 252–53.
89   Above note 59 at para. 84.
90   *Ibid.* at para. 85.
91   *Ibid.* at para. 84.
92   *R. v. Haynes* (1997), 121 C.C.C. (3d) 1 at 23 (B.C.C.A.).

Similarly, in *Mattel Inc. v. 3894207 Canada Inc.*, a public opinion survey did not meet the relevance test because the question posed was broader than the material issue the court was interested in, leaving the survey results uselessly ambiguous.[93]

4.4)   Precondition 3—A Properly Qualified Expert

4.4 (a)   The Qualification Requirement

To offer expert testimony the particular witness must, of course, be an expert in the field in which they are testifying. "Expertise" is a modest status that is achieved when the expert possesses special knowledge and experience going beyond that of the trier of fact in the matter testified to. In *R. v. R.(W.D.)* the trial judge erred when refusing to allow a defence witness who did not have clinical experience with sexual assault victims to testify about problems with the accuracy of repressed memories of sexual abuse. The expert had greater knowledge and experience than the trier of fact.[94] Where this threshold exists, deficiencies in expertise can affect the weight of the expert evidence, but not its admissibility. In *R. v. Fisher*,[95] for example, the forensic DNA analyst was permitted to report random match statistics even though she was not a population geneticist. The practice of assigning statistics using resource material was standard in her field. Her lack of special training in statistics went to the weight of her opinion alone.[96] It is only where deficiencies in training are pronounced enough to undermine the claim to superior knowledge in a specialized area that they will preclude admissibility.[97]

To be clear, the question is not simply whether the witness is an expert. It is whether the witness has the expertise to offer an opinion in the relevant area. In *McMillan v. Regional District Health Board* an orthopedic surgeon, a man of obvious expertise, was not shown to have the specific expertise needed to determine the cause of a rotator cuff injury.[98] By contrast, in *McPherson v Bernstein (No. 2)* a general surgeon was qualified to offer an expert opinion on standards of care expected by obstetrician/gynecologists because he had researched and published about cancer treatment and breast examination, the relevant area.[99]

---

93   (2006), 268 D.L.R. (4th) 424 (S.C.C.).
94   (1994), 35 C.R. (4th) 343 (Ont. C.A.).
95   (2003), 179 C.C.C. (3d) 138 (Sask. C.A.).
96   *Ibid.* at 152.
97   See, for example, *R. v. Thomas* (2006), 207 C.C.C. (3d) 86 (Ont. S.C.J.).
98   [2000] S.J. No. 121 (Q.B.).
99   (2005), 76 O.R. (3d) 133 (S.C.J.).

4.4 (b) Enforcing the Qualification Requirement

"It is trite law that expert witnesses should not give opinion evidence on matters for which they possess no special skill, knowledge or training . . . ."[100] The precise area of expertise of the witness should therefore be defined at the *voir dire*, and witnesses should not be permitted to offer opinion evidence on matters beyond their established expertise.[101] The Goudge Inquiry in Ontario found, for example, that the failure to hold disgraced child pathologist Charles Smith to the scope of his demonstrated expertise contributed to his ability to offer misleading opinion evidence that led to a rash of wrongful convictions.[102] It is not, however, an appealable error for experts to offer opinions outside of their established qualifications where their expertise, although not presented during a *voir dire*, is nonetheless clear.[103]

4.4 (c) Must an Expert Be Independent and Impartial to Qualify?

Parties in an adversarial system select the expert witnesses whose opinions will favour their case. Not surprisingly, at times expert witnesses have acted as little more than hired guns. There is a body of opinion that the "expertise" requirement to admissibility should be used to curb this by excluding the testimony of partial experts, even when they have the technical knowledge. For example, in *Deemar v. College of Veterinarians of Ontario* the Ontario Court of Appeal upheld the decision of a discipline committee to refuse to qualify as an expert a former college employee who, while employed, had administered the complaint against Deemar but was now offering to provide expert testimony on his behalf.[104] The report she had prepared smacked of advocacy. The Ontario Court of Appeal upheld the decision of the college to refuse to consider her testimony, saying that "the party tendering the proposed witness must satisfy the [tribunal] that he or she possesses not only the necessary expertise, but also the requisite independence as well."[105]

---

100 *Johnson v. Milton (Town)* (2008), 91 O.R. (3d) 190 at para. 50 (C.A.).

101 See, for example, *Vigoren v. Nystuen* (2006), 266 D.L.R. (4th) 634 at 655 (Sask. C.A.).

102 See *R. v. Abbey*, above note 59 at para. 64, citing Ontario, Inquiry into Pediatric Forensic Pathology in Ontario, *Report: Policy and Recommendations*, vol. 3 (Toronto: Queen's Printer, 2008) [The Goudge Report].

103 *R. v. Marquard* (1993), 25 C.R. (4th) 1 (S.C.C.), and see *R. v. Colas* (2001), 161 C.C.C. (3d) 335 (Ont. C.A.).

104 Above note 48; see also *United City Properties Ltd. v. Tong*, [2010] B.C.J. No. 145 (S.C.) and *R. v. Docherty*, [2010] O.J. No. 3460 (S.C.J.).

105 *Deemar v. College of Veterinarians of Ontario*, *ibid.* at para. 21. Where the term "tribunal" appears in the above-quoted passage, the Ontario Court of Appeal

There is sense in this. An expert who assumes an advocacy role is not performing the role of an expert witness.[106]

Still, the more conventional view is simply to treat indications of partiality as matters of weight, not admissibility. It is also becoming increasingly common internationally for courts to create protocols requiring experts to assert, before testifying, that they understand their role is to assist the court and to present their evidence impartially.[107] It may be that measures such as these, rather than disqualification, will continue to be used to control partiality, but exclusion is a viable option and the qualification requirement is a fitting place to enforce impartiality and independence standards.

4.5) Precondition 4 — The Absence of an Exclusionary Rule

Just because expert testimony passes the *Mohan* test does not permit the expert to offer testimony that breaches other rules of admissibility. To be admissible there must be an "absence of any other exclusionary rules" prohibiting the testimony being offered. For example, in *R. v. Pascoe* the evidence was excluded because of the danger it would be used solely to show that the accused was, as a result of his character, the kind of person to commit the alleged crime.[108]

The evidence in *R. v. Mohan* was excluded in part because its admission would offend the exclusionary rule that applies where an expert purports to testify that an accused person is not capable of committing the offence charged.[109] That exclusionary rule is avoided only if "the personality profile of the perpetrator group [is] sufficiently complete to identify distinctive psychological elements that were in all probability present and operating in the perpetrator at the time of the offence."[110] Although it is not necessary for the "standard profile" to contain an exhaustive inventory of personality traits, it must provide with "workable precision what exactly distinguishes the . . . perpetrator from other

---

actually said "trier of fact." The court misspoke; admissibility decisions are, of course, made by the trier of law, not the trier of fact.

106 *Perricone v. Baldassara*, [1994] O.J. No. 2199 at para. 17 (Gen. Div.). In this case the court did not exclude the expert evidence but gave it no weight.

107 See also David M. Paciocco, "Taking a 'Goudge' out of Bluster and Blarney: An 'Evidence-based Approach' to Expert Testimony" (2010) 13 Can. Crim. L. Rev. 135.

108 (1997), 5 C.R. (5th) 341 (Ont. C.A.).

109 Above note 12 at 256.

110 *R. v. J.(J.-L.)*, above note 41 at para. 40.

people."[111] The evidence Dr. Mohan offered fell short. Similarly, in *R. v. J.(J.-L.)* the Supreme Court of Canada held that expert evidence that persons who would sodomize a young child would frequently or habitually exhibit characteristics absent in the accused did not portray a distinctive enough profile to warrant admissibility.[112]

4.6)   The Gate-keeping Function

If these four preconditions—necessity, logical relevance, a properly qualified expert, and the absence of an exclusionary rule" —are satisfied, the expert evidence will be admitted provided it survives the gate-keeping function during which the trial judge determines whether the benefits of admissibility outweigh its costs. Admissibility is not an "all or nothing proposition. . . . The trial judge may admit part of the proffered testimony, modify the nature or scope of the proposed opinion, or edit the language used to frame the opinion."[113] In other words, so much of the expert evidence that satisfies the *Mohan* standards should be admitted, even if other features of the testimony have to be jettisoned or altered.

4.6 (a)   Determining the Benefits

The "benefits" inquiry is simply an examination of probative value. The more probative the evidence, the greater the benefit of admitting it. As always, the probative value of evidence is a function of how influential the evidence may be if it is accepted, and how believable it is.[114]

As Justice Charron recognized in *R. v. K.(A.)*, the potential influence that expert evidence can have on the case depends on how cogent the evidence is in proving the thing it is offered to prove and how live the issue it addresses is in the proceedings.[115] In *R. v. Pascoe*, for example, evidence diagnosing the accused as a homosexual pedophile could not make the grade because the expert could not provide a useful profile of homosexual pedophiles that could assist the jury in understanding the accused's intention.[116] While intent was a central issue, the cogency of

---

111 *Ibid.* at para. 44.
112 *Ibid.* See also *R. v. McClenaghan* (2008), 437 A.R. 247 (C.A.), where a defence expert impermissibly said that the accused did not have the character or propensity for violence.
113 *R. v. Abbey*, above note 59 at para. 63.
114 See chapter 2, section 4.2.
115 Above note 35.
116 Above note 108.

the evidence was marginal. It provided only minimal support for the inference sought to be made from it.

The influence of the expert evidence also turns on the extent to which the opinion is founded on proven facts.[117] This is because the opinion must relate to the evidence in the case to have utility. As will be seen below in this chapter, an opinion that is predicated on factual assumptions that are not firmly established by evidence may be worth little or even no weight.[118]

When it comes to determining how believable the expert evidence is, courts will tread softly. This is because it is up to the trier of fact to decide whether to believe what a witness is saying. Still, courts may properly consider the impartiality or the objectivity of the expert,[119] and in extreme cases can even take into account specific credibility problems in the delivery of expert evidence, such as inconsistencies in the expert's position.[120] Unless credibility problems with the witness are severe they are not apt to cause exclusion.

Courts are much more comfortable, however, when considering whether the theory or technique the expert witness is using is "reliable"[121] enough to warrant admitting. To be admissible, expert evidence must always achieve a threshold level of reliability sufficient to warrant placing it before the trier of fact,[122] and it is an important part of the gate-keeping function to assure that this threshold level is met. Once that threshold is achieved, the more reliable the evidence is, the greater the benefits of its admissibility will be.

In spite of this, courts do not always inquire into the reliability of the expert methods being used. They are pragmatic. If the expert is testifying in a familiar area, there is generally no need to conduct a reliability inquiry. Courts tend to do so only where experts offer novel theories or employ non-established techniques,[123] or where familiar forms of expertise are meaningfully challenged.[124] What will be required to meet the reliability threshold will depend on the nature of the evidence. When the opinion that is presented purports to be based

---

117 Above note 35.
118 See the discussion in this chapter, section 6, "The Presentation and Evaluation of Expert Evidence."
119 *R. v. Abbey*, above note 59 at para. 87.
120 *Ibid.* at para. 142.
121 Scientists tend to use the term "validity" to describe this same concept.
122 *R. v. Abbey*, above note 59 at para. 130. In *R. v. Terceira*, above note 41 at 378 (Ont. C.A.) the court called for proof of reliability on the balance of probabilities.
123 *R. v. Trochym*, above note 55 at para. 31.
124 See the discussion in this chapter, section 5, "Novel and Challenged Science."

in science, the factors considered in the influential American decision of *Daubert v. Merrell Dow Pharmaceutical*[125] will normally be consulted. *Daubert* focused intently on the scientific method as the key inquiry relating to the reliability of expert propositions. The scientific method includes not only testing the underlying hypotheses relied on by the expert to see if they can be falsified, and the establishment of known rates of error, but also peer review and publication as well as "general acceptance in the relevant academic community."[126] In *R. v. Dimitrov*, for example, the hypothesis that footprint impressions left in boots can be linked by wear patterns to the feet of a suspect could not be validated using scientific principles, and the evidence was excluded.[127] The degree of compliance with the scientific method is equally important where a witness relies on "behavioural science," or any claim to "a connected body of demonstrated truths or . . . observed facts systematically classified and more or less connected together by a common hypothesis operating under general laws."[128] So, in *R. v. Ranger* scientific principles were utilized to assess the reliability of criminal profiling evidence, and it was found wanting.[129] And in *R. v. Trochym* the Supreme Court of Canada used the scientific method standards from *Daubert* to test the reliability of hypnotically induced evidence, and found it to be wanting.[130]

"Scientific validity is not [however] a condition precedent to the admissibility of expert opinion evidence."[131] This is because not all expertise purports to rest in science. For example, police officers can acquire expertise through experience and training in the practices of drug traffickers, or in the composition and identification of gangs,[132] but they are hardly applying the principles of science. Forensic accountants can

---

125 113 S. Ct. 2786 (1993). It was the *Daubert* decision that no doubt inspired the development of the *Mohan* test.

126 For a careful exploration of reliability focusing on the scientific method, see *R. v. Murrin*, [1999] B.C.J. No. 2715 (S.C.).

127 (2003), 181 C.C.C. (3d) 554 (Ont. C.A.), leave to appeal to S.C.C. refused, [2004] S.C.C.A. No. 59.

128 *R. v. McIntosh*, above note 72 at 392.

129 See *R. v. Ranger*, above note 28. "Criminal profile" evidence is testimony purporting to identify why a crime was committed, or by whom. It is to be distinguished from criminal staging evidence, directed at what happened at the crime scene, which is more apt to be admissible: *R. v. Klymchuk*, above note 82. In *R. v. J.(J.-L.)*, above note 41, scientific principles were also used to test the claim that a general offender profile could exclude a particular accused who did not share that profile.

130 *R. v. Trochym*, above note 55 at 236.

131 *R. v. Abbey*, above note 59 at para. 109. And see the influential American case of *Kumho Tire Co. v. Carmichael*, 143 L. Ed. (2d) 238 (1999) (U.S.S.C.).

132 *R. v. Wilson* (2002), 166 C.C.C. (3d) 294 (Ont. S.C.J.).

provide useful testimony interpreting financial information[133] and appraisers can establish values,[134] although these witnesses are in no way engaging in acts of scientific explication. The proper question to be answered where the expertise does not depend on the principles of science is whether experience and research permit the expert to develop a specialized knowledge that is sufficiently reliable to justify placing before the trier of fact.[135] The focus is on what constitutes "a reliable basis in the knowledge and experience of [the relevant] discipline."[136] In R. v. Abbey, for example, the expert evidence had to do with the meaning of teardrop tattoos in a gang culture. The expert was a sociologist who had studied the culture of urban street gangs in Canada. He did not purport to be offering principles of science when describing why gang members wear the kind of tattoo the accused had. The court therefore did not use compliance with the scientific method to test the reliability of his evidence. Instead it consulted a range of factors, noting that there is no closed list of appropriate considerations. Those factors included whether the expert's field is a recognized discipline or area of specialized training; the degree of quality assurance measures in the field; if data is used how accurate is it apt to be [including whether it was gathered for the purposes of litigation] and how accurately it has been recorded; and the extent to which the reasoning process used by the expert can be explained.

As part of the reliability inquiry the *Abbey* court also encouraged an examination of the quality of the expert *witness* as well as quality of the performance of the expert in that case. The court considered the expert's own qualifications as well as the extent to which the expert used methods accepted within the field, and the degree to which boundaries and limits established in the field were honoured.

This latter inquiry was a departure from prior Ontario Court of Appeal authority. In R. v. Terceira the Ontario Court of Appeal had previously held that the quality and practices of the particular laboratory using DNA technology were matters of weight for the trier of fact, and not circumstances to be considered in assessing reliability.[137] The decision in *Abbey* to consider such factors at the admission stage is nonetheless appropriate. If the gate-keeping function is to prevent inaccurate or unreliable information from being admitted, one would think that relative inexperience or poor practices should be relevant, since they can

---

133   R. v. Wood, [2001] N.S.J. No. 75 (C.A.).
134   City of Saint John v. Irving Oil Co., [1966] S.C.R. 581.
135   R. v. Abbey, above note 59 at para. 117.
136   Kumho Tire Co. v. Carmichael, above note 131 at 252.
137   R. v. Terceira, above note 41.

undermine the reliability of evidence as readily as poor theory can. The *Abbey* approach also finds support in *R. v. J.(J.-L.)* where the Supreme Court of Canada considered the quality of the practices of the particular expert in evaluating reliability, including the failure of the expert to prepare case-specific scenarios for testing the accused, and the fact that he did not supervise the testing.[138] In the United States, *Federal Rules of Evidence*, rule 702(3) makes it clear that an important reliability consideration is whether the expert has applied the principles and methods reliably to the facts of the case.

The law is therefore settled. The "benefit" of the admission of expert evidence that is to be evaluated is an amalgam of (1) the cogency of the evidence, (2) the importance of the issues the evidence addresses, and (3) the believability of the evidence. "Believability" includes not only the impartiality and credentials of the expert, but also the quality of the expert's performance in the case. Where the evidence is novel or the reliability of the theories and techniques used have been subject to realistic challenge, the benefit analysis will also include an assessment of the integrity of those theories or techniques. The nature of that inquiry will depend on whether the expert opinion purports to rest in scientific principles.

4.6 (b) Identifying the Costs

Having assessed the benefits of the evidence, the judge is then in a position to weigh the value in hearing the opinion against the costs that may arise from its presentation. Those costs are simply the negative consequences that admitting the expert evidence are apt to produce.

Those negative consequences include practical considerations such as the undue consumption of time, the diversion of attention from real issues in the case,[139] or the inability of the opposing party to cope with expert evidence offered by a party having a distinct resource advantage, such as the Crown in a criminal proceeding.[140] If the evidence is prejudicial in nature, this also increases the costs of its admission. The "most important danger," far more prevalent in jury trials, is that the trier of fact "will be unable to make an effective and critical assessment of the evidence. The complexity of the material underlying the opinion, the expert's impressive credentials, the impenetrable jargon in which the opinion is wrapped

---

138 *R. v. J.(J.-L.)*, above note 41.

139 *R. v. M.(W.)* (1997), 115 C.C.C. (3d) 233 (B.C.C.A.); *R. v. K.(A.)*, above note 35, and see *R. v. Clark* (2004), 182 C.C.C. (3d) 1 at paras. 104–13 (Ont. C.A.), for a good illustration of an evaluation of the costs of admitting expert "crime scene analysis" evidence on the facts of the case.

140 *R. v. Abbey*, above note 59 at para. 91.

and the cross-examiner's inability to expose the opinion's shortcomings may prevent an effective evaluation of the evidence."[141]

In assessing the costs associated with the presentation of expert evidence, a court will consider whether procedural safeguards such as jury directions, cross-examination, editing of the expert opinion, or the provision of notice and discovery can eliminate or reduce the relevant risks.[142] The court should also consider whether the evidence can be presented in less "conclusionary" or inflammatory terms than proposed. For example, the Kaufman Commission into the wrongful conviction of Guy Paul Morin noted the tendency of forensic experts to testify that hair and fibre samples linked to the scene "matched" those linked to the accused. To claim a match comes too close to suggesting that the hair or fibre is linked to the accused, when no expert can rule out the prospect of coincidental similarities. The expert should instead describe the similarities between the suspect and subject samples and offer reliable testimony as to the frequency with which, or the probabilities of, samples exhibiting those same characteristics.

5. NOVEL AND CHALLENGED SCIENCE

Expert evidence will be treated as "novel science" where there is no established practice among courts of admitting evidence of that kind, or where the expert is using an established scientific theory or technique for a new purpose. In order to be admissible, "novel science" must:

- *be essential in the sense that the trier of fact will be unable to come to a satisfactory conclusion without the assistance of the expert;*
- *be subjected to special scrutiny with respect to its reliability; and*
- *satisfy an even stricter application of the "necessity" and "reliability" inquiries where the expert opinion approaches an ultimate issue in the case.*

Even where there is an established practice of admitting a kind of expert evidence, if the underlying scientific theory or technique is challenged and that challenge is realistic either because that theory

---

141   *Ibid.* at para. 90.
142   See *R. v. Murrin*, above note 126 at para. 53. See the Honourable Fred Kaufman, C.M., Q.C., *The Commission on Proceedings Involving Guy Paul Morin*, vol. 1 (Toronto: Ontario Minister of the Attorney General, 1998) at 338–39. And see *R. v. Klymchuk*, above note 82 at para. 62.

> *or technique has not previously been closely scrutinized, or because of changes in the base of knowledge, the expert evidence should not be admitted without confirming the validity of the underlying assumptions.*

The "dramatic growth in the frequency with which [expert witnesses] have been called upon in recent years . . . led to an ongoing debate about suitable controls on their participation, precautions to exclude junk science, and the need to preserve and protect the role of the trier of fact."[143] As a result, courts have developed safeguards that apply where scientific theories or techniques may realistically be unreliable. Where areas of expert testimony are well established and familiar, there is generally little need to be concerned about this. Where the "science" is not established, however, there is an increased risk that "expert" witnesses will be presenting worthless or misleading information to triers of fact who may be unable to identify it as such and who will defer to the "expert" because of the expert's credentials. Where the science or theory is "novel," three particular requirements are therefore imposed:

- although the "necessity" requirement is not to be applied too strictly for established science, with respect to "novel science" the opinion evidence must be "essential in the sense that the trier of fact will be unable to come to a satisfactory conclusion without the assistance of the expert";[144]
- there must be a "special scrutiny" of reliability undertaken;[145] and
- "the closer the evidence [about a novel scientific technique] approaches an opinion on an ultimate issue, the stricter the application . . . ."[146] Where the evidence relates directly to the ultimate issue, "very careful scrutiny" is required.[147]

Exactly when this more intense examination will be called for is not entirely settled because "novel science" has not been authoritatively defined. Justice Bastarache suggested in a dissenting judgment in *R. v. Trochym* that "[a] scientific technique or knowledge will be considered 'novel' in two situations; when it is new, or when the application of recognized scientific knowledge or technique is new,"[148] as it was in *R. v. J.(J.-L.)* where a scientific instrument generally accepted for use in the

---

143 *R. v. J.(J.-L)*, above note 41 at para. 25.
144 *R. v. Mohan*, above note 12 at 225.
145 *Ibid.*
146 *Ibid.*; *R. v. J.(J.-L.)*, above note 41 at para. 37.
147 *R. v. Pascoe*, above note 108 at 357.
148 See above note 55 at para. 133.

treatment of pedophiles was considered to be novel science when it was employed in an effort to diagnose pedophilia.[149]

There is some modest ambiguity in defining novel science as new science. On the one hand, the theory or technique can be "new" within the scientific community. This is the standard used in *Wolfin v Shaw*,[150] and it was the "relatively recent history" of "dental ergonomics" that led to it being treated as novel in *Best v. Paul Revere Life Insurance Co.*[151] The "new" within the scientific community standard was also implicitly applied in *R. v. J.(J.L.)*, given that the Court there appeared to accept that use of the scientific instrument in question to treat pedophiles would not have been novel.

On the other hand, a theory or technique that has long been offered within the scientific community may be new or novel to courts, and some courts have used this as the standard of novelty. In *R. v. Dimitrov*, for example, the Ontario Court of Appeal treated footprint impression identification evidence as novel science, remarking that it has not been routinely presented in court.[152]

Since the "novel science" concept is meant to service the gate-keeping function relating to admissibility, it is sensible to employ this latter standard. As the majority noted in *R. v. Trochym*, there is a difference between reliability for the purposes of a profession, and sufficient reliability for use in a court of law.[153] Since what is being tested by the novel science doctrine is forensic reliability, the relevant question should naturally focus on the novelty of admission. Moreover, asking whether the admission of the evidence in question is novel performs a pragmatic function. As the *Trochym* majority observed, where admissibility is well established, judges can rely on past practice to assume that the technique or science is reliable enough to warrant admission.[154]

Using familiarity of admission as the trigger for novel science scrutiny must be made subject to one important caveat. Canadian courts have, on occasion, established a practice of admitting kinds of expert evidence that have subsequently been shown to be unreliable. It happened with the optical comparison of hair samples, once routinely admitted, but now understood to be dangerous.[155] It also happened with

---

149 *R. v. J.(J.-L.)*, above note 41.

150 *Wolfin v. Shaw* (1998), 43 B.C.L.R. (3d) 190 at 196 (S.C.).

151 [2000] M.J. No. 415 (C.A.).

152 Above note 127 at para. 40.

153 Above note 55 at para. 37.

154 *Ibid.* at para. 32.

155 The reliability and relevance of this kind of evidence was called into question in Kaufman, *The Commission on Proceedings Involving Guy Paul Morin*, above note

"recovered memory syndrome." Although not strictly speaking an expert evidence situation, it happened, as well, with hypnotically induced evidence. In *R. v. Trochym*, after subjecting the established practice of refreshing witness memories with hypnosis to strict scrutiny, the Supreme Court of Canada held that hypnotically induced evidence is too unreliable to admit. The majority remarked that "even if it has received judicial recognition in the past, a technique or science whose underlying assumptions are challenged should not be admitted in evidence without first confirming the validity of those assumptions."[156]

Of course, where there is a history of admitting a type of expert evidence, a bald-faced challenge should not be enough to require courts to conduct searching reliability inquiries. There should be a basis for the challenge. In *R. v. Olscamp*[157] the challenge to the established practice of admitting child abuse accommodation syndrome had an air of reality to it because the theory had not previously been explored. Similarly, as the *Trochym* Court recognized, changes in the store of scientific knowledge can make a challenge to established categories of evidence appropriate.[158]

It is therefore fair to say that special scrutiny will be called for when expert evidence is predicated upon a theory or technique that is novel in the sense that courts have not developed an established practice of admitting it, or where an established practice is being put to a novel use, or where there is a realistic basis for challenging the underlying theory.

6. THE PRESENTATION AND EVALUATION OF EXPERT EVIDENCE

Depending on the circumstances, there are a variety of ways in which expert evidence will be presented.

6.1) Expert Training

At times, expert witnesses simply provide general, background information to the trier of fact that is useful in assessing evidence. This can

---

142 at 311–24. In Manitoba a review has since uncovered four cases where DNA analysis subsequently contradicted hair-comparison evidence that had been relied on by prosecutors to support murder convictions. See *R. v. Bennett* (2003), 19 C.R. (6th) 109 (Ont. C.A.).

156 Above note 55.

157 Above note 57.

158 Above note 55 at para. 32.

be done without the expert commenting on the particular case. For example, an expert might simply advise the trier of fact of such general matters as the phenomenon that abused children may well continue to associate with their abusers.[159] This information enables the trier of fact to generate its own conclusions based on the facts it finds.

6.2) Expert Opinions Based Wholly on Personal Observations

Most often experts offer their interpretation of a given set of facts. At times the expert may be a witness to the facts forming the foundation for their opinion, such as the burn expert in *R. v. Marquard* who examined the burn before diagnosing it.[160] These witnesses will testify as eyewitnesses to the underlying facts, and then offer an expert opinion as to what those facts signify. As explained earlier, the expert evidence rules apply solely to the opinions offered. They do not apply to the testimony about the facts the expert has personally observed unless the observations in question could not have been made without expertise.[161]

6.3) Expert Opinions Based in Whole or in Part on Hearsay or Inadmissible Information

At other times, the expert witness will conduct an investigation prior to trial that includes interviewing witnesses or reading documents, and then offer an opinion based on the facts they have "found." In other words, these expert witnesses rely in whole or in part on "hearsay" to form their opinions. In *R. v. Lavallee*, for example, the psychiatrist diagnosed the accused as suffering from battered woman's syndrome based on conversations with the accused, her mother and consultation of hospital admission records.[162] Since it is essential for the trier of fact to know the basis for an expert opinion so that the opinion can be evaluated, it is permissible for expert witnesses to relate any inadmissible information that they have relied on, including hearsay. The inadmissible information that the trier of fact learns about in this way is to be used solely to enable the trier of fact to evaluate the opinion, but not as proof of facts.[163] In *Lavallee* the testimony of the expert about what he

---

159   *R. v. K.(A.)*, above note 35.

160   Above note 103.

161   See the discussion in section 1, "The General Exclusionary Rule and its Exceptions," above in this chapter.

162   (1990), 76 C.R. (3d) 329 (S.C.C.).

163   *R. v. Abbey* (1982), 29 C.R. (3d) 193 (S.C.C.).

had been told about the accused's history of abuse could not be used as proof of the events she and her mother had described when interviewed by him. The expert's description of those conversations came in solely so that the basis for his opinions could be understood.

Paradoxically the fact that an expert opinion based on hearsay is admissible does not always mean that the trier of fact is entitled to rely on that opinion. The Supreme Court of Canada stated in *R. v. Abbey* that although an opinion based on inadmissible information may be received, "[b]efore *any* weight can be given to [the] expert's opinion, the facts upon which the opinion is based must be found to exist" on the basis of admissible evidence.[164] In other words, while the expert can testify based on hearsay information, before the rier of fact may rely on that opinion there must be admissible evidence that proves that the hearsay information the expert witness relied upon in making that opinion was true. In this way there will be an evidentiary foundation for accepting the expert's opinion.

This "rule in *Abbey*" was interpreted by some to mean that the *entire foundation* for an opinion had to be confirmed by independent evidence accepted by the trier of fact before that opinion could be used by the trier of fact. In *R. v. Lavallee*,[165] however, the rule in *Abbey* was explained to mean that although it is necessary for the facts supporting the opinion to be found to exist based on admissible evidence, it is not necessary to establish each and every fact that the expert relied upon. "[A]s long as there is *some* admissible evidence to establish the foundation for the expert's opinion," that opinion can be accepted, although a judge must warn the jury that the more the expert relies on facts not proved in evidence, the less weight the jury may attribute to the opinion.[166] Where an opinion is based *mainly* on information not proved by admissible evidence it is appropriate for a judge to direct a jury that the opinion is entitled to no weight.[167]

In determining whether a sufficient foundation has been presented to enable an opinion to be given weight, it is important to bear in mind whether the hearsay supporting the foundation is admissible or not. In other words, the expert may have consulted only admissible business records. If the hearsay foundation offered by the expert witness satisfies

---

164   *Ibid.* at 214 [emphasis added].

165   Above note 162.

166   *Ibid.* at 362 [emphasis added]. See also *R. v. Palma* (2000), 149 C.C.C. (3d) 169 (Ont. S.C.J.), for a helpful discussion of the rule.

167   *R. v. Scardino* (1991), 6 C.R. (4th) 146 (Ont. C.A.); *R. v. Grandinetti* (2003), 178 C.C.C. (3d) 449 (Alta. C.A.); *R. v. Warsing* (2002), 167 C.C.C. (3d) 545 (B.C.C.A.).

hearsay exceptions, the necessary foundation can be established by the expert directly and it will be up to the trier of fact to decide whether it considers that admissible hearsay foundation to be reliable, and the opinion worthy.

Moreover, the Supreme Court of Canada has indicated that if an expert obtains and acts on information of a kind that is within the scope of his expertise and which does not come from a party to the litigation, the trier of fact is free to weigh the opinion even if that information does not meet established hearsay exceptions. In *R. v. B.(S.A.)*,[168] for example, the DNA expert relied on international guidelines to determine whether a non-matching test result that contradicted five other results was a mutation that should be disregarded. It was not necessary to call evidence from the experts who established the "mutation" guidelines to permit the trier of fact to rely, at its discretion, on the DNA expert's testimony. Similarly, in *City of Saint John v. Irving Oil Co.* there was an adequate foundation for the opinion of an appraiser when he relied on the ordinary kinds of sources appraisers consult in determining value, even though technically those sources were hearsay information.[169] In effect, the customary reliance on disinterested information by experts imbues that information with sufficient reliability to permit the trier of fact to decide whether to act on the opinion. By contrast, where the expert opinion is based on information derived from an interested party to the litigation, that hearsay foundation has to be proved by admissible evidence.[170]

6.4) Expert Opinions Secured by Hypothetical Questions

Frequently, expert witnesses who have not conducted their own investigation are asked to offer an opinion on a proper inference arising from the actual facts of the case or to make an expert observation relating to evidence that has been presented in court. Of course, the facts of the case are for the trier of fact to determine, not the expert. Unless those facts are uncontested,[171] (such as where the material facts are not in dispute or where the expert is commenting on the significance of an item of real evidence that has been admitted) it is inappropriate to have the expert listen to the evidence to form a conclusion as to the

---

168 (2003), 231 D.L.R. (4th) 602 (S.C.C.).
169 Above note 134.
170 See *R. v. Worrall* (2004), 19 C.R. (6th) 213 (Ont. S.C.J.), where the authority is explained and applied.
171 *Bleta v. R.* (1964), 44 C.R. 193 (S.C.C.).

facts upon which their opinion will be based.[172] The party calling the witness should present the expert with a hypothetical factual scenario that reflects the facts the party hopes that the trier of fact will find, always bearing in mind that "before any weight at all can be given to an expert's opinion, the facts upon which the opinion is based must be found to exist."[173] If the trier of fact finds that the facts contained in the hypothetical exist, the opinion can be applied. If the trier of fact finds facts materially inconsistent with the hypothetical, the opinion becomes useless. For example, if the expert in the Ontario Court of Appeal case of *R. v. Abbey* was asked to offer an opinion on the significance of a teardrop tattoo worn by a member of an urban street gang and there had been no evidence linking Mr. Abbey to an urban street gang, the expert's opinion would have been useless.

While it will often be appropriate for experts to relate their opinions to the specific facts of a case by responding to hypothetical questions in this fashion, the practice of doing so heightens the risks associated with expert testimony. This is because the expert is not only training the trier of fact about how to interpret evidence using expert techniques. The expert is offering the conclusion he or she would draw based on the facts they have been offered. This increases the risk that the trier of fact may simply adopt the expert's conclusion without critical analysis. It is obviously important before this risk is taken to ensure that the expertise is capable of supporting the conclusion offered. In *R. v. K.(A.)*, for example, the state of learning about the behaviours exhibited by sexually abused children was insufficient to enable the expert to respond to a hypothetical question about whether the complainant had been sexually abused. By contrast, the state of learning was sufficient to enable the expert to reply that the kinds of misbehaviours described in a hypothetical question could be the result of sexual abuse. This more modest conclusion, supported by the state of knowledge in the field, was important in educating the jury about what to make of the defence claim that the complainant's behaviours suggested she was not a credible person.[174] At times it is not the state of learning that prevents the use of hypotheticals but rather the balance between necessity and prejudice. In *R. v. Reid* the expert could have adequately educated the jury about the impact that battered woman's syndrome could have on the disclosure patterns of a witness without going so far as to offer

---

172 *Thorndycraft v. McCully* (1994), 20 O.R. (3d) 373 (Gen. Div.).

173 *R. v. J. (J.-L.)*, above note 41 at para. 59.

174 Above note 35.

opinions on the significance of hypothetical questions that tracked the particular facts of the case.[175]

6.5) Presenting the Expert Evidence and Explaining the Evidence to Juries

"If the testimony [of an expert] is highly technical, counsel, who has called the expert witness, should ask the witness to explain himself in language the layman can understand."[176] This is not only good advocacy. The Supreme Court of Canada has positively discouraged trial judges from attempting to translate expert evidence into simpler language to assist jurors, as this can be a "potentially hazardous task" that can cause the technical evidence to lose its precision.[177] When a judge does choose to "wade into the waters of interpreting expert testimony" for a jury, "he must exercise great care to impress upon the jury that his interpretation is only an opinion which they may either accept or reject."[178] If the expert evidence is recapped in a misleading way, either during a jury direction or in a decision rendered by a judge alone, reversible error can occur.

7. THE USE OF WRITTEN AUTHORITIES TO EXAMINE AND CROSS-EXAMINE THE EXPERT

Technically, books and articles are hearsay when they are being relied upon as providing accurate information. Although expertise is often garnered by reading the factual claims and opinions of others, this is inherent in the nature of study. The hearsay foundation for expertise is not treated, therefore, as problematic. On the other hand, the rules of evidence do not permit reliance on books and articles in the examination or cross-examination of experts unless certain criteria are met. The expert can refer to and even quote from other authorities while testifying in chief so long as he adopts the opinions contained in those authorities as his own by expressing his agreement with them. In theory, the trier of fact is then being presented with his opinion, and not that of the author.

---

175   Above note 27.
176   *R. v. Thériault*, [1981] 1 S.C.R. 336 at 342.
177   *R. v. Daley* (2007), 226 C.C.C. (3d) 1 at 32 (S.C.C.).
178   *Ibid.* at 33.

The expert can be cross-examined using texts, articles, and studies, but according to established law, only where she acknowledges that the works being used are authoritative. Where she acknowledges the authority of the work, if she adopts the opinions of the author they become part of her evidence. Where she acknowledges the authority of the work but rejects its conclusions, she can be asked to explain why, and her responses can be of relevance to the credibility of the opinion she offers.[179]

In *R. v. Marquard*, the Supreme Court of Canada was asked to modify this rule to allow authorities to be used in cross-examination even if the expert does not recognize their authority, so long as the reliability of the work is established independently or by judicial notice.[180] This is the rule used by a number of American courts. Under the Canadian approach, an expert unfamiliar with the authorities in his field cannot be confronted with them. In effect, the ignorance of the expert insulates him from having to explain the inconsistency of his views with the opinions of others. The *Marquard* Court was able to avoid resolving the question of whether the proposed rule is preferable to the strict Canadian approach because the technique used by the Crown failed to meet even the more liberal standard.[181]

8. SPECIAL STATUTORY PROVISIONS

A number of sections relating to expert evidence are contained in the various provincial Evidence Acts. Two kinds of provision are of particular importance. The first imposes limits on the number of experts who can be called without leave of the court. The number who can be called as of right varies between three[182] and five[183] for those jurisdictions limiting the number of experts. The sections are obviously intended to keep trials from degenerating into contests between experts, judged according to who can produce the most.

---

179 *R. v. Anderson* (1914), 22 C.C.C. 455 (Alta. C.A.); *Cansulex Ltd. v. Reed Stenhouse Ltd.* (1986), 70 B.C.L.R. 189 (S.C.).

180 Above note 103 at 20–21.

181 Madam Justice L'Heureux-Dubé, dissenting on other grounds, expressed favour with the more liberal approach: *ibid.* at 36–37.

182 *Alberta Evidence Act*, s. 10; *Manitoba Evidence Act*, s. 25, New Brunswick, *Evidence Act*, s. 23; Northwest Territories, *Evidence Act*, s. 10; Ontario, *Evidence Act*, s. 12; Yukon Territory, *Evidence Act*, s. 9.

183 Saskatchewan, *The Evidence Act*, s. 48.

The second kind of provision permits reports by certain experts to be filed with the court without the need to call the expert. Some of these provisions apply to any kind of expert,[184] while others are confined to qualified medical practitioners.[185] These sections provide notice and disclosure requirements and give the opposing party the right to insist that the expert be produced for cross-examination. If a party calls an expert where a report would have sufficed, most of these sections provide expressly that an order for costs can be made against that party.

In criminal cases, certificates of analysis conducted by experts relating to blood and breath samples in alcohol driving cases,[186] or the analysis of narcotics,[187] are admissible without the need to call the expert. In each case leave of the court is needed to compel the attendance of the expert for cross-examination. Section 657.3 of the *Criminal Code* permits expert reports, supported by affidavit, to be admitted on any issue in lieu of calling the witness, although the court retains the discretion to require the witness to testify in chief or to be cross-examined. The provisions also impose notice and disclosure obligations relating to expert reports, including on the accused, although for reasons having to do with the principle of a case to meet[188] while the Crown must give disclosure within a "reasonable period before trial," the accused need not furnish the actual expert report until the close of the Crown case. It has been held that there is no authority under section 657.3 to exclude expert evidence for non-compliance.[189]

---

184 British Columbia, *Evidence Act*, s. 10; New Brunswick, *Evidence Act*, s. 50; Northwest Territories, *Evidence Act*, ss. 11, 12, & 13.

185 Ontario, *Evidence Act*, s. 52; *Manitoba Evidence Act*, s. 50; Prince Edward Island, *Evidence Act*, s. 33; Saskatchewan, *The Evidence Act*, s. 32.

186 Sections 258(1)(e)–(i) of the *Criminal Code*, above note 16.

187 Section 51(1)–(3) of the *Controlled Drugs and Substances Act*, S.C. 1996, c. 19.

188 See chapter 8, section 1, "Introduction."

189 *R. v. Horan* (2008), 240 O.A.C. 313 at 324 (C.A.).

CHAPTER 7

PRIVILEGE

1. GENERAL PRINCIPLES

Privilege, as a rule of evidence, arises at trial and belongs to a "witness." The witness, although required to take the stand, by virtue of privilege can refuse to answer certain questions or refuse to produce certain documents. In *Descôteaux v. Mierzwinski*, the Supreme Court of Canada recognized that a "privilege" or a "right to confidentiality" was a "substantive rule" giving a person protection from disclosure of communications outside the trial setting.[1] *Descôteaux v. Mierzwinski* concerned solicitor-client communications, but there is little reason why this substantive rule should not apply to all privileges, providing protection for confidential communications inside and outside the courtroom.

Privilege, unlike other rules of exclusion, is not designed to facilitate the truth-finding process. In fact, privilege is inimical to the search for truth in that it leads to the loss of otherwise relevant and reliable evidence. It is for this reason that the finding of a privilege is to be exceptional. Dean Wigmore provided these words of caution:

> It follows, on the one hand, that *all privileges of exemption from this duty are exceptional*, and are therefore to be discountenanced . . . judges and lawyers are apt to forget this exceptional nature. The presumption

---

1   (1982), 70 C.C.C. (2d) 385 (S.C.C.).

against their extension is not observed in spirit. The trend of the day is to expand them as if they were large and fundamental principles, worthy of pursuit into the remotest analogies. This attitude is an unwholesome one. The investigation of truth and the enforcement of testimonial duty demand the restriction, not the expansion, of these privileges.[2]

Compelling reasons must exist before a privilege is recognized. There must be some overriding social concern or value that warrants the loss of probative evidence.[3] Such a determination is more a matter of policy than of proof. The assumption underlying a privilege is that it does indeed go to protect some societal interest, which is an assumption not open to ready proof. For example, with respect to a privilege for religious communications, how does one assess the importance or need to preserve such confidences? In *R. v. Gruenke*, the Supreme Court of Canada rejected the creation of a blanket privilege for religious communications.[4] However, L'Heureux-Dubé J., in dissent, was of the view "that there is a human need for a spiritual counsellor, a need which, in a system of religious freedom and freedom of thought and belief, must be recognized" and "must supercede [sic] the truth-searching policy."[5] How does one prove or challenge this view?

What is involved is a balancing of the broader "social interest" against the principle that courts should be provided and have available *all* relevant evidence. To this end, Wigmore fashioned four conditions to serve as the foundation for determining all such privileges whether claimed or established:

(1) The communications must originate in a *confidence* that they will not be disclosed.

(2) This element of *confidentiality must be essential* to the full and satisfactory maintenance of the relation between the parties.

(3) The *relation* must be one which in the opinion of the community ought to be sedulously *fostered*.

(4) The *injury* that would inure to the relation by the disclosure of the communications must be *greater than the benefit* thereby gained for the correct disposal of litigation.[6]

---

2   J.H. Wigmore, *Evidence in Trials at Common Law*, 3d ed. rev. by J.T. McNaughton, vol. 8 (Boston: Little, Brown, 1961) s. 2192 [emphasis in original].

3   *R. v. Gruenke* (sub nom. *R. v. Fosty*) (1991), 8 C.R. (4th) 368 at 392 (S.C.C.), L'Heureux-Dubé J.

4   *Ibid.*

5   *Ibid.* at 403.

6   Wigmore, above note 2, s. 2285 [footnotes omitted].

The "Wigmore test" represents a "utilitarian" approach to privilege, in that the privileges are created to serve the greater public good.[7] For example, the fact that a communication is made in confidence is not, standing alone, enough to create a privilege.[8] Take the situation where you share an intimate secret in confidence with a friend, and that conversation becomes relevant in a subsequent proceeding. The communication was made in confidence, but the broader social value in preserving and maintaining friendships is not sufficient to override the need to present the relevant evidence at trial. Nevertheless, in recent years confidentiality or "protection of privacy" has been advanced as a sufficient justification to found a privilege.[9] The "privacy" model has the potential to greatly broaden the scope for finding privileges—far more so than Wigmore would accept under his "utilitarian" model.[10]

1.1)   "Class" Privileges and "Case-by-Case" Privileges

The Supreme Court of Canada in *R. v. Gruenke* made a distinction between "class" and "case-by-case" privileges.[11] For a class privilege there is a *prima facie* presumption that the communications are privileged and inadmissible. The party urging admission must show why the communications should *not* be privileged. Class privileges are few in numbers. Two of the most significant are: (1) at common law—solicitor-client communications, and (2) under statute—spousal communications. A third less-defined class privilege applies to settlement discussions between actual or contemplated litigants. With a case-by-case privilege there is a *prima facie* assumption that the communications are not privileged and are admissible. The party urging exclusion must show why the communications are privileged. In order to determine whether privilege applies in a particular case, the Court accepted the "Wigmore test" as a "general framework."

1.2)   Waiver of Privilege

A unique feature of privilege is that the right to claim or to waive the privilege belongs to its "holder"—for whose benefit the privilege was

---

7   E.W. Cleary, ed., *McCormick on Evidence*, 3d ed. (St. Paul, MN: West, 1985) s. 171.

8   *D. v. National Society for the Prevention of Cruelty to Children*, [1978] A.C. 171 at 218, Lord Diplock.

9   See *R. v. Gruenke*, above note 3, L'Heureux-Dubé J. (dissenting).

10   See, for example, *V.(K.L.) v. R.(D.G.)*, [1994] 10 W.W.R. 105 (B.C.C.A.), where a privilege was found in diary entries. Leave to appeal to the Supreme Court of Canada was granted; however, the case settled and was never heard.

11   Above note 3.

created—and it is essential to identify who actually holds the privilege. An issue arises when "government" is the holder. In a narrow sense the holder of the privilege is the executive council of government. Such an interpretation would essentially insulate government from any claim of waiver by its civil servants. A more palatable interpretation is to apply the principle of distributed governmental authority; whereby a privileged communication may be waived by a civil servant acting within that person's proper authority and responsibilities.[12]

The holder may be a party to the litigation or an ordinary witness. Where a witness is the holder, none of the parties have the right to assert the privilege, and none of the parties are harmed if a trial judge erroneously overrides a witness's claim for privilege—only the witness has been harmed. In this situation, neither party can appeal the error, because the erroneous decision has harmed the witness, not the parties. On the other hand, should a trial judge erroneously uphold a privilege, evidence has been lost, and this loss may give the party deprived of the evidence a ground of appeal.

As mentioned, the "holder" may waive the protection of the privilege and disclose the information. Certain courts have stated that the waiver must be clear and must be done in complete awareness of the result.[13] The waiver may be made expressly, or may be found by implication. An implied waiver is not based solely on finding an implied intention on the part of the holder to waive the privileged communications, but is also based on considerations of fairness and consistency. As Wigmore noted, "A privileged person would seldom be found to waive, if his intention not to abandon could alone control the situation."[14] For example, a party to an action may choose to disclose a portion of a privileged communication with his lawyer that is favourable to his cause. In these circumstances, fairness dictates that the entire content of the communication on that same matter should be disclosed. In other words, a party cannot use privilege "both as a sword and a shield—to waive when it inures to her advantage, and wield when it does not."[15]

The issue of implied waiver often arises when one party puts their state of mind into issue. For example, they allege that they acted in good faith upon the advice of legal counsel. In this situation, the party cannot at once make the assertion of good faith, without disclosing the advice. This was exactly the case in R. v. Shirose where the accused brought an application for a stay of proceedings on the basis that the

---

12   *Nova Scotia (Transportation & Infrastructure Renewal) v. Peach*, 2011 NSCA 27.
13   *R. v. Perron* (1990), 75 C.R. (3d) 382 (Que. C.A.).
14   Wigmore, above note 2, s. 2327.
15   *Bone v. Person* (2000), 145 Man. R. (2d) 85 at para. 14 (C.A.).

police conduct was illegal and constituted an abuse of process.[16] Undercover RCMP officers were involved in a reverse sting, in which they offered to sell narcotics to suspected drug traffickers. The police obtained legal advice as to the legality of the reverse sting operation. In response to the stay application the RCMP alleged that they did not act in an abusive way, in part because of the legal advice received. The Supreme Court of Canada found an implied waiver, requiring the disclosure of the advice received by the RCMP.

1.3)   Inadvertent Disclosure of Privileged Information

What of inadvertent disclosures? By definition, such disclosures are unintentional and do not constitute valid waivers of privilege. Nevertheless, the traditional common law position has been that the privilege is lost and the communication is admissible. This result is based on three different rationales. First, there is the principle that privilege protects the source of the information, and not the information *per se*. Second, privileges are narrowly construed by the common law courts in order to minimize the loss of evidence.[17] Third, those involved in the privileged relationship are obliged to safeguard their communications, and if they do not, then so be it, and the privilege is lost.

The leading example of the traditional common law approach is *Rumping v. D.P.P.*, where the accused was convicted of murder.[18] The accused wrote a letter to his wife, essentially confessing to the murder. The letter was intercepted and admitted into evidence at his trial. Under statute, neither the husband nor the wife could be called to testify as to the contents of the letter, but this restriction did not preclude the admission of the letter itself through third parties. Even if the letter had been stolen by the third party, it was still admissible at trial.

Modern decisions are not so unforgiving, and greater protection is accorded to the privileged communications both inside and outside the courtroom. This approach flows from the Supreme Court of Canada's decision in *Descôteaux v. Mierzwinski*, where the Court made it clear that privilege was a "substantive rule" designed to protect the confidentiality of communications. Accordingly, we see that the courts are affording greater protection to inadvertently disclosed privileged information. In fact, there have been a number of court decisions where counsel are removed as solicitors of record when they become aware of

16   (1999), 133 C.C.C. (3d) 257 (S.C.C.).

17   With respect to solicitor-client communications, see *Calcraft v. Guest*, [1898] 1 Q.B. 759 (C.A.).

18   [1962] 3 All E.R. 256 (H.L.).

and decide to make use of privileged documents inadvertently sent to them by mistake.[19] These decisions show that the courts are prepared to protect the privilege and chastise counsel for taking advantage of inadvertent mistakes.

In civil cases, disclosure does not automatically result in the loss of the privilege; nor will it be automatically protected. It is a matter of case-by-case judgment. For example, if the person claiming the privilege knew of the disclosure, remained silent, and allowed the person in receipt of the information to rely upon it, then a court may very well find that the privilege is lost.[20] In *Metcalfe v. Metcalfe* the Manitoba Court of Appeal held that the starting point is that a court should protect the confidentiality of privileged communications as much as possible. However, inadvertently disclosed information can be used where the communications are important to the outcome of the case and there is no reasonable alternative form of evidence that can serve the same purpose.[21]

Different principles apply in criminal cases. Full answer and defence considerations in a criminal case discourage courts from using privacy interests to suppress information that may assist the accused; even though they might suppress similar information in a civil case.[22] On the other hand, when dealing with solicitor-client privilege in a criminal context, where privilege usually inures to the benefit of the accused, Justice Arbour remarked in *R. v. Fink* that "[u]njustified, or even accidental infringements of the privilege erode the public's confidence in the fairness of the criminal justice system. This is why all efforts must be made to protect such confidences."[23] There are also statutory provisions that are relevant. Subsection 189(6) of the *Criminal Code* affords statutory protection for otherwise privileged information that is intercepted—a recognition that in our day and age electronic eavesdropping is such that few confidences are safe from being overheard.

19   *Celanese Canada Inc. v. Murray Demolition*, [2006] 2 S.C.R. 189; *Chan v. Dynasty Executive Suites Ltd.*, 2006 CanLII 23950 (Ont. S.C.J.).

20   *Chapelstone Developments Inc. v. Canada*, 2004 NBCA 96. See also *Royal Bank of Canada v. Lee* (1992), 127 A.R. 236 (C.A.).

21   *Metcalfe v. Metcalfe* (2001), 198 D.L.R. (4th) 318 (Man. C.A.).

22   See *M.(A.) v. Ryan* (1997), 143 D.L.R. (4th) 1 at 14 (S.C.C.), and the discussion below in section 2.2, "Innocence at Stake."

23   (2002), 167 C.C.C. (3d) 1 at para. 49 (S.C.C.).

2. SOLICITOR-CLIENT PRIVILEGE

A communication between a solicitor and a client, of a confidential nature and related to the seeking, forming, or giving of legal advice, is privileged information.

There is no privilege for communications that are themselves criminal or that are made with a view to obtaining legal advice to facilitate the commission of a crime or fraud.

The privilege may also be overridden where it would result in the withholding of evidence that might enable an accused to establish his innocence, or where public safety is at risk.

Solicitor-client privilege arises because lawyers have made themselves indispensable to the administration of justice. The central rationale for according this privilege was stated by Justice Cory as follows:

> Clients seeking advice must be able to speak freely to their lawyers secure in the knowledge that what they say will not be divulged without their consent. It cannot be forgotten that the privilege is that of the client, not the lawyer. The privilege is essential if sound legal advice is to be given in every field. It has a deep significance in almost every situation where legal advice is sought whether it be with regard to corporate and commercial transactions, to family relationships, to civil litigation, or to criminal charges. Family secrets, company secrets, personal foibles, and indiscretions all must on occasion be revealed to the lawyer by the client. Without this privilege clients could never be candid and furnish all the relevant information that must be provided to lawyers if they are to properly advise their clients. It is an element that is both integral and extremely important to the functioning of the legal system. It is because of the fundamental importance of the privilege that the onus properly rests upon those seeking to set aside the privilege to justify taking such a significant step.[24]

The privilege belongs to the client and is for the client and not the solicitor to waive, although the client may authorize his solicitor to disclose the information. Trial judges are also called upon to ensure that lawyers, who disclose confidential communications, do so only with the express consent of the client.[25]

Safeguarding solicitor-client privilege lies at the heart of the successful challenge to section 488.1 of the *Criminal Code*. This section outlined

---

24   *Smith v. Jones* (1999), 132 C.C.C. (3d) 225 at para. 46 (S.C.C.); see also *Blank v. Canada (Minister of Justice)*, 2006 SCC 39 at para. 26.

25   *Geffen v. Goodman Estate* (1991), 81 D.L.R. (4th) 211 (S.C.C.).

a procedure for dealing with documents seized from lawyers, pursuant to a search warrant. The problem with the section was that by default, when a lawyer failed to claim privilege, the privilege was lost and this could occur without the client's knowledge. This in the words of Justice Arbour was the section's "fatal feature."[26] The section was found to be unconstitutional and as a result struck down. To fill the void, the Court went on to craft a regime for searches, which included the requirement that "every effort must be made to contact the lawyer and the client."[27]

Wigmore outlined the scope of solicitor-client privilege in the following terms:

> (1) Where legal advice of any kind is sought (2) from a professional legal adviser in his capacity as such, (3) the communications relating to that purpose, (4) made in confidence (5) by the client, (6) are at his instance permanently protected (7) from disclosure by himself or by the legal adviser, (8) except the protection be waived.[28]

The privilege protects confidential communications that arise on contact. There is no need for a formal retainer. The client's contacts with the lawyer's secretary or clerk are also privileged. So long as the purpose of the contact is the seeking of legal advice, the communications are protected. The contact must be a perceived professional one; casual conversation will not suffice.[29]

Communications involving salaried lawyers, in-house counsel, and government lawyers pose special problems. These lawyers have a variety of functions — some law-related and some not. Solicitor-client privilege will protect communications where legal advice is sought; it will not protect advice given by lawyers on matters outside the law. For example, in private practice many lawyers are valued more for their business sense than for their legal acumen. No solicitor-client privilege attaches to advice on purely business matters. Each situation must be assessed on a case-by-case basis. The courts need to examine the nature of the relationship, the subject matter of the advice, and the circumstances in which it is sought and rendered.[30]

---

26   *R. v. Fink*, above note 23 at para. 39.

27   *Ibid.* at para. 49.

28   Wigmore, above note 2, s. 2292. This statement of the law has been quoted with approval by the Supreme Court of Canada in a number of cases. See, for example, *Descôteaux v. Mierzwinski*, above note 1 at 398, and *R. v. Shirose*, above note 16 at 288.

29   *Cushing v. Hood*, 2007 NSSC 97; aff'd 2008 NSCA 47.

30   *R. v. Shirose*, above note 16 at 289, and *Pritchard v. Ontario (Human Rights Commission)* (2004), 19 C.R. (6th) 203 at para. 20 (S.C.C.).

The communications must be intended to be confidential. There-fore, the presence of an unnecessary third party undermines such in-tent. Having said this, a solicitor may certainly have more than one client and so long as the information is shared among those with a "common interest" or "joint interest" it will remain privileged to the outside world. However, should a dispute arise among the parties the privilege is inapplicable and the respective parties may demand dis-closure.[31] The common interest exception has been expanded to cover those situations in which a fiduciary or like duty has been found to exist between the parties, such as a trustee-beneficiary, fiduciary as-pects of Crown-aboriginal relations, and certain types of agency rela-tions. The key is that the parties have the "self-same interest" or share a common goal.[32] In *Pritchard v. Ontario Human Rights Commissioner* a complainant wanted access to a legal opinion given to the commission on her claim. She cited "joint interest." The Supreme Court of Canada found that the common interest exception did not apply because there was no shared interest between the commission and the complainant. The commission was a disinterested gatekeeper in complaints and not the advocate for the complainant.[33]

The privilege protects "communications" and there is a real issue as to what is captured within that term. In *Maranda v. Richer* the RCMP sought a search warrant to seize the fees and disbursements made by a client to a lawyer.[34] The Crown argued that such information was not privileged. This was a critical point in that the Supreme Court in *R. v. Fink* had held that: "No search warrant can be issued with regards to documents that are known to be protected by solicitor-client privilege."[35] The Crown argued that the gross amounts of fees paid were a "pure fact" and not a communication. The Court rejected the distinction between "fact" and "communication." Rather, the Court adopted a functional ap-proach; it was sufficient if the "fact" arose out of the solicitor-client relationship and is connected to that relationship. Where this occurs there is a presumption that the "fact," "information," or "communica-tion" is privileged. It will then be up to the challenging party, in this case the Crown, to show that disclosure of the information would not violate the confidentiality of the relationship.

The question also arises as to whether the identity of a client is intended to be confidential. In *Fink* the Supreme Court noted: "The

---

31   See *R. v. Dunbar* (1982), 138 D.L.R. (3d) 221 at 245 (Ont. C.A.).
32   *Pritchard v. Ontario (Human Rights Commission)*, above note 30 at para. 24.
33   *Ibid.* at para. 22.
34   (2003), 178 C.C.C. (3d) 321 (S.C.C.).
35   Above note 23 at para. 49.

name of the client may very well be protected by solicitor-client privilege, although this is not always the case."[36] In ordinary circumstances, the client's name and address are not in any way intended to be kept confidential.[37] However, this is not the situation when the client goes to a lawyer specifically in order to protect his identity. For example, a hit-and-run driver goes to see a lawyer seeking advice, and perhaps to act as a means to see that the victims are compensated. In these circumstances, the client certainly wants to keep his identity confidential to the rest of the world.[38]

Similarly, the privilege cannot be used to shield the client from disclosing otherwise non-privileged material. For example, the client facing a tax audit cannot send her financial records to a lawyer and seek refuge from disclosure; the privilege does not apply to documents that existed prior to the solicitor-client relationship. Nor does the privilege apply to physical objects, such as a smoking gun or stolen property—these objects are not "communications"—although the communications that take place between the lawyer and the client about these items are privileged. As one court put it, "A lawyer is not a safety-deposit box."[39] The notorious videotapes in Paul Bernardo's murder trial make the point.[40] These "indescribably horrible" videotapes showed the young murder victims being forced to participate in various sexual acts. Bernardo instructed his lawyer, Ken Murray, to take possession of these videotapes, which were hidden in his home. Murray, who had access to Bernardo's home, retrieved the tapes from their hidden location. He should not have done so. Murray's discussions with Bernardo about retrieving the tapes were covered by privilege, but the tapes were not. The videotapes pre-existed the solicitor-client relationship and they ultimately had to be turned over to the Crown.

It is said for solicitor-client privilege that "once privileged, always privileged." The privilege survives the relationship, and survives the death of the client. An exception is made for will cases, where the execution, contents, or validity of a will is in dispute. The Supreme Court of Canada expanded this exception to include the validity of a trust instrument where the settlor was deceased.[41] The fundamental principle

---

36 *Ibid.* at para. 28.

37 See *Autorité des marchés financiers v. Mount Real Corporation*, 2006 QCCQ 14479 at paras. 30–37.

38 *Thorson v. Jones* (1973), 38 D.L.R. (3d) 312 (B.C.S.C.).

39 *Keefer Laundry Ltd. v. Pellerin Milnor Corp.*, 2006 BCSC 1180 at para. 61.

40 *R. v. Murray* (2000), 144 C.C.C. (3d) 289 (Ont. S.C.J.). Murray was charged with attempt to obstruct justice by concealment of the videotapes and was acquitted.

41 *Geffen v. Goodman Estate*, above note 25.

is that in such cases the interests of the client are indeed furthered by the disclosure of the confidences.

In *R. v. Jack* the Manitoba Court of Appeal seized upon this principle to admit otherwise privileged communications in a murder prosecution.[42] Jack was on trial for the murder of his wife, whose body was never found. At issue was her state of mind immediately prior to her disappearance. Three days before her disappearance, she went to see a family law lawyer. The Crown called the lawyer to prove her state of mind and future intentions. In these circumstances, the court found that it was in the interests of both the client and the administration of justice that the communications be admitted into evidence.

2.1) Communications in Furtherance of Crime or Fraud

The privilege will not protect communications that are in themselves criminal or else are made with a view to obtaining legal advice to facilitate the commission of a crime.[43] This is not an "exception" to but a "negation" of solicitor-client privilege. Such communications are not part of the professional relationship. Only communications made for the legitimate purpose of obtaining lawful legal advice are privileged. The privilege is designed to facilitate the administration of justice and is not intended to assist in the aiding and abetting of criminal activities. Therefore, no privilege will attach where the client, for a criminal or fraudulent purpose, either conspires with his solicitor or deceives him. The key will be the client's intent and purpose. The client's intention is paramount because the law will not discourage clients from seeking legal advice in good faith even regarding transactions that ultimately turn out to be illegal.[44]

A distinction is to be made between "future" crimes and "past" crimes. The privilege will not extend to communications where the client's purpose is to commit a future crime or fraud. On the other hand, the privilege will protect communications involving the litigation of past crimes. Similarly, the seeking of legal advice to avoid committing future wrongs is also protected.

The suggestion of criminal or fraudulent wrongdoing is a serious allegation. Accordingly, the party raising the allegation must provide an evidentiary foundation. Courts often speak of the need to "give colour

---

42   (1992), 70 C.C.C. (3d) 67 at 91 (Man. C.A.).

43   *Descôteaux v. Mierzwinski*, above note 1 at 413.

44   See *R. v. Shirose*, above note 16 at paras. 55–64, and *Blue Line Hockey Acquisition Co. v. Orca Bay Hockey Ltd.*, 2007 BCSC 143 at para. 34 .

to the charge."[45] A mere allegation is insufficient. It takes more than evidence of a crime and proof of an anterior consultation with a lawyer.[46] Should an evidentiary foundation be met, then the recommended procedure is for the trial judge to vet the material or evidence. Upon such a review, the evidence should only be disclosed if it can fairly support an inference of criminal or fraudulent intent.

This "negation" of solicitor-client privilege is most often framed in terms of criminal or fraudulent wrongdoing. However, the argument is made that the privilege should not apply whenever communications are made in furtherance of "any unlawful conduct," which would include torts, breach of contract, regulatory offences and abuse of process applications.[47] In principle, these communications are not within the scope of professional privilege at all, in that it is no part of a solicitor's duty, innocently or otherwise, to further any breach of duty or wrongful act.

The Supreme Court of Canada in *Blank v. Canada* commented that privilege would not protect from disclosure evidence of abuse of process or "similar blameworthy conduct." In the words of Justice Fish, a privilege "is not a black hole from which evidence of one's own misconduct can never be exposed to the light of day."[48] This comment was made with respect to "litigation privilege"; however, in principle it would seem applicable to solicitor-client privilege as well. All privileges are created in the public interest and it is contrary to the effective administration of justice to use the privilege to shield criminal, fraudulent, or abusive misconduct. Applying this principle, in *Dublin v. Montessori Jewish Day School* the exception was recognized for claims involving intentional infliction of emotional harm.[49]

The "crime and fraud" exception was also extended by the High Court of Australia in *Attorney-General (N.T.) v. Kearney* to a case of abuse of process by the Northern Territory government. Essentially the government sought legal advice on how to thwart legitimate aboriginal land claims. Justice Gibbs observed that such a purpose ran counter to the public interest underlying the privilege in the first place. He stated:

> It would be contrary to the public interest which the privilege is designed to secure—the better administration of justice—to allow it to be used to protect communications made to further a deliberate

---

45   *Coe v. Sturgeon General Hospital District No. 100* (2000), 274 A.R. 313 (Q.B.).

46   *R. v. Shirose*, above note 16 at 294.

47   In *Goldman, Sachs & Co. v. Sessions*, 1999 CanLII 5317 (B.C.S.C.) the court applied the exception for a civil abuse of process claim. See also *Hallstone Products Ltd. v. Canada*, 2004 CanLII 16272 (Ont. S.C.J.).

48   *Blank v. Canada (Minister of Justice)*, above note 24 at para. 44.

49   *Dublin v. Montessori Jewish Day School* (2007), 85 O.R. (3d) 511 (S.C.).

abuse of statutory power and by that abuse to prevent others from exercising their rights under the law.[50]

2.2)   Innocence at Stake

In Canada no privilege, including solicitor-client, is absolute. Having said this, the privilege will be rigorously protected and it is in only rare instances that the privilege will be overridden as a last resort. Disclosure of a privileged solicitor-client communication will only be ordered where absolutely necessary. The absolute necessity test "is as restrictive a test as may be formulated short of an absolute prohibition in every case."[51] The law recognizes two exceptions to the solicitor-client privilege: (1) the "innocence at stake" exception and (2) the "public safety exception." Each will be discussed below.

Privileges will yield to the accused's right under section 7 of the *Charter* to make full answer and defence, where they stand in the way of an innocent person establishing his or her innocence. "Our system will not tolerate the conviction of the innocent."[52] The Supreme Court of Canada in *R. v. Brown* outlined the "*McClure* test" as follows:

A)   The Threshold Test:

To satisfy the threshold test, the accused must establish that:

1)   the information he seeks from the solicitor-client communication is not available from any other source; and
2)   he is otherwise unable to raise a reasonable doubt.

If the threshold test is not met the privilege stands and the judge need go no further. If the threshold has been satisfied, the judge should proceed to the innocence at stake test, which has two stages:

B)   The Innocence at Stake Test:

Stage 1: The accused seeking production of the solicitor-client communication has to demonstrate an evidentiary basis to conclude that a communication exists that could raise a reasonable doubt as to his guilt.

Stage 2: If such an evidentiary basis exists, the trial judge should examine the communication to determine whether, in fact, it is likely to raise a reasonable doubt as to the guilt of the accused.

---

50   (1985), 61 A.L.R. 55 at 64 (H.C.A.).
51   *Goodis v. Ontario (Ministry of Correctional Services)*, 2006 SCC 31 at para. 20.
52   *R. v. McClure* (2001), 151 C.C.C. (3d) 321 at 334 (S.C.C.).

It is important to distinguish that the burden in the second stage of the innocence at stake test (likely to raise a reasonable doubt) is stricter than that in the first stage (could raise a reasonable doubt).

If the innocence at stake test is satisfied, the judge should order disclosure of the communications that are likely to raise a reasonable doubt.

The onus is on the accused to establish each element of the test on a balance of probabilities.[53]

Brown provides a good example both of the test at work and of the difficulties presented in its practical application. Brown was charged with murder. Circumstantial evidence linked him to the murder, along with a confession allegedly overheard by a jailhouse informant. Prior to his trial, Brown brought a motion to compel production of "third-party" solicitor-client communications that had taken place between a man named Benson and his lawyers. The foundation for the application was a statement from Donna Robertson, Benson's girlfriend, that Benson had told her that he had killed the victim and confessed as much to his lawyers. Benson and Robertson had a stormy relationship, and they were drinking heavily at the time of the confession. Robertson went to the police. The police investigated, but found no other evidence linking Benson to the murder. The motion's court judge granted the defence motion and ordered production of certain documents, otherwise protected by solicitor-client privilege, to the defence. Benson appealed directly to the Supreme Court of Canada under section 40(1) of the *Supreme Court Act*.[54] The Supreme Court of Canada overruled the judge's decision and in so doing the Court expanded upon the *McClure* procedure.

First, as a preliminary matter, it must be determined whether solicitor-client privilege applies. If there is no privilege, there is no need to look for an exception to the privilege. There was some evidence that Benson had waived his privilege and this should have been ruled upon by the judge before moving to a *McClure* hearing.

Second, in both the "threshold test" and in the "innocence at stake test" there is a requirement that the accused have some knowledge of "information" or "communications." In *Brown*, Robertson's evidence provided the basis to suspect that the privileged information existed. In most cases this will be absent. Mere speculation as to what a file might contain is insufficient.[55]

---

53   [2002] 2 S.C.R. 185.
54   R.S.C. 1985, c. S-26.
55   *R. v. McClure*, above note 52 at 337.

Turning to the threshold test, the first component is one of "necessity"; before violating solicitor-client privilege other sources of the "information" must be explored. The Court explained that "information" means more than simple knowledge of a fact; it means that the accused does not have access to other information that is admissible at trial.[56] Turning to the facts in *Brown*, the Court had to determine whether the information sought, namely Benson's confession, was available from another source. The other source was Donna Robertson's testimony. The problem was that having Robertson repeat Benson's confession would be hearsay. The trial judge had serious concerns about the admissibility of this evidence, both because Benson and Robertson had been drinking at the time and because of their stormy relationship. Interestingly, the Supreme Court Justices were not as convinced that Robertson's evidence was inadmissible. The majority noted that "some rules of evidence may be applied with something less than their usual degree of rigour," in order to avoid a wrongful conviction.[57] In a concurring opinion, Justices Arbour and L'Heureux-Dubé went even further and wrote:

> Logic, principle and policy dictate that if one of the most stringent exclusionary rules, the solicitor-client privilege, is to yield to concerns about convicting an innocent person, other exclusionary rules, such as the hearsay rule, should yield first.[58]

In any event, the message is clear that trial judges should determine the admissibility of other potential sources of the information before overriding the privilege.

The second element of the threshold test is whether the accused can raise a reasonable doubt in any other way. This too goes to necessity. If the accused can be acquitted on some other basis, then there is no need to violate solicitor-client privilege. For example, if the accused could raise a reasonable doubt at his trial on the question of *mens rea* by access to the solicitor-client file, but could also raise a reasonable doubt by raising alibi or identification, then it would be unnecessary to use the solicitor-client file.[59]

The Court suggested that, in the usual case, it is preferable to delay the *McClure* application until the end of the Crown's case. This would then allow the trial judge a better opportunity to assess the strength of the Crown's case, and to determine whether the accused's innocence is,

---

56 *R. v. Brown*, above note 53 at para. 35.
57 *Ibid.* at para. 42.
58 *Ibid.* at para. 117.
59 *R. v. McClure*, above note 52 at 336.

in fact, at stake. If the judge believes that the Crown has failed to prove its case beyond a reasonable doubt, the application should be denied. If the trial judge believes that the Crown has made a strong case, but that the defence may be able to raise a reasonable doubt through its evidence, she may again decide to deny or postpone the application. It is open to the defence to bring *McClure* applications at different times throughout the trial.

The motion court judge in *Brown* was very troubled by this aspect of the threshold test. He questioned how a judge was to do this without usurping the jury's function. Therefore, he concluded that *McClure* was simply imposing on trial judges an obligation to consider whether there is a genuine danger of wrongful conviction. He was wrong. Justice Major, writing the majority decision, reiterated that the trial judge should only allow the *McClure* application when the judge is of the view that the accused will be unable to raise a reasonable doubt without the evidence protected by the privilege. If there is or may be some evidence upon which a reasonable jury, properly instructed, could acquit, the *McClure* application should be denied.

With respect, the requirement that the accused has to show that he cannot otherwise raise a reasonable doubt without disclosure of the solicitor-client confidence is thoroughly unworkable.[60] It puts defence lawyers in a position of having to argue that their case is not strong enough to avoid conviction. Particularly in a judge alone trial, if they fail in getting access to the information, they have prejudiced their position by denigrating their own case. Even leaving this aside, in a judge alone trial this requirement compels the judge effectively to prejudge guilt. In a jury trial, all the judge can do is guess what a jury will do. It is all speculative. If the judge guesses "acquittal," and is wrong, and the jury convicts, then the accused has been denied his opportunity to provide his "innocence at stake" evidence. Presumably, appeal courts may then be called upon to examine the *McClure* application anew.

Turning to the "innocence at stake" test, stage one is the precursor to getting the trial judge to examine the communication. In stage two, the judge examines the communication. The communications may be oral or written. Rather than requiring counsel to testify, the Court in *Brown* suggested that amplification of the record should be done by way of an affidavit for the benefit of the trial judge.

Both stages of the innocence at stake test speak of raising "a reasonable doubt about the accused's guilt." This phrase was interpreted

---

60   The difficulties in applying the *McClure* test are outlined in *R. v. Schertzer*, 2008 CanLII 1952 at paras. 13–24 (Ont. S.C.J.).

narrowly by the Court in *McClure* and in *Brown*. Usually it means that the otherwise unavailable evidence goes directly to one of the elements of the offence. It cannot be ordered to bolster or corroborate evidence that is already available to the accused. Nor should it be ordered to advance ancillary attacks on the Crown's case, such as by impugning the credibility of Crown witnesses. In *Brown*, the Court ruled that if Robertson's testimony about Benson's confession was held to be admissible, then it would already be available. Moreover, the Court was unimpressed with the fact, acknowledged by it, that a jury was apt to be more inclined to trust the confession by Benson to his lawyers than the drunken admission made to his estranged and angry girlfriend. In the words of Justice Major, "The quality of the evidence is not a factor."[61] With respect, it ought to be. In many cases credibility is central to the trial. Depriving the accused of access to evidence that disproves credibility or reliability is as dangerous to the prospect of wrongful conviction as depriving the accused of access to evidence supporting an affirmative defence.

It is understandable that the Court wants to protect solicitor-client relationships as far as possible, but the test developed in *McClure* and *Brown* is unduly restrictive. The fundamental principle is that innocent people ought not to be convicted. Yet, the Court, somewhat cynically, acknowledged "that a failed *McClure* application may precede a wrongful conviction."[62] The Court suggested recourse to section 690 of the *Criminal Code* and appealing to royal prerogative. A fairer and more reasonable recourse would have been to loosen the restrictions in both the threshold test and the innocence at stake test.

Finally, what of protecting the third party, whose privileged communications are now produced? The Court in *Brown* set forth a number of safeguards:

- The judge should order production of only those communications that are necessary to allow the accused, whose innocence is otherwise at stake, to raise a reasonable doubt as to his guilt. Any portions of the communications that are not necessary to raise a reasonable doubt as to the guilt of the accused should not be disclosed.
- The communications produced are not to be turned over to the Crown. If the accused decides not to use the communications as evidence, then they will never come to the Crown's attention.
- If the communications are used by the accused, the privilege holder is protected under the *Charter* by "use immunity and derivative use

---

61   *R. v. Brown*, above note 53 at para. 71.
62   *Ibid.* at para. 56.

immunity."[63] This means that the privilege holder's communications and any evidence derived therefrom cannot be used in a subsequent case against the privilege holder.

2.3) Public Safety

In *Smith v. Jones* the Supreme Court of Canada recognized a "public safety" exception to solicitor-client privilege.[64] When public safety is involved and death or serious bodily harm is imminent, solicitor-client privilege should be set aside. The accused was charged with aggravated sexual assault on a prostitute. His counsel referred him to a psychiatrist, in preparation of a guilty plea. During his interview with the psychiatrist the accused described in detail his plan to kidnap, rape, and kill prostitutes. The psychiatrist informed defence counsel that the accused was a dangerous individual and would, more likely than not, commit future offences. The psychiatrist subsequently contacted counsel to inquire about the case. When he was informed that his concerns would not be addressed, he went to court for a declaration that he be entitled to disclose the communications made to him by the accused. Solicitor-client privilege attached, because at the time the psychiatrist was acting as the lawyer's agent in interviewing and assessing the client.

In determining when public safety outweighs solicitor-client privilege, there are three factors to consider — clarity, seriousness, and imminence:

- First, is there a clear risk to an identifiable person or group of persons?
- Second, is there a risk of serious bodily harm or death?
- Third, is the danger imminent?[65]

All the surrounding circumstances will have to be taken into consideration in determining whether the threat to public safety outweighs the need to preserve solicitor-client privilege.[66]

The Supreme Court of Canada went on to find that the danger in this case was sufficiently clear, serious, and imminent to override the privilege. Justice Cory then allowed the psychiatrist to provide to the authorities both his opinion as to the danger posed by the accused and those communications relevant to the imminent risk of serious harm or death. In the result, the accused's confession as to what he did and his intent could be disclosed. Justice Major, in dissent, would have limited

---

63 See chapter 8, sections 3.2 and 3.5.
64 *Smith v. Jones*, above note 24.
65 *Ibid.* at 248.
66 *Ibid.* at 251.

disclosure only to the psychiatrist's opinion. His concern was that the accused's own words would now be used against him to his detriment. In Justice Major's view, it is one thing to warn the authorities, but it is quite another thing to use the accused's own words against him. This is precisely what came to pass. The accused, Leopold, was sentenced as a dangerous offender, largely on the privileged communications made to his defence psychiatrist.[67]

It is implicit that the public interest exceptions recognized for solicitor-client privilege are available for all other privileges. Justice Cory termed solicitor-client the "highest privilege recognized by the courts"; therefore, if it must yield to the public interest in seeing that the innocent are not convicted or that the public are kept safe, then all other privileges must so yield as well.

The more flexible Canadian approach to privilege—"once privileged, not always privileged"—is in stark contrast to the approaches adopted in the United States and in Great Britain, where their highest courts have opted for certainty over flexibility. The United States Supreme Court in *Swidler & Berlin v. United States* was asked to override solicitor-client privilege following the death of the client where the information sought pertained to a criminal investigation.[68] The majority rejected any balancing of interests in determining whether or not to uphold a privilege and, accordingly, the Court ruled that the privilege survived the death of the client.[69] In a similar vein, the House of Lords in *R. v. Derby Magistrates' Court* overturned earlier lower court decisions to rule that solicitor-client privilege was "absolute"—with no exceptions.[70]

3. LITIGATION PRIVILEGE

Communications between a lawyer and third persons are privileged if, at the time of the making of the communication, litigation was commenced or anticipated and the dominant purpose for the communication was for use in, or advice on, the litigation.

---

67 *R. v. Leopold* (2001), 155 C.C.C. (3d) 251 (B.C.C.A.). See also D. Clayton, "*R. v. Leopold*: The Public Safety Exception and Defence Counsel as Confidential Informant" (2001) 43 C.R. (5th) 319.

68 118 S. Ct. 2081 (1998).

69 In dissent, Justice O'Connor wrote that "a criminal defendant's right to exculpatory evidence or a compelling law enforcement need for information may, where the testimony is not available from other sources, override a client's posthumous interest in confidentiality." *Ibid.* at 2088.

70 [1996] 1 A.C. 487 (H.L.).

In the course of providing legal advice to a client, a lawyer will need to interview witnesses, consult with experts, and undertake copious research on the law—to name but a few tasks. The lawyer accumulates a great deal of information and the claim of privilege is made, often under the rubric of solicitor-client privilege. This term is a misnomer. Client confidences may or may not be involved. Consider this situation:

In a personal injury action the lawyer for the plaintiff hires an investigator to find and interview potential witnesses to the accident. The investigator uncovers a number of witnesses and obtains signed statements from each.

In this situation there are no client confidences involved. The witnesses are giving a statement with little or no expectation that it will be kept confidential. In fact, they no doubt anticipate being called to testify and to tell all. The statement, if it is privileged, has nothing to do with solicitor-client confidentiality; rather, the material is protected by way of litigation privilege, which is also called "work product," "solicitor-third party," or "anticipation of litigation" privilege.

3.1) The Rationale for the Privilege

It had been argued that litigation privilege was but a branch of solicitor-client privilege. This argument was laid to rest in *Blank v. Canada*. In the words of Justice Fish it is preferable to recognize that they are "distinct conceptual animals" and not "two branches of the same tree."[71] Litigation privilege is separate and distinct from solicitor-client privilege in the following ways:

- The rationales underlying the two privileges are different. Solicitor-client privilege exists to protect the relationship; litigation privilege exists to facilitate the adversarial process. This privilege is based on the adversary system, which encourages the opposing parties to prepare their respective cases as best they can. The parties would be loath to do so if they had to turn over the fruits of their preparation to the other side.[72]
- Solicitor-client privilege exists any time a client seeks legal advice, whether or not litigation is involved. Litigation privilege applies only in the context of litigation.
- Solicitor-client privilege is permanent and survives the termination of the relationship. Litigation privilege is temporary and ends with

---

71   *Blank v. Canada (Minister of Justice)*, above note 24 at para. 7.
72   *Regional Municipality of Ottawa-Carleton v. Consumers' Gas Ltd.* (1990), 74 D.L.R. (4th) 742 (Ont. Div. Ct.).

the litigation. Once the litigation is over there is no longer a need to maintain the adversarial protection.

- Solicitor-client privilege is meant to protect client confidences. Litigation privilege does not require that the communications be made in confidence.
- Solicitor-client is recognized as the "highest" privilege, not lightly to be overridden. Litigation privilege is far more likely to be truncated.

In *Blank*, the key issue was whether litigation privilege had expired or was protected permanently under the rubric of solicitor-client. Blank and a company he was associated with were initially prosecuted by the federal government for pollution offences. The charges eventually were dropped. Mr. Blank then began a long saga in the courts by suing the government in damages for fraud, conspiracy, perjury, and abuse of its prosecutorial powers. He wanted disclosure from the government of documents related to the earlier pollution prosecutions. The government claimed that they were privileged by way of solicitor-client. The Supreme Court of Canada found that the documents were caught by litigation privilege and that the privilege ended with the litigation. However, the Court did go on to recognize that the privilege may transcend the particular litigation. Closely related litigation may still be ongoing and in this case the litigation privilege continues. Justice Fish explained the parameters of "litigation" in the following terms:[73]

> At a minimum, it seems to me, this enlarged definition of "litigation" includes separate proceedings that involve the same or related parties and arise from the same or a related cause of action (or "juridical source"). Proceedings that raise issues common to the initial action and share its essential purpose would in my view qualify as well.

The example given in *Blank* was that of the urea formaldehyde insulation litigation. In the 1980s the federal government confronted litigation across Canada arising out of its urea formaldehyde insulation program. The parties were different and the specifics of each claim were different but the underlying liability issues were common across the country.[74]

In *Blank* the documents at issue originated in the criminal litigation, which had ended. The civil litigation sprung from a different judicial source and was unrelated to the criminal prosecution, which gave rise to the privilege.[75] Accordingly, it was found that the documents were not

---

73   *Blank v. Canada (Minister of Justice)*, above note 24 at para. 39.
74   *Ibid.* at para. 40.
75   *Ibid.* at para. 43.

caught by litigation privilege and ought to be disclosed. Following *Blank* it has also been found that litigation privilege arising from a civil case was not protected in a criminal prosecution arising from the same incident.[76]

The line between litigation privilege and solicitor-client privilege blurs at times. It is well settled that solicitor-client privilege can extend to certain third-party communications. The law often speaks in terms of these third parties being "agents" of either the solicitor or the client. The clearest example is where the third party merely acts as a channel or conduit of communication between the client and the solicitor, as with a translator or messenger. Solicitor-client privilege also extends to communications where the third party employs an expertise in assembling and explaining information provided by the client. For example, solicitor-client privilege applies when the lawyer engages an expert to examine the client. In this situation the expert is an agent of the lawyer, and the client's statements to the expert are as privileged as if they were made to the lawyer herself.[77] "Agency" for our purposes is not to be determined under the law of agency. Justice Doherty suggests a functional approach, where the court looks for the true nature of the function that the third party was retained to perform.[78] That function must be essential to the existence or operation of the solicitor-client relationship. In *Smith v. Jones* it was essential that the expert examine and explain the client's mental condition for the lawyer. On the other hand, if the third party is only authorized to gather information from outside sources, the third party's function is not essential to the maintenance or operation of the solicitor-client relationship and does not fall under that privilege. For example, a private investigator engaged to investigate and interview witnesses is a gatherer of information, but the fruits of his investigation do not fall within solicitor-client privilege. The solicitor-client privilege is intended to allow the client and lawyer to communicate in confidence. It is not intended to protect communications or other material simply deemed useful by the lawyer in advising the client.[79]

Litigation privilege is designed to establish a "zone of privacy" for the preparation of litigation and no more.[80] The competing trend is towards

---

76   *R. v. Bidzinski*, 2007 MBQB 138, but see *contra R. v. Kea*, 2005 CanLII 45973 (Ont. S.C.J.).

77   See *R. v. Perron*, above note 13, and *Smith v. Jones*, above note 24.

78   *General Accident Assurance Co. v. Chrusz* (1999), 180 D.L.R. (4th) 241 at 282 (Ont. C.A.).

79   See the discussion by Doherty J.A., *ibid.* at 282–85.

80   R.J. Sharpe, "Claiming Privilege in the Discovery Process" in Law Society of Upper Canada Special Lectures, *Law in Transition: Evidence* (Toronto: De Boo, 1984) at 165.

greater disclosure both in civil cases and on the part of the Crown in criminal cases. Therefore, under the rules of civil procedure in a number of jurisdictions, the plaintiff in the scenario above would have to disclose the identity of witnesses contacted.[81] The other side is free to go and contact the witnesses—there is no privilege in witnesses. However, the signed statement obtained by the investigator and now in the possession of the plaintiff's lawyer is protected by litigation privilege.

Litigation privilege is less "sacred" than solicitor-client privilege. In the words of one court, "Litigation privilege does not enjoy such a place on the altar of the proper administration of justice."[82] The zone of privacy sought to be protected through litigation privilege is narrower. *R. v. Uppal* underscores this point.[83] Individuals being tried separately for the same offence as Uppal were given copies of witness statements that Uppal had secured when preparing his defence. The trial judge reasoned that the witness statements could assist these individuals in defending themselves when cross-examining these witnesses and that their disclosure would not prejudice Uppal. This was enough to override litigation privilege even though a solicitor-client privilege could not have been set aside using such reasoning. One final point: litigation privilege requires an adversarial process. In *Hudson Bay Mining and Smelting Co. v. Cummings* the Manitoba Court of Appeal found that litigation privilege did not attach to transcripts of interviews conducted by Crown counsel in preparation for an inquest.[84] The court ruled that an inquest is a fact-finding, non-adversarial proceeding, where the Crown counsel acts impartially in the public interest. There was, therefore, no need for counsel to have a zone of privacy.

3.2)   The Dominant Purpose Test

Litigation party privilege attaches to information obtained by the solicitor or the agent for the solicitor from third persons, if made for the purpose of litigation either commenced or anticipated. The leading case is *Waugh v. British Railways Board*.[85] The plaintiff's husband was employed by the defendant board and he died in a collision between two

---

81   See, for example, Ontario, *Rules of Civil Procedure*, R.R.O. 1990, Reg. 194, r. 31.06(2).

82   *Llewellyn v. Carter*, 2008 PESCAD 12 at para. 25. See also *Davis v. MacKenzie*, 2008 NBCA 85.

83   *R. v. Uppal*, [2003] B.C.J. No. 2480 (S.C.).

84   *Hudson Bay Mining and Smelting Co. v. Cummings*, 2006 MBCA 98.

85   [1980] A.C. 521 (H.L.). For a similar example of where "labelling" is not determinative of the purpose see *Gallant v. Capital Health Region*, 2004 BCSC 1107, where a nurse made note of an incident primarily to cleanse her conscience, but

locomotives. As was common practice, an internal report was prepared for the board. The head of the report contained the wording: "For the information of the board's solicitor: This form is to be used by every person reporting an occurrence when litigation by or against the B.R.B. is anticipated." The defendant board claimed privilege over the report and refused to make it available to the plaintiff. In the circumstances, it is clear that the report really had two purposes: (1) railway operation and safety, and (2) obtaining legal advice in anticipation of litigation. In order to determine whether the report was privileged, the House of Lords canvassed a variety of tests. At the time, the High Court of Australia approved the "sole purpose test."[86] This test provides the widest amount of disclosure. A document will only be privileged when its "sole purpose" is for litigation or anticipated litigation. In *Waugh*, using this test, the report obviously would have to be disclosed. A second test is that of the "dominant purpose." Under this test a document may be prepared with more than one purpose in mind, but the "dominant purpose" must be that of litigation before the privilege will attach. A third test is that of a "substantial purpose." Under this test, the obtaining of information in anticipation of litigation may be a purpose, but need not be the main, primary, or dominant purpose for preparing the document. So long as litigation either anticipated or commenced is a "substantial purpose," the document is privileged. This test provides the widest net for privilege and results in the least disclosure of information. Arguably, if this test were applied in *Waugh*, the report would be privileged. The House of Lords accepted the "dominant purpose" test and, in the case on appeal, notwithstanding the wording of the form, the Court ruled that the report was not prepared with the dominant purpose of obtaining legal advice in anticipation of litigation and it was to be disclosed to the plaintiff. Dominant purpose is the accepted test in Canada.[87]

3.3) The Status of Copies

An unresolved issue concerns the status of copies of otherwise public or non-privileged documents. If the originals are not privileged, should the copies, now in the lawyer's brief, be privileged? This issue was al-

---

on the advice of her nurse manager marked the note, "Confidential in Anticipation of Litigation."

86   *Grant v. Downs* (1976), 135 C.L.R. 674 (H.C.A.). In *Esso Australia Resources Ltd. v. The Commissioner of Taxation* (1999), 74 A.L.J.R. 339 (H.C.A.) the Court adopted the "dominant purpose test."

87   See *Blank v. Canada (Minister of Justice)*, above note 24 at para. 60.

luded to in *Blank*, but was left for another day as it was not explicitly argued or raised in the appeal.[88]

There are two general responses, well reflected in the decision *Hodgkinson v. Simms*.[89] The majority in that case found the copies to be privileged, largely premised on the principle that counsel need to be able to prepare the case in confidence that the information they collect will be protected. The dissent, citing the trend towards greater disclosure, would not protect copies, where the originals would not be protected. This issue, however, should not be dealt with in an "all or nothing" fashion. *Regional Municipality of Ottawa-Carleton v. Consumers' Gas Ltd.* provides a good example. In that case one side sought disclosure from the other of (1) corporate search records, which contained the names of officers and servants of the corporations, and (2) copies of articles and papers, the result of literature searches conducted by counsel.[90] The Ontario Divisional Court held both were privileged, yet really these are two very different types of materials and should be dealt with differently. As a matter of principle, copies of documents, merely collected or gathered by the lawyer for potential use in the litigation, should not be privileged. That would include the corporate search results above. For example, the lawyer speaks to a witness, who immediately after the accident wrote a statement down as a memory aid. The lawyer copies the statement. The original is not privileged, nor should the copy be. If the witness simply gave the statement over to the lawyer, and no copying was involved, the statement would have to be disclosed. In this instance the lawyer is acting as a collector of information. Other copies flow from the research, skill, and knowledge on the part of the lawyer. Legal research is a classic example. The legal cases that are reviewed, selected, copied, and highlighted reach into the lawyer's mind and go to reveal the lawyer's case theory. That would include the literature search results above in *Consumers' Gas*. Unlike the corporate search documents, these ought to be privileged. This approach respects the principles underlying the need for a "zone of privacy."[91] The following is an apt statement of principle to be applied:

> I think that the result in any such case depends on the manner in which the copy or extract is made or obtained. If it involves a selective

---

88   *Ibid.* at para. 64.
89   (1988), 55 D.L.R. (4th) 577 (B.C.C.A.). This debate was also raised, but not resolved, in *General Accident Assurance Co. v. Chrusz*, above note 78.
90   Above note 72.
91   For a discussion on this issue, see *Edgar v. Auld* (2000), 184 D.L.R. (4th) 747 (N.B.C.A.), and *General Accident Assurance Co. v. Chrusz*, above note 78.

copying or results from research or the exercise of skill and knowledge on the part of the solicitor, then I consider privilege should
apply . . . . Otherwise, I see no reason, in principle, why disclosure
should be refused of copies of documents which can be obtained
elsewhere, and in respect of which no relationship of confidence, or
legal professional privilege exists.[92]

In *Blank*, Justice Fish gave a judicial nod of approval to this approach:
"Extending the privilege to the gathering of documents resulting from
research or the exercise of skill and knowledge does appear to be more
consistent with the rationale and purpose of the litigation privilege."[93]

3.4)   The Implied Undertaking Rule

Documents disclosed on discovery are not free to be used by the receiving party for purposes other than the present litigation. For example, the receiving party is not free to disclose the documents to the
public—unless those documents are revealed in open court; nor may
they use the documents in other litigation. Documents exchanged on
discovery are subject to an "implied undertaking" that they are for use
only in the present action.[94] The rationale for the implied undertaking
rule is twofold.[95] First, the discovery process in civil cases amounts to
a state-sanctioned invasion of privacy. Litigants are compelled by the
rules of civil procedure to reveal documents and to answer questions
in discovery. Therefore, the courts limit the use of the compelled information to the particular litigation. Second, by assuring litigants that
the information they provide will not be used in collateral matters encourages more complete and candid discovery. Essentially, the implied
undertaking rule means that "whatever is disclosed in the discovery
room stays in the discovery room unless eventually revealed in the
courtroom or disclosed by judicial order."[96]

---

92   *Nickmar Pty. Ltd.* v. *Preservatrice Skandia Insurance Ltd.* (1985), 3 N.S.W.L.R. 44
     at 61–62 (S.C.), Wood J. as quoted in *General Accident Assurance Co.* v. *Chrusz,*
     above note 78 at 287.

93   *Blank* v. *Canada (Minister of Justice),* above note 24 at para. 64. In *Blank,* it was
     stated that the Ontario Court of Appeal in *Chrusz* rejected the above approach
     (para. 63). Such is not the case. *Chrusz* is a lengthy decision involving three dif-
     ferent judgments and there was no plurality on this issue. See *Ontario (Ministry
     of Correctional Services)* v. *Goodis,* 2008 CanLII 2603 at para. 61 (Ont. Div. Ct.).

94   For a summary on implied undertakings and the leading cases from across
     Canada, see R.L. Buckler, "Expressing the Implied Undertaking Rule" (1998) 56
     The Advocate 35.

95   *Juman* v. *Doucette,* 2008 SCC 8.

96   *Ibid.* at para. 25.

This rule is found under common law and under the court rules in Manitoba, Ontario, and Prince Edward Island. The undertaking is made to the court, and the sanction for a breach is contempt. A party who seeks to make use of the disclosed documents for other purposes may make a motion to the court seeking leave to do so. Before granting relief from the undertaking, the court must be satisfied "that the interests of justice outweigh any prejudice that would result to a party who disclosed evidence."[97] The applicant, who seeks relief against an implied undertaking, must demonstrate on a balance of probabilities the existence of a public interest of greater weight than the values the implied undertaking rule is designed to protect, namely privacy and the efficient conduct of civil litigation.[98]

In balancing of the above competing interests the Supreme Court of Canada in *Juman v. Doucette* outlined the following guides:

- The implied undertaking rule is, of course, not absolutely protected, but should not be too readily set aside.
- It is important to identify the competing values at stake in the particular case. For example, concerns over public safety may well trump the implied undertaking rule. On the other hand, concerns over self-incrimination speak to the need for greater protection.
- Prejudice to the parties should be considered. Where discovery material in one action is sought to be used in another action with the same or similar parties and the same or similar issues the prejudice to the litigant is "virtually non-existent and leave will generally be granted." On the other hand, courts have generally not favoured attempts to use the discovered material for extraneous purposes or for actions wholly unrelated to the original proceeding.[99]
- The implied undertaking rule ought not to shield contradictory testimony. "An undertaking implied by the court (or imposed by the legislature) to make civil litigation more effective should not permit a witness to play games with the administration of justice."[100]

An open issue is whether there is a similar implied undertaking rule to cover information disclosed by the Crown to the defence in criminal proceedings. For example, assume that an accused is charged

---

97 Ontario, *Rules of Civil Procedure*, above note 81, r. 30.1.01 (8).

98 *Juman v. Doucette*, above note 95 at para. 32.

99 See, for example, *Goodman v. Rossi* (1995), 24 O.R. (3d) 359 (C.A.).

100 *Juman v. Doucette*, above note 95 at para. 41. Under the various provincial statutes, the implied undertaking rule does not prohibit the use of evidence to impeach the testimony of a witness. See, for example, Ontario, *Rules of Civil Procedure*, above note 81, r. 30.1.01(6).

with sexual assault. The Crown is required by law to disclose all relevant information in its possession to the defence. Included in the disclosed material are a number of statements made by the complainant to investigators. The accused is acquitted at trial. The accused now brings an action in defamation against the complainant and wants to use the statements she gave to investigators. May he do so? The Ontario Court of Appeal examined this issue in *P.(D.) v. Wagg* without deciding it.[101] Justice Rosenberg made a number of observations:

- That the civil "implied undertaking rule" under common law or statute does not apply to criminal disclosure because the rule is concerned with compulsion through the civil discovery process.
- That a guiding principle is that because a party is given access to and use of documents for a particular purpose there is necessarily an implication that they will not be used for any other purpose.
- That there are important policy reasons for recognizing an implied undertaking rule with respect to disclosure of materials to the defence in a criminal case. Notably there is concern that highly personal information about third parties is made available to the defence.
- That, whilst it is true, third parties must accept intrusion in the interests of achieving a proper result in the criminal case, the law should provide them with some reasonable protection against use of the information for entirely different purposes.
- That the disclosing bodies, namely the Crown and police, be given notice so that they may resist any production if necessary.
- That where one party is in possession of the Crown brief material, fairness generally dictates that it be produced to the other side.
- That any information that was used in court should generally be produced, subject to special concerns (such as confidential medical records).

Without deciding the issue the court has provided valuable guidelines. As noted by Justice Rosenberg, Great Britain has codified the implied undertaking rule in criminal proceedings.[102] Certainly he sees the value of recognizing the same in Canada. Courts do seem to be moving in that direction.[103]

---

101 (2004), 184 C.C.C. (3d) 321 (Ont. C.A.).
102 *Criminal Procedure and Investigations Act 1996* (U.K.), 1996, c. 25, s. 17.
103 See *Wong v. Antunes*, 2009 BCCA 278; *R. v. Basi*, 2011 BCSC 314.

4. SPOUSAL PRIVILEGE

> *No husband is compellable to disclose any communication made to*
> *him by his wife during their marriage, and no wife is compellable*
> *to disclose any communication made to her by her husband during*
> *their marriage.*

At common law, spouses were not competent to testify because of their interest in the case. Therefore, the issue of a spousal privilege, which would allow a spouse to refuse to answer questions that would reveal communications made between spouses, really did not arise. This situation changed in the mid- and late 1800s, when spouses were made competent and compellable by legislation. Accompanying this legislation was the creation of a spousal privilege. The privilege is provided for in subsection 4(3) of the *Canada Evidence Act*, which reads:

> No husband is compellable to disclose any communication made to
> him by his wife during their marriage, and no wife is compellable
> to disclose any communication made to her by her husband during
> their marriage.

The various provincial Evidence Acts contain a similar provision.[104] In Alberta the legislation includes communications between "adult interdependent partners"; presumably this covers common law relationships.[105] The Alberta move is a questionable expansion of the privilege (see below).

It is important to separate competency from privilege. The former may prevent the person from testifying at all; with the latter, the person must testify but may refuse to answer certain questions under the claim of privilege. At times, courts mix the two. The Quebec Court of Appeal did so in *R. v. St-Jean*.[106] The accused was charged with incest, and this charge made his wife a competent and compellable witness for the prosecution under subsection 4(2) of the *Canada Evidence Act*. The wife, while testifying, sought privilege from answering a question as to something said to her by her husband. The court held that "in cases where a spouse is competent and compellable, he or she may testify about *all* aspects of the case." With respect, this ruling fails to separate

---

104 See British Columbia, *Evidence Act*, s. 8; *Manitoba Evidence Act*, s. 8; New Brunswick, *Evidence Act*, s. 10; Newfoundland and Labrador, *Evidence Act*, s. 6; Nova Scotia, *Evidence Act*, s. 49; Ontario, *Evidence Act*, s. 11; Prince Edward Island, *Evidence Act*, s. 9; Saskatchewan, *The Evidence Act*, s. 7.

105 *Alberta Evidence Act*, s. 8.

106 (1976), 34 C.R.N.S. 378 (Que. C.A.).

competency from privilege. The rendering of a spouse competent to testify should not sweep aside the privilege.

The decision of the Ontario Court of Appeal in *R. v. Zylstra* is to be preferred.[107] Prior to calling the spouse of the accused, the defence sought an advance ruling as to whether the spouse could assert privilege under subsection 4(3) of the *Canada Evidence Act*. The Ontario Court of Appeal held that the privilege could be asserted, but that it would have to be asserted in the presence of the jury; otherwise, the jury could well be confused as to why the Crown was not pursuing certain obvious lines of cross-examination. The court also held that when the privilege was asserted, then a special instruction was called for. The court was not prepared to lay down any hard-and-fast rule, but suggested that the following instruction was a minimum requirement:

- The privilege in s. 4(3) is a statutory privilege which all legally married witnesses are entitled to assert in a trial; and
- The privilege is one that belongs to the witness, not the accused person, and, as such, the decision whether to assert or waive the privilege lies with the witness, not the accused.

A number of rationales have been put forth to justify spousal privilege: it preserves harmony between the spouses; it encourages the sharing of confidences between spouses; and it is suggested that the invasion of private marital communications is an indelicate undertaking not to be sanctioned. None of these justifications are particularly compelling. The question better asked is: If there were no privilege, would marital communications or marital harmony be inhibited? There is little evidence to suggest that they would. For this reason, spousal privilege has been abolished in England for both civil and criminal cases.[108] Canada should do the same.[109]

However, in Canada, the statutory privilege still stands. It protects communications made "during the marriage." Pre-marriage and post-marriage communications are not protected.[110] Moreover, the privilege, unlike that for solicitor-client, ends with the marriage. Simply put, the

---

107   *R. v. Zylstra* (1995), 41 C.R. (4th) 130 (Ont. C.A.).
108   *Civil Evidence Act 1968* (U.K.), 1968, c. 64, s. 16(3), and *Police and Criminal Evidence Act 1984* (U.K.), 1984, c. 60, s. 80(9).
109   See chapter 10, section 3, "The Competency and Compellability of Spouses" for a further discussion on this point. See as well L. Stuessser, "Abolish Spousal Incompetency" (2007) 49 Crim. R. (6th) 49.
110   See *R. v. Couture*, [2007] S.C.J. No. 28 at para. 41, where the Court held that communications made prior to a marriage would not be privileged.

statute applies to a "husband" and "wife"; it does not apply to widows/widowers or divorcees.

The statute also protects "any communication." This wording raises a number of issues. Consider the following problem:

The accused is charged with the murder of his twelve-year-old niece. At breakfast on the day of the murder, the accused told his wife that he was going over to his sister's house after work. His wife observed him return home at around 6:00 p.m. His clothes were covered in blood. He immediately went to the laundry room and washed his clothes. He told her, "I killed Sally [the niece], but don't tell anyone." The wife is a competent and compellable witness under subsection 4(4) of the *Canada Evidence Act*. Is there privilege over what she was told at the breakfast table? Over what she observed? Over her husband's confession?

Solicitor-client privilege and other privileges are intended to protect "confidential" communications. The breakfast table statement is an ordinary statement and, when made, certainly was not intended to be confidential. Other family members may well have been seated around the table at the time. Wigmore was of the view that the essence of spousal privilege, like other privileges, was to protect confidences only.[111] But the statute does not confine the privilege to "confidential communications," and there is authority that "any communication" means exactly that and protects all spousal communications whether intended to be confidential or not.[112]

Can the wife be compelled to testify to what she observed? "Communication," as we have seen for hearsay statements, may include words as well as actions. The Supreme Court of Canada in *Gosselin v. R.* refused to give communication a broad interpretation and held that the section did not make privileged a spouse's observations.[113]

Finally, assuming that the wife was more than prepared to testify to all that she saw and was told by the accused, can the accused claim privilege to prevent her from relating his confession? No. The privilege is held by the spouse receiving the communication and not by the spouse who made it, even though the husband fully expected that his confession would be kept confidential.[114]

---

111 Wigmore, above note 2, s. 2336.
112 *MacDonald v. Bublitz* (1960), 31 W.W.R. 478 (B.C.S.C.).
113 (1903), 33 S.C.R. 255.
114 Lord Reid in *Rumping v. D.P.P.*, above note 18 at 259, stated: "It is a mystery to me why it was decided to give this privilege to the spouse who is a witness." See also *R. v. Couture*, above note 110 at para. 41.

5. SETTLEMENT NEGOTIATION PRIVILEGE

There exists a "class" privilege to protect settlement discussions. The discussions must be made during the course of settlement negotiations, for the purpose of settlement, and are not intended to be disclosed or used against the parties should the negotiations fail. The fundamental purpose underlying the privilege is to encourage settlement. The privilege applies to both civil settlement discussions and criminal resolution discussions. The privilege applies not only to the parties involved in the negotiations, but also protects communications from being disclosed to third parties.

The privilege is subject to exceptions. The starting point is that settlement discussions are privileged. Where the existence of an agreement, or the terms of a settlement are at issue, or the negotiation discussions give rise to a cause of action, the privilege may be overridden. The privilege may also be overridden where there exists a compelling public interest to do so.

5.1) The Nature and Scope of the Privilege

The law of evidence has long accepted a "privilege" for "without prejudice communications" or "settlement discussions." As a general proposition, oral or written communications made during settlement discussions for the purpose of settlement are not admissible in evidence.[115]

The privilege is in place primarily as a matter of public policy to encourage litigants to settle their disputes without the need to go to trial. Communications made for the purpose of settlement are protected from disclosure; otherwise few parties would engage in such settlement discussions for fear that any concessions or statements made could be used against them if no settlement is reached. A second rationale for the rule—occasionally cited—is the express or implied agreement of the parties themselves that communications in the course of their negotiations should not be admissible in evidence.[116]

Most of the leading cases on settlement negotiation privilege involve private civil disputes. However, in principle the public policy

---

115 *I. Waxman & Sons Ltd. v. Texaco Canada Ltd.* (1968), 67 D.L.R. (2d) 295 (Ont. H.C.J.), aff'd (1968), 69 D.L.R. (2d) 543 (Ont. C.A.); *British Columbia Children's Hospital v. Air Products Canada Ltd.* (2003), 224 D.L.R. (4th) 23 (B.C.C.A.).

116 See *Meyers v. Dunphy*, 2007 NLCA 1.

generators for such a privilege apply equally in criminal cases and protection of plea negotiations is well recognized in criminal cases.[117]

There is some uncertainty as to the exact form of the privilege. The prevailing view is that settlement discussions are caught by a blanket "class" privilege and that discussions made during and for the purpose of settlement are *prima facie* privileged.[118] A counter position is that a privilege for settlement discussions falls to be decided on a "case-by-case" basis. In other words, the party seeking the protection of the privilege would need to show that the communications ought to be privileged given the particular case.[119] The case-by-case approach requires a balancing of the need for the disclosure of the communications versus the detrimental effects that could befall the negotiating parties.

A class privilege is the preferred approach. First, it provides, as a starting point, the greatest protection in accordance with the public policy interest to encourage settlement. The party seeking disclosure has to convince the court to override the privilege. Second, it complies with the parameters set by the Supreme Court of Canada for the recognition of a class privilege. In *R. v. Gruenke*, Chief Justice Lamer observed that a class privilege would only be appropriate where the protected communications "are essential to the effective operation of the legal system" and that "such communications are inextricably linked with the very system which desires the disclosure of the communication."[120] Arguably these essentials hold true for settlement discussions. Without settlement the administration of justice would be brought to an overburdened halt. Third, a blanket privilege provides greater certainty in application.

The privilege will be recognized when three preconditions exist:

1) A litigious dispute must be in existence or within contemplation;
2) The communication must be made with the express or implied intention that it would not be disclosed to the Court in the event that negotiations failed.
3) The purpose of the communication must be to attempt to effect a settlement.[121]

---

117 See, for example, *R. v. Bernardo*, [1994] O.J. No. 1718 (Gen. Div.); *R. v. Delorme* (2005), 198 C.C.C. (3d) 431 (N.W.T.S.C.); *R. v. Lake*, [1997] O.J. No. 5447 (Gen. Div.); *Forest Protection Ltd. v. Bayer A.G.* (1998), 84 C.P.R. (3d) 187 at para. 24 (N.B.C.A.).

118 *Middelkamp v. Fraser Valley Real Estate Board* (1992), 96 D.L.R. (4th) 227 (B.C.C.A.); *Brown v. Cape Breton (Regional Municipality)*, 2011 NSCA 32.

119 "Case-by-Case" privilege is discussed in section 6 of this chapter.

120 Above note 3 at para. 32.

121 *Meyers v. Dunphy*, above note 116 at para. 12, quoting from J. Sopinka, S. Lederman, & A. Bryant, *The Law of Evidence in Canada*, 2d ed. (Markham, ON: Butterworths, 1999) at para. 14.207.

The use or overuse of the phrase "without prejudice" is not required nor is it conclusive.[122] The substance and context of the communication has to be considered. For example, in *Histed v. Law Society of Manitoba* correspondence was exchanged between lawyers as to the appointment of a case management judge. In one of the letters the lawyer made disparaging remarks about a number of judges. The phrase "Strictly Confidential and Without Prejudice" was written on the top of the letter in question. The lawyer in receipt of the letter forwarded it on to the Law Society. At the disciplinary hearing the lawyer who wrote the offending letter claimed settlement privilege. The Court of Appeal gave short shrift to this argument and found that the letter was about process and had nothing to do with settlement.[123]

The privilege applies not only to the parties involved in the negotiations; preventing one from using admissions made against the other. It also protects communications from being revealed to third parties.[124] Take the common situation where plaintiff A sues two separate defendants B and C. A settles with B. C now seeks disclosure of the agreement and relevant admissions made between A and B. The privilege protects the communications between A and B and it also protects the disclosure of the completed settlement.[125]

5.2) Overriding the Privilege

The onus lies on the party seeking disclosure of communications otherwise caught under settlement privilege to prove an exception. Settlement privilege is not as sacrosanct a privilege as solicitor-client privilege. It is not considered a substantive rule of law or a fundamental civil right.[126]

Having said this, it is also the case that there exists a compelling public interest in the encouragement of settlement; hence the recognition of a class privilege in the first place. Therefore, in order to override the privilege, a compelling case needs to be made. "An applicant for disclosure will have to demonstrate that there are compelling policy

---

122 *TDL Group Ltd. v. Zabco Holdings Inc.*, 2008 MBQB 86.

123 *Histed v. Law Society of Manitoba*, 2007 MBCA 150 at para. 33 (C.A.), leave to appeal to S.C.C. refused, [2008] S.C.C.A. No. 67.

124 See, for example, *Middelkamp v. Fraser Valley Real Estate Board*, above note 118.

125 Final settlements are protected in British Columbia and Nova Scotia, but there are *contra* decisions in Manitoba and Alberta. See *Dos Santos v. Sun Life Assurance Co. of Canada* (2005), 249 D.L.R. (4th) 416 at para. 15 (B.C.C.A.); and *Brown v. Cape Breton (Regional Municipality)*, above note 118.

126 *Histed v. Law Society of Manitoba*, above note 123 at para. 35.

reasons to invoke an exception to the general rule."[127] The result is that exceptions are "narrowly defined and seldom applied."[128]

A key factor will be the relevancy and use to be put of the communications sought. The public policy basis of the rule is to prevent anything said in settlement negotiations being relied upon as an admission against their maker. Simply put, the privilege protects admissions.[129] Accordingly, throughout the case law, when a settlement communication is sought to be produced in order to be used to the prejudice of its maker, the courts have been vigilant to see that the communication is protected.[130]

On the other hand, where the communication sought is not to be used against its maker and there is little or no prejudice, then the compelling public policy purpose underlying the rule is not triggered and courts are more inclined to override the privilege. For example, in *R. v. Bernardo*, Justice Lesage ordered the production of negotiation communications between the Crown and the key Crown witness in the case, Karla Homolka. In the circumstances, the information sought was not going to be used against her in any subsequent prosecution. She was already sentenced for her involvement in the murders and was no longer at any risk of prejudice.[131]

Some case authority seems to suggest that relevancy standing alone is enough to found an exception to the privilege. It is argued that communications are admissible if they are being introduced for any relevant purpose other than as an admission against the negotiating parties.[132] Relevancy is too low a threshold.[133] All privileges result in the loss of otherwise relevant evidence. In addition to relevancy, the party seeking to override the privilege must establish "that admission of the otherwise privileged communications is necessary, either to achieve the agreement of the parties to the settlement, or to address a compelling or overriding interest of justice."[134]

---

127 *Heritage Duty Free Shop v. Canada (Attorney General)*, 2005 BCCA 188 at para. 31.
128 *Ibid.* at para. 25.
129 See, for example, *Unilever plc v. The Proctor & Gamble Co*, [2001] 1 All E.R. 783 (C.A.).
130 See, for example, *R. v. Lake*, above note 117. *Lake* was a case involving potential prejudice to an accused. Similarly, courts recognize that prejudice may also inure to the Crown. See *R. v. Steinhoff*, [2003] O.J. No. 3398 (Ct. J.); *R. v. Bernard*, 2002 ABQB 747.
131 Above note 117.
132 See *Muller v. Linsley & Mortimer*, [1996] P.N.L.R. 74 (C.A.).
133 *Dos Santos v. Sun Life Assurance Co. of Canada*, above note 125 at para. 21.
134 *Meyers v. Dunphy*, above note 116 at para. 26.

The case law recognizes a number of exceptions. In *Meyers v. Dunphy*, the following were cited as "established exceptions":[135]

1. whether without prejudice communications have resulted in a concluded compromise agreement;
2. to show that an agreement apparently concluded between the parties during negotiations should be set aside on the ground of misrepresentation, fraud, or undue influence;
3. where a clear statement made by one party to negotiations, and on which the other party is intended to act and does in fact act, may be admissible as giving rise to an estoppel;
4. if the exclusion of the evidence would act as a cloak for perjury, blackmail, or other unambiguous impropriety, but such an exception should only be applied in the clearest cases of abuse of a privileged occasion;
5. in order to explain delay or apparent acquiescence in responding to an application to strike out a proceeding for want of prosecution but use of the letters is to be limited to the fact that such letters have been written and the dates at which they were written;
6. whether the claimant had acted reasonably to mitigate his loss in his conduct and conclusion of negotiations for the compromise of proceedings brought by him; and
7. where an offer is expressly made "without prejudice except as to costs."

The listed exceptions should not be applied in a mechanistic way; rather, they should be analyzed in light of the purpose and principles underlying the rule.[136] In *Meyers v. Dunphy* at issue was a missed limitation period. The plaintiff sought to introduce settlement negotiations as an acknowledgment of a cause of action, which would act to reset the limitation clock and allow the action to proceed. The court refused to override the privilege and rejected the notion that there exists a "limitation period" exception. Rather, it found that what was being sought to be introduced was an admission against the defendant and absent compelling reasons was not admissible.

There is no definite list of compelling interests such to override the privilege. Certainly, in criminal cases accused persons can rely upon the need to make full answer and defence.[137] Nor is the privilege intended to protect threats made, unlawful and abusive communications,

---

135 *Ibid.* at para. 20. This list was taken from Lord Walker's judgment in *Unilever plc v. The Proctor & Gamble Co*, above note 129.

136 *Ibid.* at para. 19.

137 See, for example, *R. v. Delorme*, above note 117.

or to shield perjury. Any privilege is created in the public interest and such communications are contrary to that public interest.[138]

Dos Santos v. Sun Life Assurance provides a good example of the law at work.[139] The plaintiff reached a mediated settlement for injuries arising from a car accident. Sun Life provided long-term disability benefits to the plaintiff and had a subrogated claim to monies recovered. A global settlement sum was revealed. Sun Life wanted to know the portion attributed to long-term disability. The plaintiff claimed privilege over the settlement discussions and break down of the global sum. It was accepted that such discussions were caught by settlement privilege. However, an exception to the privilege was found based on the public interest to prevent excessive and unjust enrichment. Moreover, the court went on to consider the "chilling" effect that its decision would have on settlement discussions and found that it would have none. The plaintiff was still receiving her "just" compensation; she was not entitled to an unjust award.

In summary, from the case law there appears to be certain guiding factors in finding an exception. First, if the settlement or discussions surrounding a settlement are at issue, then presumably the privilege does not apply. This is recognized in the first three exceptions in the above list. Second, relevancy and prejudice need to be considered. Where settlement discussions are being introduced as admissions courts are more protective than if the discussions have another relevancy. Where there is potential prejudice to the makers, the courts are more protective of the privilege. Where there is little or no prejudice, there is less need to protect the privilege. Third, there needs to be a compelling public interest to override the protection; the privilege is founded in the public interest and may have to give way to the public interest.

6. "CASE-BY-CASE" PRIVILEGE

Certain communications will be privileged on a "case-by-case" basis using the "Wigmore Four" criteria:

1) *The communications must originate in a confidence that they will not be disclosed.*

2) *This element of confidentiality must be essential to the full and satisfactory maintenance of the relation between the parties.*

---

138 *R. v. Legato* (2002), 172 C.C.C. (3d) 415 (Que. C.A.) — the privilege could not be used to shield perjury.

139 Above note 125.

3) *The relation must be one which in the opinion of the community ought to be sedulously fostered.*

4) *The injury that would inure to the relation by the disclosure of the communications must be greater than the benefit thereby gained for the correct disposal of litigation.*

Claims for privilege are made by professionals of all kinds—journalists, accountants, clerics, physicians, psychiatrists, social workers, counsellors, mediators—and, at times, others in non-professional relationships seek to protect certain confidences, such as those between a parent and a son or daughter.[140] For the most part, the courts have resisted these claims of privilege, fundamentally because expansion of privilege results in the loss of much valued evidence.

The Supreme Court of Canada has made it abundantly clear that creation of new "class" privileges by the courts will be rare indeed; if new class privileges are created it will be through legislative action. In *R. v. Gruenke*, the Court refused to recognize a new class privilege for religious communications.[141] Chief Justice Lamer, for the majority, wrote:

> As I have mentioned, a *prima facie* privilege for religious communications would constitute an exception to the general principle that all relevant evidence is admissible. Unless it can be said that the policy reasons to support a class privilege for religious communications are as compelling as the policy reasons which underlay the class privilege for solicitor-client communications, there is no basis for departing from the fundamental "first principle" that all relevant evidence is admissible until proven otherwise.[142]

On the other hand, the Court was prepared to recognize privileges on a "case-by-case" basis, an approach to privilege first alluded to by the Supreme Court in *Slavutych v. Baker*.[143] Determination of privilege in a given case was to be guided by Wigmore's four criteria:

1) The communications must originate in a *confidence* that they will not be disclosed.

2) This element of *confidentiality must be essential* to the full and satisfactory maintenance of the relation between the parties.

---

140   See *People v. Fitzgerald*, 422 N.Y.S. 2d 309 (Co. Ct. 1979).

141   Above note 3. By statute in Newfoundland and Labrador and Quebec, there is a privilege for clergy: Newfoundland and Labrador, *Evidence Act*, s. 8; Quebec, *Charter of human rights and freedoms*, R.S.Q. c. C-12, s. 9.

142   *R. v. Gruenke*, ibid. at 386.

143   (1975), 38 C.R.N.S. 306 (S.C.C.).

3) The *relation* must be one which in the opinion of the community ought to be sedulously *fostered*.
4) The *injury* that would inure to the relation by the disclosure of the communications must be *greater than the benefit* thereby gained for the correct disposal of litigation.

In *M.(A.) v. Ryan* the Supreme Court went through all four of the Wigmore criteria, and the decision is instructive as it sheds light on how to apply those criteria.[144] The defendant, Dr. Ryan, had been the plaintiff's psychiatrist. The plaintiff was seventeen years old at the time. In the course of treatment, Dr. Ryan had sexual relations with her. Arising from these acts, he was convicted of indecent assault. The plaintiff brought a civil action. She alleged that his conduct caused her severe mental distress and anguish, and left her with lasting psychological and emotional trauma. Dr. Ryan did not deny the sexual activity but still contended that it was consensual and in any event did not cause the emotional or psychological trauma as alleged. The plaintiff went to see another psychiatrist, and she was very concerned about keeping her communications with her new psychiatrist confidential. During the examination for discovery of the plaintiff, the defendant requested production of the second psychiatrist's records and notes. The claim of psychiatrist-patient privilege was raised.

At the initial lower court hearing, the Master found that the communications did not originate in confidence because both the plaintiff and her psychiatrist recognized that notwithstanding their desire for confidentiality, the record of their sessions might someday be ordered by a court to be disclosed. In other words, they recognized that their communications could not be absolutely protected. Justice McLachlin, writing for the majority, found that the mere possibility that the communications might have to be divulged did not change the fact that they were made in confidence. Absolute protection could not be given and was not required.

Turning to whether the element of confidentiality was essential to the relationship, the psychiatrist's evidence established both that confidentiality was essential to the psychiatrist-patient relation in general, and that it was particularly necessary in order to assist the plaintiff. That the relation ought to be sedulously fostered was accepted by the Court with the following observation: "The mental health of the citizenry, no less than its physical health, is a public good of great importance."[145]

---

144 (1997), 143 D.L.R. (4th) 1 (S.C.C.).
145 *Ibid.* at 11.

In terms of the fourth requirement—that the injury to the relation caused by the disclosure must be greater than the benefit gained by the correct disposal of litigation—Justice McLachlin observed that the balancing involved not only the short-term interests of the specific parties, but the long-term injury to the professional relationship in general. This is important because in certain instances, the particular psychiatrist-patient relationship may have already come to an end and there is no longer a need to protect that specific relationship. Nevertheless, the profession has an interest, and other patients have a continuing interest, to see that their communications are protected. Justice McLachlin wrote:

> The interests served by non-disclosure must extend to any effect on society of the failure of individuals to obtain treatment restoring them to healthy and contributing members of society. Finally, the interests served by protection from disclosure must include the privacy interest of the person claiming privilege and inequalities which may be perpetuated by the absence of protection.[146]

The interests sought to be protected were also to reflect *Charter* values, the right to privacy under section 8, and the right under section 15 of every person to equal treatment and benefit of the law.

On the other side of the equation, the need to find the truth in litigation before the court, Justice McLachlin wrote:

> It follows that if the court considering a claim for privilege determines that a particular document or class of documents must be produced to get at the truth and prevent an unjust verdict, it must permit production to the extent required to avoid that result.[147]

Justice McLachlin went on to note that the interest in disclosure by a defendant in a civil case is less compelling than the interest of an accused in a criminal case: "The defendant in a civil suit stands to lose money and repute; the accused in a criminal proceeding stands to lose his or her very liberty."[148] The result is that a privilege is less likely to be protected in a criminal case, and that in the vast majority of criminal cases the public interest in the correct disposal of charges will prevail.

Letourneau v. Clearbrook Iron Works Ltd. is a rare example where a case-by-case privilege was found.[149] The case involved an alleged infringement of patent. The defendant wanted to examine the plaintiff/inventor about conversations that he may have had with his common

---

146 *Ibid.*
147 *Ibid.* at 12.
148 *Ibid.* at 14.
149 *Letourneau v. Clearbrook Iron Works Ltd.*, [2004] F.C.J. No. 1796 (F.C.).

law partner about his invention. The plaintiff claimed privilege. Spousal privilege was not applicable. The judge turned to case-by-case privilege and found that one existed. Of note is that the evidence sought to be obtained was "exceedingly marginal" versus the potential injury to the couple's long-standing relationship. Given the rather tenuous relevancy, if any, of the information to be had the result seems sound.

Finally, should the balancing of competing interests favour disclosure, then the court should consider whether or not full disclosure is necessary. Partial disclosure may achieve the ends of justice. It is open to the courts to limit the number of documents to be disclosed, edit out non-essential material, and impose conditions on those who may see and have access to the materials. At the end of the day in *Ryan*, this is precisely what the Supreme Court of Canada ordered. The psychiatrist's notes and records of consultations with the plaintiff were to be disclosed, but not the psychiatrist's notes to herself. Conditions were attached: Dr. Ryan could not see the materials; inspection was confined to the defendant's solicitors and expert witnesses; copies were not to be made; and disclosure to other people was not permitted.

Ryan underscores the problem with the case-by-case approach in that it sacrifices certainty. Individuals involved in confidential relationships are not able to predict whether their communications will or will not be protected. Uncertainty of protection makes any privilege precarious. For example, in *Ryan*, notwithstanding that the plaintiff could demonstrate a "compelling interest in protecting the communications," they were ordered to be disclosed. It is interesting to note that the Supreme Court of the United States in *Jaffee v. Redmond*, a case decided a few months before *Ryan*, accepted a "class" or "absolute" privilege for psychotherapist-patient communications.[150] In so doing, the majority of the Court rejected any notion of case-by-case or "*ad hoc*" privilege as being little better than no privilege at all.

In response to *Jaffee v. Redmond*, Justice McLachlin replied:

> I for one cannot accept the proposition that "occasional injustice" should be accepted as the price of the privilege. It is true that the traditional categories of privilege, cast as they are in absolute all-or-nothing terms, necessarily run the risk of occasional injustice. But that does not mean that courts, in invoking new privileges, should lightly condone its extension.[151]

---

150 *Jaffee v. Redmond*, 116 S. Ct. 1923 (1996).
151 *M.(A.) v. Ryan*, above note 22 at 12.

It follows that the Supreme Court of Canada will decline to create any new class privileges. If ever a class privilege were to be recognized, *Ryan* was the case. It involved a clearly identifiable relationship between professional psychiatrist and patient in a context where the need for confidentiality was strong. The message is clear: the Supreme Court of Canada favours flexibility over certainty.

In terms of procedure, the judge is to determine the privilege in a *voir dire* or hearing.[152] The burden rests on the person seeking to exclude the evidence on the basis of privilege. Presumably as part of that hearing, the court will be informed as to the evidence sought to be excluded; otherwise, the court cannot properly weigh the "benefit thereby gained for the correct disposal of litigation." The judge is called upon to consider "the circumstances of the privilege alleged, the documents, and the case."[153] Although it is not essential that the judge examine every document, where necessary to the proper determination of the claim for privilege, examination must be undertaken.[154]

6.1) Journalist-Source Case-by-Case Privilege

In *R. v. National Post* the Supreme Court of Canada recognized that journalist-source privilege is available on a case-by-case basis.[155] The Court applied the Wigmore four and found that the criteria applied equally to the maintenance of the confidentiality of the identity of a source—even though the intent of the source in going to the journalist was to publicize the information provided.

In terms of the third criterion (fostering of the relationship in the public good), the Court noted some flexibility in analysis. The problem being that there is no accreditation of journalists. The Court mused that there may well be a different weighing of a relationship between a source and a blogger as opposed to a source and a professional journalist.

As with most case-by-case privileges, the primary area of contention will be under the fourth criterion, which does "most of the work." The court must weigh the value to the public of the relationship in question against any countervailing public interest, such as the investigation of a particular crime or litigation of a particular matter.[156] In the weighing process suggested areas to consider include:

---

152 *R. v. Gruenke*, above note 3 at 390.
153 *M.(A.) v. Ryan*, above note 22 at 15.
154 *Phillips v. Watson*, 2007 ABCA 144.
155 *R. v. National Post*, 2010 SCC 16. See also *Globe and Mail v. Canada (Attorney General)*, 2010 SCC 41.
156 *R. v. National Post*, ibid. at para. 58.

- "the nature and seriousness of the offence under investigation";[157] (In *National Post* the Crown argued that the existence of any crime vitiated the privilege. The Court rejected that proposition as being too broad.)
- the centrality to the dispute of the evidence sought;
- the potential probative value of the information;
- the type of information sought; (In *National Post* the information sought was physical real evidence as opposed to "compelling" a journalist to disclose a source.)
- the purpose of the investigation; ("There may be circumstances where the criminal investigation appears to be contrived to silence improperly the secret source, and in such cases the court may decline to order production."[158])
- whether the facts, information or testimony are available from another source;[159]
- the degree of public importance of the story and whether the story is already in the public domain.

In *R. v. National Post* it was argued that once the first three criteria were met the onus should shift to the party seeking disclosure to show why on a balance of probabilities that disclosure should be ordered—as opposed to the party seeking to establish the privilege in the first place. The Court gave this argument short shrift. Until the media establish all four criteria no journalist-source privilege arises.

7. PROTECTION OF THIRD-PERSON RECORDS IN CRIMINAL CASES

In criminal cases, the Crown has a duty to turn over to the defence all relevant information in its possession. Third parties are under no such duty. The accused must apply to the court for the production of third-party records. In sexual offence cases, there is a special legislated procedure the accused must comply with before the trial judge orders a complainant or witness to produce specified records to the accused. If the records have already been turned over to the Crown, they are not to be disclosed to the accused unless the

157 *Ibid.* at para. 61.
158 *Ibid.* at para. 62.
159 See *Globe and Mail v. Canada (Attorney General)*, above note 155 at para. 62.

complainant or witness waives their protection or the trial judge orders production.

In a criminal case, the Crown is obliged to disclose to the accused all relevant information that it has in its possession. In the words of Justice Sopinka, "the fruits of the investigation which are in the possession of counsel for the Crown are not the property of the Crown for use in securing a conviction but the property of the public to be used to ensure that justice is done."[160] The threshold of "relevancy" for Crown disclosure is low; if the information is of some use to the defence, then it should be disclosed. The duty to disclose is triggered by a request and does not require an application to the court.[161]

The broad duty of disclosure is premised on two assumptions: (1) that the material in possession of the prosecuting Crown is relevant to the accused's case and (2) that this material will likely comprise the case against the accused. The accused, therefore, has a prevailing interest in obtaining disclosure of all relevant material in the Crown's possession for the purpose of making full answer and defence.[162]

This does not mean that all information that the Crown has must be turned over. The Crown has a discretion to refuse to make disclosure on the grounds that the information sought is clearly irrelevant, privileged or its disclosure is governed by law. Where the Crown exercises this discretion, the Crown bears the burden of satisfying the trial judge that the information is privileged or irrelevant. Any privilege claimed, however, cannot unduly limit the right of the accused to make full answer and defence. In fact, information in the possession of the Crown that is clearly relevant and important to the ability of the accused to raise a defence *must* be disclosed to the accused, regardless of any potential claim of privilege.[163]

The Crown's obligation to disclose to the accused all relevant information applies only to information in the possession or control of the prosecution. In short, "the law cannot impose an obligation on the Crown to disclose material which it does not have or cannot obtain."[164] The disclosure regime attaches to the prosecuting entity; it does not attach to the "Crown" as a whole and other non-involved state agencies or departments.[165] The police, although separate and distinct in law from

---

160 R. v. *Stinchcombe* (1991), 8 C.R. (4th) 277 at 283 (S.C.C.).

161 For an excellent summary of the law see R. v. *McNeil*, 2009 SCC 3.

162 *Ibid.* at para. 20.

163 R. v. *O'Connor* (1995), 44 C.R. (4th) 1 at 18 (S.C.C.).

164 R. v. *McNeil*, above note 161 at para. 22.

165 *Ibid.*

the "Crown," have a corollary duty to disclose to the Crown all relevant information in their possession. In this way, for disclosure purposes the police and Crown are to be regarded as one.[166]

Prior to *R. v. McNeil* the corollary duty on the police applied solely to the "fruits of the investigation" —things discovered or collected by the police while investigating the offence. In *R. v. McNeil* the Supreme Court of Canada extended the reach of this "first party" or *Stinch-combe* disclosure. McNeil was charged and convicted of multiple drug charges. The arresting officer was the Crown's main witness. Prior to sentencing, the accused learned that the arresting officer was facing disciplinary proceedings and criminal charges involving drug-related misconduct on another occasion. The accused sought production of all documents related to the officer's misconduct. The Crown argued that these records were not the "fruits of the investigation" and that to secure them McNeil would have to meet the *O'Connor* test for the disclosure of "third-party" records. The Court reasoned that where the Crown or the police are aware that relevant information exists, they should secure it as part of the investigation. Where police misconduct records of officers playing a material role in an investigation are either related to or could reasonably impact on the case against the accused, then they should be retrieved and treated as "first-party" information and disclosed in accordance with the obligations under *Stinchcombe*. Accordingly, when put on notice of potentially relevant information, Crown counsel are under a "duty to inquire" and obtain the information if it is reasonably feasible to do so.[167]

The scope of "duty to inquire" has yet to be fleshed out. It certainly applies to government records. However, Justice Doherty in *R. v. Darwish* outlined the following parameters:[168]

- an accused does not have a freestanding constitutional right to an adequate investigation of the charges against him or her;
- an accused also does not have a constitutional right to direct the conduct of the criminal investigation of which he or she is the target;
- nor does the disclosure right, as broad as that right is, extend so far as to require the police to investigate potential defences.

Another area of uncertainty concerns the Crown counsel's own "work product" — notes, memoranda, research, observations, and interview records prepared in anticipation of trial. For example, in *R. v.*

---

166 *Ibid.* at para. 25.
167 *Ibid.* at para. 49.
168 *R. v. Darwish*, 2010 ONCA 124, leave to appeal to S.C.C. refused, 2010 CanLII 61140 (S.C.C.).

Bernardo, the Crown was required to turn over to the defence information on the details and negotiations that took place between the Crown and Karla Homolka, which led to her famous (or infamous) plea bargain and partial grant of immunity.[169] The information that needs to be disclosed will certainly depend upon the issues in the case; however, one helpful distinction is to differentiate matters of opinion, such as trial strategy, which would be exempt from disclosure, from matters of fact, such as witness statements, which would need to be disclosed.[170]

Different considerations apply to information in the hands of third parties. These people are strangers to the prosecution and are under no duty to assist the defence—hence the distinction between "first-party" and "third-party" disclosure. Third-party production, unlike Crown disclosure, requires a weighing of competing rights. The accused's right to make full answer and defence must be weighed against the third party's right to privacy. Moreover, requests for production are most commonly raised in sexual offence prosecutions and pertain to information about the complainants, which may be highly personal. These requests raise fundamental concerns about our traditional notions of relevancy, trial fairness, and equality under the law. The law has evolved to the point where there are two regimes for third-party production in criminal cases, the statutory regime in sections 278.1 to 278.91 of the *Criminal Code* which applies in sexual offence cases, and the regime in *R. v. O'Connor* which applies in other cases.[171] *O'Connor* involved a sexual offence prosecution, but provoked the passage of sections 278.1 to 278.91, which has limited its application.

7.1) The Common Law: *R. v. O'Connor*

R. v. O'Connor was the first attempt by the Supreme Court of Canada to strike a balance between an accused's right to full answer and defence and a third party's right to privacy.[172] O'Connor was a former Roman Catholic priest charged with sexual offences committed against former students. The defence sought disclosure of the complainants' entire medical, counselling, and school records. At the time the prosecution did not have any of these records.

---

169 *R. v. Bernardo*, above note 117, Lesage J.

170 See *Report of the Attorney General's Advisory Committee on Charge Screening, Disclosure, and Resolution Discussions* (Ontario: Queen's Printer, 1993) (Chair: G.A. Martin) at 252. This distinction was recognized in *Hudson Bay Mining and Smelting Co. v. Cummings*, above note 83 at paras. 62–63 (C.A.).

171 Above note 163.

172 *Ibid.*

The *O'Connor* Court used constitutional principles to develop a two-step procedure for production of third-party records. In step 1, the accused must convince the trial judge that the information sought is "likely to be relevant." This threshold of proof was termed "significant" but not "onerous." The relevance threshold at this stage was set simply to prevent the defence from engaging in speculative fishing expeditions. "Likely relevant" under *O'Connor* means that there is "a reasonable possibility that the information is logically probative to an issue at trial or the competence of a witness to testify."[173] If the trial judge is satisfied that the information sought is likely to be relevant, then the information is produced to the judge for review. If the information does not meet the necessary threshold of relevance, then the analysis stops and no production order will issue. At this stage, there is no balancing of competing interests or rights. In step 2, the trial judge is to examine the records to determine whether, and to what extent, they should be produced to the accused. It is at this stage that the trial judge is to balance competing interests.

In *R. v. O'Connor* a majority in the Supreme Court went on to find that documents or records provided to the Crown by complainants or other third parties lost any cloak of confidentiality or privilege that might have otherwise applied. The material became "public property," which now needed to be disclosed to the accused.[174]

The procedure to be followed in an *O'Connor* application is as follows:[175]

1) The accused first obtains a *subpoena duces tecum* under sections 698(1) and 700(1) of the *Criminal Code* and serves it on the third-party record holder. The subpoena compels the person to whom it is directed to attend court with the targeted records or materials.

2) The accused also brings an application, supported by appropriate affidavit evidence, showing that the records sought are likely to be relevant in his or her trial. Notice of the application is given to the prosecuting Crown, the person who is the subject of the records and any other person who may have a privacy interest in the records targeted for production.

---

173   *R. v. McNeil*, above note 161 at para. 33.

174   As will be seen below in this chapter, legislation has reversed this holding in *O'Connor* as it applies to sexual offences — delivery of documents or records to the Crown by a sexual offence complainant or third party in a sexual offence case is not to be taken as a waiver. In other contexts, though, this observation in *O'Connor* continues to apply as a matter of principle.

175   As outlined in *R. v. McNeil*, above note 161 at para. 27.

3) The *O'Connor* application is brought before the judge seized with the trial, although it may be heard before the trial commences. If production is unopposed, of course, the application for production becomes moot and there is no need for a hearing.

4) If the record holder or some other interested person advances a well-founded claim that the targeted documents are privileged, in all but the rarest cases where the accused's innocence is at stake, the existence of privilege will effectively bar the accused's application for production of the targeted documents, regardless of their relevance. Issues of privilege are therefore best resolved at the outset of the *O'Connor* process.

5) Where privilege is not in question, the judge determines whether production should be compelled in accordance with the two-stage test established in *O'Connor*. At the first stage, if satisfied that the record is likely relevant to the proceeding against the accused, the judge may order production of the record for the court's inspection. At the next stage, with the records in hand, the judge determines whether, and to what extent, production should be ordered to the accused.

With respect to the second-step balancing, Justice Charron suggests that the touchstone is "true relevancy" of the sought after information.[176] If upon inspection the trial judge finds the material clearly irrelevant the application is dismissed. If, however, upon inspection the trial judge finds the material is relevant "the accused's right to make full answer and defence will, with few exceptions, tip the balance in favour of allowing the application for production."[177] Justice Charron explained:[178]

> In effect, a finding of true relevance puts the third party records in the same category for disclosure purposes as the fruits of the investigation against the accused in the hands of the prosecuting Crown under *Stinchcombe*. It may be useful to pose the question in this way: If the third party record in question had found its way into the Crown prosecutor's file, would there be any basis under the first party *Stinchcombe* disclosure regime for not disclosing it to the accused? If the answer to that question is no, there can be no principled reason to arrive at a different outcome on the third party production application.

176　*Ibid.* at paras. 41–42.

177　*Ibid.*

178　*Ibid.* at para. 42. See also David M. Paciocco, "*Stinchcombe* on Steroids: The Surprising Legacy of *McNeil*" (2009) 62 C.R. (6th) 26.

Privacy interests are not discarded. Rather, they are considered in tailoring the disclosure. It is open to the courts to craft conditions on the release of the information that balance the accused's right to full answer and defence and the privacy interests of the third parties.[179]

7.2)   Legislation: Third-Party Records in Sexual Offences

As indicated, legislation soon followed in response to the Supreme Court's decision, dealing with the production of third-party records in sexual offence cases, leaving *O'Connor* to apply in non-sexual offence prosecutions. On its face, this legislation, found in sections 278.1 to 278.91 of the *Criminal Code*, rejects the *O'Connor* test, notwithstanding that the *O'Connor* test was developed in reliance on constitutional principles. However, the legislation was upheld by the Supreme Court in *R. v. Mills*.[180] Through creative interpretation the Supreme Court managed to read down the legislation so that it could pass constitutional muster and not infringe the accused's right to make full answer and defence.

The legislation is broad in scope. It applies to both complainants and witnesses. Section 278.1 defines "record" as including "any form of record that contains personal information for which there is a reasonable expectation of privacy." The section goes on to list a broad array of "records," including medical, counselling, education, employment, and social services records. Indeed, virtually all government records are caught because the section 278.1 list includes records whose privacy is protected by statute, and all jurisdictions have aggressive privacy legislation. If the record that is sought in a case is listed, an objectively reasonable expectation of privacy is presumed. The party seeking the record therefore has the onus of rebutting that presumption.[181] In short, just because the kind of record sought is listed does not mean it will be protected but it is presumed that it will be. It should also be kept in mind that the Court in *Mills* emphasized that only records that "truly raise a legally recognized privacy interest are caught and protected."[182]

Unlike a "privilege" where the presence of a third party may well negate the finding of confidentiality, a reasonable expectation of privacy may still be found notwithstanding the presence of third persons. For

---

179   An example of possible conditions is found in the statutory regime, below in this chapter, *Criminal Code*, R.S.C. 1985, c. C-46, s. 278.7(3).
180   (1999), 139 C.C.C. (3d) 321 (S.C.C.).
181   *R. v. R.C.* (2002), 163 C.C.C. (3d) 3 (Ont. C.A.).
182   Above note 180 at 372. The Court in *Mills* cited *R. v. Regan* (1998), 174 N.S.R. (2d) 230 (S.C.), where the judge opined that otherwise public school or employment records would be outside the legislation.

example, a person still has a reasonable expectation of privacy over disclosures made in group therapy sessions—albeit somewhat reduced.[183]

The legislation applies even though the witness or complainant may have turned over the records to the prosecution, *contra O'Connor*. In these situations, the Crown is under a duty to notify the accused that it has such a record in its possession, but it is not to disclose the record's contents unless the witness waives the protection or the court so orders (see section 278.2).

The legislation does not apply to records already in the possession of the accused. Simply put, the defence has no need to seek "compelled production of the personal information"; they have it. As clearly stated by Justice Binnie in *R. v. Shearing*, the legislation is concerned about production of personal information records and not about admissibility.[184]

The legislation adopts the two-step procedure from *O'Connor* in form, but changes it significantly.[185] The first step remains—the accused must convince the trial judge to review the record. The threshold for this first step has changed; it is stricter than under *O'Connor*. Unlike *O'Connor* there are two components that must be met—the "relevance inquiry" and the "interests of justice" inquiry. Even the relevance inquiry is stricter. As with *O'Connor* the second step of the procedure involves judicial inspection, but again, the standards are stricter.

7.2 (a)   Step 1: Getting Inspection—The Relevance Inquiry

The relevance inquiry requires that the record "is likely relevant to an issue at trial or to the competence of a witness to testify." This formula has been interpreted to require "that there is a reasonable possibility that the information is logically probative,"[186] either to "the material issues in the case (that is, the unfolding of events) [or] evidence relating to the credibility of witnesses and to the reliability of other evidence in the case."[187]

It is important to remember when conducting this relevance inquiry that "[t[he *Mills* regime is tailored to counter speculative myths, stereo-

---

183   *R. v. R.C.*, above note 181 at para. 52.

184   *R. v. Shearing* (2002), 165 C.C.C. (3d) 225 at para. 95 (S.C.C.). See also *R. v. T.C.* (2004), 189 C.C.C. (3d) 473 (Ont. C.A.).

185   See *R. v. McNeil*, above note 161 at paras. 30–32.

186   *R. v. Mills*, above note 180 at para. 124.

187   *R. v. O'Connor*, above note 163 at para. 22. Although *O'Connor* was not interpreting s. 278.1 when offering this clarification, it was defining the same phrase, "an issue at trial or the competence of the witness to testify." In *R. v. Mills, ibid.*, the Court relied on that passage in interpreting the meaning of "likely relevance" in s. 278.1.

types, and generalized assumptions about sexual assault victims and about the usefulness of private records in sexual assault proceedings."[188] To prevent inappropriate arguments, section 278.3(4) states that "any one or more of the following assertions by the accused are not sufficient on their own to establish that the record is likely relevant." The section lists eleven assertions. On their face, they cover virtually every conceivable relevancy for third-party records, and if read literally would block any review of the records. Keep in mind that defence counsel are arguing in the dark in that they have not seen the contents of the records, and that the objective is to have a judge inspect the records to see whether they do, indeed, contain important, relevant information. The Court in *Mills* therefore rejected the "plain reading" of this section. Instead the Court chose the "constitutional reading" of the statute. The Court explained that section 278.3(4) "does not entirely prevent an accused from relying on the factors listed, but simply prevents reliance on bare 'assertions' of the listed matters, where there is no other evidence and they stand 'on their own.'" What the section requires is that the accused be able to point to "case-specific evidence or information" that shows the record is likely relevant to an issue at trial.[189] "Case-specific evidence or information" does not require the accused to show the precise manner in which the targeted document would be used at trial, lest the accused person, who has not seen the documents, is placed in an impossible Catch-22 position.[190] It does, however, require an evidentiary foundation that actually demonstrates a reasonable possibility that the document will contain relevant information, as opposed to a bald assertion that it could.

It will not be easy to lay the proper foundation. The keepers of the record and those to whom it relates are not compellable witnesses at the hearing (see section 278.4). The Court in *Mills* is of the view that means are available through Crown disclosure; the statements of complainants and witnesses are not caught by the legislation (see section 278.1) and will have to be disclosed to the defence. Furthermore, the defence can look to their own witnesses and the cross-examination of Crown witnesses, at both the preliminary and at trial. On this last point, it anticipates that the respective judges will allow the defence some latitude in exploring the records involved—without divulging their specific contents. Questions that touch upon the "private or personal domain," or the "intensely private aspects" of the witness's life contained in the

---

188 *R. v. McNeil*, above note 161 at para. 31.

189 Above note 180 at 380.

190 See *R. v. McNeil*, above note 161 at para. 33, where the Court makes this point in the context of *O'Connor* applications.

record are not permitted. Questions that do not implicate the "private domain" are permitted.[191] Justice Hill suggests that it would be open to the defence to examine upon the timing of the relevant entries, the degree of the writing (narrative or summary) or nature of the entries (detailed history or recording of feelings and emotions). In fact, should the defence not take advantage of their opportunity to do so this may be held against them in any subsequent motion for production.[192]

7.2 (b)   Step 1: Getting Inspection — The "Interests of Justice" Inquiry

Besides demonstrating that the information is "likely to be relevant," the accused must convince the trial judge that production of the record to the judge for inspection is "necessary in the interests of justice." This requires that the trial judge, without having seen the record, balance the accused's right to make full answer and defence against the right to privacy and equality of the complainant or witness. Under *O'Connor* this balancing would only occur in step 2, after the judge had decided to review the material. Section 278.5(2) lists eight factors to consider, five of which come from the majority's judgment in *O'Connor*:

(a)   the extent to which the record is necessary for the accused to make a full answer and defence;

(b)   the probative value of the record;

(c)   the nature and extent of the reasonable expectation of privacy with respect to the record;

(d)   whether production of the record is based on a discriminatory belief or bias;

(e)   the potential prejudice to the personal dignity and right to privacy of any person to whom the record relates;

(f)   society's interest in encouraging the reporting of sexual offences;

(g)   society's interest in encouraging the obtaining of treatment by complainants of sexual offences; and

(h)   the effect of the determination on the integrity of the trial process.

The Court recognized that the balancing required under the section runs counter to *O'Connor*, but relied on judges to interpret and apply the section in a constitutional manner. Accordingly, the factors listed in section 278.5(2) are not to be "conclusively assessed." The trial judge is directed merely to "consider" and "take into account" the factors listed. As a final protection for the accused, the trial judge is always

---

191   *R. v. B.(E.)* (2002), 57 O.R. (3d) 741 at para. 40 (C.A.).

192   *R. v. M.(D.)* (2000), 37 C.R. (5th) 80 (Ont. S.C.).

free to make whatever order is "necessary in the interests of justice."[193]
If the application establishes likely relevance, but the judge is left uncertain as to whether its production is necessary to make full answer
and defence, then the judge should rule in favour of inspecting the
document. The Court's advice is, when in doubt—inspect.

7.2 (c)   Step 2: Inspection

Step 2 involves the review by the trial judge of the record and the determination as to whether or not the record, or part of the record, should
be produced to the accused. In deciding whether or not to order production the same balancing factors considered earlier are once again
to be taken into account. Three of the factors listed were expressly rejected by the majority in *O'Connor* for consideration at the production
stage. These factors include:

- society's interest in encouraging the reporting of sexual offences;
- society's interest in encouraging the obtaining of treatment by complainants of sexual offences; and
- the effect of the determination on the integrity of the trial process.

It was argued that these factors unfairly altered the balance against
the accused. In *Mills* the Court responded that these factors, like the
others in the list, have no controlling weight and are merely to be "taken
into account" as part of the trial judges' wide discretion in this area.

Certainly it is the case that the new legislation provides far more
protection for witnesses and complainants in sexual cases than any
other case-by-case privilege. The fact that it covers personal records
reflects that the legislation is aimed at preserving privacy as opposed to
protecting a privileged relationship.[194] Unlike a case-by-case privilege,
the onus is also on the accused to gain access to the records, rather
than on the witness or complainant to protect their privacy.

8.   PUBLIC INTEREST IMMUNITY

> *Government documents and information may be protected from
> disclosure when a judge determines that the public interest in
> preserving the confidentiality of the information prevails over the*

---

193 *Ibid.*
194 For example, the courts are willing to protect diaries and journals. These records are not tied to the preservation of any relationship. See *R. v. D.W.L.* (2001),
156 C.C.C. (3d) 152 (N.S.C.A.).

public interest in seeing that litigants have access to all relevant evidence.

It has long been recognized that certain information regarding governmental activities should not be disclosed in the public interest. The protection of this information was once referred to as "Crown privilege," but is now better described as "public interest immunity." It differs from a "privilege" in three respects:

1) The protection is not "owned" by the Crown. Should the Crown fail to object, others, including the presiding judge, may do so in order to safeguard the "public interest."
2) It is said that the Crown cannot waive the protection.[195]
3) Its primary purpose, unlike for a privilege, is to protect information and not a relationship. Therefore, once the protection is given, no secondary sources may reveal the information.[196]

Public interest immunity is recognized both at common law and under statute. We will first examine the origins and nature of this protection in the common law, from which we can better understand and appreciate the statutory regime.

8.1) The Common Law

Under the common law, public interest immunity gives protection to a broad array of government and public body interests, security concerns, cabinet decision making and police matters. The court is called on to balance two competing public interests. On the one hand, it is in the public interest that the administration of justice should not be frustrated by the withholding of relevant information. On the other hand, there are certain government secrets that should not be disclosed in the public interest. In a criminal action, "public interest immunity cannot prevent the disclosure or bar the admissibility of documents that can enable the accused to resist an allegation of crime or to establish innocence."[197]

The immunity is available in both civil and criminal actions. In a civil action should the protection be rejected, then the state must dis-

---

195 See *Phipson on Evidence*, 16th ed. (London: Sweet & Maxwell, 2005) ss. 25–13. This is too rigid a statement. To hold that the Crown is completely incapable of waiving any objection places the litigant opposing the Crown in the untenable position of being unable to rely on the Crown's actions or undertakings. See *Leeds v. Alberta (Minister of the Environment)* (1990), 69 D.L.R. (4th) 681 (Alta. Q.B.).
196 *R. v. Snider*, [1954] S.C.R. 479 at 487.
197 *A.(L.L.) v. B.(A.)* (1995), 103 C.C.C. (3d) 92 at para. 51 (S.C.C.), L'Heureux-Dubé J.

close the information. In a criminal action should the protection be rejected, and the information is material to the case, then the Crown must choose: either the information is disclosed or the charges are stayed.

In the past the need for government secrecy was seen as paramount and, if a minister of the Crown claimed privilege, it was granted by the courts. The role of government has changed. Arms of government now are involved in a wide variety of activities in society. The result is a decline in the perceived need for government secrecy and the demise of absolute protection. Today the courts, under the common law, no longer take the minister's claim for privilege as final and conclusive. The opinion of the minister must be given due consideration, but, in the end, it is for the court and not the Crown to determine the issue.[198]

In the usual case, it is the Crown who objects to the disclosure of information, and this is done by way of an affidavit of the appropriate minister or government official. In certain cases, however, such as those involving police concerns, no affidavit is filed and the objection is dealt with by way of evidence from the police officer involved and submissions by counsel. Generally, the objection is based on either the "class" or "content" of the documents. Class objections are concerned with protecting certain types of documents. For example, the government may stake its claim for immunity on the basis that what is sought to be protected are "cabinet documents." The information is not particularized at all. Class claims usually rely on concerns about candour. The "candour argument" is that confidentiality is essential to ensure full, free, and frank discussion of matters of public importance. A second argument put forth is the fear of political interference and harassment should internal documents be prematurely disclosed.[199] Suffice it to say the courts are not enamoured with claims of class protection and, "generally speaking, a claim that a document should not be disclosed on the ground that it belongs to a certain class has little chance of success."[200] By contrast, a "content" objection seeks to protect specific information "contained" in the documents. Specific concerns are raised, and the courts have a far better understanding as to why the particular information ought not to be disclosed.

The affidavit or evidence provided in support of the objection should be as helpful as possible in identifying the interest sought to be protected. The court can in some cases determine the issue based on the minister's statement alone. For example, the statement may raise

---

198 *Carey v. Ontario* (1986), 35 D.L.R. (4th) 161 at 171 (S.C.C.).
199 *Ibid.* at 176–77.
200 *Ibid.* at 175.

concerns of national security or defence, and the court may hold these concerns sufficient without even looking at the documents in dispute. But, in cases of doubt, the judge has the discretion to inspect the documents and should do so.

Carey v. Ontario is the leading case on the common law approach to public interest immunity.[201] This was a civil action that revolved around the failure of a resort in Northwestern Ontario, in which the government had become involved. Carey alleged breach of contract and deceit against the government. He subpoenaed various Cabinet documents that dealt with the funding of the resort. The government claimed these Cabinet discussions were absolutely protected as a "class," and in the supporting affidavit very little information was given as to what was contained in these documents. In the Supreme Court, Justice La Forest confirmed that, under the common law, these documents were not absolutely protected. The judgment then went on to address how courts are to deal with these claims.

It was argued in *Carey* that the judge ought not to inspect the documents unless the party seeking disclosure can show a "concrete ground for belief" that the material contains information that would substantially assist the party seeking production. The difficulty with this position, as was pointed out by Justice La Forest, is that the party seeking disclosure is in the dark as to what information is to be had. In the case on appeal the documents dealt precisely with the dispute now before the court, and on this basis Justice La Forest was prepared to find that they were likely to assist Carey's case. He certainly rejected imposing any rigorous prerequisites to the court's inspection of the documents. "[C]ommon sense must be allowed to creep into the picture," he wrote, and the best way for a judge, where doubt exists, to balance competing interests is to look at the disputed documents and see what they actually contain.[202]

In terms of balancing the competing interests, *Carey* provides a list of considerations:

- the level of decision making;
- the nature of the policy discussions;
- the particular contents of the documents;
- the time when the document or information is to be revealed;
- the importance of the case;
- the need or desirability of producing the documents to ensure that the case can be adequately and fairly presented;

---

201 *Ibid.*
202 *Ibid.* at 193.

- whether or not the allegations involve government misconduct;[203] and
- the ability to ensure that only the particular facts relating to the case are revealed.

There is no question that *Carey* represents a move away from government secrecy to more openness. Mr. Justice La Forest provided these final words:

> Divulgence is all the more important in our day when more open government is sought by the public. It serves to reinforce the faith of the citizen in his governmental institutions. This has important implications for the administration of justice, which is of prime concern to the courts.[204]

The common law applies to matters within provincial jurisdiction and to claims of privilege brought by the provincial governments, as was the case in *Carey*. Under federal jurisdiction, legislation has been passed but, as we will see in the next section, the common law has not been entirely displaced by the legislation.

The common law position, whereby the courts have the ultimate say over all types of government claims of protection, can now be compared to the immunity under statute. Sections 36.1 to 39 of the *Canada Evidence Act* apply. These statutory provisions have been amended in the wake of September 11, by the *Anti-terrorism Act*.[205] Section 37 permits the confidentiality of information to be protected on the basis of any "specified public interest." Section 38, in turn, is to be used to protect the confidentiality of "sensitive information" or "potentially injurious information." "Sensitive information" includes any information possessed by the government relating to international relations, national defence, or national security. "Potentially injurious information" is information not in the possession of the government, the disclosure of which could injure international relations, national defence, or national security. Section 39, which was not amended by the *Anti-terrorism Act*, protects Cabinet and Cabinet committee confidences, discussions, and communications.

---

203 In *Carey v. Ontario, ibid.* at 188, Mr. Justice La Forest wrote: "The purpose of secrecy in government is to promote its proper functioning, not to facilitate improper conduct by the government."

204 *Ibid.*

205 S.C. 2001, c. 41, s. 43.

8.2) Section 37: Issues of a Specified Public Interest

Section 37 deals with the protection of information relating to "specified public interests." This means that objection can be taken on any ground of public interest specified in the objection. Objection can be undertaken under section 37 only by a government official (see section 36.1). The application for non-disclosure is to be made to a superior court, or a federal court. Provincial trial courts cannot hear section 37 applications.

Section 37 is concerned with "disclosure of information." It is reactive, in the sense that it is designed to prevent disclosure of objected to information. It is not "proactive" in the sense of protecting already disclosed information.[206]

If the court hearing the application concludes that the disclosure of the information "would encroach upon a specified public interest" that information can be released, but only if the public interest in disclosure outweighs the importance of the specified public interest, and the judge should craft appropriate conditions to limit encroachment of the specified public interest to the extent possible.

Section 37, therefore, includes the balancing of the "public interest in disclosure" against the "importance of the specified public interest." Section 37.3 goes on to expressly recognize the accused's right to a fair trial and that the judges hearing the application may order, in appropriate cases, that certain charges against the accused be dismissed or stayed.

The court that is to resolve a section 37 application can receive inadmissible evidence to assist it. If, in order to limit encroachment, information is released in a form that would not be admissible, the court may make an order permitting its introduction into evidence. This is a unique power, since the court making the order may not be a trial court; one judge makes orders relating to admissibility that are binding on another.

Prior to the amendments, courts found that section 37 had not displaced the common law. The amendments have not changed this. What this means is that it is still open to the Crown to object to disclosure under the common law. An objection under the common law will not trigger the section 37 process. Most importantly, although the section does not provide for provincial courts to hear "an objection made under section 37," this does not preclude the provincial courts, either in the course of a preliminary inquiry or a trial, from hearing a claim for im-

---

206 See *Dominion Investments (Nassau) Ltd. v. R.*, 2005 FC 1397.

munity under the common law. In fact, such a procedure is to be encouraged.[207] This will save the inconvenience of adjourning the matter to be heard in the superior court of the province, as is required under the section. Take the example where the police object to disclosure of how they conducted the surveillance of an accused on the ground that it will compromise future investigations. If the provincial court judge upholds the immunity, then there is no need to proceed to the superior court to protect the immunity. If the provincial court judge denies the immunity and orders disclosure, then the Crown can still object under section 37. The objections are separate and distinct. The section 37 objection would then need to be heard in the superior court. The hearing in the superior court would amount to a reconsideration of the application anew and not as a review of the provincial court judge's decision.[208]

In *R. v. Pilotte* the Ontario Court of Appeal held that a section 37 application was a separate and distinct proceeding from the trial proper.[209] The court noted that the separate nature of the inquiry is apparent given the separate appeal process outlined in the statute. An appeal lies to the Federal Court of Appeal or the provincial Court of Appeal, but must be brought within ten days of any determination. Moreover, it matters not that the same superior court judge could be presiding over both the trial and application. The trial is adjourned and the application heard. Where the objection to the production of the information is made by a person not a party to the proceeding, for example in *Pilotte* objection was made by a minister of the Attorney General of Canada and not the Crown prosecutor, then the application has to be determined under section 37; there is no common law option.[210]

8.3) Section 38: National Security Issues

Section 38 is a more aggressive provision, dealing with national security questions. It imposes obligations on the Crown, defence, plaintiff, defendant, or on any government official from whom disclosure is sought, to notify the attorney general of Canada in writing of any possibility that sensitive information or potentially injurious information is expected to be disclosed during a proceeding. The judge at the

---

207 See *R. v. Lam* (2000), 148 C.C.C. (3d) 379 (B.C.C.A.); *R. v. Richards* (1997), 115 C.C.C. (3d) 377 (Ont. C.A.); and *R. v. Pilotte* (2002), 163 C.C.C. (3d) 225 (Ont. C.A.), leave to appeal to S.C.C. refused (2003), 170 C.C.C. (3d) vi (S.C.C.).

208 *Canada (A.G.) v. Sander* (1994), 90 C.C.C. (3d) 41 (B.C.C.A.).

209 *R. v. Pilotte*, above note 207. See also *R. v. Omar*, 2007 ONCA 50 at para. 22.

210 *R. v. Pilotte*, *ibid.* at para. 45.

proceeding where the disclosure is anticipated is to be informed, and once informed, must prevent the disclosure.

Depending on the nature of the information, either the attorney general or the minister of national defence is empowered to authorize the disclosure of the information, or to enter into a disclosure agreement with the interested party. If disclosure is not made in this way, the attorney general, or the person seeking the information, or the record holder, is authorized to apply to the Federal Court, Trial Division, for an order with respect to disclosure. The application is a confidential, *ex parte* application, and the judge will determine whether to hold a hearing and who should be permitted to make representations. It is prohibited for anyone to even disclose that a section 38 application has been made. This can lead to the absurd result that decisions under appeal before the Federal Court may not even be disclosed to counsel arguing another case in the same court.[211]

Pursuant to subsection 38.11(1), the hearings shall be heard in private. In *Toronto Star Newspapers Ltd. v. Canada* this provision was read down so as only to apply to *ex parte* applications.[212] The court held that the mandatory requirement to exclude the public from sessions when there existed no risk that national security information or foreign confidences could be disclosed was overbroad and violated the open court principle. The judge hearing the application must determine three issues:[213]

1) is the information sought to be disclosed relevant or not in the usual sense of the *Stinchcombe* rule, that is to say it may reasonably be useful to the defence;

2) if the information is relevant then the judge must determine whether the disclosure of the information would be injurious to international relations, national defence or national security; and

3) upon a finding that the disclosure would result in injury, the judge must determine whether the public interest in disclosure outweighs in importance the public interest in non-disclosure.

The third step contemplates a case-by-case balancing of competing interests and there is no additional burden on an accused to establish an innocence at stake exception.[214] Rather the party seeking disclosure of

---

211 See the comments of Lutfy C.J. in *Ottawa Citizen Group Inc. v. Canada*, 2004 FC 1052.

212 *Toronto Star Newspapers Ltd. v. Canada*, 2007 FC 128.

213 Refer to ss. 38.06.

214 *Canada (Attorney General) v. Khawaja*, 2007 FC 490 at para. 93.

the information bears the burden of proving that the public interest is tipped in its favour.[215]

The judge is not to order disclosure if it would be injurious to international relations or national defence or national security to do so, unless the public interest in disclosure outweighs the importance of the relevant public interest. The judge is also required to impose conditions to limit the injury that disclosure could cause. The judge can order all or some of the information to be disclosed, or can require a written admission of facts relating to the information to be handed over. Again, inadmissible evidence can be received during the hearing. The judge's decision can be appealed to a judge of the Federal Court of Appeal.

What is mandated under section 38 is a bifurcated scheme. Unlike section 37, this section confers jurisdiction to the Federal Courts. Provincial superior courts do not have jurisdiction—in terms of the disclosure application. Trial judges, however, do have the power and responsibility to "protect the right of the accused to a fair trial" under subsection 38.14, which includes the power to stay proceedings if need be. The Federal Court controls disclosure; the trial court controls trial fairness. This bifurcation scheme may be clumsy, inefficient, and invite delay, but according to the Supreme Court of Canada in R. v. Ahmad it is constitutional.[216]

Subsection 38.13 provides the attorney general of Canada with an override power, in the form of a certificate, if the judge conducting the hearing or appeal does order disclosure. That certificate can prohibit the relevant judge from disclosing the information, or it can provide terms for disclosure. The certificate lasts for 15 years. The only avenue of appeal from this certificate is entirely illusory. It is an appeal to a single judge of the Federal Court of Appeal who is not authorized to balance competing interests, or to inquire into whether the judges' disclosure order that is the subject of the certificate was reasonable, or even correct. According to subsection 38.13(8), the Federal Court of Appeal judge can override the certificate only if the judge determines that some or all of the information subject to the certificate "does not [in fact] relate to information obtained in confidence from, or in relation to a foreign entity, or to national defence or security." In other words, so long as the information protected by the certificate is relevant to those protected areas, the appeal judge must uphold the certificate.

---

215 *Ribic v. Attorney General of Canada* (2003), 185 C.C.C. (3d) 129 (F.C.A.), leave to appeal to the S.C.C. refused.
216 *R. v. Ahmad*, 2011 SCC 6.

Section 38 represents a marked departure from the common law. There is little evidence that the changes introduced were necessary. There is no evidence that the old section was somehow inadequate or being abused. On the other hand, today the concern of abuse is real. Government loves secrecy, and under the guise of "potentially injurious information" or "sensitive information" many spurious claims for protection can be made. The courts will need to be vigilant to see that claims brought under section 38 strictly comply with the terms of the Act and have merit.

8.4) Section 39: Cabinet and Committee Information

The final statutory provision relating to public policy immunity is section 39. It was not amended under the *Anti-terrorism Act*. There was no need to make it stronger. It protects confidences of the Queen's Privy Council for Canada, essentially cabinet and committees of cabinet. "Confidences" include: proposals, recommendations, discussion papers, agenda, deliberations, decisions, communications between ministers relating to government decisions or policy and draft legislation. This information is absolutely protected. A minister or Clerk of the Privy Council files a certificate with the court indicating that the information falls with the "class." Provided that the certificate on its face brings the information within the designated class it is protected, without the judge examining or hearing the information.

As Chief Justice McLachlin observed in *Babcock v. Canada*, section 39 provides greater protection than at common law.[217] Once information is certified it "shall" not be disclosed. There is no balancing of interests between the need for confidentiality and the need for disclosure. The scope of judicial review under section 39 is limited to ensuring that the certification is valid. Four principles were identified by the Supreme Court in *Babcock*:

1) The certification must be done by the Clerk of the Privy Council or a minister of the Crown.
2) The information must fall within the categories described in section 39(2).
3) The power exercised must flow from the statute and must be issued for the *bona fide* purpose of protecting Cabinet confidences in the broader public interest.

---

217   (2002), 3 C.R. (6th) 1 (S.C.C.).

4) Section 39 applies to "disclosure"; where a document has already been disclosed section 39 no longer applies. Section 39 cannot be applied retroactively to documents already produced.

Chief Justice McLachlin went on to explain that:

> The function of the clerk under the Act is to protect Cabinet confidences, and this alone. It is not to thwart public inquiry nor is it to gain tactical advantage in litigation. If it can be shown from the evidence or the circumstances that the power of certification was exercised for purposes outside those contemplated by s. 39, the certification may be set aside as an unauthorized exercise of executive power . . . .[218]

The Court also reiterated that waiver does not apply. The fact that the government may have released some documents does not prevent the Crown from protecting the non-disclosed under section 39. In other words, there is no implied waiver. In answer to the concern that selective disclosure of documents may be used unfairly as a litigation tactic, the Court responded that "[s]elective disclosure designed to prevent getting at the truth would not be a proper exercise of the Clerk's or minister's s. 39 powers."[219] Moreover, it would be open to a court to draw adverse inferences from the refusal to disclose information.

Two ancillary points ruled upon by the Court in *Babcock* were: (1) that the section 39 review applies to tribunals as well as courts and (2) that there was no basis upon which to find that section 39 was unconstitutional.

The key point from *Babcock* is that even given the "absolute" wording of the statute there remains an important judicial review function. As the Chief Justice stated, "even language this draconian cannot oust the principle that official actions must flow from statutory authority clearly granted and properly exercised."[220]

9. PROTECTION OF INFORMANT'S IDENTITY

The common law protects the identity of an informant from disclosure in a criminal or a civil proceeding. This is recognized as a fixed rule. It is subject to only one exception, imposed by the need to demonstrate the innocence of an accused person.

---

218 *Ibid.* at para. 25.
219 *Ibid.* at para. 36.
220 *Ibid.* at para. 39.

An informant's identity is protected, as a fixed rule of law. Whether to disclose the informant's identity is not, as with government secrets, a matter of discretion for the judge. There is no balancing of interests to see whether or not the privilege exists in a given case. If you like, the decision has been made: the public interest is best served by protecting the identity of informants. It is accepted that informants play an important role in solving crimes, particularly drug-related offences. It is further accepted that the informants need to conceal their identities both for their own protection and to encourage others to come forward with information.[221] Given these two rationales, it follows that the privilege is not for the Crown or the informant alone to waive. A valid waiver of the privilege requires the consent of both.[222]

The rule protects the informant's identity; it does not protect the information provided. However, the information should not be divulged where to do so threatens to reveal the informant's identity. In the case of anonymous tips, where it may be impossible to determine which details of the information provided by an informer will or will not result in that person's identity being revealed, then none of those details should be disclosed.[223]

The rule, although fixed, is not absolute. The one and only exception to the rule protecting the informant's identity is where the evidence is needed to demonstrate the innocence of an accused person. "All other purported exceptions to the rule are either applications of the innocence at stake exception or else examples of situations in which the privilege does not actually apply."[224] It follows that there is no exception in civil cases. Nor will such a claim succeed at a preliminary inquiry, since the presiding judge is not called upon to determine the innocence or guilt of the accused.[225] The Supreme Court of Canada in *R. v. Scott* outlined in more specific detail where the exception would apply. Each of these situations goes to establish the accused's innocence or a defence. Where the informant is a material witness, his or her identity must be revealed. Similarly, the informant's identity must be revealed where the informant has acted as an *agent provocateur*, and the accused provides an evidentiary basis for the defence of entrapment. The law distinguishes between an "informant" and an "agent."

---

221 See *R. v. Scott* (1990), 2 C.R. (4th) 153 at 167 (S.C.C.); *Named Person v. Vancouver Sun*, 2007 SCC 43 at para. 18.

222 See *R. v. Leipert* (1997), 112 C.C.C. (3d) 385 (S.C.C.); *Named Person*, *ibid.* at para. 25.

223 *R. v. Leipert*, *ibid.* at 398.

224 *Named Person*, above note 221 at para. 29.

225 *R. v. Richards*, above note 207 at 380.

An informant merely furnishes information to the police; an agent acts on the direction of the police and goes into the field to participate in the illegal transaction in some way.[226] The identity of informants is strongly protected, whereas the identity of agents is not.[227] The innocence at stake exception also applies where the accused seeks to establish that a search was not undertaken on reasonable grounds and therefore contravened section 8 of the *Charter*.[228] This last exception has been extended to cases where wiretap authorizations are challenged.[229]

In determining whether or not the accused's innocence is at stake, the courts are utilizing the "innocence at state test" from the Supreme Court of Canada's decision in *McClure*.[230] The following procedure is outlined:

- First, the accused must show some basis to conclude that without the disclosure sought his or her innocence is at stake.
- If such a basis is shown, the court may then review the information to determine whether, in fact, the information is necessary to prove the accused's innocence.
- If the court concludes that disclosure is necessary, the court should only reveal as much information as is essential to allow proof of innocence.
- Before disclosing the information to the accused, the Crown should be given the option of staying the proceedings.
- If the Crown chooses to proceed, disclosure of the information essential to establish innocence may be provided to the accused.[231]

As can be seen, the identity of informants is much more likely to be protected than claims under public interest immunity. This is well illustrated in the debate over the status of "surveillance post privilege." This issue arises often in undercover drug operations. A police officer takes up a location and observes the drug transactions. The Crown wants to protect the "identity" of the location in order to hide, in many cases but not all, the identity of those who co-operated with the police. In some instances no "co-operating person" is involved and the police simply want to protect an investigatory technique. In this case, protection of the location clearly falls within public interest immunity. In *R. v.*

---

226 *R. v. A.*, [2007] N.B.J. No. 272 at para. 19 (Q.B.).
227 *R. v. Babes* (2000), 146 C.C.C. (3d) 465 (Ont. C.A.).
228 *R. v. Scott*, above note 221 at 315.
229 *Dersch v. Canada (A.G.)* (1990), 80 C.R. (3d) 299 (S.C.C.).
230 See section 2.2, "Innocence at Stake," above in this chapter. *R. v. Marshall*, 2005 CanLII 30051 at paras. 101–4; *R. v. Deol*, 2006 MBCA 39.
231 *R. v. Leipert*, above note 222 at 398.

Thomas it was held that there was no distinction to be made between protecting the identity of an informant and the identity of a location, which would expose members of the public to danger.[232] However, in *R. v. Lam*, while it was admitted that the policy considerations supporting the two claims for protection are essentially the same, it was held that they are distinct.[233] The key distinction was that an informant's involvement in a case usually begins and ends with the "tip" to the police. However, the evidence of a police officer, who asserts "surveillance post privilege" is often crucial to the case. Without disclosure, the accused may be denied the means to adequately challenge the officer's observations. Therefore, the court was more comfortable to have a trial judge weigh the competing interests, rather than finding a more conclusive informant's protection.

---

232 *R. v. Thomas* (1998), 124 C.C.C. (3d) 178 (Ont. Gen. Div.).
233 Above note 207; see also *R. v. Richards*, above note 207; *R. v. Hernandez*, 2010 BCCA 514.

CHAPTER 8

SELF-INCRIMINATION

1. INTRODUCTION

The common law has long treated it as unfair to "conscript" or force an accused person to be his own betrayer in a criminal case. As a matter of principle, it is believed that a person should not be required to answer an allegation made against him unless and until the Crown has charged him and established "a case to meet" during trial by presenting evidence supporting the allegation. Until then, he should not have to dignify the allegation with a response. In modern times this notion is "intimately linked to our adversarial system of criminal justice and the presumption of innocence."[1] It is a vestige of the revulsion that was felt over the ancient courts of Star Chamber, which would detain suspected enemies of the state on mere suspicion, compel them to swear an oath, and then require them on pain of punishment to answer questions asked about what they were thinking or what they believed. The idea that self-incrimination is offensive rests, therefore, on ideas about privacy and the inherent dignity of individuals.[2] It is also about the abuse of state power and the risk that compelling accused persons to respond can produce unreliable information.[3] Hence, the principle against self-incrimination supports "limits on the extent to which an accused person can be used

---

1   *R. v. Henry* (2005), 202 C.C.C. (3d) 449 at para. 2 (S.C.C.).
2   *R. v. D'Amour* (2002), 4 C.R. (6th) 275 at para. 35 (Ont. C.A.).
3   *R. v. B.(S.A.)*, [2003] 2 S.C.R. 678 at para. 57.

as a source of information about his or her own criminal conduct."[4] At its heart it is about choice. Individuals should be free to "choose whether to co-operate with the state and, if they choose not to, [they should] be left alone by the state"[5] unless and until the Crown proves that they have violated a pre-existing rule of law.

In order to vindicate the principle against self-incrimination, the common law developed a number of precise rules, including the privilege against self-incrimination (the right of any witness in any proceeding to refuse to answer questions that may incriminate them), the right of accused persons to decide whether to testify at their own trials, and the rule excluding involuntary confessions. As can be seen, each of these rules is concerned with "testimonial" self-incrimination[6]—situations where accused persons are made to act like witnesses against themselves by speaking about their own guilt. For more than a hundred years, the principle against self-incrimination provided no protection in cases of non-testimonial conscription—situations where suspects were made to participate in the investigation against them through some physical act such as giving a blood sample,[7] blowing into a breathalyzer,[8] or standing in a police line-up.[9] Confining self-incrimination protection to testimonial compulsion in this way was not arbitrary. It was done in recognition of the fact that whereas compelled statements may well prove to be untrue, the reliability of authentic real evidence is not affected by the manner in which it is obtained. Moreover, forcing testimonial self-incrimination arguably involves a particularly odious breach of privacy as it requires individuals to expose their thoughts and ideas, and "the mind is the individual's most private sanctum."[10] Finally, when a person speaks about his guilt, he is creating new, previously unavailable evidence that will assist the Crown, which is not the case when he is required to hand over pre-existing real evidence.

With the advent of the *Charter* the self-incrimination concept grew. This happened initially in the context of section 24(2) of the *Charter*. Section 24(2) requires judges to exclude unconstitutionally obtained

---

4   *Ibid.* at para. 33.

5   *R. v. D'Amour*, above note 2 at para. 34.

6   The concept of "testimonial self-incrimination" is explained in *Marcoux v. R.* (1976), 29 C.R.N.S. 211 (S.C.C.).

7   *Quebec (A.G.) v. Begin* (1955), 21 C.R. 217 (S.C.C.).

8   *Curr v. R.* (1972), 18 C.R.N.S. 281 (S.C.C.).

9   *Marcoux v. R.*, above note 6.

10 *R. v. F.(S.)* (1997), 120 C.C.C. (3d) 260 at 309 (Ont. Gen. Div), rev'd in part on other grounds (2000), 182 D.L.R. (4th) 336 (Ont. C.A.).

evidence if its admission would bring the administration of justice into disrepute. The Court accepted that given the importance of self-incrimination principles, if unconstitutionally obtained evidence is self-incriminatory it should ordinarily be excluded. Before long the Court began to use the term "self-incrimination" to describe restricted forms of real evidence that are intimately connected to the accused—things like breath samples[11] and blood samples[12] and participation in line-ups[13] and to treat these forms of evidence the same as compelled testimonial self-incrimination for the purposes of exclusion.[14] This extension was no doubt grounded in the notion that if the underlying idea is that individuals should be able to choose whether to participate in their own conviction, these forms of evidence, each of which requires the compelled participation of the accused to obtain, should be treated the same as compelled statements.

In 2003 the high-water mark of the self-incrimination concept was reached when this broader conception of self-incrimination was recognized outside of section 24(2). *R. v. B.(S.A.)* involved a constitutional challenge to DNA warrants which compel persons to produce bodily samples for analysis. The Supreme Court of Canada observed that the principle against self-incrimination applies to compulsion relating both to "products of the mind and products of the body."[15]

More recently the Supreme Court of Canada has backtracked. In 2009 in *R. v. Grant* it held that its earlier section 24(2) authority "wrongly equates bodily evidence with statements."[16] The Court made it clear that "communicative" information warrants greater legal protection than other forms of compelled participation. This casts doubt about whether non-communicative forms of conscription should now be treated as constituting self-incrimination.

It is evident, therefore, that the self-incrimination concept is unstable. Indeed, the Supreme Court of Canada has observed that the self-incrimination principle "has a limited scope and requires different things at different times."[17] Fortunately, most cases can be resolved using fixed and reliable rules. There are two categories of clear rules

---

11   *R. v. Dyment*, [1988] 2 S.C.R. 417.
12   *R. v. Therens*, [1985] 1 S.C.R. 613.
13   *R. v. Leclair*, [1989] 1 S.C.R. 3.
14   See chapter 9, section 6.2, "Rejected Practices," and section 6.4 (b), "Bodily Evidence."
15   *R. v. B.(S.A.)*, above note 3 at para. 34.
16   *R. v. Grant*, 2009 SCC 32 at para. 105. See chapter 9, section 6, "Requirement 2: The Effect of the Admission on the Repute of the Administration of Justice."
17   *R. v. B.(S.A.)*, above note 3 at para. 57.

that vindicate the principle against self-incrimination, rules that apply during formal proceedings (sheltering under the general heading, the "privilege against self-incrimination"), and rules that relate to conscription occurring outside of formal proceedings (falling under the rubric of the "right to silence").[18] These rules are canvassed in this chapter. In *R. v. B.(S.A.)* the Supreme Court of Canada also adapted a broad purposive analysis that can be used to identify whether the principle against self-incrimination is offended outside of the established rules, both in cases of testimonial or non-testimonial compulsion involving evidence emanating from the body or the use of the body. The vague and indeterminate principles to be used in identifying whether problematic self-incrimination has occurred outside of the established or settled rules will be canvassed near the end of this chapter.[19]

A few things are clear, though. First, however broadly the self-incrimination concept is applied, it will lead to the more aggressive protection of "compelled communicative evidence" involving involuntary oral or written statements created as a result of an investigation, than of other forms of compelled participation. Second, with the exception of bodily samples intimately linked to the accused, the self-incrimination concept simply does not apply to pre-existing items of real evidence that are capable of being gathered without the participation of the accused. There is ample settled authority, for example, that the principle against self-incrimination is not violated where the accused is compelled to hand over existing documents.[20] Bodily samples aside, the self-incrimination concept, however broad or narrow, has to do with compelled participation in the *creation* of information and not with the compulsory disclosure of pre-existing information.[21] Third, the self-incrimination concept provides protection only against incrimination, not against other uses of compelled information. In *R. v. Weitnz*, for example, the British Columbia Court of Appeal held that self-incrimination principles were not implicated where a driver was made to blow into the face of an officer investigating impaired driving because the officer's observations could not be used at the trial as evidence that the accused had committed an offence. The officer's observations could be used solely to enable the officer to decide whether there was lawful

---

18   In *R. v. Hebert* (1990), 77 C.R. (3d) 145 at 180 (S.C.C.), the Court adopted this terminology.

19   See section 6, "A Principled Approach to Self-incrimination," below in this chapter.

20   See, for example, *Thomson Newspapers Ltd. v. Canada (Director of Investigation and Research)* (1990), 54 C.C.C. (3d) 417 (S.C.C.).

21   See, for example, *R. v. D'Amour*, above note 2 at para. 37.

authority to arrest the accused and compel the accused to provide a breath sample.[22]

2. THE PRIVILEGE AGAINST SELF-INCRIMINATION (FORMAL PROCEEDINGS)

At common law the "principle against self-incrimination" supported only two self-incrimination rules. The first was the "privilege against self-incrimination" which enabled witnesses to refuse to answer questions in a formal proceeding if their answers would tend to incriminate them. The second rule prevented the Crown from calling the accused as a witness during his own trial. Until a little over 100 years ago, this second rule did not exist. This is because the accused was not allowed to testify at all, even if he wanted to, due to concerns that his obvious interest would cause him to testify falsely. When the accused was finally made competent, he was made competent only for the defence, thereby giving rise to the non-compellability protection.

At the same time that this non-compellability rule was adopted, the common law "privilege against self-incrimination" was removed by statute. It was replaced by rules giving witnesses a protection (as opposed to a privilege) against self-incrimination, under which they would be made to answer self-incriminating questions on the understanding that their answers could not be used to incriminate them in a subsequent proceeding. In effect, the witnesses were given what is often referred to as "use immunity."

These self-incrimination rules have been modified by the *Charter*. "The jurisprudence of our [Supreme] Court on self-incrimination developed such that three procedural safeguards emerged, use immunity, derivative use immunity, and constitutional exemption."[23] In essence, the *Charter* now provides witnesses with an aggressive form of the "use immunity" described above, as well as a new "derivative use immunity" which can cause not only the testimony of a witness to be protected, but even other evidence derived from, or found as a result of, that testimony. The third procedural safeguard referred to, the "constitutional exemption," includes the common law non-compellability of accused persons

---

22   R. v. *Weintz* (2008), 59 C.R. (6th) 195 (B.C.C.A.), leave to appeal to S.C.C. refused, [2008] S.C.C.A. No. 362.

23   R. v. *Bagri* (*sub nom. An Application under s. 83.28 of the Criminal Code*) (2004), 184 C.C.C. (3d) 449 at para. 70 (S.C.C.).

at their trials but extends further to provide "a complete immunity from testifying where proceedings are undertaken or predominantly used to obtain evidence for the prosecution of the [suspect] witness."[24] These three constitutional "self-incrimination" protections, "use immunity," "derivative use immunity," and "constitutional exemptions," as well as their related common law and statutory rules, are described later in this chapter.

3. THE SELF-INCRIMINATION PROTECTION OF WITNESSES

If the accused does not testify at his trial, his testimony from an earlier proceeding cannot be used against him at that trial, regardless of whether he was the accused or a mere witness at the earlier proceeding.

Even if the accused does testify at his trial, his testimony from an earlier proceeding cannot be used against him at that trial if he was compellable as a witness at the earlier proceeding.

If the accused does testify at his trial, his testimony from an earlier proceeding can be used to cross-examine him at that trial provided he was not compellable as a witness at the earlier proceeding.

By way of exception to these rules, if the accused is being prosecuted because it is alleged that it was an offence for him to testify as he did at an earlier proceeding (such as in a prosecution for perjury or obstruction of justice for giving misleading answers), then the Crown is free to prove his earlier, allegedly criminal testimony.

3.1) Statutory Use Immunity

As indicated, at common law witnesses had the right to refuse to answer questions during their testimony if the answer would tend to incriminate them. The *Canada Evidence Act*, in section 5, removed this right. In place of the privilege to refuse to answer, it now provides protection to those who are forced to reveal information tending to show that they have committed offences. While witnesses can still be prosecuted for the offences their testimony reveals, under section 5 the incriminating answers they give cannot be used against them during that subsequent prosecution for any purpose, whether as an admission of the offence charged or to contradict answers those witnesses may give at their sub-

---

24 *Ibid.*

sequent trial.[25] In effect witnesses are given "use immunity," as a *quid pro quo* for losing their common law privilege to refuse to answer. As Justice Arbour has explained:

> [W]hen a witness who is compelled to give evidence in a proceeding is exposed to the risk of self-incrimination, the state offers protection against the subsequent use of that evidence against the witness in exchange for his or her full and frank testimony.[26]

To be clear, the "use immunity" protection provided by the *Canada Evidence Act* relates only to those answers that amount to self-incriminating admissions at the time the previous testimony is being given. It does not extend to other testimony witnesses may give. As a simple example, assume that a corporate director who is charged criminally with fraud testified as a witness at the previous criminal trial of another person. Any admissions the corporate director made at that earlier trial about participating in the fraud would be excluded, but evidence by the corporate director acknowledging his corporate directorship would not be, as there is nothing incriminating in admitting the corporate offices held.

Provincial and territorial statutes have also universally removed the common law privilege to refuse to answer, replacing it with use immunity. The nature of that use immunity varies, however, from jurisdiction to jurisdiction. Alberta and the three territories mimic the *Canada Evidence Act* and offer use immunity only if the compelled self-incriminating testimony is being used in a subsequent provincial prosecution to incriminate the witness, whereas the balance of the provinces effectively prevent any subsequent use of the self-incriminating testimony, including in civil proceedings.

To gain the "use immunity" protection provided under section 5 of the *Canada Evidence Act* and in some provinces,[27] a witness must invoke it expressly by stating her awareness or fear that the particular answers may tend to incriminate her.[28] Certainly under the *Canada Evidence Act* and probably in those provinces where objection is required the witness need not invoke the protection for every question

---

25 *R. v. Noël* (2002), 5 C.R. (6th) 1 at para. 33 (S.C.C.), citing *R. v. Wilmot*, [1940] 3 D.L.R. 358 (Alta. C.A.).

26 *R. v. Noël, ibid.* at para. 21, cited with approval in *R. v. Henry*, above note 1 at para. 22.

27 Objection is required to trigger the use immunity in British Columbia, Manitoba, Newfoundland, Nova Scotia, Ontario, Prince Edward Island, and Saskatchewan.

28 *R. v. Noël*, above note 25 at paras. 32 and 37, citing *R. v. Côté* (1979), 50 C.C.C. (2d) 564 (Que. C.A.).

but can do so with respect to a series of related questions.[29] It will be up to the judge at the subsequent trial to decide ultimately whether the testimony objected to was incriminating at the time the testimony was being given, and therefore protected by the section.

Section 13 of the *Charter* gives easier access to "use immunity" than section 5 of the *Canada Evidence Act* and in those provincial jurisdictions where objection is required. Witnesses are entitled to be protected by 13 as a matter of constitutional right whether they claim it or not, and whether or not they appreciate at the time they are answering that their responses are self-incriminating.

Although the matter is not yet settled, the preferred view is that section 13 of the *Charter* has made section 5 of the *Canada Evidence Act* redundant. While there is nothing in law preventing a statute from extending the protection of a constitutional rule, and the language of section 5 appears to support a broader interpretation, section 5 should not be given broader reach than section 13 for at least three reasons. First, section 13 has the same theoretical foundation as the statutory provisions. In *R. v. Henry* the Court repeated with approval a passage from *R. v. Noël* where it had earlier advised that "section 13 . . . is best understood by reference to section 5 of the *Canada Evidence Act*" and its *quid pro quo* purpose.[30] Second, the *R. v. Henry* Court noted that section 13 was "intend[ed] to extend s. 5 of the *Canada Evidence Act* to give further and better effect to this [common] purpose";[31] it would be inconsistent with that observation to read section 5 as housing broader protection than section 13 does. And third, as will be seen, the primary motivation for recent developments in the interpretation of section 13 was to prevent section 13 from being used to enable an accused person to give a version of events to a trier of fact while hiding from the trier of fact that she has previously offered a different account of those same events under oath. If section 5 of the *Canada Evidence Act* is interpreted more broadly than section 13 there will be cases where section 5 produces this undesirable effect. It would be perverse to read a statutory provision that fills the same function as the *Charter* provision in a way that frustrates the policy limits the Court has imposed on the *Charter* provision. There should therefore be no need or benefit in invoking the protection of the *Canada Evidence Act*; the best view is that section 5 of the *Canada Evidence Act* has become otiose because its function has been subsumed by section 13, which provides the same limited protec-

---

29 *R. v. Noël*, *ibid.* at paras. 37 and 38, citing *R. v. Mottola*, [1959] O.R. 520 at 526 (C.A.).

30 *R. v. Henry*, above note 1 at para. 22.

31 *Ibid.* at para. 23.

tion. Given that section 13 applies solely where the witness is subsequently being prosecuted, however, it remains prudent to invoke the protection of the relevant provincial evidence act in those provinces that provide civil use immunity if objection is taken.

3.2) Constitutional Use Immunity — Section 13 of the Charter

3.2 (a)   The Rules of Constitutional Use Immunity Introduced
Section 13 provides:

> A witness who testifies in any proceedings has the right not to have any incriminating evidence so given used to incriminate that witness in any other proceedings, except in a prosecution for perjury or for the giving of contradictory evidence.

Although this provision does not protect accused persons against adverse inferences being drawn from an earlier *refusal* to testify or answer questions,[32] it does provide significant protection for answers that have been furnished in testimony at earlier proceedings. In identifying the scope of that protection, care has to be taken in reading the section 13 cases decided prior to *R. v. Henry*.[33] In *Henry* the Supreme Court of Canada resiled from much of its own previously settled section 13 authority. It took this unusual step because its case law had become too complex and impractical. After *Henry* much of the *dicta* in earlier decisions must now be regarded as wrong, and at least one of the older cases decided by the Court, *R. v. Mannion*,[34] would have had a different outcome were it to be litigated under the new rules.

The new rules derived from *R. v. Henry*[35] are easy to state and illustrate:

1) If the accused does not testify at his trial, his testimony from an earlier proceeding cannot be used against him at that trial, regardless of whether he was the accused or a mere witness at the earlier proceeding.

Example: Dubois testified at his first trial and admitted that he killed the deceased, but claimed he acted in self-defence. His conviction at that first trial was overturned. At Dubois' retrial a section 13 violation occurred when the

---

32   *Ibid.*
33   *R. v. Ervin* (2003), 176 C.C.C. (3d) 152 (Alta. C.A.).
34   *R. v. Mannion* (1986), 53 C.R. (3d) 193 (S.C.C.).
35   *R. v. Henry*, above note 1.

trial judge permitted the Crown to use, as part of its case, admissions made by Dubois in his first trial that he struck the fatal blow: *R. v. Dubois*.[36]

2) Even if the accused does testify at his trial, his testimony from an earlier proceeding cannot be used against him at that trial if he was compellable as a witness at the earlier proceeding.

Example: Noël testified as a compellable witness at his brother's murder trial. When he was testifying Noël implicated himself in the killing. At Noël's subsequent trial for his part in the murder, section 13 was violated because the Crown was allowed to cross-examine Noël using extracts from the testimony Noël had given at his brother's trial.[37]

3) If the accused does testify at his trial, his testimony from an earlier proceeding can be used to cross-examine him at that trial provided he was not compellable as a witness at the earlier proceeding.

Example: Henry testified as a witness at his first trial on charges of murder. His conviction at that trial was set aside. Henry testified again at his second trial on those same charges, giving a different account. The Crown was permitted to cross-examine Henry at his second trial, using his testimony from the first trial: *R. v. Henry*.[38]

3.2 (b)   The Field of Operation of the Constitutional Use Immunity Rules

In order to receive protection, the testimony of the accused must occur in some "other proceedings" relative to the trial at which the protection is invoked. A broad interpretation is given to the term "other proceedings." In *R. v. Dubois*[39] the Crown argued that section 13 was immaterial to the case because Dubois' retrial was not an "other proceeding" relative to his first trial, as both trials were conducted on the same indictment. The Court disagreed, concluding that the term had to be defined broadly to fulfil section 13's underlying mission.[40] Since *Dubois* it has come to be accepted that a bail hearing, preliminary inquiry, and even

---

36   *R. v. Dubois* (1985), 48 C.R. (3d) 193 (S.C.C.). While the result of the decision has been upheld, some of the reasoning in this case was disapproved of in *R. v. Henry*, above note 1.

37   *R. v. Noël*, above note 25. While the result of the decision has been upheld, the reasoning the *Noël* Court used, and much of its *dicta*, has now been rejected.

38   *R. v. Henry*, above note 1.

39   *R. v. Dubois*, above note 36.

40   That mission is described below in this chapter and includes preventing the Crown from conscripting the accused as a witness against himself by using his

a *voir dire* within a trial, are "other proceedings" relative to the trial itself. The same is true, of course, of an earlier independent proceeding such as a civil trial (including an examination for discovery conducted at the earlier trial) or an administrative hearing at which evidence is taken under formal process.

Where, then, do the protections against using testimony from such "other proceedings" apply? That protection is offered only at proceedings that are brought in an effort to impose penal consequences on the person whose earlier testimony is sought to be used against him. This will typically be a criminal case but includes any trial at which a person is being prosecuted for an offence. The application of section 13 is limited in this way because its base function is to prevent the use of earlier testimony to "incriminate" an accused. Section 13 therefore does not give protection in civil or purely administrative cases,[41] For this reason, in *Knutson v. Saskatchewan Registered Nurses Assn.*,[42] section 13 did not prevent the earlier testimony of a witness from being used against her during an administrative, disciplinary proceeding.

3.2 (c) The Constitutional Use Immunity Rules Explained

Where the accused does not testify at his trial
As indicated, if the accused does not testify at his trial, his testimony from an earlier proceeding cannot be used against him, regardless of whether he was the accused or a mere witness at that earlier proceeding. He has absolute use immunity. This was the outcome of the Supreme Court of Canada's first section 13 decision, *Dubois v. R.*[43] The Court reasoned that if the Crown could prove all or even parts of its case by using testimony that the accused furnished in an earlier proceeding, it would be tantamount to using the accused as a Crown witness during his own trial. This would subvert both the principle of a "case to meet" and the constitutional right of the accused under section 11(c) not to testify at that trial, things that section 13 is dedicated to preventing.

Where the accused does testify at his trial
Under the rule just described (Where the accused does not testify at his trial) it is not possible for the Crown to use earlier testimony from

---

earlier testimony as part of the Crown's case, thereby effectively compelling a version of events from the accused.

41   In some cases, section 7 of the *Charter* will extend "use immunity" protection to proceedings where, strictly speaking, the accused is not being incriminated. See the discussion in this chapter in section 3.5, "Use Immunity under Section 7."

42   (1990), 90 Sask. R. 120 (C.A.).

43   *R. v. Dubois*, above note 36.

the accused as part of its case. In some cases the Crown may, however, use the earlier testimony of the accused to cross-examine him where he chooses to testify in his own defence. The Crown may do so only if the accused was not compellable at the early proceeding and chose to give that earlier testimony. The Crown may not do so if the accused was compellable at that earlier proceeding.[44]

This was not always the law. In the pre-*Henry* authority a different approach was taken. It is important to describe this now obsolete law so that earlier case law will not confuse.

When the Supreme Court of Canada first interpreted section 13 it held that the Crown could cross-examine an accused person using her earlier testimony, whether the accused person was compellable or not at the proceeding where that earlier testimony was given. The Crown's ability to do so was not unlimited. The Crown could not cross-examine an accused person using her earlier testimony in an effort to produce positive evidence of guilt — this "incrimination purpose" was prohibited.[45] The Crown could, however, use the earlier testimony to cross-examine the accused in order to demonstrate that the accused was not a reliable witness — this "impeachment purpose" was permissible.[46] This distinction was adopted because the text of section 13 prohibits only the use of previous testimony "to incriminate" the accused. It does not, on its face, prohibit the use of that testimony for impeachment purposes.

In 2002, the approach of examining the purpose of the cross-examination to determine whether it was permissible fell out of favour and was discarded. This happened primarily because it was easy for the Crown to put incriminating admissions made in earlier testimony be-

---

44   *R. v. Henry*, above note 1.

45   For example, in *R. v. Mannion*, above note 34, s. 13 was held to have been violated when the Crown used Mannion's testimony from his previous trial to contradict his claim at his current trial that he was unaware of the rape allegations against him when he left Edmonton. The Crown was cross-examining Mannion on that testimony with the aim of getting him to admit that he fled because of the criminal allegation against him. If true, this could stand as circumstantial evidence of his guilt on the theory that an innocent man would have no reason to flee. The Crown's cross-examination was therefore for the purpose of incriminating Mannion. Note: This decision has been overruled by *R. v. Henry*, above note 1.

46   In *R. v. Kuldip* (1990), 1 C.R. (4th) 285 (S.C.C.) the Crown was permitted to cross-examine Mr. Kuldip to show he gave inconsistent answers at his two trials relating to the description of a particular police officer. Those answers contained no information showing that Kuldip fled the scene of the accident, as was being alleged against him. The Crown was simply trying to show that Kuldip was an unreliable witness.

fore the jury by cross-examining the accused about them under the pretence that those admissions were simply being used for impeachment purposes when their real impact was to show guilt. In *R. v. Noël*,[47] for example, 80 percent of Mr. Noël's cross-examination involved challenging his testimony where he was declaring his innocence by using incriminating admissions he had made during the trial of his brother; all done, it was said, solely to show that Noël was an unreliable witness. By 2002 it had also come to be accepted that a jury direction admonishing the jury to use a cross-examination in which earlier admissions of guilt were put to the accused solely to test his credibility and not as evidence of his guilt was unrealistic. So the *Noël* Court decided to modify the approach. It held that cross-examination on the prior testimony of the accused would be impermissible not only when its purpose was to incriminate the accused, but also where the cross-examination could possibly have that effect. As a result, the accused could be confronted only with earlier testimony that was about things that were innocuous on the issue of guilt.

From the outset, the *Noël* approach was controversial. The main objection was that the rule indirectly gave constitutional protection to false testimony on the crucial issues in the case by permitting the accused to: volunteer one story at his or her first trial, have it rejected by the jury, then after obtaining a retrial on an unrelated ground of appeal volunteer a different and contradictory story to a jury differently constituted in the hope of a better result because the second jury is kept in the dark about the inconsistencies.[48]

And so, in 2007 the Court reversed itself in *R. v. Henry*. The line between permissible and impermissible cross-examination would no longer turn on purpose or effect. Instead, it now depends on whether the accused was a compellable witness at the proceeding where she gave the previous testimony.

In an important sense this new approach has narrowed the protection of section 13. It is now permissible to cross-examine any accused person who is being retried with evidence he gave at his earlier trial. Based on the rules articulated, it should also now be permissible to cross-examine any accused person with testimony he gave at his own bail hearing, his preliminary inquiry or during a *voir dire* in his case. And when cross-examination is permitted, subject to other rules of evidence, his earlier testimony can be used both to impeach and incriminate him.

---

47   Above note 25.
48   *R. v. Henry*, above note 1 at para. 2.

Yet, at the same time, this new approach has broadened the protection in other cases. Even though the language of section 13 prohibits the use of previous testimony only where it is being used "to incriminate," under the new regime there is now a complete bar on using earlier compellable testimony; compellable testimony cannot be used either to incriminate or to impeach a witness at her subsequent trial. The *Henry* Court, having declared it impossible to distinguish cross-examination that would only impeach from that which would incriminate, had no choice but to take this approach. Pragmatics trumped text because the language of the provision called for a distinction that proved unworkable in practice.

Theoretical controversy

While the decision in *R. v. Henry* is an intensely practical one, the Court did offer a principled justification for its approach. It reasoned that the "consistent theme in the s. 13 jurisprudence is that 'the purpose of s. 13 . . . is to protect individuals from indirectly being *compelled* to incriminate themselves.'"[49] That being so, if the accused testifies freely at the first proceeding and then freely takes the stand during his trial, there is no relevant compulsion; he was neither compelled to give the evidence that is being now being used against him, nor was he being compelled to take the stand to face it.[50] The Supreme Court of Canada in *Henry* was of the view that in its own earlier decisions it had lost sight of this, and so it corrected the error; section 13 protects compelled testimony and nothing more. The *Henry* Court wanted, however, to avoid delving into difficult questions about whether, at the early proceeding, the accused wanted to testify or did so only because of compulsion; in keeping with its pragmatic approach the Court held that for the purposes of section 13, "evidence of compellable witnesses should be treated as compelled even if their attendance was not enforced by subpoena."[51]

In truth, the theoretical foundation used by the *Henry* Court to develop its three basic rules is controversial. First, the Court accepted the position that had matured in *R. v. Noël* that section 13 can best be understood as a constitutional commitment to the same *quid pro quo* promise that had been made when section 5 of the *Canada Evidence Act* was passed,[52] but then arguably misapprehended the nature of that promise. In *Noël* the bargain contemplated was the exchange of use immunity for the loss of the privilege to refuse to answer self-

---

49   *Ibid.* at para. 22.
50   *Ibid.* at para. 42.
51   *Ibid.* at para. 34.
52   *Ibid.* at para. 22.

incriminating questions. That right to refuse to answer was taken away from all witnesses, not just those who are compelled to take the stand. If section 13 does rest in *quid pro quo* reasoning all witnesses, having lost the privilege the common law gave them to refuse to answer self-incriminating questions, should arguably get the "use immunity" in return. The *Henry* decision is in fact inconsistent with *quid pro quo* theory. The Court glossed over this by reading passages from *Noël* that read contextually could only have been alluding to compulsion *to testify about self-incriminating matters*, as though they referred instead to compulsion to take the witness stand.

Second, the absolute use immunity that the *Henry* Court confirmed for all accused persons who do not testify during the trial in question, even though they chose to testify at the earlier proceeding, is inconsistent with the waiver thinking that underlies the balance of the Court's reasoning. Put another way, why are those who *chose* to take the stand at their first trial treated as being *compelled* to self-incriminate where the answers that they *ex hypothesi chose* to give by taking the stand at that earlier proceeding are tendered against them as part of the Crown's case at their later trial? This is not explained.

Third, there is the long-standing paradox, perpetuated in *Henry* through its reaffirmation of *Dubois* that it is considered impermissible indirect conscription for the Crown to try to use the voluntary testimony given by the accused in an earlier proceeding, but it is not considered impermissible indirect conscription for the Crown to use the voluntary pre-trial confessions made by the accused to the police.

Still, in spite of its theoretical failings and the damage that is done to the text of section 13 the rules developed in *Henry* bear the considerable virtue of being both realistic and clear.

3.3) Exceptions: Perjury and Similar Cases

Section 13 provides exceptions to its general rule that earlier testimony cannot be used to incriminate a witness. The provision specifically excludes prosecutions for "perjury and for the giving of contradictory evidence" from its reach. The reason is simple. If a Crown prosecuting perjury or contradictory evidence charges was to be prohibited by section 13 from using the earlier testimony of a witness to incriminate that witness it would be impossible to prosecute perjury or contradictory evidence cases. This is because the earlier testimony is the very *actus reus* of such offences. The exception for "perjury and for giving contradictory evidence" has been interpreted purposively to allow the Crown to use the earlier testimony of an accused to incriminate him in any prosecution against him where his earlier testimony forms the *actus reus* of the offence he is alleged to have committed.[53]

3.4) Derivative Use Immunity

Occasionally, the testimony of a compellable witness will lead to the discovery of other evidence, sometimes known as "derivative evidence." For example, a compellable witness may testify at the trial of an accomplice that together they robbed a store and threw the gun into the bush at a particular location. If that compellable witness is later prosecuted for robbery, his testimony cannot be used against him at his trial because of section 13. That section would not prevent the admission of the gun if it was thereafter discovered by the police, however, because the gun is not testimony.

In some cases, section 7 of the *Charter* can be used at the subsequent proceeding to fill the breach left by section 13 to exclude evidence derived from the earlier testimony of a compellable witness. This will occur where the authorities are attempting to use evidence against the accused that they would not have found but for his earlier compelled testimony. Although the burden is initially on the accused to prove that the evidence would not have been discovered without the testimony, that burden can effectively be shifted to the Crown. If the accused can show a plausible connection between his testimony and the discovery of the evidence, the court will expect the Crown to prove on the balance of probabilities that the evidence would have been discovered even without the testimony. If the Crown cannot do so, the derivative evidence is excluded. This burden shift occurs because, as a practical matter, the Crown is in a better position than the accused to lead evidence about the investigation.[54]

The case of *R. v. Z.(L.)*[55] provides an example. There the Crown used compelled testimony Z.(L.) gave in a related criminal proceeding to persuade a witness, Mr. Borba, to give a statement against Z.(L.). The Crown then offered Mr. Borba's statement as evidence at Z.(L.)'s trial, pursuant to a hearsay exception. In other words, it offered evidence against Z.(L.) that it had derived from Z.(L.)'s earlier compelled testimony. The Ontario Court of Appeal held that the trial judge should have given Z.(L.) derivative use immunity by excluding the hearsay state-

---

53   *R. v. Staranchuk* (1983), 36 C.R. (3d) 285, aff'd (*sub nom. Staranchuk v. R.*) (1985), 47 C.R. (3d) 192 (S.C.C.).

54   *R. v. S.(R.J.)* (1995), 36 C.R. (4th) 1 (S.C.C.), explained in *British Columbia Securities Commission v. Branch* (1995), 38 C.R. (4th) 133 (S.C.C.).

55   *R. v. Z.(L.)* (2001), 155 C.C.C. (3d) 152 (Ont. C.A.).

ment. Of interest, the Ontario Court of Appeal did not act as though it was applying a set rule. Instead, it treated derivative use immunity as discretionary. The trial judge had erred in applying that discretion because it had been unfair to compel Z.(L.) to testify at the related criminal proceeding in the first place; it was clear from the transcript of the examination of Z.(L.) that the primary reason he had been called as a witness at that criminal proceeding was to find out about Z.(L.)'s own role in the crime. This was an abusive use of the subpoena power which undermined Z.(L.)'s self-incrimination protection. The Crown should not derive any benefit from that strategy. The court held that the derivative evidence should therefore have been excluded from Z.(L.)'s trial.

3.5) Use Immunity under Section 7

There are cases where "use immunity" is conferred even though the evidence is not being used to incriminate the accused at the proceedings. This is done not under section 13, but under section 7 of the *Charter.* In *R. v. Bagri*[56] the Supreme Court of Canada held that this will occur if the Crown tries, at a deportation or extradition hearing of an individual, to use testimony or derivative evidence obtained from that individual through an "investigative hearing." Investigative hearings, created as part of the government's anti-terrorism initiatives, enable the state to compel witnesses to testify before a judge in order to furnish information useful in the investigation of a past or apprehended terrorist offence. While the statute provides for use immunity and derivative use immunity in subsequent prosecutions, given the international nature of anti-terrorism measures these protections could easily be rendered illusory by deporting or extraditing the witness to another jurisdiction for trial, along with his investigative hearing evidence. Self-incriminating information secured from the witness in Canada could then be used in a foreign trial to incriminate the witness, without the Canadian protection being available. Even though a person is not being incriminated at a deportation or extradition hearing, section 7 therefore steps in to provide indirect protection against this happening. As indicated, it prevents testimony and derivative evidence obtained from a witness at an investigative hearing from being used at a deportation or extradition hearing against that witness.[57]

---

56   Above note 23.

57   This indirect way of preventing self-incrimination is only partially effective. If there is enough other evidence to extradite or deport the subject apart from the investigative hearing testimony, the subject could still find himself facing his own investigative hearing testimony in the foreign jurisdiction.

3.6)   Cross-examination about Immunity

The protection granted by section 13 raises the spectre that other persons can falsely admit at the trial of an accused that they, and not the accused, committed the offence yet avoid having their admissions admitted against them or used to cross-examine them if they themselves are later tried. In *R. v. Jabarianha*[58] the Crown wanted to dull the credibility of the testimony of a defence witness who took the stand to claim that he was solely responsible for the theft that Jabarianha was implicated in by cross-examining this defence witness in an effort to show that he knew that section 13 left him little to lose if he falsely "took the rap." The Supreme Court of Canada held that the trial judge erred by permitting the Crown to cross-examine the defence witness about his knowledge of section 13. The Court reasoned that, generally, the probative value of this line of cross-examination will be low because section 13 does not provide complete protection for witnesses. The witness can still be charged and tried on other evidence, or charged with perjury if their admission is false. The incomplete protection furnished by section 13 reduces the risk that a witness, even knowing about section 13, would falsely implicate himself because of that section.[59]

The Court added that the low-probative value of this kind of questioning will tend to be outweighed in most cases by the prejudice it will cause. This line of questioning treats the enjoyment of a constitutional right as an *indicum* of dishonesty, and could well lead to objections based on solicitor-client privilege. Together the low-probative value and high prejudice generally require exclusion.

The Supreme Court of Canada did not foreclose this line of cross-examination in all cases. It conceded that in rare circumstances, such as where the Crown can prove a plot to lie, or a decision to lie to obtain

---

58   *R. v. Jabarianha*, [2001] S.C.J. No. 72.

59   The *Jabarianha* decision, *ibid.*, predated *R. v. Henry*, above note 1. When *Jabarianha* was decided, the pre-*Henry* rules therefore applied. According to the law as it then was, a witness who testified at the trial of another that he himself committed the offence could be cross-examined about that testimony at his own subsequent trial for impeachment purposes. The *Jabarianha* Court considered this risk to lessen the incentive for witnesses to rely on s. 13 to shield themselves when making false admissions of responsibility at the trial of another. This, in turn, lowered the probative value in questioning witnesses about their knowledge of s. 13. Since *Henry*, however, those who admit guilt at the trial of another are now given complete use immunity; as compellable witnesses they will never be faced with their testimony from that earlier trial if they themselves are subsequently tried for the offence they admit to. It is therefore possible to argue that *Jabarianha* should be reconsidered, but given the balance of the reasoning in the case, its outcome is unlikely to change.

favours, the balance might shift and this line of cross-examination might become permissible.

In *R. v. Noël* the Court made it clear that similar prohibitions apply with respect to section 5 of the *Canada Evidence Act*; as a general rule a witness cannot be cross-examined about her knowledge that section 5 could be used to shelter incriminating admissions from later being used against her.[60]

4. THE NON-COMPELLABILITY OF ACCUSED PERSONS AT THEIR OWN TRIALS

Accused persons, other than corporations, cannot be compelled to testify against themselves at their own trials. As a general rule, however, accused persons can be compelled to testify at other proceedings, even when those other proceedings deal with the same subject matter as the charges they are accused of.

In rare cases, however, even those merely suspected of crimes as well as those formally accused may be protected from having to testify at proceedings that touch upon their allegedly criminal activity, such as public inquiries or coroner's inquests; if the sole purpose in calling suspects as witnesses at such a proceeding is to obtain self-incriminatory information from them to assist in investigations against them, they cannot be forced to testify. Beyond this restriction, the law is not certain. It appears to be that if there is a legitimate public interest in having the evidence of a witness at a proceeding, the witness will be required to testify unless the predominant purpose in calling him was to obtain self-incriminatory evidence against him. In non-penal proceedings governed by the provincial Evidence Acts, the parties can be forced to testify by the opposing parties.

4.1)   Competence and Compellability outside the *Charter*

At common law, accused persons were disqualified from testifying at their own criminal prosecution because of their interest in the outcome. Subsection 4(1) of the *Canada Evidence Act* now makes it permissible for them to testify on their own behalf, although they are not made compellable by the Crown. "An accused who chooses to testify is compelled by law, like any other witness, to answer the questions

---

60   *R. v. Noël*, above note 25.

put to him [even if those answers are self-incriminatory], and there are serious legal consequences [including being convicted of contempt of court] for failing to comply with the law."[61] Moreover, where an accused refuses to answer questions, it would certainly impact on his credibility.

Provincial Evidence Acts vary. All make the parties to a proceeding competent witnesses. Most make the parties compellable as well in civil proceedings, although they cannot be made to testify against themselves in provincial prosecutions.[62] Others purport to make the defendant a compellable witness even in the prosecution of a provincial offence.[63]

4.2) Subsection 11(c) of the *Charter*

Subsection 11(c) of the *Charter* has overtaken the law relating to the non-compellability of accused persons charged with offences. Even in those provinces where the Evidence Acts make the defendant compellable in his own prosecution, subsection 11(c) would operate to prevent this compulsion from happening. Subsection 11(c) provides:

Any person charged with an offence has the right . . .

(c) not to be compelled to be a witness in proceedings against that person in respect of the offence.

Of note, even though subsection 11(c) confers protection on "persons"—a term usually interpreted to include corporations—corporate accused cannot rely on this provision. This is because the inanimate nature of corporations prevents them from experiencing the indignity of compelled self-incrimination. This means that senior officers of a corporation are compellable against that corporation, notwithstanding subsection 11(c).[64]

---

61   *R. v. Arradi*, [2003] 1 S.C.R. 280 at para. 34.
62   *Alberta Evidence Act*, s. 4(3); British Columbia, *Evidence Act*, s. 7; New Brunswick, *Evidence Act*, ss. 5 and 9; Newfoundland and Labrador, *Evidence Act*, ss. 2 and 4(a); Nova Scotia, *Evidence Act*, ss. 45 and 48; Yukon Territory, *Evidence Act*, s. 3; Saskatchewan, *The Evidence Act*, ss. 35(1) & (2); Ontario, *Evidence Act*, s. 8, and the *Provincial Offences Act*, R.S.O. 1990, c. P.33, s. 46(5).
63   Prince Edward Island, *Evidence Act*, s. 4; Northwest Territories, *Evidence Act*, s. 3; *Manitoba Evidence Act*, s. 4.
64   *R. v. Amway Corp. (sub nom. Canada v. Amway of Canada Ltd.)* (1989), 68 C.R. (3d) 97 (S.C.C.). Corporate officers are also compellable against their corporation at common law: *R. v. Judge of the General Sessions of the Peace for the County of York, Ex parte Corning Glass Works of Canada Ltd.* (1971), 16 D.L.R. (3d) 609 (Ont. C.A.), and see *R. v. Amca Sales Ltd.*, [2000] N.S.J. No. 71 (Prov. Ct.).

The protection under subsection 11(c) is available to natural persons only when they are "charged with an offence." This clearly includes individuals who are being prosecuted for criminal or quasi-criminal offences, even under provincial statute.[65] Yet the phrase, "charged with an offence," goes farther. Whether a person is charged with an offence, is a matter of substance, not form. The real question is whether the relevant proceedings have penal consequences. A police officer facing a professional discipline hearing that could have resulted in his incarceration was treated as having been charged with an offence.[66] Moreover, "the concern whether proceedings are [penal] in nature is concerned not with the *nature of the act* which gave rise to the proceedings, but the *nature of the proceedings* themselves."[67] In *Martineau v. Canada (Minister of National Revenue—M.N.R.)*,[68] for example, subsection 11(c) was not available during a *Customs Act* forfeiture proceeding, even though the unpaid duty had been assessed because the subject was alleged to have contravened the law by making false statements. What mattered was that the forfeiture proceedings were designed to operate as a civil recovery mechanism for the unpaid duty, not to punish or stigmatize him.

Assuming an individual is charged with an offence in the relevant sense, "[t]hree conditions must be met . . . to benefit from the protection against self-incrimination under s.11(c) of the *Charter*: (1) the person must be compelled to be a witness (2) in proceedings against that person (3) in respect of an offence."[69]

When is a person compelled to be a "witness"? A witness is someone who furnishes testimony at a formal proceeding. A person who is subject to compulsion during an interrogation at a police station is therefore not a witness. Subsection 11(c) does not catch informal admissions or confessions, even if they are compelled. Separate rules handle this situation.[70] Subsection 11(c) would, however, catch a pretrial discovery proceeding.[71]

The second requirement, that the proceedings are "against" the person, is again, a question of substance. Technically, Martineau was the plaintiff when he sued for a review of a customs forfeiture notice that led

---

65 *Martineau v. Canada (Minister of National Revenue—M.N.R.)*, [2004] S.C.J. No. 58 at para. 21.

66 *R. v. Wigglesworth*, [1987] 2 S.C.R. 541.

67 *R. v. Shubley*, [1990] 1 S.C.R. 3 at 18–19.

68 Above note 65.

69 *Ibid.* at para. 67.

70 See the discussion later in this chapter at section 5.4, "The 'Confession Rule.'"

71 *Martineau v. Canada (Minister of National Revenue—M.N.R.)*, above note 65 at para. 70.

to his compelled testimony, but that forfeiture hearing related to an assessment notice that the state had initiated. The Supreme Court of Canada therefore treated the proceedings as being against Martineau.[72] Had he otherwise qualified for the protection of subsection 11(c), the fact that he had launched the suit would not have been a problem for him.

A proceeding can be against more than one person; therefore, subsection 11(c) would prevent co-accused at a joint trial from forcing each other to testify.[73]

The third requirement, "in respect of the offence," has been interpreted broadly. It requires that there be "'some connection' between the offence and the proceedings."[74] Since the forfeiture against Martineau arose because he was alleged to have committed customs offences, the forfeiture hearing was "in respect of the offence," even though Martineau was not being tried for the offence at that hearing. This means that had Martineau been charged with a customs offence and subjected to a separate forfeiture proceeding, he would have been able to use subsection 11(c) to avoid being examined for discovery at that forfeiture proceeding. *Martineau* therefore establishes, for the first time, albeit in *obiter dictum*, that subsection 11(c) protection is not confined to the proceeding at which the accused is being tried for the offence.

The question that arises is how far does its protection extend? The language used by the Supreme Court of Canada in *Martineau* is decidedly broad, but it cannot be that a person charged with an offence can rely upon subsection 11(c) to claim non-compellability at independent proceedings into the same event that comprises the alleged offence, such as civil proceedings, public inquiries, or the separate trials of co-accused persons. If this was intended, the *Martineau dictum* would override a significant body of authority to the contrary.[75] The *obiter dictum* should therefore be understood in light of the facts of the case, and read as extending the protection of subsection 11(c) to situations where there is a substantive connection between the two proceedings. The substantive link between the offence and the forfeiture proceeding in *Martineau* was intimate and unique, because the right to civil forfeiture that was being claimed against Martineau required an allegation that a customs offence had been committed (even if it was not being prosecuted). Moreover, had Martineau been charged the state would have been responsible for instituting both proceedings.

---

72   *Ibid.*

73   *R. v. Clunas* (1992), 11 C.R. (4th) 238 (S.C.C.).

74   Above note 65.

75   See the discussion later in this chapter at section 4.3, "Section 7 and 'Constitutional Exemptions' from Testifying."

4.3)   Section 7 and "Constitutional Exemptions" from Testifying

In rare cases, section 7 will buttress subsection 11(c) and enable a witness who is a suspect to avoid testifying. This is because it is contrary to the principles of fundamental justice to compel a person to testify at a proceeding, even where he is not accused, if this is being done in order to obtain incriminating information from him. Put simply, the state power to compel testimony is not to be used as a substitute for a criminal investigation.[76] In *R. v. Bagri* the Supreme Court of Canada dubbed the relevant protection a "constitutional exemption" from testimony. The right to this constitutional exemption arises where "the predominant purpose" of calling a person at a hearing is "to obtain information or evidence for the prosecution of the witness."[77] The Court intimated that had the investigative hearing power been used in that case to investigate the witness with a view to his own possible prosecution, the constitutional exemption would have applied to prevent that investigation hearing from taking place.

The approach taken in the *Bagri* case is consistent with *dictum* in *Phillips v. Nova Scotia (Commission of Inquiry into the Westray Mine Tragedy)*[78] where Justice Cory expressed the view that a predominant purpose test should be used to determine whether a suspect called to testify at a proceeding will be entitled to quash a subpoena. In *British Columbia Securities Commission v. Branch*,[79] however, a majority of the Court had earlier suggested that a witness would not receive a constitutional exemption even if the predominant purpose in compelling his testimony was to have him disclose his own criminality, unless his testimony at that proceeding would actually prejudice him in his subsequent trial. The Court also remarked on how the possibility of prejudice from having to testify is seriously lessened by the use immunity and derivative use immunity protections that would ultimately be available to an accused. There is therefore some uncertainty about whether a showing of prejudice is required to gain a constitutional exemption, but the more recent authority suggests not. First, the *Bagri* case furnishes an unequivocal affirmation that a straightforward predominant purpose test should be used, and no mention of prejudice is made. Second, in *R. v. Jarvis* the Supreme Court of Canada used a predominant purpose test

---

76   *British Columbia Securities Commission v. Branch*, above note 54.
77   Above note 23 at para. 72.
78   (1995), 98 C.C.C. (3d) 20 at 55–56 (S.C.C.). And see *R. v. Cadagan*, [1998] O.J. No. 3724 at para. 16 (Gen. Div.).
79   Above note 54 at 143.

without a showing of prejudice in determining whether the state could use a statutory power to compel a suspect to answer self-incriminating questions outside of a formal proceeding.[80] Parallel reasoning suggests that no prejudice requirement attaches to the constitutional exemption in cases where the predominant purpose in calling a suspect as a witness in a formal proceeding is to make him speak about his own guilt.

While this is an important right, it has to be recognized that it will be difficult for potential witnesses to enjoy it. Normally, as in *Nova Scotia (Minister of Community Services) v. M.(D.J.)*, the testimony will be sought at another proceeding for a legitimate reason, and not predominantly to enforce self-incrimination.[81] Even where there is reason for concern, it will be a rare case where the accused can show on the balance of probabilities that the predominant reason for his compulsion is to make him speak about his own criminality. In *R. v. Z.(L.)*, discussed earlier in this chapter,[82] Z.(L.) tried to quash his subpoena to testify at the related trial but was unable to persuade the court that the predominant reason he was being called there was to speak about his own role in the offence.[83] It was only after he had testified that the transcript showed that Z.(L.) was right about this.[84] By then, of course, the constitutional exemption had become academic because Z.(L.) had already been forced to testify.

Is it possible that there is a residual discretion that can enable a subject in an appropriate case to acquire a constitutional exemption even where the Crown's predominant purpose in calling her is not to extract self-incriminatory evidence? In *Phillips*, Justice Cory suggested there was. According to Justice Cory, even if the Crown has a legitimate purpose in calling the witness, a subject can resist testifying if her testimony would undermine her right to a subsequent fair trial, taking into account that she will be provided with use and derivative use

---

80 (2002), 6 C.R. (6th) 23 (S.C.C.), and see section 6, "A Principled Approach to Self-incrimination," below in this chapter.

81 (2002), 224 D.L.R. (4th) 701 (N.S.C.A.), leave to appeal to S.C.C. refused, [2002] S.C.C.A. No. 473. The government wanted to register D.J.M. in its child abuse registry. He brought an application to review that decision, coupled with a disclosure application. He sought a constitutional exemption from having to testify at that disclosure application but he failed as he was not being compelled for the predominant purpose of securing his self-incrimination but rather to enable the judge to decide the motion.

82 See the discussion at section 3.4, "Derivative Use Immunity," above in this chapter.

83 *R. v. Z.(L.)*, [1997] O.J. No. 788 (Ont. C.A.).

84 *R. v. Z.(L.)*, above note 55.

immunity.[85] There remains some uncertainty, however, about whether this *obiter dictum* reflects the law. No mention of this possibility was made in *Branch* where the Court first discussed constitutional exemptions. Still, it would be a sensible rule. It is flexible, it is in keeping with the contextual approach favoured by the Court, it is an approach that recognizes the reality that the effect of state action can compromise a constitutional right even where state action is undertaken for a proper purpose, and it provides a means to vindicate the central constitutional right to a fair trial.

4.4) Adverse Inferences from the Failure to Testify

4.4 (a)   Adverse Inferences by Trial Courts

The failure of the accused to testify cannot be used as evidence of his guilt, although, where the evidence in the case already shows the accused to be guilty beyond a reasonable doubt, the trier of fact may use the failure of the accused to testify to conclude that the accused has no explanation that could raise a reasonable doubt.

Even though the accused has a constitutional right not to testify, it is often inadvisable for the accused to refrain from doing so. This is because, as a practical matter, where the Crown case calls out for an answer and where common sense suggests that the accused would be able to provide an answer if there was one, jurors are apt to consider the failure of the accused to testify to be additional proof of guilt.[86] In spite of this, it is an error of law for triers of fact, be they juries or judges sitting alone, to draw inferences of guilt from the failure of an accused person to testify in a criminal case. The reason is simple. If the law endorsed this kind of reasoning, it would severely undercut the right not to testify. As Justice Sopinka explained in the leading case of *R. v. Noble*: "[If adverse inferences are permitted] [t]he failure to testify tends to place the accused in the same position as if he had testified and admitted his guilt. . . . [T]his is tantamount to conscription of self-incriminating communicative evidence and is contrary to the underlying purpose of the right to silence."[87]

---

85   *Phillips v. Nova Scotia (Commission of Inquiry into the Westray Mine Tragedy)*, above note 78, as explained in *R. v. Cadagan*, above note 78 at para. 17.

86   In civil proceedings, it is permissible for the trier of fact to infer in such a case that the reason the party did not testify is that their evidence would have harmed their case: *Vieczorek v. Piersma* (1987), 58 O.R. (2d) 583 (C.A.); *Connor v. Shaparrall Ltd.* (1998), 34 C.C.E.L. (2d) 208 (Ont. Gen. Div.).

87   *R. v. Noble* (1997), 6 C.R. (5th) 1 at 41 (S.C.C.).

In *Noble*, the judge incorrectly drew an adverse inference because of the failure of the accused to testify in a trial that arose after an apartment manager apprehended a young man who was attempting to jimmy a car. At trial the manager was unable to identify Noble as the man he had apprehended. Based on examination of a driver's licence photo that the manager had seized from the suspect, however, the trial judge believed Noble to be the perpetrator. In convicting him, the trial judge commented that the failure of Noble to testify, given his obvious likeness to the photograph, "certainly may add to the weight of the Crown's case on the issue of identification."[88] The Supreme Court of Canada held that the judge erred by reasoning in this fashion. Justice Sopinka ruled for the majority that a trier of fact that is not convinced of guilt beyond a reasonable doubt on the evidence cannot use the failure of the accused to testify as if it were additional proof of guilt. "Belief in guilt beyond a reasonable doubt must be grounded on the testimony and any other tangible or demonstrative evidence admitted during the trial," not on the fact that the accused exercised his right not to testify.[89]

Justice Sopinka did not say in *Noble* that the failure to testify could never be considered by the trier of fact. He indicated that where an accused is already shown by the evidence to be guilty beyond a reasonable doubt, a trier of fact may use the accused's failure to testify to conclude that the accused has no explanation that could raise a reasonable doubt.[90] In truth, this permissible inference is rather pointless. It is settled law that a reasonable doubt cannot be a speculative doubt. It would therefore be wrong, in any event, for a trier of fact to conjecture about exculpatory explanations that do not arise from the evidence. Moreover, the concession that a judge can use silence to infer that the accused has no answer to the Crown's case so long as the judge does not use silence as affirmative proof of guilt permits the rule in *Noble* to be easily avoided. In *R. v. Hall*, for example, the Ontario Court of Appeal upheld a conviction where a judge relied on pre-*Noble* authority and said outright that she was drawing an adverse inference. The Court of Appeal held that the judge had not actually drawn an adverse inference but instead was simply noting that the accused offered no explanation in the face of a case sufficient on its own to support his conviction.[91]

On its face it seems curious that the Supreme Court of Canada would feel the need to identify a permissible inference that serves to do no more than to counter impermissible speculation and open the door

---

88   *Ibid.* at 36.
89   *Ibid.* at 41.
90   *Ibid.* at 41–42.
91   *R. v. Hall* (2007), 83 O.R. (3d) 641 (C.A.).

to avoiding the rule, but the decision by Justice Sopinka to do so can be explained historically. Case law prior to *Noble* had suggested that judges and juries can, in fact, consider the failure of the accused to testify.[92] There is also settled case law to the effect that judges and Crowns are free to comment on the failure of the accused to testify in judge alone trials,[93] again, suggesting that the failure to testify must have some relevance. Moreover, there is long-standing case law permitting accused persons who are seeking to cast blame on a co-accused to invite jurors to consider the failure of the co-accused to testify.[94] These lines of authority are predicated entirely on the existence of some legitimate use that can be made of the failure of an accused to take the stand. By describing a permissible inference, albeit a totally anemic one, the *Noble* Court was able to reconcile its view that the failure to testify cannot be proof of guilt, with existing case law and practices suggesting that the failure to testify can be relevant. Be that as it may, the important point emerging from *Noble* is that it is now settled that the failure to testify cannot be used as a factor to assist in proving the guilt of the accused beyond a reasonable doubt. It can be used solely for the unimportant purpose of concluding that an accused person, already proven guilty, has no answer to the charge.

Those pre-*Noble* decisions that permitted adverse inferences held that where the evidence led by the Crown invites but does not impel inculpatory inferences, and where the accused would be in a position to enlighten the trier of fact about whether exculpatory inferences are to be preferred, the failure to testify can be used to assist the court in deciding to draw the inculpatory inferences. Before such an inference could be drawn, the Crown case would have to enmesh the accused in highly incriminating circumstances.[95]

We prefer this approach for two reasons. It probably describes what triers of fact actually do in such cases, and it respects what we consider to be the centrally important principle relevant to this controversy—the "principle of a case to meet." By the time the Crown has presented a case powerful enough either to call out for an answer by the accused or to have him risk conviction by not responding, the Crown's obligation to establish a case to meet will have been satisfied.

---

92   See, for example, *R. v. Johnson* (1993), 79 C.C.C. (3d) 42 (Ont. C.A.).

93   *R. v. Binder* (1948), 6 C.R. 83 (Ont. C.A.); *R. v. B.* (1993), 117 N.S.R. (2d) 356 (C.A.).

94   See, for example, *R. v. Cuff* (1989), 49 C.C.C. (3d) 65 (Nfld. C.A.); *R. v. Naglik* (1991), 65 C.C.C. (3d) 272 (Ont. C.A.), rev'd on other grounds (1993), 23 C.R. (4th) 335 (S.C.C.).

95   See, for example, *R. v. Johnson*, above note 92.

It is important to appreciate that when the failure to testify is relied on in such circumstances, it is not the silence alone that is being used as a presumptive indicator of guilt. The force of the evidence that has been presented is relied on, coupled with a logical inference that arises naturally from the failure to answer by someone who would have an answer, were one to exist. This was the view of Justice Lamer, who dissented in *Noble*.

In *R. v. Wang* the Ontario Court of Appeal attempted to resurrect this approach when it said, "[T]he absence of an explanation can be a feature of the trial which can assist the trier of fact in determining what reasonable inferences can be drawn from the evidence adduced."[96] As attracted as we are to the reasoning in *Wang*, it is impossible to reconcile with *Noble*. The *Wang* approach describes what the trial judge did in *Noble*, yet he was overturned for having done it. Using the failure to testify as a factor in selecting what inferences to draw from evidence unquestionably involves using the failure to testify as data that assists in determining whether the Crown has reached the level of proof beyond a reasonable doubt, something the *Noble* majority disapproved of.

The one clear exception to the prohibition of using the failure to testify as positive data in deciding whether a reasonable doubt exists pertains to alibi cases. Adverse inferences are permitted to be drawn against the credibility of an alibi if the accused does not provide reasonable notice of the alibi to the Crown in advance of the trial, or if the accused does not testify in support of his alibi.[97]

4.4 (b)   Inferences by Appeal Courts

In *Noble*, Justice Sopinka expressed the opinion that these same rules apply to appeal courts, but left "for another day any final conclusion as to whether . . . silence may be treated as a make-weight by an appellate court."[98] This reservation stems from the fact that it is common for appeal courts, when deciding whether an error of law has caused a miscarriage of justice or whether a verdict is unreasonable, to support their conclusions by reference to the failure of the accused to testify.[99] Justice Sopinka therefore left open the possibility that appeal judges can use the failure to testify as additional proof of guilt because the presumption of innocence, which supports the bar on adverse inferences at trial,

---

96   *R. v. Wang*, [2001] O.J. No. 1491 at para. 44 (C.A.).
97   *R. v. Vezeau*, (1977), 34 C.R.N.S. 309 (S.C.C.); *R. v. Noble*, above note 87.
98   *R. v. Noble*, *ibid.* at 55.
99   See, for example, *R. v. Corbett* (1973), 14 C.C.C. (2d) 385 (S.C.C.); *R. v. Steinberg*, [1931] O.R. 222 (C.A.); *R. v. B.(J.N.)* (1989), 68 C.R. (3d) 145 (Man. C.A.), aff'd [1991] 1 S.C.R. 66.

operates with much less vigour on appeal after the accused has already been convicted. Appeal courts nonetheless seem insecure about the proper use of silence. In *R. v. D.D.T.*, for example, the Ontario Court of Appeal did not use silence as a makeweight adding to the inference of guilt but said it was applying the same pointless inference that *Noble* approved for trial judges, namely, noting the failure of the accused to testify in order to conclude that there is nothing to undercut the logically available inference of guilt that arises from the evidence.[100] It is time for the law to be settled. Either it should hold that no adverse inferences are appropriate either at the trial or appeal level, or alternatively, that the failure to testify provides an appropriate basis for choosing to draw inculpatory inferences at either level where the evidence enmeshes the accused in highly incriminating circumstances that he would be able to explain if he is innocent.

4.5) Commenting on the Failure to Testify

Subsection 4(6) of the *Canada Evidence Act* prohibits the Crown and the judge from commenting on the failure of the accused (or the failure of the spouse of the accused) to testify. In spite of its broad wording, a majority of the Supreme Court of Canada held in *McConnell v. R.* that a reference to the failure of the accused to testify will only be considered a "comment" for the purpose of subsection 4(6) if, in context, it suggests that the accused's silence is a cloak of guilt.[101] As a result, even adverse comments that do not invite this particular inference may be permissible. In *R. v. Diu*,[102] for example, Lam won the right to retake the stand because Diu held back information when cross-examining him. Yet Lam chose not to do so. The trial judge pointed this out when instructing the jury on how to respond to the unfair tactic by Diu. This comment effectively neutralized Lam's ability to argue that the information Diu held back should not be trusted because he had not had a fair opportunity to confront it. Yet the Ontario Court of Appeal held that section 4(6) was not breached. The trial judge's comment did not invite the inference that Lam was using his silence as a cloak for his guilt. It did no more than assist the jury in the proper evaluation of the evidence. Comments become inappropriate only if they suggest that "there is evidence the accused could give and which he has failed to give."[103]

---

100 (2010), 257 O.A.C. 258 (C.A.).
101 (1968), 4 C.R.N.S. 269 at 274–75 (S.C.C.); *R. v. Avon* (1971), 4 C.C.C. (2d) 357 (S.C.C.).
102 *R. v. Diu*, [2000] O.J. No. 1770 at paras. 177–79 (Ont. C.A.).
103 *R. v. Wright*, [1945] S.C.R. 319 at 324.

Neutral comments, simply alluding in passing to the fact that the accused has not testified, are therefore not prohibited by subsection 4(6). Such comments have often been held to be appropriate.[104] Indeed, in *Noble*, Justice Sopinka made a point of saying that subsection 4(6) does not prevent a judge from telling a jury that the evidence on a particular issue is uncontradicted, since this is not an invitation to rely on the failure of the accused to testify but rather an instruction to the jury "that it need not speculate about possible contradictory evidence."[105] In *R. v. Biladeau* the Crown went too far, however. The Crown not only noted that the complainant's evidence was uncontradicted but remarked that it is difficult to determine the knowledge of the accused because "he did not testify so he can't be asked directly."[106] This latter comment crossed the line.

Remarkably, until recently the prevailing view was that section 4(6) prohibited positive comments by trial judges.[107] In *R. v. Prokofiew*[108] the Ontario Court of Appeal found a way around this problematic interpretation. It observed that remarks by Supreme Court of Canada judges supporting this view were *obiter dicta* and it construed earlier Supreme Court authorities as permitting judges to explain to juries that the accused has the right not to testify and that this cannot affect their deliberations. This view of the law makes sense. Although the Ontario Court of Appeal cannot overturn the Supreme Court of Canada, *Prokofiew* has found a way out of an undesirable situation. Look for its interpretation of the law to gain broad acceptance.

Regardless of the nature of the comment—whether favourable or not—there are three situations where subsection 4(6) does not apply. First, subsection 4(6) does not prevent defence counsel from commenting favourably on the failure of the accused to testify; it is routine for defence counsel to explain the right of the accused not to testify when the accused has exercised that right, although, in the absence of evidence, defence counsel should not explain why the accused chose not to take the stand.[109] Second, as a concession to the liberty interest of accused persons, subsection 4(6) does not even prevent an accused

104 See *R. v. Potvin* (1989), 68 C.R. (3d) 193 (S.C.C.); *Diggs v. R.* (1987), 57 C.R. (3d) 163 (N.S.S.C.A.D.).

105 *R. v. Noble*, above note 87 at 50.

106 (2008), 93 O.R. (3d) 365 (C.A.).

107 *R. v. Noble*, above note 87. See *R. v. Bush*, [2001] B.C.J. No. 2020 (C.A.), leave to appeal to S.C.C. refused, [2001] S.C.C.A. No. 600, and see *R. v. Naglik*, above note 94 at 347 (S.C.C.); *R. v. Cuff*, above note 94.

108 (2010), 256 C.C.C. (3d) 355 (Ont. C.A.).

109 *R. v. Smith* (1997), 37 O.R. (3d) 39 (C.A.).

who is attempting to assign blame to a co-accused from commenting on the failure of the co-accused to testify, so long as the comment does not invite the jury to speculate or draw unwarranted inferences.[110] Third, subsection 4(6) does not apply at all in the case of a trial by a judge alone, where even the Crown can comment adversely on the failure of the accused to testify.[111] The distinction between jury trials and judge alone trials rests in the belief that the role of subsection 4(6) is to prevent prejudice to the accused that could arise if undue emphasis was given to the failure to testify. While undue emphasis might be given by a jury that is openly invited to consider the failure of the accused to testify, a judge is not apt to blow this failure out of proportion, so there is no need to insulate the judge from such comments.

4.6)   Tactical Compulsion

During the course of a trial, accused persons may come to feel that they have no choice but to testify because of the strength of the evidence against them. Any compulsion to testify in such cases is not the result of law, but arises because of the force of circumstances, or the weight of the evidence. The compulsion is "tactical" and not "legal" because it is not imposed by law but rather is the product of choice in the face of compelling circumstances. In formal settings, self-incrimination protection under either section 11(c) or section 7 extends only to "legal compulsion," cases where a rule of law or a judicial ruling purports to force the accused to provide self-incriminatory evidence.

In *R. v. Darrach*[112] the accused argued that section 276.1 of the *Criminal Code* was unconstitutional because it was forcing him to testify. Section 276.1 provides effectively that if an accused wishes to present evidence of a complainant's prior sexual experience in a sexual offence case, he must provide an evidentiary foundation demonstrating the need and propriety of doing so. Since *Darrach* wished to present evidence about prior sexual contact between himself and the complainant, and because complainants are not compellable witnesses during section 276.1 hearings, *Darrach* would have to take the stand in order to meet his section 276.1 burden. He urged that this was forcing him to testify, contrary to section 11(c) and the principle against self-incrimination housed in section 7. The Supreme Court of Canada held that neither sections 7 nor 11(c) of the *Charter* were violated because *Darrach* was not compelled to testify by law. He was compelled, if at all, only by his

110   *R. v. Naglik*, above note 94.
111   *R. v. Binder*, above note 93; *R. v. B.*, above note 93.
112   *R. v. Darrach* (2000), 148 C.C.C. (3d) 97 at 121–24 (S.C.C.).

tactical choice to attempt to produce this evidence, and because of the factual circumstance that he happened to be the only available source of the necessary information. Self-incrimination protection exists with respect to legal and not tactical compulsion.

Similarly, in *R. v. Warsing* the fact that as a practical matter the accused would have to testify to furnish the factual foundation for the opinion of an expert witness did not constitute legal compulsion,[113] nor does it offend self-incrimination principles for courts to be suspicious of automatism defences,[114] or claims of psychological detention in the absence of defence evidence.[115]

5. PRE-TRIAL RIGHTS TO SILENCE

The central animating "right to silence" principle is that the accused is entitled to choose whether to speak to persons in authority. Adverse inferences cannot generally be drawn against an accused person because of his pre-trial silence for if they were allowed, those adverse inferences would deprive the accused of any meaningful choice to refrain from speaking.

Where the accused does speak there are a series of rules for determining whether those statements, or the evidence those statements lead to, can be admitted. The function of these rules is to protect the principle of choice by distinguishing those cases where the accused makes an integral choice to speak from those cases where that choice is not integral or truly voluntary.

The Common Law
The rule that is most often implicated is the common law "voluntariness rule." It applies generally to statements made by the accused to persons he knows or reasonably believes to be in authority. To satisfy the voluntariness rule and have such statements admitted against the accused, the Crown must establish beyond a reasonable doubt, in all of the circumstances, that the will of the accused to remain silent was not overborne by inducements, oppressive circumstances, the lack of an operating mind, or a combination of such things. In short, a confession will not be admissible if it is made under circumstances that raise a reasonable doubt as to its voluntariness.

---

113   (2002), 167 C.C.C. (3d) 569 (B.C.C.A.).
114   *R. v. Stone*, [1999] 2 S.C.R. 290 at para. 183.
115   *R. v. Nicholas* (2004), 182 C.C.C. (3d) 393 at paras. 38–51 (Ont. C.A.).

Not all efforts to persuade the accused to speak are improper. As a result, not all inducements will cause a confession to become inadmissible. What are problematic are "quid pro quo" promises or threats that by their nature raise a doubt about whether they caused the accused to speak against his will.

Even in the absence of "quid pro quo" promises or threats, voluntariness can be undermined by "oppressive circumstances," things such as depriving the accused of food, clothing, water, sleep, or medical attention, denying the accused access to counsel, or engaging in intimidating or prolonged questioning. The concern is that mistreatment like this can sap the will of the accused to resist requests for information.

The voluntariness of a statement will also be undermined where there is a reasonable doubt about whether the speaker had an "operating mind" sufficient to enable the accused to make a meaningful choice whether to speak. Unlike "inducements" and "oppression," "operating mind" considerations do not ordinarily relate to police conduct. An accused will fail to have an operating mind if he or she does not, because of intoxication, mental illness, injury or other cause, possess the limited degree of cognitive ability necessary to understand what he or she is saying, or to comprehend that his or her statements may be used in proceedings against him or her. Even if an accused suffering some diminished mental ability has an operating mind in this narrow sense, his subjective mental condition will nonetheless be relevant in determining whether any inducements or oppressive circumstances caused by persons in authority caused him to speak involuntarily.

Examining these factors alone or in conjunction, where the circumstances in which a confession has been made raise a reasonable doubt as to whether the will of the accused to choose to speak has been overborne, the voluntariness rule requires that the confession be excluded.

In the interests of protecting the integrity of the administration of justice, and altogether apart from the foregoing factors, a confession may also be considered "involuntary" and inadmissible if it is obtained by police trickery that, while "neither violating the right to silence nor undermining voluntariness per se, is so appalling as to shock the community."

Section 7

Section 7 of the Charter supplements the common law protections described above by giving constitutional recognition to the right of *accused persons to choose whether to speak to persons in authority. This has resulted in several discrete rules that can cause the exclusion of evidence that would have been admissible at common law under the voluntariness rule.*

Undercover/Detained Statements

Section 7 can cause the exclusion, for example, of statements surreptitiously and actively elicited from detained suspects by state agents. The Charter rejects such statements because active elicitation by undercover state agents will deprive detained suspects of the ability to make an effective choice whether to speak to the authorities.

Statutorily Compelled Statements

Section 7 will also require the exclusion, in proceedings that incriminate the accused, of some statements that the accused has been obliged by law to make. Not all statutorily compelled statements are excluded. Courts will make context-based decisions. They will look for (1) the existence of real coercion in making the statement, (2) the existence of an adversarial relationship at the time the statement is made, (3) any risk that the statement will be unreliable, and (4) the risk that the statutory authority to compel statements may lead to abuse of power. The presence or absence of these factors will be evaluated together to decide whether admission of the statement would compromise the purposes underlying the principle against self-incrimination. Those purposes include the protection of persons against making unreliable confessions, and the protection of personal autonomy and dignity.

Derivative Evidence

Prior to the Charter, the common law would have permitted real evidence discovered as a result of an involuntary confession to be admitted along with so much of the confession that the discovery of the real evidence confirmed to be true. It is likely that this rule has now been changed to conform to Charter principles, causing the exclusion of the entire involuntary statement as well as all otherwise undiscoverable evidence found as a result of the confession. Whether the common law has changed in this way or not, it is settled that section 7 of the Charter can produce this same effect by supplementing the common law and causing the exclusion of both the entire involuntary statement as well as evidence derived from it.

The Redundant General Constitutional Right to Silence

Apart from these discrete rules, section 7 of the Charter has not caused wholesale modification to the common law. This is because the general constitutional right to silence will be satisfied in any case where the accused makes the choice to speak to authorities, or in other words, makes a voluntary statement. As a result, in cases other than detained/undercover statements and statutorily compelled statements, the Charter right to silence is redundant to the common law voluntariness rule. Since the Crown carries the heavy burden of proving voluntariness under the common law voluntariness rule and the accused bears the burden of establishing a Charter violation, the accused will generally be better off relying on the common law rule than attempting to invoke this general section 7 right to pre-trial silence.

Remedial Exclusion of Statements for the Breach of Other *Charter* Rights

There are other more general Charter rights distinct from the section 7 right to pre-trial silence that can result in the exclusion of statements made by the accused. Violations of the right to counsel represent the most common basis under the Charter for excluding statements. Where the accused establishes on the balance of probabilities that her statement was obtained in violation of a Charter right such as the right to counsel, or as the result of arbitrary detention, the statement is apt to be excluded under section 24(2) of the Charter, even if that statement was voluntary. Real evidence derived from statements obtained in violation of the Charter may, in some cases, be excluded as well.

5.1) General

Recently the Supreme Court of Canada observed "that the common law right to silence simply reflects the general principle that absent statutory or legal compulsion, no one is obliged to provide information to the police or respond to questioning."[116] This observation is reminiscent of the theory that was used prior to the *Charter* to explain that the sole self-incrimination protections recognized in Canadian law at the time were the protection (as opposed to privilege) of witnesses against self-incrimination and the non-compellability of accused persons at their own trials, and to support the view that the involuntary confessions

---

116 *R. v. Singh*, [2007] S.C.J. No. 48 at para. 27.

were excluded because of concern for their reliability, and not because their admission would violate any affirmative right to silence. While the underlying notion that the right to silence reflects the absence of a legal obligation to speak is still being rehearsed from time to time, what has changed is that the law does give affirmative protection to the right to silence, including prior to trial. We now exclude involuntary confessions, and at times even other evidence that such confessions lead to, in large measure because of self-incrimination concerns. There are also other related but discrete constitutional rules that positively impel the exclusion of pre-trial statements that accused persons were compelled to make against their will. The place to begin an examination of the law that supports the pre-trial right to silence, however, is with those cases where the accused does remain silent.

5.2) Where the Accused Does Remain Silent

Both the common law and section 7 of the *Charter* confer the right to remain silent at the investigative stage. This right "exists at all times against the state" and "applies anytime [the accused] interacts with a person in authority, whether detained or not."[117] Given this "right to silence," a decision by the accused not to speak will ordinarily be irrelevant at his trial; silence is as consistent with the exercise of that right as it is with the guilty desire to conceal the truth. The Crown is therefore generally barred from proving the silence of the accused, either as part of its case in chief or when cross-examining the accused as a witness,[118] and the law prohibits "irrelevant" adverse inferences from being drawn against the accused because of pre-trial silence, whether those inferences are relied upon to show guilt, or to undermine the credibility of the accused as a witness.[119]

This "right to silence" is robust enough that the accused does not waive it by providing information selectively; as the Supreme Court of Canada said in *R. v. Turcotte*, "[a]n individual is free to provide some, none, or all information he or she has."[120] Turcotte walked into a police station and told the police to send a car to a ranch where he worked, that they should put him in jail and that there was a rifle in his truck, but he refused to tell the police why the car should be sent (three men had been murdered) or to make any further statements. His "right to

---

117 *R. v. Turcotte* (2005), 200 C.C.C. (3d) 289 at para. 51 (S.C.C.).

118 *R. v. Chambers* (1990), 80 C.R. (3d) 235 (S.C.C.).

119 *R. v. Cones* (1999), 143 C.C.C. (3d) 355 (Ont. C.A.), and see *R. v. Wojcik*, [2002] 3 C.R. (6th) 92 (Man. C.A.).

120 *R. v. Turcotte*, above note 117 at para. 52.

silence" survived his selective disclosures and prevented adverse inferences from being drawn against him from his decision not to say more.[121]

Exceptionally, in spite of the general prohibition on proving that the accused remained silent there are cases where the trier of fact can learn that the accused did so because there will be "a real relevance and proper basis for [the] admission" of silence by the accused.[122]

At times silence by the accused is admitted as a necessary part of the narrative surrounding admissible evidence. In *R. v. Turcotte*, for example, it was proper for the Crown to prove that *Turcotte* refused to answer questions, for it would have been impossible to prove the admissible voluntary statements he made without narrating the entire conversation, including where he had refused to respond.[123] The sole use that his silence could be put to in that case was to permit the admissible statements to be understood. In other words, Turcotte's silence proved nothing on its own. In *R. v. Stevenson* the Crown was permitted to ask a Crown psychiatrist about the refusal of the accused to be interviewed. Had that questioning not been allowed, the jury would be left wondering why the Crown psychiatrist's opinion rested on a less complete foundation than the opinion that would be offered by the defence psychiatrist.[124]

The tactics the accused uses can also open the door to proof of the accused's silence and permit it to be used for limited, evidentiary purposes. For example, if the accused claims while testifying to have co-operated with the police, or to have shared particular information with them that he did not, his silence can be proved in rebuttal.[125] Similarly, in *R. v. W.(M.C.)*,[126] the defence suggested in court that the police had failed to investigate properly and therefore missed discovering the real perpetrator, one "J.B." This opened the door to the Crown leading evidence about who was questioned by the police, including W.(M.C.). When W.(M.C.) decided in the face of this that he should explain why he remained silent, this opened the door further for the Crown to cross-examine him about why he did so.

Alibi cases are a classic, well-established example of when the conduct of the defence can open the door to proof of silence. An alibi defence is presented when the accused claims he was elsewhere and was

---

121 See also *R. v. G.(L.)* (2009), 250 O.A.C. 266 (C.A.).
122 *R. v. Chambers*, above note 118 at para. 54.
123 *R. v. Turcotte*, above note 117 at para. 51 (S.C.C.).
124 *R. v. Stevenson* (1990), 58 C.C.C. (3d) 464 (Ont. C.A.).
125 See the examples provided in *R. v. Turcotte*, above note 117 at para. 49.
126 *R. v. W.(M.C.)* (2002), 3 C.R. (6th) 64 (B.C.C.A.).

not implicated in the crime for which he has been charged.[127] If the accused does not provide reasonable notice of an alibi sufficient to enable the police an opportunity to investigate the alibi, this failure can affect the weight of the alibi evidence.[128] Reasonable notice of an alibi includes information about the whereabouts of the accused at the time, and the names of the witnesses to the alibi.[129] Where the police already have this information, no adverse inference will be appropriate, even if the accused does not provide formal notice.[130] Moreover, silence at the time of arrest is not sufficient to ground this inference.[131] Reasonable notice will normally be required only after the accused has had an opportunity to consult counsel, and after counsel has had an opportunity to consider the matter, arguably in light of full disclosure.

Where the Crown is permitted to prove the accused's pre-trial silence, the trial judge is obliged to direct a jury about "the proper purpose for which the evidence was admitted, the impermissible inferences that must not be drawn from the evidence of silence, the limited probative value of silence, and the dangers of relying on such evidence."[132]

The right to silence is not as well protected where it is a co-accused, rather than the Crown, who wants to prove the failure by the accused to speak to authorities. This is because, unlike the Crown, accused persons have the right to make full answer and defence.[133] An accused who is trying to cast blame on a co-accused is therefore permitted to cross-examine a testifying co-accused about his or her failure to tell their exculpatory story to the police.[134] In an effort to compromise between the right of full answer and defence of the accused and the constitutional right of silence of the co-accused, the Supreme Court has held,

---

127 *R. v. Wright* (2009), 254 O.A.C. 55 at para. 24 (C.A.). It is improper to draw adverse inferences based on absence of notice for other forms of denial by the accused, such as a denial of knowledge of possession of a firearm (*R. v. Rohde* (2009), 246 C.C.C. (3d) 18 (Ont. C.A.)), or a denial to operating the vehicle in a driving offence (*R. v. Pavlov* (2009), 289 Nfld. & P.E.I.R. 19 (N.L.C.A.)). Attempts to draw adverse inferences by characterizing such denials as "near alibis" are wrong.

128 *R. v. Cleghorn*, [1995] 3 S.C.R. 175.

129 *Ibid.* at para. 32, Major J., dissenting on other grounds.

130 *R. v. Wright*, above note 127 at para. 24.

131 *Ibid.* at para. 25; *R. v. Cones*, above note 119 at 363 (Ont. C.A.).

132 *R. v. Turcotte*, above note 117 at para. 58.

133 For example, an accused may cross-examine a co-accused about his propensity to commit offences, or may use a statement made by him to persons in authority, without having to establish its voluntariness. See *R. v. Kendall* (1987), 57 C.R. (3d) 249 (Ont. C.A.); *R. v. Pelletier* (1986), 29 C.C.C. (3d) 533 (B.C.C.A.); *R. v. Jackson* (1991), 9 C.R. (4th) 57 (Ont. C.A.), aff'd on other grounds (1993), 26 C.R. (4th) 178 (S.C.C.).

134 *R. v. Crawford* (*sub nom. R. v. Creighton*) (1995), 37 C.R. (4th) 197 at 213 (S.C.C.).

however, that the pre-trial silence of the co-accused can be used solely to challenge her credibility but not as evidence of her guilt.[135] The judge must provide a complex jury direction, explaining such matters as the existence of the right to silence, the right of full answer and defence, and the limited use that can be made of the pre-trial silence of the co-accused. She must also advise the jury that silence may not, in fact, be relevant to credibility, but may simply reflect legal advice received by the co-accused.

5.3) Admissions by the Accused

"[S]tatements made by an accused are admissions by an opposing party litigant, and thus fall into an exception to the hearsay rule."[136] Where those statements have been made to ordinary persons, such as the family or friends of the accused, they are admissible at the behest of the Crown to prove the truth of their contents. Statements by accused persons that have been made to "persons in authority," such as police officers, however, are not so easily admitted in evidence in a criminal case. To be admitted those statements must satisfy the "confession rule.

5.4) The "Confession Rule"

5.4 (a)   The General Significance of R. v. Oickle

The "confession rule" is meant to ensure that statements made by the accused to persons in authority are admitted into evidence only where the accused has made a meaningful choice to speak.[137] This is because confessions obtained in the absence of meaningful choice have resulted in many miscarriages of justice.[138] Requiring "meaningful choice" not only reduces the risk that unreliable evidence will be admitted, but also preserves the fairness of the adversarial criminal trial process, and vindicates the right of the accused to remain silent.[139]

At the same time, not all means used to persuade accused persons to admit guilt are improper.[140] Police questioning is seen to be a legitimate and effective tool of criminal investigation,[141] and exclusionary practices that are too aggressive can squander important proof. The mission

---

135 R. v. Crawford, ibid.

136 R. v. T.(S.G.), [2010] S.C.J. No. 20 at para. 20.

137 R. v. Hebert, above note 18.

138 R. v. Oickle, (2000), 147 C.C.C. (3d) 321 at 341–45 (S.C.C.).

139 Ibid.

140 Ibid. at 349.

141 Ibid. at 341.

of the law is to get the balance right. This goal and continued uncertainty about how the relevant rules operate caused the Supreme Court of Canada in *R. v. Oickle* to recast the law relating to the voluntariness of confessions. Speaking generally, the Court did with the law of confessions in *Oickle* what it has done with many other rules of proof. It rejected resort to fixed and narrow rules so that a contextual approach that will be neither overinclusive or underinclusive can be applied.[142] The *Oickle* case is therefore significant. So, too, is the firm, overriding advice provided by the Court to those who apply the voluntariness rule; the animating objective in this contextual approach is to respect the "twin goals" of protecting the rights of accused persons "without unduly limiting society's need to investigate and solve crimes."

In broad terms, the rule adopted by the *Oickle* Court is simply this: "a confession will not be admissible if it is made under circumstances that raise a reasonable doubt as to voluntariness [on the part of the person making the admission]."[143] Not only will the involuntary statements initially given be inadmissible. So, too, will any subsequent statements made to persons in authority where the factors that tainted the involuntary statement are still operating at the time of the subsequent statement, or where the making of the involuntary statement was a substantial factor in the decision to make the subsequent statement.[144] This is called the "derived confessions rule." For example, if the police refer to the earlier involuntary confession to persuade the subject that there is no point in remaining silent, any subsequent confession would be excluded.

The "confession rule" inquiry is to be contextual and specific, turning on the factors particular to the case[145] and will involve consideration of "the making of threats or promises, oppression, the operating mind doctrine, and police trickery."[146] While the Supreme Court of Canada has emphasized the importance of understanding voluntariness "broadly" and avoiding "fixed and narrow rules" the voluntariness rule does operate differently, depending on context. In other words, the law relating to threats and oppression can give rise to different practices and concerns than the operating mind doctrine, which in turn differs from the police trickery inquiry.

The heart of the law is captured in the following general proposition:

---

142 *Ibid.* at 345.
143 *Ibid.* at 353.
144 *R. v. I.(R.) and T.(E.)*, [1993] 4 S.C.R. 504.
145 *R. v. Singh*, above note 116 at para. 35.
146 *R. v. Spencer* (2007), 217 C.C.C. (3d) 353 at para. 12 (S.C.C.).

[I]n order for most statements made to a person in authority to be
admissible the Crown must establish beyond a reasonable doubt in
light of all the circumstances that the will of the accused to choose
whether to speak has not been overborne by inducements, oppressive
circumstances, or the lack of an operating mind. In addition, there
must not be police trickery that unfairly denies the accused's right
to silence.

The components of the rule can be further refined, as follows:

5.4 (b)   "In order for most statements . . . to be admissible . . ."

It is not every statement made by the accused to a person in authority
that must be shown to be voluntary before the Crown can prove it. For
example, if a statement is the *actus reus* of an alleged offence, such as
a false complaint in a public mischief charge,[147] or words of refusal by
an accused charged with refusing to provide a breath sample,[148] the
Crown need not prove those words to have been voluntary. Similarly, as
a matter of practice voluntariness *voir dires* are not generally conducted
with respect to statements made under statutory compulsion, where
different considerations apply.[149]

Apart from exceptional cases like these, the voluntariness rule applies to the bulk of statements made to persons in authority. It applies
both to full confessions ("I was driving the car and I left the scene after
the accident because I wanted to avoid liability") and to less complete
admissions by accused persons ("I own the car that was in the accident"). The voluntariness rule applies whether statements are inculpatory or exculpatory, and whether they are offered to establish the
truth of their contents, or simply to cross-examine the accused in order
to show inconsistency between those statements and the accused's in-
court testimony.[150]

5.4 (c)   ". . . statements made to a person in authority . . ."

As a general rule, the voluntariness rule applies only to statements made
to "persons in authority." Since "persons in authority" will be understood by the accused to have coercive power it is believed their actions
are more apt to influence the accused into providing false confessions

---

147 *R. v. Stapleton* (1982), 66 C.C.C. (2d) 231 (Ont. C.A.).
148 *R. v. Zerbeski* (1982), 66 C.C.C. (2d) 284 (Sask. Q.B.).
149 See the discussion in section 5.7 (b), "Statutorily Compelled Statements," below
    in this chapter.
150 *R. v. Piché* (1971), 12 C.R.N.S. 222 (S.C.C.).

than are the actions of non-state agents.[151] Moreover, those adversarial rights that are protected by the voluntariness rule, including the right to silence, are tenable against the state; since the voluntariness rule is not designed to limit the conduct of private individuals, it need not apply where their conduct has induced statements.

Speaking objectively, "person[s] in authority" are "those formally engaged in the arrest, detention, examination or prosecution of the accused."[152] The most obvious examples are police officers and prison guards, but the concept can include more remote participants such as doctors assigned to investigate and report suspected cases of child abuse.[153] There are, however, important nuances in the way the concept of "person in authority" is applied. Although authoritative case law has yet to say so clearly, it is inevitable that the "persons in authority" analysis differs depending on whether the voluntariness concern in the case at hand is with (1) inducements or oppressive circumstances, (2) the operating mind doctrine, or (3) with police trickery. For ease of explanation these classic involuntariness categories will be approached out of their usual order.

"Police trickery" cases

The "police trickery" branch of the voluntariness rule — which can cause exclusion where the conduct in question would shock the community — should operate only if the person whose conduct in question is in fact a state agent. This follows naturally given that the purpose of exclusion in such cases is with the impact that the conduct of authorities can have on "the integrity of the criminal justice system."[154]

"Inducement" and "oppression" cases

Where the concern is with the impact that inducements or oppressive conduct may have had on the choice of the accused to speak, a purely objective standard is inappropriate. It is settled law that the operative "person in authority" question in such cases is "whether the accused, based on his [reasonable] perception of the recipient's ability to influence the prosecution believed either that refusing to make a statement to the person would result in prejudice, or that making one would result in favourable treatment."[155] This subjective focus follows from the

---

151 *R. v. Singh*, above note 116 at para. 40.

152 *R. v. Hodgson* (1998), 18 C.R. (5th) 135 (S.C.C.).

153 *R. v. Laidley* (2001), 41 C.R. (5th) 123 (Ont. S.C.J.).

154 *R. v. Spencer*, above note 146 at para. 12; *R. v. Oickle*, above note 138 at para. 35.

155 *R. v. Grandinetti*, 2005 SCC 5, [2005] 1 S.C.R. 27 at paras. 38 and 42, aff'g (2003), 178 C.C.C. (3d) 449 (Alta. C.A.).

theory that it is the power of persons in authority that creates the real risk of unreliable confessions; if the accused does not believe that the recipient of the statement has authority, no power imbalance will be operating and the voluntariness rule need not apply.

Thus, in *Rothman v. R.*,[156] statements made by Rothman to an undercover police officer who was posing as a fellow prisoner did not have to satisfy the voluntariness rule, given that Rothman did not believe that the officer was a "person in authority." And in *R. v. Grandinetti*[157] undercover police officers were not persons in authority, even though they told Grandinetti that they could protect him from potential charges. The crucial point was that these undercover officers did not claim to be acting on behalf of any state authority but had offered instead to use corruption to influence the course of the prosecution.

Because a subjective standard is used in inducement and oppression cases, it is even possible for persons with no real authority to satisfy the "person in authority" test. In *R. v. Wells*,[158] for example, the accused was alleged to have made statements to the father of a boy he was suspected of having sexually assaulted. The father approached Wells after meeting with the police to see if he could make Wells say anything. A threat was made and Wells admitted his guilt. Since the father's police meeting raised the spectre that he may have been acting as a police agent when he approached Wells, the trial judge had erred by not considering whether Wells believed him to be a person capable of influencing the course of the prosecution.

"Operating mind" cases

In "operating mind" cases the "person in authority" requirement is even more nuanced. As will be described later in this chapter,[159] there are two distinct situations, those where the functioning of the mind affects the influence that inducements or oppression have (the "inhibited operation of the mind cases"), and those cases where the concern is that the mind of the accused is simply not operating because of its own internal or subjective state (the "pure inoperative mind cases"). In the "inhibited operation of the mind cases" the subjective approach just described would be appropriate as the inquiry is interested in the impact that the power of authority can have on the accused, given his mental condition. In the "pure inoperative mind cases," however, concerns

---

156 (1981), 20 C.R. (3d) 97 (S.C.C.).

157 Above note 155.

158 (1998), 18 C.R. (5th) 181 (S.C.C.).

159 See the discussion below in section 5.4 (h), "the will of the accused has not been overborne . . . by *the lack of an operating mind*."

about the malfunctioning of the mind of the accused are self-standing. They operate independently of anything any person in authority may have done. The concern is with the impact of subjective conditions such as intoxication, mental illness, or the impact of physical trauma on the brain, making it irrelevant whether the person receiving the statement was a person in authority.

Procedure and persons in authority
Other than in "pure inoperative mind cases" a *voir dire* into voluntariness need not be held unless the person receiving the statement is a person in authority according to the relevant standard. It is settled law that if the statement was made to a police officer or prison official or guard, a *voir dire* should be held unless it is waived by the accused through an admission of voluntariness. By contrast, to receive the protection of a *voir dire* when the statement was made to *undercover* police officers or to persons who are not objectively in authority, the accused must point to some evidence suggesting that he or she believed the person to whom the statement was made was a person in authority. There must be a realistic basis for believing that the person may have been acting "in concert with the police or prosecutorial authorities, or as their agent."[160] If this is so, the burden then shifts to the Crown to try to avoid having to prove voluntariness by establishing, "beyond a reasonable doubt . . . that the accused did not reasonably believe the person to whom the confession was made was a person in authority . . . ."[161]

5.4 (d)   "the Crown must establish beyond a reasonable doubt, in light of all of the circumstances . . ."

In order to prove a statement caught by the voluntariness rule there are two standards of proof that apply. First, the Crown must meet the modest burden of presenting evidence capable of satisfying a reasonable trier of fact that the statement was made.[162] This does not require that statements be proved verbatim, but judges do have the discretion to exclude statements that are poorly recorded.[163] Second, the Crown must prove beyond a reasonable doubt that if such a statement was in fact made it was made voluntarily.[164] This is a heavy burden that

---

160   *R. v. T.(S.G.)*, above note 136 at para. 24.
161   *R. v. Grandinetti*, above note 155 at para. 37; *R. v. Hodgson*, above note 152.
162   *R. v. Gauthier* (1975), 27 C.C.C. (2d) 14 at 20 (S.C.C.).
163   *R. v. Melnychuk* (2008), 432 A.R. 290 (C.A.).
164   *R. v. Oickle*, above note 138 at para. 353. As intimated by the different burdens, the voluntariness of a statement, and whether that statement was made, are separate issues. Accordingly, a concession by the defence of voluntariness for the

requires the Crown to remove all and any reasonable doubt that the statement was made as a result of factors such as improper *quid pro quo* inducements, oppression, or because the accused's mind was not "operating." The Crown will also have to show that there was no police trickery or misconduct in securing the statement that would shock the public. These evaluations are to be done "in all of the circumstances." In general a "court should strive to understand the circumstances surrounding the confession and ask if it gives rise to a reasonable doubt as to the confession's voluntariness, taking into account all aspects of the rule."[165]

The combination of the heavy burden that is placed on the Crown and the need for the judge to evaluate all of the circumstances means that the Crown will not succeed if there are *material* gaps in the *voir dire* evidence relating to what was said or what happened during the interrogation. While the Crown is not required to call as a witness every person in authority who had any dealings with the accused, there have been cases where reasonable doubt has been left about voluntariness because the Crown failed to call material witnesses who could describe what happened when they were in the company of the accused.[166]

Videotaping the entire process surrounding the making of statements has obvious advantages. Generally it would enable courts to monitor interrogation practices, deter police impropriety and, in the case at hand, to make a more informed judgment on the voluntariness issues.[167] In spite of these advantages, taping interrogations is not a prerequisite to admissibility.[168] This certainly makes sense where taping is not feasible[169] but there are those who argue that where videotaping is possible there should be a strict rule requiring exclusion if the police fail to tape an interrogation in its entirety.[170] The law, however, has not

---

purpose of dispensing with a *voir dire* cannot be taken as an admission that the statement was in fact made: *R. v. Reid* (2003), 18 C.R. (6th) 350 at para. 65 (Ont. C.A.).

165   *R. v. Oickle, ibid.* at 354–55. For a good illustration of how myriad factors can combine to cause exclusion, see *R. v. Walsh* (2002), 4 C.R. (6th) 341 (N.S.S.C.).

166   *Thiffault v. R.* (1933), 60 C.C.C. 97 (S.C.C.), and see by way of example the contrasting facts in *R. v. Woodward* (1975), 23 C.C.C. (2d) 508 (Ont. C.A.) and *R. v. Settee* (1974), 22 C.C.C. (2d) 193 (Sask. C.A.). See also *R. v. Menezes* (2001), 48 C.R. (5th) 163 (Ont. S.C.J.).

167   *R. v. Oickle*, above note 138 at 344–45.

168   *Ibid.*

169   See, for example, *R. v. Wareham* (2003), 16 C.R. (6th) 172 (Ont. S.C.J.).

170   Justice Peter de C. Cory, *The Inquiry Regarding Thomas Sophonow* (Winnipeg: Queen's Printer, 2001) at 19, online at Manitoba Justice: www.gov.mb.ca/justice/publications/sophonow.toc.html; Lee Stuesser, "The Accused's Right to Silence:

gone this far. The Ontario Court of Appeal has been the most aggressive among Canadian appellate courts, holding that where recording facilities are available and an officer expects a discussion about the offence to occur, "in most circumstances the failure to record will render the confession suspect."[171] In British Columbia unrecorded statements are not immediately suspect. Traditional assessments of credibility and reliability are used to evaluate voluntariness unless particular concerns are raised about the state of the record, in which case the failure to videotape where possible can raise suspicion.[172] Meanwhile, in Manitoba even less importance is attached to the failure to videotape. In *R. v. Ducharme*[173] the Manitoba Court of Appeal, while endorsing the desirability of taping, expressed the view that the Ontario position is inconsistent with *Oickle*.

Even where a failure to record is insufficient to raise a reasonable doubt about voluntariness, there is authority requiring judges in Ontario and British Columbia to warn a jury to consider the absence of a proper recording in deciding whether to rely on the police version of the alleged statement.[174]

The following discussion explains precisely what it is that the Crown must prove beyond a reasonable doubt where a *voir dire* is required.

5.4 (e)   ". . . the Crown must establish . . . that the will of the accused has not been overborne . . ."

From time to time, courts have declared the importance of causation to the voluntariness rule. Statements were to be excluded only if there was a basis for doubting whether the accused would have made the statement, absent the improper pressure.[175] In practice, trial courts rarely gave emphasis to this, excluding statements whenever improper inducements or conduct was detected. In *Oickle*, causation has now been reinforced as a central consideration. Speaking specifically about "inducements," but no doubt making a statement of general application, the Court said:

> [An effort by the police to convince suspects to make admissions] becomes improper only when the inducements [or other improper

---

No Doesn't Mean No" (2002) 29 Man. L.J. 149; and David Tanovich, "Annotation: *R. v. Ducharme*" (2004) 20 C.R. (6th) 333.

171 *R. v. Ahmed* (2002), 7 C.R. (6th) 308 at para. 14 (Ont. C.A.); and see *R. v. Moore-McFarlane* (2001), 160 C.C.C. (3d) 493 (Ont. C.A.).

172 *R. v. Crockett* (2002), 7 C.R. (6th) 300 (B.C.C.A.).

173 *R. v. Ducharme* (2004), 20 C.R. (6th) 332 (Man. C.A.).

174 *R. v. Swanek* (2005), 28 C.R. (6th) 93 (Ont. C.A.); *R. v. Narwal* (2009), 248 C.C.C. (3d) 62 at para. 49 (B.C.C.A.).

175 See, for example, *R. v. Fitton* (1956), 24 C.R. 371 (S.C.C.).

pressure], whether standing alone or in combination with other factors, are strong enough to raise a reasonable doubt about whether the will of the subject has been overborne.[176]

This inquiry requires an examination both of the intensity of the pressure, and the ability of the particular accused to resist that pressure. Given that the ultimate focus is on the voluntariness of the decision or choice by the accused to speak, it is understandable that the law would focus on the impact that inducements or oppression or tricks would have on the accused, given his personal characteristics and experiences, even though this effectively permits different strategies to be employed by the police for different accused persons. An illustration of the impact that this individualized inquiry can have is provided by the post-*Oickle* case of *R. v. M.(C.).*[177] There a statement made by a young offender was admitted in spite of a number of alleged inducements. The court did not believe the comments made by the police had functioned as inducements to the accused, largely because the accused had previous convictions and was familiar both with the workings of the court system and the kind of sentences handed out for the offence he was charged with. The focus on context holds out the possibility that similar importuning by the police may have rendered statements by an inexperienced offender involuntary.

5.4 (f)   ". . . the will of the accused has not been overborne by inducements . . ."

The "*Ibrahim* rule," dealing with inducements, once expressed the entire law relating to confessions. That rule required that the Crown prove that a statement was voluntary "in the sense that it has not been obtained from [the accused] either by fear of prejudice or hope of advantage exercised or held out by a person in authority."[178] "Fear of prejudice" related to express or implied threats that would be carried out if the accused did not co-operate, while "hope of advantage" described promises of benefit to be accorded in exchange for testimony. What *Ibrahim* focused on were *quid pro quo* consequences inspiring the choice to speak.

While the *Ibrahim* rule no longer provides an adequate description of the relevant rule, the presence of inducements raising "fear of prejudice" or "hope of advantage" will still feature in most cases where confessions are excluded. Speaking of "inducements" the *Oickle* Court said,

---

176 *R. v. Oickle*, above note 138 at 349.
177 *R. v. M.(C.)*, [2001] N.S.J. No. 144 (C.A.).
178 *Ibrahim v. R.*, [1914] A.C. 509 at 609 (P.C.).

"[t]he most important consideration in all cases is to look for a *quid pro quo* offer by interrogators, regardless of whether it comes in the form of a threat or a promise."[179] Depending on the circumstances, those *quid pro quo* inducements can serve to undermine voluntariness, whether the threats or promises relate to the accused or to someone closely connected to the accused.[180] Indeed, an inducement can render a confession involuntary even though the inducement arises only implicitly from the actions of a person in authority who does not intend to offer hope or to raise fear.[181]

It bears emphasis that not all inducements will render a confession or admission involuntary, and that not all inducements to persuade the accused to speak are inappropriate. In *R. v. Spencer* a majority of the Supreme Court of Canada ruled that even though the police effectively promised the accused that he could visit his girlfriend if he talked, the trial judge was entitled to find that this inducement was not strong enough to render the statement involuntary; Mr. Spencer was an "aggressive," "mature and savvy participant" who had himself attempted to secure deals with the police and who played on a level playing field with the police during the taped interview.[182] The ultimate question will be whether the inducements are strong enough, either alone or in combination with other factors, "to raise a reasonable doubt about whether the will of the subject has been overborne."[183]

Although speaking of a subject's "will" being "overborne" seems dramatic, in the words of Justice Fish, the rule does not require that the accused lose "any independent, meaningful ability to choose to remain silent."[184] Were that so, the inducement bar would add nothing to the oppression doctrine. More importantly, the purpose of the rule in expunging dangerous confessions would be defeated by such a high standard. It is clear from the authority that the question is whether the accused's will to remain silent was lost because it was the unreasonable or unfair pressure of the inducement rather than a freely made choice to speak that "caused or led to the statement."[185]

---

179 *R. v. Oickle*, above note 138 at 350.

180 *Ibid.* at 346.

181 *R. v. Alexis* (2002), 163 C.C.C. (3d) 387 (B.C.C.A.).

182 *R. v. Spencer*, above note 146 at paras. 20–21.

183 *R. v. Oickle*, above note 138 at 349.

184 *R. v. Spencer*, above note 146 at para. 32. Justice Fish was dissenting when he used this language, but the dissent was prefaced on a disagreement about how the trial judge reasoned, and not a disagreement with the majority over what the law is.

185 *Ibid.* at para. 14.

The *Oickle* Court, solely by way of non-exhaustive illustration and without intending to cast doubt on the need to look at the totality of the circumstances, gave the following guidance:

- any confession that is the product of outright violence is involuntary;[186]
- suggestions such as "it would be better to confess" may or may not result in a finding of involuntariness — central in that determination is whether, in context, such words would tend to be taken as a veiled threat;[187] and
- spiritual or moral inducements will generally not produce an involuntary confession because the inducement offered is not within the control of the police.[188]

Speaking of "hope of advantage" inducements, the Court said:

- "an explicit offer by the police to procure lenient treatment in return for a confession is clearly a very strong inducement, and will warrant exclusion in all but exceptional circumstances;"[189]
- where an accused person has been subjected to such intense and prolonged questioning that he would become convinced that no-one will believe his protestations of innocence, *holding out the possibility* of a reduced charge or sentence in exchange for a confession would raise a reasonable doubt;[190] and
- an offer of psychiatric help or other counselling in exchange for a confession is not generally as strong an inducement as an offer of leniency.[191]

The application of these principles in *Oickle* itself illustrates how difficult they can be in application; reasonable people might disagree on whether a comment amounts to an inducement. Justice Arbour provided a strong dissent in the case, finding, as had a majority of the

---

186 R. v. *Oickle*, above note 138 at 347. Indeed, where a police assault has occurred it is so serious that its effect may be assumed to linger for hours after. See R. v. *Sabri* (2002), 4 C.R. (6th) 349 (Ont. C.A.).

187 R. v. *Oickle*, ibid. at 347–48.

188 *Ibid.* at 349. The same is true of "self-imposed" threats; the accused in R. v. *Carpenter*, [2001] B.C.J. No. 95 (C.A.), leave to appeal to S.C.C. refused, [2002] S.C.C.A. No. 302, was encouraged to admit that he had swallowed heroin so that he could get medical help given the risk this would present to his health.

189 R. v. *Oickle*, ibid. at 346. See R. v. *Nugent* (1988), 42 C.C.C. (3d) 431 (N.S.S.C.A.D.) (promise that the charge would be reduced to manslaughter); R. v. *Bégin* (2002), 6 C.R. (6th) 360 (Que. C.A.) (promise of protection while in custody).

190 R. v. *Oickle*, ibid. [emphasis added].

191 *Ibid.*

Nova Scotia Court of Appeal, that the police had suggested that Oickle could get help if he confessed, that if he confessed to all of the arson fires suspected against him the charges could be bundled up, and that if he did not confess, his girlfriend would be treated as a suspect and subjected to an unpleasant investigation. The majority of the Supreme Court of Canada disagreed, concluding that none of the comments could be taken as *quid pro quo* threats or promises.

5.4 (g)   "the will of the accused has not been overborne . . . by oppressive circumstances . . ."

It gradually came to be accepted that a confession may be excluded as involuntary where it is the product of an atmosphere of oppression created by the authorities, even though there have been no improper inducements.[192] This remains the case after *Oickle*, but again, the ultimate question will be whether the oppressive circumstances, either alone or in conjunction with inducements or other circumstances, raise a reasonable doubt about whether the will of the accused was overborne. The *Oickle* Court identified two psychological mechanisms that can produce this result, the "stress-compliant confession [made] to escape [the oppressive] conditions," and the phenomenon by which the oppressed accused comes to doubt his own memory and to believe the relentless allegations made by the police.[193] Relevant circumstances that can create an atmosphere of oppression include deprivation of food, clothing, water, sleep, or medical attention, denying access to counsel, or excessively aggressive, intimidating questioning for a prolonged period.[194] *R. v. Hoilett*[195] provides an example. Hoilett, who was intoxicated, was left naked in a cold cell for two hours before being provided with inadequate clothing. He was awakened in the middle of the night after only one hour's sleep and interrogated, nodding off five times during the questioning. He was refused a tissue to wipe his nose and warmer clothing. His confession to a sexual assault was excluded because of the oppressive circumstances in which the confession was made.

---

192   *Hobbins v. R.* (1982), 27 C.R. (3d) 289 (S.C.C.); *R. v. Owen* (1983), 4 C.C.C. (3d) 538 (N.S.S.C.). See *R. v. S.(M.J.)*, [2000] A.J. No. 391 (Prov. Ct.), where oppression was found, based on the use by the police of the common "Reid technique" of interrogation, which includes befriending, baiting, minimizing the seriousness of the offence, rejecting protestations of innocence, changing the subject when the desired answer is not obtained, and using "themes." The judge in *S.(M.J.)* described the term "themes" as a polite way of describing outright falsehoods such as "we've cleared everyone else."

193   *R. v. Oickle*, above note 138 at 350.

194   *Ibid.* at 351.

195   *R. v. Hoilett* (1999), 136 C.C.C. (3d) 449 (Ont. C.A.).

Although it is not *per se* improper for the police to lie[196] or to confront accused persons by claiming to have evidence they do not, using this tactic can contribute to an oppressive interrogation. The *Oickle* Court described this as a dangerous ploy that can contribute, along with other factors, to an involuntary confession.[197] In dissent, Justice Arbour concluded that the false claim by the police, that the polygraph that Oickle had failed was infallible, created an oppressive atmosphere. The majority felt that this was too isolated an indiscretion to undermine the voluntariness of the statement provided by Oickle. In *R. v. Hammerstrom*,[198] a trial judge excluded a murder confession made by a suspect who reasonably believed himself to be detained, and who, in his despondent and emotional condition brought on by aggressive questioning, came to believe that protests of his innocence would be futile because the police had deceived him into believing that he was caught at the crime scene by security cameras.

It has been held that before a statement will be involuntary because of oppression, the statement must result from external pressure rather than from the subjective fear or timidity of the accused.[199] This merely means that there must be actual oppressive circumstances. It does not mean that subjective considerations that would make a person more vulnerable to mistreatment are irrelevant; all of the circumstances must be examined, with the objective of identifying whether the will of the subject has been overborne.

5.4 (h) "the will of the accused has not been overborne . . . by the lack of an operating mind."

In time it came to be accepted that, to be admissible, statements must be the product of an "operating mind." For example, in *Ward* it was held that a statement made by someone suffering from shock after an accident could not be admitted because it was not the product of an operating mind.[200] The same has been said of a hypnotized statement.[201] Intoxicated confessions may also be excluded on this basis, and so too might confessions by some individuals suffering from mental disorders.

---

196 *R. v. Cook*, [1998] 2 S.C.R. 597 at para. 60.

197 *R. v. Oickle*, above note 138 at 351.

198 (2006), 43 C.R. (6th) 346 (B.C.S.C.). An appellate court did not have an opportunity to consider this aggressive application of the oppression doctrine, as Mr. Hammerstrom was ultimately convicted on other evidence: [2006] B.C.J. No. 3317 (S.C.).

199 *Hobbins v. R.*, above note 192.

200 *Ward. v. R. (sub nom. R. v. Ward)* (1979), 10 C.R. (3d) 289 (S.C.C.).

201 *Horvath v. R.* (1979), 7 C.R. (3d) 97 (S.C.C.).

The mere fact of intoxication[202] or mental illness,[203] or other conditions that could impair one's cognitive function is not enough to require exclusion. In *R. v. Whittle*[204] the Court explained that the focus is on whether the accused has truly been able to make a choice to make the statement:

> The operating mind test . . . requires that the accused possess a limited degree of cognitive ability to understand what he or she is saying and to comprehend that the evidence may be used in proceedings against [him]. . . . In determining the requisite capacity to make an active choice, the relevant test is: Did the accused possess an operating mind? It goes no further and no inquiry is necessary as to whether the accused is capable of making a good or wise choice or one that is in his or her own interest.[205]

Statements made by Whittle, a schizophrenic, confessing to murder were admitted even though he was "very mentally unstable," at times actively hallucinating. He felt an inner compulsion to confess because of voices in his head and he could not keep himself from speaking. The statements were admissible because Whittle had the cognitive ability to understand what he was saying and he knew that the statements could be used against him.

Justices of the Supreme Court of Canada have, on more than one occasion, stressed that "the operating mind should not be understood as a discrete inquiry completely divorced from the rest of the confession rule."[206] It is "just one application of the general rule that involuntary confessions are inadmissible."[207] With respect, these passages are unfortunate because the "operating mind" authority just outlined can only be understood as discrete or different from other involuntariness cases. The concern in these cases is with the impact that some intrinsic condition affecting the functioning of the mind of the accused has on his capacity to make voluntary statements. The concern is not with the conduct of authorities. In *Ward v. R.*,[208] for example, the "shock" that undermined the voluntariness of the confession was caused by an accident, not by any police impropriety, and had Whittle been mentally ill enough not to know what he was saying, his confession would

---

202 See, for example, *R. v. Bennett*, [2005] O.J. No. 4035 (S.C.J.).
203 See, for example, *R. v. Ristine* (2007), 48 C.R. (6th) 13 (Ont. S.C.J.).
204 *R. v. Whittle* (1994), 32 C.R. (4th) 1 (S.C.C.).
205 *Ibid.* at 20.
206 *R. v. Oickle*, above note 138 at 351; *R. v. Spencer*, above note 146 at para. 12.
207 *R. v. Oickle*, *ibid.* at 352.
208 Above note 200.

no doubt have been rejected even though the police treated him fairly. Given this, there is no reason or sense in such cases in imposing the general rule's "person in authority" requirements, or in looking for acts by state agents such as inducements or oppression. These "pure inoperative mind cases" are discrete, and they do operate outside of the general voluntariness rule.

There are, however, cases where the diminished mental capacity of the accused—whether caused by substances abuse, injuries, or illness—should be examined within the general voluntariness rule. In these "inhibited operation of the mind cases" although the accused does suffer some mental impairment, he is able to understand what he is saying and that what he says can be used against him as evidence. Still, his diminished mental faculties will nonetheless be an important factor in deciding whether any improper inducements or any oppressive conduct by state agents caused him to lose the will to resist speaking. This is how Hoilett's[209] alcohol impairment factored into the oppression analysis in that case. His intoxication did not deprive him of an operating mind, but contributed to a finding of involuntariness because his impairment made him vulnerable and impeded his will to resist. In such cases there has to be regard to the "persons in authority" requirement and there must be a search for conduct by persons in authority that contributes to involuntariness.

5.4 (i)   "Police Trickery"

A confession may be considered "involuntary" and inadmissible if it is obtained by police trickery that, while "neither violating the right to silence nor undermining voluntariness *per se*, is so appalling as to shock the community."[210] This inquiry is not dependent on a finding that the will of the accused has been overborne. It is separate from considerations relating to inducements, oppression, and the exploitation of an inoperative mind because its primary objective is to maintain the integrity of the criminal justice system.[211] In excluding confessions on this basis, courts are to be wary not to unduly limit police techniques. As a result, not all lies told by the police or all "tricks" employed by them will require exclusion. Examples provided by the *Oickle* Court of conduct that would shock the conscience and therefore require exclusion included posing as a priest or a legal aid lawyer and injecting truth serum into a diabetic accused under the pretense it is insulin.[212]

---

209   Above note 195.
210   *R. v. Oickle*, above note 138 at 353.
211   *Ibid.* at 352.
212   *Ibid.* at 353.

A "trick" that induced a confession but was not shocking enough to require exclusion occurred in *R. v. Rowe*.[213] The police gave reward money to a Jamaican spiritualist who then used a ritual to induce Rowe to confess; it was important that the accused had not undertaken the ritual for personal spiritual purposes but had done so in the belief that the spiritualist could assist him in avoiding apprehension. And in *R. v. Omar*[214] it was held that the "Mr. Big" scam (in which accused persons are tricked into bragging about their criminal exploits as a way to gain favour with undercover police officers posing as gangsters) was not a trick that would shock the public.

The "shocks the conscience" test was initially developed by Justice Lamer in his concurring judgment in *Rothman v. R.*[215] He had in mind two objectives that would be served by this test. First, he was concerned with conduct that was so seriously unfair that it would warrant excluding even reliable confessions because their admission would bring the administration of justice into disrepute. Second, he was concerned about the risk that tricks could produce unreliable confessions. He reasoned that if a confession was unreliable it would have to be excluded because of the principle against self-incrimination. He reasoned that if an unreliable confession was to be admitted, the accused would have no choice but to take the stand to explain that confession away. This, he felt, would offend self-incrimination principles by effectively depriving the accused, who would be forced onto the stand to deny an unfairly induced and unreliable confession, of his right not to be compelled to testify.

Justice Lamer's complex theory requires mention here because, in quoting from *Rothman*, the *Oickle* Court appears to have lost sight of the distinction that Justice Lamer drew between excluding reliable and unreliable confessions. In describing the "correct approach" in *Oickle*, the Court quoted a passage from *Rothman* that was meant to pertain only to the second basis for exclusion, and not to serve as the general test for exclusion. That passage said:

> [A] statement before being left to the trier of fact . . . should be the subject of a *voir dire* in order to determine . . . whether the authorities have done or said anything that could have induced the accused to make a statement that might be untrue.[216]

213 *R. v. Rowe* (2006), 208 C.C.C. (3d) 412 (C.A.).
214 *R. v. Omar* (2007), 84 O.R. (3d) 321 (C.A.).
215 *Rothman v. R.*, above note 156.
216 *R. v. Oickle*, above note 138 at 352, citing *Rothman v. R.*, *ibid.*

Because it was described by the *Oickle* Court as housing the "correct approach," this passage could mistakenly be taken by some as confining the exclusion of statements produced by "police tricks" to those tricks that, by their nature, could produce false statements. This limitation would be impossible to reconcile with the examples used in *Oickle*. Both a confession to an imposter priest and a statement to an imposter legal aid lawyer are offensive not because such conduct can induce statements that might be untrue. Indeed, statements obtained in these ways are likely to be true. Who goes to confession and makes up sins? Who tries to mislead his own lawyer by making false inculpatory statements? What is offensive is that the conduct that produces such statements, whether those statements are true or not, shocks the conscience because it so far removed from acceptable and decent police conduct. Given that the *Oickle* Court affirmed that this branch of the voluntariness test is aimed at "the more specific objective of maintaining the integrity of the criminal justice system," this passage should not be treated as housing the test. Instead, the standard outlined elsewhere in the *Oickle* decision should be used: confessions may be excluded if they are obtained by "police trickery, though neither violating the right to silence nor undermining voluntariness *per se*, is so appalling as to shock the community."[217]

5.5)   Statements under the *Youth Criminal Justice Act*

Children are particularly vulnerable. As a result, special rules apply to statements made by persons under the age of eighteen. Subject to narrow statutory exceptions, the Crown has to prove both voluntariness and material compliance with section 146 of the *Youth Criminal Justice Act*,[218] beyond a reasonable doubt,[219] before statements made by a young person can be admitted. The statute provides "informational," "consultation," and "attendance" rights. The "consultation" and "attendance" rights are best described first. They entitle a young person to speak to, and have present during questioning, not only a lawyer, but also their parents, relatives, or other appropriate adults. The "informational" component requires that the young person be made aware of those rights, that they need not speak, and that any statement they make can be used as evidence against them. This information has to be delivered in age-appropriate language suitable to the apparent level of

---

217 *R. v. Oickle, ibid.* at 353.
218 S.C. 2002, c. 1.
219 *R. v. H.(L.T.)*, [2008] S.C.J. No. 50.

understanding of the young person. Indeed, the person in authority is obliged to take reasonable steps to ensure that the young person understands, failing which the statement will not be admitted.[220]

5.6) The General Discretion to Exclude

Independently of the voluntariness rule judges have residual discretion to exclude confessions or admissions. The general power that judges have to exclude evidence where its probative value is outweighed by the risks of prejudice it presents can be used to exclude even voluntary confessions obtained by persons in authority.[221] Beyond this matters become more difficult. There is important and credible authority recognizing that judges have a discretion operating outside of the voluntariness rule to exclude confessions on broader grounds, namely to preserve trial fairness. In *R. v. Wells* the B.C. Court of Appeal decided that this discretion could exclude confessions obtained by violence or threats by someone who is not in authority.[222] And in *R. v. Laidley* the trial judge claimed discretion to exclude voluntary confessions obtained by individuals he found to be persons in authority based on broad fairness concerns.[223] The trial judge considered it unfair that a child abuse team appointed within a hospital to identify and report child abuse did not inform the accused about the purpose of their interview, and he was troubled by the inconsistent testimony given by members of that team about their role.

The existence of such a broad discretion is in keeping with Supreme Court of Canada decisions in *R. v. Harrer*[224] and *R. v. Terry*.[225] In those cases the Court endorsed a general power in judges to exclude technically admissible evidence in order to preserve trial fairness. Both of these cases dealt with statements obtained by foreign officers who were not subject to the *Charter*. Unfortunately, in an effort to leave flexibility, the Supreme Court of Canada furnished little guidance as to the criteria and standards to be employed in identifying trial fairness. This lack

---

220 *Ibid.*

221 See, for example, *R. v. Sodhi* (2003), 179 C.C.C. (3d) 60 (Ont. C.A.).

222 (2003), 12 C.R. (6th) 185 (B.C.C.A.).

223 (2001), 41 C.R. (5th) 123 (Ont. S.C.J.). The trial judge purported to ground that authority in sixty-year-old *obiter dictum*, but in an annotation to the case, (2001) 41 C.R. (5th) 124, Professor R.J. Delisle defended the discretion on the basis of *R. v. Harrer* (1995), 42 C.R. (4th) 269 (S.C.C.), discussed immediately below.

224 *Ibid. Harrer* and the trial fairness discretion are discussed below in chapter 9, section 8, "Excluding Unfairly Obtained Evidence in the Absence of a *Charter* Violation."

225 [1996] 2 S.C.R. 207.

of guidance raises important questions. First, in *Oickle* the Supreme Court of Canada adopted a "shocks the conscience" test for addressing trickery by persons who are in authority.[226] Can a different and possibly less restricted discretion operate as an alternative basis for excluding confessions on the basis of misconduct, whether taken by persons in authority or not? Second, in *R. v. Grandinetti* when the Supreme Court of Canada endorsed the power to exclude confessions rendered unreliable by the actions of persons who are not in authority it did not invoke *Harrer* or the "shocks the conscience" standard but relied instead on yet another body of law—the common law and *Charter*-based power of courts to remedy abuses of process.[227] It can, therefore, be said with confidence that courts do possess the power outside of the voluntariness rule to exclude confessions, but the standards for applying that discretion await clarification.

5.7)   Section 7 of the *Charter*

Like the common law, the *Charter* protects the right to silence; it has been recognized that the right to remain silent is a principle of fundamental justice guaranteed by section 7.[228] While both regimes pursue the same basic objectives, Justice Iacobucci warned in *R. v. Oickle* with respect to the common law and *Charter* regimes that "[i]t would be a mistake to assume that one subsumes the other entirely."[229] The *Charter* has indeed supplemented or added to the common law protections, but only in discrete areas. As already observed, section 7 of the *Charter* is violated if the accused is cross-examined about why he failed to give a statement to the police. Section 7 has made other contributions to the law relating to the admissibility of confessions.

5.7 (a)   Undercover/Detained Statements

It was held in *R. v. Hebert*[230] that the section 7 right to silence of a detained person is contravened where an undercover state agent (either a police officer or an informant planted by the police) actively elicits a statement from the accused. In such cases, the statement is likely to be excluded under subsection 24(2) of the *Charter*.

Hebert had told the police he did not wish to speak to them. The police nonetheless planted an officer in his cell, who posed as a fellow

---

226 See the discussion above in this chapter at section 5.4 (i), "'Police Trickery.'"
227 Above note 155 at para. 36.
228 See *R. v. Hebert*, above note 18.
229 Above note 138 at 340.
230 Above note 18.

prisoner. The officer managed to get Hebert to speak. This effectively deprived Hebert of "the right to make a free and meaningful choice as to whether to speak to the authorities or to remain silent,"[231] and the confession was excluded.[232] In R. v. Liew the Supreme Court of Canada affirmed that this doctrine applies, whether or not the accused advises the police that he does not wish to speak.[233]

The rule in Hebert is not contravened every time a detained accused person makes a statement to an undercover state agent. It will be violated only if the undercover state agent causes the accused to make incriminating comments that he would not otherwise have made. Two sets of factors are useful in testing "the relationship between the state agent and the accused to determine whether there was a causal link between the conduct of the state agent and the making of the statement by the accused."[234]

The first set of useful factors relates to the nature of the exchange, and asks whether the exchange that produced the incriminating statements was akin to an interrogation. If so, the Hebert rule has been offended. An exchange does not have to involve overbearing or oppressive questioning to become akin to an interrogation. It can become akin to an interrogation where the undercover state agent engages in a form of conversation that has the effect of provoking admissions and where that form of conversation is not one that would ordinarily be engaged in by someone in the role the undercover state agent is playing. If, on the other hand, the undercover state agent simply permits a conversation to develop naturally, in the fashion that someone in the role he is playing would converse, then any admissions that are made by the detainee will simply be the product of the detainee's voluntary choice to speak. In short, if the undercover agent goes outside of his assumed role, he may have begun to actively elicit statements, thereby offending the rule.

The second set of factors has to do with the exploitation of a relationship of trust. Whenever an accused person makes self-incriminatory admissions to another, he takes the risk that the other will breach the confidence and provide evidence against him. Where, however, the accused has a special relationship with a person, the risk of betrayal that the accused is choosing to take may be low. It is considered unfair for state agents to exploit such relationships in order to secure admis-

---

231   Ibid. at 186.
232   This, of course, is different than the result at common law. See Rothman v. R., above note 156.
233   R. v. Liew, [1999] 3 S.C.R. 227 at para. 44.
234   Ibid. at para. 46.

sions. Hence, if the state agent assumes a special relationship with the accused that is of such a nature that it would cause the accused to reasonably believe that his statements would not end up in the hands of the authorities, and the state agent thereby obtains admissions, the *Hebert* rule is violated.[235]

It should be apparent given the nature of the test and of the factors consulted that the determination of whether there is a causal link is fact-based and unpredictable. In *Liew* no such link was found, even though the undercover officer posed questions and moved the conversation to a more incriminating subject. The Court reasoned, over the strong dissent of Chief Justice Lamer, that the accused had initiated the discussion, and the questions and change of subject followed naturally from the train of the conversation. Nor was the Court persuaded that the act of the police officer in posing as a drug dealer arrested in the same transaction as Liew created a sufficient special relationship to ground a violation. Liew's statements were therefore admitted.

It is important to understand that the *Hebert* rule is subject to strict limits. It does not mean that an accused person cannot be interviewed in the absence of his counsel where those rights have otherwise been respected. If the accused chooses to volunteer information as the result of police persuasion short of denying him the right to choose, there is no breach of his right to silence. Moreover, the protection applies solely to those who are subject to the coercive power of the state, namely, those individuals who have been arrested, charged, or who are being detained.[236] The rule does not apply to voluntary statements made by detained persons to fellow inmates who are not state agents, since the rule is directed at state action.

5.7 (b)   Statutorily Compelled Statements

In some cases, section 7 prevents the Crown, in prosecuting the accused, from using statements that the accused has made because of what is, or what the accused reasonably perceives to be, a legal obligation to speak. Since the common law does not impose obligations to speak to persons in authority, the source of that legal compulsion will invariably be statutory. There are, in fact, a number of statutes that require persons to furnish information to state agents, usually in a regulatory context. In *R. v. White*[237] the accused was required, under a statute that regulates the operation of motor vehicles, to identify herself as the driver

235 *R. v. Broyles* (1991), 9 C.R. (4th) 1 (S.C.C.). And see *R. v. Liew, ibid.*

236 *R. v. Noble*, above note 87 at 39.

237 *R. v. White*, [1999] 2 S.C.R. 417. And see *R. v. Powers* (2006), 213 C.C.C. (3d) 351 (B.C.C.A.).

of a motor vehicle that had been involved in an accident. The Supreme Court of Canada prevented the Crown from using this statement when White was prosecuted criminally for failing to remain at the scene of an accident. Note that section 7 did not permit Ms. White to refuse to make the statutorily required statement. It provided her with "use immunity." The statement could not be used against her in a proceeding in which she was being prosecuted criminally.

White does not hold that all statutorily compelled statements must be excluded in this way. Protection arises only if the admission of the statement would compromise the purposes underlying the principle against self-incrimination. These purposes include protection from unreliable statements and the prevention of the use of state power in a manner that diminishes personal autonomy and dignity. In deciding whether a compelled statement will have such results, factors to be considered include whether the statement is the product of "real coercion," whether there is an adversarial relationship at the time, whether the risk of unreliable confessions is presented, and whether the legislation increases the risk of state abuse. Therefore, persons who voluntarily enter a regulated activity where information must be gathered to maintain the regulatory scheme, and who furnish that information at a time when they are not in an adversarial relationship with the state, will not be protected.[238] Since White had no real choice but to drive, she did not effectively choose to enter a regulated regime. Moreover, she was in an adversarial position to the state when she made her statement. The nature of the state authority undermined her voluntariness, jeopardizing the reliability of the confession she gave and presenting a risk of state abuse. In *R. v. Jones*[239] the Ontario Court of Appeal held that the admission of statutorily compelled statements made to a customs officer would not contravene the underlying purpose protected by self-incrimination principles because no one who enters a country reasonably expects to be left alone. In a sense, there is not the ordinary reasonable expectation of privacy of information.

5.7 (c)   Derivative Evidence

At common law, the "rule in *R. v. St. Lawrence*" provides that where an involuntary confession leads to the discovery of real evidence, that real evidence is admissible as is so much of the confession as is confirmed

---

238   *R. v. Fitzpatrick* (1995), 43 C.R. (4th) 343 (S.C.C.).
239   (2006), 41 C.R. (6th) 84 (Ont. C.A.).

to be true by the discovery of the real evidence.[240] In *R. v. Sweeney*,[241] a post-*Charter* case, the accused confessed to a robbery and disclosed where the gun was hidden. The trial judge found the confession to be involuntary but then relied on the common law rule in *R. v. St. Lawrence* to admit not only the gun, but the confession itself.[242] Sweeney challenged that decision by asking the Ontario Court of Appeal to overrule *R. v. St. Lawrence* to reflect *Charter* values. The court agreed that the common law had indeed been modified,[243] but did not decide the case on that basis. Instead, Justice Rosenberg, speaking for the court, held that section 7 of the *Charter* was violated when the police obtained an involuntary confession from Sweeney, who was detained at the time.[244] The admissibility of the confession would therefore turn, not on the common law and the rule in *R. v. St. Lawrence*, but on the operation of section 24(2) of the *Charter*. Applying that section, the court held that the entire confession should have been excluded, notwithstanding what would have happened at common law.

Sweeney did not ask for the gun to be excluded, but it bears notice that the gun would have been "derivative evidence" within the meaning of section 24(2) jurisprudence, and although its exclusion was not assured under section 24(2), it too may have been excluded.[245]

5.7 (d)   Section 7 and the Right to Silence

Apart from the three areas just described ("undercover/detained statements," "statutorily compelled statements," and "derivative evidence") the *Charter* principle protecting the right to silence has not added to the common law voluntariness rule; if the common law voluntariness rule is satisfied there will be no breach of section 7's general right to silence

---

240 *R. v. St. Lawrence* (1949), 93 C.C.C. (3d) 376 (Ont. H.C.J.), approved in *R. v. Wray*, [1971] S.C.R. 272.

241 (2000), 147 C.C.C. (3d) 247 (Ont. C.A.).

242 Technically, the trial judge erred even under the common law rule. He admitted the entire statement and should have admitted only those parts confirmed by the real evidence.

243 Justice Rosenberg commented, without deciding, that at the very least, the common law had to be modified to give the trial judge the discretion to exclude the entire involuntary statement, notwithstanding its confirmation by the discovery of real evidence. Indeed, he remarked that it would be only in highly exceptional cases that a judge should refrain from exercising that discretion.

244 The court included the "detention" requirement out of an abundance of caution because the comments of Justice McLachlin from *R. v. Hebert* (above note 18) that the court was relying on were made in the context of detained persons. It seems clear that if the *Charter* is offended by the obtainment of involuntary confessions by state agents, that will be so whether the subject is detained or not.

245 See the discussion below in chapter 9, section 6.4 (d), "Derivative Evidence."

because the accused will have exercised the choice to speak, and that is what section 7 protects.[246] As a result, even though the voluntariness rule itself has acquired constitutional status as a principle of fundamental justice,[247] there will be no point in invoking the constitutional version. This is not only because it is redundant. It is mainly because, as between the two regimes, the common law rule gives the accused better value; whereas the common law rule imposes the heavy onus on the Crown of proving voluntariness beyond a reasonable doubt, if the *Charter* rule is used the accused has to establish involuntariness. The common law will therefore exclude confessions more readily.

In *R. v. Singh*[248] the accused tried to persuade the Supreme Court of Canada to use the constitutional principle to support a new rule that would make it contrary to the *Charter* for the police to continue to question a detained subject who says he does not want to speak. Singh urged that a "right to silence" is pointless if the police can ignore it and try to get an accused, who is attempting to enjoy that right, to give it up. A majority of the Court denied that there was such a rule and the admission of Singh's statement was upheld even though Singh had repeatedly told the police he wanted to exercise his right to silence. The Court emphasized that the constitutional right is to remain silent; it is not a right not to be spoken to or questioned by state authorities. While the accused cannot be obliged to speak, police are free both to question the accused and, within the limits of the voluntariness rule, to attempt to persuade him to speak.[249] The trial judge had found that in spite of Singh's protests he had made a voluntary choice to speak, and the trial judge's decision was entitled to deference.

The *Singh* Court did hold, however, that even though the constitutional right to silence had not changed the voluntariness rule, the failure to warn a suspect who the police have reasonable grounds to believe committed an offence about her right to silence[250] is an important consideration. In *R. v. Brown* such failure supported an involuntariness finding.[251] *Singh* also held that persistent, futile efforts made by

---

246 *R. v. Singh*, above note 116 at para. 25; *R. v. Hebert*, above note 18 at 184; *R. v. Timm* (1998), 131 C.C.C. (3d) 306 (Que. C.A.), aff'd [1999] 3 S.C.R. 666; *R. v. Rhodes* (2002), 3 C.R. (6th) 21 (B.C.S.C.), especially para. 110.

247 *R. v. Whittle*, above note 204 at 14.

248 *R. v. Singh*, above note 116.

249 *R. v. Hebert*, above note 18 at 184; *R. v. Oickle*, above note 138 at 341–45 and 349.

250 *R. v. Singh*, above note 116 at para. 32. The Court explained that the warning should be given in any case where a police officer would prevent the accused from leaving the questioning room or the officer's presence if the accused tried to do so.

251 (2010), 268 O.A.C. 168 at para. 10 (C.A.).

an accused person to invoke their right to silence can also influence voluntariness determinations.[252] For example, in *R. v. Otis* the failed attempt by the accused to invoke his right to silence contributed to the exclusion of the confession.[253] Otis had only limited cognitive ability and, despite his clear insistence on his right to silence on four occasions, the police forced him to endure continued interrogation until he collapsed emotionally and confessed.[254] By contrast, in *R. v. Roy*, even though the accused had insisted on his right to silence, his readiness to furnish selective information showed that he continued to choose what to say.[255]

5.7 (e)   Derived Confessions to Persons Not in Authority

The "derived confessions rule," introduced above in this chapter, clearly applies where the subsequent statement has been made to a person in authority.[256] It also applies where accused persons describe an involuntary confession they had made to persons in authority, when speaking to someone not in authority.[257] That subsequent conversation will also be inadmissible lest it be used to disclose the involuntary confession.

There remains uncertainty over whether the "derived confessions rule" applies where the accused person does not simply narrate their involuntary confession to a person not in authority, but makes another statement about the events. The fact the accused already spoke to the police may have influenced their choice to speak about what happened to the person not in authority. Still, in *R. v. T.(S.G.)* the Supreme Court of Canada chose not to resolve whether the derived confessions rule applies in such cases.[258] The majority did suggest, however, that it may be best to use the section 7 voluntariness rule under the *Charter* and to treat the subsequent statement as derivative, unconstitutionally obtained evidence.[259]

---

252 *R. v. Singh*, above note 116 at para. 53.
253 (2000), 151 C.C.C. (3d) 416 at para. 56 (Que. C.A.), leave to appeal to S.C.C. refused, [2000] S.C.C.A. No. 640.
254 *Ibid.* at 435–36 (Que. C.A.).
255 (2003), 15 C.R. (6th) 282 (Ont. C.A.)
256 See this chapter, Section 5.4. The "Confession Rule."
257 *R. v. G.(B.)*, [1999] 2 S.C.R. 475, as explained in *R. v. T.(S.G.)*, above note 136 at paras. 31–32.
258 *R. v. T.(S.G.)*, *ibid.* at para. 33.
259 *Ibid.* See chapter 9, section 6.4 (d), "Derivative Evidence."

6. A PRINCIPLED APPROACH TO SELF-INCRIMINATION

6.1) The Principles to Consider

As described throughout this work, a principled approach is being taken in most areas of the law of evidence. Established fixed rules are being supplemented or even replaced by flexible rules that involve the application of general standards to determine admissibility. The same trend is occurring with the law of self-incrimination. The Supreme Court of Canada has developed a principled approach for determining whether, outside of the fixed rules, additional self-incrimination protection is warranted. This approach builds on the factors first identified in the "statutorily compelled statements" area. It is most clearly illustrated in the decision in *R. v. B.(S.A.)*,[260] a case involving a constitutional challenge to the DNA warrant regime.

B.(S.A.) argued that the DNA warrant legislation was unconstitutional because it compelled him to furnish a DNA sample that, by its nature, is so intimately tied to his person that the legislation effectively requires him to self-incriminate. In rejecting this claim the factors used in the statutory compulsion case of *R. v. White*[261] were rearranged by the Court, with the key question becoming whether, in the relevant context, the search for the truth outweighs self-incrimination concerns about the abuse of state power.[262] Dealing first with the "search for the truth," the Court observed that DNA evidence is reliable and important evidence, advancing the ability of a court to make accurate factual findings. Unlike in the case of compelled statements that may well be untrue, this factor agitated in favour of admissibility. The counterbalancing "abuse of state power" consideration could be measured by examining the extent of the compulsion being exercised, the degree to which the state and the subject were in an adversarial position at the time the evidence was being gathered, and any circumstances that might increase the risk of abuse of power, including the degree of invasion required. The Court held that while the compulsion of a warrant is great and the adversarial position high during a criminal investigation, the safeguards attached to the warrant and the safe, as well as relatively unobtrusive, way DNA can be obtained lessened the risk of abuse of power to the point where the balance favoured discovering the truth over the self-incrimination concerns of the accused.

---

260 *R. v. B.(S.A.)*, above note 3.
261 [1999] 2 S.C.R. 417.
262 *R. v. B.(S.A.)*, above note 3 at para. 60.

In *R. v. Osmar* the Ontario Court of Appeal found that self-incrimination principles are not contravened where officers pose as underworld figures and induce criminal confessions from their targets by persuading them that they will be brought on board if they show their criminal *bona fides* and loyalty by describing their criminal past. The court held that there is no "real coercion" in such cases, and no increased risk of unreliability relating to the abuse of state power.[263]

A similar albeit looser application of this approach can be seen in *R. v. Jarvis*.[264] Jarvis was attempting to invoke self-incrimination protections to prevent taxing authorities from using information that they had gathered in his prosecution. He argued that they were abusing their regulatory power to demand information in order to assist in identifying tax liability by using those powers for the purpose of obtaining evidence from him to use in prosecuting him. The Supreme Court of Canada found that, on the facts, Revenue Canada had not done so, but the Court agreed that had the government acted as alleged it would have acted improperly. Invoking the kind of approach it had taken in *White* and would later take in *B.(S.A.)*, the Court held that where the relationship between the taxpayer and the government becomes sufficiently adversarial, self-incrimination protection arises. This will occur when the predominant purpose of the government in seeking information is to assist in prosecuting or incriminating the accused. At that point, "no further statements may be compelled by the taxpayer . . . for the purpose of advancing the criminal investigation."[265] Similarly, the protection against unreasonable search and seizure under section 8 of the *Charter* intensifies, requiring the government to use warrants to obtain documentation.

Thus, it would be a mistake to confine self-incrimination concepts to the established rules. The principle of self-incrimination can be invoked in a variety of contexts to exclude evidence, depending on whether the search for the truth outweighs self-incrimination concerns about the abuse of state power.

6.2) The Principled Approach and Non-testimonial in Court Self-incrimination

An area where this approach can assist in settling the law involves cases where the accused is called upon during his trial, not to testify but to

---

263 (2007), 84 O.R. (3d) 321 (Ont.C.A.).
264 *R. v. Jarvis* (2002), 6 C.R. (6th) 23 (S.C.C.).
265 *Ibid.* at para. 96. See also paras. 84 and 88.

perform some physical act, such as displaying his hands to a witness, or standing or walking. The accused is not being asked to act as a witness in such cases so subsection 11(c) would not seem to apply. In *R. v. Cyr* a trial judge claimed the authority to force Mr. Cyr to remove his shirt and display a tattoo, although the judge recognized that if the accused were to refuse, the remedy would not be to forcibly undress him but rather to allow the trier of fact to draw an adverse inference against him.[266] And in *R. v. Ouelette*[267] the Alberta Court of Appeal drew an adverse inference against the accused for not taking the initiative of rolling up his sleeve to demonstrate that he did not have the tattoo that the arresting constable described. The court reasoned that if Ouelette did not have that tattoo, he would have done so, and held that since not demonstrating a tattoo is different from not testifying, there is no bar on drawing adverse inferences in such cases. Still, there is an element of conscription in expecting the accused to participate actively in the trial in this way that the law has yet to come to grips with. A court could settle whether this is an appropriate response by using the factors employed in *R. v. B.(S.A.)* to balance the search for the truth against self-incrimination concerns. The contribution that observing the accused can make to the search for the truth can vary intensely from case to case. On the other side of the equation, the adversarial position between the Crown and the accused is never higher than it is during trial. Moreover, although the degree of compulsion may seem modest given that force will not be applied against the accused, the prospect of an adverse inference would exert significant pressure on the accused. Finally, while there is little room for abuse of state authority given the presence and protection of the judge, depending upon what is being asked, the incursion into privacy may be significant. A context-based, principled analysis of this kind could produce different resolutions in different cases.

7. SUBSECTION 10(B)

Subsection 10(b) of the *Charter* provides detained persons with the right "to retain and instruct counsel without delay and to be informed of that right." It exists in large measure to protect the self-incrimination rights of detainees by giving them the opportunity to become informed of their rights and obligations as well as to receive advice on how to ex-

---

266 *R. v. Cyr* (1997), 6 C.R. (5th) 75 (B.C.S.C.).
267 *R. v. Ouellette* (2005), 200 C.C.C. (3d) 353 (Alta. C.A.).

ercise them.[268] This does not make subsection 10(b) a substitute for the voluntariness rule. Even if subsection 10(b) is complied with, confessions can still be excluded as involuntary. This is because arming the accused with information about his rights does not assure that he will ultimately be able to enjoy those rights.[269]

By the same token, even if statements are otherwise voluntary, there are cases where they will be excluded because of subsection 10(b) violations. Indeed, it is not uncommon for statements or other evidence provided by the accused to be excluded because of subsection 10(b) violations.

Subsection 10(b) imposes both "informational" and "implementational" duties on the police. When any of these obligations have been violated, the evidence may be excluded under subsection 24(2).

- The informational component requires the detainee to be informed both of the right to retain and instruct counsel without delay and of the existence of the legal aid and duty counsel system in place in the jurisdiction.[270]
  - » Where there are special circumstances indicating that a detainee may not understand the subsection 10(b) caution, such as language difficulties or apparent mental disorder, the police must take reasonable steps to ensure that the detainee understands the information provided.[271]
  - » It is a violation of subsection 10(b) for the police to belittle the accused's lawyer with the express goal or effect of undermining the accused's confidence in, and relationship with, defence counsel.[272]
- The implementational component imposes the obligation on the police, when the accused has indicated a desire to consult counsel, to provide a reasonable opportunity to do so, including providing privacy for that consultation.
  - » Most significantly, it requires the police to refrain from eliciting evidence from the detainee until he or she has had a reasonable opportunity to consult with counsel (absent urgent circumstances).[273]
  - » That right lapses where the accused has not been reasonably diligent in exercising it.[274]

---

268 R. v. *Bartle* (1994), 33 C.R. (4th) 1 (S.C.C.).
269 R. v. *Holmes* (2002), 7 C.R. (6th) 287 (Ont. C.A.)
270 R. v. *Bartle*, above note 268.
271 R. v. *Baig* (1987), 61 C.R. (3d) 97 (S.C.C.).
272 R. v. *Burlingham* (1995), 38 C.R. (4th) 265 (S.C.C.).
273 R. v. *Manninen* (1987), 58 C.R. (3d) 97 (S.C.C.).
274 R. v. *Tremblay* (1987), 60 C.R. (3d) 59 at 62 (S.C.C.).

» Section 10(b) includes the right to consult counsel of one's choice, unless it is not possible to do so within a reasonable time (given all of the circumstances), in which case detainees are expected to exercise their right by calling another lawyer.[275]

> The right to consult counsel does not include the right to have counsel present during custodial interrogation. The assumption is that once armed with knowledge of their rights after consulting counsel, detained persons are free to make their own choices about how to exercise those rights.[276]

» Although there is no general right to be given a second or subsequent opportunity to consult counsel, there is an obligation to facilitate such contact where a change in circumstances makes this additional opportunity necessary "to fulfill the purpose of section 10(b) of providing the detainee with legal advice on the choice whether to cooperate with the police investigation."[277] This obligation will be breached if "it becomes clear, as the result of changed circumstances, that the initial advice, viewed contextually, is no longer sufficient or correct" and the police fail to provide this additional opportunity by recautioning the detainee and facilitating consultation if it is desired.[278] For example, these rights can be triggered if:

> non-routine procedures such as polygraphs or police line-ups are attempted;[279]
> the investigation takes on a new or more serious turn as events unfold;[280]
> events indicate that the detainee who has "waived" his rights may not have understood them;[281] or
> a detainee, who has previously asserted the right to counsel and has been unable to contact counsel despite diligent efforts, indicates that they no longer want legal advice.[282]

It is possible for detained persons to waive their rights to counsel and to provide self-incriminating information without enjoying the right to counsel and without a *Charter* violation occurring. The Supreme Court of Canada has repeatedly indicated that the standard for

---

275 *R. v. Willier*, 2010 SCC 37 at para. 35.
276 *R. v. Sinclair*, 2010 SCC 35 at para. 2.
277 *Ibid* at para. 53.
278 *Ibid.* at para. 57.
279 *Ibid.* at para. 50.
280 *Ibid.* at para. 52.
281 *Ibid.* (known as the "*Prosper* warning").
282 *R. v. Willier*, above note 275 at para. 32.

waiver will be high, especially when it has not been expressed. When there has been a breach of the informational obligation, a waiver is unlikely to occur because detainees cannot be expected to make informed choices absent full information.[283]

Despite insistence that the waiver standard is high, the Court in R. v. *Whittle* equated the standard for waiving the right with the operating mind test:

> The accused must be [shown to be] capable of communicating with counsel to instruct counsel, and understand the function of counsel and that he or she can dispense with counsel even if this is not in the accused's best interests. It is not necessary that the accused possess analytical ability.[284]

Whittle was found to have validly waived his right to counsel, despite his mental disorder. The trial judge had erred by imposing a more stringent awareness of the consequences test, which had focused inappropriately on Whittle's ability to act in his own best interests.

---

283 R. v. *Bartle*, above note 268.
284 Above note 204 at 21.

CHAPTER 9

IMPROPERLY OBTAINED EVIDENCE

1. THE EVOLUTION OF THE INADMISSIBILITY OF SOME IMPROPERLY OBTAINED EVIDENCE

1.1) The Common Law

With the exception of involuntary statements, the probative value of evidence does not change because it was obtained illegally. If a court is interested in finding out whether the accused committed the crime charged, throwing out perfectly good evidence because of how it was discovered therefore seems self-defeating. For this reason, the notion that evidence should be excluded simply because it has been illegally obtained has always been controversial. The great American jurist Benjamin Cardozo captured this sentiment with his caustic paraphrase of the American exclusionary rule: "The criminal is to go free because the constable has blundered."[1]

In order to avoid the loss of perfectly good proof and distorted factual findings the common law generally refused to reject evidence because of how it was obtained. Even statements obtained in violation of the voluntariness rule were traditionally excluded not because that rule had been violated but because of the concern that induced statements are unreliable. It was this thinking that led common law

---

1   *People v. Defore*, 150 N.E. 585 at 587 (N.Y.C.A. 1926).

courts to reject involuntary statements but to accept any real evidence that was discovered as a result of those statements. In the leading Canadian common law case of R. v. Wray,[2] for example, the Court excluded Wray's involuntary confession but admitted the firearm that Wray's statements permitted the police to find. Wray's protest that this was unfair and that judges should have the authority to exclude illegally obtained evidence was repudiated. The Supreme Court of Canada said that it was not unfair to admit the gun into evidence as it was reliable proof that would produce an accurate rather than unfair verdict. In taking this approach the common law courts were not saying that they did not care if police officers broke the law. They were saying that at the trial of the accused, the issue is not whether the police officers acted legally; the issue is whether the accused acted illegally, and relevant reliable evidence on that question should be admitted. The time to deal with the illegality of police conduct is in other legal proceedings about the police officer's conduct.

The reality, though, was that prosecution and disciplinary action against police officers were rare. As a result, police illegality was most often left unaddressed. Many believed that this harmed the repute of the administration of justice. Citizens were prosecuted for breaking the law, but police illegalities were ignored. The Law Reform Commission of Canada therefore recommended that judges have the discretion to exclude illegally obtained evidence,[3] but to no avail. It was not until 1982 that things changed with the proclamation of the *Charter* and the adoption, in section 24(2), of an exclusionary rule for unconstitutionally obtained evidence.

1.2) The *Charter*

Since the *Charter* will be violated by almost any illegal investigative technique, most evidence obtained illegally by state agents is now subject to potential exclusion under section 24(2), Canada's constitutional exclusionary rule.[4] This rule, which criminal lawyers have come to

---

2   *R. v. Wray*, [1971] S.C.R. 272.

3   Law Reform Commission of Canada, *Report—Evidence* (Ottawa: Law Reform Commission, 1977) s. 15 of Draft Evidence Code.

4   All illegal searches contravene s. 8 of the *Charter* (*R. v. Collins*, [1987] 1 S.C.R. 265) and all illegal detentions violate s. 9 of the *Charter* (*R. v. Grant*, 2009 SCC 32 at paras. 54–57). The *Charter* imposes legal obligations relating to statements through s. 7 (see the discussion at chapter 8, section 5.6) where the right to silence is preserved, and s. 10 where the right to counsel is provided (see the discussion at chapter 8, section 7).

take for granted, was not easily born. Indeed, early drafts of the *Charter* would have perpetuated the common law position by providing expressly that the exclusion of evidence would *not* be a remedy for unconstitutional conduct. These early drafts reflected an aversion to an American style rule that excluded crucial evidence, even as a result of minor violations. At Parliamentary hearings, civil libertarians, offended by the empty promise of constitutional rights without remedy, fought against this thinking and lobbied for an exclusionary rule. After much debate, a compromise was reached. It was agreed that unconstitutionally obtained evidence would be excluded, but only in those cases where its admission would bring the administration of justice into disrepute.[5] As a result, the characteristic feature of the Canadian constitutional exclusionary rule is that some unconstitutionally obtained evidence is excluded, while other unconstitutionally obtained evidence will be admitted. It all depends on whether the admission of the unconstitutionally obtained evidence in question will bring the administration of justice into disrepute.

Although this formula—whether admission of the evidence would bring the administration of justice into disrepute—achieved a compromise, on its own it offers little real guidance. Canadian courts have therefore struggled with when to exclude evidence. This struggle has produced an unstable jurisprudence. Back in 1995 Justice Sopinka described the "incremental evolution in the jurisprudence in this area."[6]

When the *Charter* was initially proclaimed, trial courts excluded little evidence. Then the Supreme Court of Canada signalled that the exclusionary remedy should be taken seriously.[7] By 1997, in *R. v. Stillman*,[8] the Court had developed an approach which led to the quasi-automatic exclusion of unconstitutionally obtained "conscriptive evidence"—statements, bodily samples, or evidence derived from the use by the accused of his body such as by compelled participation in police line-ups. This aggressive and rigid approach provoked criticism,[9] and

---

5   "August 28, 1980 Draft." See Roy Romanow, John Whyte, & Howard Lesson, *Canada . . . Notwithstanding* (Toronto: Carswell/Methuen, 1984) at 256.

6   *R. v. Burlingham*, [1995] 2 S.C.R. 206 at para. 154, Sopinka J.

7   *Hunter v. Southam Inc.*, [1984] 2 S.C.R. 145, adopted an aggressive, purposive interpretation of the *Charter* and imposed high standards for police searches, while *R. v. Therens*, [1985] 1 S.C.R. 613, rejected established and narrow notions of detention and, over the strong objection of Justice McIntyre, excluded the results of alcohol testing in an impaired driving case.

8   (1997), 5 C.R. (5th) 1 (S.C.C.).

9   See *R. v. Richfield* (2003), 14 C.R. (6th) 77 (Ont. C.A.); *R. v. Petri* (2003), 171 C.C.C. (3d) 553 (Man. C.A.), and *R. v. Dolnychuk* (2004), 184 C.C.C. (3d) 214 (Man. C.A.).

by June 2009 the Supreme Court decided to "revisit" this "important and contentious" area of criminal law and take a "fresh look at the framework [it had] developed for the resolution" of exclusionary issues. This occurred in the groundbreaking decisions of *R. v. Grant*[10] and *R. v. Harrison*,[11] where the two-box approach was rejected. Even though the kinds of factors considered then continue to remain similar now,[12] and there is debate about how significantly this development has changed admission patterns,[13] a new mode of analysis, described in this chapter, was adopted. As a result, it is perilous to rely on early decisions without viewing them carefully though the lens of what *R. v. Grant* and *R. v. Harrison* now say. The last word has yet to be written. The incremental evolution of section 24(2) jurisprudence is likely to continue.

1.3)   A Complex of Theories for Exclusion under Section 24(2)

There is no doubt that the evolving conceptions of the exclusionary rule found over time in Canadian jurisprudence reflect different levels of tolerance for the rejection of probative proof. Yet this is not the sole reason for the instability in the authority. Courts have also struggled because the *Charter* is ambiguous as to its underlying exclusionary theory. Specifically, section 24 empowers courts to grant "remedies" for *Charter* violations. This suggests that we exclude in order to compensate the accused for the wrong done to him. At the same time, section 24(2) is found among the "enforcement" provisions of the *Charter*, suggesting that exclusion is done to impel future compliance by deterring the police. Meanwhile, section 24(2) focuses not on the original violation but on the effect that admitting the evidence would have on the trial, including arguably, whether admission would undermine trial fairness. For its part, the triggering test for exclusion seems aimed at protecting the reputation of courts by empowering judges to avoid the harm that may occur if they are seen to condone unconstitutional acts

---

10   *R. v. Grant*, above note 4.
11   *R. v. Harrison*, 2009 SCC 34.
12   *R. v. Beaulieu*, [2010] S.C.J. No. 7.
13   See Mike Madden, "Marshalling the Data: An Empirical Analysis of Canada's Section 24(2) Case Law in the Wake of *R. v. Grant*" (2011) 15 Can. Crim. L. Rev. 229. This article canvasses reported cases and describes exclusionary patterns. The author acknowledges deficiencies in the sample and analytical method employed. Most significantly, the article identifies relatively high rates of exclusion by trial judges across all kinds of cases (75 percent).

by accepting the fruits of *Charter* violations. In other words, the test seems to reflect a "condonation theory" for exclusion.[14]

It is not surprising that this complex net of apparent exclusionary objectives has confused the authority, since, in law, purpose can and does drive outcomes, and each of these objectives suggests different approaches to exclusion. For example, a remedial rationale emphasizes causation and de-emphasizes the negative impact that exclusion might have on the process and the blameworthiness of the police. An enforcement rationale, on the other hand, would highlight blameworthiness of the police, and be relatively disinterested in causation. Meanwhile, a fair trial theory would focus on the way evidence operates at trial, while a condonation theory would turn primarily on the seriousness and significance of the breach.

Not surprisingly, as the jurisprudence has matured, the emphasis given to the exclusionary rationales has vacillated. Over the years, the Supreme Court of Canada has claimed that section 24(2) operates to "oblige law enforcement authorities to respect the exigencies of the *Charter*,"[15] yet has also said that section 24(2) is not intended to punish illegal police conduct.[16] For more than two decades the jurisprudence emphasized the goal of preventing "improperly obtained evidence from being admitted to the trial process when it impinges upon the fairness of the trial."[17] Now, with the decision in *R. v. Grant*, that "fair trial" theory has been pushed aside. Currently, the "main concern" behind exclusion is seen to be the need to "preserve public confidence in the rule of law and its processes."[18] The key concept that drives the present law is therefore "condonation theory." The more serious the violation and the more significant the intrusion into the constitutionally protected interests of the accused, the greater the need for courts to distance themselves from the violation by excluding the evidence. As for the deterrence of improper police conduct, it is not now an operative goal that drives exclusionary decisions. To the extent that excluding evidence inspires compliance with the *Charter*, this is nothing more than a happy side-effect.[19]

---

14   *R. v. Buhay* (2003), 10 C.R. (6th) 205 at para. 70, quoting *R. v. Collins*, above note 4 at 208.

15   *R. v. Burlingham* above note 6 at para. 25; *R. v. Buhay*, *ibid.* at para. 71.

16   *R. v. Grant*, above note 4 at para. 70.

17   *R. v. Burlingham*, above note 6 at para. 25.

18   Above note 4 at para. 73.

19   *Ibid.*

2. THE CURRENT LAW INTRODUCED

2.1) The Law Summarized

Subsection 24(2) provides:

> **24.** (1) Anyone whose rights or freedoms, as guaranteed by this Char-
> ter, have been infringed or denied may apply to a court of competent
> jurisdiction to obtain such remedy as the court considers appropriate
> and just in the circumstances.
>
> (2) Where, in proceedings under subsection (1), a court con-
> cludes that evidence was obtained in a manner that infringed or de-
> nied any rights or freedoms guaranteed by this Charter, the evidence
> shall be excluded if it is established that, having regard to all the
> circumstances, the admission of it in the proceedings would bring
> the administration of justice into disrepute.

This provision is the primary basis for excluding evidence under the
Charter.[20] A party seeking exclusion on the basis that evidence has been
obtained unconstitutionally must therefore satisfy the court on the balance of probabilities that each of the components of subsection 24(2)
have been met. Where those preconditions are satisfied, the evidence
must be excluded. Where they are not, it cannot be excluded by way of
a *Charter* remedy, even though the evidence may have been obtained
unconstitutionally. In propositional form, the law provides that

> *Accused persons must apply to the trial court to have unconstitu-*
> *tionally obtained evidence excluded. Before a court can even con-*
> *sider whether to exclude the evidence, the applicant must establish,*
> *on the balance of probabilities, that her* Charter *rights have been*
> *breached by a state agent. If the accused is successful, the court will*

---

20 In *R. v. Therens*, above note 7 at 647, Le Dain J. (dissenting on another point),
   described s. 24(2) as the sole exclusionary remedy. It has since been recognized
   that judges have discretion to exclude evidence under s. 24(1) to remedy abuses
   of process, where a stay of proceedings is not appropriate: *R. v. Caster* (2001),
   159 C.C.C. (3d) 404 at 412 (B.C.C.A.). Section 7, which guarantees that life,
   liberty or security of the person will only be deprived in accordance with the
   principles of fundamental justice, can also produce the exclusion of evidence.
   In *R. v. White*, [1999] 2 S.C.R. 417, for example, the Supreme Court of Canada
   held that the admission of statutorily compelled statements made by the accused would violate s. 7 because the use of the evidence by the Crown at trial
   would contravene fundamental self-incrimination principles. The evidence was
   excluded not to *remedy* a *Charter* breach but rather to prevent a *Charter* breach
   from occurring. See the discussion in chapter 8, section 5.7 (b), "Statutorily
   Compelled Statements."

go on to consider whether each of the two exclusionary require-
ments has been met:

The First Requirement: *"obtained in a manner"*

Evidence can be excluded under subsection 24(2) solely where
it has been "obtained in a manner" that breached the Charter
rights of the applicant. Although a non-remote causal connection
between the breach and the discovery of the evidence will satisfy
the "obtained in a manner" requirement, a causal connection is
not strictly required. Instead a generous approach is to be taken.
Courts should examine whether there is a sufficient connection,
given temporal, contextual, and/or causal factors, for it to be said
that the breach and the discovery are part of the same transaction
or course of conduct. Where this is so, the evidence has been taint-
ed by the Charter breach, satisfying the "obtained in a manner"
requirement.

The Second Requirement: *"The admission of the evidence in all of*
the circumstances [c]ould bring the administration of justice into
disrepute."

Where evidence has been obtained in a manner that violates the
Charter, *a court will exclude it if (1) the breach is serious enough*
and (2) the impact on the Charter-*protected interests of the accused*
is significant enough to (3) outweigh society's interest in the adjudi-
cation of the case on its merits. In conducting this balancing exer-
cise, the court is to assess each of these three factors to determine
whether a reasonable person, fully informed of the all of the cir-
cumstances and the values underlying the Charter, *would conclude*
that the admission of the evidence could bring the administration of
justice into disrepute. When asking this question, the focus is on the
damage that condoning the Charter *violation by accepting its fruits*
for admission could do to the long-term interest in maintaining the
integrity and public confidence in the justice system.

The seriousness of the breach — *Gauging the seriousness of*
the Charter-*infringing state conduct involves assessing the blame-*
worthiness of the conduct. This focuses most intently on the state
of mind of the officer about Charter *compliance, but extends to*
include systemic or institutional failures in Charter *compliance.*
Moreover, the Charter-*infringing state conduct will be more ser-*
ious where it is part of a larger pattern of Charter *violations com-*
mitted during the investigation of the accused.

The significance of the impact — *The measure of the signifi-*
cance of the impact of the violation on the accused is gained by

examining the nature and degree of intrusion of the Charter *breach into the* Charter-*protected interests of the accused. The way the impact is assessed varies with the kind of evidence sought to be admitted:*

a. Statements — *Generally speaking, the degree of intrusion that occurs when statements are unconstitutionally obtained is high. This is because the right of the accused to choose whether to speak to authorities is aggressively protected. As a result, unconstitutionally obtained statements are presumptively inadmissible. The significance of the impact can be reduced where there is a sound basis for concluding that the accused would have spoken in any event, or where the breach is so technical as to have no real effect on the decision to speak.*

b. Bodily Samples — *The degree of intrusion that is caused when bodily samples are secured depends upon the extent to which privacy, bodily integrity, and human dignity are compromised given the nature of the samples and the manner in which they are secured.*

c. Non-bodily Physical Evidence — *The significance of the impact of the violation where non-bodily physical evidence is obtained turns primarily on the manner of discovery and the degree to which the manner of discovery undermines the* Charter-*protected privacy interests of the accused, although privacy interests related to the nature of the non-physical evidence also fall to be considered.*

d. Derivative Evidence — *For "derivative evidence," typically real evidence that is discovered as a result of unconstitutionally obtained statements, the significance of the impact of the violation will turn on the* Charter *breach used to obtain the statement that led, in turn, to the derivative evidence. Since "derivative evidence" comes from unconstitutionally obtained statements, that degree of intrusion will generally be significant, unless*

  i. *the breach had no real impact on the* Charter-*protected interest of the accused to make an informed choice about whether to speak to the authorities;*

  ii. *it can confidently be said that the statement in question would have been made notwithstanding the* Charter *breach; or*

  iii. *it can confidently be concluded that there is a likelihood that the derivative evidence would have been discovered*

> *even had there been no Charter violation. Where this con-*
> *clusion can be made, the significance of the intrusion var-*
> *ies with the degree of likelihood that discovery would have*
> *occurred in any event.*

Society's Interest in Adjudication on the Merits— *The weight*
to be accorded to society's interest in the adjudication of the case
on its merits varies according to (1) the reliability of the evidence
and (2) the importance of that evidence to the case for the Crown.
While the seriousness of the offence is also a "valid consideration,"
it in fact contributes little to the outcome since both society's inter-
est in deciding a case on its merits and its vital interest in having
a justice system that is above reproach, are heightened, effectively
neutralizing the importance of the seriousness of the offence as a
factor material to the exclusionary decision.

2.2) The Law Illustrated

In *R. v. Grant*[21] police officers who engaged in "neighbourhood policing" in a high-crime school area stopped, obstructed his path, and
questioned Mr. Grant because he stared at them and fidgeted with his
coat and pants in a way that made them suspicious. This constituted a
"detention" because a reasonable person in Mr. Grant's position would
conclude by reason of this police conduct that he had no choice but to
comply with their requests or demands. That detention was unlawful
and therefore unconstitutional contrary to section 9 of the *Charter* because the police lacked reasonable grounds to suspect that Mr. Grant
had committed an offence—the operative standard for investigative
detentions and for detentions conducted during neighbourhood policing. Moreover, the informational obligations under section 10(b) of
the *Charter* were breached since the officers did not advise Mr. Grant
upon detaining him of his right to counsel. The Court nonetheless
ruled that a handgun— "derivative evidence" obtained "temporally and
causally" as a result of Mr. Grant's unconstitutionally obtained statements—was admissible in evidence. The Court found it admissible
in evidence because the breach was not serious enough to undermine
public confidence in the administration of justice, in part because the
officers believed they were acting lawfully and the law of detention in
neighbourhood policing situations was unclear at the time and called
for close judgment. Moreover, the police conduct was not abusive, nor
was there any basis for a finding of racially discriminatory practices,

---

21 *R. v. Grant*, above note 4.

notwithstanding that Mr. Grant was a person of colour. However, the impact of the section 9 breach on Mr. Grant's *Charter*-protected interests, while not severe, was more than minimal. Specifically, the detention did not involve physical coercion and was not carried on in an abusive manner. Meanwhile the impact of the section 10(b) breach was significant. Mr. Grant was deprived of the advice necessary to make an informed choice whether to speak, while the police officers were probing for answers to justify a search. The gun would not have been discovered had Mr. Grant not admitted to possessing the weapon. On the other hand, the gun was highly reliable evidence essential to a determination of the case on its merits. While the impact of the breach on Mr. Grant's *Charter*-protected interests weighed strongly in favour of exclusion, the public interest in the adjudication of the case on its merits weighed strongly in favour of admission. Since the facts did not support a clear outcome, the Supreme Court of Canada deferred to the trial judge's decision to admit the gun into evidence.

In *R. v. Harrison*,[22] a police officer on highway patrol stopped a vehicle that initially attracted his attention because it did not have a front licence plate as required by Ontario law. After the police officer turned to pursue and stop the oncoming vehicle he noticed that it was an Alberta vehicle, which did not require a front licence plate. He testified that he nonetheless chose to pull the vehicle over because abandoning the detention might have affected the integrity of the police in the eyes of observers, an explanation that the trial judge disbelieved. The police officer ran a computer check on the licence and determined it was rented in British Columbia. Aware that drug couriers often use rental vehicles; and because the vehicle was traveling at the posted speed limit in an area where traffic customarily exceeded the speed limit (a mode of driving the officer interpreted as suspicious) the police officer had a hunch that the vehicle was carrying drugs. On approaching the vehicle he determined that the driver had a suspended licence. He arrested the driver and then searched the vehicle, ostensibly as a search "incidental to arrest," which he claimed to have conducted to find the missing driver's licence. This claim was incredible given that the discovery of the licence itself was irrelevant to the charge of driving with a suspended licence. The officer then discovered boxes in the cargo area, containing 35 kilograms of cocaine. This evidence was obtained in a manner that violated the *Charter* because the detention that occurred when the police officer directed the vehicle to stop was arbitrary, contrary to section 9 of the *Charter*, as it was not a routine,

---

22 *R. v. Harrison*, above note 11.

random traffic stop but was done unlawfully as an investigation in the absence of reasonable grounds to believe that an offence had occurred. Moreover, the search of the vehicle was illegal and therefore contrary to section 8 of the *Charter*, as it was not a valid search incidental to the arrest. These breaches led directly to the discovery of the evidence.

The breaches were serious and not to be condoned lightly. The officer's conduct showed a reckless and blatant disregard for *Charter* rights, aggravated by the officer's misleading in-court testimony. Moreover, the departure from *Charter* standards was "major in degree" since "reasonable grounds for the stop were entirely non-existent."

The impact on the *Charter*-protected interests of the accused was significant, although not egregious, interfering with the expectation accorded to all drivers to be left alone subject to valid highway traffic stops or other lawful detentions.

The evidence was highly reliable and crucial to the Crown case, which favoured admissibility. In applying section 24(2), the trial judge erred in principle in admitting the evidence by giving undue emphasis to this third factor while neglecting the importance of the other inquiries, which strongly supported exclusion. The Supreme Court of Canada therefore gave the trial judge's decision no deference. The Court came to the conclusion that the stop and search of the vehicle without any semblance of reasonable grounds, aggravated by the misleading testimony, was so reprehensible, and the impact of the breach was significant enough to require the Court to dissociate the justice system from these flagrant *Charter* breaches, notwithstanding the public interest in the truth-seeking function of the criminal trial process. The evidence was therefore excluded.

The process that led to these decisions, and the law that was applied in deciding whether to exclude the evidence, is explained below.

3. THE APPLICATION FOR EXCLUSION

3.1) The Technical Components Introduced

Accused persons must apply to the trial court to have unconstitutionally obtained evidence excluded. Before a court can even consider whether to exclude the evidence, the applicant must establish, on the balance of probabilities, that his Charter rights have been breached by a state agent.

The phrase in subsection 24(2), "Where, in any proceedings under subsection (1)," makes it clear that the exclusionary remedy operates only after the preconditions of subsection 24(1) have been complied with. Subsection 24(1) requires:

(i) an application to,

(ii) a court of competent jurisdiction,

(iii) brought by "anyone whose rights or freedoms, as guaranteed by the *Charter*, have been infringed or denied.

3.2) The Application

A number of appellate courts have supported the proposition that impromptu *Charter* applications should not be made.[23] Still, practices vary. Some courts require formal notices of motion to be served and filed. Others allow mere submissions to suffice. Often these applications are dealt with during a *voir dire* conducted at the start of the trial, particularly in jury cases. Sometimes the *voir dire* is held during the trial, at the time the evidence is presented.

Whatever procedure is in use in the jurisdiction or court in question, it remains true that criminal courts have traditionally been reluctant to deny relief because of procedural flaws. This is because substance is generally considered to be more important than form when it comes to the rights of accused persons.[24] It also happens occasionally that the *Charter* breach does not become apparent before the evidence in the case unfolds. Hence, the "application" requirement is not always applied rigorously. Indeed, it has been held that where "uncontradicted" evidence discloses a significant *Charter* violation, the trial judge is obliged to enter into an inquiry to determine whether that infringement occurred, even in the absence of an application by the aggrieved individual.[25] This is particularly so where the accused is unrepresented.[26]

3.3) A Court of Competent Jurisdiction

The application must be made to "a court of competent jurisdiction." "[A] court of competent jurisdiction . . . is a court that has jurisdiction over the person and the subject matter and has, under the criminal or penal law, jurisdiction to grant the remedy."[27] For the purposes of the

---

23   See, for example, *R. v. Kutynec* (1992), 70 C.C.C. (3d) 289 (Ont. C.A.); *R. v. Loveman* (1992), 71 C.C.C. (3d) 123 (Ont. C.A.); *R. v. Dwernychuk* (1992), 77 C.C.C. (3d) 385 (Alta. C.A.), leave to appeal to S.C.C. refused, [1993] 2 S.C.R. vii.

24   See, for example, *R. v. Blom* (2002), 167 C.C.C. (3d) 332 (Ont. C.A.).

25   *R. v. Arbour* (1990), 4 C.R.R. (2d) 369 (Ont. C.A.).

26   *R. v. Travers* (2001), 154 C.C.C. (3d) 426 (N.S.C.A.).

27   *R. v. Mills* (*sub nom. Mills v. R.*) (1986), 52 C.R. (3d) 1 at 42 (S.C.C.).

remedy of exclusion of unconstitutionally obtained evidence, this will be the trial court. Even though any superior court can be a court of competent jurisdiction for the purpose of granting *Charter* relief, subsection 24(2) applications are brought before the trial court, typically at the time the impugned evidence is being offered for admission. Canadian courts have disapproved of holding "suppression hearings" before the start of a trial.

The significant limitation that is posed by the "court of competent jurisdiction" requirement is that judges conducting preliminary inquiries cannot exclude evidence as a subsection 24(2) remedy.[28] The jurisdiction of preliminary inquiry judges is derived exclusively from statute and does not include the power to grant *Charter* relief. Hence, accused persons are sometimes committed to stand trial at a preliminary inquiry after the admission of unconstitutionally obtained evidence that will not be admissible at their trials. Similarly, judicial officers conducting bail hearings and parole board panels are not courts of competent jurisdiction that can refuse to consider information on the basis that it has been obtained unconstitutionally.[29] Unconstitutionally obtained evidence can therefore be used without regard to section 24(2) during bail hearings and parole board panels. Adjudicators, however, are now recognized to have discretion outside of the *Charter* to exclude evidence that would undermine the fairness of the proceeding, a point that will be returned to below.[30]

3.4) The Applicant's *Charter* Rights Are Violated

Before an accused can seek to have evidence excluded under subsection 24(2), she first must establish on the balance of probabilities that her *Charter* rights have been infringed or denied. Apart from the need to marshal sufficient evidence to meet that standard of proof, this raises two related obstacles. First, it is the accused's own *Charter* rights that must be violated.[31] In *R. v. Paolitto*, the accused could not rely on subsection 24(2) to exclude handwriting samples that had been obtained from an accomplice in violation of the accomplice's right to counsel.[32] Most often this limitation arises in search cases. In *R. v. Edwards*,[33] for

---

28   *R. v. Hynes* (2001), 159 C.C.C. (3d) 359 (S.C.C.).

29   *Mooring v. Canada (National Parole Board)* (1996), 45 C.R. (4th) 265 (S.C.C.).

30   See the discussion at section 8, "Excluding Unfairly Obtained Evidence in the Absence of a *Charter* Violation," below in this chapter.

31   *R. v. Edwards* (1996), 45 C.R. (4th) 307 (S.C.C.); *R. v. Belnavis*, [1997] 3 S.C.R. 341.

32   (1994), 91 C.C.C. (3d) 75 (Ont. C.A.).

33   Above note 31.

example, the accused did not have a reasonable expectation of privacy in his girlfriend's apartment because he was merely a frequent visitor who did not contribute to accommodation costs and had no right to exclude others from the premises. As a result, he could not rely on subsection 24(2) to seek to exclude evidence that was discovered during a search of the apartment, even though that search contravened his girlfriend's constitutional rights.

Second, the *Charter* right must be violated by a state agent. In *R. v. Harrer*,[34] the accused claimed that a statement she made to American authorities should be excluded because the American authorities did not respect the requirements of subsection 10(b), the *Charter's* right to counsel provision. The court held that even if this were so, subsection 24(2) could not be relied upon because the American authorities whose conduct was being impugned were not Canadian state agents.[35] Similarly, the conduct of private individuals, which would have been contrary to the *Charter* had they been acting on behalf of the state, will not amount to a *Charter* breach and cannot support a subsection 24(2) application. In *R. v. Shafie*,[36] for example, a private investigator hired by the employer of a person suspected of theft was not required to provide a subsection 10(b) right to counsel warning before questioning the suspect because the investigator was not a state agent. Hence, subsection 24(2) could not be used to exclude the "uncautioned" statement.

In some cases it will be possible to extend access to the exclusionary remedy beyond those cases where police officers have violated directly the *Charter* rights of individuals. A medical doctor who took a vial of blood from a suspect at the request of the police has been held

---

34   (1995), 42 C.R. (4th) 269 (S.C.C.).

35   Since *Harrer*, *ibid.*, was decided, the Supreme Court of Canada held in *R. v. Hape* (2007), 220 C.C.C. (3d) 161 (S.C.C.) that the *Charter* does not apply to Canadian state agents operating in a foreign jurisdiction unless that foreign jurisdiction consents to the application of Canadian law. The thinking is that since Canada is helpless to enforce its standards in foreign legal jurisdictions, it would be impractical to expect Canadian officers conducting joint investigations to insist on Canadian standards during those joint investigations. The *Charter* will apply where Canadian state agents participate abroad in breaches of international (as opposed to domestic) law, since the principles of international law and comity are not offended when the *Charter* is used to preserve internationally recognized legal standards: *Canada (Justice) v. Khadr*, 2008 SCC 28. The Court also reserves the right to exclude evidence obtained in foreign jurisdictions where, given the way in which it was obtained, its admission would affect the fairness of the trial. A relevant consideration is whether foreign legal standards have been respected. See the discussion at section 8, "Excluding Unfairly Obtained Evidence in the Absence of a *Charter* Violation," below in this chapter.

36   (1989), 68 C.R. (3d) 259 (Ont. C.A.).

to be a state agent.[37] The test for whether a civilian will be treated as a state agent, thereby enabling a section 24(2) application to be brought, is whether the act said to be a *Charter* violation would have taken place in the form and in the manner which it did but for the involvement of a state agent. In *R. v. M.(M.R.)* it was held, using this test, that a school principal was not a state agent when he searched a student for drugs after requesting a police officer to be present because the principal would have searched the student in the form and manner he did even if the police had not been present. It was important that the principal initiated the search and was acting under his authority to maintain discipline and security in the school.[38] A private citizen will also be acting as a state agent if their primary purpose in acting is to discover evidence with a view to criminal charges.[39] It has also been held that the arrest of a citizen is a governmental function, whether that arrest is conducted by a police officer or a private citizen. The private citizen exercises his powers of arrest on behalf of the state and, therefore, an unreasonable search pursuant to such an arrest may lead to the exclusion of the evidence found.[40]

4. WHERE THE APPLICANT'S *CHARTER* RIGHTS HAVE BEEN VIOLATED

Where the applicant succeeds in establishing that her *Charter* rights have been infringed or denied by a state agent, two further preconditions must be met before the evidence is excluded. First, the applicant must establish that the evidence she wants the court to exclude has been "obtained in a manner that infringed or denied" her *Charter* rights. Second, the applicant must persuade the court that "in all of the circumstances, the admission of the evidence in the proceedings would bring the administration of justice into disrepute."

---

37   *R. v. Pohoretsky*, [1987] 1 S.C.R. 945.

38   *R. v. M.(M.R.)* (1998), 129 C.C.C. (3d) 361 at 376 (S.C.C.), and see *R. v. Buhay*, above note 14.

39   *R. v. Chang* (2003), 180 C.C.C. (3d) 330 at paras. 14–16 (Alta. C.A.).

40   *R. v. Lerke* (1986), 49 C.R. (3d) 324 (Alta. C.A.). The Supreme Court of Canada expressly reserved on this point in *R. v. Asante-Mensah*, [2003] S.C.J. No. 38 at para. 77.

5. REQUIREMENT 1: "OBTAINED IN A MANNER"

Evidence can be excluded under subsection 24(2) solely where it has been "obtained in a manner" that breached the Charter rights of the applicant. Although a non-remote causal connection between the breach and the discovery of the evidence will satisfy the "obtained in a manner" requirement, a causal connection is not strictly required. Instead, a generous approach is to be taken. Courts should examine whether there is a sufficient connection, given temporal, contextual, and/or causal factors, for it to be said that the evidence has been tainted by the Charter breach.

5.1) "Obtained in a Manner" and the Sufficiency of the Connection

The phrase "obtained in a manner" requires that the applicant establish a connection between the *Charter* breach and the discovery of the evidence. The purpose of this requirement is to ensure that evidence will be excluded under subsection 24(2) only if the discovery of the evidence can be linked in a meaningful way to the *Charter* violation.[41] "[T]he sufficiency of the connection between the *Charter* breach and the subsequent obtaining of the evidence . . . can only be determined by a case-specific factual inquiry."[42] The "decisive question" is whether the evidence has been tainted by the *Charter* breach. As the Supreme Court of Canada explained in *R. v. Wittwer*:[43]

> In considering whether a statement is tainted by an earlier *Charter* breach, the courts have adopted a purposive and generous approach. It is unnecessary to establish a strict causal relationship between the breach and [the evidence. The evidence] will be tainted if the breach and the impugned [evidence] can be said to be part of the same transaction or course of conduct. The required connection between the breach and the [evidence] may be "temporal, contextual, casual or a combination of the three."

While such fact-specific inquiries invariably produce a complicated jurisprudence, in the overwhelming majority of cases the "obtained in

---

41   *R. v. Goldhart* (1996), 48 C.R. (4th) 297 (S.C.C.).
42   *R. v. Simon*, [2008] O.J. No. 3072 at para. 69 (C.A.).
43   *R. v. Wittwer*, [2008] 2 S.C.R. 235 at para. 21.

a manner" requirement does not become a real issue because a causal link between the breach and the discovery of evidence is obvious.

5.2)   Cases with a Causal Connection

A "causal connection" is established where the unconstitutional investigative technique leads to the discovery of the evidence. For example, items found with an unconstitutional warrant meet the test. So, too, do statements that are made during an interview that is being conducted in breach of the right to counsel, or breath samples that are obtained during an arbitrary detention. "Derivative evidence" can also meet the test. Unconstitutionally obtained evidence is "derivative" when it is discovered as the result of finding other unconstitutionally obtained evidence, or where its relevance becomes apparent only because of the *Charter* breach. In *R. v. Burlingham*, for example, a gun that was discovered as a result of the confession made by the accused to the police after his right to counsel had been violated was derivative evidence that was ultimately excluded along with the confession.[44]

Even where there is a factual connection between the breach and the discovery of the evidence, where that connection is so remote or attenuated that the factual connection is not material, evidence will not be "obtained in a manner" that violated the *Charter* and therefore cannot be excluded under section 24(2). In effect, while the *Charter* breach is an antecedent to the discovery of the evidence, it is not the material cause of its discovery. In *R. v. Goldhart*,[45] for example, the police learned of a witness during an unconstitutional search. In a sense, the witness's testimony was evidence that became available as a result of the *Charter* breach, yet no "causal connection" was found. The Supreme Court of Canada held that this factual connection was too remote given that simply finding the witness did not make the testimony available. What made the testimony available in a meaningful sense was the decision of the witness to co-operate and his agreement to provide testimony. Had the witness not done so, his discovery during the search would have led to no evidence.

---

44   Above note 6 at 286. Although derivative evidence is almost invariably "real" or physical evidence, such as the gun in *Burlingham*, *ibid.*, it need not be. In *R. v. Burlingham*, derivative evidence included a statement made by the accused to his girlfriend, which he would not have made had it not been for his unconstitutionally obtained confession.

45   Above note 41. And see *R. v. White* (2007), 47 C.R. (6th) 271 (Ont. C.A.), where the relevant breach, the failure to inform White of the reason for his detention, did not contribute to the seizure of the evidence.

5.3)   Cases without a Causal Connection

"So long as a violation of [a *Charter* right] precedes the discovery of evidence,"[46] if the *Charter* violation and the discovery of the evidence can be characterized as "integral parts of the same transaction" the "obtained in a manner" test will be met even in the complete absence of a causal connection between the violation and the discovery of the evidence.[47] Temporal and contextual factors can make the necessary link. The decision in *R. v. Strachan*[48] is illustrative. In that case the police discovered narcotics at Strachan's apartment during the proper exercise of a valid warrant. While the search was being conducted, the police violated Strachan's right to counsel by refusing to allow him to call a lawyer. The Crown argued that even though there had been a breach of the right to counsel, the narcotics could not be excluded because that *Charter* violation had nothing to do with their discovery. It urged that in the absence of a causal connection between the breach and the discovery, it could not be said that the evidence was obtained in a manner that infringed the *Charter*. The Supreme Court of Canada disagreed. Chief Justice Dickson feared that to require a causal connection test to be satisfied in every case would make the law too rigid to respond to the varied circumstances in which the admission of evidence could bring the administration of justice into disrepute. The Court therefore held that so long as the discovery of the evidence is part of the "chain of events during which the *Charter* violation occurred," and the connection is not too remote, it can be said that the evidence was obtained in a manner that infringed the *Charter*. Both the breach (the section 10(b) violation) and the discovery of the evidence (the narcotics) were part of the same transaction: the search of the home. Similarly, in *R. v. Flintoff*,[49] a breath sample obtained from a suspected impaired driver met the test because the man had been needlessly strip-searched during the course of the detention that led to the production of that sample. Both the breach (the strip search) and the discovery of the evidence (the breath sample) were part of the same chain of events: the detention.

Although the *Strachan* case said that the breach must precede the discovery of the evidence, and this is the received view,[50] it is arguable that the temporal connection test can be met in some cases where this

---

46   *R. v. Strachan* (1988), 67 C.R. (3d) 87 at para. 45 (S.C.C.).
47   *R. v. Goldhart*, above note 41 at 310.
48   Above note 46.
49   (1998), 16 C.R. (5th) 248 (Ont. C.A.).
50   See, for example, *R. v. Pettit* (2003), 179 C.C.C. (3d) 295 at para. 20 (B.C.C.A.), and *R. v. LaChappelle* (2007), 226 C.C.C. (3d) 518 at paras. 45–47 (Ont. C.A.).

is not so. In *R. v. Therens*, in a passage cited in *Strachan*, La Forest J. said the temporal connection test could be met if the breach "preceded, *or occurred in the course of, the obtaining of evidence.*"[51] The French text of subsection 24(2) appears to contemplate the power in courts to address breaches that are linked to the same event, but occur after the discovery of the evidence. There are also sound reasons of policy for leaving this door open. Assume that the police discover marijuana during a lawful and reasonable pat-down search, and then publicly and needlessly go on to strip search the suspect. Is a court to be deprived of the power to exclude the evidence because of the sequence of events? To insist on the breach preceding the discovery of evidence as an absolute precondition to exclusion means that *ex hypothesi* evidence can be admitted even where its admission would bring the administration of justice into disrepute, just because of the order in which things happened to occur.

It is important to appreciate that a temporal connection between the breach and the discovery of the evidence will not suffice. There must also be a contextual connection. The test would not have been met in *Strachan* if the drugs had been discovered during an independent search at a bus station locker, even if the search was occurring at precisely the same time that Strachan was being deprived of his right to counsel at home. What is required is that there be a sufficiently important factual or contextual connection between the breach and the discovery of the evidence to make it possible to say that the breach and the discovery of the evidence are part of the same chain of events. In *Strachan*, the accused sought to enjoy his right to counsel precisely because of the search that eventually produced the evidence, hence the connection. In *Flintoff*, the police conducted the strip search while processing the accused for the breath test. In neither case could it be said that the breach led to the discovery of the evidence, but in each it was possible given the factual relationship between the breach and the discovery of the evidence to treat them as integral parts of the same transaction.

5.4)   An Overall Evaluation

As *R. v. Wittwer*[52] made clear, in applying the generous, purposive "obtained in a manner" test, the key inquiry is whether there is a sufficient connection that the evidence has been tainted by the breach. Even though "contextual" or "temporal" links can suffice, it remains true

---

51   Above note 7 at 649 [emphasis added].
52   Above note 43.

that the absence of causation can make the link between the breach and the evidence so attenuated that temporal and contextual factors are inadequate. For example, the Court in *Goldhart* found any temporal connection between the discovery of Mayer during the unconstitutional search and his testimony during the trial to be too remote to meet the "obtained in a manner" test. It was not the passage of time that made it so; any "temporal link between the illegal search and the testimony . . . [was] greatly weakened by the intervening events of Mayer's voluntary decision to cooperate with the police, to plead guilty and to testify."[53]

At times the link is broken because events after the initial breach effectively make the breach immaterial, before the evidence is discovered. The New Brunswick Court of Appeal held in *Ouellette v. New Brunswick*[54] that there was no temporal connection between the breach that occurred when the police failed to read Ouellette his rights to counsel properly, and the breath sample Ouellette furnished shortly thereafter. The chain between the breach and the discovery of the evidence was broken when Ouellette in fact managed to speak to a lawyer before blowing into the breathalyzer. Although it is possible to argue that in *Ouellette*, as in *Flintoff*, the breach and the obtainment of the evidence were both part of the transaction or event in which Ouellette was detained in order to provide a sample, *Ouellette* is distinguishable. When Ouellette spoke to a lawyer, the failure by the police to properly advise Ouellette of his right to contact counsel became moot, denuding the breach of its status as an integral part of the detention transaction. In effect, any "taint" was gone.

Things were different in *R. v. Wittwer*.[55] Wittwer confessed before properly being given his right to counsel warning. When the police realized their error a few hours later, Wittwer was given a proper warning by a new officer. He then made a "new" statement, which the Crown wanted to present as evidence. The Court held that, even though Wittwer received a proper warning before this "new" statement, the fact that Wittwer said nothing incriminating until the new officer mentioned that he was aware of Wittwer's first statements, forged a causal

---

53 Above note 41 at 312.
54 (1996), 2 C.R. (5th) 223 (N.B.C.A.). *R. v. Simon*, above note 42, provides a particularly aggressive example of how subsequent events can break the link between the evidence and the breach. Simon was not given a proper right-to-counsel warning before furnishing a DNA sample. The court held that breach to be moot because the DNA consent form Simon signed gave him all of the information he needed to make an informed decision about whether to give the sample, even in the absence of legal advice.
55 Above note 43.

link and left the temporal link intact between the initial breach and the ultimate statement.

Even though the absence of causation can and does influence some temporal or contextual connection decisions, the ability to rely on temporal and contextual connections serves to inject flexibility into the "obtained in a manner" inquiry. It increases the prospect of the "obtained in a manner" requirement being satisfied. As the Court said in *Goldhart*, where "the temporal connection . . . [is] so strong that the *Charter* breach is an integral part of a single transaction . . . a causal connection that is weak or even absent will be of no importance."[56] The temporal connection will be strong enough to accomplish this where, as in *Strachan* and *Flintoff*, there is a meaningful factual nexus other than causation between the breach and the discovery of the evidence.

6. REQUIREMENT 2: THE EFFECT OF ADMISSION ON THE REPUTE OF THE ADMINISTRATION OF JUSTICE

6.1) The Mode for Assessing Disrepute under the Current Law

Where evidence has been obtained in a manner that violates the Charter, a court will exclude it if (1) the breach is serious enough and (2) the impact on the Charter-protected interests of the accused is significant enough to (3) outweigh society's interest in the adjudication of the case on its merits. In conducting this balancing exercise, the court is to assess each of these three factors to determine whether a reasonable person, fully informed of the all of the circumstances and the values underlying the Charter, would conclude that the admission of the evidence could bring the administration of justice into disrepute. When asking this question, the focus is on the damage that condoning the Charter violation by accepting its fruits for admission could do to the long-term interest in maintaining the integrity and public confidence in the justice system.

The Court in *R. v. Grant* held that where the accused applies to exclude evidence that has been "obtained in a manner" that violates the *Charter*, courts must gauge (1) the seriousness of the *Charter*-infringing state conduct, (2) the impact of the *Charter* breach on the *Charter*-protected

---

56 Above note 41 at 310–11.

interests of the accused, and (3) society's interest in the adjudication of the case on its merits.[57] "The evidence on each [of these three] line[s] of inquiry must [then] be weighed in the balance"[58] by the trial judge[59] to determine whether a reasonable person, fully informed of all of the circumstances and the values underlying the *Charter*, would conclude that the admission of the evidence would[60] bring the administration of justice into disrepute," based not on "the immediate reaction to the individual case," but given the "long-term" interest in "maintaining the integrity of, and public confidence in, the justice system."[61] This requires courts to look beyond the immediate case at the broader implications. For example, in *R. v. Payette*[62] the Crown urged that evidence secured by an unconstitutional sniffer-dog search of an automobile should be admitted because the search was transitory and the contraband detected was reliable. The court recognized that these factors pertain in all sniffer-dog automobile searches. If given too much weight they would lead to the routine admission of such evidence, thereby harming the repute of the administration of justice.

As the Supreme Court of Canada recognized in *R. v. Harrison*, this "balancing exercise" is "a qualitative one, not capable of mathematical precision."[63] It is not a simple question of counting whether there are more "pro-exclusionary" than "pro-inclusionary" factors.[64] Although technically section 24(2) *obliges* judges to exclude the evidence in any case where its admission could bring the administration of justice into disrepute (the section says that the evidence "shall be excluded") the imprecision inherent in determining the impact of admission on the repute of the administration of justice requires trial judges to exercise discretion or judgment. As a result, "[p]rovided the judge has considered

57   Above note 4 at para. 71.
58   *R. v. Harrison*, above note 11 at para. 36.
59   *R. v. Grant*, above note 4 at para. 127.
60   Prior to *R. v. Grant*, it was settled law that, although the English version of s. 24(2) asks whether admission "would" bring the administration of justice into disrepute, the word "would" must be read as if it said "could." This is because "could" is a more accurate translation of the equally authoritative French version, and the interpretation that best advances the purpose of ensuring a fair process for the accused is to be preferred: *R. v. Collins*, above note 4 at 287–88. The *Grant* decision uses the word "would" without commenting on this point, but gives no reason to assume that it has rejected the overall standard for exclusion. For this reason the propositions contained in this chapter replace the word "would" with the legally conventional term "could."
61   *R. v. Grant*, above note 4 at para. 68.
62   (2010), 259 C.C.C. (3d) 178 at para. 42 (B.C.C.A.).
63   Above note 11 at para. 36.
64   *Ibid.*

the correct factors considerable deference should be accorded to [the trial judge's] decision."[65] Where, however, the trial judge "has fallen into error in principle, a material misapprehension of the evidence relevant to the ruling [has occurred] or a clearly unreasonable conclusion [has been arrived at]," the appellate court may "perform the s. 24(2) calculation afresh and determine the admissibility of the evidence."[66] As indicated above, in *R. v. Harrison* the trial judge "placed undue emphasis on the third line of inquiry" and inappropriately converted the inquiry into "a simple contest between the degree of police misconduct and the seriousness of the offence."[67] This is what freed the appellate court, the Supreme Court of Canada, to conduct its own evaluation of whether section 24(2) required exclusion.

6.2) Rejected Practices

The *Grant* test applies to all kinds of evidence and regardless of the *Charter* breach. As indicated in the introduction to this chapter,[68] prior to *Grant* the law was otherwise. Courts, applying the "*Collins/Stillman* framework"[69] before *Grant* ultimately rejected it, took a markedly different approach to whether admission would bring the administration of justice into disrepute, depending on the kind of evidence at issue. In effect, evidence would notionally be put into one of two "boxes," depending upon whether it was "compelled conscriptive" evidence or not. Compelled conscriptive evidence would go into Box 1 and would be excluded unless the Crown could prove that the evidence would have been discovered without breaching the *Charter*. No consideration would be given to how serious the breach was or how much damage exclusion would do to the reputation of the administration of justice. By contrast, non-compelled or non-conscriptive evidence would fall into Box 2 and be excluded only if, given the seriousness of the violation, more harm would be done to the repute of the administration of justice by admission than by exclusion.

This now obsolete "two-box" approach had been built on a "fair trial" theory that borrowed heavily from self-incrimination concepts. The Supreme Court of Canada reasoned in the *Collins/Stillman* line of cases that since a "fair trial" demands that the Crown prove its case without calling the accused as a witness, a trial would become unfair if the Crown could

---

65   *R. v. Grant*, above note 4 at para. 127.
66   *R. v. Harris* (2007), 49 C.R. (6th) 220 at para. 50 (Ont. C.A.).
67   Above note 11 at para. 37.
68   See this chapter, section 1.1, "The Common Law."
69   As it is called in *R. v. Grant*, above note 4 at para. 60.

indirectly co-opt the accused as a witness by presenting out-of-court statements obtained from the accused in violation of the *Charter*. Since it will always damage the repute of the administration of justice to conduct unfair trials, such evidence would almost automatically be excluded. In time, this thinking expanded beyond "testimonial self-incrimination" (incrimination through the use of statements made by the accused) to include other forms of "conscripting" the accused to participate in the investigation against him. It came to be held that a trial would be rendered unfair by admitting samples taken unconstitutionally from the body of the accused; or by compelling the accused to act (to use his body) to create evidence, such as by participating in identification line-ups or doing re-enactments; or by using evidence derived from other conscriptive evidence, such as the gun found after the accused describes its location to the police in an unconstitutionally obtained statement. It was only when the Crown could prove "discoverability" (i.e., that the constitutionally obtained compelled conscriptive evidence would have been discovered even without the *Charter* breach) that the admission of these kinds of evidence would not render a trial unfair.

The July 2009 decision in *R. v. Grant* made the "two-box," *Collins/Stillman* framework obsolete by rejecting the fair trial theory upon which it was based. The Court reasoned that this fair trial theory is inconsistent with the fair trial concept used more generally in the law, which is a "multi-faceted and contextual concept," meant to "satisfy the public interest in getting at the truth, while preserving basic procedural fairness to the accused."[70] Moreover, the near-automatic exclusion of compelled conscriptive evidence was irreconcilable with section 24(2)'s command to judge the impact of admission on the repute of the administration of justice by "having regard to all the circumstances."[71] Finally, it produced anomalous results.[72] It was more apt to cause the exclusion of a plucked hair than real evidence secured from a demeaning and objectionable body cavity or strip search.[73]

Care must therefore be exercised in relying on pre-*Grant* case law, as a number of its practices have now been rejected. The *Grant* court not only abolished the "two-box" approach and jettisoned the *Collins/Stillman* fair- trial theory, the Court has also:

- rejected the equation of self-incrimination and other conscriptive evidence;

---

70   *Ibid.* at para. 65.
71   *Ibid.* at para. 60.
72   *Ibid.* at para. 106.
73   *Ibid.* at para. 103.

- reduced the role "discoverability" plays; and
- marginalized the reliance that can be placed on the seriousness of the offence as a relevant factor in section 24(2) reasoning.

These changes will be discussed as they arise for consideration in the detailed description of the *Grant* framework that follows.

6.3)   Step 1 in Assessing Disrepute — Gauging the Seriousness of the *Charter*-infringing State Conduct

The seriousness of the breach — *Gauging the seriousness of the Charter-infringing state conduct involves assessing the blameworthiness of the conduct. This focuses most intently on the state of mind of the officer about* Charter *compliance, but extends to include systemic or institutional failures in* Charter *compliance. Moreover, the* Charter-infringing *state conduct will be more serious where it is part of a larger pattern of* Charter *violations committed during the investigation of the accused.*

This "first line of inquiry"[74] under the *Grant* test of gauging the seriousness of the *Charter*-infringing state conduct is undertaken to determine how important it is for courts to dissociate themselves from the unconstitutional conduct. The underlying theory is that while, in some measure, a court will be seen to condone a *Charter* breach if it admits the fruits of that breach, the degree of harm caused will vary depending upon the seriousness of the breach. "The more severe or deliberate the state conduct that led to the *Charter* violation, the greater the need for courts to dissociate themselves from that conduct, by excluding evidence linked to that conduct."[75]

In this first line of inquiry the "seriousness of the breach" refers to the "gravity of the state conduct."[76] The degree of harm the *Charter* breach does to the legitimate interests of the accused is dealt with separately, in the second line of inquiry. Essentially, there are three clear considerations that will colour the seriousness of the breach: (1) the blameworthiness of the conduct, (2) the degree of departure from *Charter* standards, and (3) the presence or absence of "extenuating circumstances." As will be described, while this "first inquiry concerns the police conduct in obtaining the [evidence],"[77] where the police con-

---

74   *Ibid.* at para. 72.
75   *Ibid.*
76   *Ibid.* at para. 73.
77   *Ibid.* at para. 124.

duct reflects institutional or systemic concerns, this will increase the seriousness of the violation.[78]

6.3 (a)   Blameworthiness of the Conduct

Officer Conduct

The *Grant* Court has recognized that "good faith" by a police officer will "reduce the need for the court to dissociate itself from the police conduct," while "willful or flagrant disregard of the *Charter* by those very persons who are charged with upholding the right in question may require the Court to dissociate itself from such conduct."[79] Even before *Grant* "[t]he relative good faith or bad faith by the police [was] one of the most important factors in determining the seriousness of a *Charter* breach."[80] As a result, pre-*Grant* authority on the blameworthiness of the conduct continues to give guidance.

While some decisions have attempted to pigeonhole the actions of the police as either good or bad faith, it is more useful to place the actions of the police along a fault line.[81] This is because a lack of good faith cannot be equated with bad faith,[82] and both good faith and bad faith can be more or less unreasonable.

It is important to appreciate at the outset that where the police officer's breach lands on this fault line relates to the officer's belief in *Charter* compliance, not to her ulterior motives for violating the *Charter*. Good faith does not exist simply because an officer believes it is necessary to breach the *Charter* in order to catch a suspected criminal. In *R. v. Kokesch* the Court remarked that "the unavailability of other constitutionally permissible, investigative techniques is neither an excuse nor a justification for constitutionally impermissible investigative techniques."[83] In all cases, to be a good faith breach, an officer must honestly but mistakenly believe that she is respecting the *Charter*. Moreover, that belief must be "reasonable."[84] Where a particular case fits on that "good faith" spectrum depends on the circumstances that make the belief reasonable.

---

78   See this chapter, section 6.3 (a), "Blameworthiness of the Conduct."
79   *R. v. Grant*, above note 4 at para. 75.
80   *R. v. Washington*, (2007), 52 C.R. (6th) 132 at para. 78 (B.C.C.A.).
81   *R. v. Kitaitchik* (2002), 166 C.C.C. (3d) 14 at para. 41. (Ont. C.A.).
82   *R. v. Smith* (2005), 199 C.C.C. (3d) 404 (B.C.C.A.).
83   *R. v. Kokesch*, (1990), 1 C.R. (4th) 62 at 67 (S.C.C.), a passage affirmed in *R. v. Stillman*, above note 8 at 49, and see *R. v. Buhay*, above note 14 at para. 36.
84   *R. v. Buhay*, *ibid.* at para. 59.

Since officers are not expected to anticipate or predict the outcome of *Charter* challenges yet to be taken, the most compelling cases of good faith are those where an officer relies on an existing legal rule that is yet to be declared unconstitutional. So, officers relying on writs of assistance[85] and upon warrantless wiretaps[86] were held to be acting in good faith even though the sections authorizing those investigative techniques were ultimately struck down.

A less pronounced form of good faith can exist where the law that was breached was obscure or highly technical, or involved the exercise of close judgment. In such cases, the finding of "good faith" is premised on a "reasonable misunderstanding of the law."[87] In *R. v. Grant* the seriousness of the failure by the police to recognize that they had effectively detained Grant was mitigated because the point at which encounters become detentions is not always clear, and the officers did not have the guidance of the standards for detention that the *Grant* Court developed for situations such as the one the officers faced, namely, in the context of "neighbourhood policing" as opposed to investigating specific crimes.[88]

Of more controversy are cases where the officer's honest mistake of law occurs where the law is not complex but where the legal question is open or unsettled. It has been held that it is possible for an officer to act in good faith even if his actions breach guidelines established in a subsequent authoritative decision,[89] but there is controversy about whether this should be considered good faith, or merely ignorance of the law.[90] If this is to be a form of "good faith" it must surely be at the lowest end of that spectrum.

One moves off the "good faith" spectrum where the officer *should have known* about the relevant *Charter* limit. The best that the Crown can hope for in such cases is a finding that there is an "absence of bad faith."[91] This may be a fitting label in cases where the law is little known or controversial, but where the constitutional limit the officer is ignorant of is basic and settled, the breach moves unequivocally into the bad faith

---

85   *R. v. Sieben* (1987), 56 C.R. (3d) 225 (S.C.C.); *R. v. Hamill* (1987), 56 C.R. (3d) 220 (S.C.C.).

86   *R. v. Sanelli* (1990), 74 C.R. (3d) 281 (S.C.C.).

87   *R. v. Wong* (1990), 1 C.R. (4th) 1 at 19 (S.C.C.).

88   As a result of the guidance provided for in *Grant*, the Court cautioned that similar conduct would not as justifiable in the future: above note 4 at para. 133, and see also paras. 40–42.

89   *R. v. B.(B.W.)* (2002), 4 C.R. (6th) 24 (B.C.C.A.).

90   See the debate between the judges in *R. v. Washington*, above note 80.

91   *R. v. Silveira*, [1995] 2 S.C.R. 297; *R. v. Wise* (1992), 11 C.R. (4th) 253 at 269 (S.C.C.).

zone and is an aggravating factor. Where established judicial decisions from courts with jurisdiction in the relevant province settle constitutional questions,[92] or where the Supreme Court of Canada has settled a legal question,[93] it is manifestly unreasonable for the police to remain ignorant of them and this will increase the seriousness of the breach. In *R. v. Kokesch*, the Court refused to treat an inadvertent violation as being in good faith because the need for a search warrant to invade the privacy of a residence, even to conduct a perimeter search, should have been clear to the officers in light of established decisions requiring warrants to enter private property.[94] The more notorious and settled the limit is, the more aggravating. Indeed, the failure to adhere to obvious constitutional limits, such as by detaining a motorist without any reasonable grounds as occurred in *R. v. Harrison*, may betray a reckless disregard of *Charter* standards and be treated as "brazen" and "flagrant" violation falling at the "serious end of the spectrum."[95] In *R. v. Feeney*, the decision of an officer to conduct a search in the absence of a subjective belief that there were reasonable and probable grounds to enter the residence was held to be "flagrant" because if the officer did not know about the law relating to warrantless searches, he should have known it.[96]

Carelessness also pushes cases to the "bad faith" end of the spectrum. In *R. v. Morelli* the officer's fault level was high because of the "careless drafting" that led to an "unacceptable" failure to discharge the heavy obligation of ensuring that *ex parte* warrant affidavits are accurate and fair.[97] And in *R. v. Dhillon* the fact that the officer was rushed did not excuse his carelessness in including inaccurate information in a warrant application or prevent the breach from being serious.[98] And in *R. v. Burke* the decision of the officer not to bother to confirm the identity of the subject wrongfully arrested on an outstanding warrant was characterized as a bad faith breach.[99]

---

92 In *R. v. Grant* (1993), 24 C.R. (4th) 1 (S.C.C.), the Court held that the police in British Columbia were entitled to rely on statutory authority that had been struck down in Ontario because it had not been struck down by the British Columbia Court of Appeal. Ontario officers could not have relied reasonably upon that same provision.

93 *R. v. Silveira*, above note 91.

94 Above note 83 at 72, Sopinka J.; *R. v. Mann* (2004), 185 C.C.C. (3d) 308 at para. 55 (S.C.C.), and see *R. v. Calderon* (2004), 188 C.C.C. (3d) 481 at para. 96 (Ont. C.A.).

95 Above note 11 at paras. 23 & 24.

96 (1997), 115 C.C.C. (3d) 129 at 171 (S.C.C.).

97 *R. v. Morelli*, [2010] S.C.J. No. 8.

98 (2010), 260 C.C.C. (3d) 53 at paras. 49–50 (Ont. C.A.).

99 *R. v. Burke* (2009), 312 D.L.R. (4th) 196 (Que. C.A.).

At the bad faith extreme of the fault line are cases where the violation is wilful. In *R. v. Burlingham*, in order to prevent the accused from benefiting from the right to counsel, the police purposefully required him to decide whether to accept a "deal" before his lawyer became available.[100] Similarly, in *R. v. Clarkson* the breach was particularly serious because the police insisted on interviewing the accused while she was impaired, knowing that if they waited for her to become sober, she would probably decide to consult counsel and then fail to provide a statement.[101] In *R. v. Buhay*, the officer showed "blatant disregard" for the accused's *Charter* rights when he conducted a warrantless search after concluding that he did not have the grounds to obtain a warrant.[102] In *R. v. Grant*, the Court made it clear that "derivative evidence," being real evidence discovered as a result of unconstitutionally obtained statements, must be excluded where there is reason to believe the police deliberately abused their power to get the statement in the hope it would lead to derivative evidence.[103] It is evident that wilful *Charter* violations will generally require exclusion.

Of interest, the assessment of the blameworthiness of the relevant conduct is not confined to the time of the breach but extends, as well, to the officer's testimony about *Charter* compliance. The Court held in *R. v. Harrison* that the fact that a police officer attempted to mislead the Court about his *Charter* compliance "was properly a factor to consider as part of [the seriousness] inquiry."[104] To admit unconstitutionally obtained evidence that an officer lies about directly undermines section 24(2)'s goals of preserving "the integrity of the judicial system and the truth-seeking function of the courts."[105] This thinking no doubt extends as well to misleading information provided in search warrant or wire tap applications and other sworn investigative declarations.

Institutional and Systemic Conduct
There is some confusion over whether the fault line should be drawn with sole reference to the investigating officer's frame of mind. There

---

100 Above note 6.
101 [1986] 1 S.C.R. 383.
102 Above note 14 at para. 60. See also *R. v. Sandhu*, [2009] O.J. No. 4106 (S.C.J.), where the officer, aware he did not have grounds for a warrant, conspired with a Ministry of Transport official to have the ministry official use his regulatory powers of inspection to open the door of a transport to facilitate the officer's criminal investigation.
103 Above note 4 at para. 128.
104 Above note 11 at para. 26. See also the judgment of Iacobucci J., albeit dissenting in the result, in *R. v. Belnavis*, above note 31 at para. 93.
105 *R. v. Harrison*, ibid.

are cases that find good faith on the part of officers who have complied with defective internal policy directives or have received bad legal advice before acting. In *R. v. Wong*,[106] for example, the admission of the evidence was aided by the fact that the police officers obtained legal advice before unlawfully installing video-surveillance cameras. In *R. v. Généreux*,[107] the decision to admit the evidence was assisted because the defective practice of establishing reasonable grounds for a warrant used by the police was standard in the province of Quebec. This line of authority is problematic. It is difficult to reconcile with the notion that where the law is settled, it is unreasonable to remain ignorant of *Charter* standards. Moreover, its perverse effect is to enable the Crown to reduce the seriousness of the violation by a police officer by relying on constitutional errors made by other, often more responsible, state agents. Fittingly, in *R. v. Stillman*, the majority found no mitigation for the *Charter* violation that occurred after the police relied on erroneous and incomplete legal advice from the Crown's office.[108] We suggest that *Stillman* represents the better view. This is particularly so in light of the recent comment in *R. v. Harrison* that "evidence of systemic or institutional abuse will aggravate the seriousness of the breach and weigh in favour of exclusion, [while] the absence of such a problem is hardly a mitigating factor."[109] The failure by law enforcement agencies as a whole to respond to *Charter* rules is therefore a relevant consideration. This being so, there is little that can be said for permitting individual police officers to invoke poor institutional advice or bad institutional practices in an effort to mitigate the seriousness of their breaches.

Pattern of Violations

Just as systemic or institutional abuse will aggravate the seriousness of a *Charter* breach, so too will a pattern of illegality. The more violations there are, the more likely there will be disrepute caused by admission of the unconstitutionally obtained evidence.[110] This is because a pattern of violations, whether of constitutional or "non-constitutionalized"

---

106 Above note 87.

107 (1992), 70 C.C.C. (3d) 1 (S.C.C.).

108 Above note 8. See also *R. v. Schedel* (2003), 12 C.R. (6th) 207 (B.C.C.A.), and *R. v. Lau* (2003), 12 C.R. (6th) 296 (B.C.C.A). The trial judges in these cases had found police officers who executed searches to be acting in good faith when following a Vancouver Police Policy to break down the door when warrants are being executed for "grow-ops." The Court of Appeal held that the trial judges erred in mitigating the breaches in this way. The policy actually aggravated the breaches, as it was developed in flagrant disregard of the law and the *Charter*.

109 Above note 11 at para. 25.

110 *R. v. Chiasson* (2006), 37 C.R. (6th) 43 (S.C.C.).

rights,[111] demonstrates a lack of respect for the rule of law, thereby exacerbating the seriousness of any constitutional violations that occur.[112]

6.3 (b)   Degree of Departure from *Charter* Standards

According to *R. v. Grant*, section 24(2) exists so that "courts, as institutions responsible for the administration of justice, [do not] effectively condone state deviation from the rule of law by failing to dissociate themselves from the fruits of the unlawful conduct."[113] That being so the more significant the deviation is, the more compelling the case for exclusion will be.

It is therefore important to determine whether the breach is substantial or merely technical. For example, it is a substantial violation of the right to counsel not to advise a detainee about the availability of legal aid when he has expressed concern about his ability to afford a lawyer,[114] but it is not as serious to fail to advise a person being searched incidental to arrest of his right to counsel before commencing that search.[115] In *R. v. Harrison* the Court held that the seriousness of the violation was "exacerbated" because the officer departed from *Charter* standards to a major degree. It was not simply a case of the officer misjudging whether reasonable grounds for the stop existed. Reasonable grounds were "entirely non-existent."[116] By contrast, a departure from constitutional standards will be less major where the legal defect is simply technical in nature.[117] In *R. v. Wise*,[118] for example, the *Charter* violation was not considered to be serious because of its technical nature where the police installed an electronic tracking device,

---

111   In *R. v. Stillman*, above note 8 at 49, the pattern relied on to make the *Charter* breach more serious included disregard for the protection provided by the law to young offenders.

112   *R. v. Feeney*, above note 96 at 173. See also *R. v. Calderon*, above note 94 at para. 93.

113   *R. v. Grant*, above note 4 at para. 72.

114   *R. v. Brydges* (1990), 74 C.R. (3d) 129 (S.C.C.).

115   *R. v. Debot* (1989), 73 C.R. (3d) 129 (S.C.C.). This is because, while the police must give detainees immediate information about their *Charter* rights before conducting a search, the police may search the detainee before giving the detainee an actual opportunity to speak to counsel. If the opportunity to speak to counsel is in fact provided at the first reasonable opportunity after the search, the failure to advise the suspect before the search that this will happen is a highly technical omission.

116   Above note 11 at para. 24.

117   *R. v. Caslake*, [1998] 1 S.C.R. 51; *R. v. Belnavis*, above note 31; *R. v. Feeney*, above note 96.

118   *R. v. Wise*, above note 91.

unaware that their warrant had expired. Still, some technical defects can be significant, as in *R. v. Genest*[119] where the officer who was to execute a warrant was not named, no times were listed for its execution, and it did not include a list of objects to be searched for.

The overall manner in which the police conduct themselves can also influence the assessment of how far removed they are from respecting appropriate *Charter* standards. In *R. v. Grant* the seriousness of the violation would have been greater had the officers behaved abusively during the detention, or had the detention occurred because of racial profiling.[120]

The departure from *Charter* standards will also be more intense when the vulnerability of the accused is exploited. In *R. v. Evans*,[121] the right to counsel violation was rendered more serious because the accused was mentally challenged, while in *R. v. Clarkson* the vulnerability of the intoxicated detainee exacerbated the breach.[122]

6.3 (c)   Extenuating Circumstances — Necessity and Emergency

In *R. v. Grant*, the Court recognized that "extenuating circumstances . . . may attenuate the seriousness of the police conduct that results in a *Charter* breach."[123] Although no extenuating circumstances operated in either *Grant*, or its companion case, *R. v. Harrison*, previous case law that no doubt still applies demonstrates the "necessity" and "emergency" concepts.

Specifically, it has been held that "necessity" in breaching the *Charter* to preserve evidence can diminish the seriousness of the *Charter* violation. Perhaps the key factor enabling the Court in *R. v. Silveira* to conclude that the serious home invasion by the police was sufficiently mitigated to allow for the admission of the evidence was the real risk that the evidence would have been lost or destroyed if the police had not acted as they did.[124] Two important points need to be made, however. First, as the Court stated in *R. v. Feeney*, more is needed than the simple fact that "[a]fter any crime is committed, the possibility that evidence might be destroyed is inevitably present."[125] There must be some particular foundation for the belief in urgency or necessity in the case at hand, such as existed in *Silveira* after the very public arrest of the

---

119 (1989), 67 C.R. (3d) 224 (S.C.C.).

120 Above note 4 at para. 133.

121 (1991), 4 C.R. (4th) 144 (S.C.C.).

122 Above note 101.

123 *R. v. Grant*, above note 4 at para. 75.

124 *R. v. Silveira*, above note 91 at 374, Cory J.

125 Above note 96 at 169.

accused. The likelihood that Silveira's co-conspirators knew of his arrest raised the realistic spectre that any contraband at his house would be destroyed or removed before the police could arrive. Second, the urgency of preserving evidence should not be understood as reducing the seriousness of intentional, as opposed to inadvertent, *Charter* violations. It is important, for example, that in *Silveira* the officers were not aware that they were violating the *Charter* by securing the home. The majority was careful to point out that after its decision, "[t]he police must now know that exigent circumstances do not provide an excuse for failing to obtain a warrant."[126]

In "emergency" cases, where public or police safety is at stake, a more generous approach is taken. For example, in *R. v. Strachan*,[127] the fact that the initial delay in providing the right to counsel was caused by the desire of the police to get a potentially volatile situation under control assisted in justifying the ultimate admission of the evidence. In *R. v. Golub*, where the police entered a residence without warrant after receiving a report that the accused had an Uzi submachine gun, the Ontario Court of Appeal held that, if this constituted a *Charter* breach at all, the seriousness of the breach was significantly mitigated by the urgent need to ensure public safety.[128]

6.4)   Step 2 in Assessing Disrepute — Gauging the Impact of the *Charter* Violation on the *Charter*-protected Interests of the Accused

The significance of the impact — *The measure of the significance of the impact of the violation on the accused is gained by examining the nature and degree of intrusion of the* Charter *breach into the* Charter-protected *interests of the accused. The way the impact is assessed varies with the kind of evidence sought to be admitted:*

a.   Statements — *Generally speaking, the degree of intrusion that occurs when statements are unconstitutionally obtained is high. This is because the right of the accused to choose whether to speak to authorities is aggressively protected. As a result, unconstitutionally obtained statements are presumptively inadmissible. The significance of the impact can be reduced where there is a sound basis for concluding that the accused*

---

126   *R. v. Silveira*, above note 91 at 374, Cory J.
127   Above note 46.
128   *R. v. Golub* (1997), 9 C.R. (5th) 98 (Ont. C.A.).

would have spoken in any event, or where the breach is so technical as to have no real effect on the decision to speak.

b.   Bodily Samples—*The degree of intrusion caused when bodily samples are secured depends upon the extent to which privacy, bodily integrity, and human dignity are compromised given the nature of the samples and the manner in which they are secured.*

c.   Non-bodily physical evidence—*The significance of the impact of the violation where non-bodily physical evidence is obtained turns primarily on the manner of discovery and the degree to which the manner of discovery undermines the Charter-protected privacy interests of the accused, although privacy interests related to the nature of the non-physical evidence also fall to be considered.*

d.   Derivative evidence—*For "derivative evidence," typically real evidence that is discovered as a result of unconstitutionally obtained statements, the significance of the impact of the violation will turn on the Charter breach used to obtain the statement that led, in turn, to the derivative evidence. Since "derivative evidence" comes from unconstitutionally obtained statements, that degree of intrusion will generally be significant, unless*

   i.   *the breach had no real impact on the Charter-protected interest of the accused to make an informed choice about whether to speak to the authorities;*

   ii. *it can confidently be said that the statement in question would have been made notwithstanding the Charter breach; or*

   iii. *it can confidently be concluded that there is a likelihood that the derivative evidence would have been discovered even had there been no Charter violation. Where this conclusion can be made, the significance of the intrusion varies with the degree of likelihood that discovery would have occurred in any event.*

"This [second] inquiry focuses on the seriousness of the impact of the *Charter* breach on the *Charter*-protected interests of the accused."[129] The more those interests are harmed by the *Charter* violation, the greater the case for exclusion. It is meant to address "the danger that admitting the evidence may suggest that *Charter* rights do not count thereby negatively impacting on the repute of the administration of justice."[130]

---

129   *R. v. Grant*, above note 4 at para. 76.
130   *Ibid.* at para. 109.

The more intrusive the breach is, the greater the danger to the repute of the administration of justice in appearing to discount *Charter* rights.

While the *Grant* decision rejected the fair trial theory that drove the *Collins/Stillman* framework, this did not make the kinds of evidence being tendered immaterial. Indeed, the kind of evidence secured is a key consideration in assessing the degree of intrusion. This is because the degree and nature of intrusion tends to vary between different kinds of proof. The common law has long reacted more strongly to compelling statements than it does to compelling bodily samples such as fingerprints, breath samples, or even blood samples. Meanwhile the law has long been more reticent to compel bodily samples than it has been in restricting the seizure of property. These values are reflected in the *Grant* decision, which, in discussing how the degree of intrusion is to be measured, breaks things down according to the kind of evidence secured. Of course, the nature of the investigative technique employed will also colour the degree of intrusion into the *Charter*-protected interests of the accused. According to the *Grant* decision, the measure of the degree of intrusion will also be affected by the role the *Charter* breach played in making the evidence available. Certainly, in the case of statements and "derivative evidence," and probably in the case of all kinds of evidence, if the Crown would have had the impugned evidence even without the breach, the breach is considered to be less intrusive and exclusion is less likely to occur. In keeping with the structure of the *Grant* decision, the method for evaluating the intrusiveness of the breach will be described for each kind of evidence identified by the court. It will then be fitting to take a closer look at causation and discoverability issues.

6.4 (a)   Statements

"Statements by the accused engage the principle against self-incrimination, 'one of the cornerstones of our criminal law.'"[131] The *Grant* judges accepted that the unconstitutional obtainment of statements from the accused tends to undercut the ability of the accused to "make a meaningful . . . choice [about] whether to speak, the related right to silence, and most importantly, the protection against testimonial self-incrimination."[132] This is a significant intrusion into an individual's interest in liberty and autonomy.[133] For this reason (and because statements may prove unreliable), the Court held that there is a presumption that statements obtained in breach of the *Charter* will be excluded.[134]

---

131 *Ibid.* at para. 89.
132 *Ibid.* at para. 95.
133 *Ibid.*
134 *Ibid.* at para. 92.

While that presumption can be overcome when the balance of the factors favour admission, the "centrality of the protected interest . . . against testimonial self-incrimination" will in most cases favour exclusion of statements taken in breach of the *Charter*.[135]

There will be exceptional cases where this presumption in favour of excluding statements will not operate. First, the *Grant* Court noted that technical *Charter* breaches that do not prevent the accused from being informed of his choice to speak or from exercising that choice will have a lesser impact on an accused's protected interest.[136]

Second, the Court made it clear that the impact of the breach will be lessened when there is no causal link between the breach and the statement. Some statements are made spontaneously and independently of the breach. Others would have been made regardless of the breach. The *Grant* Court cited, as an example, *R. v. Harper*.[137] In that case, statements made subsequent to a defective right to a counsel warning were admitted into evidence because before being detained, the accused had already blurted out that he was the one the police were looking for, and he invited the police to take him away. *R. v. Hachez*[138] provides another example. Hachez declined to contact counsel when advised of his right to do so, and he then confessed to the crime for which he was arrested. The police then changed the focus of their interrogation by asking him about other crimes. Before doing this they should have re-advised him of his right to counsel, but they did not do so. Hachez's confession to other crimes was nonetheless ultimately admitted into evidence because the trial judge was satisfied that Hachez would have continued to speak even if he had been re-advised of the right to counsel.[139] Of course, attempting to determine whether an accused would have spoken "even if" his *Charter* rights had been respected is dangerous and conjectural. Indeed, the Quebec Court of Appeal was not comfortable applying this kind of reasoning in *R. v. Auclair*.[140] Fittingly, the *Grant* Court has now affirmed that discoverability should be applied only in those exceptional circumstances where it can be said *confidently*

---

135 *Ibid.* at para. 98.
136 *Ibid.* at para. 96.
137 (1994), 33 C.R. (4th) 61 (S.C.C.).
138 (1995), 42 C.R. (4th) 69 (Ont. C.A.); and see *United States of America v. Yousef* (2003), 178 C.C.C. (3d) 286 (Ont. C.A.).
139 What is important in each of these cases is that the accused understood his basic right to counsel and to remain silent. These cases involved informational breaches only. In *R. v. Auclair* (2004), 183 C.C.C. (3d) 273 at paras. 58–68 (Que. C.A.), it was held that the "even if" doctrine should not be used unless the accused is shown to have understood his rights.
140 *Ibid.*

that the statement in question would have been made notwithstanding the *Charter* breach.

6.4 (b)   Bodily Evidence

Perhaps the greatest change wrought by *R. v. Grant* is its approach to bodily evidence. The Court held that the *Collins/Stillman* fair trial theory "wrongly equates bodily evidence with statements." The *Grant* Court found that equation to be erroneous because bodily samples, unlike statements, are not "communicative."[141] They are not, therefore, "self-incriminatory" in the way that statements are. The accused whose bodily samples are taken is not being used as a "witness" against himself. Statements create new information, but bodily samples exist. When we take offence at unconstitutionally obtained bodily samples, we are not so much reacting to the compelled participation by the accused in the investigation as we are to the violation of the privacy and dignity of the person that obtaining the evidence involves.[142] Significantly, the nature and degree of the violation of privacy and dignity will fluctuate with the "wide variation between different kinds of bodily evidence."[143] As the Court noted, "[a]t one end of the spectrum, one finds the forcible taking of bodily samples or dental impressions (as in *Stillman*). At the other end of the spectrum lie relatively innocuous procedures such as fingerprinting or iris-recognition technology."[144] As a result, under the *Grant* regime there is no presumption favouring the exclusion of bodily evidence, as there is with statements. The importance of the nature and degree of intrusion is "better addressed [on a case-by-case basis] by reference to the interests in privacy, bodily integrity and human dignity"[145] and by the nature of the technique used to secure those samples. For example, in *R. v. Ramage* the intrusion was modest because the bodily sample was discarded urine.[146]

The largest impact of *Grant* is occurring in alcohol driving cases. On a day to day basis samples secured in alcohol driving offences have historically been the most common subject of *Charter*-exclusion applications. This is because *Charter* breaches are common in alcohol driving cases, and alcohol driving charges are common and frequently litigated. These cases invariably involve detentions that trigger *Charter* obligations, and the law surrounding alcohol driving investigations

---

141   *R. v. Grant*, above note 4 at para. 105.
142   *Ibid.*
143   *Ibid.* at para. 103.
144   *Ibid.* at para. 109.
145   *Ibid.* at para. 104.
146   (2010), 77 C.R. (6th) 134 (Ont. C.A.).

is complex. Courts applying the *Collins/Stillman* framework almost automatically excluded such samples, thereby destroying the Crown case, often because of "minor" violations. The *Grant* decision has now changed this. It characterizes the collection of breach samples as "relatively non-intrusive," and uses them as an illustration of intrusions that are "less severe in terms of privacy, bodily integrity and dignity," and more apt to result in admission.[147] This does not mean that breath samples will be routinely admitted.[148] It does, mean, however, that their admissibility is determined in all of the circumstances and they are less readily excluded than was once the case.

6.4 (c) Non-bodily Physical Evidence

When it comes to non-bodily physical evidence, the degree of intrusion is primarily influenced by the nature of the search or seizure that produces the evidence, and how compromising that search or seizure is of the privacy interests of the accused. Some personal searches or seizures, including body-cavity searches[149] and strip searches,[150] represent more serious intrusions into privacy rights than other personal searches, such as "pat-down" or "frisk" searches.[151] Meanwhile, unreasonable pat-down or frisk searches of one's person tend to be more offensive than property searches, while searches of one's home[152] are more serious than searches of one's office or car[153] or the sleeping quarters in a transport truck,[154] or of one's locker in a school.[155]

---

147 *R. v. Grant*, above note 4 at paras. 106 and 111.

148 Indeed, while bearing in mind its methodological limitations, Madden's empirical analysis revealed no perceptible difference between the frequency of exclusion of breath samples and statements. Madden, "Marshalling the Data," above note 13.

149 See *R. v. Greffe* (1990), 75 C.R. (3d) 257 (S.C.C.) where a sigmoidoscope was used. Body cavity searches include "a physical inspection of the detainee's genital or anal regions" but not the mouth: *R. v. Golden* (2001), 159 C.C.C. (3d) 449 at 473 (S.C.C.).

150 "A strip search is properly defined as . . . the removal or rearrangement of some or all of the clothing of a person so as to permit a visual inspection of a person's private areas, namely genitals, buttocks, breasts (in the case of a female), or undergarments." *R. v. Golden, ibid.* It is apparent that even the degree to which a strip search violates privacy interests can vary.

151 "Frisk" or "pat down" searches do not involve the removal of clothing: *R. v. Golden, ibid.*

152 *R. v. Silveira*, above note 91.

153 *R. v. Wise*, above note 91; *R. v. Caslake*, above note 117; *R. v. Belnavis*, above note 31.

154 *R. v. Nolet*, 2010 SCC 24.

155 *R. v. M.(M.R.)*, above note 38. See *R. v. Tessling*, [2004] 3 S.C.R. 432 at paras. 20–24 where an illustrative hierarchy of expectations of privacy is furnished.

Of course, the degree of intrusion can even vary within a particular kind of search. In *R. v. Golden*, for example, the Supreme Court of Canada described a number of features that can change the intrusiveness of a strip search, including where it took place, the nature of the physical contact, and the relative sex of the subject and those who participate in or are present for the search.[156]

The intensity of the privacy interest can also be affected by the nature of the objects searched or seized. Searches that reveal highly personal documents containing core information, for example, are more intrusive of privacy interests than searches that may, for example, uncover ordinary articles of clothing. In *R. v. Morelli* the Court remarked that "it is difficult to imagine a search more intrusive, extensive or invasive of one's privacy than the search or seizure of a personal computer."[157]

6.4 (d)   Derivative Evidence

"Derivative evidence" was defined in *R. v. Grant* as "physical . . . evidence discovered as a result of an unlawfully obtained statement."[158] Generally speaking, where derivative evidence is being evaluated for admission, the negative impact of the breach on the *Charter*-protected interests of the accused will be high. This will be because the relevant breach is the one that produced the statement, which in most cases will have "impinged upon a free and informed choice" by the accused as to whether to speak.[159] This is true not only of involuntary statements, but also of breaches of "the section 10(b) right to counsel, which protects the accused's interest in making an informed choice whether to speak to the authorities."[160] "Where that interest was significantly compromised by the breach, this factor will strongly favour exclusion."[161]

The *Grant* decision recognized that "discoverability" may reduce the intrusiveness of the violation. Where reasonable conclusions can be drawn about "discoverability," it plays "a useful role . . . in assessing the actual impact of the breach on the protected interests of the accused," by enabling "courts to assess the strength of the causal connection between the *Charter*-infringing self-incrimination and the resultant evidence."[162] "The more likely it is that the evidence would have

---

156 Above note 149.

157 Above note 97 at para. 2.

158 Above note 4 at para. 116. As indicated, it is possible for statements to be derivative evidence: see note 44 above.

159 *R. v. Grant*, above note 4 at para. 66.

160 *Ibid.*

161 *Ibid.*

162 *Ibid.* at para. 122.

been obtained even without the statement, the lesser the impact of the breach."[163] Where "it cannot be determined with any confidence wheth- er evidence would have been discovered in absence of the statement, discoverability will have no impact on the s. 24(2) inquiry"[164] and the intrusiveness of the breach is apt to be treated as high.

6.4 (e) Discoverability and Causation

As can be seen, if a *Charter* breach does not lead to the discovery of the evidence sought to be excluded, or that evidence would have been dis- covered even without the breach, the intrusion into *Charter*-protected interests is considered to be mitigated.[165] *R. v. Grant* spoke specifically about the impact of discoverability only when discussing the admis- sion of statements and derivative evidence. However, causation and discoverability are relevant factors affecting the intrusiveness of the breach, regardless of the kind of evidence at stake.

In *R. v. Nolet* the Court used discoverability as a factor in admit- ting real evidence discovered as the result of an unconstitutional illegal inventory search of a transport truck. It reasoned that had the officers continued their constitutionally valid search incidental to arrest they would have "readily discovered" that evidence.[166] This is consistent with pre-*Grant* authority. In *R. v. Strachan*, for example, the fact that the right to counsel breach did not lead to the discovery of the narcot- ics assisted the Court in concluding that the admission of the evidence would not bring the administration of justice into disrepute.[167] Similarly, unreasonable searches have long been considered less serious where

---

163 *Ibid.*

164 *Ibid.*

165 Is it theoretically sound for the *Grant* decision to have treated causation and discoverability as bearing on the degree of the intrusiveness of the breach? The matter in issue is supposed to be the intrusiveness of the breach *on the* Charter- *protected interests of the accused*: *R. v. Grant*, above note 4 at para. 76. The *Charter* does not protect accused persons against the discovery of probative evidence, or the prospect of facing a stronger case. The *Charter* is intended instead to protect, for example, privacy interests, the liberty of movement, or the right to make an informed choice to speak. The degree of intrusiveness of the breach should there- fore arguably turn on the nature of the investigative violation and not on what the breach happened to make available. A better explanation for the relevance of causation and discoverability is arguably the third analytical factor about to be discussed, namely, "society's interest in adjudication on its merits." It is more costly to society to exclude evidence the Crown would have had even without the breach. To do so not only removes the fruits of the breach, but also causes the loss to the Crown of evidence it would have without the *Charter* violation.

166 *R. v. Nolet*, above note 154 at para. 54.

167 Above note 46.

there would have been reasonable grounds for the warrantless search or for the defective search warrant.[168]

The same holds true for bodily samples. In *R. v. Connors*,[169] for example, the police illegally took Connors' fingerprints when they arrested him. He was then charged with impaired driving. Since the police had the authority to compel Connors to give his prints after he had been charged, the prints would have been obtained even without the breach and they were ultimately admitted into evidence.

Although analysed when evaluating the degree of intrusiveness of the breach, discoverability and causation questions are closely related to the bad faith continuum. In the pre-*Grant* case law, discoverability would not enhance admissibility if the police knew they could have obtained the evidence without violating the *Charter* or if they failed to make a "sincere effort to comply with the *Charter*."[170] In such cases, the blameworthiness of the *Charter* violation would be aggravated because the *Charter* violation would be gratuitous. Similar principles should operate post-*Grant*. Discoverability is not a pro-inclusionary factor for bad faith breaches.

6.5) Step 3 in Assessing Disrepute—Judging Society's Interest in an Adjudication on the Merits

> Society's Interest in Adjudication on the Merits—*The weight to be accorded to society's interest in the adjudication of the case on its merits varies according to (a) the reliability of the evidence and (b) the importance of that evidence to the case for the Crown. While the seriousness of the offence is also a "valid consideration," it in fact contributes little to the outcome since both society's interest in deciding a case on its merits, and its vital interest in having a justice system that is above reproach, are heightened, effectively neutralizing the importance of the seriousness of the offence as a factor material to the exclusionary decision.*

"The third line of inquiry relevant to the s. 24(2) analysis asks whether the truth-seeking function of the criminal trial process would be better served by admission of the evidence or by its exclusion."[171] Measuring

---

168 *R. v. Buhay*, above note 14 at para. 65; *R. v. Brooks* (2003), 15 C.R. (6th) 319 (Ont. C.A.); *R. v. Caslake*, above note 117 at para. 34.

169 (1998), 14 C.R. (5th) 200 (B.C.C.A.).

170 See *R. v. Buhay*, above note 14 at para. 63; *R. v. Feeney*, above note 96 at para. 76; *R. v. Dyment*, [1988] 2 S.C.R. 417 at 440.

171 *R. v. Grant*, above note 4 at para. 79.

the damage to the truth-seeking function permits courts to determine "whether the vindication of the specific *Charter* violation through the exclusion of evidence extracts too great a toll on the truth-seeking goal of the criminal trial."[172]

There are two central factors in examining the impact of exclusion on the truth-seeking function: (1) the reliability of the evidence, and (2) the importance of the evidence to the prosecution case.

6.5 (a)   The "Reliability of the Evidence"

The *Grant* Court noted that "reliability of the evidence is an important factor" in determining the impact that exclusion will have on the public interest in truth-finding. "If a breach (such as one that effectively compels the suspect to talk) undermines the reliability of the evidence this points in the direction of exclusion of the evidence."[173] This is because there is no public interest in the admissibility of unreliable evidence. In contrast, "exclusion of relevant and reliable evidence may undermine the truth-seeking function of the justice system and render the trial unfair from the public perspective, thus bringing the administration of justice into disrepute."[174]

In its early section 24(2) decisions the Supreme Court of Canada had not featured reliability. Indeed, in 1995 in *R. v. Burlingham* a majority of the Court rejected reliability as a central consideration in section 24(2) jurisprudence, rebuffing an attempt by Justice L'Heureux-Dubé to develop a guiding "reliability principle."[175] This resistance did not last long. Justice Cory agreed with Justice Doherty of the Ontario Court of Appeal in the 1997 decision in *R. v. Belnavis* that the more reliable and probative the evidence, the greater costs of its exclusion.[176] Indeed, in *R. v. White* the evidence at issue was reliable and proved the guilt of the accused to a virtual certainty, prompting the Ontario Court of Appeal to hold that even if the trial judge had been right about the *Charter* breach, it would have been an error to have excluded the evidence.[177]

It is important to appreciate that the reliability factor is not a return to the common law approach exemplified in *R. v. Wray*.[178] As the *Grant* Court put it, "[t]he view that reliable evidence is admissible regardless

---

172   *Ibid.* at para. 82.
173   *Ibid.* at para. 81.
174   *Ibid.*
175   Above note 6 at para. 85 (L'Heureux-Dubé J.), paras. 37–39 (Iacobucci J.), and para. 146 (Sopinka J.).
176   *R. v. Belnavis*, above note 31 at 84.
177   *R. v. White*, above note 45.
178   Above note 2.

of how it was obtained . . . is inconsistent with the *Charter*'s affirmation of rights. More specifically, it is inconsistent with the wording of s.24(2), which mandates a broad inquiry into all the circumstances, not just the reliability of the evidence."[179] As *R. v. Harrison* shows,[180] where the breach is serious enough and its impact significant, the reliability of the evidence will not save it from exclusion.

6.5 (b)   The Importance of the Evidence

"The importance of the evidence to the prosecution's case is another factor to be considered in this line of inquiry."[181] This is because the exclusion of evidence "may impact more negatively on the repute of the administration of justice where the remedy effectively guts the prosecution."[182]

Even under the *Collins/Stillman* framework this was an important pro-inclusionary consideration. In *R. v. Silveira*, for example, the Court supported its decision to admit the evidence because "[t]he evidence at issue . . . was vitally important if not crucial to the prosecution of the case."[183] Exclusion would have substantially diminished the strength of the Crown's case. In some respects this is curious. It appears to endorse exclusion as a remedy, provided it will have no real effect. In *R. v. Buhay*, however, the Supreme Court of Canada cautioned against treating the fact that evidence is crucial to the Crown case as automatically requiring that the evidence be included.[184] Even if evidence is crucial, exclusion will occur if a *Charter* breach is serious enough or its impact on *Charter*-protected interests is significant enough. This is in keeping with the goal of protecting the long-range interests of justice, and not making the exclusionary decision solely by considering the case at hand. The point is simply this. The more crucial the evidence is, the more serious or significant the breach must be for exclusion to occur.

6.5 (c)   The Seriousness of the Offence

Under the *Collins/Stillman* framework, the seriousness of the offence was an important consideration in determining how much damage ex-

---

179   *R. v. Grant*, above note 4 at para. 80.
180   Above note 11. See the outline of the decision in section 2.2, "The Law Illustrated," above in this chapter.
181   *R. v. Grant*, above note 4 at para. 83.
182   *Ibid.*
183   Above note 91 at 375. See also *R. v. Plant* (1993), 24 C.R. (4th) 47 (S.C.C.). Paradoxically, in *R. v. Smith* (1991), 4 C.R. (4th) 125 (S.C.C.), the Court justified admitting an unconstitutionally obtained statement made by the accused, in part because he was not prejudiced by its admission. There was ample other evidence to show that it was he who had discharged the gun.
184   Above note 14 at para. 71; *R. v. Mann*, above note 94 at para. 57.

clusion would do to the repute of the administration of justice. The thinking was that the more serious the offence is, the greater the costs of exclusion will be. In *R. v. Silveira*, for example, the significant quantity of hard drugs involved, coupled with the catastrophic effect of drug use on society, helped to encourage the Court to receive the fruits of the illegal search.[185] In *R. v. Colarusso* the appalling circumstances in which the impaired driving occurred justified the admission of the evidence.[186] This is not to say that the exclusion of evidence did not occur in serious cases. In the homicide cases of *R. v. Feeney*[187] and *R. v. Stillman*[188] the Supreme Court of Canada excluded important evidence to remedy *Charter* violations. The breaches were simply too serious to condone. Still, seriousness of the offence was treated as a standard pro-inclusionary consideration in the pre-*Grant* case law.

The *Grant* majority has now made the seriousness of the offence largely immaterial to section 24(2). It affirmed that section 24(2)'s goals "operate independently of the type of crime for which the individual stands accused,"[189] and noted that the section addresses the long-term interests of the administration of justice and not the immediate impact on how people view the justice system.[190] The majority disagreed with Justice Deschamps, who, in her concurring decision, considered the seriousness of the offence to be a very important consideration. Curiously, the majority allowed that the seriousness of the offence may be a "valid consideration," but then effectively neutralized its impact by noting that seriousness "has the potential to cut both ways."[191] "The public has a heightened interest in seeing a determination on the merits where the offence is serious, [but] it also has a vital interest in having a justice system that is above reproach, particularly where the penal stakes for the accused are high."[192] This "cuts-both-ways" observation effectively undercut the seriousness of the offence as a factor of influence. In *R. v. Grant*, the Court found that the seriousness of the gun charges was not of much assistance because the public safety concerns were met by Mr. Grant's argument that "the seriousness of the offence makes it all the more important that his rights be respected."[193] Meanwhile, in *R. v.*

185 Above note 91 at 384; *R. v. Jacoy* (1988), 66 C.R. (3d) 336 (S.C.C.).
186 [1994] 1 S.C.R. 20.
187 Above note 96.
188 Above note 8.
189 Above note 4 at para. 84.
190 *Ibid.*
191 *Ibid.*
192 *Ibid.*
193 *Ibid.* at para. 139.

Harrison the Court discounted the seriousness of drug charges involving 35 kilograms of cocaine, an appalling amount of the drug, because this factor "must not take on disproportionate significance."[194] It has to be wondered why the seriousness of the offence was recognized as a valid consideration if it will in fact have no material bearing on the outcome.

It also has to be wondered whether the law relating to the seriousness of the offence described in *Grant* reflects actual practice. In *R. v. Chuhaniuk*, for example, the British Columbia Court of Appeal commented on the seriousness of large-scale grow operations in explaining why unconstitutionally obtained evidence was admissible.[195] Cases to date also suggest that handguns continue after *Grant* to be less apt to be excluded than other forms of real evidence.[196] It will no doubt be difficult for courts, charged with the obligation to consider the impact exclusion will have on the reputation of the administration of justice, to disregard the nature of the allegations they are trying.[197]

7. EXCLUDING EVIDENCE UNDER SECTION 24(1) OF THE *CHARTER*

Section 24(2) applies only where unconstitutional investigation produces evidence. Evidence can be excluded under section 24(1) in one and possibly two other situations.

First, exclusion can occur under section 24(1) to remedy *Charter* violations that do not occur at the time the evidence is obtained, but which relate to that evidence. This form of exclusion is available, for example, to remedy an abuse of process by the Crown that affects the ability to evaluate evidence,[198] or where the Crown breaches the *Charter* by failing to disclose. The standards for exclusion are high. In *R. v. Bjelland*, the Supreme Court of Canada ruled that "under s.24(1) . . . exclusion is only available as a remedy where its admission would result in an unfair trial or would otherwise undermine the integrity of the justice system," and where a "less intrusive remedy cannot be fash-

---

194 Above note 11 at para. 34.
195 (2010), 261 C.C.C. (3d) 486 (B.C.C.A.).
196 See Madden, "Marshalling the Data," above note 13. However, the rates of excluding hard drugs are high, based on the available sample.
197 See David M. Paciocco, "Section 24(2): Lottery or Law—The Appreciable Limits of Purposive Reasoning" (2011) 57 Crim. L.Q. [forthcoming].
198 See *R. v. Caster*, above note 20 at 412 (B.C.C.A), and *R. v. Mahar*, [2009] O.J. No. 4082 (S.C.J.).

ioned to safeguard the fairness of the trial process and the integrity of the justice system."[199] Curiously, when the impact of exclusion on the fairness of the trial and the integrity of the criminal justice system are considered, the seriousness of the offence is a relevant and proper consideration under section 24(1),[200] even though it is a neutral factor under section 24(2).

Second, exclusion may also be occurring under section 24(1) where the very receipt of the evidence by a court would breach the *Charter,* such as where the admission of statutorily compelled statements would compromise self-incrimination principles.[201] This was the approach taken in *R. v. White,* where the trial judge used section 24(1) to reject the statutorily compelled evidence.[202]

Justice Iacobucci chose not to interfere with this reasoning, but did leave open the possibility that exclusion should occur automatically under section 7. There is merit in this. Since it would be a *Charter* violation to admit such evidence, the court should arguably reject it without regard to the remedial provision. Indeed, section 24(1) provides for discretionary relief, something that is inappropriate where the receipt of the evidence would, *ex hypothesi*, constitute the *Charter* breach. When derivative evidence obtained from the compelled testimony is excluded under section 7, exclusion is not treated as a remedy. It occurs without resort to sections 24(1) or 24(2). This is the preferred view—where admission itself would violate the *Charter* (for example, because it would contravene self-incrimination principles to admit it) exclusion should be automatic independently of section 24(1).[203]

8. EXCLUDING UNFAIRLY OBTAINED EVIDENCE IN THE ABSENCE OF A *CHARTER* VIOLATION

Until relatively recently, courts disclaimed the authority to exclude evidence because it was obtained illegally or unfairly where the *Charter* had not been violated.[204] It is now settled that courts can, in fact,

---

199 *R. v. Bjelland*, [2009] S.C.J. No. 38 at paras. 3 and 19.
200 *Ibid.* at para. 27.
201 See the discussion in chapter 8, section 5.7 (b), "Statutorily Compelled Statements."
202 Above note 20.
203 See the discussion in Paciocco, "Section 24(2): Lottery or Law," above note 197.
204 *R. v. Wray*, above note 2. See the discussion in chapter 2, section 5, "The Exclusionary Discretion."

exclude evidence because of how it was obtained, even in the absence of a *Charter* breach. The power to do so had been recognized in passages in a number of cases[205] but remained controversial until the Supreme Court of Canada decision in *R. v. Harrer*,[206] where the authority to exclude unfairly obtained evidence received a clear endorsement. For the sake of clarity, this discretion will be referred to as "non-24(2) unfair trial exclusion" in the following discussion.

Harrer involved an application by the accused to exclude statements made to American authorities while she was being detained in the US. Although the American authorities complied with the requirements of the law in the US, had a Canadian peace officer conducted an interview in the same fashion, the accused's right to counsel would have been violated. It was nonetheless impossible for Harrer to rely on the *Charter*'s exclusionary remedy in subsection 24(2) because there had been no misconduct by Canadian state agents and therefore no *Charter* breach. The Court noted, however, that had the actions of the American authorities been such as to render the admission of the evidence unfair, the evidence should nonetheless be excluded. In the circumstances of *Harrer*, the evidence was ultimately received, but the discretion to exclude was given unambiguous endorsement. Justice McLachlin, in her concurring opinion, grounded the discretion in the common law,[207] although Justice La Forest, writing for the majority, went further. In his view, the discretion to exclude evidence to preserve the fairness of a trial in a criminal case is actually a matter of obligation. Where, in all of the circumstances, admission of the evidence would render a trial unfair, subsection 11(d) of the *Charter* imposes a duty on the trial judge to exclude it to preserve the integrity of the trial. Members of the Court have since held that section 7 produces much the same effect; it would violate principles of fundamental justice for a court to admit evidence where that admission would render the trial unfair.[208]

The Supreme Court of Canada recognized that this "non-24(2) unfair trial exclusion" could be used where the person who acts illegally

---

205   See, for example, *R. v. Potvin* (1989), 68 C.R. (3d) 193 (S.C.C.); *R. v. Hebert* (1990), 77 C.R. (3d) 145 (S.C.C.); *R. v. S.(R.J.)* (1995), 36 C.R. (4th) 1 at 83–84 (S.C.C.).

206   Above note 34.

207   In *R. v. Buhay*, above note 14 at para. 40, the Court referred to this power as a common law discretion. Its antecedents are controversial. See Michael C. Plaxton, "Who Needs Section 24(2)? Or: Common Law Sleight-of-Hand" (2003) 10 C.R. (6th) 236.

208   *R. v. Cook*, [1998] 2 S.C.R. 597. On this thinking, the fair trial exclusion occurs because admission of the evidence would violate the *Charter*. Again, as a matter of principle no resort should be required to the *Charter*'s remedies provision in such cases. Exclusion takes place outside of section 24.

or unfairly is a private actor, like a security guard.[209] It would be avail-able as well, where the accused does not have standing to rely on sub-section 24(2) because it is the rights of another that have been violated. Courts have, however, taken a stringent view of when maltreatment of a witness or co-accused could render the trial of an accused unfair, thereby triggering "non-*Charter* unfair trial exclusion."[210] It has been used successfully, however, to support the principle against self-con-scription where the state has tried to use information it is authorized to gather for a limited purpose or for a different or improper purpose. In *R. v. Milne*,[211] for example, the Ontario Court of Appeal used "non-24(2) unfair trial exclusion" to prevent sobriety tests from being relied upon as proof of impairment where they were obtained without advising the accused of her right to counsel. Although it is not a *Charter* breach for officers to ask drivers who have consumed alcohol to perform such tests without advising them of the right to counsel, the demonstrably justifiable provincial law that permits this to occur contemplates that the test results will be used solely to enable the officer to determine if there are reasonable grounds to make a breath demand. The court held that a trial would be rendered unfair if this self-conscripting evidence, which the law allows to be obtained for a limited purpose, was subse-quently used by the Crown as actual proof of impairment.[212]

Unfortunately, the "non-24(2) unfair trial exclusion" authority leaves the framework for determining when exclusion should occur vague and undefined. The cases have invited courts to conduct an un-structured case-by-case evaluation involving a "careful balancing of all competing interests" to see whether a fair trial, "one which satisfies the public interest in getting at the truth, while preserving basic proced-ural fairness to the accused,"[213] could be conducted were the evidence to be admitted. This is a legal test without normative standards. Courts considering "non-24(2) unfair trial exclusion" tend to rely on the fol-lowing factors for consideration:[214]

a) whether the manner of obtaining the evidence renders it unreliable;
b) whether the evidence, by its nature, could be misleading;

---

209 *R. v. Buhay*, above note 14 at para. 40.
210 See, for example, *R. v. Caster*, above note 20, and *R. v. Hyatt* (2003), 9 C.R. (6th) 378 (B.C.C.A.).
211 (1996), 48 C.R. (4th) 182 (Ont. C.A.), approved in *R. v. Orbanski*, [2005] 2 S.C.R. 3 at para. 58.
212 But see *R. v. Gunn* (2010), 253 C.C.C. (3d) 1 (Sask. C.A.).
213 *R. v. Harrer*, above note 34 at 288.
214 *R. v. Harrer*, ibid.; *R. v. Cook*, above note 208 at 46; *R. v. Brunczlik* (1995), 103 C.C.C. (3d) 131 (Ont. Ct. Gen. Div.).

c) the seriousness of the misconduct; and

d) whether, as a result of the unfair conduct, the accused is compelled to incriminate himself.

Where the case involves the actions of state agents in another juris-diction, a relevant consideration is whether the authorities respected the legal standards within that jurisdiction, and even where this is so, whether those legal standards would be anathema to a Canadian con-science.[215]

It must be remembered when conducting this inquiry that there are important differences between section 24(2) exclusion and "non-*Char-ter* unfair trial exclusion." The goals differ. Whereas the "non-24(2) unfair trial exclusion" is dedicated to ensuring a fair trial that "satis-fies the public interest in getting at the truth, while preserving basic procedural fairness to the accused,"[216] section 24(2) is used to protect "the integrity of the judicial system and the truth-seeking function of the courts."[217] Section 24(2) is driven by fear that admission will be seen to condone *Charter* breaches, while the "non-*Charter* unfair trial" exclusion operates where there is no *Charter* breach. A different focus is therefore required.

Still, courts applying the "non-24(2) unfair trial exclusion" who seek a more structured approach can do so by borrowing the analytical structure adopted in *Grant*. This can be done without undermining the differences between the two exclusionary rules by conducting a three-part inquiry into (1) the seriousness of the misconduct, (2) the degree of intrusiveness of the misconduct, and (3) society's interest in an ad-judication on the merits, before asking whether a reasonable person, fully informed of all of the circumstances and the values at stake would conclude that the admission of the evidence would produce a trial that does not properly balance the public interest in getting at the truth, while preserving basic procedural fairness to the accused.

9. IMPROPERLY OBTAINED EVIDENCE AND CIVIL CASES

The general common law rule that relevant evidence is admissible re-gardless of how it has been obtained applies in both civil and criminal

---

215 *R. v. Harrer, ibid.* at 290.

216 *Ibid.* at 288.

217 *R. v. Harrison*, above note 11 at para. 26.

cases. While this rule has been displaced by the *Charter*, the *Charter's* exclusionary remedy is tenable only against the state. The conventional view is that subsection 24(2) is therefore available only in criminal cases and in civil cases conducted before courts of competent jurisdiction where the state seeks to rely on unconstitutionally obtained evidence, but not in private civil proceedings.[218]

Judges conducting civil trials do, however, have an exclusionary discretion. This discretion should be exercised consistently with *Charter* values and can therefore result in the exclusion in private civil litigation of unconstitutionally obtained evidence.[219] In *Mooring v. Canada (National Parole Board)*[220] the Supreme Court of Canada recognized that the duty of fairness that applies to public authorities to make administrative decisions can, depending on the case, require the exclusion of unconstitutionally obtained evidence based on concerns related both to fairness and reliability. Had the police misconduct been egregious, the parole board review panel may have been obliged to exclude the evidence. In *Thomsen v. Alberta (Transport and Safety Board)*[221] it was also held that an administrative tribunal under its duty of fairness *must* consider the source of evidence or information, including whether it was gathered in breach of the *Charter*, and decide whether to exercise its discretion to receive the evidence.

In exercising this discretion, context is critical. In *R. v. Daley*, dealing with proceeds of crime legislation even in a criminal milieu, the Alberta Court of Appeal indicated that a section 24(2) analysis would not include the criminal law's trial fairness doctrine that excludes automatically conscriptive evidence because the notion "makes little sense in [a] proceeding where there are no charges, no accused and no risk of conviction."[222] The Ontario Court of Appeal made the same point in *P.(D.) v. Wagg*.[223] Even though the automatic exclusion of conscriptive evidence has now been rejected for section 24(2) cases, the under-

---

218 *Monsanto Canada Inc. v. Schmeiser* (2002), 218 D.L.R. (4th) 31 (Fed. C.A.); but see the *obiter dictum* of Rosenberg J.A. in *P.(D.) v. Wagg* (2004), 184 C.C.C. (3d) 321 at paras. 59–60 (Ont. C.A.), leaving open the possibility that *Charter* remedies like exclusion of evidence may be available in a civil action between private citizens on the basis that state action is satisfied where it was a state agent who infringed the *Charter*.

219 *P.(D.) v. Wagg*, *ibid*. See also *Seddon v. Seddon*, [1994] B.C.J. No. 1729 (S.C.).

220 Above note 29.

221 *Thomson v. Alberta (Transportation and Safety Board)* (2003), 178 C.C.C. (3d) 508 at para. 68 (Alta. C.A.).

222 [2001] A.J. No. 815 at para. 37.

223 Above note 218 at paras. 62–70.

lying point made by these courts remains true. Practices developed in criminal cases should not be mimicked in civil cases without regard for the differences in interests, concerns, and principles between criminal and civil litigation.

CHAPTER 10

METHODS OF PRESENTING EVIDENCE

1. THE CALLING OF WITNESSES

Our trial system is based on the calling of witnesses and, as a general rule, the court is entitled to every person's evidence, provided the person is competent to testify.[1] Competency means that the person is qualified or capable of giving evidence. Should the person not wish to testify, he can be forced or compelled to do so. The person is served with a subpoena. A *subpoena ad testificandum* requires that the person attend to give evidence. A *subpoena duces tecum* requires not only that the person attend to give evidence but that the person also bring anything in his possession or control that relates to the charge and, more particularly, those things specified in the subpoena. Should the person fail to attend, a warrant may be issued for his arrest and the person may be found guilty of contempt of court.[2]

At common law, many potentially valuable witnesses were rendered incompetent to testify. The common law judges were concerned about the giving of inaccurate or perjured testimony. Therefore, at common law people were precluded from testifying on grounds of interest, infamy (should the witness have a criminal history), infancy, insanity, disbelief in a Supreme Being, and marriage. Fortunately, most of the common law rules barring certain persons from testifying have been

---

1   *R. v. National Post*, 2010 SCC 16 at para. 1.
2   See *Criminal Code*, R.S.C. 1985, c. C-46, ss. 698–708.

swept aside by statute. For example, all the provincial Evidence Acts have a provision comparable to section 3 of the *Canada Evidence Act*, which reads:

> A person is not incompetent to give evidence by reason of interest or crime.

Today, for the most part, all potential witnesses are allowed to testify—warts and all; their frailties are left as a matter of credibility for the trier of fact to assess. However, vestiges of the common law remain with respect to children and with respect to the calling of spouses of accused persons.

2. COMPETENCY GENERALLY

In criminal cases, governed by the Canada Evidence Act *there are two competency regimes. Section 16 of the Act applies to adult witnesses and section 16.1 applies to child witnesses under the age of fourteen years.*

Adult Witnesses
Under section 16 persons over the age of fourteen are presumed competent to testify. An inquiry into their competency will be undertaken by the court only when the proposed witness's competency is challenged and the court is satisfied that there is an issue as to the person's capacity to testify under oath or affirmation.

Capacity under section 16 requires understanding of an oath or affirmation and whether the witness is able to communicate the evidence. Understanding of an oath or affirmation involves an understanding of the additional moral obligation to speak the truth in court. An ability to communicate the evidence involves the capacity to perceive, remember, and communicate the evidence.

Should the witness understand the nature of the oath or solemn affirmation and be able to communicate the evidence, the witness will then be allowed to testify under oath or affirmation.

Should the witness not understand the nature of the oath or affirmation, but have the necessary capacity to give evidence, the witness may testify on promising to tell the truth.

Child Witnesses
Under section 16.1 of the Canada Evidence Act all child witnesses under the age of fourteen years are presumed competent to testify.

> *An inquiry into their competency will be undertaken by the court when the proposed witness's competency is challenged or when the court is satisfied that there is an issue as to the child's capacity to understand and respond to questions.*
>
> *No child witness will take an oath or solemn affirmation. They will be permitted to testify on promising to tell the truth and no inquiry will be allowed as to their understanding of the nature of a promise to tell the truth.*
>
> *A child's evidence taken by way of a promise to tell the truth shall have the same effect as if it were taken under oath.*

Competency involves two aspects: capacity and responsibility. The witness must have the capacity to observe, recollect, and communicate. Is the witness capable of observing what was happening? Is the witness capable of remembering what he or she observes? Can the witness communicate what he or she remembers?[3] Beyond these requirements, the witness must also accept and be aware of the responsibility to testify in a truthful manner.

The applicable statutory provisions reflect these dual themes of capacity and responsibility. They address issues of capacity and responsibility by establishing tests to determine whether witnesses are entitled to give testimony under oath or affirmation, or as unsworn evidence. Should a witness fail to qualify under these tests, the witness will be held incompetent to testify.

At common law, a witness could only testify under oath and it was the inquiry into the ability to swear an oath that served as the check into both the capacity and responsibility of witnesses. Only children of "tender years," those under fourteen, would typically be tested, as those beyond tender years were presumed to be competent. If a tested witness did not understand the "nature and consequences of an oath," the witness would be found incompetent to give evidence.

Before 1987 the legislation across Canada was fairly similar. The statutes provided for children of "tender years" who did not "understand the nature of an oath" to give unsworn evidence, provided they "possessed sufficient intelligence" and understood the "duty of speaking the truth." If the evidence was taken in such an "unsworn" fashion, then corroboration of the child's testimony was required: no case was to be decided on a child's unsworn evidence alone. This statutory scheme remains in effect in a number of the provinces.[4] In 1987 the *Canada Evidence Act* was

---

3   *R. v. Marquard* (1993), 25 C.R. (4th) 1 at 10 (S.C.C.).
4   *Alberta Evidence Act*, s. 19; Nova Scotia, *Evidence Act*, s. 63; New Brunswick, Newfoundland, and Ontario have removed the requirement for corroboration:

amended and the requirement for corroboration was repealed.[5] In 2005 the Act was amended again and created an entirely separate regime to deal with the competency of child witnesses under the age of fourteen. The new regime does away with much of the formality and abstraction that made the competency inquiry difficult to apply to children.

Therefore, in a criminal trial we now have two competency regimes: section 16 of the *Canada Evidence Act* applies for adult witnesses, who are over fourteen years of age, and section 16.1 applies for children, who are under fourteen years of age. In order to appreciate the separate procedures involved it is valuable to examine section 16 first, because prior to 2006 it also applied to child witnesses. Deficiencies in its process prompted section 16.1, which was passed to facilitate the testimony of child witnesses by streamlining and simplifying the competency process for children.[6]

2.1) Competency of Adult Witnesses

Witnesses over the age of fourteen are presumed competent. For proposed witnesses over the age of fourteen, an inquiry into their competency will be undertaken only when a challenge is made and the court is satisfied that there is an issue as to the proposed witness's mental capacity.[7] Subsection 16(1) provides:

> 16(1) If a proposed witness is a person of fourteen years of age or older whose mental capacity is challenged, the court shall, before permitting the person to give evidence, conduct an inquiry to determine
> (a) whether the person understands the nature of an oath or a solemn affirmation; and
> (b) whether the person is able to communicate the evidence.

Where the answer to both questions inquired into is yes, the witness can swear an oath or affirm. Where the answer to the first question is no, but the second yes, the witness will be permitted to give unsworn

---

New Brunswick, *Evidence Act*, s. 24; Newfoundland and Labrador, *Evidence Act*, s. 18.1; Ontario, *Evidence Act*, s. 18.2. Prince Edward Island has no applicable statute and falls under the common law, where the child must either be sworn or is incompetent to testify.

5   The 1987 approach is in place in British Columbia, *Evidence Act*, s. 5; *Manitoba Evidence Act*, s. 24; Saskatchewan, *The Evidence Act*, s. 12.

6   In *R. v. D.I.*, 2010 ONCA 133, leave to appeal to S.C.C. granted, 2010 CanLII 62505 (S.C.C.), it was held that adults with developmental disabilities were to be treated under the adult regime in s. 16.

7   *Canada Evidence Act*, s. 16(5).

evidence. Where the answer to the second question is no, the witness will be declared incompetent.

The section 16 inquiry begins with a challenge to the mental capacity of the proposed witness and the burden rests with the challenger to satisfy the court that there is an issue as to the capacity of the witness to testify (see section 16(5)). The inquiry provided by section 16 is usually conducted in front of the jury, since matters of competency will also assist the jurors in weighing the witness's evidence. The trial judge has a discretion to conduct the inquiry in the absence of the jury where there exists a possibility of prejudice to the accused should the witness be found not competent to testify.[8] Expert witnesses may be called, such as a psychiatrist, who is familiar with the witness and may assist the trial judge in interpreting what he has seen or heard from the witness. However, competency is not a matter for the experts. As Justice Binnie observed in *R. v. Parrott*, determining the competency of a would-be witness is not a matter outside the experience and knowledge of a judge, rather "it is the very meat and potatoes of a trial court's existence."[9] At the conclusion of the inquiry the judge then rules on the witness's competency, and "a large measure of deference is to be accorded to the trial judge's assessment of a child's capacity to testify."[10]

As indicated, during the inquiry, two criteria are examined: whether the witness "understands the nature of an oath or solemn affirmation," and whether the witness is able to "communicate the evidence." The second inquiry, the ability to "communicate the evidence," is the "capacity" inquiry. It establishes the threshold for competence to testify. Any witness who fails to meet this part of the test will be prohibited from testifying. It will therefore be addressed first.

In *R. v. Marquard*, the Supreme Court of Canada was called upon to clarify the meaning of "communicate the evidence." At issue was the capacity of a young child to testify. The defence argued that the judge must test the child's ability to perceive and interpret the events in question at the time they took place, as well as the child's ability to recollect accurately and communicate the events at trial. The Crown argued that the only requirement was that the child now be able to communicate her evidence, all other matters of testimonial capacity being excluded. Madam Justice McLachlin (as she then was) chose a middle course between these two extremes. What she outlines is a general inquiry into capacity, and not a specific inquiry into the witness's ability to have

---

8   *R. v. Ferguson* (1996), 112 C.C.C. (3d) 342 (B.C.C.A.).

9   *R. v. Parrott* (2001), 150 C.C.C. (3d) 449 at 472 (S.C.C.). See also *R. v. Morrissey*, [2003] O.J. No. 5960 (S.C.J.).

10   *R. v. Marquard*, above note 3 at 11.

observed and to have remembered the specific incident now before the court. She wrote as follows:

> It is necessary to explore in a general way whether the witness is capable of perceiving events, remembering events and communicating events to the court . . . . It is not necessary to determine in advance that the child perceived and recollects the very events at issue in the trial as a condition of ruling that her evidence be received. That is not required of adult witnesses, and should not be required for children.[11]

The inquiry into understanding "the nature of an oath or solemn affirmation" is about "responsibility." It is meant to determine whether there is any way to get hold of the conscience of the witness. What is required is that the oath in some way gets a hold on the witness's conscience, "that there is an appreciation of the significance of testifying in court under oath."[12] The Ontario Court of Appeal in *R. v. Leonard* outlined the following test:

> The child's understanding of the moral obligation must include:
> (i)   an appreciation of the solemnity of the occasion;
> (ii) an understanding of the added responsibility to tell the truth *over and above* the duty to tell the truth as part of the ordinary duty of normal social conduct;
> (iii) an understanding of what it means to tell the truth *in court*;
> (iv) an appreciation of what happens, in both a practical and moral sense, when a lie is told *in court*.[13]

Should such an understanding be exhibited, the witness will testify under oath or solemn affirmation (see section 16(2)). Should no such understanding be found, but the witness has satisfied the "ability to communicate the evidence" threshold, the witness may still testify on "promising to tell the truth" (see section 16(3)). Before a witness is permitted to testify on promising to tell the truth, however, more is required than a simple ability to communicate the evidence. The witness must also understand what a promise to tell the truth is, and the witness must know what it means to tell the truth. Although these last two conditions are not expressed in the legislation, they are implicit. This is because a promise to tell the truth would be an empty gesture if the witness did not have such understanding.[14] It is therefore necessary for the trial judge to make some inquiry, and to satisfy himself of these things

---

11   *Ibid.* at 10.
12   *R. v. Khan* (1990), 79 C.R. (3d) 1 at 7 (S.C.C.).
13   *R. v. Leonard* (1990), 54 C.C.C. (3d) 225 at 227 (Ont. C.A.) [emphasis in original].
14   *R. v. McGovern* (1993), 88 Man. R. (2d) 18 at 21 (C.A.).

before permitting the witness to give unsworn evidence. The tests are not exacting, however. To promise to tell the truth, "the witness need only understand the duty to speak the truth in terms of ordinary everyday social conduct"[15] and "understand the obligation to tell the truth in giving his or her evidence."[16] In essence, then, the difference between a witness who is permitted to swear or affirm, and one who must give unsworn evidence, is that the witness who is permitted to swear or affirm appreciates the added responsibility of telling the truth in court and the solemnity of the court process, whereas the witness who gives unsworn evidence appreciates only the ordinary duty of speaking the truth after promising to do so. The difference is subtle, to say the least.

The problem is that "truth and "promise" are abstract concepts, difficult to explain or define. There is certainly no need in law to ask for definitions in order to resolve whether the witness "understands the duty to speak the truth in terms of ordinary everyday social conduct." Nor should the witness have to define what a "promise" is in a technical sense; what is required is that the witness understand the obligation to tell the truth in giving evidence. More importantly, the witness must ultimately commit to tell the truth. There is a difference between understanding what a promise is, and actually promising to do so.[17] Studies show that promising to tell the truth has greater effect on the accuracy of evidence than a cognitive understanding of the meaning of truth and of promise.[18]

The Ontario *Evidence Act* goes further than the *Canada Evidence Act*, by providing yet another option. It enables unsworn evidence to be given without a promise to tell the truth.[19] Those witnesses who can communicate the evidence but who do not understand what it means to speak the truth can still testify, provided the trial judge concludes, as a matter of discretion, that the evidence is "sufficiently reliable" to receive.

2.2) Competency of Child Witnesses

Prior to 2006 the above section 16 inquiry was mandatory for all child witnesses under the age of fourteen. That has now changed. Children,

---

15   *R. v. A.(K.)* (1999), 137 C.C.C. (3d) 554 (Ont. C.A.)—this phrase is widely accepted by the courts.

16   *R. v. Rockey* (1996), 110 C.C.C. (3d) 481 (S.C.C.).

17   *R. v. B.(R.J.)* (2000), 33 C.R. (5th) 166 (Alta. C.A.).

18   N. Bala *et al.*, "A Legal and Psychological Critique of the Present Approach to the Assessment of the Competence of Child Witnesses" (2000) 38 Osgoode Hall L.J. 409 at 444.

19   Ontario *Evidence Act*, s. 18.1(3).

like adults, are presumed to have the capacity to testify (see section 16.1(1)). The focus has changed in terms of receiving children's evidence, from one of admissibility to reliability.[20]

An inquiry will be proceeded with if the child's capacity is challenged, in which case the challenger has the burden of satisfying the court that there is an issue as to the child's capacity (see section 16.1(4)). Or, it seems that the court, on its own volition, may raise the matter if satisfied that there is an issue as to the child's capacity (see section 16.1(5)). The formalism and abstraction associated with section 16 have been swept aside. There is no need to inquire into the child's understanding of what it means to swear an oath. Under section 16.1(2) a child witness shall not take an oath or solemn affirmation. Children will be permitted to testify upon promising to tell the truth (see section 16.1(6)). Moreover, the child shall not be asked any questions regarding their understanding of the nature of the promise to tell the truth (see section 16.1(7)).[21] This makes sense as the notion of a "promise" is conceptual; one may know what it means but have real difficulty in articulating that meaning.[22]

When competency is an issue the focus is on the child's capacity to "understand and respond to questions" (see section 16.1(5)). Arguably, this narrows capacity to the ability to communicate and removes the abilities to recollect and observe as identified in *Marquard* earlier in this chapter. However, at least one court has concluded that an ability to "understand and respond" includes the abilities to recollect and observe.[23] The section speaks of "the court" conducting the inquiry, and the procedure usually followed is for the judge to lead the examination, with counsel being invited to ask any supplemental questions.[24] There is, however, no requirement that the trial judge conduct the actual questioning. In many cases, it would be more appropriate for counsel who are familiar to the child to ask the questions of the child.[25]

The evidence of a child witness given by way of a promise is to have the same effect as if it were taken under oath (see section 16.1(8)). This too makes sense. It removes the stereotypical thinking that a child's

---

20   See *R. v. J.Z.S.*, 2008 BCCA 401 at para. 53, aff'd 2010 SCC 1, in which the Court upheld the constitutionality of s. 16.1.

21   See N. Bala, K. Lee, & R. Lindsay, "*R. v. M.(M.A.)*: Failing to Appreciate the Testimonial Capacity of Children" (2001) 40 C.R. (5th) 93.

22   For an example of a futile examination into the meaning of a promise, see *R. v. M.A.M.*, 2001 BCCA 6 at paras. 32–41.

23   *R. v. S.J.*, [2006] CarswellBC 3523 (Prov. Ct.), aff'd 2007 BCSC 900.

24   For an example of the process, see *R. v. Leonard*, above note 13.

25   *R. v. Peterson* (1996), 47 C.R. (4th) 161 (Ont. C.A.).

evidence is inherently suspect. A child's evidence is to be approached in the same way as that of an adult witness on an individual basis. In *R. v. W.(R.)*, Madam Justice McLachlin (as she then was) stated:

> [W]e approach the evidence of children not from the perspective of rigid stereotypes, but on what Wilson J. called a "common sense" basis, taking into account the strengths and weaknesses which characterize the evidence offered in the particular case.[26]

3. THE COMPETENCY AND COMPELLABILITY OF SPOUSES

The rule of spousal incompetency applies only where there is a valid and subsisting marriage. The rule does not apply to "common law" relationships or where the couple, although legally married, are irreconcilably separated.

In a civil case, any party or the spouse of any party is a competent and compellable witness for any party to the action.

In a criminal case, the spouse of an accused is a "competent" witness for the defence. The spouse of an accused is also a "competent and compellable" witness for the Crown where the accused is charged with offences listed in subsections 4(2) and 4(4) of the Canada Evidence Act. The spouse of an accused is also "competent" to testify for the Crown under the common law exception, which is preserved by section 4(5) of the Canada Evidence Act. The common law exceptions apply when: (1) the accused is charged with an offence involving the spouse's person, health, or liberty; (2) even though there is no charge, evidence reveals that the accused threatened the spouse's person, liberty, or health; or (3) violence, cruelty, or threats are made against the spouse's child. There is an issue as to whether a spouse is "compellable" under common law; the preferred view is that the spouse on being found competent is also compellable.

At common law the parties and their spouses in a civil case and the accused and spouse in a criminal case were not competent to testify. This rule has been abolished in civil cases; parties and their spouses

---

26   (1992), 74 C.C.C. (3d) 134 at 143–44 (S.C.C.). Moreover, s. 659 of the *Criminal Code*, above note 2, which was enacted in 1993, states:

> 659. Any requirement whereby it is mandatory for a court to give the jury a warning about convicting an accused on the evidence of a child is abrogated.

are both competent and compellable to testify and, in fact, may well be called to do so by the opposing side. In criminal cases, under subsection 4(1) of the *Canada Evidence Act*, the accused and the spouse are made competent to testify for the defence. The accused may not be called to testify by the prosecution.[27] The spouse may, in certain circumstances, be called by the prosecution to give evidence. Subsections 4(2) and 4(4) of the *Canada Evidence Act* make the spouse "competent and compellable" to testify for the prosecution where the accused is charged with certain listed offences. Subsection 4(2) lists sexual offences and crimes against the marriage, such as polygamy (section 293). Subsection 4(4) is concerned with crimes that involve harm or violence to children. These lists are far from logical. For example, why may the spouse be called to testify where the victim of a murder is under fourteen years of age, but may not testify when the victim is over the age of fourteen? The enactment of these sections indicates a trend towards the erosion of spousal incompetency.

This trend is also evident in the common law exception, which is preserved in subsection 4(5) of the *Canada Evidence Act*. At common law the spouse could testify in cases that involved the spouse's "person, liberty, or health." Obviously, if spouses were not allowed to testify they could well be victimized in secret with complete immunity.[28] The exception applies, however, even when the spouse is not the "charged" victim. In *R. v. Schell* the accused was charged with first degree murder in an alleged contract killing.[29] The Crown sought to call his estranged spouse to testify as to a conversation in which the accused admitted to the killing. The accused had also told his wife that if she said anything she or her children could be shot. The court found it absurd to confine the common law "threat" exception to situations where the accused is actually charged with the threat against the spouse. No useful purpose is served. Surely once such a threat is made there is little marital harmony to preserve and there is every need to provide protection to the spouse. For similar reasons this exception has been expanded to include crimes of violence or threats of violence against the spouse's children.[30]

At common law and under statute, the rule applies to "spouses"; there must be a valid marriage. Those in a "*de facto*" or "common law"

---

27   See chapter 8, section 4, "The Non-compellability of Accused Persons at their Own Trials," which addresses the issue of competency and compatibility in provincial prosecutions.

28   J.H. Wigmore, *Evidence in Trials at Common Law*, rev. J.T. McNaughton, 3d ed., vol. 8 (Boston: Little, Brown, 1961) s. 2239.

29   *R. v. Schell* (2004), 188 C.C.C. (3d) 254 (Alta. C.A.).

30   *R. v. MacPherson* (1980), 52 C.C.C. (2d) 547 (N.S.C.A.).

relationship cannot invoke the rule and may be called as ordinary witnesses.[31] The marriage must be valid and subsisting at the time the
spouse is called to testify. Therefore, the spouse is rendered incompetent to testify as to events that may have occurred before the marriage.
Conversely, should the marriage come to an end, the ex-spouse is now
competent to testify. The two most cogent rationales put forth to justify
the rule are as follows: (1) the protection of marital harmony, and (2)
the natural repugnance in compelling a wife or husband to assist in
convicting the other.[32] In *R. v. Salituro*, the Supreme Court of Canada
ruled spousal incompetency did not apply where, although there was
a valid marriage in law, the spouses were irreconcilably separated. As
Iacobucci J. noted, where spouses are irreconcilably separated, "there
is no marital harmony to be preserved." The burden of proof is on the
Crown to invoke this exception, satisfying the court on a balance of
probabilities.[33] The threshold does not require the Crown prove that
the parties will never reconcile in the future. Rather, the test is whether
there exists no "reasonable prospect of reconciliation" at the time the
witness is testifying.[34] The test is necessarily a subjective determination.
Obviously, the spouse's stated intention is very important, but the objective evidence may well be such that even though the spouse says "we
might reconcile in the future" the objective evidence says otherwise.

   Salituro was concerned simply with the question of "competency."
Mrs. Salituro wanted to testify against her husband, who was charged
with forging his wife's signature on a cheque payable jointly to her and
to him. Mr. Salituro's defence was that his wife authorized him to do
so. Mrs. Salituro denied that she had done so. In the circumstances,
the spousal incompetency rule barred a willing witness from testifying.
Iacobucci J. found this to be an affront to the values in the *Charter* accorded to human dignity and to the right of individual choice. He went
on to muse that in principle it was perhaps appropriate that all spouses
should be competent witnesses under all circumstances.[35] As Chief Justice Burger observed in *Trammel v. United States*:

> When one spouse is willing to testify against the other in a criminal
> proceeding—whatever the motivation—their relationship is almost
> certainly in disrepair; there is probably little in the way of marital

---

31   *R. v. Duvivier* (1991), 64 C.C.C. (3d) 20 (Ont. C.A.).

32   *R. v. Salituro* (1991), 9 C.R. (4th) 324 at 340 (S.C.C.). Two other rationales that have
not survived are that (1) a spouse is incompetent because, in law, husband and
wife are one, and (2) they are disqualified because their interests are identical.

33   *R. v. Jeffrey* (1993), 25 C.R. (4th) 104 (Alta. C.A.).

34   *R. v. Schell*, above note 29 at para. 32.

35   Above note 32 at 340.

harmony for the privilege to preserve. In these circumstances, a rule of evidence that permits an accused to prevent adverse spousal testimony seems far more likely to frustrate justice than to foster family peace.[36]

What if, in the circumstances, Mrs. Salituro had not wanted to testify? Could she be compelled to do so by the Crown? In *Trammel*, the United States Supreme Court left the choice with the witness spouse; if she wanted to testify, she could; if not, she could not be compelled to testify. Mr. Justice Iacobucci made it quite clear that *Salituro* was not concerned with the question of "compellability," although he expressed the view that had it been necessary to decide this question, "the possibility that a competent spouse would be found also to be compellable is a *real* one."[37] He then referred to the decision of the Yukon Court of Appeal in *R. v. McGinty*, where the spouse was found to be not only a competent but a compellable witness for the Crown.[38] The Alberta Court of Appeal in *R. v. Schell* is the most recent of courts to endorse the view that compellability flows from competence.[39] This is the correct route to follow. Leaving the choice to testify with the spouse, who remember is competent under the law because of violence or threats made against her, would only serve to exacerbate matrimonial discord and provide incentive for further violence aimed at convincing her not to testify. It is better for the spouse to be faced with no choice, as is the case with any other witness.

Does the spousal incompetency rule apply to out-of-court statements? Yes. In *R. v. Couture* the Supreme Court held that an out-of-court statement made by a spouse to the police would undermine the spousal incompetency principle and for that reason ought to be excluded.[40] In *Couture* the police took the spouse's statement for the express purpose of introducing it in evidence against the spouse's husband. The state was doing indirectly what it could not do directly, which is to say call the spouse to testify. In other cases, the state may not be involved in undermining the spouse's incompetency. For example, a husband is charged with the murder of a drinking companion and a witness heard the spouse cry out, "Husband stop hitting him. You'll kill him." This statement by the spouse may well be admitted as a spontaneous utterance and not offend the spousal incompetency principle.

---

36   445 U.S. 40 at 52 (1980) [footnotes omitted].
37   Above note 32 at 343 [emphasis added].
38   (1986), 52 C.R. (3d) 161 (Y.C.A.).
39   Above note 29 at para. 75. See also *R. v. Aziga*, 2008 CanLII 53841 (Ont. S.C.J.).
40   *R. v. Couture*, 2007 SCC 28 at paras. 63–72.

The Supreme Court has made it clear that any substantial change in the law respecting spousal incompetency must be made by Parliament. The Court has also made it clear that the existing law is in an unsatisfactory state and that reform is needed. Such reform has been urged upon Parliament for decades. It is time for Parliament to act. As the court in *Schell* observed:[41]

> Given the current definitions of "spouse" and "marriage" and the broad application of *Canadian Charter of Rights and Freedoms* values, whether such distinctions remain supportable is an open question. Moreover, of greater legal and societal significance is whether this common law rule remains valid in the 21st century. On its face, it appears to run contrary to basic *Charter* values that accord individuals dignity and an entitlement to participate equally in society, including being able to testify in a court of law. The *Charter* jurisprudence on gender equality, sexual orientation, marital status, the redefinition of "marriage" and "spouse," and security of the person, all raise the prospect that the rule as currently framed might not survive *Charter* scrutiny.

The greatest pressure is to expand the definition of "spouse" to include common law relationships. In *R. v. Martin* the trial judge extended the spousal incompetency rule to persons in common law relationships. The ruling was overturned on appeal. The Court of Appeal held that such a major change in the law should be left to Parliament and not the courts.[42] What to do? The problem is that if you expand the definition of spouse to include common law relationships the result is the loss of more and more evidence. It is not in the interests of the criminal justice system to deny the Crown access to valuable witnesses especially when, as Wigmore noted many years ago, there is so little proof that the spousal competency rules have any real affect upon preserving marital harmony.[43] Queensland recently abolished spousal competency and privilege.[44] This is the simplest, cleanest, and most logical way to go. In a criminal prosecution the interests of justice demand that we have access to the evidence of all witnesses — save the accused.

---

41   Above note 29 at para. 29.
42   *R. v. Martin*, 2009 SKCA 37.
43   Wigmore, above note 28, s. 2228.
44   *Evidence Act 1977* (Qld.), s. 8.

4. EXAMINATION IN CHIEF

Most evidence is presented in the form of oral evidence. Oral evidence, or testimony, is obtained from witnesses through the answers they provide to questions posed by the lawyers. The questions are not evidence. Only the answers are, coupled with as much of the question as is necessarily incorporated into the response of the witness. For example, if a lawyer says "I understand you are eight years old" and the witness replies "yes," the testimony of the witness is that she is eight years old.

Witnesses are not simply invited to take the stand and tell their story as they see fit. Questions are used to structure the presentation of evidence, to keep the information the witness provides relevant, to help ensure that only admissible evidence is given, and, for strategic purposes (subject to the ethical limit that counsel cannot attempt to mislead the court), so as to allow a party to be selective in the information that is sought from the witness.

4.1) Examination in Chief Defined

"Examination in chief," or direct examination, as it is called in the United States, describes the phase in the testimony of a witness where that witness is being questioned by the party who has called her. It can also describe the method of questioning that the party calling a witness is entitled to use under normal circumstances.

4.2) The Method of Questioning During Examination in Chief

The party calling a witness should generally use open-ended as opposed to leading questions. Although the answers to leading questions are not inadmissible, the fact that they were obtained by leading questions may affect their weight. There are two kinds of leading questions. The first kind suggests the answer to the witness. The second kind presupposes the existence of a fact not presented by that witness in evidence. This second kind of leading question is never permissible unless the presupposed matter is not contested. There are numerous situations where the first kind of leading question is appropriate. These include

- *introductory or undisputed matters,*
- *the identification of persons or things,*
- *the contradiction of statements made by another,*

- *complicated or technical matters,*
- *where leave has been obtained to cross-examine a witness as adverse or hostile,*
- *where the witness is having difficulty answering the question and leave has been obtained to lead the witness,*
- *where the question will refresh the memory of a witness and leave has been obtained to lead the witness, and any other case where leave has been obtained to lead the witness, in the interests of justice.*

4.2 (a)   Open-ended Questions

It is what the witness has to say that is of importance, not what the lawyer wants the witness to say. Often witnesses called by a party will be sympathetic or favourable to that party. This can cause them, wittingly or not, to provide answers consistent with the express or implied suggestions of that party's lawyer. Even where witnesses are truly neutral, the lawyer who has called them will typically know what information they have to offer and may be inclined to control unfairly the evidence they provide. Limits are therefore placed on the way that questions can be asked by the party who has called a witness. In particular, the lawyer is to ask open-ended questions. For example, "Who was with you?" "What happened next?" "When did you first notice that?" "Where were you at 8:00 a.m.?" "Why did you go there?" "Could you please describe the man you have just referred to?"

Open-ended questioning enables the witness to tell his own story and reduces the influence of the lawyer. Answers to open-ended questions are often persuasive and credible because the responses will be natural and are likely to be seen to be independent and untainted. Depending on who the witness is, well-organized open-ended questions are therefore the best way strategically to present the evidence.

4.2 (b)   "Leading" Questions

It is generally impermissible for the party who has called a witness to ask that witness leading questions.[45] Broadly speaking, there are two kinds of leading questions. "Leading questions are questions that suggest an answer or assume a state of facts that is in dispute."[46] A question can be leading in the first sense whether it directly or indirectly suggests the answer. For example, the question "I take it you checked your rear-view mirror before changing lanes?" is leading because it directly

---

45   *Maves v. Grand Trunk Pacific Ry. Co.* (1913), 6 Alta. L.R. 396 at 404–5 (C.A.).
46   *R. v. E.M.W.*, 2011 SCC 31 at para. 9.

suggests the answer. Even the question "Did you look in your rear-view mirror before changing lanes?" is leading. It suggests the answer indirectly because, when asked by the lawyer who called the witness and considered in context, the witness may conclude that, whether it happened or not, it would have been a good thing to have checked the rear-view mirror. This approach can influence the answer that is provided. Even an honest but lazy or nervous witness may assent to suggestive questioning. A proper way to determine whether caution-ary steps were taken by the driver who testifies that he changed lanes would be to ask simply, "What, if anything, did you do before you com-pleted the lane change?" In *R. v. E.M.W.* the Court did not consider binary questions—those posing alternatives that a witness can select between—to be leading. Binary questions asked in that case included "Less than ten [times]? More than five or less than five?" "Was he on the inside or outside of your clothes when he was doing this?"[47]

The second kind of leading question, those that "assume a state of facts that is in dispute," are posed in a way that presupposes the existence of a fact that has not been testified to by the witness. For ex-ample, the question "What happened after you put your turn signal on?" would be improper if the witness had not provided testimony that he had put his turn signal on. This kind of question can confuse the trier of fact, potentially leading it to believe that facts have been testified to which have not been. It can embarrass the witness, who may choose to respond only to the question asked rather than challenge the accuracy of the implied fact. Or, like the first kind of leading question, it can sug-gest to the witness that the implied fact actually occurred.

A more egregious form of this type of leading question not only presupposes facts but is also calculated to manipulate the answer un-fairly. The classic example is, "Have you stopped beating your wife?"

Leading questions that presuppose the existence of a fact that has not been testified to by the witness are never proper, unless there is no controversy about the presupposed fact. Such questions do not invite comment on the presupposed fact. Insofar as that fact is concerned, they are not really questions at all. This kind of leading question is not even permissible during cross-examination. By contrast, "the degree of con-

---

47 *Ibid.* In *R. v. E.M.W.*, the witness was a child who was having difficulty answering completely open-ended questions. As explained immediately below, more latitude is given when questioning children who are having difficulty testifying. Binary questions are more apt to be suggestive than fully open-ended questions, since the choice of alternatives can narrow the range of possible responses. Ideally, they should be avoided for ordinary witnesses who can respond to more general questions such as "How many times did this happen?"

cern that may arise from the use of leading question[s] [that merely suggest the answer] will depend on the particular circumstances and the rule is applied with some flexibility."[48] Indeed, in some cases this kind of leading is not only proper but is the preferred method of obtaining testimony during examination in chief. Although it would be wrong to consider that there is a closed list of exceptions, the following are examples of when leading questions can be asked during examination in chief:

- in introductory or undisputed matters;[49] for example, "I understand you are a plumber?"
- in identifying persons or things; for example, "Have you ever seen this gun before?"
- in contradicting statements by another; for example, "If Mrs. Jones said that you were driving the car at 7:00 p.m., would that be correct?"
- when the matter is complicated or technical; for example, "I understand that the DNA has to be extracted from the blood cells before you can begin to analyze it."
- when leave has been obtained to cross-examine your own witness as "adverse" or "hostile."[50]

Judges have discretion to remove the ban on questions that suggest the answer where it is necessary to do so in the interests of justice.[51] They may do so, for example, where

- the witness, because of age, language or mental challenge, is having difficulty answering the question;[52] for example, "Did Uncle Fred talk to you about a secret?"
- the question will refresh the memory of a witness who is having difficulty recalling;[53] for example, [Witness provides list of persons

---

48   *R. v. Rose* (2001), 153 C.C.C. (3d) 225 at para. 9 (C.A.).

49   "[T]he *general* rule is that in examining one's own witness—not that no leading questions must be asked, but that *on material points* one must *not* lead his own witness but that on points that are *merely introductory and form no part of the substance* of the inquiry one should lead." *Maves v. Grand Trunk Pacific Ry. Co.*, above note 45 at 406 [emphasis in original].

50   See chapter 11, section 6.4, "Cross-examination of One's Own Witness."

51   *Reference re R. v. Coffin* (1956), 23 C.R. 1 at 18 (S.C.C.); *R. v. Rose*, above note 48 at para. 9.

52   See *R. v. E.M.W.*, above note 46. Use of leading questions when examining children may be unavoidable. It may, however, diminish the weight that can be given to the evidence, and where key evidence is secured in a suggestive way, it can destroy the case altogether. See *R. v. Caron* (1994), 94 C.C.C. (3d) 466 (Ont. C.A.).

53   "[T]he rule against leading ought to be relaxed where non-leading questions fail to bring the mind of the witness to the precise point on which his evidence is desired, and it may fairly be supposed that this failure arises from a temporary

present omitting to mention his sister, whom he has previously told counsel about] "Did you see your sister that night?"

The rules of court in a number of Canadian jurisdictions confirm this approach for civil cases, allowing leading questions to be used if "a witness appears unwilling or unable to give responsive answers."[54]

Even outside of these categories, it is important to realize that whether a question is leading is a matter of degree and often calls for the exercise of some judgment. For example, "You checked your mirror before changing lanes, didn't you?" is leading compared with "Did you check your mirror?" This question, in turn, is leading compared with "What precautions did you take to ensure that it was safe to change lanes?" which itself is leading compared with "What happened next?"

As this second last example reveals, it is an over-simplification to make the common claim that leading questions are those that invite a "yes" or "no" answer. Most do, but many do not. The key in identifying such questions is whether, in context, they suggest the response.

In practice, leading questions are not always objected to, particularly where the matter is uncontested or unimportant. Even where a question that is leading enough to be objectionable has been asked inappropriately, the answer provided is not "inadmissible." However, the fact that the answer was obtained by a leading question is likely to diminish the weight that it is given. In *R. v. Rose* the trial judge permitted such egregious leading that it contributed substantially to a finding that there was an appearance of bias against the accused, requiring a new trial.[55]

5. REFRESHING MEMORY

5.1) Generally

Testifying is an unnerving experience for most people. This stress can increase the natural human tendency to forget things that are in fact stored in the human memory. A memory, however, can be jarred in a

---

inability to remember." *Maves v. Grand Trunk Pacific Ry. Co.*, above note 45 at 408. See also *R. v. Shergill* (1998), 13 C.R. (5th) 160 at 170 (Ont. Gen. Div.), aff'd on other issues, [2001] O.J. No. 3489 (C.A.).

54 Ontario, *Rules of Civil Procedure*, R.R.O. 1990, Reg. 194, r. 53.01(4); Manitoba, *Court of Queen's Bench Rules*, Man. Reg. 553/88, r. 53.01(2); British Columbia, *Supreme Court Rules*, B.C. Reg. 221/90, r. 40(21); Prince Edward Island, *Civil Procedure Rules*, r. 31.03(2) & (3) (unwilling witnesses or adverse parties); Nova Scotia, *Civil Procedure Rules*, r. 31.03(2) & (3) (unwilling witnesses and adverse parties).

55 Above note 48.

number of ways. "[A] song, a scent, a photograph, an allusion, even a past statement known to be false" can revive a memory.[56] More commonly, written statements believed to record facts accurately are relied upon to refresh a faded memory. The law enables counsel, subject to limits, to attempt to refresh the memory of a witness.

5.2)   Prior to Trial

Witnesses are generally free to use whatever means they choose to refresh their memories prior to trial, although the means used can affect the weight that is given to their evidence. By way of exception, testimony, such as post-hypnosis evidence (testimony on a matter about which the witness's memory has been refreshed using hypnosis) that has been generated using unproven "scientific" memory enhancing techniques is prima facie inadmissible. Before such testimony can be received, the party presenting it will be obliged to demonstrate that the relevant technique possesses the threshold of reliability required for "novel science" in the expert opinion evidence context.

As a general rule, witnesses are free to use whatever means they choose to refresh their memories, although the means used can affect the weight the evidence is given.[57] Opposing counsel is therefore entitled to explore what means, if any, were undertaken to refresh a witness's memory prior to trial. Where documents or real items have been consulted, the trial judge has discretion to order them to be produced to opposing counsel.[58]

As an exception to this general rule, post-hypnosis evidence (testimony on a matter about which the witness's memory has been refreshed using hypnosis) is *prima facie* inadmissible because currently post-hypnosis evidence does not have the kind of "reliable foundation" needed for

---

56   *United States v. Rappy*, 157 F.2d 964 at 967 (2d Cir. 1946).

57   See *R. v. Dilling* (1993), 24 C.R. (4th) 171 (B.C.C.A.), leave to appeal to S.C.C. refused (1994), 31 C.R. (4th) 406 (S.C.C.), where just before trial a police officer examined a photograph of the suspect that she had originally seen shortly after his arrest and upon which she had written his name. In *R. v. B.(K.G.)* (1998), 125 C.C.C. (3d) 61 (Ont. C.A.), it was held that no objection could be taken to witnesses, prior to court, rereading years after the event statements they had given to the police.

58   *R. v. Monfils* (1972), 4 C.C.C. (2d) 163 (Ont. C.A.). There is authority to the contrary (see, for example, *R. v. Kerenko* (1964), 45 C.R. 291 (Man. C.A.)), although, in the interests of full evaluation of the testimony, the *Monfils* approach is undoubtedly the better one.

"novel science." The Court arrived at this view in *R. v. Trochym*[59] because the impact of hypnosis on human memory is not well understood. The prevailing current view is that "hypnosis makes people more suggestible [and] that any increase in accurate memories during hypnosis is accompanied by an increase in inaccurate memories [and] that hypnosis may compromise the subject's ability to distinguish memory from imagination, and that subjects frequently report being more certain of the content of post-hypnosis memories, regardless of their accuracy."[60] This makes witnesses who have had their testimony hypnotically refreshed more difficult to cross-examine, and gives their evidence a dangerous allure of confidence. As a result, it has been held that post-hypnosis evidence is to be excluded absent proof by the party who is seeking to rely on it of a change in the underlying scientific assumptions about its reliability. The witness may testify on those matters on which their memory has not been refreshed by hypnosis provided the probative value of that testimony outweighs the potential prejudicial effect of the hypnosis, including its potential tainting impact on topics that are not touched, and the extent to which the exclusion of hypnotically induced memories will impair cross-examination on other matters. Where such evidence is admitted, the judge must warn the jury of the potential frailties of post-hypnosis evidence and give proper instructions on the weight of the testimony.[61]

Prior to *Trochym* some courts had admitted the testimony of witnesses who have been injected with sodium amytol, a supposed "truth serum,"[62] in an effort to improve their memories. It is now clear that before testimony secured using this or any other "scientific" memory enhancing technique is admitted, the party presenting the proof will be obliged to demonstrate that the technique possesses the threshold reliability required of novel science.

5.3) During Trial

Past Recollection Recorded
A witness may, with leave of the court, refresh her memory in court from a document or an electronic record that was recorded reliably. The witness must use the original, if it is available, but where it is not,

---

59   (2007), 43 C.R. (6th) 217 (S.C.C.).

60   *Ibid.* at para. 40.

61   *Ibid.* at para. 64.

62   *R. v. Allen (No. 2)* (1979), 46 C.C.C. (2d) 477 (Ont. H.C.J.). In *R. v. Moore* (1990), 63 C.C.C. (3d) 85 (Ont. Gen. Div.), a taped statement obtained from an accused who claimed no independent memory of the incident while she was under the influence of sodium amytol was admitted into evidence pursuant to the hearsay exception in *R. v. Khan,* above note 12.

an authenticated copy can be relied on. If the record is a document created by the witness, it must have been created at a time when the memory of the witness was sufficiently fresh to be vivid and probably accurate. If the record is a document created by another, or an electronic recording, that document or recording must have been reviewed by the witness at a time when his memory was sufficiently fresh to be vivid and probably accurate. The witness can rely on the document or electronic record to assist in presenting his testimony only if the witness is able to assert that the document or recording accurately represents his recollection at the time it was made.

Present Recollection Revived
Subject to an exclusionary discretion where doing so would be too suggestive, a witness may consult any document while testifying. As long as the document sparks an actual recollection of the event recorded, the witness can present oral testimony about the event remembered.

Transcripts and Depositions
A court may allow witnesses who cannot recall matters they have previously testified about to be shown transcripts of their earlier testimony or their depositions. There is no contemporaneity requirement, nor is there a need for the witness to have read over the transcript and to have verified that it accurately recorded her testimony.

As described above, questions alluding to events may stimulate the memory of a witness. Or counsel may even obtain leave to ask leading questions of her witness when the memory cannot otherwise be stimulated and it is in the interests of justice to permit such questions. Most often, documents will be relied upon.

5.3 (a)   Past Recollection Recorded
Provided certain prerequisites are met, a rule generally known as "past recollection recorded" permits witnesses to use, in court, documents (such as business records, or memoranda of events) or electronic recordings,[63] to assist them while giving their testimony. "The admission of past recollection recorded is an exceptional procedure and the conditions precedent to its reception should be clearly satisfied."[64]

First, this rule should not be used to permit a witness to use any document or electronic recording unless the witness actually needs to

---

[63]   R. v. Mills, [1962] 3 All E.R. 298 (C.A.), and in R. v. Fliss, 2002 SCC 16, the Court endorsed the use of a transcript made from an electronic recording.

[64]   R. v. Fliss, ibid. at para. 64.

have his memory refreshed. In *R. v. McCarroll* the fact that the witness was obviously lying when asserting memory problems prevented the Crown from showing the witness their prior statement. This is sensible.[65] The refreshing memory rules are intended to facilitate the supply of testimony that would otherwise be unavailable, not to bolster the testimony witnesses are able to give in any event or to give them a script for their testimony. Nor should this rule be used to enable a party to control the evidence his witness will supply. In *R. v. Rose* the Crown presented a Crown witness with her written statement as soon as she took the stand and tried to use the record as a script for the testimony. This was inappropriate, and amounted to improperly leading the witness.[66]

Relying on *Wigmore on Evidence*, the Supreme Court of Canada has described the prerequisites that apply where the witness does require to have their memory refreshed, and the doctrine of "past recollection recorded" is relied on:

1) The past recollection must have been recorded in some reliable way.

2) At the time [he made or reviewed the record, his memory] must have been sufficiently fresh and vivid to be probably accurate.[67]

3) The witness must be able now to assert that the record accurately represented his knowledge and recollection at the time [he reviewed it]. The usual phrase requires the witness to affirm that he "knew it to be true at the time."

4) The original record itself must be used, if it is procurable.[68]

---

65   (2008), 241 O.A.C. 316 (C.A.).

66   Above note 48.

67   We have modified the passage from *Fliss* by inserting the information in the square brackets, to reflect well understood components of the rule.

68   *R. v. Fliss*, above note 63 at para. 63. Whether the requirement that the memory be fresh and vivid (the "reasonable contemporaneity requirement") is met, is a matter of degree. In *R. v. Donovan* (1991), 65 C.C.C. (3d) 511 (Ont. C.A.), a child sexual assault complainant was allowed to review notes she had made from a two-year-old tape-recorded statement, which itself was recorded two years after the alleged incident. The generous approach to admission of child evidence inspired the decision. Where the tape is a videotaped statement, however, the Ontario Court of Appeal has expressed doubt about whether the rule should be available. Parliament has provided expressly under s. 715.1 of the *Criminal Code*, above note 2, for the use of such statements and the requirements of that section arguably should not be circumvented by using rules relating to refreshing memory: *R. v. McBride* (1999), 133 C.C.C. (3d) 527 (Ont. C.A.). The *McBride* court also held that although exact contemporaneity between the record and the event is not required for refreshing one's memory, where there is reason to be concerned that a witness may have been tainted by the influence of others between the event and the recording, this may defeat the ability of the witness

Each requirement is important. In *R. v. Wilks*[69] the Manitoba Court of Appeal overturned a verdict because the trial judge permitted a witness to rely on a trial summary he had prepared from pre-existing computer records, without attesting that the trial summary accurately recorded his knowledge at the time of the events recorded. And in *R. v. Fliss* the trial judge erred when permitting a police officer to present a complete, verbatim transcript of an intercepted conversation as representing his "refreshed" memory. The officer had no memory at the time the transcript was made of everything that had been said, so the rule could not be satisfied.[70] Although described as exceptional, this procedure is routinely used to enable police officers to use their police notes; given the precise nature of the evidence police officers have to provide and the repetitive nature of the work they do, police officers frequently require assistance to recall matters of detail pertaining to particular investigations. The usual series of questions is often presented in a leading fashion, and tends to follow this model:

"Do you wish to refer to your notes?"
"Do you need them to refresh your memory?"
"Were those notes made by you?"
"Were they made near the time of the events that they record?"
"Was your memory fresh at the time?"
"Do the notes accurately reflect your memory at the time?"
"Have there been any changes to those notes since then?"

Counsel then asks the court for permission to allow the witness to review the notes.

Once a witness has reviewed a document that contains "past recollection recorded," the information contained in the record does not become evidence in the case unless the witness incorporates the information into her testimony, or unless the document is admitted under some other rule of evidence, such as a business records exception to the hearsay rule.

It is not entirely accurate to refer to this procedure as "refreshing" the memory of the witness. There is no requirement that the witness

---

to use that record to refresh her memory. The decision in *R. v. Silvini* (1991), 9 C.R. (4th) 233 at 247 (Ont. C.A.), in keeping with concerns about full answer and defence, reflects a generous approach to the contemporaneity requirement where the accused is the witness.

69 (2005), 35 C.R. (6th) 172. (Man. C.A.).

70 By reading portions from the transcript that the witness could neither recall nor authenticate, the witness was effectively using a non-authenticated transcript as the evidence.

who has viewed the document actually recall the event before testifying to it. It is permissible for him to testify that he does not remember, but that he knew the facts at the time the record was made and that they were accurately recorded. In this way, the recorded fact, which he does not remember, gets incorporated into his oral testimony. This is what occurred in the leading case of *Fleming v. Toronto Ry. Co.*,[71] where a witness who earned his living inspecting railway cars could not have been expected to remember his routine act of having inspected a particular railway car many months before. His oral testimony that the record was accurate and that it showed that he inspected the subject car was evidence that the inspection occurred.

Since "past recollection recorded" permits witnesses who have no personal memory of an event to rely on the contents of the record and to incorporate the contents of the record into their testimony, it is artificial to suggest that the witness is the immediate source of the evidence. The witness, who has no personal memory of the details and facts recorded, is vouching for the record, but it is the record that is supplying those details and facts. For this reason, many believe that "past recollection recorded" is actually a hearsay exception, with those portions of the record incorporated into the testimony serving as the evidence.[72] This is more realistic than pretending that the testimony of a witness who is simply parroting the document is original testimony. Recognizing this also reaffirms the importance of ensuring strict compliance with the prerequisites to the rule—effectively, they furnish the kind of necessity and reliability requirements that operate for other forms of hearsay evidence.

In spite of the fact that the doctrine permits witnesses to testify to facts they formerly knew but no longer recall, the prevailing practice is for a witness who is being asked to refresh her memory to read the

---

71   (1911), 25 O.L.R. 317 (C.A.).

72   *R. v. Eisenhauer* (1998), 123 C.C.C. (3d) 37 at 74–75 (N.S.C.A.), leave to appeal to the S.C.C. refused, [1998] S.C.C.A. No. 144, and see *R. v. Wilks*, above note 69. In *R. v. Rouse* (1977), 39 C.R.N.S. 135 (B.C.C.A.), aff'd (*sub nom. McInroy v. R.*) (1978), 5 C.R. (3d) 125 (S.C.C.), the majority of the British Columbia Court of Appeal treated past recollection recorded as a hearsay exception. The Supreme Court of Canada expressly refrained from deciding the point. See also the comments of Kerans J. in *R. v. Meddoui* (1990), 2 C.R. (4th) 316 at 323–24 (Alta. C.A.), aff'd without discussion of this issue, [1991] 3 S.C.R. 320. Based on this view, Justice Cromwell makes a compelling case in *Eisenhauer* that the use of "past recollection recorded" should not be confined to cases where there is a total memory loss. There should, in our view, however, be a sufficient degree of memory loss to satisfy the necessity principle normally used for the admission of hearsay evidence, before resort can be had to "past recollection recorded."

document to herself. Her attention can be drawn to relevant portions and, having refreshed her memory, she will then be asked relevant questions. It is generally considered inappropriate to simply ask the witness to read from the document.[73]

This practice makes perfect sense if it is intended to keep witnesses from reading in parts of the document that they do not recall or cannot authenticate as having been accurately recorded at the time. On the other hand, a witness who does not recall the details in question after reviewing the record should be allowed to read from the record those portions that she can attest were recorded accurately and verified as accurate at the time. To make the witness present this information as independent oral testimony, as though it is her own current recall, is misleading. The trier of fact should know that the witness is relying entirely on the record. What better way to signal that than to have the witness read the relevant passages? Since the record is the real source of the evidence, what is the harm? Indeed, in many cases it will be impossible for the witness to do anything other than read from the record; consider the witness in *Fleming v. Toronto Ry. Co.*[74] who was being asked to recall the identification numbers on a railway car, information he depended entirely on the record to be able to provide. In practice, where details are important, witnesses typically read directly from the documents.

Having said this, in *R. v. Fliss*, in a concurring judgment in which she concluded that the requirements of "past recollection recorded" had been met, Madame Justice Arbour said that in the particular circumstances of that case the trial judge contravened the common law rule by permitting the witness to read the document into the record, *verbatim.*[75] This was sensible given that the document was a transcript of a conversation; there is no way the witness could actually verify that every word recorded was accurate based on his memory, even the day after the conversation. All he could reasonably be expected to certify was that when he reviewed the transcript while his memory was fresh, the conversation transcribed was, in essence, as he had remembered it. As a general proposition, where a witness has not personally recorded

---

73   Although in *R. v. Rouse, ibid.*, the Crown read to the witness from the document. The British Columbia Court of Appeal split on whether this was proper, and the majority of the Supreme Court of Canada declined comment. Since the evidence is to be the evidence of the witness, having counsel read the document seems inappropriate. See *R. v. Green* (1994), 32 C.R. (4th) 248 (Ont. Gen. Div.), where Ferguson J. had evidence of past recollection recorded read to the jury.

74   Above note 71.

75   Above note 63 at 11.

information, and where that information cannot be verified with precision, it should not be read into evidence, nor should the witness while testifying refer to the information that is not recalled or that was not authenticated with precision when his memory was fresh.

Although the conventional view is to the contrary,[76] some courts, recognizing that the document is actually the source of the evidence, permit the document itself to be admitted as an exhibit.[77] Where the document is the font or source of the information, permitting it to be filed as an exhibit is sensible unless the document contains otherwise inadmissible information, information that the witness cannot authenticate, or there is legitimate concern that it will be given undue weight if provided to a jury in the form of an exhibit.[78]

5.3 (b) Present Recollection Revived

Wigmore contended that there is a need to distinguish between cases where a witness relies on a record he authenticates as being an accurate recording ("past recollection recorded") and those cases where, having seen the record, the witness now professes to recall the matter or details recorded ("present recollection revived"). He urged that different rules should apply in these two situations. The distinction has come to be accepted in Canada.[79] The primary significance of the distinction is that for cases where a review of the record does not inspire an actual recall of the facts recorded, the rigid requirements just described, those applicable to "past recollection recorded," are to be insisted upon. The document is in substance the evidence, and must therefore meet the requirements of time, verification, and accuracy of the past recollection recorded rule. If a witness views a record, however, and has her present

---

76   *Young v. Denton* (1927), 21 Sask. L.R. 319 (C.A.).

77   This is the rule in New Zealand: *R. v. Naidanovici*, [1962] N.Z.L.R. 334 (C.A.). See *R. v. Simons* (1991), 68 C.C.C. (3d) 97 (Alta. Q.B.). The authors of *The Law of Evidence in Canada* support this position for "past recollection recorded." See J. Sopinka, S.N. Lederman, & A.W. Bryant, *The Law of Evidence in Canada*, 2d ed. (Toronto: Butterworths, 1999).

78   Professor Delisle takes the view that a document used as "past recollection recorded" should not go to the jury because of the undue influence that an exhibit which is merely testimony in a different form could have on a jury. Annotation to *R. v. Green* (1994), 32 C.R. (4th) 248 at 249, relying on *R. v. McShannock* (1980), 55 C.C.C. (2d) 53 (Ont. C.A.).

79   *R. v. Fliss*, above note 63 at para. 45; *R. v. Bengert (No. 2)* (1979), 15 C.R. (3d) 21 (B.C.S.C.), aff'd (1980), 15 C.R. (3d) 114 (B.C.C.A.); *R. v. B.A.J.* (1994), 90 C.C.C. (3d) 210 (Nfld. C.A.), rev'd on other grounds (1995), 98 C.C.C. (3d) 95 (S.C.C.); *R. v. Simons*, above note 77; *R. v. Green*, above note 73; *R. v. Cook*, [2006] M.J. No. 195 (C.A.).

memory revived and then testifies about the event, the record is not the evidence. Her testimony, based on her actual memory, is. The record was nothing more than an *aide memoire*, a trigger. As original testimony, the information supplied by the witness can be cross-examined on as effectively as any other original testimony. The cross-examiner is entitled and able to explore the extent to which the witness actually recalls matters, or actually depended on the record for that information. That being so, there is no reason why the document that is used as the memory trigger should have to meet the strict requirements of time, verification, and accuracy.

R. v. Heydon[80] provides an example. A lawyer kept jottings of comments made to him by his client. Six months later, when approached by investigators in a criminal matter, he made a complete memorandum. When the lawyer was called to testify and sought to rely on that complete memorandum rather than on the timely jottings, defence counsel objected because the memorandum was not made at a time when the lawyer's memory was fresh and vivid, but was constructed in reliance on his earlier notes. At best, the witness was trying to rely on a memorandum that itself depended on the lawyer refreshing his memory from still other documents. The court held that the lawyer should nonetheless be entitled to review that memorandum. The decision is compelling to the extent that viewing the document would add to the witness's ability to testify by sparking his independent recall.

Despite the apparent risks of permitting witnesses to rely on documents that do not have the safeguards associated with "past recollection recorded," other safeguards should make it allowable for witnesses to testify about facts they claim to remember. In *R. v. Shergill*,[81] it was held that before allowing a witness in court to review a statement that does not meet the requirements of the "past recollection recorded" doctrine, the trial judge should examine the risks involved, including the reliability of the statement, its potential to convey erroneous information, how much time passed between the event and the record, and how suggestive the record is. If the risks are too pronounced, the attempt to revive the memory should not be permitted. In the circumstances of *Shergill*, the court refused to allow a lay witness to review a police officer's notes about an interview with that witness, but allowed the witness to review a transcript of his evidence taken during the preliminary inquiry.

Of course, where a record viewed by a witness does not spark his memory, no use should be made of it unless the record is admissible

---

80   *R. v. Heydon*, [1999] O.J. No. 4614 (Gen. Div.).
81   Above note 53.

under some other rule of evidence. Even if the document does spark the memory of the witness, the witness should not read from the record in chief, as the record is not the evidence; it is merely an *aide memoire*, and in no circumstances should the party using the record to spark a recollection be entitled to make that record an exhibit. Opposing counsel should be able, however, to use that record for the purposes of cross-examination,[82] and the judge should have the discretion to make that record an exhibit if required to enable the trier of fact to understand or fully appreciate the cross-examination.

5.3 (c)   Transcripts and Depositions

It is also settled that a court may allow witnesses who cannot recall matters they have previously testified about to be shown transcripts of their earlier testimony or their depositions.[83] These transcripts are not subject to the contemporaneity requirement for past recollection recorded. Nor is there a need for the witness to have read over the transcript and to have verified that it accurately recorded her testimony.[84] Again, the prevailing view is that the witness should be provided with the document, should read silently from it, and then answer questions about the event without reading from the document itself.[85]

5.3 (d)   Refreshing Memory with Unconstitutionally Obtained Evidence

In *R. v. Fliss*,[86] a police officer refreshed his memory in court using the transcript of an electronic interception that was held to have been obtained in violation of section 8 of the *Charter* and was thereby excluded from evidence. The Supreme Court of Canada suggested in *obiter dictum* that the officer would have been entitled to refresh his memory prior to trial using that transcript. Moreover, the Court did not take issue with the propriety of the witness refreshing his memory from that transcript in court according to the doctrine of "past recollection recorded." With respect, the decision is troubling. Even though notionally it is the witness's testimony and not the record that is the evidence, if the witness's

---

82   *R. v. Shergill*, *ibid*. In cases of "past recollection recorded" opposing counsel is entitled to inspect any record a witness is using in court to refresh his memory, and to cross-examine the witness using that record: *R. v. Alward* (*sub nom. Alward v. R.*) (1976), 39 C.R.N.S. 281 (N.B.C.A.), aff'd (1977), 39 C.R.N.S. 281 at 306 (S.C.C.).

83   See, for example, *R. v. S.(S.)*, [1997] O.J. No. 361 (Gen. Div.).

84   *Reference re R. v. Coffin*, above note 51 at 18–20; *R. v. Shergill*, above note 53.

85   *R. v. Laurin (No. 5)* (1902), 6 C.C.C. 135 (Que. K.B.).

86   Above note 63.

testimony is derived from an unconstitutionally obtained record, the relevant testimony should, in principle, be treated the same as unconstitutionally obtained derivative evidence; whether resort can be had to the record to refresh the witness's memory should be assessed to determine whether doing so would, in the circumstances of the case, bring the administration of justice into disrepute.

6. CROSS-EXAMINATION

The opportunity to cross-examine in order to test or to challenge a witness's evidence is a vital part of the adversary process. In a criminal case, the Supreme Court of Canada has affirmed that the accused has a right to cross-examine witnesses for the prosecution—without significant and unwarranted constraint—as an essential component of the right to make full answer and defence.[87] Cross-examination has two basic goals: (1) eliciting favourable testimony from the witness, and (2) discrediting the testimony of the witness. The practice in Canada is to follow the "English Rule," which allows the cross-examiner to inquire into any relevant matter, as compared with the "American Rule," where cross-examination is limited to subjects or topics that were covered in examination in chief and to matters relating to the witness's credibility.[88]

6.1) The Method of Questioning in Cross-examination

The use of leading questions in cross-examination is permitted; however, the use of leading questions becomes improper where the witness proves partisan to the cross-examiner's side.

The cross-examiner presumably questions a witness partisan to the other side. In this situation, the witness is not as susceptible to suggestion, and leading questions are not improper. On the contrary, they are entirely permissible, and counsel are well advised to lead as a means of controlling the testimony of these adversary witnesses. The asking of leading questions in cross-examination may become improper when the witness is in fact biased in favour of the cross-examiner. For example, the plaintiff in an action against a defendant company calls one of the defendant's employees to testify. In this circumstance, the employee

---

87   *R. v. Lyttle* (2004), 180 C.C.C. (3d) 476 (S.C.C.).
88   *Federal Rules of Evidence*, Rule 611. See also *R. v. Burgar*, 2010 ABCA 318 at para. 17.

may prove to be very loyal to the defendant, and defendant counsel may be prohibited from asking leading questions in cross-examination.[89]

6.2) Cross-examination on Credibility

Each witness who takes the stand puts his or her credibility into issue, and counsel in cross-examination are free to discredit or to "impeach" the witness's credibility.

As indicated, the cross-examiner may question on any relevant matter. Counsel are allowed to explore any matter directly related to the facts in issue and to probe areas affecting the credibility of witnesses. All witnesses when they take the stand put their credibility into issue. Cross-examiners, therefore, are free to discredit or "to impeach" a witness's credibility. Wigmore likened impeachment to "explanation."[90] The witness has made an assertion in examination in chief, and in cross-examination counsel seeks to *explain away* that evidence. The witness's evidence is explained away either by discrediting the witness or by discrediting the testimony, or both. An attack on the witness goes to the witness's veracity. An attack on the testimony goes to the accuracy of the witness's testimony. Cross-examination designed to impeach a witness may focus on a number of areas:

- by showing bias, prejudice, interest, or corruption;
- by attacking the character of the witness through raising prior convictions, prior bad acts, or poor reputation;
- by contradicting the witness through previous inconsistent statements;
- by challenging the witness's capacity to observe, recall, and communicate accurately;
- by putting contrary evidence to the witness; and
- by showing that the witness's evidence is contrary to common experience.

In general, when a cross-examiner asks a question relating purely to credibility, the witness's answer is final. This practice is called the collateral facts rule, which prohibits the presenting of evidence to contradict a witness on a collateral matter.

---

89   *Mooney v. James*, [1949] V.L.R. 22 at 28.
90   J.H. Wigmore, *Evidence in Trials at Common Law*, rev. J.H. Chadbourn, 3d ed., vol. 3A (Boston: Little, Brown, 1970) s. 874.

6.3) Limitations on Cross-examination

6.3 (a) Generally

> *Cross-examining counsel are bound by the rules of relevancy and are barred from resorting to harassment, misrepresentation, repetitiousness or, more generally, from putting questions whose prejudicial effect outweighs their probative value. In addition, counsel are not to ask questions that cast aspersions on a witness or suggest contrary facts unless the cross-examiner has a "good faith" basis for the question.*

Although the ambit of cross-examination is broad and counsel are given wide latitude, this is not to say that "anything goes." The trial judge has a discretion to check the cross-examination if it becomes irrelevant, prolix, or insulting.[91] Moreover, as a matter of professional conduct, counsel must not "needlessly abuse, hector or harass a witness."[92] Accordingly, there are certain limits placed on the questions that counsel can ask. While it is true that the questions asked are not evidence — only the answers given — it is also true that suspicions are raised by the mere asking of the question. There is power in innuendo. For example, the accused calls a friend to testify as an alibi witness. The Crown in cross-examination asks, "You've lied for the accused before, haven't you?" Although the witness denies the accusation and the denial is the evidence, the suggestion has been made. Is it a proper suggestion? That depends on whether the cross-examiner has a basis for asking the question. The cross-examiner must have a "good faith basis" for the suggestion. In *R. v. Lyttle*, Justices Major and Fish explained:

> a "good faith basis" is a function of the information available to the cross-examiner, his or her belief in its likely accuracy, and the purpose for which it is used. Information falling short of admissible evidence may be put to the witness. In fact, the information may be incomplete or uncertain, provided the cross-examiner does not put suggestions to the witness recklessly or that he or she knows to be false. The cross-examiner may pursue any hypothesis that is honestly advanced on the strength of reasonable inference, experience or intuition. The purpose of the question must be consistent with the lawyer's role as an officer of the court: to suggest what counsel

---

91   *R. v. Anderson* (1938), 70 C.C.C. 275 (Man. C.A.). See also *R. v. Lyttle*, above note 87, and *R. v. Peazer* (2005), 200 C.C.C. (3d) 1 at para. 23 (Ont. C.A.).

92   Canadian Bar Association, *Code of Professional Conduct* (Ottawa: Canadian Bar Association, 2009) Chapter IX, Rule 2(k).

genuinely thinks possible on known facts or reasonable assumptions is in our view permissible; to assert or to imply in a manner that is calculated to mislead is in our view improper and prohibited.[93]

Does the cross-examiner need to adduce evidence to support the suggestions made? No. There had been confusion spawned by the Supreme Court's decision in R. v. Howard, which some courts interpreted as requiring counsel to prove the facts asserted.[94] The Supreme Court in Lyttle put this interpretation to rest. The Court clarified that Howard was a case where counsel sought to cross-examine on "inadmissible" evidence and that the ratio of Howard is that counsel are not allowed to cross-examine on irrelevant or inadmissible matters. There is a crucial difference between questions that relate to and rely on inadmissible evidence and cross-examination on unproven facts. As the Court noted, it is not uncommon for counsel to believe that something is true, without being able to prove that it is so.[95] Therefore, counsel do have a right to cross-examine on relevant and otherwise admissible areas—without proof—provided they have a "good faith basis."

Where a certain line of questioning appears to be tenuous or suspect and imputations are raised, the trial judge may enter into a voir dire to seek and obtain counsel's assurance that a good faith basis exists for putting the questions. Such a voir dire also alerts the judge and counsel to the potential need for a caution to the jury that the witness's answers given in response to the questions is the evidence and that there is no evidence before them to support the allegations made.[96]

The key parameters are relevancy and materiality. Counsel should be allowed to pursue relevant and material lines of questioning and trial judges ought not prevent counsel from exploring relevant issues.[97] However, the scope of cross-examination is by necessity contextual. Relevancy and materiality are not fixed concepts, but are fluid and change with the issues at hand and the type of hearing involved. In certain circumstances, limits may be placed on cross-examination to ensure that the trial is effective, efficient, and fair to both sides.[98]

Some cross-examinations of necessity take time. In R. v. Lowe the defence argued that cross-examination of an accused for nineteen days

---

93   R. v. Lyttle, above note 87 at para. 48.

94   R. v. Howard (1989), 48 C.C.C. (3d) 38 at 46 (S.C.C.).

95   R. v. Lyttle, above note 87 at para. 47.

96   R. v. Lyttle, ibid. at para. 52. See also R. v. Wilson (1983), 5 C.C.C. (3d) 61 at 76–78 (B.C.C.A.).

97   R. v. Peazer, above note 91 at para. 23.

98   R. v. Snow (2004), 190 C.C.C. (3d) 317 at para. 24 (Ont. C.A.). See also R. v. Mitchell, 2008 ONCA 757.

was excessively long, to the point of being oppressive. The Court of Appeal disagreed. The cross-examination in that case was lengthy—but relevant. Chief Justice Finch wrote, "In assessing the propriety of cross-examination, the law distinguishes between cross-examination that is 'persistent and exhaustive', which is proper, and cross-examination that is 'abusive,' which is not."[99]

6.3 (b)   Limits on Crown Counsel in Cross-examination of the Accused

It is improper for Crown counsel to ask the accused as to the veracity of Crown witnesses and it is improper for Crown counsel to question the accused as to otherwise inadmissible bad act evidence.

Justice Cory in *R. v. Logiacco* stated that the Crown prosecutor "must be a symbol of fairness."[100] Restraint is especially required in the cross-examination of the accused and certain lines of questioning are simply not permitted.[101]

It is improper to ask the accused about the veracity of Crown witnesses. This is well illustrated in the rather notorious case of *R. v. Ellard*.[102] The accused was charged with the brutal "swarming" death of Reena Virk. The accused denied committing the fatal assault upon the victim. Credibility was the critical issue in the case. The accused testified and in cross-examination was repeatedly asked questions along these lines:

- Why would that Crown witness lie?
- What reason would she have to accuse you?
- What motive does she have to make this up?

The accused was convicted of the murder, but because of this line of questioning a new trial was ordered. The problem with this line of questions is that they suggest an onus upon the accused to provide a motive and in so doing they undermine the presumption of innocence.[103]

A second prohibited area of questioning concerns discreditable conduct on the part of the accused. As with any witness, the accused puts his credibility into issue. Ordinary witnesses can be questioned as to their discreditable conduct and associations, unrelated to the matters

---

99 *R. v. Lowe*, 2009 BCCA 338 at para. 51.

100 *R. v. Logiacco* (1984), 11 C.C.C. (3d) 374 at 379 (Ont. C.A.).

101 See *R. v. E.M.W.*, 2010 NSCA 73 at 47.

102 *R. v. Ellard* (2003), 172 C.C.C. (3d) 28 (B.C.C.A.).

103 See *R. v. Rose*, above note 48 at para. 27, and *R. v. Kusk* (1999), 132 C.C.C. (3d) 559 (Alta. C.A.).

at trial; accused persons cannot.[104] This practice protects the accused from the introduction of bad character evidence by way of cross-examination. For example, in *R. v. C.(W.)*, the accused was charged with sexual assault on a young girl.[105] The accused testified and, in cross-examination, Crown counsel repeatedly suggested that the accused was a satanist and that as a part of his religion he practised child abuse. The accused emphatically denied any involvement in satanism. The Ontario Court of Appeal found that the cross-examination was not only improper but "destroyed the necessary appearance of fairness," and directed a new trial.

It is especially important that Crown counsel have a good faith basis before cross-examining an accused upon contradictory evidence. It is accepted that if evidence is too unreliable to be tendered in the Crown's case, or if the Crown doubts its veracity, it should not be used in cross-examination of an accused, because such evidence would be incapable of providing a good faith basis for suggestions in cross-examination.[106] Where the Crown's good faith foundation is challenged on reasonable grounds, and the suggestion put to the accused may be unfairly prejudicial, the proper course is for the Crown or defence to seek a *voir dire* on the propriety and scope of any questions to be asked.

Even when the accused introduces good character evidence, cross-examination is not unlimited. In *R. v. M.M.* the accused, on trial for incestuous sexual assaults on one of his daughters, testified in examination in chief that he was a decent husband and father.[107] The cross-examination then "plumbed the depths of misbehaviour, or suggestions of it, long before and long after the period of the alleged assaults." It included questions as to whether the accused was involved in an act of bestiality when he was a child. In this instance the cross-examination exceeded the bounds of what was proper and the trial became unfair. Certainly it is open to the Crown to cross-examine the accused on discreditable incidents to neutralize and offset his assertion that he was a "decent husband and father"; however, opening the door to character is not a licence to destroy the accused.

Cross-examination that is directly relevant to prove the falsity of the accused's evidence does not fall within the ban, notwithstanding that it may incidentally reflect on the accused's character by disclosing discreditable conduct on his part. Nor does the prohibition apply

---

104 *R. v. Davison* (1974), 20 C.C.C. (2d) 424 (Ont. C.A.), leave to appeal to S.C.C. refused (1974), 20 C.C.C. (2d) 424n (S.C.C.).

105 (1990), 54 C.C.C. (3d) 37 (Ont. C.A.).

106 *R. v. Mallory*, 2007 ONCA 46 at para. 254.

107 (1995), 102 Man. R. (2d) 312 (C.A.).

when the discreditable conduct is a part of the case. For example, in *R. v. Cameron* the accused was charged with murder.[108] The accused was a drug trafficker, the deceased was a customer, and the altercation leading to the death involved a dispute over drugs. In this situation the accused's disreputable lifestyle was a necessary part of the context or background and was obviously before the jury. The accused took the stand, and the jury was instructed that it could consider this lifestyle as bearing on the accused's credibility as a witness.

6.4) Failure to Cross-examine: The Rule in *Browne v. Dunn*

> *A party who intends to impeach an opponent's witness must direct the witness's attention to that fact by appropriate questions during cross-examination. This is a matter of fairness to the witness. If the cross-examiner fails to do so, there is no fixed consequence; the effect depends upon the circumstances of each case. The court should first see if the witness can be recalled. If that is not possible or appropriate, the weight of the contradictory evidence or submission may be lessened, or such evidence may be rejected in favour of the testimony of the opponent's witness.*

It is not required that every witness be cross-examined; however, in certain instances fairness demands that it occur. Where counsel intends to impeach the witness by presenting contradictory evidence, the evidence should be put to the witness. It is especially unfair to a witness to adduce evidence that casts doubt on his veracity when he has not been given an opportunity to deal with that evidence.[109] Besides being fair, challenging a witness also assists the trier of fact in assessing credibility. The rule requiring cross-examination was laid down in *Browne v. Dunn*, where Lord Herschell stated:

> My Lords, I have always understood that if you intend to impeach a witness you are bound, whilst he is in the box, to give him an opportunity of making any explanation which is open to him; and, as it seems to me, that is not only a rule of professional practice in the conduct of a case, but is essential to fair play and fair dealing with witnesses.[110]

---

108 (1995), 96 C.C.C. (3d) 346 (Ont. C.A.).

109 *R. v. K.(O.G.)* (1994), 28 C.R. (4th) 129 (B.C.C.A.); *R. v. Verney* (1993), 87 C.C.C. (3d) 363 (Ont. C.A.).

110 (1893), 6 R. 67 at 70 (H.L.). See also *R. v. Lyttle*, above note 87 at para. 64.

Some examples illustrate violations of the rule:

- A Crown witness testifies that the accused attacked the victim without provocation and slashed the victim with a broken beer bottle. The accused testifies that he merely pushed the victim, who fell and cut himself on broken glass on the floor. The accused's version of events was never put to the Crown witness.
- Three Crown witnesses testify that they were sexually assaulted in a similar manner by the accused. In closing argument defence counsel suggests that the three witnesses colluded. The suggestion of collusion was never put to any of the witnesses.
- The plaintiff seeking insurance monies for a burned-out boat is not cross-examined by the insurer's counsel on a statement allegedly made to a friend prior to the fire in which the plaintiff said, "It would be best if my boat was torched so I could collect the insurance." The insurer now seeks to call the friend to tell the court about the statement.

In order to comply with the rule, counsel is not required to slog through every single detail to be contradicted. The necessary unfairness that triggers the rule only arises when there is a failure to cross-examine on central features or significant matters. Arguably all of the examples above concern "central" issues. The fundamental question is whether the witness was given an opportunity to respond to the cross-examiner's contrary position and not necessarily all the details.[111]

How should the court deal with the failure by counsel to confront a witness with contradictory evidence? There is no prescribed consequence. The effect depends on the circumstances of each case and is within the discretion of the trial judge.[112] For example, the failure may be remedied by recalling the witness and having the contradiction put to her. Nor is the trier of fact obliged, as a matter of law, to weigh the failure to cross-examine against the cross-examining party, but may certainly do so.[113] Furthermore, the rule does not go so far as to preclude the calling of contrary evidence.[114] In *R. v. McNeill*, Justice Moldaver suggests that the first option to explore is that of recalling the witness.[115] If it is practical and appropriate to recall the witness, that

---

111 See *R. v. Carter* (2005), 199 C.C.C. (3d) 74 (B.C.C.A.) and *R. v. Marshall* (2005), 200 C.C.C. (3d) 179 (Ont. C.A.).

112 *Palmer v. R.* (1979), 14 C.R. (3d) 22 (S.C.C.); *R. v. Werkman* (2007), 219 C.C.C. (3d) 406 (Alta. C.A.); *Gardiner v. R.*, 2010 NBCA 46.

113 *R. v. MacKinnon* (1992), 72 C.C.C. (3d) 113 (B.C.C.A.).

114 *R. v. Caskenette* (1985), 63 A.R. 232 (C.A.).

115 (2000), 144 C.C.C. (3d) 551 (Ont. C.A.). Justice Moldaver also felt it was improper for the Crown to cross-examine the accused on his counsel's failure to

option should be put to the aggrieved party. If the aggrieved party declines the offer, then no special instruction need be given to the jury regarding the failure of cross-examination. If it is not practical or appropriate to recall the witness, then it is within the judge's discretion to give a special instruction to the jury. If one is warranted, the jury should be told that in assessing the weight to be given to the uncontradicted evidence, they may properly take into account the fact that the witness was not questioned about it and may, as well, take that into account in assessing the credibility of that witness.

Ultimately, in egregious cases, stronger options are still meted out by the courts. For example, in *R. v. Christensen* the Crown asked no questions of the accused in cross-examination, even though credibility was a central issue in the case.[116] The accused's version appeared to be reasonable and, in the circumstances of the case, the failure to cross-examine was tantamount to an acceptance of the accused's version. He was acquitted. In this case it was the prosecution's failure. The rule in *Browne v. Dunn* is one of fairness and it is entirely fair that courts should be more rigorous in protecting an accused.

It should also be noted that should counsel fail to confront a witness with a prior inconsistent statement, this violates the procedure for proper impeachment on these statements (see the third example above). Under sections 10 and 11 of the *Canada Evidence Act* and the provincial equivalents, before being allowed to contradict a witness by introducing prior inconsistent statements, counsel must lay a proper foundation, which includes confronting the witness in cross-examination with the making of the inconsistent statements.[117]

6.5) The Collateral Facts Rule

The "collateral facts rule" prevents the calling of evidence to contradict the answers of an opponent's witness, whether given in chief or on cross-examination, on "collateral matters." What constitutes a "collateral fact" is open to debate. There are two general approaches.

1) The Wigmore Test: *Could the fact, as to which error is predicated, have been shown in evidence for any purpose independently of the contradiction? This test includes facts relevant to*

---

confront the witness with the contradictory evidence. The accused should not be held responsible for the tactical decisions or oversights of defence counsel.

116 (2001), 46 C.R. (5th) 371 (B.C.S.C.).

117 See section 6.7, "Prior Inconsistent Statements, " below in this chapter.

> *a material issue and facts that go to discredit a witness's credibility.*
>
> 2) The Phipson Test: *Proof may only be given on matters relevant directly to the substantive issues in the case. Proof of contradiction going to credibility is prohibited unless it falls within certain exceptions.*

A Proposal: *The allowing of evidence to contradict a witness's testimony is a matter best left to the discretion of the trial judge. In exercising this discretion, the trial judge is to weigh the benefits of receiving the evidence against any potential prejudice caused. Contradiction should be allowed where the probative value and nature of the contradictory evidence is such that it is not outweighed by the counterbalancing policy concerns and, in the case of defence evidence, the counterbalancing concerns must significantly outweigh the value in receiving the evidence.*

The impeachment of a witness may begin in cross-examination, but does not necessarily end there. Consider the following example.

The accused is charged with the robbery of a bank. An eyewitness identifies the accused as the robber. The defence has evidence that this eyewitness was drinking all day at a local bar, had no more money, and went to the bank. The waitress who served the eyewitness specifically remembers him because he returned to the bar and told everyone about the robbery. In cross-examination the defence questions the eyewitness about his drinking. If he admits to drinking heavily, then the impeachment is complete, and there is no need to call the waitress. But if he denies that he had too much to drink, then the defence will want to call the waitress to contradict his evidence. The issue is whether the defence can do so.

The collateral facts rule forbids the calling of evidence to contradict the answers given by an opponent's witness about "collateral" facts. The contradiction usually arises from an answer given in cross-examination, so the rule is often stated: "A witness's answer on a collateral matter to a question asked in cross-examination is final." However, the rule is not confined to answers given in cross-examination; it is now understood to apply to the contradiction of any answers, whether provided in chief or on cross-examination.[118]

Evidence that goes to prove a contradiction has some probative value in that it may make it more probable that the witness is not tell-

---

118 *R. v. Krause* (1986), 54 C.R. (3d) 294 (S.C.C.).

ing the truth or is not accurate about the facts in issue.[119] Therefore, the rule is not based on lack of relevancy or probative value. Rather, the rule is based on policy considerations. Primarily, it is a rule of trial efficiency. Allowing proof on collateral matters may confuse the trier of fact by engaging distracting side issues, may take undue time to develop, and may unfairly surprise a witness who will not be prepared to answer the collateral evidence.

The difficulty with the collateral facts rule is in application and in deciding what is or is not a collateral fact. The leading case is *A.G. v. Hitchcock*, where Pollock C.B. outlined the following test:

> [I]f the answer of a witness is a matter which you would be allowed on your part to prove in evidence—if it have such a connection with the issue, that you would be allowed to give it in evidence—then it is a matter on which you may contradict him.[120]

Hitchcock has spawned two different approaches to collateral facts. Wigmore rephrased the test from *Hitchcock* as follows: "Could the fact, as to which error is predicated, have been shown in evidence for any purpose independently of the contradiction?"[121] In other words, if the only basis for presenting the evidence is that it contradicts the opponent's witness, it is inadmissible, but if it assists the trier of fact in some other way, it is admissible. This assistance includes facts relevant to a material issue and facts that go to discredit a witness's credibility. If we return to our example of the eyewitness to the robbery, the evidence of drinking goes to impeach the witness's ability to have perceived the incident accurately. Under this test, the evidence has "independent" relevance beyond proving that the witness lied or was mistaken about his drinking. Within this approach, McCormick would allow proof of a third type of fact—the "linchpin" fact. This is a fact that, standing alone, is trivial and is collateral, but which, if contradicted, brings into question the witness's entire evidence.[122]

The second approach, illustrated in Phipson's text, is more restrictive.[123] It prohibits proof of contradiction going to credibility. Proof may only be given on matters relevant directly to the substantive issues in the case. We see this approach in the Supreme Court of Canada's

---

119 See M. Rosenberg, "Developments in the Law of Evidence: The 1992–93 Term—Applying the Rules" (1994) 5 Sup. Ct. L. Rev. (2d) 421 at 431.

120 (1847), 154 E.R. 38 at 42 (Ex. Ch.).

121 Wigmore, above note 90, s. 1003 [emphasis in original].

122 E.W. Cleary, ed., *McCormick on Evidence*, 3d ed. (St. Paul, MN: West, 1984) s. 47.

123 *Phipson on Evidence*, 16th ed. (London: Sweet & Maxwell, 2005) at s. 12–47.

decision in *R. v. Krause*, where McIntyre J. explained that a matter is collateral where it is

> not determinative of an issue arising in the pleadings or indictment or not relevant to matters which must be proved for the determination of the case, [and] no rebuttal will be allowed.[124]

Under this view, evidence about the credibility of a witness is collateral, and a party cannot call evidence to contradict a witness on a collateral matter unless it fits within one of several stated exceptions. These include proof of (1) bias, interest, or corruption; (2) previous convictions; (3) evidence of reputation for untruthfulness; or (4) expert evidence on problems that could affect the reliability of the witness's evidence. The difficulty with the Phipson approach is that it invites the "pigeonholing" of evidence and, if rigidly applied, excludes valuable evidence going to credibility.

In deciding on what collateral test to apply, we need to turn to first principles. The collateral facts rule is not based on lack of relevancy or probative value, otherwise the questions asked would not be allowed. Allowing proof on collateral matters is excluded because it may confuse the trier of fact by engaging distracting side issues, may take up too much valuable court time, or may unfairly surprise a witness, who is not prepared to answer questions on "collateral" matters. Where the evidence sought to be admitted has sufficient value, or the competing concerns are absent, the evidence is not collateral. The generally recognized "exceptions" illustrate the point. Bias, interest, and corruption all go directly to the witness's credibility and are important in assessing the witness's evidence. Physical or mental defects that go to the witness's reliability are important. The witness's reputation for truthfulness goes to the heart of the witness's evidence. The exception for prior convictions may have less relevance, but there is ease of proof; all that a party need do is file the certificate of conviction.

Categorizing is not the correct approach. Instead of looking at the "type" of relevancy of the offered evidence, we need to look at the value of the evidence. The key question ought to be: Is the evidence offered of sufficient value and of sufficient importance to the issues before the court that we ought to hear it having regard to the necessary court time required, potential confusion of issues, and any unfairness and prejudice to the witness?

The eschewing of "categories" in favour of a more flexible approach is consistent with the trend that we see in other areas in the law of evi-

---

124 Above note 118 at 301.

dence. For example, the law with respect to similar fact evidence has abandoned the category approach and now concentrates on the probative value of the evidence versus its potential prejudice.[125] In the law of hearsay, no longer are the courts required to force fit the evidence into recognized hearsay exceptions. The evidence may be received provided it meets the principles of necessity and reliability.[126] Similar flexibility ought to apply with respect to the collateral facts rule.[127]

Wigmore, after listing the "recognized exceptions" to the finding of collateral facts, opined:

> In general, the exclusionary rule is too strictly enforced. "Everything," said Lord Denman, "is material that affects the credit of the witness." The discretion of the trial court should be left to control. It is a mistake to lay down any fixed rule which will prevent him from permitting such testimony as may expose a false witness. History has shown, and every day's trials illustrate, that not infrequently it is in minor details alone that the false witness is vulnerable and his exposure is feasible.[128]

So too in a more recent edition of *Phipson on Evidence* there is an acknowledgment that the English courts may be moving to a more liberal approach to the admission of collateral fact evidence.[129]

Treating the collateral facts rule as a discretionary device would also clarify the law. Technically, the collateral facts rule determines whether parties can call evidence to contradict collateral answers that have been received. It is not the rule to be used to determine whether questions that provoke collateral answers should be permitted. Yet courts frequently cite the collateral facts rule as a basis for refusing to permit collateral questions to be asked during cross-examination,[130] even though the practice of asking collateral questions that might bear on credibility is widespread.[131] Recognizing that in both contexts the ultimate question is really whether probative value outweighs prejudice would clarify thinking. Of necessity, the trial judge in ruling on

---

125 See chapter 3, "Character Evidence: Primary Materiality."
126 See chapter 5, section 1, "Principles Underlying the Exceptions."
127 See David M. Paciocco, "Using the Collateral Facts Rule with Discretion" (2002) 46 Crim. L.Q. 160.
128 Wigmore, above note 90, s. 1005.
129 *Phipson on Evidence*, above note 123, ss. 12–46.
130 See, for example, *R. v. Riley* (1992), 11 O.R. (3d) 151 (C.A.), leave to appeal to S.C.C. refused (1993), 13 O.R. (3d) xvi (S.C.C.); *R. v. W.(B.A.)* (1991), 59 O.A.C. 325, rev'd [1992] S.C.R. 811; *R. v. Schmidt*, [2001] B.C.J. No. 3 (C.A.).
131 See this chapter, section 6.2, "Cross-examination on Credibility."

collateral facts exercises a large measure of discretion. A good example of the law at work is found in the Ontario Court of Appeal's decision in *R. v. Riley*.[132] In this case, defence counsel wanted to cross-examine the complainant about an allegation of sexual assault she had made against another man on another occasion, which the defence claimed was false. The defence proposed to call the other man who would testify that he had been acquitted of charges brought against him by the complainant. The Court of Appeal agreed with the trial judge that this line of questioning and proposed evidence was "collateral" and ought not to be allowed. The concern is obvious—the trial would expand into a re-litigation of the other charge. However, the court did go on to say that if the defence were in a position to establish a pattern of fabrication of similar allegations of sexual assault against other men through evidence that the complain-ant either recanted her earlier accusations or that they are demonstrably false, then the result may well be different.[133] "Proven fabrication" has far greater relevancy than an "alleged fabrication," which makes the evi-dence both worth hearing, and, at the same time, avoids the pitfall of a time-consuming "re-trial" on the issue.

At a time when we are attempting to shed the shackles of rigid, technical rules about proof, there is something unsettling in a rule that operates by "typing" the evidence. The solution is both simple and familiar. Whether "collateral" questions can be asked, and "collat-eral" answers contradicted, should depend on nothing more than the case-by-case assessment by the trial judge as to whether it is worth it. Contradiction should be allowed where the probative value and nature of the contradictory evidence is such that it is not outweighed by the counterbalancing policy concerns and, in the case of defence evidence, the counterbalancing concerns must significantly outweigh the value in receiving the evidence.

Nevertheless, the *Phipson* approach has a strong tradition in Canada and the various exceptions are well recognized by the courts. Therefore, these exceptions are outlined and examined below in this chapter.

6.5 (a) Bias, Interest, Corruption

In *A.G. v. Hitchcock* the defendant, a maltster, was charged with breach-ing the revenue laws.[134] The key witness against the defendant was asked in cross-examination whether he had ever received a bribe, ever

---

132 Above note 130. See also *R. v. Hicks*, [2009] O.J. No. 743 (S.C.J.).

133 This *dictum* was described as an exception under the collateral facts rule by Finlayson J.A. in *B.(A.R.)* (1998), 18 C.R. (5th) 241 at para. 15 (Ont. C.A.).

134 Above note 120.

said he had received a bribe, and whether he had ever said he had been offered a bribe. The defendant then proposed to contradict the witness by showing not that he had received a bribe, not that he had said that he had received a bribe, but that on some occasion he had said that he had been offered a bribe. The court found this to be collateral. Had the defendant proof that the witness had actually received a bribe, a fact denied by the witness, the proof would have been allowed. It is accepted that partiality, bias, or corruption colours a witness's entire testimony; therefore, such evidence is always relevant and is not collateral.[135]

6.5 (b)   Previous Convictions

This exception is recognized under statute and allows for questioning on prior convictions. Should the witness deny or refuse to answer, the cross-examining party may then prove the convictions. To a certain extent this exception is based on ease of proof and the conclusive nature of that proof. It will be examined in more detail in the section that follows.

6.5 (c)   Reputation as to Trustworthiness

The common law long recognized the practice of allowing evidence of bad reputation to discredit a witness's testimony. It is true, however, that such evidence was rarely adduced. The witness called to impeach the credit of another was to be asked the following litany of questions:

1. Do you know the reputation of the witness as to truth and veracity in the community?
    If the answer is "yes" the questioning proceeds.
2. Is that reputation good or bad?
    If the answer is "bad" a final question is permitted.
3. From that reputation [or from your own knowledge], would you believe the witness on oath?[136]

The witness was not to give evidence of specific acts.

The general principles underlying this exception and its limitations were stated by Lord Pearce in the following terms:

> On the one hand, the courts have sought to prevent juries from being beguiled by the evidence of witnesses who could be shown to be, through defect of character, wholly unworthy of belief. On the

---

135 *R. v. McDonald*, 2007 ABCA 53 at para. 12 (C.A.). For a more thorough review of the collateral fact rule and the bias, interest, corruption exception, see *Nicholls v. The Queen*, [2005] HCA 1 at paras. 61–73, McHugh J.

136 *R. v. Clarke* (1998), 18 C.R. (5th) 219 at 235 (Ont. C.A.).

other hand, however, they have sought to prevent the trial of a case becoming clogged with a number of side issues, such as might arise if there could be an investigation of matters which had no relevance to the issue save in so far as they tended to show the veracity or falsity of the witness who was giving evidence which *was* relevant to the issue. Many controversies which might thus obliquely throw some light on the issues must in practice be discarded, because there is not an infinity of time, money and mental comprehension available to make use of them.[137]

In *R. v. Gonzague*, the Ontario Court of Appeal, following English precedent, held that it was permissible to have the witness express a personal "opinion" as to the veracity of another witness.[138] In *R. v. Taylor*, the same Court of Appeal extended the law one step further and allowed these "credit" witnesses to testify as to the *basis* of their opinions, which necessarily involved the description of specific incidents.[139] The court relied on English text writers; however, these writers supported no such extension of the law. In fact, one of the writers states the law as follows:

> The impeaching witness, cannot, in direct examination, give particular instances of the other's falsehood or dishonesty, since no man is supposed to come prepared to defend all the acts of his life.[140]

What actually occurred in the *Taylor* trial should give us cause to reconsider the court's ruling. Twenty defence witnesses testified that they would not believe the testimony of the complainants. They described for the court various tales of far-fetched stories of sexual assaults made by the complainants. In reply, the landlord and fiancé of one of the complainants were called and they stated that they would believe her testimony given under oath. As well, two expert witnesses were called who expressed the opinion that one of the complainants exhibited symptoms of sexual abuse and that sexually abused children tend to have a rich fantasy life. Borrowing Lord Pearce's words, the trial became "clogged with a number of side issues."

In *R. v. Clarke* the Ontario Court of Appeal came to reconsider its earlier decisions in *Gonzague* and *Taylor* concerning evidence of a witness's reputation for veracity. Rosenberg J.A. was most concerned about this type of evidence in cases where the outcome rests upon the evi-

---

137   *Toohey v. Metropolitan Police Commissioner*, [1965] 1 All E.R. 506 at 511 (H.L.).
138   *R. v. Gonzague* (1983), 34 C.R. (3d) 169 (Ont. C.A.).
139   (1986), 55 C.R. (3d) 321 (Ont. C.A.).
140   *Phipson on Evidence*, above note 123, ss. 12–50.

dence of a single witness. In his view, in these cases an expression of opinion as to that witness's veracity is a comment on the ultimate issue, and there is concern that the jury will defer to or overvalue that opinion on the theory that the reputation witness obviously knows the witness better than the jurors. Therefore, with respect to the third question in the litany—"would you believe the witness on oath?"—Rosenberg J.A. held that the accused does not have the absolute right to ask that question and "that in most cases the trial judge would be justified in refusing to permit that question to be asked."[141] Moreover, the trial judge also has a discretion to prohibit witnesses called to testify on the first two "reputation" questions. However, according to Rosenberg J.A., it would be extremely rare to exclude the general reputation questions because they do not specifically address the witness's veracity in the case before the jury and therefore do not have the same tendency to usurp the jury's function as does the third question.

6.5 (d)   Expert Opinion on the Reliability of a Witness

In *Toohey v. Metropolitan Police Commissioner*, the House of Lords ruled that expert evidence could be called to show physical or mental problems that make the witness incapable of giving reliable evidence. "Such evidence is not confined to a general opinion of the unreliability of the witness, but may give all the matters necessary to show not only the foundation of and reasons for the diagnosis but also the extent to which the credibility of the witness is affected."[142]

6.6)   Cross-examination on Prior Convictions

> *Any witness, including the accused, may be questioned as to prior convictions. However, with respect to an accused, the court has a discretion to disallow such questions weighing the probative value of the evidence against its potential prejudice. The factors considered in exercising this discretion include the nature of the conviction, similarity to the charge now before the court, age of the conviction, and fairness in the trial.*

Section 12 of the *Canada Evidence Act* provides that any witness, including the accused, may be questioned as to whether he has been convicted of any offence. The provincial Evidence Acts contain a similar

---

141   *R. v. Clarke*, above note 136 at 236.
142   Above note 137 at 512.

provision, although the wording varies.[143] If the witness either denies the fact or refuses to answer, then the cross-examiner may prove the conviction.

It is accepted, as a general proposition, that a prior criminal conviction may bear on credibility. It is also well established that the trial judge is under a duty, in cases where the accused has been cross-examined as to prior convictions, to instruct the jury regarding the limited permissible use it can make of such evidence.[144] The extent to which the Crown may use prior convictions is also carefully circumscribed. "Conviction" is strictly construed, with the result that the accused cannot be cross-examined on a "discharge." Similarly findings of misconduct in a disciplinary proceeding are not "convictions" under the section.[145] Moreover, the accused may only be examined as to the fact of the conviction and the sentence imposed, but not concerning the conduct or facts that led to the conviction. Nor can the accused be asked whether he testified on the prior occasion.[146]

The above limitations apply to accused persons who testify and do not apply to ordinary witnesses. Section 12 does not place a limitation on the well-established principle that an ordinary witness may be cross-examined with respect to discreditable conduct. The fact the conduct has resulted in a criminal conviction will usually enhance the probative value of the cross-examination. Therefore, the ordinary witness may be cross-examined on the facts underlying the criminal conviction. The only limit is that of relevancy and propriety.[147]

In *R. v. Corbett*, the Supreme Court of Canada recognized that trial judges have a discretion whether to allow cross-examination of an accused on prior convictions.[148] When the accused has a lengthy criminal

---

143 *Alberta Evidence Act*, s. 24; British Columbia, *Evidence Act*, s. 15; *Manitoba Evidence Act*, s. 22; New Brunswick, *Evidence Act*, s. 20; Newfoundland and Labrador, *Evidence Act*, s. 13; Nova Scotia, *Evidence Act*, s. 58; Ontario, *Evidence Act*, s. 22; Prince Edward Island, *Evidence Act*, s. 18; Saskatchewan, *The Evidence Act*, s. 18.

144 *R. v. Corbett* (1988), 64 C.R. (3d) 1 at 15 (S.C.C.). See also *R. v. Grams* (2004), 187 C.C.C. (3d) 448 (B.C.C.A.).

145 *R. v. Stevely* (2001), 152 C.C.C. (3d) 538 (Sask. Q.B.).

146 *R. v. Corbett*, above note 144 at 21.

147 *R. v. Miller* (1998), 131 C.C.C. (3d) 141 (Ont. C.A.). See also *R. v. Gassyt* (1998), 127 C.C.C. (3d) 546 (Ont. C.A.), where the court drew a distinction between cross-examination of a witness on the existence of an outstanding charge and cross-examination on the underlying facts of the charge. Cross-examination on the fact of a charge will not be permitted without a proper foundation being laid to establish its relevance [usually to show a possible motivation to seek favour with the prosecution].

148 Above note 144.

record, the defence may seek to prohibit cross-examination on only certain of the most prejudicial convictions. For example, in *R. v. Leland* the accused was charged with murder and the trial judge refused to allow cross-examination on prior convictions for violent offences, but allowed cross-examination on convictions involving dishonesty.[149] The probative value of the evidence of conviction is assessed against its potential prejudice in the given case.[150] Unlike with the admissibility of bad character evidence, there is no presumption against the admissibility of the accused's criminal record when he or she chooses to testify. To the contrary, the criminal record is accepted as being relevant to credibility and in the usual case cross-examination should be allowed. In other words, it is for the accused to show that the prejudice is such that to allow the cross-examination would undermine the accused's right to a fair trial. This decision is necessarily a matter within the discretion of the trial judge and is not to be lightly overturned on appeal.[151] Justice La Forest advanced four factors to consider in exercising the discretion:

1) The nature of the previous conviction: a conviction for perjury or for fraud is far more telling about a person's honesty and integrity than a conviction for assault.

2) How similar the previous conviction is to the offence now charged: the concern here is of prejudice. Justice La Forest was of the view that "a court should be very chary of admitting evidence of a previous conviction for a similar crime."[152]

3) The remoteness or nearness of the previous conviction: convictions occurring long before and followed by a blameless life should generally be excluded.

4) Fairness: where the accused attacks the credibility of the Crown witnesses and credibility is at issue, it would be unfair to insulate

---

149 (1998), 17 C.R. (5th) 62 (B.C.S.C.).

150 See *R. v. Saroya* (1994), 36 C.R. (4th) 253 at 255 (Ont. C.A.), where it was held that the trial judge erred in balancing "the right of an accused to a fair trial and the right of the jury to have all the evidence before them." See also *R. v. P.(G.F.)* (1994), 29 C.R. (4th) 315 at 322 (Ont. C.A.), where the court ruled it was an error to exclude an accused's criminal record only "as a last resort."

151 *R. v. N.A.P.*, 2002 CanLII 22359 (Ont. C.A.).

152 The Law Commission of England and Wales conducted a review of the impact of various prior convictions. It was found that certain offences, like indecent assault on a child, can be particularly prejudicial to an accused, *whatever the offence charged*. Great Britain, Law Commission, *Evidence in Criminal Proceedings: Previous Misconduct of a Defendant (Consultation Paper No. 141)* (London: HMSO, 1996).

the accused from his own criminal past. To allow this would present a distorted view to the jury.[153]

In terms of an attack on the credibility of Crown witnesses there is a distinction between an attack on the good character of a witness and challenging the accuracy and reliability of the witness. The former engages the *Corbett* concerns for trial fairness and the latter does not to the same degree.[154] A *Corbett* application is to be made by the defence before calling evidence and after the close of the Crown's case. The Supreme Court of Canada in *R. v. Underwood* applied the case-to-meet principle to the timing of the application.[155] The defence has a right to know, before calling evidence, whether or not the accused's prior convictions will be raised in cross-examination should the accused testify. This bears directly on the decision whether or not to put the accused on the stand.

A *voir dire* is to be held. In the *voir dire*, besides informing the trial judge of the prior convictions, the defence is to reveal the evidence it intends to call. This provides a context for the trial judge to assess the probative value versus the potential prejudice raised by the prior convictions. Chief Justice Lamer in *Underwood* made it clear, however, that the purpose of the *voir dire* is not "defence disclosure."[156] All that is required is a "context." In cases where the defence is fairly obvious or otherwise has been revealed, then disclosure need not be given. The *Corbett* ruling is subject to modification should the defence fail to disclose evidence or depart significantly from what was disclosed on the application and the new evidence would have had a material impact on the original decision. If the judge rules that the cross-examination should be allowed, the defence may then decide not to call the accused or to call the accused and raise the prior convictions in examination in chief in order to soften the blow.

R. v. Maracle is a good example of what not to do.[157] The accused was on trial for a vicious sexual assault in which a fourteen-year-old girl was abducted and repeatedly sexually assaulted. The accused had a lengthy criminal record including two prior convictions for sexual assault. The trial judge conducted a *Corbett* hearing and ruled that the Crown would not be permitted to cross-examine the accused on the prior convictions for sexual assault. Defence counsel led the remainder

---

153 *R. v. Corbett*, above note 144 at 52–55.
154 *R. v. Bomberry*, 2010 ONCA 542 at para. 50.
155 (1998), 121 C.C.C. (3d) 117 (S.C.C.).
156 *Ibid.* at 122.
157 *R. v. Maracle*, 2006 CanLII 4152 (Ont. C.A.).

Methods of Presenting Evidence 451

of the accused's record in direct examination. In cross-examination Crown counsel referred the accused back to the convictions covered in direct and asked: "That's not the totality of your convictions?" The accused answered, "No, it's not." Such a question is both misleading and highly prejudicial. It is misleading because the jury would now be left with the impression that the defence was not completely forthright in the direct examination. More importantly it was very prejudicial in that the jury would necessarily speculate as to the undisclosed convictions. Something was being hidden from them and it must be bad—very bad. Such speculation could well be more damning than cross-examining on the actual convictions. At least if the prior convictions are raised the trial judge is required to give a strong limiting instruction. How do you limit speculation?

Thus far we have been referring to *Corbett* applications in criminal cases, and there is no question that it is in these cases where cross-examination on prior convictions will most often arise. Yet, cross-examination on prior convictions is also provided for in civil cases and, although the liberty interest of an accused may not be at stake, there still remain valid concerns about potential prejudice. In other words, there is a place for *Corbett* applications in civil cases. This is well illustrated in the case of *Hutton v. Way*.[158] The plaintiff brought a personal injury action for damages, which was heard before a jury. The defendant was allowed to admit into evidence a "stale dated criminal record" committed by the plaintiff when he was a teenager for sexual assault on a female, dangerous driving, and possession of marijuana. The Ontario Court of Appeal found that the only result of this evidence was to paint the plaintiff as a sex offender, and it worked. The court went on to find that the verdict reflected a "certain meanness of spirit." According to the court, a *Corbett* application should have been held and the convictions should have been excluded.

6.7) Prior Inconsistent Statements

Witnesses may be impeached using prior inconsistent statements. The prior inconsistent statements go only to credibility and are not evidence of their truth unless they are adopted by the witness. Before counsel will be allowed to contradict a witness by proving a prior inconsistent statement, fairness demands that the statement be put to the witness.

---

158 (1997), 105 O.A.C. 361 (C.A.).

Witnesses may be impeached by adducing evidence that they have made statements inconsistent with their present testimony. The inconsistency shows an *"undefined capacity to err."*[159] That the witness has erred on a particular point may bring into question the accuracy or the veracity, or both, of the witness's entire testimony. The inconsistent statement goes only to credibility or reliability and is not introduced for its truth unless the witness adopts the prior statement as true, or it is admissible under a hearsay exception; of particular importance is the hearsay exception created in *R. v. B.(K.G.)*.[160] When a prior inconsistent statement is introduced, the jury should be instructed as to its proper use.

Sections 10(1) and 11 of the *Canada Evidence Act* govern the questioning on, and proof of, prior inconsistent statements in criminal matters. These provisions are replicated in the respective provincial Evidence Acts.[161]

Essentially sections 10 and 11 require that the cross-examiner give the witness notice of the statement. This is done primarily out of fairness to the witness in that the witness is given an opportunity to explain any contradiction or inconsistency either in cross-examination or in re-examination. A second rationale is that it saves time. The witness when confronted with the former statement may admit making it and thus save the cross-examiner from calling other witnesses to prove the making of the statement.[162]

Both sections speak of "witness," which includes parties in civil cases and the accused in criminal cases. Section 10 deals with statements in writing, reduced to writing or recorded, and section 11 deals with prior inconsistent statements made orally.[163] Section 10 requires that the statement be "made by the witness." This would include written statements acknowledged or adopted by the witness, but would not include, for example, a police officer's notes of a conversation with the witness—such a conversation would fall under section 11.

Section 10 does away with the common law rule that required the cross-examiner to show the witness the writing before questioning on

---

159 Wigmore, above note 90, s. 1017 [emphasis in original].

160 (1993), 19 C.R. (4th) 1 (S.C.C.). See chapter 5, section 2, "Prior Inconsistent Statements."

161 *Alberta Evidence Act*, ss. 22 & 23; British Columbia, *Evidence Act*, ss. 13 & 14; *Manitoba Evidence Act*, ss. 20 & 21; New Brunswick, *Evidence Act*, ss. 18 &19; Newfoundland and Labrador, *Evidence Act*, ss. 11 & 12; Nova Scotia, *Evidence Act*, ss. 56 & 57; Ontario, *Evidence Act*, ss. 20 & 21; Prince Edward Island, *Evidence Act*, ss. 16 & 17; Saskatchewan, *The Evidence Act*, s. 19.

162 *R. v. G.P.* (1996), 4 C.R. (5th) 36 (Ont. C.A.).

163 In *R. v. G.P.*, *ibid.* at 50, Rosenberg J.A. expressed the view that s. 11 applies to both oral and recorded statements.

its contents. The common law rule was much criticized as it completely negated the cross-examiner's tactical ability to surprise the witness. The witness would see the inconsistency coming and could adjust his testimony accordingly. Section 10 authorizes cross-examination on the writing without it being shown to the witness. But if there is any difficulty or confusion by reason of the writing not being shown to the witness, the judge has the power to stop the cross-examination on the writing unless it is shown to the witness.[164]

Section 10 refers to "previous statements"; however, it is implicit that the section is concerned with "inconsistent" prior statements. The entire purpose of the section is to impeach the credibility of the witness through contradictory proof, and this will occur only when the statement is "inconsistent" with the witness's present testimony. A liberal standard is encouraged, and McCormick provided the following test for "inconsistency": "[C]ould the jury reasonably find that a witness who believed the truth of the facts testified to would have been unlikely to make a prior statement of this tenor?"[165]

The impeachment of a witness using prior inconsistent statements involves four steps:

1) Counsel has the witness *confirm* the present testimony. The purpose here is to make the testimony clear in order to highlight the inconsistency.
2) The witness is then confronted with the making of a prior statement.
3) The prior inconsistent statement is then put to the witness showing the contradiction. Usually the cross-examiner reads the prior inconsistent statement out loud for the record, the court, and the witness.
4) Finally the witness may be asked to *adopt* the prior inconsistent statement for its truth. If the witness refuses to do so, then the statement goes only to credibility, unless of course the witness is a party or an accused, which makes the statement admissible for its truth as an admission.

In confronting the witness with the making of a prior written statement, the cross-examiner asks the witness to identify the writing. Opposing counsel is shown the statement and provided with a copy. If the statement was made orally, "the circumstances of the supposed statement, sufficient to designate the particular occasion," must be put to the witness. This requires that cross-examining counsel advise the

---

164 R. v. *Rodney* (1988), 46 C.C.C. (3d) 323 (B.C.C.A.).
165 *McCormick on Evidence*, above note 122, s. 34.

witness of the time, place, and person involved in the prior statement and draw the witness's attention to the substance of the statement. In rare circumstances counsel need not be so specific. When the witness, for example, categorically denies stating anything of the sort to anyone, then it may well be needlessly time-consuming to require counsel to put a number of contradicting statements to the witness. The trial judge also has a discretion to admit proof of the prior inconsistent statement even if section 11 has not been strictly complied with.[166]

After being given notice of the statement, the witness is asked whether or not he made it. If the witness admits to making the written or oral statement, there will be no need to call evidence to prove its making. If the witness does not admit to making the statement, then the cross-examiner may be allowed to call evidence, as part of her case, to prove the statement.

Not every inconsistent statement may be proven. The witness may only be contradicted on those statements "relative to the subject-matter of the case." This clause is meant to prevent contradiction on "collateral" matters.[167] As is the case with the collateral facts rule, there are differences of opinion as to what this means. This phrase has been interpreted narrowly, confining proof of prior inconsistent statements to those relating directly to a fact in issue or to matters that are relevant to credibility, independent of the fact that they are inconsistent.[168] Other courts have interpreted it more broadly. In *R. v. Eisenhauer*, for example, the Nova Scotia Court of Appeal ruled that the section simply requires that the inconsistency be "sufficiently connected to the material issues in the case,"[169] in other words, that it be worth hearing. This broader approach is more in keeping with the practice in trial courts and is consistent with the more flexible approach that we favour with respect to the collateral facts rule.

Where section 10 has been employed, the writing has been used only for the purpose of impeaching the witness on the inconsistencies, and the relevant portions of the writing that go to explain or qualify those inconsistencies have been put to the witness. There is no further need for the entire document to be made an exhibit. This is particularly important where counsel is using one portion of a document to impeach the witness, but other portions of the document are extremely damaging to the cross-examiner's case. Section 10 provides that the trial judge

---

166 *R. v. G.P.*, above note 162 at 51.
167 *R. v. Krause*, above note 118. See section 6.5, "The Collateral Facts Rule," above in this chapter.
168 *R. v. Varga* (1994), 90 C.C.C. (3d) 484 (Ont. C.A.).
169 Above note 72 at 61.

may "make such use of [the writing] for the purposes of the trial as the judge thinks fit." This discretion should not be used to introduce prior inconsistent statements as a matter of course simply because there has been some cross-examination on them. The inconsistencies are on the record. Much will depend, however, on the extent of the use made of the writing. If there has been extensive cross-examination on the writing, it may be necessary to have the statement marked as an exhibit so that the court, counsel, and the jury may properly understand the extent to which the witness has been contradicted or impeached.[170]

Even if the requirements of sections 10 and 11 are complied with the trial judge has an overriding discretion to prohibit the cross-examiner from calling evidence to prove the prior inconsistent statement where the potential prejudice in calling the evidence exceeds its probative value.[171]

6.7 (a)   Prior Inconsistent Statements of Accused or Parties

Prior inconsistent statements of accused or parties to an action are treated differently from those of other witnesses. Such statements by an accused or a party may be used as evidence going to the substantive issue of guilt, and not just credibility. They are admissions. Accordingly, there is no need for instructions to the jury limiting the use they can make of these prior inconsistent statements; nor is there a requirement that the accused or party adopt the statements before they can be considered as evidence against them.[172] Having said this, there is concern should the Crown hold back certain statements to be used in anticipation of the accused testifying. The Crown cannot split its case. "[T]he law regards it as unfair for the Crown to lie in wait and to permit the accused to trap himself."[173]

Given that the Crown cannot split its case, generally speaking, prior statements first tendered by the Crown in cross-examination will not be inculpatory. Otherwise they should have been tendered as part of the Crown's case. The statements usually only go to the accused's credibility (should the accused testify inconsistent with the prior statements). However, there is controversy as to the actual use that can be made of the prior inconsistent statements. In R. v. McKerness the Ontario Court of Appeal held that a prior inconsistent statement introduced in the cross-examination of an accused only goes to credibility

---

170   R. v. Rodney, above note 164.

171   R. v. Dooley, 2009 ONCA 910 at para. 159.

172   R. v. Mannion, [1986] 2 S.C.R. 272 at 277–78; R. v. Tran, 1999 BCCA 535 at para. 24.

173   R. v. Drake (1970), 1 C.C.C. (2d) 396 at 397 (Sask. Q.B.).

and was not admissible on the substantive issues.[174] This appears to run counter to the principle outlined earlier in this section that statements, if admitted to being made by the accused, are admissions and admissible as proof of the truth of their contents.[175]

As a further protection, an accused also may not be cross-examined on a statement ruled inadmissible either because it was involuntary or because it was excluded under subsection 24(2) of the *Charter*. For example, in *R. v. Calder* the accused, a police officer, gave a statement.[176] He was not informed of his right to counsel by the officers who took the statement. The trial judge found a breach of subsection 10(b) of the *Charter* and the statement was excluded under subsection 24(2). The accused took the stand and gave evidence that contradicted his earlier statement. The Crown argued that the circumstances had now changed and that the statement ought to be rendered admissible to impeach the accused's credibility during cross-examination. It may have been unfair to tender the statement obtained in violation of his *Charter* rights as substantive evidence, but the situation is different when the accused chooses to testify and puts his credibility in issue. The trial judge refused to allow the otherwise inadmissible statement to be used for such a purpose and the Supreme Court of Canada agreed. Admittedly Sopinka J., writing for the majority, did say that in "very limited circumstances" the Crown may be allowed to cross-examine the accused on such a statement. Yet, it is difficult to imagine what these special circumstances might be.[177]

6.8) Incomplete Cross-examinations

> *A cross-examination that is cut short does not necessarily result in the loss of the testimony already given. There is no set consequence and the matter is within the discretion of the trial judge.*

Witnesses can become unresponsive in cross-examination, some even die, or become otherwise unavailable, with the result that the cross-examination is either incomplete or not possible at all. What is the consequence?

There is no set consequence. The right to cross-examine a witness, although fundamental to our trial process, is not absolute or limitless.

---

174 *R. v. McKerness*, 2007 ONCA 452.
175 See *R. v. Krause*, above note 118; *R. v. Brooks* (1986), 28 C.C.C. (3d) 441 (B.C.C.A.).
176 (1996), 46 C.R. (4th) 133 (S.C.C.).
177 See also *R. v. Cook* (1998), 128 C.C.C. (3d) 1 (S.C.C.).

Accordingly, the inability to cross-examine does not necessarily render the witness's testimony that is given inadmissible.[178] Certainly, there is concern about ensuring a fair trial; however, there is no definite test in determining whether an accused has been deprived of the right to make full answer and defence. The matter is within the trial judge's discretion to be exercised with a view to ensuring fairness to the accused, to the Crown and to the pursuit of truth.[179]

In exercising this discretion three relevant considerations serve as a guide:

1) the reasons for the incomplete cross-examination;
2) the impact of the lack of cross-examination; and
3) possible ameliorative action.[180]

With respect to the reasons for the loss of cross-examination consideration is given to the fault of the witness, calling party and cross-examiner. Unforeseen death or illness of a witness attributes no fault. In this situation authority supports admitting the testimony already given; only its weight is undermined.[181] On the other hand, deliberate conduct of the witness to frustrate the cross-examiner speaks against receiving the witness's testimony. The "fault" analysis should not be applied in an inflexible manner to child witnesses. Flexibility and common sense must be applied when considering the consequences of a child witness becoming unresponsive during cross-examination.[182] Judges need to consider whether the child's unresponsiveness is the result of the nature of the process and whether appropriate steps have been taken to reduce the child's discomfort. For example, the child could testify outside the courtroom or through the use of a screen pursuant to section 486.2 of the *Criminal Code* or a support person could be provided using section 486.1 of the *Criminal Code*.

The judge may also consider the fault of the cross-examiner. The manner of questioning may have prompted the unresponsiveness. For example, questions may be asked of a child that are not clear or age appropriate.

The second consideration looks to the impact of the lack of cross-examination. What is looked for is prejudice to the cross-examiner. The likelihood of complete capitulation by the witness is not the standard

---

178 *R. v. Cameron* (2006), 208 C.C.C. (3d) 481 at paras. 21 and 37 (Ont. C.A.).

179 *Ibid.* at para. 22.

180 *R. v. Hart* (1997), 135 C.C.C. (3d) 377 (N.S.C.A.).

181 *R. v. Yu* (2002), 171 C.C.C. (3d) 90 at para. 13 (Alta. C.A.), leave to appeal to S.C.C. refused, [2003] S.C.C.A. No. 321.

182 *R. v. Hart*, above note 180 at 400.

required to show prejudice. It is sufficient to identify areas where the witness is vulnerable to attack had the cross-examination been complete.[183] A measure of speculation is required. The trial judge needs to make an assessment of the likely impact or value of the cross-examination had it been allowed to continue. The following questions need to be considered:

- How important is the evidence? The more important the evidence to the prosecutor's case, the more reluctant the trial judge should be to allow it to be given without full cross-examination.
- Can the trier of fact evaluate the evidence? The presence or absence of corroborative evidence may assist in the evaluation of the witness's testimony.
- How much cross-examination, if any, was complete and what was the context and effect of that cross-examination?
- Are there significant areas of cross-examination left unchallenged?
- Was counsel able to cross-examine on inconsistencies?

The list is not exhaustive; all the circumstances must be looked to in the context of the witness's testimony and the trial itself.

Finally, before concluding that the trial has become unfair or whether there has been a denial of the right to full answer and defence, the trial judge should consider whether the limitation on cross-examination can be remedied or at least ameliorated. For example, the trial judge should consider whether the difficulty with the witness is likely to be permanent. If there is a reasonable prospect of the witness becoming responsive in a reasonable period of time, consideration should be given to the postponement of the trial, having regard to the accused's right to a timely trial.[184] Furthermore, the trial judge ought to consider placing less weight upon the evidence given the lack of cross-examination and an appropriate instruction to the jury to that effect.[185]

7. REAL EVIDENCE

7.1) General Principles

Real evidence refers to tangible items exhibited to the judge or jury. This evidence may be directly linked to the occurrence (such as "the murder weapon") or may be "demonstrative evidence," which

---

183 *R. v. Duong*, 2007 ONCA 68 at para. 34.
184 *R. v. Hart*, above note 180 at 413.
185 *R. v. Cameron*, above note 178 at para. 36.

refers to aids used to help witnesses better illustrate or explain their evidence. The evidence is admissible provided it is properly authenticated. The trial judge must be satisfied that there is a sufficient basis to support the identification of the exhibit, its continuity, and its integrity.

Real evidence may also be excluded where its potential to arouse undue prejudice outweighs its probative value.

Our trial system is based on an oral tradition. Most evidence is introduced through the testimony of witnesses, which means that the evidence is received secondhand in that the trier of fact must rely upon the testimonial capacity and sincerity of the witnesses. By contrast, "real" evidence is received firsthand—it is direct—as the triers of fact rely on their own senses to draw conclusions. Observing the demeanour of witnesses is an informal type of real or direct evidence. In other situations, the real evidence is formally placed before the court. One form of real evidence involves "original" things that allegedly played a part in the action now before the court, and it is to this evidence that the phrase "real evidence" usually is applied. For example, in a murder case, the jury is shown the alleged murder weapon, the torn clothes of the victim, a bloody glove found near the body, and numerous photographs of the scene. A second type of real evidence, usually called "demonstrative evidence," involves the use of visual aids to illustrate or explain. This evidence is used to assist a witness in the giving of testimony. In our murder case, a map may be introduced that will help the witnesses explain, and the judge or jury understand, the location of various sites referred to in testimony. An expert called may use a chart or diagram to explain blood typing or DNA matching. Another expert may use an anatomical model to explain the wounds suffered by the victim. The expert may then go on to demonstrate how, in her opinion, the victim was killed. As can be seen, demonstrative evidence is a testimonial aid and is not original evidence of what occurred. For this reason the common question asked of the witness before admitting this evidence is: "Would that diagram (map, chart, graph, model) help you in explaining your testimony to the jury?" Or, "Would that diagram (map, chart, graph, model) aid the jury in understanding your testimony?"

Real evidence, as with any evidence, must be relevant and otherwise admissible. The relevance of real evidence is inextricably linked to its authenticity. For example, in our murder case, the introduction into evidence of the bloody glove, which connects the accused to the murder, will have relevance only if it is indeed the same glove taken from the murder scene. Forensic tests may also be conducted on the

the validity of these tests rests on preserving the integrity of
xhibit—showing that the exhibit has not been tampered with or
erwise contaminated. The obligation is on the Crown to provide a
ufficient foundation for the reception of the glove into evidence. The
Crown must establish the "continuity" of the exhibit in that the exhibit
is accounted for from pick-up at the scene to presentation in court. The
police officer, who found the glove at the scene, the detective, who then
took possession of the glove, and the identification officer, who ultimately assumed the care and custody of the glove, will all have to be
called. The calling of these witnesses may be dispensed with where opposing counsel concedes the authenticity or continuity of the evidence.
The trial judge rules on the admissibility of the exhibit. The threshold
of proof is not high. The trial judge must be satisfied that there is evidence to support the conclusion that the item of real evidence is what
the party claims. Once admitted, the trier of fact makes the final determination as to authenticity and determines what weight to attach to
the evidence.

The second concern is with undue prejudice. Visual, tangible evidence has powerful impact. The trial judge, as a matter of discretion,
may exclude the real evidence if its prejudicial effects outweigh its probative value. The prejudice may relate to inflaming emotional passions
or to the potential for misleading the trier of fact. In our murder case,
the judge may exclude autopsy photographs of the victim if the photographs are particularly gruesome and of minimal probative value. For
example, there may be no issue as to the cause of death; the only issue
is identification, about which the autopsy photographs have no value.
Compare this to *R. v. Muchikekwanape*, where the Manitoba Court of
Appeal upheld the admissibility of a particularly graphic photograph
of the deceased in a first degree murder case.[186] The Crown theory was
that the accused had beaten the victim to death and then had thrown
her body into a nearby river. The defence theory was that the deceased,
who was very intoxicated, had fallen down the river embankment. A
"terrible" photograph of the deceased's face, taken at the autopsy, was
admitted into evidence for the purpose of showing the extent of the
dislocation of the bones in her face. The photograph had specific probative value and was relied upon by the respective experts who gave
contrasting opinions on the cause of death. In these circumstances, the
trial judge identified the proper purpose for admitting the photograph
and also warned the jury against its improper use.

---

186 *R. v. Muchikekwanape* (2002), 166 C.C.C. (3d) 144 (Man. C.A.).

7.2)   Views

Should it be impractical to bring the evidence to the court, the court may go to the evidence by way of a view. The trial judge has the discretion whether or not to undertake a view.[187] The value in conducting a view must be weighed against the inconvenience and disruption necessitated in essentially moving the court participants to the site.

Preserving a record as to what occurs and what is said during the course of a view is a concern. Sometimes attempts are made to conduct views without commentary. This is impractical in most instances. Some explanation will almost inevitably be required. Therefore, a recommended practice is to have a court reporter present to record any commentary and which also allows for the parties and the judge to put on the record what is occurring. The view record could also be preserved through videotaping.[188]

One issue that arises is the purpose of a view. The Ontario Court of Appeal in *Chambers v. Murphy* said that it was "well settled and beyond all controversy that the purpose of a view by a Judge or jury of any place is 'in order to understand better the evidence.'"[189] *Murphy* involved an automobile accident that occurred at the intersection of two highways. The defendant had testified that his vision was obstructed. There was no evidence to the contrary. The judge and counsel viewed the scene and, based on his own observations, the judge rejected the defendant's claim that his vision was blocked. The Court of Appeal said the rejection was "unwarranted" in that the judge was effectively relying on his own evidence. The Manitoba Court of Appeal in *Meyers v. Manitoba* rejected this limitation.[190] The court concluded that the observations of the trier of fact made during a view were evidence. The court quoted from Lord Denning in *Buckingham v. Daily News Ltd.*, where he said:

> Everyday practice in these courts shows that, where the matter for
> decision is one of ordinary common sense, the judge of fact is en-

---

187 See, for example, *Criminal Code*, above note 2, s. 652; Ontario, *Rules of Civil Procedure*, above note 54, r. 52.05.

188 In one case a judge tried to avoid having any untoward commentary during a view by having a script prepared in advance. Not only is this most unworkable, but it puts counsel to considerable time and work to prepare. The judge also then gave the option of having a court reporter present and having the view audio- and videotaped. The latter option is the far more sensible approach. See *Edmonton v. Lovat Tunnel Equipment Inc.* (2000), 258 A.R. 92 (Q.B.).

189 [1953] 2 D.L.R. 705 at 706 (Ont. C.A.). See also *Triple A Investments Ltd. v. Adams Brothers Ltd.* (1985), 56 Nfld. & P.E.I.R. 272 (Nfld. C.A.); *R. v. Welsh* (1997), 120 C.C.C. (3d) 68 (B.C.C.A.).

190 (1960), 26 D.L.R. (2d) 550 (Man. C.A.).

titled to form his own judgment on the real evidence of a view, just as much as on the oral evidence of witnesses.[191]

Mr. Justice Schultz in the Manitoba Court of Appeal then went on to state a far broader proposition, which would apply to all real or demonstrative evidence:

> I think it is a matter of everyday practice in our Courts that scale models, or similar objects, are tendered and accepted as real evidence. Such evidence may offer stronger and more convincing proof of the fact claimed than the oral evidence of witnesses. The Judge who views them in the court room is in no different position there than when, with all the necessary safeguards and conditions met, he views them outside the court room.[192]

This statement of the law as it applies to views or other real evidence is sound. It is illogical to ask judges or jurors to ignore what they have observed.[193]

7.3)   Photographs and Videotapes

The admissibility of photographs or videotapes depends upon (1) their accuracy in truly representing the facts; (2) their fairness and absence of any intention to mislead; and (3) their verification on oath by a person capable of doing so.[194] The person verifying the authenticity of the photographs or videotapes need not be the photographer. An eyewitness of the scene or events may confirm that the photograph or videotape is a fair and accurate reproduction. This is true even if the photograph of the scene is taken well after the events, as long as a witness testifies that it is a fair and accurate reproduction of the scene *as it looked at the time of the incident.*

A good case to illustrate the concerns about accuracy and fairness is *R. v. Maloney (No. 2).*[195] In a National Hockey League game, Maloney, who played for the Detroit Red Wings, got involved in a fight with a Toronto Maple Leaf player. During the course of the fight, Maloney repeatedly smashed the Toronto player's head into the ice. Maloney was charged with assault causing bodily harm. The Crown sought to intro-

---

191   [1956] 2 All E.R. 904 at 914 (C.A.).

192   *Meyers v. Manitoba,* above note 190 at 558.

193   For a thorough discussion on this issue, see G.S. Lester, "Tendering a View and a Demonstration on a View in Evidence" (1997) 19 Advocates' Q. 345.

194   *R. v. Creemer* (1967), 1 C.R.N.S. 146 at 154 (N.S.C.A.).

195   (1976), 29 C.C.C. (2d) 431 (Ont. G.S.P.).

duce videotapes taken of the game. Certain of the videotapes were out of sequence or in slow-motion and the trial judge refused to admit them because they distorted the true reality and speed of what occurred.

R. v. Penney provides another example.[196] In this case a seal hunter was charged under the Marine Mammals Regulations with failing to kill a seal in a manner designed to kill it quickly. The charge was laid after Fisheries officials received a videotape taken by an animal rights group. Prior to being turned over to the authorities it had been in the possession of a professional editing studio for approximately ten months. The videotape had in fact been transferred from the camera format twice to the format now shown. The trial judge refused to admit the videotape and the Newfoundland Court of Appeal agreed. The court held that as a precondition to admissibility the proponent must establish that the videotape has not been altered or changed. In coming to this conclusion, the court recognized that "[c]urrent technology is such that it is not difficult for a competent person to alter visual evidence."[197] The court also found that the Crown had failed to establish that the video was an accurate representation of the facts. The cameraman had only filmed selected short sequences of what he described as the "gory stuff." Time codes were not recorded on the tape. Sequence and timing may not always be relevant, but in the context of this case, where the accused was being charged with failing to kill "quickly," timing was important. The approach taken by the court in Penney is a valid one. A videotape of the "actual incident" is powerful evidence, and care needs to be taken to see that before it is admitted the videotape is not materially altered and fairly depicts the incidents.

As alluded to earlier, photographs or videotapes are powerful pieces of evidence, and they may be excluded where they would serve to inflame the minds of the jurors against the accused. The issue is not so much how grotesque or shocking the photographs or videotapes are, but their probative value. Today, we are exposed to more violence in more graphic detail, and are less likely to be swayed by terrible images, than in years gone by. Therefore, there should be few cases where photographs or videotapes are excluded because of their inflammatory prejudice—provided they have probative value to the case making them worth seeing.[198]

Videotapes, in particular, are now capturing on tape the actual incidents, as occurred in Maloney and Penney. This evidence is highly

---

196 R. v. Penney, 2002 NFCA 15.
197 Ibid. at para. 17.
198 See R. v. Teerhuis-Moar, 2010 MBCA 102.

probative and the Supreme Court of Canada in *R. v. Leaney* held that
the judge may rely on his own viewing of a videotape taken of a crime
to establish identification.[199] We might take this as a matter of common
sense, but one theory advanced for the reception of photographs and
recordings is that the videotapes have no independent probative value.
They rest on and must be associated with the testimony of a witness.[200]
This issue arose in *R. v. Nikolovski*, where the accused was charged with
a number of offences arising from the robbery of a convenience store.[201]
A surveillance camera captured the robbery on videotape. The victim
of the robbery was unable to identify the accused, even after reviewing
the videotape. The judge, too, viewed the videotape, but had "no doubt"
that the accused was the man who committed the robbery. The videotape was of very good quality and showed the robber for approximately
30 seconds. The sole issue on appeal was whether it was open to the
trial judge to rely on her own comparison of the robber on the videotape and the accused in the court. There were no other witnesses who
identified the man on the videotape as the accused. In other words, the
videotape was not associated with the testimony of any witness and
would have to stand on its own. The Ontario Court of Appeal ruled that
the videotape needed to be associated with a witness. On appeal, the
Supreme Court of Canada rejected this approach and in no uncertain
terms stated that a videotape, once authenticated, can stand on its own
as a "silent witness." Justice Cory wrote:

> So long as the videotape is of good quality and gives a clear picture
> of events and the perpetrator, it may provide the best evidence of the
> identity of the perpetrator. It is relevant and admissible evidence that
> can by itself be cogent and convincing evidence on the issue of iden-
> tity. Indeed, it may be the only evidence available. For example, in
> the course of a robbery, every eyewitness may be killed yet the video
> camera will steadfastly continue to impassively record the robbery
> and the actions of the robbers. Should a trier of fact be denied the
> use of the videotape because there is no intermediary in the form of
> a human witness to make some identification of the accused? Such
> a conclusion would be contrary to common sense and a totally un-
> acceptable result.[202]

---

199 (1989), 71 C.R. (3d) 325 (S.C.C.).
200 Wigmore, above note 90, vol. 3, s. 790.
201 (1996), 3 C.R. (5th) 362 (S.C.C.).
202 *Ibid.* at para. 22.

Although it is open to triers of fact to make an identification based solely on the videotape evidence, they must exercise caution in doing so. Special instructions and procedures are warranted.[203]

An emerging issue concerns the admissibility of videotape re-en-actments. In *R. v. Latimer* the Crown introduced into evidence a video-tape re-enactment where Latimer "walked through" the killing of his daughter and showed how he had done so.[204] This is a confession by the accused. Provided it was made voluntarily there is little danger of misleading emphasis or unfairness to the accused. However, it is quite different for the police, or any party for that matter, to create their own video version of events and present that to the court. There is a real concern as to prejudice. The party is being allowed to repeat their ver-sion of events in a powerful and visual way. Yet, this is precisely what was done in *R. v. MacDonald*.[205] The police were involved in a "take-down" of the accused that went awry and the accused was shot. The police prepared a videotape re-enactment of the takedown and it was admitted at trial. On appeal it was found that the trial judge had erred. Although the Ontario Court of Appeal was not prepared to impose a rigid ban on their admissibility, the decision makes it quite clear that courts should be very careful before admitting such evidence.

The court approved a case-by-case analysis, where the probative value of the videotape re-enactment is weighed against its prejudicial effect. In balancing the prejudicial and probative value of the video re-enactment, the court suggested that trial judges should consider the video's relevance, its accuracy, its fairness, its necessity, and whether what it portrays can be verified under oath. The court noted that a video's probative value rests on the accuracy of its re-enactment of un-disputed facts. Emphasis on "undisputed" facts is important. The more. a video relies on "disputed" facts, the less valuable it becomes. Should a video simply reflect one side's version of events it becomes a most dangerous type of evidence.

In *MacDonald* the video was both inaccurate and "one-sided." As a consequence, the video was highly prejudicial. In the words of the court, "The video permitted the prosecution to put before the jury its own version of what occurred, distilled into a neatly packaged,

---

203 *Ibid.* at 31–32. See also *R. v. Turpin*, 2011 ONCA 193.

204 *R. v. Latimer* (1997), 112 C.C.C. (3d) 193 (S.C.C.).

205 *R. v. MacDonald* (2000), 146 C.C.C. (3d) 525 (Ont. C.A.). See also *R. v. Waliza-dah*, 2007 ONCA 528, leave to appeal to S.C.C. refused, 2008 CanLII 42343 (S.C.C.).

compressed, and easily assimilated sight and sound bite."[206] Essentially the re-enactment became an extra witness for the Crown.[207]

The court in *MacDonald* was correct to exclude the video because of its unfair prejudice; however, there are other more fundamental concerns about the type of evidence presented in the case. Under the cloak of "demonstrative evidence," the Crown was introducing otherwise inadmissible evidence. The video re-enactment either violated the hearsay rule or the rule barring prior consistent statements.[208] The video amounted to little more than a visual out-of-court statement compiled from the officers. We would not allow the officers to file their respective statements as evidence. Why should a videotape re-enactment, which is a statement, be any different? Do not be deceived by the format. "Demonstrative" evidence is intended to aid witnesses in giving their evidence; it is not intended to allow witnesses to repeat their testimony.

What is needed is care. Re-enactment evidence or "experiment evidence" if sufficiently accurate and fair may well assist the trier of fact. A standard of perfection is not required.[209] Charron J.A. (as she then was) expressed the law as follows:

> In a nutshell, experiment evidence, if it is relevant to an issue in the case, should generally be admitted, subject to the trial judge's residuary discretion to exclude the evidence where the prejudice that would flow from its admission clearly outweighs its value.[210]

7.4) Documents

Documents may be authenticated in a variety of ways: calling the writer, calling a witness who saw the document signed, calling a witness who is familiar with the writer's handwriting, by comparison of the writing in dispute with a writing proved to the satisfaction of the court to be genuine, by the calling of experts, or through an admission by the opposing party.[211] Circumstantial evidence may also point to the genuineness of the document. For example, letters received in reply to an earlier correspondence are accepted as being made by the send-

---

206 *R. v. Macdonald*, *ibid.* at para. 48.

207 This phrase is taken from *Lopez v. State*, 651 S.W. 2d 413 (Tex. App. 1983), which provides a brief but powerful critique of such evidence.

208 See chapter 11, section 4, "Prior Consistent Statements."

209 *R. v. Walizadah*, above note 205 at para. 49.

210 *R. v. Collins* (2001), 160 C.C.C. (3d) 85 at para. 21 (Ont. C.A.).

211 See *Canada Evidence Act*, s. 8. In *R. v. Abdi* (1997), 116 C.C.C. (3d) 385 (Ont. C.A.), it was held that s. 8 did not oust the common law rule that the trier of fact may compare disputed handwriting with proved handwriting.

er.[212] A second example is that of ancient documents, generally more than 30 years old, which are admissible provided the circumstances raise no suspicions and the documents are produced from a source that would normally have custody of them. In addition, under statute, a wide variety of public and judicial records are admissible without proof of genuineness.[213]

The use of documents at trial is also guarded by the best evidence rule. The best evidence rule requires that the original of a document be tendered when a party seeks to prove the contents of that document. Secondary evidence, by way of copies or the testimony of witnesses, is inadmissible. The rule is sensible in that we are all aware that the wording of a document provides its meaning, and if that wording is changed, either through accident or design, the meaning of the document may also be fundamentally altered. For example, in a dispute over the terms of a contract, the "best evidence" is to submit to the court the original contract. In other cases, it may be desirable to tender the original, but it is not essential. For example, in a dispute over a debt, the defendant says that he repaid the loan by cheque. In this case, the content of the cheque is not at issue and there is no "requirement" that the original cheque be tendered, although it would be a valuable piece of evidence. At trial the defendant may testify that the debt was paid, bank records may be produced showing a photocopy of a cancelled cheque, and other witnesses who were present when the defendant repaid the money may also testify. The best evidence rule, or perhaps better stated, "the original documents" rule, as it exists today, is confined to cases where a party has the original document and could produce it, but does not. The party may satisfy the court that the original is lost, destroyed, or is otherwise in the possession of another and cannot be obtained.[214] Moreover, under statute, the rule has also been relaxed to allow for the introduction of copies in certain instances.[215] Flexibility is urged: "An over-technical and strained application of the best evidence rule serves only to hamper the inquiry without at all advancing the cause of truth."[216]

---

212 *Stevenson v. Dandy*, [1920] 2 W.W.R. 643 (Alta. C.A.).
213 See, for example, *Canada Evidence Act*, ss. 19–25.
214 R. Delisle, D. Stuart, & D. Tanovich, *Evidence: Principles and Problems*, 8th ed. (Scarborough, ON: Thomson Carswell, 2007) at 409.
215 See *Canada Evidence Act*, s. 29 (financial records), s. 30(3) (business records), s. 31 (government and "corporate" records).
216 *R. v. Betterest Vinyl Manufacturing Ltd.* (1989), 52 C.C.C. (3d) 441 at 448 (B.C.C.A.).

7.5) Computer-generated Evidence

The admissibility of computer-generated evidence generally falls to be decided within the traditional frameworks of the law of evidence, although the *Canada Evidence Act* now has a new provision dealing with the authentication of electronic documents as do certain provinces.[217] This section will consider three types of computer-generated evidence: records, models, and re-creations.

Most businesses now rely on computers to store their records. Where these records rely on human input, hearsay concerns apply and an exception needs to be found. Most computer records are admissible under the business records exception. The statutes are phrased in broad terms. For example, under the Ontario statute "record includes any information that is recorded or stored by means of any device."[218] The *Canada Evidence Act* (section 30(3)) distinguishes between "record" and a "copy," whereby adducing a copy in lieu of the record requires an affidavit of authenticity. It is sometimes argued that a computer "printout" is not a record but a copy. This technical construction is unwarranted and for good reason has not been accepted by the courts, and now has been addressed in section 31.2 of the *Canada Evidence Act*.[219] A further technical argument raised against the admissibility of computer records, and correctly dismissed, is that the printout is not created contemporaneously or reasonably contemporaneously with the events recorded. The printout, however, merely retrieves information stored in the computer. It is the time of input that is critical and not the time of retrieval. For example, the police may retrieve information from a computer as part of an investigation. This does not make the information inadmissible under section 30(10) of the *Canada Evidence Act* as being "a record made in the course of an investigation or inquiry." The information was "made" when it was inputted.[220] Nor must the witness called to introduce the record be a computer expert. It is enough that this witness has knowledge as to the contents of the records, how they are kept, secured, and retrieved.[221] The reliability of these computer records is shown from the fact that the business relies on them to conduct its day-to-day affairs.

---

217   *Canada Evidence Act*, ss. 31.1–31.8; *Alberta Evidence Act*, ss. 41.1–41.8; New Brunswick, *Evidence Act*, ss. 47.1 and 47.2; Nova Scotia, *Evidence Act*, ss. 23A–23H; Ontario, *Evidence Act*, s. 34.1.

218   Ontario, *Evidence Act*, s. 35(1).

219   *R. v. Bicknell* (1988), 41 C.C.C. (3d) 545 (B.C.C.A.).

220   *R. v. Hall*, 1998 CanLII 3955 (B.C.S.C.).

221   *Ibid.*

Some information, which is self-generated by the computer, is not hearsay at all—for example, trace calls obtained from telephone company records. The machine creates the information. Since there is no human input, the traditional hearsay concerns do not apply. This information should be treated as original or real evidence, with the only question being one of accuracy and reliability of the information-generating process.[222]

A good example of the need for reliability is found in the case of *R. v. Gratton*, which concerned the admissibility of a printout from the sensing diagnostic module (SDM) of a truck driven by the accused that was involved a tragic traffic accident that claimed five lives.[223] A civilian collision analyst downloaded the information from the SDM, which showed that the truck's speed was 74 m.p.h. five seconds prior to the deployment of the vehicle's air bag with reduced speed up to the point of deployment. Unfortunately, the witness could only tell the court what the printout said. He knew very little about how the SDM worked, did not know how to test the reliability of the unit, and knew nothing as to the unit's rate or margin of error. In the absence of expert evidence as to the reliability of SDM technology the information downloaded was ruled inadmissible.

Computers can create wonderful visual aids. One form of computer-generated visual aid is that of a three-dimensional model. In fact, one computer animation program known as A.D.A.M. (acronym for Animated Dissection of Anatomy for Medicine) brings *Gray's Anatomy* to life through three-dimensional anatomical images.[224] This type of evidence is demonstrative in nature. It is used to aid in the giving of testimony. As with any demonstrative evidence, counsel must establish a proper foundation in that:

1) the expert's testimony is relevant and admissible and the model relates to that evidence;
2) the expert whose testimony the model illustrates is familiar with it;
3) the model fairly and accurately reflects the expert's evidence to which it relates; and
4) the model will aid the trier of fact in understanding or evaluating the expert's evidence.[225]

---

222 J.W. Strong, ed., *McCormick on Evidence*, 4th ed. (St. Paul, MN: West, 1992) at 505–6. See also *R. v. Spiby* (1990), 91 Cr. App. R. 186 (Eng. C.A.).

223 *R. v. Gratton*, 2003 ABQB 728.

224 See A. Thapedi, "A.D.A.M.—The Computer Generated Cadaver: A New Development in Medical Malpractice and Personal Injury Litigation" (1995) 13 J. Marshall J. Computer & Info. L. 313.

225 This list is modified from R. Bain & D. Broderick, "Demonstrative Evidence in the Twenty-First Century" in J.C. Tredennick, Jr. & J.A. Eidelman, eds., *Winning with*

In *R. v. Suzack and Pennett* a computer-generated model was made into a video and used to illustrate various bullet wounds and injuries suffered by a murdered police officer.[226] An expert pathologist then used the model to explain the angle of entry and exit of the bullets and the sequence of shots. Using the computer model was far less inflammatory than using photographs of the victim. Provided that the expert can attest to the accuracy of the model and any graphics incorporated in it, there is no need to call the computer programmer or artist.

A computer re-creation is in some respects like a video re-enactment, except that it re-creates objects moving through space by applying the laws of physics to the mass, velocity, acceleration, and friction of the objects to project what occurred. In this case the evidence will be subjected to greater scrutiny.

When a computer re-creation is introduced the reliability of the computer program should be assessed. The data used should be reviewed. Counsel should examine what information was included and what was left out. In other words the computer program will need to pass the test for the admissibility of "novel science" and the criteria from *Mohan* should be applied.[227]

There are few cases in Canada where this type of evidence has been discussed. In *Owens v. Grandell* a re-creation was used by an accident reconstruction expert to explain how an accident occurred.[228] The court conducted a careful review of the evidence. The computer programmer was called and the court was walked through the preparation and creation of the simulation.

Owens v. Grandell was a case involving mechanical, physical objects, and the movement of vehicles. In *Green v. Lawrence* it was sought to introduce a re-creation involving the interaction of human beings.[229] At issue was whether the police used excessive force in arresting and subduing the plaintiff, who suffered a fracture of the spine and was rendered a quadriplegic. The re-creation was not tied to the evidence of the plaintiff's medical expert. Rather, it was supposedly a re-creation of the events using a computer program. Justice MacInnes applied the *Mohan* criteria. He accepted that the creator of the re-creation was an expert in computer re-creations and that the program used was accurate.

Computers: Trial Practice in the 21st Century, Part 1 (Washington, DC: American Bar Association, 1991) 369 at 374.

226 *R. v. Suzack and Pennett*, [1995] O.J. No. 4237 (Gen. Div.). See also *R. v. Scotland*, [2007] O.J. No. 5304 (S.C.J).

227 See chapter 6, section 5, "Novel and Challenged Science."

228 [1994] O.J. No. 496 (Gen. Div.).

229 (1996), 109 Man. R. (2d) 168 (Q.B.).

However, he excluded the evidence because it failed to provide a sufficient degree of reliability and faithfulness in the reproduction of the scene. It was too "subjective." As a result, the visual re-creation of the events would be misleading and too prejudicial.[230]

8. JUDICIAL NOTICE

8.1) Judicial Notice of Facts

Judicial notice is the acceptance by a court, without the requirement of proof, of any fact or matter that is so generally known and accepted in the community that it cannot be reasonably questioned, or any fact or matter that can readily be determined or verified by resort to sources whose accuracy cannot reasonably be questioned.

It is important to distinguish between taking judicial notice of "adjudicative facts" and "legislative facts." Judicial notice, as outlined, applies to adjudicative facts, which are facts to be determined in the litigation between the parties. Legislative facts are also admitted without the need for proof. However, legislative facts are those that have relevance to legal reasoning and the law-making process and involve broad considerations of policy. Legislative facts assist in determining questions of law and are not intended to assist in resolving questions of fact.

Judicial notice also includes "social framework facts," which provide a context for the judge to consider and apply the evidence in a given case. This information may be provided to the court by experts where necessary, or may be accepted by the trial judge as a matter of common knowledge in the community. The social framework facts will only have relevance if linked to the evidence in the particular case.

Certain facts do not need to be proven. Indeed, much in every case is already known. Judges and jurors bring with them vast knowledge, understanding, and experience that they are expected to use. We know that children can drown in lakes; we need no proof of that. We also know that alcohol can impair a person's faculties; we need no proof of that. Much is simply accepted as part of human experience, as a matter

---

230 Justice MacInnes ended his decision with these parting words of advice: "In my view, counsel would be well advised to critically consider whether evidence of this kind (or expert evidence of any kind on any issue) is truly necessary given the cost both in dollars and time, to the litigation process." *Ibid.* at para. 20.

of common sense, for which no proof is needed and to which nothing is said. When the silence is broken and the acceptance of a matter of common knowledge is urged or disputed, the issue of judicial notice arises. However, keep in mind that there is no bright line that divides judicial notice from common sense.

Judicial notice dispenses with the need for proof of facts that are clearly uncontroversial or beyond reasonable dispute. Facts judicially noticed are not proved by evidence under oath. Nor are they tested by cross-examination. Therefore, the threshold for judicial notice is strict: a court may properly take judicial notice of facts that are either: (1) so notorious or generally accepted as not to be the subject of debate among reasonable persons; or (2) capable of immediate and accurate demonstration by resort to readily accessible sources of indisputable accuracy.[231]

What is looked to is general knowledge within the "community" where the trial is held. For example, in a Kenora, Ontario courtroom judicial notice is taken that there are numerous cottages on the Lake of the Woods. Judicial notice of this same fact may not be taken in a Toronto courtroom. On appeal none of the members of the panel hearing the case may be familiar with Kenora, but that is of no moment; the appellate court must look to what is or is not the local community's common knowledge.[232] Moreover, should one of the justices actually have a cottage on Lake of the Woods and have a detailed knowledge of that area, it is equally clear that the judge is not justified in acting on that personal knowledge, unless, once again, it can be seen to be common knowledge within the local community.[233]

Two purposes are advanced to justify judicial notice, and each affects the possible scope of the doctrine. One rationale is that it is a means to expedite the trial process—a tool of convenience designed to shorten and simplify trials. Professor Thayer wrote:

> Taking judicial notice does not import that the matter is indisputable. It is not necessarily anything more than a *prima facie* recognition, leaving the matter still open to controversy . . . . In very many cases, then, taking judicial notice of a fact is merely presuming it, *i.e.*, assuming it until there shall be reason to think otherwise. Courts may judicially notice much which they cannot be required to notice.[234]

---

231 *R. v. Find* (2001), 154 C.C.C. (3d) 97 at para. 48 (S.C.C.).
232 *R. v. Potts* (1982), 26 C.R. (3d) 252 (Ont. C.A.).
233 *Ibid.*
234 J.B. Thayer, *A Preliminary Treatise on Evidence at the Common Law*, reprint of 1898 ed. (New York: Augustus M. Kelly, 1969) at 308–9.

A second rationale, advanced by Professor Morgan, is that judicial notice is based on the need to protect the credibility of the judicial system. Under this model, judicial notice applies only to "indisputable" facts that, if not accepted by the court, would bring the judicial system into disrepute.[235] According to Morgan, once judicial notice is taken, the matter is "indisputable" — final. Morgan's stricter view of judicial notice is accepted in Canada. We see this in the Supreme Court of Canada's decisions in *R. v. Find*[236] and *R. v. Spence*.[237]

8.1 (a)   Adjudicative Facts

The above outline of judicial notice applies to what are termed "adjudicative facts."[238] Adjudicative facts are the facts to be determined in the particular case. They address such questions as "who did what, where, when, how, and with what motive or intent."[239] For example, judicial notice has been taken that camels are domestic animals,[240] that generally speaking the cost of raising children increases as the children grow older,[241] or that cigarettes are more expensive in Manitoba than Ontario.[242]

Judicial notice is also taken of facts that are commonly before the courts and that are, if you like, of common knowledge in the court community, such as that police officers usually take notes or that legal aid is available to eligible persons.[243]

It is also accepted that judicial notice may be taken of facts previously found by other courts.[244] In *R. v. Paszczenko* it was held that based on the practice and precedent of literally hundreds of cases courts are entitled to take judicial notice of two assumptions underlying toxicology reports in impaired driving cases: (1) an accepted elimination of alcohol rate and (2) that there is a plateau effect where elimination of the alcohol remains constant for a time.[245]

---

235 E.M. Morgan, "Judicial Notice" (1944) 57 Harv. L. Rev. 269.
236 *R. v. Find*, above note 231.
237 *R. v. Spence*, 2005 SCC 71.
238 K. Davis, "An Approach to the Problems of Evidence in the Administrative Process" (1942) 55 Harv. L. Rev. 364.
239 C. L'Heureux-Dubé, "Re-examining the Doctrine of Judicial Notice in the Family Law Context" (1994) 26 Ottawa L. Rev. 551 at 554.
240 *McQuaker v. Goddard*, [1940] 1 All E.R. 471 (C.A.).
241 *Ivey v. Ivey* (1996), 153 Sask. R. 157 (Q.B.).
242 *R. v. MacLaurin* (1996), 30 W.C.B. (2d) 93 (Man. Prov. Ct.).
243 *R. v. Muzurenko*, [1991] N.W.T.J. No. 248 (Terr. Ct.).
244 See *R. v. Koh* (1998), 42 O.R. (3d) 668 at 679 (C.A.).
245 *R. v. Paszczenko*, 2010 ONCA 615 at para. 66.

Finally, judicial notice of adjudicative facts extends to facts capable of ready determination by resort to sources of indisputable accuracy. Although the facts discovered may not be generally known, their accuracy is easily verified by going to sources that ordinary, reasonable people would consult. Common examples include reference to calendars to match days and dates, or to maps to determine distance and location.

In *R. v. Krymowski* the Supreme Court of Canada recognized that dictionary meanings were another "source of indisputable accuracy."[246] The issue in the case was whether the terms "Gypsy" and "Roma" were interchangeable. Dictionary meanings were relied on and the Court concluded that the trial judge should have taken judicial notice that "Gypsy" referred to "Roma."

8.1 (b) Legislative Facts

A second type of judicial notice applies to "legislative facts," which are "facts" that have relevance to legal reasoning and the law-making process and involve broad considerations of policy.[247] They are not directed at resolving a specific factual issue in the case before the court. Rather, they are resorted to when the courts are asked to make law, which is a matter that transcends the particular dispute and is of general social importance. For example, where the constitutionality of a statute is being considered and a section 1 inquiry is undertaken, the obligation of the court is to consider the standards of a free and democratic society, which is not a question of fact relating to the allegation against the accused. In *R. v. Clayton* the Supreme Court of Canada took judicial notice of statistics on firearm use and violent crimes from Department of Justice published reports.[248] The information was used to determine whether or not investigation of gun-related criminal activity was of pressing and substantial concern.

Legislative facts are amorphous and are not likely to be "indisputable." We see them in the decisions of the Supreme Court of Canada where the Court is called upon to rule on the constitutionality of a law, or when interpreting a statute, or when asked to either extend or restrict a common law rule. In these cases the Court relies on a wide variety of social science research and study. Much of the information is provided to the Court by counsel; however, much is not.[249] It is one

---

246 *R. v. Krymowski*, 2005 SCC 7 at para. 22.
247 *Report of the Federal/Provincial Task Force on Uniform Rules of Evidence* (Toronto: Carswell, 1982) at 44.
248 *R. v. Clayton* (2007), 281 D.L.R. (4th) 1 (S.C.C.).
249 The Supreme Court has been criticized for conducting its own research outside of the adversary process. See C. Baar, "Criminal Court Delay and the *Charter*:

thing for the Supreme Court of Canada to refer to a vast array of social science material in determining the law, but it is quite another matter for a trial judge to do the same in determining a question of fact. This is exactly what the trial judge did in *R. v. Desaulniers*.[250] The accused was charged with two counts of sexual assault involving two young girls. In his defence, Desaulniers called a psychologist and a psychiatrist. The psychiatrist had testified that it is "a well recognized phenomenon in young children this ability to make up stories." The trial judge rejected this evidence and relied on findings contained in the *Badgley Report* (the *Report of the Committee on Sexual Offences Against Children and Youths in Canada*) and in a book entitled *Abus sexuels* (*Sexual Abuse*). These works were not put in evidence through the Crown calling its own expert witnesses, or by way of cross-examination of the defence experts. True, the Supreme Court of Canada has referred to the *Badgley Report* on at least five occasions, but in each of these the Court was using the report in determining what the law should be. What the trial judge was doing in *Desaulniers* was to use the report to challenge the expert's credibility—an "adjudicative fact."

A second troubling aspect about *Desaulniers* is that it deals with expert evidence. Judicial notice and expert evidence are not compatible. Judicial notice, as outlined, deals with matters of notorious common knowledge; on the other hand, expert evidence is called precisely because the expert has knowledge beyond the ken of the ordinary person. In *Desaulniers*, the trial judge conducted his own research outside of the trial process, and then used that research to impeach the testimony of the expert, who was given no opportunity to challenge or to answer what the judge was doing. This flies in the face of our adversarial system, which is premised on the adducing and testing of evidence in open court. Moreover, the judge is venturing into areas of specialized knowledge, with none of the expertise.[251] In the end, the Quebec Court of Appeal found that the trial judge had erred. The court wrote:

> There is no doubt that judicial notice can only and must only bear on facts which are either of public notoriety, or which can easily and readily be verified, for example in a dictionary. Judicial notice would

The Use and Misuse of Social Facts in Judicial Policy Making" (1993) 72 Can. Bar Rev. 305.

250 (1994), 93 C.C.C. (3d) 371 (Que. C.A.), leave to appeal to S.C.C. refused (1995), 93 C.C.C. (3d) vi (note) (S.C.C.).

251 In *R. v. Lalonde* (1995), 37 C.R. (4th) 97 (Ont. Gen. Div.), the trial judge took judicial notice of battered wife syndrome and then applied that syndrome to the case on trial, without any expert evidence being called! See also *R. v. Find*, above note 231 at para. 49.

not seem to extend, in the context of a criminal trial, to expert evidence or a type of existing expert evidence which was not put in evidence by one of the parties.[252]

8.1 (c)   Social Framework Facts

In recent years, "social framework facts" have emerged as a third form of judicial notice. These facts are really a hybrid of adjudicative and legislative facts. They "refer to social science research that is used to construct a frame of reference or background context for deciding factual issues crucial to the resolution of a particular case."[253] These are not "facts" in the true sense of the word; rather, they are general explanations about society or human behaviour. Usually experts are called to explain the relevant social condition. For example, in *R. v. Lavallee*, expert evidence of the psychological experiences of battered women was admitted to provide necessary background in determining whether the accused, who had shot her unarmed husband in the back of the head, did so in self-defence.[254] The expert testimony provided a framework for the defence psychiatrist's evidence that the accused feared for her life and acted in a reasonable belief that she had no choice other than to kill her husband. Similarly, in jury selection cases involving challenges-for-cause, judges have made use of expert evidence on relevant social conditions such as racism.[255] Where such expert evidence is looked to, the issues relate to the general social framework, and like "legislative facts," this information is used to develop the law in a general way and is not necessarily specific to the parties in the particular case.

It is not necessary to look to experts to explain all manner of social conditions. Much is known about human conditions and social realities that is indisputable among reasonable people. Therefore, judges already rely a great deal on "social context facts" without saying a word about judicial notice and without requiring any expert testimony. There is nothing wrong in judges doing so; we expect it of them.

Because the information relating to social context is not specific to the parties in the particular case, taking judicial notice of it does not intrude into the adversarial function in the same way that tak-

---

252 *R. v. Desaulniers*, above note 250 at 376.

253 L'Heureux-Dubé, above note 239 at 556.

254 (1990), 76 C.R. (3d) 329 (S.C.C.). It should be noted that the Court's acceptance of "battered woman syndrome" based on Lenore Walker's book has been much criticized. In *R. v. Malott* (1998), 121 C.C.C. (3d) 456 (S.C.C.), Justices L'Heureux-Dubé and McLachlin clarified that Lenore Walker's profile was too restrictive.

255 See the comments of Cory J. in *R. v. S.(R.D.)* (1997), 10 C.R. (5th) 1 at 44–45 (S.C.C.).

ing judicial notice of adjudicative facts does. For example, it would be manifestly improper for a judge to conduct research on the correlation between speed, weight, and the length of skid marks in order to decide how fast the defendant was driving. That judge would appear to be assisting the plaintiff. It is less troubling for a judge to have resort to studies demonstrating the existence of racism in resolving the more general question of whether there is racial bias in a given community, sufficient to give an air of reality to the concern that some jurors may not be impartial in judging a black accused.

The fact that judicial notice of social context facts tends to have less impact on the adversarial function does not mean that the requirements of notoriety or incontrovertibility are immaterial. Courts have to be cautious. They are far more comfortable taking judicial notice of propositions about social context that are widely understood than of novel or controversial propositions. In *R. v. Find*[256] the accused attempted to rely on judicial notice of social framework to help persuade the Supreme Court of Canada that in sexual offence cases involving children there is a realistic possibility that some jurors might be unable to adjudicate impartially and try the cases solely on the evidence. The Court was prepared to accept certain underlying facts relied on by the accused, including the prevalence of sexual abuse, that such abuse can have traumatic effects on its victims and that some victims may well become members of the jury panel, but the Court was not prepared to accept the controversial inference that the accused wanted it to draw from these facts. The Court was not persuaded that the proposition that the trauma of victimization could predispose a juror to convict in a sexual offence case either followed from those social context facts, or was incontrovertible enough on its own to be taken judicial notice of.[257]

For the social context information to have any relevance, it must be linked to the evidence in the particular case. As can be seen in *Lavallee*, the general information on battered women was linked to the accused and to the facts of that case. Without an evidentiary link, the general proposition, standing alone, is of no relevance, and in such instances it is dangerous and inappropriate to rely upon it.

8.1 (d)   The Procedure
The procedure for taking judicial notice is somewhat fluid. It is generally contemplated that the matter will be raised at trial, when counsel

256   Above note 231.
257   See also *R. v. Advance Cutting and Coring Ltd.* (2001), 205 D.L.R. (4th) 385 at para. 225 (S.C.C.).

formally asks the court to take judicial notice of certain facts.[258] In this situation, counsel have the opportunity to present argument and, if need be, to call evidence on the point. Judges may, on their own initiative, take judicial notice with no input from counsel. There will be no problem with the judge doing so if the fact taken notice of is truly "indisputable"; however, problems arise when the trial judge through his or her own independent research and study finds new information, which may be helpful but is not "undisputed." In this situation "the adversarial process requires that the court ensure that the parties are given an opportunity to deal with the new information by making further submissions, oral or written, and allowing, if requested, fresh material in response."[259] Finally, the matter of judicial notice may be raised for the first time on appeal, as an appellate court can properly take judicial notice of any matter of which the trial court may properly take notice.[260]

In terms of the test for admissibility, the Supreme Court of Canada in R. v. Spence recognized that adjudicative facts, legislative facts and social facts are not treated alike.[261] The test for accepting judicial notice of adjudicative facts is strict; there is need for notoriety or acceptance by an indisputable source. If the criteria are not satisfied, then the adjudicative fact will not be judicially recognized.[262] However, this "gold standard" is not necessarily required for legislative and social facts. Justice Binnie outlined a more elastic test based on two interrelated variables: (1) the level of notoriety and indisputability of the "fact" sought to be noticed, and (2) the significance or centrality of the "fact" in disposing of the issue. The more important the fact, the more stringent the proof required. The less important the fact, the less the need for indisputable proof to be shown.[263]

Even though the Court in Spence accepted a measure of flexibility in admitting legislative and social facts it is fair to say that the entire tenor of the decision is that judicial notice must be applied more carefully and with greater scrutiny. The Court specifically commented upon the practice of merely filing social science reports and studies as proof of the facts asserted. The Court expressed a preference for such

---

258   See G.D. Nokes, "The Limits of Judicial Notice" (1958) 74 L.Q. Rev. 59 at 66.
259   Cronk v. Canadian General Insurance Co. (1995), 25 O.R. (3d) 505 at 518 (C.A.).
       See also R. v. Peter Paul (1998), 18 C.R. (5th) 360 (N.B.C.A.), leave to appeal to
       S.C.C. refused (1998), 128 C.C.C. (3d) vi (note) (S.C.C.).
260   Varcoe v. Lee, 181 P. 223 (Cal. Sup. Ct. 1919). See also R. v. Potts, above note 232.
261   R. v. Spence, above note 237.
262   Ibid. at para. 62.
263   Ibid. at para. 60.

evidence to be introduced through expert witnesses who can be cross-examined as to the value and weight to be given the relied upon studies or reports. The Court issued this warning: "Litigants who disregard the suggestion proceed at some risk."[264]

8.2) Judicial Notice of Laws

A judge is charged with the duty of knowing the domestic statute and common law. Under the various Evidence Acts, judicial notice is to be taken of the laws of Canada and of the provinces.[265] Laws of a foreign jurisdiction must be proved, although in certain provinces judicial notice is to be taken of statutes from countries of the British Commonwealth.[266] In Manitoba, judicial notice shall be taken of the laws of any part of the Commonwealth or of the United States.[267] Most subordinate legislation, such as municipal bylaws, must be proven by official copies or certified copies.[268]

In *R. v. Schaeffer* the court was asked to take judicial notice of an ungazetted park bylaw. The court refused to do so and reiterated the law: "The basic evidentiary rules concerning subordinate legislation, such as the Bylaw, are well known. They must be proven in the absence of a statutory provision requiring or permitting judicial notice."[269]

9. SPECIAL PROCEDURES FOR CHILD WITNESSES

9.1) The Child Witness

The courtroom is not a friendly place for children. It is an adult forum, run by adults and intended for adults. Yet, as society confronts the serious social problem of crimes against children, more children are being called to the witness stand. In particular, the number of prosecutions for sexual and physical abuse of children has increased significantly in recent years. These cases bring into play their own special dynamics. The child is called upon to condemn his or her abuser—often a loved

---

264 *Ibid.* at para. 68.
265 See, for example, *Canada Evidence Act*, s. 17.
266 British Columbia, *Evidence Act*, ss. 25 & 26; *Manitoba Evidence Act*, s. 29; New Brunswick, *Evidence Act*, s. 70; Prince Edward Island, *Evidence Act*, s. 21.
267 *Manitoba Evidence Act*, s. 30.
268 See, for example, *Canada Evidence Act*, ss. 24 and 28.
269 *R. v. Schaeffer* (2005), 194 C.C.C. (3d) 517 (Sask. C.A.).

one. Moreover, the child's testimony is essential in that often there are likely to be no other witnesses to the crime; it is the child's word against the accused's. In this situation, the young complainant faces enormous stress and trauma. It is within this context that Parliament acted to facilitate the giving of evidence by children in the prosecution of sexual offences against children. A number of helpful procedures were introduced:

- the public may be excluded from the courtroom;
- a support person may be permitted to be close to the witness while testifying;
- the child may be permitted to testify outside of the courtroom or behind a screen;
- the accused will not be permitted personally to cross-examine the child witness unless the trial judge so allows;
- a publication ban may be imposed to protect the child's identity; and
- a child's videotape evidence is admissible at the trial.[270]

We will examine two of the most important reforms—namely, allowing children to testify without facing the accused, and the introduction of videotaped evidence given by child witnesses.

9.2)   Testifying Outside the Presence of the Accused

Subsection 486.2 (1) of the Criminal Code *provides that:*

> *Despite section 650, in any proceedings against an accused, the judge or justice shall, on application of the prosecutor, of a witness who is under the age of eighteen years or of a witness who is able to communicate evidence but may have difficulty doing so by reason of a mental or physical disability, order that the witness testify outside the court room or behind a screen or other device that would allow the witness not to see the accused, unless the judge or justice is of the opinion that the order would interfere with the proper administration of justice.*

Subsection 486.2 (1) applies to all witnesses, who at the time of trial are under the age of eighteen. This section must also be read with subsection 486.2 (7), which stipulates that the accused, judge, and jury must be able to watch the testimony by means of closed-circuit television or

---

270   See ss. 486–486.6 and 715.1 of the *Criminal Code*, above note 2. See also the Ontario *Evidence Act*, ss. 18.1–18.6.

"otherwise," and that the accused must be permitted to communicate with counsel while watching the testimony.

Under our law an accused has no constitutional right to "face one's accuser" and the Supreme Court of Canada has consistently upheld the constitutionality of legislation that allows a witness to testify out of the physical presence or view of the accused.[271] The fundamental purpose of a trial is to seek the truth; to that end, the legislation is designed to facilitate the obtaining of relevant evidence from children and vulnerable witnesses. Section 486.2 is but a testimonial aid, which does not preclude the testing of the witness's evidence through cross-examination.

The starting point for children under the legislation is that upon application a court "shall" grant the order, unless the order "would interfere with the proper administration of justice." There is a presumption in favour of use. Defence counsel have expressed concern over prejudice to the accused in jury trials. They argue that protecting the complainant in such a way may give the appearance that the complainant is in fear of the accused, or create the impression that the accused must really be guilty. To address these concerns, the Ontario Court of Appeal has stated that it should be the usual practice for the judge to instruct the jury

> that the use of the screen is a procedure that is allowed in cases of this kind by reason of the youth of the witnesses and that, since it has nothing to do with the guilt or innocence of the accused, the jury must not draw any inference of any kind from its use and, specifically, that no adverse inference should be drawn against the accused because of it.[272]

The Supreme Court of Canada approved of such an instruction, but declined to make it mandatory.[273]

Section 486.2(2) applies to adult witnesses; they too may apply to testify outside the courtroom or behind a screen. For adult witnesses the order is discretionary. The onus is on the witness or Crown to satisfy the court that "the order is necessary to obtain a full and candid account from the witness of the acts complained of."

---

271 R. v. Levogiannis (1993), 25 C.R. (4th) 325 (S.C.C.). See as well R. v. J.Z.S., 2008
     BCCA 401 at para. 41, aff'd 2010 SCC 1.
272 R. v. Levogiannis (1990), 2 C.R. (4th) 355 at 380 (Ont. C.A.).
273 R. v. Levogiannis, above note 271 at 339–40.

9.3)　Videotaped Evidence

Section 715.1 of the Criminal Code provides:

> *In any proceeding against an accused in which a victim or other witness was under the age of eighteen years at the time the offence is alleged to have been committed, a video recording made within a reasonable time after the alleged offence, in which the victim or witness describes the acts complained of, is admissible in evidence if the victim or witness, while testifying, adopts the contents of the video recording, unless the presiding judge or justice is of the opinion that admission of the video recording in evidence would interfere with the proper administration of justice.*

Section 715.1 is designed to achieve two main purposes. First, it aids in the preservation of evidence and the discovery of truth. The videotape preserves an early account of the child's evidence, given in a more natural setting, which may well provide the best account of what took place, an account also free from subsequent influence or suggestion. "The video record may indeed be the only means of presenting a child's evidence. For example, a child assaulted at the age of three or four years may have very little real recollection of the events a year or two later when the child is attempting to testify at trial."[274] Second, using the videotape at the trial makes it less stressful and traumatic for the child. It reduces the number of interviews that the child must undergo prior to trial in which the child faces repeated questioning, most often by strangers, usually concerning a very painful incident. At trial the child is freed from the initial need to recount the incident in direct examination, although to be sure the child will still be subject to cross-examination.

The Supreme Court of Canada in *R. v. L.(D.O.)* upheld the constitutionality of the section.[275] It was argued that the provision violated the accused's right to a fair trial in that it offended the rules of evidence against the admission of hearsay and prior consistent statements. The Court, however, found that once the child witness adopts the videotape, that evidence becomes part of the child's in-court testimony and is no longer strictly hearsay. Moreover, the traditional hearsay concerns are absent. The maker of the statement is present in court and can be cross-examined on the statement, and the court is able to see and hear the earlier statement. With respect to the general rule against the admitting of prior consistent statements, this rule of exclusion is based on

---

274　*R. v. F.(C.C.)* (1997), 120 C.C.C. (3d) 225 at 234 (S.C.C.).
275　(1993), 25 C.R. (4th) 285 (S.C.C.).

the proposition that such repetition is redundant and of no value.[276]
Under section 715.1, the videotape evidence represents the witness's
account of what occurred and, in this sense, it is of value and is not
redundant. Even in cases where the child remembers the event well
and can testify effectively, the showing of the videotape may add much
to the witness's testimony. After all, it is an account made free from the
courtroom pressures and at a time when the events would have been far
fresher in the child's mind.

The witness must "adopt" the contents of the videotape. There was
some disagreement as to what this meant. The Alberta Court of Appeal
took the view that a witness might adopt the statement, even though
she does not recall the events discussed, as long as she recalls giving
the statement and her attempt to be honest and truthful at that time.[277]
This is akin to the notion of "past recollection recorded."[278] On the
other hand, the Ontario Court of Appeal took the view that the witness
must be able to attest to the accuracy of the videotape based on the witness's present memory.[279] In other words, the witness is able to adopt
the statement as true, as opposed merely to vouching for the fact that
when it was made the witness sought to be truthful. The Ontario Court
of Appeal took this position primarily because it then enables effective
cross-examination of the complainant on the actual incident.

In *R. v. F.(C.C.)* the Supreme Court of Canada resolved the matter.[280]
Justice Cory, writing for the Court, observed that the test for adoption
needed to be consistent with the overall aim and purpose of the statute. It followed that the Ontario Court of Appeal's approach was too
restrictive. It would prevent a child who has little or no memory of the
events from adopting the video and this evidence would be inadmissible under section 715.1.

The primary concern that the Ontario Court of Appeal had was that
counsel would not be in a position to cross-examine the witness and,
therefore, the reliability of the videotape testimony could not be tested.
Justice Cory replied that "cross-examination is not the only guarantee
of reliability" and he referred to other indicia of reliability: (1) the statement is to be made within a reasonable time; (2) the trier of fact can
watch the videotape to assess demeanour, personality, and intellect of
the child; (3) the child is required to attest that she was attempting to

---

276 See chapter 11, section 4.1, "The Rule against Proof of Previous Consistent
     Statements."
277 *R. v. Meddoui*, above note 72.
278 See above in this chapter, section 5.3, "[Refreshing Memory] During Trial."
279 *R. v. Toten* (1993), 83 C.C.C. (3d) 5 (Ont. C.A.).
280 Above note 274.

be truthful at the time the statement was made; and (4) the child can be cross-examined at trial as to whether or not she was actually being truthful when the statement was made.[281] Furthermore, in situations where the child has no independent memory, the trier of fact should be given a special warning of the dangers of convicting based on the videotape alone.

In *F.(C.C.)* the child had an independent memory of the incident; however, her in-court testimony was inconsistent with portions of what she said in the videotape. Does this then render the inconsistent portions of the videotape "unadopted" and therefore inadmissible? No, said Justice Cory. The videotape along with the in-court testimony become the whole of the child's evidence. The inconsistencies go to weight, but not admissibility.[282]

Since inconsistencies go to weight, does this mean that consistency between the witness's in-court testimony and the videotape recording goes to credibility? No. The law of evidence has always treated prior inconsistent statements differently from prior consistent statements. The fact that the complainant, or any witness, makes the same statement at trial as in the videotape recording does not make the truth of that statement any more credible. The witness may "just as well be consistently lying as consistently telling the truth."[283] Consistency between the witness's own statements, therefore, cannot go to confirm or corroborate the testimony. The purpose of the videotape recording is to provide a fuller account of what occurred; it is in this way that it "augments" the in-court testimony.

Before using the videotape, there is need for a *voir dire* on its admissibility.[284] First, the videotape must be reviewed to ensure that any statements made conform to the rules of evidence. For example, in the videotape the child may recount hearsay statements of others, and these would need to be edited out of the tape. Second, the court also needs to be satisfied that the videotape was "made within a reasonable time." "What is or is not 'reasonable' depends entirely on the circumstances of a case."[285] In *R. v. L.(D.O.)*, the Supreme Court of Canada upheld the trial judge's finding that a delay of five months was not un-

---

281 *Ibid.* at 241. The Alberta Court of Appeal in *R. v. Smith* (2001), 277 A.R. 147 (C.A.) ruled that there is no adoption when the child recants and repudiates her statement.

282 *R. v. F.(C.C.)*, *ibid.* at 242.

283 *R. v. Aksidan*, 2006 BCCA 258 at para. 25. See also *R. v. K.P.S.*, 2007 BCCA 397, leave to appeal to S.C.C. refused, 2007CanLII 66734 (S.C.C.).

284 *R. v. L.(D.O.)*, above note 275 at 316.

285 *Ibid.* at 319.

reasonable. Madam Justice L'Heureux-Dubé urged courts to be mindful that children, for a variety of reasons, are apt to delay disclosure.

Let us not assume, however, that disclosure of childhood sexual assault is routinely delayed.[286] Juries are, in fact, to be instructed that "there is no inviolable rule how people who are the victims of trauma like a sexual assault will behave."[287] Yet, the Ontario Court of Appeal accepted a two-year delay as "reasonable."[288] In *R. v. S.J.L.* a delay of 45 months from the time of the incident was found to be reasonable by the trial judge, who ruled that time did not run until the abuse was disclosed.[289] The British Columbia Court of Appeal overturned her decision on appeal. The court correctly noted that this interpretation was inconsistent with both the language and the purpose of section 715.1. In Justice Cory's words from *F.(C.C.)* the "primary" goal is the creation of a record and the "subsidiary" aim is to prevent or reduce trauma. If "reasonable time" is interpreted in too relaxed a fashion it guts much of the reliability for introducing these statements. Keep in mind, the Court in *F.(C.C.)* was prepared to accept a meaning of "adoption," whereby a child may have no present memory of the incident, in part because "a videotape made shortly after the event is more likely to be accurate."[290]

Even if a videotape recording is not admissible under section 715.1 it is still possible to admit it under the principled exception to the hearsay rule. Section 715.1, as a statutory exception to the hearsay rule, does not displace the common law exceptions.[291]

Besides determining that the preconditions in the section are met, at this stage, the trial judge also has the discretion to refuse to admit the videotape into evidence if she is of the opinion that its admission would "interfere with the proper administration of justice." This discretion was inserted into the section in the 2005 statutory amendments. Yet, prior to the amendment courts had already recognized a discretion to exclude the recording where its prejudicial effect outweighs its probative value.[292] The following factors were suggested to be taken into account in exercising this discretion:

---

286 T. Moore & M. Green, "Truth and the Reliability of Children's Evidence: Problems with Section 715.1 of the *Criminal Code*" (1999) 30 C.R. (5th) 148.

287 *R. v. D.D.* (2000), 148 C.C.C. (3d) 41 at para. 65 (S.C.C.).

288 *R. v. P.S.* (2000), 144 C.C.C. (3d) 120 (Ont. C.A.), leave to appeal to the S.C.C. refused, [2000] S.C.C.A. No. 486.

289 (2001), 155 C.C.C. (3d) 338 (B.C.C.A.).

290 Above note 274 at 240.

291 *R. v. M.(D.)* (2007), 223 C.C.C. (3d) 193 at para. 20 (N.S.C.A.).

292 This same discretion is recognized with respect to the admissibility of evidence under other statutes. See s. 12 of the *Canada Evidence Act* (see above in this chapter, section 6.6, "Cross-examination on Prior Convictions") and s. 715 of

(a) the form of questions used by any other person appearing in the videotaped statement;

(b) any interest of anyone participating in the making of the statement;

(c) the quality of the video and audio reproduction;

(d) the presence or absence of inadmissible evidence in the statement;

(e) the ability to eliminate inappropriate material by editing the tape;

(f) whether other out-of-court statements by the complainant have been entered;

(g) whether any visual information in the statement might tend to prejudice the accused (for example, unrelated injuries visible on the victim);

(h) whether the prosecution has been allowed to use any other method to facilitate the giving of evidence by the complainant;

(i) whether the trial is one by judge alone or by a jury; and

(j) the amount of time which has passed since the making of the tape and the present ability of the witness to effectively relate to the events described.[293]

Justice Cory ended his judgment in *F.(C.C.)* with the following stated ideal:

> If it can reasonably be done, a sensitive judicial system should, with the aim of s. 715.1 in mind, interpret the section in a manner that will attempt to avoid further injury to children resulting from their participation in the criminal trial process. That must of course be done within the balanced bounds of always ensuring that the accused enjoys the fundamental right to a fair trial. The definitions and procedures set out in these reasons strive to achieve these aims.[294]

---

the *Criminal Code*, above note 2 (see chapter 5, section 4.3, "Admissibility under the *Criminal Code*").

293 *R. v. F.(C.C.)* , above note 274 at 243–44.

294 *Ibid.* at 245.

CHAPTER 11

SECONDARY MATERIALITY AND YOUR OWN WITNESS

1. THE BAR ON BOLSTERING THE CREDIBILITY OF YOUR OWN WITNESS

As a general rule, a party may not ask questions or present evidence solely to bolster the credibility of his own witness.

Although it may be of assistance to hear testimony about the value of the evidence that has been led in a case, there is concern that to allow this would take an undue amount of time and create distracting side issues. Until their credibility has been made an issue by the opposing party, witnesses are assumed to be trustworthy and of good character.[1] As a general rule, therefore, a party cannot initiate evidence solely to establish that his witnesses are credible. Evidence must be about the primarily material issues in the case, not about other evidence in the case. In *R. v. Siu*

---

1   *R. v. Giraldi* (1975), 28 C.C.C. (2d) 248 (B.C.C.A.), leave to appeal to S.C.C. refused (1975), 28 C.C.C. (2d) 248n (S.C.C.). This is a reference to the character of the witness for truthfulness, not a reference to the accuracy or even truthfulness of what the witness is saying in the case. In other words, while witnesses are assumed to be of good character absent evidence to the contrary, it would be wrong to presume that witnesses are giving accurate testimony in the case. The evidence of any witness must be examined on its merits. Cases where the trier of fact is unable to determine whether the evidence is accurate should be resolved according to the standards and burdens of proof, not according to a presumption that the witness is being truthful or accurate: *R. v. Thain* (2009), 243 C.C.C. (3d) 230 at para. 32 (Ont. C.A.).

this rule was contravened where a police officer stated that he believed the key Crown witness.[2] The rule was further breached when the officer testified that his belief was based in part on the offer of the Crown witness to take a polygraph test. Where a party leads inadmissible evidence to support the credibility of one of its witnesses in a jury trial, the trial judge should immediately direct the jury to disregard the evidence.[3]

At the same time, it is permissible and indeed customary to introduce a witness to the court. It is common to see witnesses provide their age and describe their family and employment status and their connection to the case. Frequently, counsel will attempt to introduce their witnesses in a way that will enhance the witness's credibility. It is a question of degree when the line is crossed between permissible introduction and impermissible "bolstering." In *R. v. Clarke*, for example, that line was crossed when a police informant testified that he was allowed to leave the prison for street visits, he was studying the Bible, he attended Alcoholics Anonymous, and he had reformed his criminal ways.[4]

2. GOOD CHARACTER EVIDENCE: THE ACCUSED AS A WITNESS

By way of exception, as an indulgence to the accused in a criminal case, the accused can prove his good character in a variety of ways. Such evidence is considered relevant both to the primarily material issue of whether the accused committed the offence charged and to the secondarily material issue of the credibility of the accused as a witness.[5] The methods for presenting such evidence on the issue of credibility are identical to those available where the good character evidence is being offered to cast doubt on the guilt of the accused.[6] In particular, the testifying accused can assert their own honesty, and other witnesses can be called to testify as to the reputation of the accused for truthfulness and veracity.[7] If the accused chooses to put their character in issue in either of these ways, the Crown will be entitled to rebut the claim to good character by cross-examining the accused or character witness, or by calling other witnesses who will testify to the accused's bad reputation for trustworthiness or sincerity.

---

2   (1998), 124 C.C.C. (3d) 301 (B.C.C.A.). And see *R. v. Austin* (2006), 214 C.C.C. (3d) 38 at 47 (Ont. C.A.).

3   *R. v. Siu, ibid.*

4   (1981), 63 C.C.C. (2d) 224 (Alta. C.A.).

5   *R. v. H.(C.W.)* (1991), 68 C.C.C. (3d) 146 (B.C.C.A.).

6   See chapter 3, section 13, "Good Character Evidence and Modes of Presentation."

7   *R. v. Clarke* (1998), 18 C.R. (5th) 219 (Ont. C.A.).

3. SECONDARILY MATERIAL EXPERT EVIDENCE

A party may call an expert witness to testify about facts relevant to the credibility of one of their witnesses where those facts are likely to be beyond the experience of the trier of fact. The rule against oath-helping prevents the expert from going so far as to testify that the witness is likely to be telling the truth.

In some cases, factors relevant to the credibility of a witness are beyond the ordinary experience and understanding of lay triers of fact. Without the assistance of experts, lay triers of fact are apt to make erroneous assumptions about credibility. For example, laypersons may not appreciate that children cannot be expected to notice time and place the way that adults do, or that sexually abused children are prone to fantasize or to retract their allegations.[8] Or they may not appreciate that the professed inability to recall can be the result of hysterical amnesia.[9] Where common experience does not provide the tools needed to assess the credibility of a witness, a party will be entitled to call an expert to provide that information, even though the testimony of the expert does nothing more than support the credibility of another witness.[10]

This practice is not without its limits. The modern rule against oath-helping prevents expert witnesses from offering the opinion that a particular witness is telling the truth. The expert can provide background information relevant to the credibility of a witness, but not information directly about the credibility of what a witness is saying.[11]

4. PRIOR CONSISTENT STATEMENTS

4.1) The Rule against Proof of Previous Consistent Statements

It is generally impermissible to prove that at some time before testifying, a witness made statements consistent with her testimony. This is

---

8   See, for example, *R. v. J.(F.E.)* (1990), 74 C.R. (3d) 296 (Ont. C.A.).

9   *R. v. Clark* (1983), 35 C.R. (2d) 357 (Ont. C.A.).

10 The law was once more guarded about admitting such evidence. See, for example, *R. v. Kyselka* (1962), 37 C.R. 391 (Ont. C.A.), and *R. v. Béland (sub nom. Béland v. R.)* (1987), 60 C.R. (3d) 1 (S.C.C.).

11 See, generally, chapter 6, section 3.3, "The Rule against Oath-helping."

because such statements are usually viewed as lacking probative value and being self-serving.[12]

Prior consistent statements tend to lack probative value because the credibility of a statement is not enhanced simply because the same statement has been made before. In the words of Twaddle J.A., "Consistency is a quality just as agreeable to lies as to the truth."[13] If admitted to show that a witness is speaking honestly the evidence of prior consistent statements is therefore of no value. On the other hand, consistency can be relevant to memory. The fact that a story is told consistently with an early version can counter any suggestion that the details being provided are the inaccurate product of a faulty memory. Notwithstanding this, the potential prejudice of allowing the testimony to be repeated supports the general rule prohibiting proof of prior consistent statements. It may gain false credence in the eyes of the trier of fact through the consistency with which it is asserted.

Prior consistent statements are "self-serving" when offered to bolster the credibility of what a witness is saying by showing that the same witness said the same thing before.[14] The Crown in R. v. S.(F.) violated this rule when he read to the jury the entire statement of a testifying witness.[15]

Where the prior statement is being offered to establish the truth of what it asserts, the hearsay rule is also infringed.[16]

As a general rule, then, the content of prior statements that are consistent with the "in-court" testimony of a witness cannot be proved by the party calling that witness. The rule can even be offended where the content of a previous consistent statement is disclosed only indirectly. In R. v. Demetrius, for example, it was considered to be proof of a prior consistent statement for the Crown to show that as a result of information received from the complainant, the police went looking

---

12 R. v. Stirling, [2008] S.C.J. No. 10 at para. 5; R. v. Dinardo, [2008] S.C.J. No. 24 at para. 36.

13 R. v. L.(D.O.) (1991), 6 C.R. (4th) 277 at 309 (Man. C.A.), rev'd (1993), 25 C.R. (4th) 285 (S.C.C.).

14 "[T]he rule against self-serving evidence" seems to extend to any evidence that is intended solely to support the credibility of a witness, such as polygraph evidence: R. v. Béland, above note 10 at 38, and see R. v. Bedgood (1990), 80 C.R. (3d) 227 (N.S.C.A.).

15 R. v. S.(F.) (2000), 144 C.C.C. (3d) 466 (Ont. C.A.). The Crown should not have read the statement to the jury, even if it had otherwise been admissible. The Crown is not a witness. Where a prior statement is admissible it is the witness who should be reading it.

16 R. v. Dinardo, above note 12 at para 36.

for Demetrius as the suspect. Even though the officer did not repeat the previous conversation, it was obvious by implication that the complainant had identified Demetrius as the attacker during that conversation, consistent with what he was saying in his testimony.[17]

There are a number of exceptional cases where prior consistent statements of witnesses can be proved. Where this is permitted, the relevance of those prior consistent statements is yielded without inferring that because the witness said the same thing before, the witness is credible. Instead, the "circumstances [in which the statements are made support other kinds of inferences that] render evidence of prior consistent statements of potential significance to the trier of fact, either with respect to the credibility of the declarant/witness or with respect to a fact in issue."[18]

If prior consistent statements are proved pursuant to an exception, it will be an error in a judge alone trial to use those statements for an improper purpose,[19] or in a jury trial if the judge fails to direct the jury adequately on their proper use.[20]

4.2) Prior Consistent Statements as Circumstantial Evidence

Occasionally the fact that a statement has been made will raise relevant and permissible inferences. For example, in *R. v. Edgar*[21] the accused claimed to have a disordered mind at the time of the killing. The words spoken by the accused after the killing were nonsensical, supporting the inference that at the time his mind was in fact disordered. Although those comments included denials of guilt consistent with his testimony at trial, the defence was permitted to prove Edgar's prior consistent statements, not to show consistency, but as circumstantial evidence of his disordered mind. As will be seen, the circumstantial value of prior consistent statements is not confined to proving the state of mind of the speaker, but where they are offered for that purpose, state of mind must of course be in issue.[22]

---

17   *R. v. Demetrius* (2003), 179 C.C.C. (3d) 26 (Ont. C.A.).

18   *R. v. Toten* (1993), 83 C.C.C. (3d) 5 at 36 (Ont. C.A.).

19   *R. v. C.(S.R.)* (2004), 188 C.C.C. (3d) 239 (P.E.I.C.A.).

20   See the discussion below in this chapter, at section 4.9, "Limiting Instructions and Prior Consistent Statements."

21   (2010), 101 O.R. (3d) 161 (C.A.), leave to appeal to S.C.C. refused, [2010] S.C.C.A. No. 466.

22   *R. v. Mathisen* (2008), 242 O.A.C. 139 at para. 104 (C.A.).

4.3)   Recent Fabrication

Prior consistent statements made by a witness are not admissible to counter the simple claim that the testimony of that witness is false.[23] If an opposing party claims, however, that the testimony of a witness has been "*recently*" fabricated, prior consistent statements that serve to rebut the allegation of *recent* fabrication will be admissible. To take an easy example, if a witness testifies to a fact and is then cross-examined about her failure to include that fact in her signed witness statement, it is implicit that the cross-examiner is suggesting that the omitted fact was made up, or added, after the point in time when the witness statement was signed. Proof that the witness had asserted that omitted fact prior to writing the statement rebuts this suggestion.[24] It should be clear that the relevance of the prior consistent statement does not come from the simple fact of consistency. It is the timing of the prior consistent statement that is important. The timing of the statement demonstrates that the version testified to is not new or "recent" as was alleged. Since the prior statement rebuts the possibility of recent concoction only if it is consistent with the impugned testimony, it will typically be necessary for the contents of the prior statement to be proved.[25] Given that they depend for their relevance absolutely on their timing, prior consistent statements are capable of rebutting an allegation of recent fabrication only where they predate the point in time at which the opposing party claims the version of events was first fabricated.[26]

It is important to appreciate that statements admitted under this exception can only be used to rebut the claim of "recent" fabrication. They cannot be relied upon either as accurate statements of what happened in their own right (their hearsay purpose) or as confirming or corroborating the in-court testimony.[27] They do not, therefore, add weight to the credibility of the testimony. The prior consistent statement is simply used to knock the "recent" fabrication challenge off the scales, returning them to the balance they had prior to the "recent" fabrication challenge. This does not mean it is wrong to recognize, in cases where recent fabrication has been alleged, that proof of a prior consistent statement has, in a narrow sense, "strengthened" or "rehabilitated" or "supported" the

---

23   *R. v. McDonald* (2000), 148 C,C.C. (3d) 273 (Ont. C.A.); *R. v. Henderson* (1999), 134 C.C.C. (3d) 131 (Ont. C.A.).

24   *R. v. Kozodoy* (1957), 117 C.C.C. 315 (Ont. C.A.).

25   *R. v. Le* (2003), 16 C.R. (6th) 375 (B.C.C.A.). By contrast, where the statement is coming in as "narrative" it will frequently be enough to prove the fact that a statement was made without disclosing its content: see section 4.8, "Narrative," below in this chapter.

26   *R. v. Sark* (2004), 182 C.C.C. (3d) 530 (N.B.C.A.).

27   *R. v. Bradford* (2002), 4 C.R. (6th) 150 (Ont. C.A.).

credibility of the witness. Specifically, the prior consistent statement strengthens the testimony by removing the challenge that has been made. This leaves the evidence stronger than it would be if that challenge remained as an accurate indictment of the testimony. The prior consistent statement does nothing, however, to make the testimony stronger than it was when originally offered. The in-court version still stands on its own after the challenge has been fended off, bearing the weight it deserves in its own right. It is therefore "permissible [in this narrow way] for [the fact that a prior consistent statement has been made] to be taken into account as part of the larger assessment of credibility."[28]

The case of R. v. Stirling is illustrative. Stirling, charged as a result of a fatal collision, was defending the case by denying he was the driver. He attacked the credibility of the Crown's key witness, Harding, by suggesting that Harding only identified Stirling as the driver to advance a civil suit Harding had brought against Stirling, and in return for the Crown dropping charges against Harding. Proof that Harding identified Stirling as the driver before commencing the civil suit and before the Crown's decision to withdraw the charges against Harding rebutted these specifically alleged motivations and, in that sense, strengthened Harding's evidence by removing those alleged motives. Harding's prior consistent statements did not, however, do anything to prove affirmatively that Harding's testimony that Stirling was driving was true. As the Supreme Court of Canada put it, "The fact that Mr. Harding reported that the appellant was driving on the night of the crash before he launched the civil suit or had charges against him dropped does not in any way confirm that the evidence is not fabricated. All it tells us is that it wasn't fabricated *as a result of* the civil suit or the dropping of the criminal charges."[29]

The recent fabrication rule has long befuddled lawyers and judges. In part this is because the term "recent fabrication" is something of a misnomer.[30] First, the alleged fabrication need not be "recent" relative to the trial or hearing; it is enough if the claim is being made that the "fabrication" occurred at or around some identifiable point in time after the event being attested to.

Indeed, even the term "fabrication" is a misnomer. As the "witness statement" example used earlier demonstrates, the rule can operate to rebut the suggestion that a witness has, over time, become confused. For this reason the definition offered in R. v. O'Connor, that "recent fabrication" is "an allegation that a person has made up a false story, after the event in question, to meet the exigencies of the case,"[31] is problematic.

---

28 R. v. *Stirling*, above note 12 at para 11.
29 *Ibid.* at para. 7.
30 *Ibid.* at para 5.
31 R. v. *O'Connor* (1995), 100 C.C.C. (3d) 285 at para. 16 (Ont. C.A.).

For the most part, though, confusion springs from the failure to hold onto the underlying function served by the exception. What is being rebutted is the suggestion that something happened at or around the point in time when the "fabrication" occurred to inspire it. When an opposing party alleges that a witness created a version of events at or after a particular point in time, they will either be expressly or implicitly suggesting that it was at or around that point in time that a motive or opportunity to provide the false account arose, or that it is inherently suspicious that the witness would not have previously mentioned the fact before that time were it true. If the party who called the witness can prove that the witness had in fact said the same thing they are now testifying to before the alleged point of invention or confusion, this rebuts the underlying challenge. *R. v. Walker* is an example of how the failure to keep in mind the function of rebuttal evidence in recent fabrication cases can cause problems. Walker testified during a voluntariness *voir dire* that the police told him that if he confessed his family would not be charged. The trial judge used the recent fabrication exception to allow the defence to prove that Walker had told this to his lawyer.[32] This exception should not have been employed to admit this evidence.[33] The Crown position was that Walker began telling this lie from the time he spoke to his lawyer. Given this, proof that Walker told his lawyer did not rebut the Crown position.

Most often, the allegation of recent fabrication or concoction will be made expressly during the cross-examination of a witness. An express allegation of recent fabrication is not necessary. It is enough if "the circumstances are such as to raise the suggestion that the accused's evidence is a recent fabrication."[34] This can occur in the pleadings, as in *Welstead v. Brown*, where the defendant claimed that the appellant and his wife "schemed, connived, planned and conspired to concoct" the claim that the defendant was the father of the child that the wife had given birth to.[35] Her spontaneous statement shortly after discovering her pregnancy tended to rebut this claim. The allegation of recent fabrication can also occur during the opening statement, or it can arise from the implications of the position adopted by the opposing party.[36] For example, an allegation of recent fabrication will be implicit in the suggestion that a witness has an improper motive to mislead the court where that motivation arose subsequent to the event being testified to.[37]

---

32   *R. v. Walker*, [2000] O.J. No. 880 (S.C.J.).

33   The prior statement should have come in under the "narrative" exception discussed below in section 4.8 of this chapter, "Narrative."

34   *R. v. Campbell* (1977), 1 C.R. (3d) 309 at 325 (Ont. C.A.).

35   [1952] 1 S.C.R. 3.

36   *R. v. Simpson* (1988), 62 C.R. (3d) 137 (S.C.C.).

37   *R. v. Campbell*, above note 34.

For example, a claim that a sexual assault allegation was prompted by a custody dispute would allow evidence that the allegation predated that dispute. Similarly, in *R. v. B.(A.J.)*,[38] an allegation of recent fabrication was found to be implicit in the defence claim that the complaint was inspired by a book she had read. In fact, she had complained of the sexual assault before reading the book. The Crown was allowed to prove this sequence of events. In *R. v. H.(J.A.)*, the defence theory was that the older sister of a teenage complainant fabricated a false allegation of sexual abuse against her to bolster the credibility of the teenager's allegations. This enabled the Crown to prove that the older sister had, in fact, complained long before the teenager had.[39]

When a party wishes to rely on a claim of recent fabrication to justify the admission of a prior consistent statement, she should announce to the court that this is what she is doing.[40] In *R.(A.E.)*, the accused appealed the decision of the trial judge to admit prior consistent statements made by the complainant. During the appeal, Crown submissions that the prior consistent statements had been properly admitted under this exception were disregarded because, at the trial, the Crown had not indicated to the trial judge that this was the basis on which it was asking the questions.[41]

4.4)   Recent Complaint in Sexual Offences

At common law, the failure of a sexual offence complainant to tell someone about her alleged victimization at the first reasonable opportunity was considered to hurt the reliability of the complaint, including any claim of non-consent. Trial judges were compelled to tell jurors of this inference in any case where "recent complaint" was not shown.[42] This requirement made it essential to allow evidence that a complainant did, in fact, make a spontaneous complaint when the opportunity presented itself. Proof of such a complaint was admissible solely to neutralize any adverse inference that might arise from the failure to complain, and not as independent proof that the offence occurred.

Section 275 of the *Criminal Code* has now abrogated these rules. They were premised on unduly rigid, stereotypical, and inaccurate assumptions about how sexual offence complainants could be expected to react

---

38   (1995), 98 C.C.C. (3d) 95 (S.C.C.).
39   (1998), 124 C.C.C. (3d) 221 (B.C.C.A.).
40   *R. v. F.(J.E.)* (1993), 26 C.R. (4th) 220 at 235 (Ont. C.A.).
41   *R. v. R.(A.E.)*, [2001] O.J. No. 3222 (C.A.).
42   *R. v. Osborne*, [1905] 1 K.B. 551 (C.C.R.); *R. v. Boyce* (1974), 28 C.R.N.S. 336 (Ont. C.A.).

to a sexual assault. As a result of section 275, it is now an error to use the failure to complain as a basis for a *presumptive adverse inference* relating to credibility or consent.[43] In the words of Justice Major in *R. v. D.(D.)*, "a delay in disclosure, standing alone, will never give rise to an adverse inference against the credibility of the complainant."[44] This does not mean that proof relating to a delay in complaining will necessarily be irrelevant and inadmissible.[45] There may be circumstances in the particular case that make it reasonable to expect that had the sexual assault occurred, the complainant would have said so earlier.[46] Where this is so, it remains proper to cross-examine the complainant about the failure to make a timely complaint. This, of course, opens the door to proof that she did complain. If made, the prior complaint comes in to negate the adverse inferences the defence sought to draw from delay, but again, it is not to be treated as positive proof that the testimony about the assault is rendered credible by the earlier allegation.[47] Despite the abrogation of the "recent complaint rule," then, recent complaints may be admissible,[48] either in this way or pursuant to other exceptions to the rule against prior consistent statements,[49] such as where recent fabrication is asserted,[50] or as part of the narrative, or pursuant to the *res gestae* or other hearsay exceptions.

4.5) Prior Consistent Admissible Hearsay

Where a prior consistent statement is found in otherwise admissible hearsay it can be proved. Because it falls within a hearsay exception, it is admissible as proof of the truth of its contents and can also be relied upon to support the credibility of the witness. Such is the case with the prior identification of persons[51] and business records.[52] This is also true where a statement meets the requirements of the case-by-case hearsay exception developed in *R. v. Khan*.[53] It is true as well with the "*res gestae*" hearsay exceptions. Although the term "*res gestae*" is

---

43   *R. v. M.(P.S.)* (1992), 77 C.C.C. (3d) 402 (Ont. C.A.).
44   *R. v. D.(D.)*, [2000] S.C.R. 275 at para. 63.
45   *R. v. Hughes* (2001), 156 C.C.C. (3d) 206 at para. 44 (B.C.C.A.).
46   *R. v. Bradford*, above note 27.
47   *Ibid.*
48   *R. v. D.(D.)*, above note 44 at para. 65.
49   *R. v. Hughes*, above note 45.
50   *R. v. Owens* (1986), 55 C.R. (3d) 386 (Ont. C.A.).
51   See chapter 5, section 3, "Prior Identifications."
52   *R. v. Anthes Business Forms Ltd.* (1974), 19 C.C.C. (2d) 394 (Ont. H.C.J.), aff'd (1975), 26 C.C.C. (2d) 349 (Ont. C.A.), aff'd [1978] 1 S.C.R. 970.
53   (1990), 79 C.R. (3d) 1 (S.C.C.). See, for example, *R. v. Pearson* (1994), 36 C.R. (4th) 343 (B.C.C.A.), where this exception was used to allow the prior com-

notoriously imprecise, it is generally understood to refer to "the facts surrounding or accompanying the transaction."[54] *Res gestae* exceptions include "excited utterances," "statements of present physical condition," "statements of present mental state," and "statements of present sense impression."[55] As is the case with evidence admitted under other hearsay exceptions, where the person who made a statement satisfying a *res gestae* exception is a witness in the proceedings, the *res gestae* statement can be used both as independent proof of the facts the statement asserts, and as evidence bolstering the credibility of the maker of the statement as a witness in the proceedings.[56]

There is no inconsistency between the general proposition that prior consistency is not evidence of truthfulness, and permitting prior consistent statements contained in admissible hearsay to be used to bolster the credibility of the maker of the statement. This is because in order to gain admissibility as hearsay, there will necessarily be some circumstances in the making of the statement that provide some indicia of reliability. The out-of-court statement therefore bears some independent stamp of reliability not generally present in the in-court testimony, which can thereby bolster the credibility of the testimony itself.

4.6)   Statements Made When Found in Possession

The *res gestae* label has also been used to allow statements made by accused persons found in possession of stolen goods[57] or illegal drugs[58] to be admitted, apparently to prove the truth of their contents.[59] The *res* of these offences, consists of the act of possession. The offence is therefore still continuing at the time that the accused person is found

---

plaints of a mentally disabled complainant to be admitted to prove the truth of their contents.

54   The term "*res gestae*" is, therefore, sometimes treated as synonymous with the term "narrative" described in chapter 2, section 6, "Relevance, Materiality, and Narration."

55   See chapter 5, section 10, "Spontaneous Statements (*Res Gestae*)."

56   In *R. v. Page* (1984), 40 C.R. (3d) 85 at 92 (Ont. H.C.J.), Ewaschuk J. would have allowed a prior complaint to be related if "the complaint was a true result of nervous excitement so as to still the complainant's reflective faculties and remove their control." Cited with approval, *R. v. Owens*, above note 50 at 389.

57   *R. v. Graham* (1974), 19 C.R.N.S. 117 (S.C.C.).

58   *R. v. Risby* (1976), 32 C.C.C. (2d) 242 (B.C.C.A.), aff'd [1978] 2 S.C.R. 139.

59   In *R. v. Graham*, above note 57, the majority described the evidence as admissible but suggested that it could be relied upon as proof of the truth of its contents solely where it becomes part of the Crown case. In other situations, the accused must testify and the relevance of the statement lies in its consistency with the testimony. In *R. v. Risby*, *ibid.*, however, no such limit was imposed.

with the items. Hence, statements made at that time occur during the transaction being inquired into.

These cases are problematic because the statements come in to prove the truth of their contents, just as excited utterances or "spontaneous statements" do. In the case of excited utterances, however, the assurance of trustworthiness is understood to arise not because the statements are contemporaneous with the event, but because they were forced from the speaker by the pressure of the moment before the prospect of concoction can realistically arise. The speaker is too caught up in the startling event to have the time for reflection necessary to make a false statement. By contrast, the rule permitting statements made when found in possession to be admitted for their truth does not require proof that the speaker was overwhelmed by the pressure of the moment. The fact that the statements are made on being found in possession is enough, even though the first instinct of someone found in possession of contraband would likely be to deny knowledge or ownership.

The possession exceptions have been explained on the basis that admission is intended to forestall the inference that it would have been natural, if possession was innocent, for the possessor to explain himself when the possession was discovered.[60] In this sense it is like the recent fabrication exception to the bar on proving prior consistent statements. Yet, statements coming in to rebut recent fabrication are not admissible to prove the truth of their contents. They simply rebut the suggestion of recent fabrication. Moreover, it has been pointed out that it would violate the constitutional right of the accused to remain silent to expect an explanation from him when he is found by the authorities in possession of contraband.[61] Despite its difficulties, the case law allowing for the admission of these statements is secure because it is of the highest authority.

4.7) Exculpatory Statements Made on Arrest

In *R. v Edgar* the Ontario Court of Appeal recently accepted that any "spontaneous out-of-court statements made upon arrest when first taxed with an accusation" can be proved by way of exception to the rule against prior consistent statements where the accused testifies.[62] Provided the accused testifies and exposes themselves to cross-examination, such statements can be proved by the accused or by other witnesses, regard-

---

60 A.W. Bryant, S.N. Lederman, & M. Fuerst, *The Law of Evidence in Canada*, 3d ed. (Markham, ON: LexisNexis, 2009) at para. 7.37.

61 See chapter 8, section 5.2, "Where the Accused Does Remain Silent."

62 Above note 21 at para. 72.

less of the charge.[63] They come in to prove "the reaction of the accused, which is relevant to credibility of the accused [due to spontaneity] and as circumstantial evidence having a bearing on guilt or innocence [given that the accused acted consistently with how one would expect innocent persons to behave]."[64] The court took a generous view of spontaneity, ruling that the exception would capture a series of statements, including one made approximately four hours after arrest.

The holding in *Edgar* is controversial. Although there was prior Supreme Court of Canada *obiter dictum* supporting the admission of exculpatory statements made on arrest,[65] the received view in Canada was that such statements are generally inadmissible.[66] *Edgar* rejected this conventional position because, using a principled approach, defence evidence should not be excluded unless prejudice substantially outweighs its probative value. Applying this calculus the court accepted that spontaneous denials of guilt can have significant probative value yet their admission raises little risk of prejudice.

There are issues that can be taken with the *Edgar* court's reasoning. First, its conclusion that denials of guilt can have significant probative value is open to debate. It is probable that both the guilty and innocent alike are apt to deny guilt when apprehended.[67] More importantly, given the right to silence, it is contrary to law for triers of fact to infer guilt from silence. It is therefore problematic that the court grounded relevance for the purposes of admissibility, in part, on the footing that denials of guilt can be useful in rebutting inferences of guilt from silence.[68] The conventional way to prevent improper inferences is to enforce legal rules preventing them, not to use the risk of improper inferences as a gateway to admissibility. Treating a denial of guilt as relevant also sug-

---

63 If this holding comes to be broadly accepted, it will subsume the "Statements Made When Found in Possession" exception.

64 Above note 21 at para. 72. In *Edgar* the circumstances made the failure of the trial judge to permit proof of these prior consistent statements under this exception a harmless error.

65 *Lucas v. R.* (1962), 39 C.R. 101 (S.C.C.).

66 *R. v. Campbell*, above note 34; *R. v. Terceira* (1998), 15 C.R. (5th) 359 (Ont. C.A.), aff'd on other grounds [1999] 3 S.C.R. 866.

67 In *R. v. Bhadwar*, [2011] O.J. No. 1541 (C.A.), the court found little probative value in such evidence in the circumstances of that case. The accused knew for five hours that he was going to be arrested, so the response was not sufficiently "spontaneous." The jury heard the denials of guilt by the accused in his testimony and because the Crown cross-examined the accused without suggesting there was anything of value to the Crown in a statement the jury learned the accused had made, there was little to be gained by proof that the accused had denied his guilt in that statement.

68 Above note 21 at para. 63.

gests that the failure to deny guilt may be indicative of guilt. This not only provides a modest basis for challenging the right to silence, but it also raises concerns in joint trials where only one accused has chosen to speak to the police upon arrest. Most significantly, the reasoning in *Edgar* draws into question the law's overall approach to prior consistent statements. The *Edgar* court found their admission to raise little risk of prejudice. It also took a generous view of their probative value by drawing inferences of credibility based on the spontaneity of an individual's factual claim, and based on theories about the circumstances in which individuals are likely to make truthful disclosures. While the court was speaking in the context of exculpatory statements made on arrest, similar kinds of reasoning can be applied with equal force to other kinds of prior consistent statements. Finally, the *Edgar* court justified admission on the basis that the speaker must testify and can therefore be cross-examined about the truthfulness of the prior consistent statement. This, of course, is true by definition for all prior consistent statements. In its attempt to protect the innocent *Edgar* could open the door to the more generous admission of inculpatory prior consistent statements. This may not be a bad thing. The point is that the implications of the *Edgar* decision remain to be seen. If it becomes settled law, the case could prove far more significant than it may seem at first blush.

4.8)   Narrative

4.8 (a)   Pure Narrative

In some cases *res gestae* statements will be admitted, although not to prove the truth of their contents. These statements form "part of the story," but fail to satisfy any of the hearsay exceptions. It may nonetheless be necessary to admit them in order to unfold the "narrative" properly. For example, in *R. v. George*,[69] it was permissible for the Crown to show that when confronted by his cousin's parents, the accused admitted that he had forced himself on his cousin. This confrontation would have made no sense to the jury unless they learned that the reason why the parents confronted the accused was because their daughter was complaining about having been sexually assaulted by him. Hence, the complaint, without its details, was admissible, but solely as background. It could not be used to support the inference that the complainant was more credible because of the prior consistent statement or to prove the truth of the complaint. Nor can such statements be used for their hearsay purpose as proof of what they allege.[70] Where it appears that

---

69   (1985), 23 C.C.C. (3d) 42 (B.C.C.A.).
70   *Ibid.*; *R. v. Jones* (1988), 66 C.R. (3d) 54 (Ont. C.A.).

a judge[71] or jury[72] may have used the contents of a statement admitted under the narrative exception to corroborate or confirm the complainant's testimony at trial, a conviction may have to be set aside.[73]

"Narrative" has become a common technique for presenting evidence about previous complaints by sexual assault complainants, particularly children. In *R. v. F.(J.E.)*,[74] the Ontario Court of Appeal was of the view that the trier of fact must have the "chronological cohesion" of a full account in order to understand the case. If they are not provided with that chronological cohesion, the story will unfold unnaturally, with distracting gaps. For example, in a case of ongoing sexual abuse, the trier needs to learn when the complainant recounted the assaults, how the assaults came to be terminated, and how the matter came to the attention of the police.

> To qualify as narrative, the witness must recount relevant and *essential* facts which describe and explain his or her experience as a victim of the crime alleged so that the trier of fact will be in a position to understand what happened and how the matter came to the attention of the proper authorities.[75]

Two important things are clear from this line of authority. First, when it is being done on a pure narrative basis, the doctrine of narrative should be used to reveal the existence of prior statements solely where it is necessary to do so. If those statements have no impact on the unfolding of events, they should not be referred to.[76] Second, only so much detail as is necessary to provide a comprehensible narration of events should be provided. Indeed, it has been said that "evidence of the prior consistent statements should only be described in general terms and should not contain much detail as details of the statement would invite the trier of fact to conclude that the witness must be telling the truth by reason of the apparent consistency with the witness' testimony."[77] "Narration" does not open the door to the repetition in court of all that is said out of court.[78]

---

71   *R. v. L.(S.)* (1999), 141 C.C.C. (3d) 93 (Ont. C.A.).
72   *R. v. R.(A.E.)*, above note 41.
73   *R. v. Dinardo*, above note 12 at para. 40.
74   Above note 40.
75   *Ibid.* at 241 [emphasis added].
76   *R. v. Hoffman* (1994), 32 C.R. (4th) 396 (Alta. C.A.); *R. v. R.(A.E.)*, above note 41 at para. 15.
77   *R. v. R.(A.E)*, *ibid.* at para. 15.
78   In *R. v. Jones*, above note 70 at 62, the background could have been explored by simply relating that "as the result of information she received from her daughter on the Wednesday [four days after the alleged event] she [the mother] contacted

It has been observed, however, that where the fact that a prior consistent statement was made is properly adduced, the accused may, if he chooses, explore the details of the complaint, although he does so at his peril. What exactly is the peril? The view has been expressed that where the details are revealed during cross-examination, the trier of fact can use them to bolster the complainant's credibility if those details prove to be consistent with her testimony.[79] With respect, this is problematic. Cross-examination should not make it permissible for triers of fact to accept the illogical inference that consistency supports credibility. The peril should be no more than the tactical one that by revealing details in cross-examination, the accused increases the risk that triers of fact could reason impermissibly by assuming that consistency confirms honesty.

4.8 (b)   Narrative as Circumstantial Evidence

There are cases where the narration of a prior consistent complaint also yields circumstantial evidence. This is why in R. v. F.(J.E) the court had continued the above quoted passage by observing:

> . . . *The fact that the statements were made* is admissible to assist the jury as to the sequence of events from the alleged offence to the prosecution so that they can understand the conduct of the complainant *and assess her truthfulness.*[80]

In effect, where the fact that a complaint was made is helpful to the trier of fact in assessing the credibility of the complainant on some basis other than the theory that consistency supports credibility, the trier of fact is entitled to take this into account.

For example, the narrative may reveal that the complainant "disclosed" the abuse only after the alleged abuser was removed from her environment. The fact and timing of the complaint in such circumstances could assist in rejecting challenges to credibility relating to any delay in reporting. In R. v. Dinardo, evidence showed the mentally challenged sexual assault complainant had difficulty situating events in time, was easily confused, and lied on occasion. The Supreme Court of Canada recognized in light of this that the "spontaneous nature of the initial complaint and the complainant's repetition of the essential elements of the allegation provide[d] important context for assessing her

---

the police." See *R. v. Albert* (1993), 19 C.R. (4th) 322 (Ont. C.A.), and *R. v. Ay* (1994), 93 C.C.C. (3d) 456 (B.C.C.A.).

79   *R. v. B.(D.C.)* (1994), 32 C.R. (4th) 91 at 99 (Man. C.A.).

80   *R. v. F.(J.E.),* above note 40 at 241 [emphasis added].

credibility."[81] In essence, the spontaneous and repetitive way the prior consistent statements were made was to be considered in evaluating whether the complainant was having trouble situating the alleged event in time, or whether she was confused about what happened. Where narrative of how a complaint came forward can logically support such inferences, it will be appropriate to provide the details necessary to support the permissible circumstantial inference.

This distinction between "using narrative evidence for the impermissible purpose of 'confirm[ing] truthfulness of the sworn allegation' and 'using narrative evidence for the permissible purpose of showing the fact and timing of a complaint, which may then *assist the trier of fact in the assessment* of truthfulness or credibility'" is a subtle but important one.[82] Bear in mind that what can be relied upon is the timing and circumstances in which the prior consistent statement was made, rather than the simple fact that the witness has said the same thing before.

4.9) Limiting Instructions and Prior Consistent Statements

Where evidence of a prior consistent statement is admitted under any of the exceptions to the general rule, "it is crucial [in most cases] that the trial judge provide a limiting instruction to [a] jury regarding the use it can make of the evidence."[83] A limiting instruction to a jury should (1) explain that prior consistent evidence cannot be used to enhance the credibility of the person making the statement since evidence does not become more credible because it has been repeated, (2) direct the jury not to use the evidence for its hearsay purpose,[84] and (3) describe any legitimate purpose for which it was admitted. As can be seen in the foregoing discussion, the legitimate use varies depending upon the exception being invoked and the circumstances of the case.

There are cases where a limiting instruction will not be required. No such direction is needed where the appropriate, limited use to which the statement should be put would be obvious to the jury,[85] or where the contents of the statement would not be helpful to the Crown,[86] or

---

81   R. v. Dinardo, above note 12 at para 39.
82   Ibid. at para 37.
83   R. v. R.(A.E.), above note 41, and see R. v. W.(A.W.), [2001] A.J. No. 347 (C.A.).
84   R. v. Austin, above note 2.
85   See the cases referred to in R. v. R.(A.E.), above note 41 and R. v. W.(A.W.), above note 83; and R. v. Clark (1995), 87 O.A.C. 178 (C.A.).
86   R. v. Johnson (2002), 166 C.C.C. (3d) 44 at paras. 55–56 (Ont. C.A.).

where the defence relies on proof of the prior consistent statement.[87] It has also been held that a limiting instruction is not required where it is clear that the prior statement was not offered as proof of what it asserts,[88] but this exception should be strictly limited to cases where the only concern is with the possible hearsay use of the prior statement. This is because there will typically be other prohibited uses that need to be addressed. For example, in most cases it is impermissible to use the prior consistent statement for the non-hearsay purpose of bolstering the in-court testimony, based on the consistency with which the story is being told.[89] A limiting instruction should not be dispensed with, therefore, unless none of the material dangers presented by prior consistent statements are present.

5. REHABILITATING THE CREDIBILITY OF YOUR OWN WITNESS

Where opposing counsel has attacked the general credibility of a witness, counsel may use approved techniques in an effort to re-habilitate that credibility. Those techniques include re-examination of the witness who has been attacked, calling evidence about the positive reputation of the witness for trustworthiness, or calling witnesses to negate or weaken expert testimony by opposing counsel relating to the hidden defects said to affect the witness.

5.1)   Relevance and Methods of Rehabilitation

Although a party cannot generally call evidence to bolster the credibility of her own witnesses, opposing counsel can open the door, allowing this to be done. As indicated, an allegation of recent fabrication can lead to proof of a previous consistent statement. The door to proof of general credibility is opened more broadly where opposing counsel makes the credibility of the witness (as opposed to the credibility of the specific testimony the witness has provided) an issue. The techniques available to opposing counsel to do so include proving the prior convictions of the witness, calling reputation or perhaps even lay opinion evidence relating to the lack of trustworthiness of the witness, calling

---

87   *R. v. Demetrius*, above note 17.
88   *Ibid.*, citing *R. v. M.(G.)*, [2000] O.J. No. 5007 (C.A.).
89   See *R. v. Divitaris* (2004), 188 C.C.C. (3d) 390 (Ont. C.A.), for example.

expert opinion evidence about the witness's hidden defects, and cross-examining him about his discreditable acts or associations.[90]

The "approved" techniques for establishing or challenging credibility are all intended to be efficient methods of proof for dealing with the issue of the credibility of a witness, once that issue has been raised. They are designed to keep the trial from becoming prolonged by detailed excursions into distracting side issues relating to the credibility of each witness. Proof by other witnesses of the specific acts of a witness indicative of credibility or a lack thereof is therefore not allowed.

While opposing counsel can cross-examine a witness about her past, specific discreditable conduct, or associations, those are collateral facts. If the witness does not admit to the suggested facts, opposing counsel is "stuck" with the answers.[91] There is therefore no evidence to rebut. If the witness admits to the suggested discreditable facts, counsel can clarify those facts in re-examination to cast them in a more benign light. Or counsel can call reputation witnesses. Counsel cannot, however, call other witnesses to the discreditable events that were admitted to.

5.2)   Softening Anticipated Evidentiary Blows

When a witness has been convicted of an offence, it is appropriate for the party who has called that witness to ask about this conviction during the evidence in chief, when the question is not being raised to impeach the witness. This allows counsel to present the witness as though there is nothing to hide, rather than allowing opposing counsel to enjoy the dramatic revelation that the witness is a criminal. Even when the accused is the witness, counsel is not considered to have placed the character of the accused into issue by asking him about his record.[92]

This kind of strategy is not confined to the criminal records of one's own witnesses. In *R. v. Thresh*[93] the Quebec Court of Appeal concluded that where it is reasonably anticipated that any fact will be presented during cross-examination to impeach one's witness, a party has the right to dull that attack by presenting the evidence during examination in chief. In *Thresh* the Crown pre-empted the defence by revealing the deal it had made with one of its witnesses to secure his testimony.

---

90   See chapter 10, section 6.5, "The Collateral Facts Rule" and section 6.6, "Cross-examination on Prior Convictions."

91   Conviction for offences is an exception. The Evidence Acts allow them to be proved, despite the fact that they are collateral, when a witness denies them. See chapter 10, section 6.6, "Cross-examination on Prior Convictions."

92   *R. v. St. Pierre* (1974), 17 C.C.C. (2d) 489 (Ont. C.A.).

93   (2003), 17 C.R. (6th) 326 (Que. C.A.).

6. CHALLENGING THE CREDIBILITY OF YOUR OWN WITNESS

A witness is "hostile" when he does not wish to tell the truth because of a motive to harm the party who has called him, or to assist the opposing party. A witness is "adverse" if the evidence he gives is unfavourable, or opposed in interest, to the party who has called him.

With the leave of the court, a party can cross-examine his own "hostile" witness. The precise scope of permissible cross-examination is not entirely settled. There are those who believe it should be confined to questions intended to discredit the testimony the hostile witness has given, and should not be used to try to get the witness to furnish substantive information that he would not furnish when being examined in chief. We disagree with this view. In our opinion, cross-examination of a hostile witness should include questions designed either to show that any harmful evidence given by that witness is not credible, or to attempt to persuade the witness to furnish evidence helpful to the party who called him.

Even if a witness is not hostile, with leave of the court a party can cross-examine him if that witness is "adverse" under the applicable Evidence Act. Again, there are those who maintain that cross-examination of an adverse witness should be restricted to questions intended to discredit the testimony that has been given, and others who believe that it should be even more confined, limited to questions about prior inconsistent statements made by the adverse witness. It is our view that neither restriction is appropriate. The cross-examination of adverse witnesses should entail any questions that challenge the evidence given by the witness or any questions intended to provoke the witness into furnishing positive testimony helpful to the party who called him.

For cases falling under the Canada Evidence Act there is yet a third path to cross-examining one's own witness, this time without the need for either a declaration of hostility or adversity. Where the witness has made a previous statement inconsistent with his testimony, the judge can grant counsel leave under subsection 9(2) to cross-examine the witness, but only about that statement. This can be done without declaring the witness adverse or hostile, provided the previous inconsistent statement was made in, or reduced to, writing, or recorded on audiotape or videotape. In addition to cross-examining the witness about that statement, counsel can prove that it was made.

Where the previous inconsistent statement is oral or where the case is covered by a provincial evidence statute, a court must

declare the witness "adverse" before allowing the previous incon-
sistent statement to be proved. In deciding whether the witness is
adverse, the previous inconsistent statement can be considered.

Counsel should attempt to refresh the memory of the witness
using appropriate techniques before seeking leave to cross-examine
the witness or to prove his previous inconsistent statements.

Under no circumstances can the party who has called a witness
attack the general credibility of that witness by leading evidence or
asking questions for the purpose of demonstrating that he is not the
kind of person who should be believed.

The common law has long taken the position that a party who calls a
witness holds that witness out as worthy of belief. As a result, if the
witness disappoints the party who called her, the law does not allow
that party to attempt to show that the witness is not a credible person. There are even strict limits on the ability of the party calling a
witness to attempt to challenge the witness in an effort to get her to
produce helpful evidence, or to neutralize any damaging testimony she
has given. These rules require reconsideration. Functionally, they are
confusing and contradictory. There is uncertainty about how the various rules fit together. From a policy perspective, the rules together may
be too restrictive.

6.1) General Attacks on Credibility

Because counsel implicitly "vouches for" the witnesses she calls, it is
never appropriate for her to attempt to challenge her own witness by
calling reputation evidence about his lack of trustworthiness, by using
his criminal record to discredit him, or by cross-examining him about
his previous discreditable acts or associations. Each of the Evidence
Acts confirms the common law by providing that "[a] party producing a
witness shall not be allowed to impeach his credit by general evidence
of bad character."[94] This does not mean that a party is bound to accept
everything its witnesses say, or to refrain from referring to things that
are established in the evidence that diminish the credibility or reliability of their witness. For example, in *R. v. Biniaris*, a Crown witness, who
was a friend of the accused, seemed anxious to accept any suggestion
being made by defence counsel during cross-examination. No error was
committed when the Crown pointed this out during submissions.[95]

---

94   See, for example, *Canada Evidence Act*, s. 9(1).
95   (1998), 124 C.C.C. (3d) 58 (B.C.C.A.), overturned on other grounds, [2000] 1
S.C.R. 381, and see *R. v. Walker* (1994), 90 C.C.C. (3d) 144 (Ont. C.A).

6.2) Calling Other Witnesses Who Contradict Your Witness

One way to attempt to neutralize the evidence of one of your own witnesses is to call other witnesses who provide a different and more helpful account. There is no limit on your ability to do so. For example, you can call two witnesses to an accident, even though one believes the car was green and the other, black. You can also ask the trier of fact to prefer the testimony of one where there is some basis for doing so.

This seemingly self-evident point is worth mentioning because of a potentially misleading provision in the *Canada Evidence Act* which has been carried into some of the provincial statutes.[96] Subsection 9(1) provides, in relevant part, that if the witness produced by a party "in the opinion of the court, proves adverse, the party may contradict him by other evidence." On its face, this suggests that before contradicting him by other evidence, it is necessary to have the court declare him "adverse." Fortunately, this apparent requirement is simply ignored as a drafting blunder.[97]

6.3) Leading Questions and Refreshing Memory

Where a witness is disappointing counsel by failing to provide expected testimony and this appears to be because he has forgotten, the techniques for refreshing memory, including asking leading questions with the leave of the court, may be of assistance.[98] In *R. v. Glowatski*,[99] after being presented with a statement that recorded his past recollection, a reluctant Crown witness adopted the accuracy of some of what he told the police. While these techniques should only be used where there is a foundation for concluding that "memory" problems may account for the failure of the witness to testify as expected, a judge has a discretion to require that counsel attempt these techniques before moving to the more invasive methods of trying to prove that the witness has previously made inconsistent statements or by attempting to cross-examine the witness.[100]

---

96 British Columbia, *Evidence Act*, s. 16; New Brunswick, *Evidence Act*, s. 17; Newfoundland and Labrador, *Evidence Act*, s. 10; Nova Scotia, *Evidence Act*, s. 55; Saskatchewan, *The Evidence Act*, s. 38.

97 *Greenough v. Eccles* (1859), 141 E.R. 315 at 353, dealing with the equivalent section.

98 See chapter 10, section 4.2 (b), "'Leading' Questions," and section 5.3, "[Refreshing Memory] During Trial."

99 (2001), 47 C.R. (5th) 230 at para. 38 (B.C.C.A.).

100 *Stewart v. R.*, [1977] 2 S.C.R. 748.

6.4) Cross-examination of One's Own Witness

Although generally a party cannot cross-examine her own witness there are rules that allow this to be done in some cases. Each of those rules, described immediately below, require the party to first obtain a formal ruling from the trial judge permitting cross-examination to occur. Unless a formal ruling has been made after the proper application of the relevant test, it is an error of law for the trial judge to permit such cross-examination.[101]

6.4 (a) The Hostile Witness

At common law, a court has the power to grant leave to a party to cross-examine their own witness when that witness is "hostile." A witness is hostile when he does not give his "evidence fairly and with a desire to tell the truth because of a hostile animus towards" the party who called him.[102] In essence, there is something motivating the witness to withhold or colour inappropriately his evidence. It is not necessary for a party to establish what this motivation is. The judge must simply be satisfied that some hostile animus exists, based on his demeanour, his general attitude, and the substance of his evidence. For example, in R. v. Haughton (No. 3),[103] a witness who had identified the accused at the preliminary inquiry was declared hostile after failing to identify him at the trial. His hostility was apparent from his failure to tell the Crown before he took the stand of his claimed belief that he had misidentified the accused at the preliminary inquiry, and from the unconvincing explanation he gave as to why he knew immediately after the preliminary inquiry that he had identified the wrong man. All too often Crown witnesses are "hostile" simply because of fear, whether reasonably held or not.

Some of the authority on hostility is quite grudging. Older case law suggested that the hostility has to be revealed through the demeanour and attitude of the witness, although this seems unduly rigid. It would mean that a witness who lies politely cannot be cross-examined, but one who bristles can be. The distorting shadow of this authority can be seen in R. v. Malik[104] where the trial judge presiding over the Air India bombing trial held that hostility is more than an interest at variance with the Crown's, but rests in an animus *against* the Crown. It appears that since Mr. Reyat's motivation for not co-operating was not animus against the

---

101 See *R. v. Rose* (2001), 153 C.C.C. (3d) 225 (Ont. C.A.); *R. v. Szpala* (1998), 124 C.C.C. (3d) 430 (Ont. C.A.); *R. v. Nicholson* (1998), 129 C.C.C. (3d) 198 (Alta. C.A.).
102 *Reference re R. v. Coffin* (1956), 23 C.R. 1 at 20 (S.C.C).
103 (1982), 38 O.R. (2d) 536 (Co. Ct.).
104 (2003), 194 C.C.C. (3d) 572 (B.C.S.C.).

Crown, but rather self-preservation by minimizing his criminal conduct, the judge declined to declare him to be hostile. With respect, if Mr. Reyat was not giving his evidence fairly because he preferred some interest in opposition to the Crown case, he should be treated as hostile regardless of his motive. After all, one of the purposes of the procedure is to provoke accurate or complete information; where examination in chief is incapable of steering a path to such evidence because a witness is not co-operating, cross-examination should be available.

6.4 (b)   The "Adverse" Witness

The common law authority to cross-examine one's own witness has been supplemented by an independent gateway to cross-examination, furnished by a perplexingly broad interpretation of subsection 9(1) of the *Canada Evidence Act*. This section does not mention the ability to cross-examine one's own witness.[105] Still, it is all but settled that if a party obtains a declaration that a witness is "adverse" under subsection 9(1), the judge can grant leave to cross-examine that witness. For example, the Ontario Court of Appeal has interpreted that section as conferring such authority in *R. v. Soobrian*,[106] as has the British Columbia Court of Appeal in *R. v. T.(T.E.)*.[107]

A witness is adverse when he is "unfavourable in the sense of assuming by his testimony a position opposite to that of the party calling him."[108] The mere existence of a material inconsistency between the earlier statement and the testimony may therefore be enough.[109] Depending on the facts, adversity can even be inferred from the "tenor of [the] evidence and inconsistencies between it and other . . . statements," made by the witness, without proof of material, inconsistent statements,[110] and without there being a hostile animus. In deciding whether a witness is adverse a court will want to consider, among other things, the demeanour and attitude of the witness, how credible the witness is, how material any inconsistencies are, and the circumstances in which they were made.[111]

---

105   See *R. v. Vivar*, [2004] O.J. No. 9 (S.C.J.), where a trial judge relied on this to reject the submission that s. 9(1) allows for cross-examination. This decision, while a compelling example of statutory interpretation, is out of the mainstream.

106   (1994), 96 C.C.C. (3d) 208 at 217 (Ont. C.A.).

107   (1991), 3 B.C.A.C. 29 at 34 (C.A.).

108   *R. v. Cassibo* (1982), 70 C.C.C. (3d) 498 at 514 (Ont. C.A.).

109   *Hanes v. Wawanesa Mutual Insurance Co. (sub nom. Wawanesa Mutual Insurance Co. v. Hanes)*, [1963] 1 C.C.C. 176 (Ont. C.A.), dealing with what is now s. 23 of the Ontario *Evidence Act*, and see *R. v. Cassibo, ibid.*

110   *R. v. Johnson*, above note 86.

111   *R. v. T.(T.E.)*, above note 107.

It is evident that the "adversity" pathway to cross-examination under subsection 9(1) is so broad as to render the more grudging common law declaration of hostility all but obsolete; it is probably the case that any hostile witness will be adverse, but not all adverse witnesses will be hostile, making the more challenging hostility declaration pointless.[112] As a result, in *R. v. Ethier*[113] the trial judge held that "adversity" must be interpreted differently depending upon whether the applicant wants to cross-examine or simply prove a prior inconsistent statement; where cross-examination is the goal, "adversity" should be interpreted to mean "hostility." Even though this approach preserves a role for the common law, it is unattractive for it means interpreting the same word in the same statute differently depending on context. Still, the decision exposes the problem with using subsection 9(1) to confer cross-examination rights.

In truth, the idea that subsection 9(1) deals with cross-examination may have resulted from confusion caused by the decision of Canadian courts that "adverse" as used in the Evidence Acts is a broader concept than common law hostility.[114] Properly understood, those decisions simply say that to get access to the statutory right to prove the previous inconsistent statements of one's own witness, counsel need not demonstrate hostility. Simple adversity is enough. Those cases do not say that the common law right to cross-examine hostile witnesses has been subsumed in the concept of adversity. Be that as it may, absent a contrary ruling from the Supreme Court of Canada, subsection 9(1) will continue to be treated as giving courts authority to allow cross-examination.

6.4 (c)   Adversity and Provincial Evidence Acts

The Evidence Acts of some provinces provide explicitly that a finding of adversity enables a court to permit counsel to cross-examine her own witness.[115] For those provincial statutes that do not, it is likely that the approach taken under subsection 9(1) applies equally to the provincial

---

112   There would be modest but continued room for the common law declaration of hostility if s. 9 cross-examination were to be confined to cases where the witness has furnished previous inconsistent statements. This is because it is possible for a witness to be hostile based on his manner during testimony, even if he has never made inconsistent statements. This was the approach taken in *R. v. Malik*, above note 104.

113   (2005), 197 C.C.C. (3d) 435 (Ont. S.C.J.).

114   See *Wawanesa Mutual Insurance Co. v. Hanes*, above note 109, rejecting the English position that "adverse" means "hostile" under the equivalent statute.

115   *Manitoba Evidence Act*, s. 19; Northwest Territories, *Evidence Act*, s. 28; Yukon Territory, *Evidence Act*, s. 27.

equivalent sections, and that they confer authority on judges to give leave to cross-examine.[116] This was the interpretation given to section 26(2) of the *Alberta Evidence Act* in *Page v. Morrison*.[117]

6.4 (d)   Special Statutory Provisions

In some cases, rules of practice applicable in civil cases may allow a party to cross-examine witnesses that he has called, without a declaration of adversity. For example, rule 53.07 of the *Rules of Civil Procedure*[118] of Ontario permits a party to call the adverse party, or a partner or corporate officer of an adverse party, and then to cross-examine them. Where rule 53.07 applies, it is the opposing party who is forbidden to cross-examine that witness because, although called by the other side, that witness is naturally favourable to the opposing party.[119]

6.4 (e)   Leave to Cross-examine

Regardless of the source of the authority, judges have the discretion to determine whether cross-examination will be allowed. Even if a witness is hostile or adverse, permission may be refused in whole or in part. For example, in *R. v. D.(C.)* the Crown was denied the right to cross-examine a witness using prior statements because they had been unfairly obtained.[120] Even the purpose for which the Crown wishes to cross-examine is material.[121] A court may refuse to give leave to the Crown to cross-examine an adverse or even hostile witness if the Crown's sole purpose in doing so is to confront the witness with prejudicial information it knows the witness will deny, as an indirect way of letting a jury know that this technically inadmissible information exists.[122]

---

116 *Alberta Evidence Act*, s. 26; British Columbia, *Evidence Act*, s. 16; New Brunswick, *Evidence Act*, s. 17; Newfoundland and Labrador, *Evidence Act*, s. 10; Nova Scotia, *Evidence Act*, s. 55; Ontario, *Evidence Act*, s. 23; Prince Edward Island, *Evidence Act*, s. 15; Saskatchewan, *The Evidence Act*, s. 38.

117 *Page v. Morrison*, [1999] A.J. No. 379 (C.A.).

118 Ontario, *Rules of Civil Procedure*, R.R.O. 1990, Reg. 194, r. 53.07.

119 *Whiten v. Pilot Insurance Co.* (1996), 132 D.L.R. (4th) 568 (Ont. Gen. Div.), appeal allowed on other grounds (1999), 42 O.R. (3d) 641 (C.A.), appeal allowed and trial judgment reinstated, 2002 SCC 18.

120 [2010] O.J. No. 4289 (S.C.J.).

121 See *R. v. Soobrian*, above note 106.

122 *R. v. Fraser* (1990), 55 C.C.C. (3d) 551 (B.C.C.A.). Where there is a reasonable prospect that the witness may accept some of the facts he will be confronted with, the cross-examination is apt to be permitted, with timely jury directions being used to ameliorate the prejudice: *R. v. Mariani* (2007), 220 C.C.C. (3d) 74 (Ont. C.A.).

6.4 (f)   The Scope of Cross-examination

Cross-examination under either a common law declaration of hostility or a declaration of adversity is "at large."[123] This means that, subject to the discretion of the trial judge to limit its scope for valid reasons and the bar on lawyers challenging the general credibility of their own witnesses,[124] cross-examination can be employed to neutralize harmful evidence by impeaching the credibility or reliability of the testimony, or to obtain helpful information from the witness.

6.4 (g)   Competing Views on the Scope of Cross-examination

There is authority to the effect that cross-examination of one's own witness is not at large in the sense we describe, but can be used only to discredit the testimony of the witness—not to attempt to get the witness to change his testimony so that it is more favourable to the party calling him.[125] This authority is based on the belief that it is unfair,[126] or inappropriate,[127] or even dangerous[128] for a party to call a witness whom he knows will testify adversely so that he can cross-examine that witness in order to intimidate him into changing his version of events. It has also been argued in the case of adverse witnesses that permitting cross-examination at large is inconsistent with the purpose of subsection 9(1), which is "witness impeachment."[129]

There are even those who view subsection 9(1) cross-examination as confined to the circumstances surrounding the making of the previous

---

123 R. v. T.(T.E.), above note 107, speaks of the scope of cross-examination under s. 9(1) as being "at large." This is the view of a number of commentators listed in M.E. Webster, "Cross-examination on a Finding of Adversity?" (1995) 38 C.R. (4th) 35, n. 2. They include Austin Cooper, Q.C; The Hon. Justice Casey Hill; Earl Levy, Q.C.; and M. Bartlett.

124 See section 6.1, "General Attacks on Credibility," above in this chapter.

125 See R. v. Soobrian, above note 106 at 215–16 (Ont. C.A.); R. v. Chisholm, [1995] O.J. No. 3300 (Ct. J.); R. v. Malik, [2004] B.C.J. No. 200 (S.C.).

126 This was the argument used in Soobrian, ibid., and Chisholm, ibid., but in each of these cases there was additional unfairness. The Crown was not trying to secure affirmative testimony about what happened from the witnesses it called, but was trying to use cross-examination to discredit them in order to suggest, without any foundation for doing so, that the accused was complicit in encouraging these witnesses to change their story.

127 See R. v. Singh (1979), 48 C.C.C. (2d) 434 at 437 (Man. C.A.).

128 See Canadian Encyclopedic Digest, 3d ed., vol. 11 (Toronto: Carswell, 1992) "Evidence" at para. 429.

129 R. v. C.(J.R.) (1996), 110 C.C.C. (3d) 373 at 382 (Sask. C.A.).

consistent statement,[130] a position supported in *R. v. Beaudry*.[131] This narrowest position is particularly problematic. It makes subsection 9(1) cross-examination all but obsolete for statements made in, or reduced to writing, since this kind of cross-examination is already permissible without a declaration of adversity under subsection 9(2).[132]

It is obvious that the law is in desperate need of reform. It is our view that reform should make clear what we believe the law to already be—that cross-examination is permitted both in cases of hostility or adversity to challenge the credibility of harmful evidence furnished by the witness in chief and to attempt to provoke the witness into providing helpful evidence that was not forthcoming during testimony in chief.

We prefer this view for four reasons. First, limiting cross-examination to challenges to credibility does not reflect clear and established practice; it is routine for a witness who is being cross-examined on a prior inconsistent statement to be asked whether the statement is true. If the witness agrees the statement is true, then the statement is not just used for impeachment purposes but becomes evidence of the truth of its contents. Second, we believe the claim that a witness can be intimidated into perjury through cross-examination by the party who called him to be exaggerated, particularly given that the witness has the protection of the court. Third, the common law assumption that a party vouches for the testimony of his witness, which underlies the restriction on challenging one's own witness, is unrealistic. There are times when parties, particularly in criminal cases, have no choice but to hope for the best and call witnesses whom they suspect are unlikely to tell the court what they may know because of fear or interest.[133] And fourth, limiting the tools available to challenge one's own witness does little to serve the search for the truth. Consider, for example, the case of *R. v. C.(J.R.)*.[134] There the Crown succeeded in having the previous out-of-court statement made by the witness admitted under the rule in *K.G.B.* for the truth of its contents. The Saskatchewan Court of Appeal held that it was unfair for the Crown to then cross-examine the witness in an effort to have him adopt the facts contained in that out-of-court

---

130 See The Hon. C. Hill, D. Tanovich, L. P. Strezos, & S.C. Hutchinson, *Canadian Criminal Evidence*, 4th ed., loose-leaf (Aurora, ON: Canada Law Book, loose-leaf release September 2003) at 18.50.40; and Webster, "Cross-examination on a Finding of Adversity," above note 123.

131 [1993] O.J. No. 703 (Gen. Div.).

132 See this chapter, section 6.5, "Previous Inconsistent Statements."

133 See R.J. Delisle, "Annotation" to *R. v. Glowatski* (2001), 47 C.R. (5th) 233, recounting the similar observation from the American *Federal Rules of Evidence* Advisory Committee.

134 Above note 129.

statement in preference to his in-court version. But consider the implications of that ruling. In such a case the defence would doubtlessly cross-examine that witness to show that the out-of-court statement is untrue. The trier of fact would be seriously disadvantaged in determining whether to rely on that out-of-court statement if no one was permitted to try to show the opposite by questioning the witness, namely that the statement was in fact true. If we are interested in the truth, the best way to achieve it is to let the trier of fact hear relevant evidence and to provide the trier of fact with the criteria for evaluating that evidence. Cross-examination produces data for decision-making that examination in chief simply cannot provide.

6.5) Previous Inconsistent Statements

A witness who disappoints the party who has called him by testifying differently from expected may ultimately provide the anticipated evidence if he is confronted with his earlier statements. Upon seeing or hearing those statements, he may adopt them as accurate and explain why his testimony differs from what he had previously said. In cases where the witness does not adopt the earlier statements, it may still be useful to prove them in order to neutralize any harmful evidence that he has provided by showing that he has given different accounts of the same event.

Despite the utility in doing so, counsel is not free simply to confront disappointing witnesses with their earlier inconsistent statements. Complex statutory provisions define when and how this is to be done. In criminal cases, or civil cases falling under the purview of the *Canada Evidence Act*, subsections 9(1) and (2) govern the admissibility of prior inconsistent statements made by a party's own witness. None of the provincial statutes has an equivalent to subsection 9(2), although, insofar as proof of prior inconsistent statements are concerned, they are all identical in substance to subsection 9(1).

Subsections 9(1) and 9(2) of the *Canada Evidence Act* provide as follows:

> 9.(1) A party producing a witness shall not be allowed to impeach his credit by general evidence of bad character, but *if the witness, in the opinion of the court, proves adverse*, the party may contradict him by other evidence, or, *by leave of the court, may prove that the witness made at other times a statement inconsistent with his present testimony*, but before the last mentioned proof can be given the circumstances of the supposed statement, sufficient to designate the particular occasion, shall be mentioned to the witness, and he shall be asked whether or not he did make the statement.

(2) Where the party producing a witness alleges that the witness made at other times *a statement in writing, reduced to writing, or recorded on audiotape or videotape or otherwise*, inconsistent with the witness's present testimony, the court may, without proof that the witness is adverse, grant leave to that party to cross-examine the witness as to the statement and the court may consider the cross-examination in determining whether in the opinion of the court the witness is adverse [emphasis added].

Together, subsections 9(1) and 9(2) have produced confusion and uncertainty.[135] This complex and cumbersome two-part provision came about because Canadian authority had suggested that in criminal cases, although curiously not in civil cases,[136] the previous inconsistent statements could not be used to assist in demonstrating "adversity" when a party was applying to get leave to prove those statements. Some courts considered that it would be circular to rely on prior inconsistent statements in an effort to gain permission to prove those same prior inconsistent statements.Subsection 9(2) was thought to correct this problem for statements made in writing, reduced to writing, or otherwise recorded, by allowing the witness to be cross-examined about them, and for this cross-examination to be taken into account by the judge in deciding whether the witness is "adverse" under subsection 9(1).[137] Through the cross-examination, the judge would learn about the earlier statement. Then, if the party seeking to prove the statement prevailed on the issue of adversity, the prior inconsistent statement could be proved during the trial itself. In other words, the subsections were seen as a two-part procedure in which each provision performed a separate function.[138]

---

135 In *R. v. Booth* (1984), 15 C.C.C. (3d) 237 at 244 (B.C.C.A.), for example, the court suggested that under s. 9(2), a court should inquire into the adversity of a witness. Yet, as the sections indicate, that inquiry is relevant solely under s. 9(1). In *R. v. Thurston* (1993), 63 O.A.C. 99 (C.A.), the trial judge applied the s. 9(2) procedure and then declared a witness adverse without looking at s. 9(1). In *R. v. Soobrian*, above note 106, counsel began to cross-examine his witness about his prior inconsistent statement without seeking leave under s. 9(2).

136 *Wawanesa Mutual Insurance Co. v. Hanes*, above note 109, rev'd on other grounds (*sub nom. Hanes v. Wawanesa Mutual Insurance Co.*), [1963] S.C.R. 154.

137 Subsection 9(2) has proved unnecessary if this was its sole purpose. It is now accepted that even prior inconsistent *oral* statements can be considered by the judge in deciding whether a witness is adverse under s. 9(1): *R. v. Cassibo*, above note 108. Prior inconsistent statements, whether oral or written, can be proved during the *voir dire* without cross-examining the witness.

138 The Ontario Court of Appeal in *R. v. Carpenter* (1982), 31 C.R. (3d) 261 took the position that ss. 9(1) and 9(2) perform distinct roles.

In theory this makes some sense and it is consistent with what is stated in the provisions. Subsection 9(1) provides for proof of previous inconsistent statements, while subsection 9(2) does not. That provision merely describes the limited form of cross-examination. Despite the apparent logic in this scheme, however, the notion that a previous inconsistent statement can be cross-examined upon under subsection 9(2) without being proved is an unsatisfactory one. This is because the subsection 9(2) cross-examination takes place in front of the jury, who are entitled to use the limited cross-examination in assessing the credibility of the witness. Invariably the witness who is being cross-examined is asked whether he made the statement, and more often than not he will testify under oath that he did. In any meaningful sense, the statement has then been "proved." The net effect is that where there has been a subsection 9(2) cross-examination and where the witness admits having made the statement, there is really no need to go on to subsection 9(1). To take just two examples, in *McInroy v. R.*[139] and *R. v. U.(F.J.)*,[140] the courts treated previous inconsistent statements as having been proved after the subsection 9(2) procedure was used, even though no subsection 9(1) applications were brought. It seems that subsection 9(2), without saying so, allows previous inconsistent statements to be "proved," at least in cases where the witness being cross-examined admits to having made them.

But what if the witness denies the statement? Does counsel then have to apply under subsection 9(1) for a declaration of adversity so that the statement can be proved by other evidence? It seems not. In *R. v. Cassibo*,[141] Martin J.A. noted that "[s]omewhat strangely s-s. (2) makes no express provision for proving the inconsistent statement if the witness denies making it, but the judicial interpretation placed upon the subsection makes it clear that such proof can be made."[142] Thus, despite the overwhelming damage it does to the language of the section, it seems that a party given leave to cross-examine under subsection 9(2) is entitled to prove the previous inconsistent statements without having to move on to subsection 9(1). According to this view, subsection 9(2) provides an alternative and easier procedure for proving previous inconsistent statements that have been made in, or reduced to, writing.

---

139 (1978), 5 C.R. (3d) 125 (S.C.C.).

140 (1994), 32 C.R. (4th) 378 (Ont. C.A.), aff'd without comment on this aspect of the case (1995), 42 C.R. (4th) 133 (S.C.C.).

141 Above note 108.

142 *Ibid.* at 520. Arguably, Martin J.A. was referring only to proving the statements during the s. 9(2) *voir dire*, but this is not the generally accepted interpretation of what he had said.

As is the case with subsection 9(1), whether the more limited cross-examination allowed by subsection 9(2) can be undertaken is a matter of discretion by the judge. The section says "the court may." In *R. v. Aitkenhead* the trial judge permitted the Crown to cross-examine a witness about a statement he made, which was found not to have been voluntary. The Manitoba Court of Appeal held that the trial judge was entitled to exercise his discretion in that way.[143] In *R. v. Dooley* the accused objected to the Crown confronting its witness with her prior inconsistent statement because it contained prejudicial admissions of abuse attributed to the accused. The court had the discretion to accede to that request. It did not because the Crown witness not only failed to give the evidence the Crown anticipated, but also had positively assisted the accused. This amplified the importance of enabling the Crown to challenge her credibility sufficiently to justify use of the prejudicial, prior inconsistent statement.[144]

6.5 (a)   Subsection 9(2) Procedure

It is important to remember that the subsection 9(2) procedure is confined to statements that have been video- or audiotaped, or made in or "reduced to writing." Subsection 9(1) includes oral statements. Although the witness need not write or sign a statement for it to be "reduced to writing,"[145] it is not enough that the record consists of the notes of a conversation written by someone other than the speaker unless that record was an accurate transcript of what was said.[146] If the statement does not meet the criteria for being made in, or reduced to, writing, a party must use subsection 9(1) before proving it.

The subsection 9(2) procedure was developed in the case of *R. v. Milgaard*.[147] That case spells out a detailed seven-stage *voir dire* process that, if satisfied, may lead to an order permitting a party to then cross-examine its witness before the trier of fact. In substance, it provides as follows:

1) Counsel advises the court that he is bringing a subsection 9(2) application.
2) If there is a jury, the jury leaves the room and a *voir dire* begins.

---

143 *R. v. Aitkenhead* (2001), 43 C.R. (5th) 392 (Man. C.A.).
144 [2009] O.J. No. 5483 (C.A.).
145 *R. v. Carpenter*, above note 138.
146 *R. v. Handy* (1978), 5 C.R. (3d) 97 (B.C.C.A.); *R. v. Morgan* (1993), 80 C.C.C. (3d) 16 at 20 (Ont. C.A.).
147 (1971), 14 C.R.N.S. 34 at 49–50 (Sask. C.A.), leave to appeal to S.C.C. refused (1971), 4 C.C.C. (2d) 566n (S.C.C.). The procedure was subsequently approved in *McInroy v. R.*, above note 139.

3) Counsel shows the judge the statement, pointing out the inconsistencies with the testimony.

4) If the judge agrees that there are inconsistencies, he invites counsel to prove the statement.[148]

5) The witness is asked if he made the statements that are recorded. If he admits that he did, the statement is proved. If he denies it, other evidence can be called to prove it.

6) Opposing counsel has the right to cross-examine the witness as well as any others called by the party seeking leave. Opposing counsel may try to show that even if the statement was made by the witness, there are circumstances that would make it improper to allow counsel to present it to the jury during cross-examination.

7) The judge, normally after inviting submissions, decides whether the statement was made and whether the ends of justice would be best attained by allowing the cross-examination.[149]

6.5 (b)   Subsection 9(1) Procedure

The procedure is similar where an application is brought under subsection 9(1), or under any of the provincial Evidence Acts, to prove either written or oral prior inconsistent statements or to cross-examine the witness. A *voir dire* is held in the absence of the jury. Because "adversity" is in issue, the nature of the evidence called will be broader than in a subsection 9(2) *voir dire*. The party seeking leave can call any evidence bearing on that issue. At the end of the *voir dire* the judge, normally with the benefit of argument, will decide whether the witness is "adverse" and whether to grant leave to allow proof of the statement and/or the cross-examination at large as part of the trial record.

Where a statement is going to be proved, counsel must advise the witness of sufficient circumstances to indicate the occasion when the statement was alleged to have been made, and then ask the witness whether he made the statement. If he denies it, the statement may be proved by other witnesses.

---

148 Even a claim by the witness that she does not recall making the previous statement can be treated as an inconsistent statement where the trial judge disbelieves the witness: *McInroy v. R.*, *ibid*. See *R. v. Fleet* (2001), 48 C.R. (5th) 28 (N.S.C.A.), where testimony of an inability to recall by a witness who had suffered memory loss as the result of a car accident was not treated as inconsistent with the fairly complete account he had provided to the police four days after the event.

149 *R. v. Carpenter*, above note 138. In *R. v. Chartrand*, [1998] 4 W.W.R. 657 (Man. Q.B.), aff'd [1998] M.J. No. 502 (C.A.), for example, it was held not to be in the interests of justice to allow cross-examination where the police had promised the witness that the prior statement was "off the record."

6.5 (c) The Use That Can Be Made of Previous Inconsistent Statements

If a prior inconsistent statement has the particularized indicia of reliability described in *R. v. B.(K.G.)*,[150] it can be admitted as proof of the truth of its contents.[151] Even if it does not, if the witness is properly confronted with the previous inconsistent statement and accepts it as true and accurate, the prior statement becomes his evidence.[152] If he does not agree that the statement is true and accurate, the version contained in the statement is not proof of the truth of its contents. It can nonetheless be used to weaken his credibility because of the inconsistent accounts he has provided.[153]

Where the statement is not admissible under a hearsay exception and not adopted by the witness as true, the trial judge must warn the jury that the previous inconsistent statement cannot be used as proof of the facts it asserts.[154]

In *R. v. Glowatski*[155] the defence argued that a "K.G.B. application" should be brought only after the Crown has shown the witness to be adverse and has exhausted the section 9 procedures. This is the procedure that was envisaged in *R. v. B.(K.G.)*.[156] It is also what normally happens; typically the party will launch and exhaust the section 9 procedures, and then at the end, notify the judge that they wish to use the statement not only to impeach the credibility of the witness, but to prove the truth of its contents. The B.C. Court of Appeal held in *Glowatski*, however, that this process is not necessary as a matter of law and it was not required on the facts of that case. The Crown witness had already admitted making the statement when it was being used to refresh the witness's memory, necessity had been established by her failure to recount what was in the earlier statement, and adequate indicia of reliability were demonstrated. In short, section 9 was satisfied without invoking the section 9 procedure.

---

150 (1993), 19 C.R. (4th) 1 (S.C.C.).
151 See chapter 5, section 2, "Prior Inconsistent Statements." This is true where the statement complies with the requirements of any hearsay exception, such as where it is contained in a business record.
152 *R. v. Deacon* (1947), 3 C.R. 265 (S.C.C.), although its weight will no doubt be affected because he has given inconsistent accounts.
153 *McInroy v. R.*, above note 139.
154 *R. v. Bevan* (1993), 21 C.R. (4th) 277 (S.C.C.).
155 Above note 99.
156 Above note 150 at 42.

CHAPTER 12

RULES RELATING TO THE USE OF ADMISSIBLE EVIDENCE

1. INTRODUCTION

In general, the trier of fact is entitled simply to apply common sense and human experience in determining whether evidence is credible and in deciding what use, if any, to make of it in coming to its finding of fact.

Exceptionally, corroboration rules and presumptions of law can control the way that particular items of evidence are used.

In most cases, the trier of fact is simply invited to apply common sense and human experience to decide whether admissible evidence is credible and to determine what use, if any, to make of it in coming to its finding of fact. This is not always so. As discussed in the introductory chapter, some rules of admissibility impose limitations on the use that can be made of admissible evidence.[1] Corroboration rules and presumptions of law, discussed in this chapter, can also control the use that triers of fact can make of certain kinds of evidence.

Corroboration rules require triers of fact to search for, and in some cases to find, independent evidence that confirms other evidence before it is relied upon. For example, subsection 19(2) of the *Alberta Evidence Act* provides that no case shall be decided on the unsworn evidence of a child of tender years unless that evidence is corroborated. This

---

1 See chapter 1, section 1.2, "Rules of Admissibility."

means that the trier of fact is legally obliged to refrain from acting on the uncorroborated, unsworn testimony of a child even where the trier of fact is firmly convinced that the child is being truthful and accurate. Similarly, the Ontario *Evidence Act* disallows any verdict from being rendered against a deceased persons' estate based solely on the uncorroborated testimony of the opposing party litigant. This means that there must be independent evidence confirming each particular claim made. In *Liu Estate v. Chau* the Ontario Court of Appeal ruled against the tenants of a deceased man, given that their defence to a rent arrears claim was based solely on their assertion that they had made the payments in cash to the landlord before he died.[2]

Strict corroboration rules are becoming less common and much less technical than they once were. They are being repealed and in some cases replaced by other rules that are intended to provide guidance to triers of fact. These rules typically require warnings to be given to the triers of fact about evidence where it is particularly dangerous, although the trier of fact remains free to act upon it.

Some presumptions of law also control the way that specific evidence is used. They can require triers of fact to find that a presumed fact exists on the evidence, even where the trier of fact might not otherwise have been satisfied about the existence of that fact. For example, where it is proved that an accused person was in the seat normally occupied by the driver of a motor vehicle, subsection 258(1)(a) of the *Criminal Code* requires the trier of fact to find that the accused was in care or control of the motor vehicle unless the accused establishes that he did not intend to drive. The trier of fact is obliged to make this finding even where it may have a reasonable doubt as to whether the accused really was in care or control of that vehicle.[3]

2. CORROBORATION AND DANGEROUS EVIDENCE

2.1) The Former Law

At common law, certain kinds of evidence were considered to be particularly unsafe. "Rules of practice" developed requiring the judge to

---

2   (2004), 236 D.L.R. (4th) 711 (Ont. C.A.).

3   Because presumptions tend to be rebuttable, they are closely linked to burdens of proof and will therefore be discussed together with the law relating to burdens of proof.

warn the jury of the dangers of convicting an accused person on the "uncorroborated" or unconfirmed evidence of certain witnesses. Moreover, judges had an obligation to describe for the jury when evidence was capable of "corroborating" the dangerous testimony, according to law. Judges even had to warn themselves in judge alone trials. According to these common law rules, triers of fact could convict in the absence of "corroboration," but only after receiving these mandatory warnings. The most important kinds of evidence singled out for this cautious treatment were the testimony of children, of accomplices to crime, and of complainants alleging sexual offences.

A number of statutes were passed making corroboration a "rule of law" in some cases, actually requiring that corroboration must exist before conviction. For example, section 133 of the *Criminal Code* provides that no person can be convicted of the offence of perjury "on the evidence of only one witness unless the evidence of that witness is corroborated in a material particular by evidence that implicates the accused."

The law of corroboration evolved into a highly technical and restrictive body of authority. Corroboration came to have a narrow meaning. Evidence would not be corroborative simply because it supported or confirmed the suspect testimony. Corroborative evidence had to be "independent," had to confirm the testimony in a material particular, and had to implicate the accused.[4] To be corroborative, circumstantial evidence had to be consistent only with guilt. In *R. v. Ethier*,[5] for example, the Crown offered evidence as corroboration during a rape prosecution that

1) human blood of a type matching the blood type of the complainant was found on the accused's shorts,
2) hair similar to the complainant's was found in his car,
3) the handle on his car was broken,
4) the accused's clothing matched the description provided by the complainant, as did the licence number,
5) she had a bruise on her left cheek,
6) she was distraught immediately after the incident, and
7) marks were found in the car consistent with the claim by the complainant that there would be foot marks on the ceiling which were made by her while she was being assaulted.

The Ontario Court of Appeal held that none of this corroborated the rape allegation. Items (5) and (6) would be some evidence to con-

---

4   *R. v. Baskerville*, [1916] 2 K.B. 658 (C.A.).
5   (1959), 31 C.R. 30 (Ont. C.A.).

firm that a rape had occurred if the injuries and emotional condition were pronounced enough, but it did not confirm the identity of the accused as the rapist. Items (3), (4), and (7) were not corroborative because their relevance depended on the testimony of the complainant. In other words, as items of evidence they were not "independent" enough to be corroborative. As for items (1) and (2), these were equally consistent with the truth as with the falsity of her allegation because her hair and blood type could get where they were without her having been raped. While all of this evidence was admissible and might well support a conviction, the trial judge erred in law by failing to tell the jury that the evidence of the complainant remained uncorroborated.

Not surprisingly, the law of corroboration was criticized because of its technicality. It was also condemned in the case of sexual offence complainants and in the case of the testimony of children as being premised on antiquated and inaccurate assumptions that these witnesses are inherently unreliable. As a result, these common law rules of practice have been abandoned and a number of the statutory corroboration requirements have been repealed.

2.2)   Statutory Corroboration Rules

Some statutory corroboration rules (such as the perjury and *Alberta Evidence Act* unsworn evidence provisions referred to above) continue to apply. The trend in criminal cases is to limit the impact of such provisions. In *R. v. B.(G.)*[6] the Supreme Court of Canada held that a section calling for a child's evidence to be "corroborated in a material particular by evidence that implicates the accused" did not require that the corroborative evidence implicate the accused. Instead it would be enough if there was independent evidence supporting the testimony needing corroboration, thereby making it safe to convict. Quoting *Vetrovec v. R.*,[7] which had dealt with common law and not statutory corroboration rules, the Court affirmed that *"[t]he important question.... is not how our trust [in the testimony] is restored, but whether it is restored at all."*[8] While the Quebec Court of Appeal held in *R. v. Neveu*[9] that it would be wrong to apply the *Vetrovec* standard to all statutory provisions regardless of their wording,[10] the court interpreted the corroboration requirement for perjury strictly such that it would apply only if the Crown's case was

---

6   (1990), 77 C.R. (3d) 327 (S.C.C.).

7   (1982), 27 C.R. (3d) 304 at 319 (S.C.C.).

8   Above note 6 at 344 [emphasis in original].

9   (2004), 184 C.C.C. (3d) 18 (Que. C.A.).

10   Sée *R. v. Thind* (1991), 64 C.C.C. (3d) 301 (B.C.C.A.), re: perjury.

based on the direct evidence of a witness rather than on circumstantial proof. In *R. v. Eriksen* the Yukon Territory Court of Appeal agreed and upheld the conviction of the accused based on his own out-of-court admissions.[11] While statutory language cannot be ignored, it is clear that the trend is to construe corroboration requirements into near oblivion. This is part of the more general movement away from technical corroboration requirements. The objective, subject to statutory limit, is to permit triers of fact to evaluate information free from inappropriate general assumptions about the lack of credibility of certain classes of evidence.

2.3) Discretionary Warnings

When the common law corroboration rules were dispensed with, they were replaced with rules giving judges the discretion to provide special warnings to jurors about the dangers of relying on the testimony of some Crown witnesses.[12] These cautions are meant to alert the jury to the risks involved.[13] They therefore apply solely in jury cases.[14] Warnings do not result in the loss of the evidence. Once trained, jurors can properly evaluate the information before them.[15]

Although the decision to warn is "discretionary" if the testimony is dangerous enough in the particular circumstances of the case a failure to give an adequate warning to a jury will constitute an error of law. The greater the concern, the more likely a warning will become mandatory.[16] In *R. v. McCarroll*, for example, it was mandatory to warn the jury about

---

11   (2006), 213 C.C.C. (3d) 374 (Y.C.A.).

12   Special warnings are not to be given for defence witnesses: *R. v. Tzimopoulos* (1986), 29 C.C.C. (3d) 304 (Ont. C.A.); *R. v. Lavallee* (2001), 42 C.R. (5th) 151 (Sask. C.A.). If a witness is "mixed," giving both favourable and unfavourable testimony, the judge has the discretion whether to give a warning: *R. v. Gelle* (2009), 244 C.C.C. (3d) 129 (Ont. C.A.). In "cut-throat" defence cases where each co-accused tries to blame the other, it may be that limited, special warnings will be appropriate: *R. v. Suzack* (2000), 141 C.C.C. (3d) 449 at para. 186 (Ont. C.A.). The risk, of course, is that cautioning the jury about believing the "witness/accused" would be prejudicial to the accused witness and could, depending on the context, offend the prohibition against discrediting the testimony of the accused because of his character.

13   *R. v. White*, [2011] S.C.J. No. 13 at para. 55.

14   *R. v. Newman* (2009), 286 Nfld. & P.E.I.R. 176 at para. 16 (N.L.S.C.A.D.). Having said this, a judge sitting alone who is not alive to the frailties of dangerous evidence will be acting in error: *R. v. Narwal* (2009), 248 C.C.C. (3d) 62 at para. 56 (B.C.C.A.).

15   *R. v. White*, above note 13 at para. 56.

16   *R. v. Brooks*, [2000] 1 S.C.R. 237 at para. 4.

a witness whose evidence was so central as to put the gun in the hands of the accused, and who lied about her outstanding fraud charges. This was particularly so because, given her role, she would likely strike the jury as the witness least implicated in events leading up to the killing.[17]

Typically special warnings are called for where there are "defects in the evidence of a witness that may not be apparent to a lay trier of fact."[18] The cases where warnings may be required include the evidence of accomplices,[19] jailhouse informants,[20] children,[21] and witnesses of unsavoury character.[22] The current approach differs from the old rules of corroboration in a number of respects. First, warnings need no longer be given for every witness falling within some predesignated category. A warning will be required where a witness plays more than a minor role in the Crown's case and where, based on an objective assessment, the court should suspect the credibility of that witness.[23] Second, the warnings are no longer confined to witnesses who fall within predefined categories. In any case where there are serious reasons to be concerned about the credibility or reliability of an important witness, a warning may be needed. Third, where a warning is required, its form is not burdened with the technical requirements that plagued the law of corroboration.

Although the strength of the required warning will vary with the circumstances, and no particular language need be used, a proper warning will tend to satisfy four characteristics. It will (1) identify the need for special scrutiny, (2) identify the characteristics that bring the evidence into question (that is, why that special scrutiny is required, including an explanation of those problems the jury might not be familiar with as laypersons), (3) caution the jury that while it can act on unconfirmed evidence it is dangerous to do so, and (4) caution the jury to look for evidence from another source that tends to show that the untrustworthy witness is telling the truth.[24] That independent evidence need not implicate the accused; in *R. v. Kehler*[25] the evidence that was treated as supportive confirmed the accomplice's description of the robbery and strengthened the jury's belief that he was a truthful witness, including about Kehler's involvement, but did not implicate Kehler.

---

17   *R. v. McCarroll* (2008), 241 O.A.C. 316 (C.A.).

18   *R. v. Sauvé* (2004), 182 C.C.C. (3d) 321 at para. 76 (Ont. C.A.).

19   *Vetrovec v. R.*, above note 7.

20   *R. v. Brooks*, above note 16.

21   See, for example, *R. v. Marquard* (1995), 25 C.R. (4th) 1 (S.C.C.).

22   *R. v. Bevan*, [1993] 2 S.C.R. 599.

23   *R. v. Brooks*, above note 16 at para. 80.

24   *R. v. Khela*, [2009] S.C.J. No. 4 at para. 37; *R. v. Smith*, [2009] 1 S.C.R. 146 at para. 14; *R. v. Hurley*, [2010] S.C.J. No. 18.

25   (2004), 19 C.R. (6th) 49 (S.C.C.).

Ultimately the question is whether the evidence is "capable of restoring the trier's faith in the relevant aspects of the witness's account."[26] The judge is also free to exercise discretion about how extensively to review potential confirming evidence, since highlighting confirmatory evidence could prove harmful to the accused.[27]

In addition to giving those relevant warnings, the judge will ordinarily have to give the jury guidance on what, in the particular case, might suffice as confirmatory evidence.[28] The need to do this and the detail required varies from case to case. In *R. v. Bevan*, for example, the Court recognized that there will be circumstances where drawing the jury's attention to confirmatory evidence that is extremely prejudicial in nature can operate to the disadvantage of the accused.[29]

2.4) Identification Cases

It has long been understood that testimony identifying a suspect can be dangerous.[30] This is particularly so where the witness does not know the suspect.[31] Judges therefore have a discretion to warn the jury of the dangers of convicting where the identification of the accused is in issue and where either the opportunity of the witness to observe was under poor conditions, or improper identification procedures (such as unfair lineups or the improper use of photo identification packets) were employed[32] or other suggestive influences have occurred.[33] Where the case depends substantially on the accuracy of eyewitness evidence, this discretion can become a duty.[34] In *R. v. Hibbert*, for example, a strong direction should have been furnished where key witnesses identified the suspect for the first time while watching televised footage of his arrest.[35]

---

26 *R. v. Khela*, above note 24 at paras. 42–43.

27 *R. v. Bevan*, above note 22 at paras. 27–29.

28 *R. v. Siu* (1998), 124 C.C.C. (3d) 301 at 325 (B.C.C.A.), and see *R. v. Dhillon* (2002), 5 C.R. (6th) 317 (Ont. C.A.), where a new trial was required because the trial judge mistakenly identified facts as potentially confirmatory when they were not.

29 *R. v. Bevan*, above note 22 at paras. 27–29.

30 See Peter DeCarteret Cory, *The Inquiry Regarding Thomas Sophonow: The Investigation, Prosecution and Consideration of Entitlement to Compensation* (Winnipeg: Manitoba Justice, 2001). For an exceptionally good summary of the principles applicable in identification cases, see *R. v. Bigsky* (2006), 45 C.R. (6th) 69 (Sask. C.A.). Concerns apply, as well, to voice identification evidence: *R. v. Quidley* (2008), 232 C.C.C. (3d) 255 at para. 36 (Ont. C.A.).

31 *R. v. Bob* (2008), 63 C.R. (6th) 108 at para. 13 (B.C.C.A.).

32 *R. v. Hanemaayer* (2008), 234 C.C.C. (3d) 3 (Ont. C.A.).

33 See, for example, *R. v. Fengstad* (1994), 27 C.R. (4th) 383 (B.C.C.A.).

34 *R. v. Candir*, [2009] O.J. No. 5485 at para. 109 (C.A.).

35 (2002), 163 C.C.C. (3d) 129 (S.C.C.).

What will be required to address problems with identification evidence varies from case to case but the specific problems with the identification evidence should be pointed out to the jury. So, too, should the general dangers of identification evidence such as "the very weak link between the confidence level of a witness and the accuracy of that witness."[36] They should be warned that mistaken identification by perfectly honest witnesses has been responsible for miscarriages of justice.[37] Where there is a notable dissimilarity between the initial description furnished by the witness and the suspect who is identified, and there is no other evidential support for that identification, that purported identification will have no probative value and juries must be told this.[38]

Given the inherently suggestive circumstances in which they occur, juries should also be cautioned about the dangers of relying on "dock identifications"[39] as positive proof of identity. "This type of identification has little probative value."[40] "The only purpose in allowing the evidence [of dock identifications] to be led is to give the . . . witnesses an opportunity to say whether or not in their opinion, the accused is the same person they saw at the offence, in order to dispel any adverse inference the jury might draw if the question were not asked, and because there is probative value in the inability of a . . . witness to identify an accused person."[41] In some cases where the first identification of the accused is made in court and there are problems with the quality of the initial observation of the suspect, juries may have to be told that the dock identification is entitled to virtually no weight.[42] This kind of direction will not be appropriate, however, where the dock identification is supported by distinctive details, prior familiarity, or previous forms of identification such as properly conducted line-ups or dock identifications.[43]

Ordinarily "identification" evidence warnings apply to the Crown case. A judge may choose to give a warning where the defence relies on identification evidence but the judge must be careful not to unfairly

---

36   *Ibid.* at para. 52.

37   *R. v. Candir*, above note 34 at para. 109.

38   *R. v. Bennett* (2003), 19 C.R. (6th) 109 at para. 96 (Ont. C.A.), leave to appeal to S.C.C. refused, 2004 CarswellOnt 1325, 2004 CarswellOnt 1326 (S.C.C.), and see *Chartier v. Quebec (Attorney General)* (1979), 9 C.R. (3d) 97 (S.C.C.). The rule was explained in *R. v. Blackman* (2007), 84 O.R. (3d) 292 at para. 29 (C.A.), aff'd on other grounds (2008), 232 C.C.C. (3d) 233 (S.C.C.).

39   A "dock identification" occurs where a witness points the accused out to the court.

40   *R. v. A.(F.)* (2004), 183 C.C.C. (3d) 518 at para. 47 (Ont. C.A.).

41   *R. v. Tebo* (2003), 175 C.C.C. (3d) 116 at para. 17 (Ont. C.A.).

42   *Ibid.* at para. 19.

43   *R. v. Ryback* (2008), 233 C.C.C. (3d) 58 at para. 121 (Ont. C.A.).

undermine the defence position, and must bear in mind that the "special care concerning eyewitness identification arises because of the danger of wrongful conviction [which] does not exist where the eyewitness evidence tends to exculpate the accused."[44]

2.5) Warnings (Cautions) in Lieu of Discretionary Exclusion

Warnings may also be used in lieu of discretionary exclusion in some cases where evidence is risky. In *R. v. White* an issue was whether a shooting was accidental (leading to a manslaughter conviction) or intentional (leading to a murder conviction).[45] The controversial evidence was testimony that White immediately fled after firing the gun. The Crown urged that this was consistent with intent to kill, not accident. Ordinarily flight is too ambiguous to lead to relevant inferences about the degree of criminal culpability. If a person is implicated in a crime he will flee regardless of how aggravated his role in that crime might be. Such evidence is therefore ordinarily excluded or the jury is directed not to draw an inference about the degree of the accused persons fault from flight.[46] The Supreme Court of Canada found the Crown's inference to be relevant in *White*, however, because it did not rest on flight alone. The reasoning was that those who would fire a gun unexpectedly would be shocked and stall before fleeing. White had not. He fled immediately. The majority recognized, however, that exceptional individuals might flee immediately even had the discharge been accidental. Still, this did not impel exclusion. While the judge could have elected to exclude the evidence as unduly prejudicial, his decision simply to warn or "caution" the jury was adequate in the circumstances.[47]

3. BURDENS OF PROOF AND PRESUMPTIONS

3.1) Introduction

The law relating to burdens of proof and presumptions is particularly complex because terminology is not used uniformly. Speaking generally, there is agreement that the term "burden of proof" is apt to describe

---

44   *R. v. Mariani* (2007), 220 C.C.C. (3d) 74 (Ont. C.A.).
45   Above note 13.
46   *R. v. Arcangioli*, [1994] 1 S.C.R. 129.
47   Above note 13 at paras. 29 and 97.

who it is that has the obligation of satisfying the adjudicator on the factual matter in issue. The term "standard of proof" is understood to describe the degree to which she must convince the adjudicator in order to discharge her "burden." Despite this distinction, it is common to see the single term "burden of proof" used to describe both the burden of proof as defined here and the standard of proof. The term "presumption" is used with even less consistency. The labels that are employed below are not all universally accepted, but are nonetheless useful in describing the general concepts.

3.2) Standards of Proof

Rules of law assign the relevant standards of proof. In a criminal case both the common law and the *Charter* require the Crown to prove the guilt of the accused beyond a reasonable doubt. In other words, the trier of fact can convict only if, at the end of the case on the basis of all admissible evidence, the trier of fact is left without a reasonable doubt on each of the elements of the alleged offence, in spite of any defences raised by the accused. Where one or more of the elements of the Crown case rest on circumstantial evidence, this standard requires that the only rational inference from the evidence shows guilt.[48]

As fundamental as the concept of "reasonable doubt" is, our courts have had difficulty defining it. Jury misdirections have been common. This prompted the Supreme Court of Canada, in *R. v. Lifchus*,[49] to take the unusual step of providing a definition for the term, in the form of a model jury charge. The model charge is as follows:

> The accused enters these proceedings presumed to be innocent. That presumption of innocence remains throughout the case until such time as the Crown has on the evidence put before you satisfied you beyond a reasonable doubt that the accused is guilty.
>
> What does the expression "beyond a reasonable doubt" mean? The term "beyond a reasonable doubt" has been used for a very long time and is a part of our history and traditions of justice. It is so engrained in our criminal law that some think it needs no explanation, yet something must be said regarding its meaning.

---

48   *R. v. Griffin*, 2009 SCC 28. This is considered to be self-evident. As a result, while the "rule in *Hodge's Case*" once required that juries be told this, it is no longer necessary in Canada for judges to train juries on how to apply the reasonable doubt concept to circumstantial evidence: *R. v. Cooper*, [1978] 1 S.C.R. 860.

49   (1997), 9 C.R. (5th) 1 (S.C.C.).

A reasonable doubt is not an imaginary or frivolous doubt. It must not be based upon sympathy or prejudice. Rather, it is based on reason and common sense. It is logically derived from the evidence or absence of evidence.

Even if you believe the accused is probably guilty or likely guilty, that is not sufficient. In those circumstances you must give the benefit of the doubt to the accused and acquit because the Crown has failed to satisfy you of the guilt of the accused beyond a reasonable doubt.

On the other hand you must remember that it is virtually impossible to prove anything to an absolute certainty and the Crown is not required to do so. Such a standard of proof is impossibly high.

In short if, based upon the evidence . . . you are sure that the accused committed the offence you should convict since this demonstrates that you are satisfied of his guilt beyond a reasonable doubt.[50]

In the subsequent case of *R. v. Starr* the majority added the following:

[A] trial judge is required to explain that something less than absolute certainty is required, and that something more than probable guilt is required, in order for the jury to convict. It will be of great assistance for a jury if the trial judge situates the reasonable doubt standard appropriately between these two standards.[51]

Neither the *Lifchus* charge nor the *Starr* modification needs to be given verbatim by trial judges. Indeed, judges might have to depart from the *Lifchus* formula if a jury, through questions to the judge, indicates that it does not understand.[52] What is required in all cases is "substantial compliance."[53] Where deviations have occurred "[i]f the charge read as a whole makes it clear that the jury could not have been under any misapprehension as to the correct burden and standard of proof then the verdict ought not to be disturbed. If on the other hand, the charge read as a whole gives rise to a reasonable likelihood that the jury misapprehended the standard of proof, the verdict should be set aside."[54]

---

50   *Ibid.* at 13–14. The model charge itself proves how easy it is to get it wrong. The words we have omitted from the last paragraph are "or lack of evidence." Since it is impossible to be satisfied of guilt based on a "lack of evidence," the Supreme Court of Canada had to grant a rehearing so that it could delete this phrase from the drafted model charge as misleading and erroneous. In effect, the Court subsequently had to overturn its own model charge. See *R. v. Lifchus, ibid.*, and *R. v. Dickhoff*, [1998] S.J. No. 646 (C.A.).

51   [2000] 2 S.C.R. 144 at para. 242.

52   *R. v. Layton*, [2009] S.C.J. No. 36.

53   See *R. v. Rhee*, 2001 SCC 71 for a summary and discussion of these cases.

54   *R. v. Lavallee*, above note 12 at para. 16.

Not surprisingly, jury directions have been upheld using this standard where judges failed to include information that was featured in the model directions.[55]While *Lifchus* and *Starr* will provide a firm point of departure, whether an appeal court finds the need to interfere where a charge is deficient will depend on "various contextual considerations which are germane" to whether there is a reasonable likelihood that the trier of fact misapprehended the standard[56]—things like the materiality of the failing given the issues in the case, or the balance of the directions that were furnished.[57]

In a case where the accused testifies the burden on the Crown is not met simply because the trier of fact disbelieves the testimony of the accused. It is possible to have no doubt that the accused has lied or is wrong, but still to be left in doubt about whether the Crown has established each of the elements of the offence according to the required standard. An innocent accused may have lied to hide some other discreditable facts or out of fear that the truth may inaccurately appear incriminating. Or the accused may be honestly mistaken. By the same token, the Crown case is not made out simply because the testimony of a complainant is preferred to the testimony of the accused. The complainant's testimony, or other evidence, must establish the allegation beyond a reasonable doubt. Indeed, in a jury trial the judge must direct the jury on these matters where the accused has testified and "credibility is a central or significant issue."[58] The suggested instruction, often referred to as the "W.(D.) warning," is as follows:

> First, if you believe the evidence of the accused, obviously you must acquit.
>
> Second, if you do not believe the testimony of the accused but you are left in reasonable doubt by it, you must acquit.
>
> Third, even if you are not left in doubt by the evidence of the accused, you must ask yourself whether, on the basis of the evidence

---

55 There are numerous such cases chronicled, for example, in *R. v. Squires* (2002), 209 Nfld. & P.E.I.R. 99 (N.L.C.A.), rev'd [2002] 4 S.C.R. 323.

56 *R. v. Taylor (C.R.)* (2001), 154 C.C.C. (3d) 273 at para. 15 (Ont. C.A.).

57 For example, in *R. v. Armstrong* (2003), 179 C.C.C. (3d) 37 (Ont. C.A.), leave to appeal to S.C.C. refused, [2003] S.C.C.A. No. 554, the failure to advise the jury that they could find doubt in the absence of evidence was not fatal where the Crown case was built on what circumstantial evidence showed, and in *R. v. Lavallee*, above note 12, the failure to situate reasonable doubt on the scale between absolute certainty and proof on the balance of probabilities did not require a verdict to be overturned given that the charge that was furnished complied in every other respect with *Lifchus* and made it clear that the jury could not convict on the balance of probabilities.

58 *R. v. Daley* (2007), 226 C.C.C. (3d) 1 at para. 106 (S.C.C.).

which you do accept, you are convinced beyond a reasonable doubt by that evidence of the guilt of the accused.[59]

This direction need not be articulated verbatim by judges. Appeal courts will not interfere with a result where in spite of the failure by a judge to intone this very formula, the jury could not have been under any misapprehension as to the correct burden.[60] It is enough if, in substance, the judge successfully communicates the general concepts relating to the standard and burden of proof, and cautions the jury "that a trial is not a contest of credibility between witnesses, and that they do not have to accept the defence evidence in full in order to acquit."[61]

As for a judge alone trial, the judge is presumed to understand the law and need not slavishly follow this formula either. "In a case that turns on credibility . . . the . . . judge must direct his or her mind to the decisive question of whether the accused's evidence . . . raises a reasonable doubt about guilt"[62] but so long as there is nothing in the record to suggest that the judge has failed to do so, appeal courts will not interfere.[63]

In a civil case, the plaintiff must establish its allegation on the balance of probabilities. Some courts and commentators have urged that the intensity of this standard varies with the matter in issue. They urge that where allegations carry increased risk of moral stigma, such as fraud, professional negligence, or sexual misconduct, courts should exercise increased caution before finding for the plaintiff. In *F.H. v. McDougall* the Supreme Court of Canada rejected this approach, saying there is only one standard and that in all cases, "the trial judge must scrutinize the relevant evidence with care to determine whether it is more likely than not that an alleged event occurred."[64]

There is no equivalent to the *W.(D.)* warning for civil cases. *W.(D.)* does not translate well to the balance of probabilities standard. In civil cases the plaintiff is entitled to win if their evidence is more credible than the defence evidence on all components of the cause of action, while the defendant will win if defence evidence is preferred to plaintiff evidence on a necessary element of the lawsuit.[65]

---

59   *R. v. W.(D.)* (1991), 3 C.R. (4th) 302 at 310 (S.C.C.).
60   *R. v. Rhee*, above note 53 at para. 21; and see *R. v. S.(J.H.)*, [2008] S.C.J. No. 30.
61   *R. v. Van*, [2009] S.C.J. No. 22 at para. 23.
62   *R. v. Dinardo* (2008), 231 C.C.C. (3d) 177 at para. 23 (S.C.C.).
63   *R. v. Y.(C.L.)*, [2008] S.C.J. No. 2; *R. v. Wadforth* (2009), 254 O.A.C. 295 at paras. 50–51 (C.A.).
64   [2008] S.C.J. No. 54 at para. 49.
65   *F.H. v. McDougall.*, *ibid.* at para. 86.

3.3)   Burdens of Proof

As indicated, the "burden of proof" describes who has the obligation of satisfying the adjudicator on a matter in issue. The party who has the burden of proof must present its evidence first and will lose the issue if it does not discharge its burden. Since the Crown in a criminal case has the burden of proving the specific criminal allegation that has been made against the accused, it is called upon to present its evidence first. Moreover, at the end of the case, the evidence must, taken together, convince the trier of fact of the guilt of the accused to the standard of "proof beyond a reasonable doubt." If it does not, the accused must be acquitted.

The "presumption of innocence" contained in subsection 11(d) of the *Charter* has been interpreted as requiring that the burden of proof in a criminal case must be on the Crown, that the accused cannot be called upon to respond until a case to meet has been presented by the Crown, and that the standard of proof required for conviction is proof beyond a reasonable doubt.[66] All these factors are intended to protect against the conviction of the innocent.

To say that the Crown bears the burden of proof in a criminal case, or that the plaintiff has the burden of proof in a civil case, is something of a simplification. In fact, the burden of proof can shift from party to party during the course of a trial, depending on the specific matter in issue at the time. For example, if the accused wishes to exclude evidence because it was unconstitutionally obtained, the burden will be on the accused to prove, on the balance of probabilities that the *Charter* violation occurred. Thus, even though the Crown always has the "ultimate burden" of proving the guilt of the accused beyond a reasonable doubt at the end of the case, there may be other burdens of proof that have to be considered.[67]

The "ultimate burden" and the kinds of particular burdens just described are burdens that have been assigned directly by rules of law. They are to be distinguished from what some people call "tactical burdens." Tactical burdens are not assigned by rules of law but arise simply because of the strength or nature of the opposing litigant's case. For example, although there is no rule of law requiring the accused to present evidence, the strength of the Crown's case may make it a practical necessity.

---

66   *R. v. Oakes* (1986), 50 C.R. (3d) 1 (S.C.C.).

67   See chapter 2, section 7, "Standards of Admissibility of Evidence," for a discussion of particular burdens relating to the admissibility of evidence.

The concept of a tactical burden can help explain some of the rules of evidence. For example, sections 276.1(2)(a) and 276.1(4) of the *Criminal Code* require accused persons who wish to prove that a sexual offence complainant has engaged in sexual activity that does not form the subject matter of the charge, to first provide evidence to support their claim that they have such evidence and that it will meet the statutory requirements for admissibility. The effect of these provisions is that an accused person who claims to be the only witness to that past sexual conduct cannot succeed in a section 276 application without swearing an affidavit himself, and taking the stand. In *R. v. Darrach*[68] the accused argued that these provisions impose an unconstitutional burden on him, effectively compelling him to testify, contrary to the presumption of innocence and section 11(c) of the *Charter*. The Supreme Court of Canada rejected this challenge on the basis that the impugned sections do not impose "legal compulsion." Nothing in the law says that Darrach must testify. He can choose to bring a section 276 application or not, and if he does choose to do so, he will be compelled not by law but because of the circumstance that he happens to be the only available witness. His burden is a tactical one, not a legal one. He is no more compelled by law than a person who chooses to take the stand during a trial because his evidence is needed to establish a defence, or to respond to a strong Crown case.

3.4)   Presumptions

3.4 (a)   The Nature of Presumptions

A substantial number of "presumptions" are provided for in statute and, to a lesser extent, by the common law. These legal rules have a significant impact on the way the trier of fact uses the evidence that has been presented. To understand the impact that presumptions have, it is necessary to distinguish between "presumptions of law" and "presumptions of fact."

A presumption of law exists automatically as a matter of law, and typically has no function other than to assign the burden of proof on an issue. The thing that is presumed by a presumption of law may not even be true as a matter of human experience. The "presumption of innocence" is the classic example. Based on guilty plea and conviction statistics, most people who are tried for an offence are in fact guilty, yet we speak about accused persons being "presumed to be innocent" because it reinforces the fact that the burden of proving guilt with

---

68   [2000] 2 S.C.R. 443 at paras. 47–52.

respect to each particular accused person rests on the Crown. Other examples of presumptions of law include the "presumption of the absence of mental disorder" housed in section 16 of the *Criminal Code*, and the common law presumptions that jurors will abide by their oath, and that judges are presumed to know the law. The "presumption that jurors will abide by their oath" is used to require parties wishing to disqualify potential jurors because of bias, to demonstrate that alleged bias.[69] The "presumption that a judge knows the law" is raised where an appellant claims that a judge made a legal error, but where the judge has not stated the legal basis for the impugned ruling.[70] In effect, a person seeking to achieve a result inconsistent with a presumption of law has the burden of showing that the presumption is not accurate. The standard needed to defeat a presumption of law will vary. To defeat the presumption of innocence, for example, the Crown must prove guilt beyond a reasonable doubt. To defeat the presumption that a judge knows the law, a party need merely prove that the judge has probably erred in law.

Even though presumptions of fact are rules of law, a presumption of fact, unlike a presumption of law, does not arise *automatically* as a matter of law. A presumption of fact arises only after a party has proved a fact required by the relevant rule. Presumptions of fact are easy to recognize. They exist where a common law or statutory rule provides, in effect, that upon proof of fact A (the basic fact), the existence of fact B (the presumed fact) will be rebuttably presumed. For example, according to section 252(2) of the *Criminal Code*, if the Crown proves that the accused left the scene of a motor vehicle accident without leaving his name and offering assistance, it is presumed that he left for the purpose of avoiding civil or criminal liability. The trier of fact must, as a matter of law, find this to be so unless there is evidence to the contrary rebutting the inference that this is why the accused left the scene of the accident. Hence, presumptions of fact are "mandatory" but "rebuttable." They are mandatory in the sense that the trier of fact must draw the presumed conclusion if the party against whom the presumption operates fails to rebut the presumed fact. They are rebuttable because they allow the party against whom the presumption operates to avoid the operation of the presumption by rebutting the presumed fact.

There are numerous presumptions of fact known to law. Most often the presumed fact follows, as a matter of human experience, so regu-

---

69   *R. v. Williams*, [1998] 1 S.C.R. 1128.
70   *R. v. Sheppard*, 2002 SCC 26 at para. 54.

larly or dependably where the basic fact exists that it is sensible to assume that the presumed fact is true where the basic fact is true, absent contrary proof. In effect, presumptions of fact operate as shortcuts to the proof of material facts. Instead of having to prove the material presumed fact, the party relying on a presumption of fact can prove the more easily established basic fact, and effectively shift the burden to the opposing party. To return to section 252(2), although there are many reasons why people might leave the scene of an automobile accident, it is almost invariably because the driver who has left wants to avoid the civil or criminal liability that might befall him if he awaits the arrival of the police. Hence there is a factual basis in human experience for the presumption.

Presumptions of fact are not always supported solely, or even mainly, because, as a matter of human experience, the presumed fact tends to follow from the existence of the basic fact. Most presumptions are supported by policy, and some depend on it entirely. For example, in a case where the requirements of subsection 258(1)(c) of the *Criminal Code* have been met, the trier of fact must find as a matter of law, in the absence of evidence to the contrary, that the concentration of alcohol in the blood of an accused was the same at the time of driving as it was at the time the breathalyzer readings were obtained. The presumption applies even though we know as a matter of fact that the presumed fact will not be true given that the human body both absorbs and metabolizes alcohol over time. Invariably, a reading taken within two hours after driving will be higher or lower than it would have been at the time of driving, depending on when the alcohol was consumed. The presumption is nonetheless supported by policy for, if it was not available, the Crown would have to call an expert toxicologist in every case to prove the blood alcohol concentration at the time of driving, and doing so with precision would be impossible.

Normally, the party seeking to rebut a presumption of fact will have to call evidence to do so. It is possible, however, for the necessary rebuttal evidence to come from the party seeking to rely on the presumption. For example, if a Crown seeking to rely on the presumption in section 252(2) presented evidence that the driver who left the scene said as he was going, "Sorry, I have to go. I have to get my son to the hospital," the presumption would be rebutted from the Crown's own case.

3.4 (b) Presumptions of Fact and the Presumption of Innocence
The standard of proof needed to rebut a presumption of fact varies. Some presumptions of fact impose a "legal burden" whereby the party must disprove the presumed fact on the balance of probabilities. For

example, subsection 362(4) of the *Criminal Code* provides that where goods are obtained with a dishonoured cheque, those goods shall be presumed to have been obtained by false pretences unless the court is satisfied by the evidence that the accused reasonably believed that the cheque would be honoured. Provisions such as this, which impose a legal burden on a party, are called "reverse onus provisions."

Other presumptions impose only an "evidentiary burden," whereby the party opposed to the presumed fact need merely raise a reasonable doubt about it. This is true of the blood alcohol provision introduced above in this chapter. If the evidence to the contrary casts a reasonable doubt on the presumed fact, the presumption falls aside. These provisions are sometimes called "mandatory presumptions."[71]

It is a matter of interpretation whether a particular presumption is a reverse onus provision, imposing a legal burden, or a mandatory presumption, imposing only an evidentiary burden. Generally, mandatory presumptions imposing a mere evidentiary burden can be identified by statutory language which provides that the presumed fact is to be inferred, "absent evidence to the contrary." By contrast, reverse onus provisions imposing a legal burden exist whenever the statute requires that the presumed fact actually be disproved. As a matter of law, where a statute imposes a burden of proof on the accused in a criminal case and where it is silent as to the standard of proof to be applied, the standard of proof needed for rebuttal is proof on the balance of probabilities.[72] Language denoting a reverse onus provision therefore includes phrases such as "if he establishes," "where he proves," "the proof of which lies upon him," or "he satisfies."

Presumptions of fact, whether they be reverse onus provisions or mandatory presumptions, can imperil the "presumption of innocence," which is constitutionally guaranteed to accused persons in criminal cases. The Supreme Court of Canada has held that any burden on an accused which has the effect of requiring a conviction in the presence of reasonable doubt contravenes the *Charter.* This is so whether the rule imposing the burden relates to an element of the offence, to a defence, or to some other matter extraneous to the offence but upon which a finding of guilt might turn.[73]

Although they are most often upheld under section 1 of the *Charter* as constituting reasonable limitations on the constitutional rights of accused persons, it is evident that all "reverse onus provisions" that

---

71   *R. v. Boyle* (1983), 35 C.R. (3d) 34 (Ont. C.A.); *R. v. Oakes,* above note 66.
72   *R. v. Oakes, ibid.*
73   *R. v. Whyte* (1988), 64 C.R. (3d) 123 (S.C.C.).

apply against the accused in a criminal case are in *prima facie* violation of the *Charter*. This is because there may be enough evidence to raise a reasonable doubt about the existence of the presumed fact, but not enough to disprove it on the balance of probabilities. In such a case the provision would still require the trier of fact to find that the presumed fact exists despite the existence of reasonable doubt. For example, section 8 of the now repealed *Narcotic Control Act*, which presumed those in possession of narcotics to be in possession for the purpose of trafficking, required triers of fact to return possession for the purpose of trafficking verdicts where the accused did not prove that he was probably not intending to traffic but where the evidence still left a reasonable doubt about why he had possession. The section was therefore of no force or effect as being contrary to subsection 11(d) of the *Charter*.[74]

Mandatory presumptions present more difficulty. On its face, it may be wondered how provisions that can be rebutted by evidence that merely raises a reasonable doubt can contravene a constitutional rule that precludes only those convictions that are made in the face of reasonable doubt. Indeed, in *R. v. Osolin* the Supreme Court of Canada asserted that a mere evidentiary burden cannot contravene subsection 11(d).[75] Yet, consider, for example, the mandatory presumption in subsection 354(2) of the *Criminal Code*. According to that provision, where an accused person is found in possession of a motor vehicle that has an obliterated serial number, it is presumed that the accused knows that the motor vehicle was stolen. This mandatory presumption can be rebutted by evidence to the contrary, whether it appears in the case for the Crown or is presented by the accused. Assume, however, that there is no evidence to the contrary. The trier of fact will be compelled by law to find that the accused knew the motor vehicle to have been stolen even though it may not be persuaded that the presence of an obliterated serial number proves the accused's knowledge of the identity of the vehicle.[76] In such a case, the mandatory presumption would have the effect of causing the conviction of the accused despite the presence of a reasonable doubt. It therefore fails the test of constitutional validity. This is what the Ontario Court of Appeal decided in *R. v. Boyle* when it struck down this part of subsection 354(2).[77] The broad statement in *Osolin* that an evidentiary burden cannot contravene subsection 11(d) is therefore incorrect.

74　*R. v. Oakes*, above note 66. The section was not saved by s. 1 as a reasonable limit on the presumption of innocence.

75　(1993), 26 C.R. (4th) 1 (S.C.C.).

76　How many of us even know where our motor vehicle serial numbers are?

77　Above note 71.

'Fortunately, there is Supreme Court of Canada authority contradicting the pronouncement in *Osolin*. In *R. v. Downey* the Court held that subsection 11(d) of the *Charter* was violated by the mandatory presumption in subsection 212(3) of the *Criminal Code*.[78] That section provides that proof that the accused lives with a prostitute is, in the absence of evidence to the contrary, proof that he lives off the avails of prostitution. The Court found that this section raised the prospect of convicting accused persons in the face of reasonable doubt because a trier of fact may well have a doubt about the livelihood of the accused, even where it is proved that he lived with a prostitute. Absent evidence to the contrary, the trier of fact would nonetheless be compelled to conclude that this is how he makes his living.[79]

3.4 (c)   Misleading Uses of the Term "Presumption"

Lawyers are not as consistent in the use of terminology as one might like. Unfortunately, cases and statutory provisions rarely state expressly that a particular presumption is a presumption of law or a presumption of fact. It is left to lawyers to make that characterization given the language and nature of the rule in question. To make matters worse, the term "presumption" is used at times to describe things that are neither presumptions of law nor presumptions of fact. For example, the term "presumption" is sometimes employed to describe factual assertions that are irrebuttable. Section 198(3) of the *Criminal Code* provides an illustration. That section presumes that a premises with a slot machine inside is a "common gaming house." On its face, it enables the Crown who has charged someone with a gaming house offence to prove that there is a slot machine in the premises, rather than that the premises is actually being used as a common game house. This is not a "presumption of fact" because the law does not allow the presumption to be rebutted. The same result could have been obtained had the drafters of the *Code* avoided the language of presumption and simply defined "common gaming house" as including a premises containing a slot machine. Then there is the "presumption that everyone knows the law." Unlike "the presumption that judges know the law," this one is not rebuttable either. The language of "presumption" is employed simply to convey that ignorance of the law is no excuse; that people are irrebuttably deemed to know the law even if they do not. It is common to refer to rules that adopt the language of "presumption" but which do not permit rebuttal, as "irrebuttable presumptions."

---

78   (1992), 13 C.R. (4th) 129 (S.C.C.).
79   Section 1 of the *Charter* was used to save this section.

The term "presumption" is also used at times, in rules that invite but do not require fact finders to infer presumed facts from the proof of particular basic facts. This kind of rule is sometimes referred to as a "permissive presumption." For example, the so-called presumption that a person intends the natural consequences of his acts is not a true presumption of fact because the trier of fact is free to reject that conclusion, even in the absence of evidence to the contrary. The same is true of the permissive presumption that a person is presumed to have knowledge of the origin of recently stolen goods. The trier of fact may, but need not, draw this inference. Where permissive "presumptions" are referred to before a jury, jurors must be made to understand that no burden is imposed on the accused.[80]

It would be better if the law avoided using the term "presumption" in these contexts. It is potentially misleading. For example, inviting a jury to apply the "presumption that persons intend the natural consequences of their act," could create the misleading impression that there is a legal burden on the accused to rebut that permissive presumption. Great care should be exercised in the use of these permissive presumptions.

3.5) The *Prima Facie* Case Standard

The *prima facie* case standard is an important example of an "evidential burden." It is used as a screening process to see whether it is justifiable and sensible to have a case go to the trier of fact who is designated by law to give an ultimate factual decision on the matter. In a criminal case, the Crown must demonstrate a *prima facie* case in order to have an accused person committed to stand trial after a preliminary inquiry.[81] At the end of the Crown's case, accused persons are entitled, on application, to a directed verdict of acquittal, if the Crown has not presented a *prima facie* case.[82] The *prima facie* case standard applies at extradition proceedings as well,[83] although, as described below,[84] it operates differently there than it does at preliminary inquiries and trials.

3.5 (a)   At Preliminary Inquiries and in Trials

In *R. v. Fontaine* the Supreme Court of Canada said that there is no *prima facie* case "unless there is evidence in the record upon which a properly instructed jury [can] rationally conclude that the accused

---

80   *R. v. Gould* (2008), 244 O.A.C. 176 at para. 1317 (C.A.).
81   *R. v. Arcuri*, [2001] 2 S.C.R. 828.
82   *R. v. Charemski*, [1998] 1 S.C.R. 679.
83   *United States of America v. Cobb* (2001), 152 C.C.C. (3d) 270 (S.C.C.).
84   See section 3.5 (b), "At Extradition Hearings," below in this chapter.

is guilty beyond a reasonable doubt."[85] This standard represents both an evolution of, and improvement on, the classic test from the *United States v. Sheppard*.[86] The ambiguously worded *Sheppard* test had been understood by some as leaving no room for evaluation of the sufficiency of proof; there would be a *prima facie* case if there was "any" evidence, no matter how weak, on each of the things the Crown had to prove in order to gain a conviction. Others accepted that the *Sheppard* test required some evaluation of sufficiency but that in undertaking that evaluation the judge should avoid considering the criminal standard of proof.[87] *Fontaine* and another Supreme Court of Canada decision, *R. v. Arcuri*,[88] have now pushed much of the uncertainty aside.

Before explaining precisely what the application of the *prima facie* test entails, it is helpful to consider the implications of a finding that there is no *prima facie* case. A judge who rules that there is no *prima facie* case prevents the case from getting to the tribunal that is, according to law, supposed to be deciding the case on its merits. A preliminary inquiry judge who refuses to commit an accused person to trial will, subject to the power of Attorneys General to issue direct indictments, be depriving the trial court of the ability to decide the case. A judge who directs a verdict of acquittal is preventing the jury from deciding the case. The operation of the *prima facie* case standard is therefore influenced heavily by rules that seek to keep the judge who is adjudicating whether there is a *prima facie* case from doing the job that another tribunal is supposed to be doing.

The first restriction, then, is that a judge deciding whether there is a *prima facie* case is to assume that all of the evidence he hears is true. He is not to trouble himself about whether he believes the witnesses or not. It is the job of the trial court or jury to decide whether witnesses are believed. For a judge to refuse to find a *prima facie* case because he does not believe the witnesses is to usurp the function of the relevant body.

The second restriction is that the judge deciding whether there is a *prima facie* case is not to "weigh" the reliability of the evidence. She should not, for example, discount the testimony of a witness because the witness had a poor opportunity to observe and could be mistaken, or has poor eyesight, or is inexperienced. The judge is to assume that

---

85   (2004), 18 C.R. (6th) 203 at para. 53 (S.C.C.).

86   [1977] 2 S.C.R. 1067.

87   In light of the unequivocal dictum in *Fontaine*, above note 85, the view articulated in *R. v. Litchfield* (1993), 25 C.R. (4th) 137 (S.C.C.), that the standard of proof does not form part of the *prima facie* case test, must now be considered to have been abandoned by the S.C.C.

88   Above note 81.

the witness is not only trying to be truthful but is succeeding in being accurate.[89]

Where there is "direct" evidence on every one of the things that the Crown must prove, the *prima facie* case standard is therefore simple. Since the judge must treat the testimony as true and accurate there will necessarily be evidence "in the record upon which a properly instructed jury could rationally conclude that the accused is guilty beyond a reasonable doubt."

Where the only evidence on one or more of the essential elements of the offence is circumstantial, things are more complex. The judge will have to engage in a restrained evaluation of the sufficiency of the circumstantial case, an evaluation the Supreme Court of Canada has described as a "limited weighing":

> In performing the task of limited weighing, the preliminary inquiry judge does not [actually] draw [ultimate] inferences from facts. Nor does she assess credibility. Rather, the judge's task is to determine whether, if the Crown's evidence is believed, it would be reasonable for a jury to infer guilt. Thus, this task of "limited weighing" never requires consideration of the inherent reliability of the evidence itself. It should be regarded, instead, as an assessment of the reasonableness of the inferences to be drawn from the circumstantial evidence.[90]

3.5 (b)   At Extradition Hearings

The *prima facie* case test described above applies at extradition hearings, subject to one important caveat. Whereas in preliminary hearings and at trials judges applying the *prima facie* case standard are to assume that the evidence presented is accurate and true, in an extradition hearing the judge has discretion to give no weight to evidence that is "unreliable." The Supreme Court of Canada gave judges this power in *United States of America v. Ferras*[91] as a result of amendments to the *Extradition Act*[92] that were unduly aggressive in streamlining the extradition process. On their face those amendments left the judge to do little more than act as a rubber stamp. The Court reasoned that it is contrary to principles of fundamental justice to deprive an accused of liberty without a fair and meaningful judicial process, which includes an assessment to reject manifestly unreliable evidence. In domestic criminal prosecutions this standard is satisfied because evidence is

---

89   *R. v. Mezzo*, [1986] 1 S.C.R. 802.
90   *R. v. Arcuri*, above note 81 at para. 3.
91   *United States of America v. Ferras* (2006), 209 C.C.C. (3d) 353 (S.C.C.).
92   *Extradition Act*, S.C. 1999, c. 18.

vetted through Canadian rules of admissibility that serve to weed out much unreliable proof, and because in domestic cases after committal or the denial of a directed verdict the truthfulness and reliability of the evidence remains to be weighed by a tribunal before a final verdict is rendered. There is no such assurance in an extradition context, hence the threshold discretion for extradition hearing judges to reject evidence that would be dangerous or unsafe to convict upon. To keep the process efficient, where evidence is "certified" under the *Extradition Act* by a foreign country it is presumed to be reliable, but if its reliability is challenged the extradition just must examine whether it has sufficient indicia of reliability to be worthy of consideration.

3.6)   The "Air of Reality" Test

Where an accused in a criminal case wants to rely on an affirmative defence[93] he must meet an "evidential burden" before the trier of fact can even consider whether that defence applies. The standard is called the "air of reality" test. Similar to the *prima facie* case standard, the air of reality test acts as a filter to prevent the ultimate decision-maker from being troubled or confused by issues that are hopelessly unrealistic. Where the air of reality test is met, then, the defence is put into issue. Indeed, where the test is satisfied a judge is obliged by law to have the trier of fact consider the defence, whether it was raised by one of the parties or not.

Satisfying the air of reality test does not, of course, resolve the issue of whether the defence will succeed. The ultimate fortunes of the defence that has been put before the trier of fact will depend on the application of the burden of proof that the defence carries. For ordinary affirmative defences, such as self-defence or provocation,[94] once the defence has been put in issue the Crown bears the burden of disproving that defence beyond a reasonable doubt. In other words, if there is a reasonable doubt about whether the defence was met, the defence succeeds.[95] For "reverse onus" defences, such as mental disorder or simple automatism,[96] the burden is on the accused to prove the defence on

---

93 Most accused persons defend themselves without presenting an "affirmative defence" by simply challenging the Crown's case as inadequate to prove guilt beyond a reasonable doubt.

94 Ordinary defences also include "belief in consent," "mistake of fact," "duress," "necessity," and "drunkenness."

95 *R. v. Cinous*, [2002] 2 S.C.R. 3, and see *R. v. Reid* (2003), 18 C.R. (6th) 350 at paras. 70–73 (Ont. C.A.), for the application of the *W.(D.)* warning to ordinary defences like self-defence.

96 Extreme intoxication is also a "reverse onus defence."

the balance of probabilities. The defence will be rejected unless the accused's claim to that defence is probably true.[97]

The air of reality test used to determine whether a defence is put into issue, asks "whether there is evidence on the record upon which a properly instructed jury acting reasonably could acquit."[98] As with the *prima facie* evidence standard, and for identical reasons, the judge applying the air of reality test is to assume that the evidence is true and that the witnesses are providing reliable information. While the judge is not to concern herself with whether the defence is likely to succeed, the judge is, in cases of circumstantial evidence, to engage in the same kind of limited weighing that the *prima facie* case requires:

> [A]uthorities . . . support a two-pronged question for determining whether there is an evidential foundation warranting that a defence be put to a jury. The question remains whether there is (1) evidence (2) upon which a properly instructed jury could acquit if it believed the evidence to be true. The second part of the question can be rendered by asking whether the evidence put forth is reasonably capable of supporting the inferences required to acquit the accused.[99]

In general, "the Judge has to say whether any facts have been established by evidence from which [the matter in issue] *may be reasonably inferred;* the jurors ought to say whether, from those facts [the matter in issue] *ought to be inferred.*[100]

The fact that there are different burdens and standards of proof attached to different defences complicates the air of reality test. Is it necessary to take the standard of proof associated with the relevant defence into account in judging whether a reasonable trier of fact "could acquit," or "conclude in favour of the accused"? It would seem so intuitively, and this was the position taken in *R. v. Stone*.[101] There is also clear *dictum* supporting this view in *R. v. Cinous*[102] and in *R. v. Fontaine* as well.[103] In spite of this, in both *R. v. Cinous*[104] and in *R. v. Fontaine*,[105] the Supreme Court of Canada insisted that the air of reality test is the same for all defences. The apparent conflict could be reconciled if what

---

97 *R. v. Fontaine*, above note 85.

98 *R. v. Cinous*, above note 95 at para. 49.

99 *Ibid.* at para. 82.

100 *Ibid.* at para. 91.

101 (1999), 24 C.R. (5th) 1 (S.C.C.).

102 *R. v. Cinous*, above note 95 at para. 177.

103 Above note 85 at 53–54.

104 *R. v. Cinous*, above note 95 at paras. 49 and 57.

105 *R. v. Fontaine*, above note 85 at paras. 57 and 70.

the Court meant was that the same test is to be used for all defences but that it applies differently depending upon the relevant standard of proof associated with the defence. It is more probable, though, that the Court meant that the same standard is to be applied. In effect, the decision is meant to signal that accused persons should not lightly be deprived of the chance to present the defence they are relying upon, and that the trier of fact can deal with deficiencies when examining defences on their merit.

CHAPTER 13

CONCLUSIONS

1. INTRODUCTION

The dominant theme in the law of evidence during the last quarter-century has been the unrelenting movement towards a principled or purposive approach. Fixed rules are now less apt to determine evidentiary issues, particularly those involving admissibility questions. Instead, the law has been structured so that broad standards are applied to the facts in question. Technicality is reduced. Context becomes everything. More sensible results can be achieved.

As sage as the movement to a principled, purposive approach is, there are important limits that should be placed on how much further things go. If we go too far, we lose the guidance and wisdom of the law. It is also important that the principles and purposes identified be protected; if they are not we will have little or no law of evidence, only power in judges to do as they think fit. As these closing observations demonstrate, these risks have to be seen and controlled. If they are, we will continue to enjoy an improved law of evidence, albeit it one that requires greater skills on the part of judges and lawyers.

2. WHY A PRINCIPLED, PURPOSIVE APPROACH WAS WISE

As is apparent throughout this book, the movement towards a principled and purposive law of evidence was inspired by the failure of technical rules. Technical rules are autocratic about outcomes. They purport to require that when a certain set of facts exist, preordained results occur. The case of *Myers v. D.P.P.*[1] has become the classic illustration in validating the wisdom of our recent movement away from technicality towards principle and purpose.

Myers and his associates were stealing cars. They took the vehicle identification numbers off wrecked vehicles of the same make and model, and put them on the stolen vehicles. They then sold the stolen vehicles as cars they had "repaired." The evidence—business records—showed this to be so because each vehicle sold as "repaired" bore the indelible engine block vehicle identification number of a stolen car, as well as non-matching moveable identification plates from damaged vehicles. Yet the House of Lords excluded the business records. They were hearsay—offered to prove the truth of their contents—and at the time no relevant hearsay exception applied.

The decision in *Myers* did not produce the "right" outcome in this sense—perfectly good evidence was rejected. Yet the decision to enforce the existing technical rules of evidence was not entirely indefensible. Applying the rules of proof regardless of the outcome respects basic ideas about the nature of law and the role of courts. In its classic form, the law values formal justice, which is achieved by treating like cases alike, more than it values particular opinions in specific cases about whether the rules produced the "right" result. This is a corollary of the rule of law, with its central notion that people should be ruled by law rather than by the wills, tastes, or perspectives of other people. In a pure rule of law system, it is expected that the judge can say "It is not my decision. I am simply applying the law." Protecting the integrity of technical rules of law can require judges to apply those rules even when they seem manifestly inappropriate in the case at hand.

This does not mean that perverse outcomes such as the one in *Myers* were ever celebrated. They were tolerated in the interests of broader considerations. If the law can be moved around to produce outcomes that are intuitively attractive to the judge, the law has been replaced with power. It is also worth remembering that while rules may be imperfect, they are built on the wisdom of ages. They were crafted based

---

1   [1965] A.C. 1001.

on experience to accomplish worthy objectives. The thinking in cases such as *Myers* is that justice can best be achieved in the long run, over more cases, by respecting rules rather than by permitting them to be disregarded and lose their influence. Finally, there was a sense that if the law is defective, it is better for legislators to fix it. Legislators pronounce rules for the future. Courts, using the common law method, cannot avoid applying a modified rule for the first time to resolve something that happened in the past. The thinking is, decide the instant case according to law and if it reveals serious problems for the quality of rules, fix them for the future.

As explained in chapter 1, several things made unbridled commitment to technicality in matters of proof intolerable, notwithstanding this imposing case. The values embraced in the *Canadian Charter of Rights and Freedoms* made it unacceptable for the technical rules of proof to operate unfairly against a particular accused person, even if those rules would produce fairer outcomes in the long run. In a constitutional democracy that protects the integrity of everyone, no accused person should be treated unfairly to preserve the integrity of rules in the long-term interests of others. The sobering realization that technical rules of proof routinely frustrated the prosecution of sexual offences was also intolerable. As *R. v. Khan* so powerfully illustrates, technicality can become indefensible.[2] It is self-destructive to allow technicality to frustrate the overall objectives of the legal system of achieving justice and protecting society. Then there are the pragmatic considerations. The laws of evidence were designed to resolve reasonably contemporary disputes where the protagonists and witnesses are readily available to tell their story. The law of evidence fails, as it did in aboriginal litigation, where this is not possible. It therefore had to be changed to operate in non-technical ways.

Similar movements away from technical, "black letter law" can be seen with the substantive law as well—consider statutory interpretation, unconscionability doctrines in the law of obligations, and the burgeoning use of fiduciary obligations and unjust enrichment concepts. Still, the movement away from technicality in the substantive law cannot match the intensity with which it has washed across the law of evidence. As these pages show, in the last quarter-century we have replaced the shopping list approach to admitting lay opinion evidence with a principled evaluation; we have endorsed broad exclusionary discretion previously denied; we have adopted a generic hearsay exception

---

2 [1990] 2 S.C.R. 531. See chapter 5, section 1, "Principles Underlying the Exceptions."

linked to the purpose of the rule and have invited the principled reconsideration of long-standing hearsay exceptions; we have rejected the
pigeon-hole approach to admitting similar fact evidence; we have given
judges a gate-keeping function to control expert opinion evidence and
have jettisoned the ultimate issue rule; we have endorsed a case-by-case
privilege and accepted a context-based approach to the loss of privilege
by accidental disclosure; we have embraced a more contextual exploration of the effects of inducements on the choice of accused persons to
speak to persons in authority, we have accepted discretion to exclude
statements where their admission would shock the conscience, and we
have accepted a principled approach to protecting self-incrimination.
We have also rejected the two-box approach to the exclusion of unconstitutionally obtained evidence. There are signs we are taking a less
technical approach to collateral facts, refreshing memory, the cross-
examination of one's own witnesses and the admissibility of prior consistent statements, trends we should arguably accelerate.[3] And we have
replaced corroboration rules with discretionary warnings. These are
only the major developments.

There are arguably three reasons why the rejection of technicality
has been so pronounced in the law of evidence. The first is that while
they are still essential to the integrity of the law, rule of law considerations do not apply with the same intensity to matters of process. One
of the virtues of ensuring that the law produces predictable outcomes
is that individuals can choose whether to act in particular ways by
examining what those outcomes are likely to be. Whether the "law
and economic theory" that drives this thinking is realistic, it has little
application to matters of procedure. Put in simple terms, an individual may consult the law before deciding how to structure a business
transaction to avoid tort or criminal implications. Change the law and
apply it to that person after the fact and the unfairness is palpable. By
contrast it is doubtful that any individuals consult the law of evidence
and act because it will be hard for others to find admissible evidence to
prove what they have done.

Second, the assumption that legislators are best placed to modify
the substantive law does not resonate when it comes to rules of proof.
These are the very tools of the trade of jurists. Jurists have the contextual experience to know what works and what does not. They know
what is right and just in matters of process because process is their
wheelhouse and their exclusive domain. Jurists therefore feel capable

---

3   The one area where we seem reluctant to embrace principle and purposes is
    "secondary materiality" where discretion performs at its best.

and are capable of modifying the rules of evidence without legislative intervention. It has always been so. Since they can respond more quickly than legislators, this comfort in moving the law using common law evolution produces more rapid change.

And third, the rules of evidence have never been stellar at predicting outcomes in any event. They are conceptually challenging. As can be seen, many of them, most notoriously the law of hearsay and character evidence, are rules of "restricted admissibility" allowing the proof for limited purposes based on sophisticated models about how individuals reason. They are always hard to apply and so outcomes are often controversial. Rules of evidence are also about facts. The application of the law is therefore endemically and unavoidably context driven. Since facts are variable, so are outcomes. As a result, the promise of the rule of law was never fully met even when the law purported to be more rigid and clear. There was therefore relatively little to lose by unharnessing the law of evidence. Indeed, fact specific questions relating to such things as relevance, probative value and prejudice were natural and fitting for the law of evidence.

There is therefore room to celebrate the reduction in technicality and rigidity in the laws of proof.

3. THE LIMITS OF PRINCIPLE AND PURPOSE

In celebrating the march to a principled, purposive approach it has always to be borne in mind that there are two components to it, not one: (1) the rejection of technicality, and (2) the ascendancy of principle and purposive analysis. These two components work in tandem. Specifically, we would not have rejected technical rules of proof and left nothing in their place. We rejected them because of the conviction that principled and purposive approaches to admissibility are better than rigid, pigeon-holed outcomes.

This is important to bear in mind because if we read the evolution of the law of evidence solely as a movement away from technicality we will move too far. This thinking can lead to the widespread rejection of rules of admissibility. There are, of course, legal systems internationally that do not use rules of admissibility, or that use them only rarely. We believe that it would impoverish our law to follow suit by jettisoning key rules of proof.

First, many of our rules of exclusion exist to pursue considerations of policy that are extraneous to the correct outcome in the case. While we discourage an overly liberal use of rules of subordinated evidence which, by their nature, undermine the accurate determinations about factual controversies (particularly when operating to the disadvantage of those accused of crimes), the litigation process does not operate in isolation. It operates in a broader world and its practices have implications, including for the privacy of individuals, the proper relationship between the state and the individual in a free and democratic society, and the integrity of the administration of justice. We will always need to control the flow of information in the interests of broader policies and principles.

Second, most of our rules of exclusion, including hearsay, opinion evidence, and character evidence rules, represent the collected wisdom about how best to achieve accurate outcomes. We know from experience that some information, or the improper use of information, can distort outcomes. These rules of non-evidence, if properly applied, therefore contribute to accurate outcomes. If we fail to apply these rules, we accept a poorer body of information.

Third, the assumption that decision-makers can weigh evidence as effectively without the assistance of rules of admissibility is suspect. Rules of admissibility have the virtue of requiring a close consideration, at the front end when evidence is first offered. If the applicable rules of evidence are applied properly this assures that a discrete and focused attempt will be made to identify the problems presented by particular items of information. There can be no assurance that items of evidence will be vetted in this way during the final deliberation process after they have been received and impressions have been created. During deliberations decision-makers are trying to cope with the case as a whole. If a close evaluation of potentially problematic evidence is to be done, it should therefore be done when it is first offered. Moreover, having rules of admissibility, particularly principled rules of admissibility, assures that the data required to properly evaluate that evidence will be made available to the decision-maker. By way of example, if a party wishing to call hearsay evidence is obliged to establish its reliability before it gains admission, there can be some assurance that a careful attempt will be made to identify all of the indicia of reliability and unreliability required to assess that evidence intelligently. If the evidence simply slides in for later evaluation there is a reduced chance that the decision-makers will be provided with the same, ample record. Simply put, the ultimate consideration given to the evidence is apt to be more poorly done if done at all.

Yet the impulse to move away from rules of admissibility is attractive. It is simpler, more efficient, and makes the law more accessible. This, of course, is why we tend not to apply rules of admissibility formally at administrative hearings. As chapter 1 indicates, we are now mimicking administrative law practices in court-based litigation. There are an increasing number of legislative initiatives that dispose of the rules of proof in a variety of court hearings. This is invariably done for reasons of administrative efficiency, and usually in contexts where the stakes are perceived, rightly or wrongly, to be relatively low.[4] The increased use of alternative dispute resolution and mediation as a prelude to court-based litigation, where rules of admissibility do not technically apply, has also become standard. This can have the effect of acculturating Canadian lawyers to informal methods of hearing. So too, can the increasing exposure of Canadian lawyers to international law and international dispute settlement bodies where rules of exclusion play little or no role. Then there is the formidable pressure to tear down technicality brought about by the proliferation of unrepresented litigants in our courts. The burgeoning cost of litigation has assured that many of those who appear to argue both civil and criminal cases will be doing so without lawyers. Lay litigants simply cannot cope on their own with the heavy conceptual demands of rules of admissibility. Together these factors can easily push us further away from our continued, heavy reliance on rules of admissibility. As a general proposition, this will impoverish our ability to resolve questions of fact.

How then, do we cope with unrepresented litigants? We do so by compromising on the adversarial model and its conception of the role of the trial judge. Judges do have a responsibility to uphold the law. As discussed in chapter 1, many tend to allow adversarial parties to control the presentation of proof by waiting for objections.[5] It is not fair to expect unrepresented litigants to object or to do so meaningfully unless they have amply been warned about the implications of their choices. We can preserve the value in having rules of exclusion in unrepresented litigant cases by having judges perform their role of enforcing the law. Expecting judges to protect unrepresented litigants in this way is far better than moving away from rules of proof to accommodate unrepresented parties. The cost of doing so would be to allow untutored, free-form litigation in crucial matters of dispute, and to deprive jurists of the benefit of the rigorous lessons of the law of evidence about when information is worth hearing and using.

---

4   See chapter 1, section 3.3, "Increased Admissibility."
5   See chapter 1, section 6.2, "Enforcement on Appeal."

4. THE PROTECTION OF PRINCIPLE AND PURPOSE

As has been repeatedly pointed out, most admissibility determinations are now "discretionary." This necessarily means that judges exercise some choice in admitting evidence. As a result, at the appeal level "deference" has become the buzzword. In virtually every major area of admissibility, including character evidence, hearsay, opinion evidence, the operation of the exclusionary discretion, the exclusion of illegally obtained evidence, and the administration of warnings about dangerous evidence, appellate courts affirm that they will give significant deference to the decisions made by trial judges. Deference has to exist, but it must be applied properly. It is applied properly by bearing in mind the difference between strong form discretion and the exercise of judgment. Strong form discretion permits decision-makers to do what they want. It is inconsistent with law. This is not what discretion means. By contrast, the exercise of judgment recognizes that reasonable people applying the proper principles of evaluation may come to different decisions. It is only within this range that deference is appropriate. If a judge has not consulted properly the principles and purposes outlined by our retooled law of evidence, the party affected has not had the benefit of the law. Appeal judges can be trusted to recognize that if deference becomes too pronounced, we will have rejected technicality without replacing it with principle. What appeal judges say when resolving evidentiary appeals guides the profession. It is therefore far better in rejecting appeals based on shortcomings in reasoning to rely on harmless error doctrines than it is to invoke deference where poor analysis has occurred but where it does not warrant an appeal remedy. Where judges misapply principled and purposive rules, or do so poorly, this should be made clear so that jurists in future cases can learn by example.

5. THE CHALLENGE

Superficially, the movement away from technicality suggests that the law is now easier to apply. The reality is that it is far more difficult to use flexible rules in an intelligent and principled way than it is to apply a technical rule without regard to its consequences. The loss of technicality brings with it the need for greater skill. This is because fixed rules permit lawyers to compel judges to reach particular outcomes; if the elements of a fixed rule are met, the judge will err if the rule is not applied. By contrast, principled rules give controlled latitude. Litigants win only when they persuade the judge. Fixed technical rules can also be more easily learned. All that is needed to apply them is to know their meaning and to recognize whether the facts fit. Things are not so easy with principled, purposive rules. The lawyer or judge must understand the underlying theory of the rules — their purposes and foundational principles. Close regard must be paid to the competing interests at stake, for those interests will form the basis for reasoned argumentation. A broader array of facts and considerations are also available for consultation. In the new law of evidence, rules must be understood in the full sense of the term, and critical and penetrating analysis of facts and context has to be performed. As we point out in the introduction the rules of evidence are therefore as complex in design and as difficult to apply as they are important. Master them and enjoy a tremendous litigation advantage. Misunderstand them at your peril and the peril of your clients. If there is one sentiment that sums up recent developments in the law of evidence it is this — things have become better, not easier.

TABLE OF CANADIAN
EVIDENCE ACTS

Canada Evidence Act, R.S.C. 1985, c. C-5

Alberta Evidence Act, R.S.A. 2000, c. A-18

British Columbia, *Evidence Act*, R.S.B.C. 1996, c. 124

Manitoba Evidence Act, C.C.S.M. c. E150

New Brunswick, *Evidence Act*, R.S.N.B. 1973, c. E-11

Newfoundland and Labrador, *Evidence Act*, R.S.N.L. 1990, c. E-16

Northwest Territories, *Evidence Act*, R.S.N.W.T. 1988, c. E-8

Nova Scotia, *Evidence Act*, R.S.N.S. 1989, c. 154

Nunavut, *Evidence Act*, R.S.N.W.T. 1988, c. E-8

Ontario, *Evidence Act*, R.S.O. 1990, c. E.23

Prince Edward Island, *Evidence Act*, R.S.P.E.I. 1988, c. E-11

Saskatchewan, *The Evidence Act*, S.S. 2006, c. E-11.2

Yukon Territory, *Evidence Act*, R.S.Y. 2002, c. 78

TABLE OF CASES

INDEX